European Yearbook of International Economic Law

More information about this series at
http://www.springer.com/series/8165

Christoph Herrmann • Bruno Simma •
Rudolf Streinz
Editors

Trade Policy between Law, Diplomacy and Scholarship

Liber amicorum in memoriam Horst G. Krenzler

Springer

Editors
Christoph Herrmann
University of Passau
Passau
Germany

Bruno Simma
Iran-United States Claims Tribunal
The Hague
The Netherlands

Rudolf Streinz
Ludwig Maximilians University Munich
Munich
Germany

European Yearbook of International Economic Law
ISBN 978-3-319-15689-7 ISBN 978-3-319-15690-3 (eBook)
DOI 10.1007/978-3-319-15690-3

Library of Congress Control Number: 2015941506

Springer Cham Heidelberg New York Dordrecht London

Printed on acid-free paper

Springer International Publishing AG Switzerland is part of Springer Science+Business Media (www.springer.com)

Horst Günter Krenzler * 26.03.1933 † 20.07.2012

List of Publications of Horst G. Krenzler

1. *Die vorläufige Anwendung völkerrechtlicher Verträge*, 1964.
2. Allgemeine Lieferbedingungen, "Heidelberger Musterverträge" Heft 38, 1968.
3. Europa und Nordamerika – Die Rolle der Europäischen Gemeinschaften in der nordatlantischen Bündnispolitik, Lecture at RIAS-Funk-Universität on 6 November 1974, Berlin.
4. Die Rolle der Kabinette in der Kommission der Europäischen Gemeinschaften, EuR (1974), pp. 75–79.
5. Die Zusammenarbeit auf dem Gebiet der Bildungspolitik in der Europäischen Gemeinschaft, EA (1975), pp. 237–242.
6. Die Zusammenarbeit der liberalen Parteien in Westeuropa: auf dem Weg zur Föderation, in: *Zusammenarbeit der Parteien in Westeuropa: auf dem Weg zu einer neuen politischen Infrastruktur?*, 1976 (together with Hans Claudius Ficker, Christian Fischer-Dieskau).
7. Exportselbstbeschränkungen – ein aktuelles Problem der Handelspolitik der Europäische Gemeinschaft, EuR (1977), pp. 177–181.
8. Das Welttextilabkommen III und die bilateralen Textilabkommen der EG, RIW (1983), pp. 423–427.
9. Entwicklungsperspektiven der Europäischen Gemeinschaft nach der Tagung des Europäischen Rates in Dublin, EA (1985), pp. 11–18.
10. Die Einheitliche Europäische Akte als Schritt auf dem Wege zu einer gemeinsamen europäischen Außenpolitik, EuR (1986), pp. 384–391.
11. Zwischen Protektionismus und Liberalismus – Europäischer Binnenmarkt und Drittlandsbeziehungen, EA (1988), pp. 241–248.
12. Zäsur in der europäischen Nachkriegsgeschichte – Berlin (West) voll in EG-RGW-Erklärungen einbezogen, DZB (1988), F 164.
13. Die Europäische Gemeinschaft und der Wandel in Mittel- und Osteuropa, EA (1990), pp. 98–96.
14. Créer l'EEE exige toute notre attention, EFTA BULLETIN 31 (Octobre–Décembre 1990) 4, pp. 19–20, Édition française (English version: Creating the EEA Requires our Total Concentration; German version: Die Schaffung des EWR erfordert unsere gesamte Konzentration).

15. Die Transatlantische Erklärung: Neue Grundlage für das Verhältnis von EG und USA, AußPol (1991), pp. 363–372 (together with Wolfram Kaiser); (English version: The Transatlantic Declaration: A New Basis for Relations between the EC and the USA).
16. Les négociations relatives à l'espace économique européen, EURO-INFO Zurich. No. 1. 15 Janvier 1991, pp. 1–2.
17. Der Europäische Wirtschaftsraum als Teil einer gesamteuropäischen Architektur, INTEGRATION Bonn 15 (1992) 2, pp. 61–71.
18. Die Rolle der Europäischen Gemeinschaft beim Weltwirtschaftsgipfel, INTEGRATION 16 (1993) 2, pp. 68–79.
19. Die gemeinsame Außen- und Sicherheitspolitik der Europäischen Union, EuR (1994), pp. 144–161 (together with Henning C. Schneider).
20. Recht und Politik der Außenwirtschaftsbeziehungen der EG, Vortrag vor dem Europa-Institut der Universität des Saarlandes, 1994.
21. Die Handelspolitik der Europäischen Gemeinschaften als Instrument der Friedenssicherung, Speech at the 60th Deutscher Juristentag 1994, Münster.
22. A new Transatlantic Agenda, European Foreign Affairs Review 1 (1996) 1, pp. 9–28 (together with Astrid Schomaker).
23. Die EU braucht eine starke Außenvertretung, EU MAGAZIN Baden Baden (1996) 7–8, pp. 18–21.
24. The Question of Consistency, in: Regelsberger/de Schoutheete/Wessels (eds.), *Foreign Policy of the European Union*, 1997, pp. 133–152 (together with Henning C. Schneider).
25. The EU and Central-East Europe: Implications of Enlargement in Stages, EUI Policy papers/RSC 1997/2.
26. Preparing for the Acquis Communautaire – Report of the Working Group on the Eastward Enlargement of the European Union, EUI Policy papers/RSC 1998/6 (together with Michelle Everson).
27. Die Reichweite der gemeinsamen Handelspolitik nach dem Vertrag von Amsterdam – eine Debatte ohne Ende?, EuR (1998), pp. 223–241 (together with Hermann da Fonseca-Wollheim).
28. Implications of the Euro for Enlargement: Report of the Working Group on the Eastern Enlargement of the European Union, EUI Policy paper/RSC 1999/3 (together with Susan Senior Nello).
29. Preparing the EU and its Institutions for Enlargement – Report of the Working Group on the Eastward Enlargement of the European Union, EUI Policy papers/RSC 1999/7 (together with Karen Elizabeth Smith).
30. EU–US Relations: More than Trade Disputes?, European Foreign Affairs Review 4 (1999) 2, pp. 153–180 (together with Gunnar Wiegand).
31. GM Food: The Next Major Transatlantic Trade War?, European Foreign Affairs Review 5 (2000) 3, pp. 287–316 (together with Anne MacGregor).
32. EU Justice and Home Affairs in the Context of Enlargement, EUI Policy papers/RSC 2001/4 (together with Kataryna Wolczuk).
33. The European Defense and Security Policy and EU Enlargement to Eastern Europe, EUI Policy papers/RSC 2001/1 (together with Milada Anna Vachudová).

34. Fortschritt oder Stagnation? – Die gemeinsame Handelspolitik nach Nizza, EuR (2001), pp. 442–461 (together with Christian Pitschas).
35. Progress or Stagnation? : The Common Commercial Policy after Nice, European Foreign Affairs Review 6 (2001) 3, pp. 291–313.
36. Recent Developments in the Regulatory Regimes for Banking, Energy and Telecommunications in the Context of the Turkish Bid for Membership of the EU, EUI Policy papers/RSC 2002/11 (together with Giacomo Luciani).
37. Die Nachkriegsentwicklung des Welthandelssystems – von der Havanna-Charta zur WTO, in: Prieß /Berrsch (eds.), *WTO-Handbuch*, 2003.
38. Public Attitudes towards the EU in Candidate Countries: Report of the Working Group on the Eastern Enlargement of the European Union, EUI Policy papers/RSC 2003/2 (together with Ania Krok-Paszkowska).
39. Die Außenhandelsbefugnisse der EU, in: Schwarze (ed.), *Der Verfassungsentwurf des Europäischen Konvents*, 2004, 1st ed., pp. 385–394.
40. Die Uruguay Runde aus der Sicht der Europäischen Union, Lecture at the Forschungsstelle für Transnationales Wirtschaftsrecht der Martin-Luther-Universität Halle-Wittenberg, 8 July 2013, Beiträge zum Transnationalen Wirtschaftsrecht Heft 32 (Oktober 2004).
41. Die Gemeinsame Handelspolitik nach dem Entwurf des Europäischen Verfassungsvertrags – ein Schritt in die richtige Richtung, RIW (2005), pp. 801–811 (together with Christian Pitschas).
42. EG-Außenwirtschaftsrecht, in: Grabitz/Hilf (eds.), *Das Recht der EU*, 2009, 40th ed.
43. A New Legal Order of International Law, in: Fastenrath/Geiger/Khan/Paulus/von Schorlemer/Vedder (eds.), *From Bilateralism to Community Interest*, 2011, pp. 1004–1023 (together with Oliver Landwehr).
44. EU-Außenwirtschaftsrecht, in: Krenzler/Herrmann (eds.), *EU-Außenwirtschafts- und Zollrecht*, May 2014, 4th ed.

Foreword

It is a good tradition of legal scholars—in particular in Germany—to honour their greatest with a special book: a *Festschrift* for celebrating a significant birthday or—on a less pleasant occasion—a *Gedächtnisschrift* after they have passed away. In the case of *Horst Günter Krenzler*, it is our great and at the same time sad honour to edit this *Liber amicorum in memoriam*, dedicated to his life and work at the European Commission and the Ludwig Maximilians University Munich, but more than that to him as a great colleague, teacher, lawyer, scholar, liberal and European!

We have tried our best to find as many former colleagues and friends of *Horst Krenzler* as possible and have benefitted a lot from referrals of others. We can only hope that we did not miss too many and apologise in every individual case. The contributions we were able to bring together, only with the collaboration and effort of all the contributors, try to touch upon all the matters *Horst Krenzler* was interested in as a lawyer, from a practical as well as a scholarly perspective. Predominantly, they treat matters of EU external relations, the common commercial policy and international economic law. Whether we have achieved to produce a book *Horst Krenzler* would have enjoyed reading is for others to judge.

The editing of a book like this would not be possible without the help of numerous other people. We are enormously grateful to the staff of *Christoph Herrmann's* Chair at the University of Passau, namely *Fiona Whiteside*, *Viktoria Sauter* and *Moritz Zegowitz*, who took care of all the proofreading and formatting. Thank you for your excellent work!

Passau, Germany
The Hague, The Netherlands
Munich, Germany
November 2014

Christoph Herrmann
Bruno Simma
Rudolf Streinz

Contents

Contributors

Katrin Arend MJur (Oxford) is an associate at Freshfields Bruckhaus Deringer LLP in Berlin, where she advises on European and international trade law. Her PhD thesis on third parties in WTO dispute settlement proceedings is submitted for publication at CUP.

Franz Blankart studied philosophy, economics and law at the Universities of Basel, Paris (Sorbonne), Exeter and Bern. In 1964, he was awarded the degree of Doctor of Philosophy (*summa cum laude*) from the University of Basel. Following banking experience, he entered the Swiss diplomatic service. He held *inter alia* the rank of Private Secretary to the Minister of Foreign Affairs and was then a member of the Swiss delegation negotiating the Free Trade Agreements with EEC/ECSC. From 1973 to 1980, he was Head of the Office for European Integration in Berne and negotiated most agreements elaborated with the Communities between 1973 and 1980 (e.g. on insurance). In June 1977, the Swiss Government granted him the rank of Minister, and in 1980, with the rank of Ambassador, he was appointed Head of the Swiss Representation to EFTA, GATT, the UNCTAD and the UN Economic Commission for Europe, and Head of the Swiss Delegation to the negotiations on commodities. Franz chaired *inter alia* the EFTA and the UNCTAD Council (TDB) and was spokesman of the Western countries (including the USA and Canada) in the ECE/UNO negotiations with the Eastern Bloc. In May 1984, he was, with the rank of Ambassador, nominated "Delegate of the Swiss Government for Trade Agreements". This function involved his role as Governor of the Inter-American Development Bank as well as bilateral relations with the whole American continent and South Africa. Moreover, he was in charge of GATT matters and World Trade, including the commercial aspects of the OECD. In 1986, he was appointed State Secretary and Director of the Federal Office for Foreign Economic Affairs. In Berne, he directed the Swiss negotiating team in the Uruguay Round and was Chief negotiator for the European Economic Area Agreement. From 2000 to 2004, he was limited partner of the private bank "Mirabaud & Cie" in Geneva. He was also a member of the Executive Council of Basel University and was a member of the Société Générale de Surveillance's ethics committee. He is a board member (Vice-President) of the BHF Bank (Schweiz) AG and was Professor at the Graduate Institute of International Studies in Geneva.

Knut Brünjes has an MA in Economics and started his career in 1977. After serving as private assistant to Otto Graf Lambsdorff, Member of the German *Bundestag*, in 1978, he became personal assistant to the German Minister of Economics. From 1980, he served in the energy division of Ministry of Economics and was appointed Head of Section for Legislative Affairs in 1982. From 1990, he was Chief of Staff for several Ministers of Economics. In 1996, he was sent to Geneva as German Representative to the WTO, and in 2000, he was appointed Head of Section for Foreign Economic Policy in Berlin, and from 2001 to present, Deputy Director-General for Trade Policy, WTO, OECD, Economic Relations with North America and Latin America in the Ministry of Economics and Energy.

Marc Bungenberg is Professor of Public Law, European Law, Public International Law and International Economic Law at the University of Siegen, Germany and visiting Professor at the Swiss Universities of Lausanne (permanent) and Lucerne. He is also Academic Council to the International Investment Law Centre Cologne. His main fields of research are European and international economic law, especially state aids, public procurement, common commercial policy and WTO law as well as of course international investment law.

Günter Burghardt served as Ambassador for the European Union to the United States from 2000 to 2005, after having accomplished a 30-year-long career with the European Commission's headquarters in Brussels. He had served, in particular, as the Commission's Director-General for External Relations under Commissioners Patten and van den Broek (1993–2000). From 1985 to 1993, he was a close aide to Commission President Jacques Delors, holding the posts of Deputy Chief of Staff and of the Commission's Political Director. During these years, he participated in major achievements of the Delors Presidency: the completion of the European Union's Internal Market Programme, the introduction of Europe's Single Currency, the Euro, the European Union's key role in helping to bring about German unification, the historic process leading to full EU membership of Europe's new democracies and the strengthening of the transatlantic partnership between the EU and the United States. From 1970 to 1985, his assignments in the Commission included various positions in the areas of internal market, environment protection, nuclear safety and innovation, and external relations. He entered the Commission as a member of the Legal Service in 1970. Günter studied law and economics in Germany, France and the UK and obtained his PhD from the University of Hamburg with a thesis on European Community Law in 1969. He retired from the European Commission in 2005 and joined the transatlantic law firm of Mayer Brown LLP as a senior counsel at their Brussels office. From 2005 to 2011, he also lectured as a guest professor at the College of Europe in Bruges and at the Law

Faculty of Ghent University, Belgium. Günter is a member of the advisory boards of "Friends of Europe", a Brussels based think tank; the Transatlantic Policy Network (Brussels/Washington, DC); the European Institute (Washington, DC) and ITINERA, a Belgian economic policy think tank.

Thomas Cottier is Professor of European and International Economic Law and the Managing Director of the World Trade Institute at the University of Bern. He was educated at the University of Bern, University of Michigan Law School, and was a visiting postdoctoral fellow at Cambridge University, UK. He taught international economic law at different Swiss Universities and abroad. Professor Cottier has written and published on a wide range of trade, European law and international law issues. His main research interests are in constitutional theory of multilevel governance and theory of international law, external relations of the EU, intellectual property, innovation and the challenges of climate change in international economic law. He managed a large national research project, NCCR Trade Regulation, from 2006 to 2013. Professor Cottier has a long-standing involvement in GATT/WTO activities. He served on the Swiss negotiating team of the Uruguay Round from 1986 to 1993, first as Chief Negotiator on dispute settlement and subsidies for Switzerland, and subsequently as Chief Negotiator on TRIPS and on IPRs in the EEA negotiations with the European Communities. He was the Deputy Director-General of the Swiss Intellectual Property Office before returning to university in 1994. He served as a member or chair of several GATT and WTO panels.

Karel De Gucht was the Trade Commissioner of the European Union (2010–2014), prior to which he served as Belgian Minister of Foreign Affairs (2004–2009) and European Commissioner for Development and Humanitarian Aid (2009–2010).

Jürgen Elvert is Jean Monnet Professor for European History at the University of Cologne and Senior Fellow at the Center for European Integration Studies, Bonn. His research interests range from modern European history to the history of ideas and institutions, maritime history, and theory and methodology of historical sciences. His publications include: *Mitteleuropa! Deutsche Planungen zur Neugestaltung Europas (1918–1945)* (1999), *Die Europäische Integration* (2012, 2nd ed.), and *Geschichte Irlands* (2014, 5th ed.).

Christian D Falkowski has over 35 years of professional international experience, mainly with the European Commission in the field of external relations and development cooperation. He opened the Commission's first diplomatic mission in Pakistan (1984), dealing with trade issues, while Horst G. Krenzler had trade responsibilities at the Commission. As head of the European Commission Delegation, Christian was Ambassador to Jordan and Yemen, Egypt and the international organisations in Vienna, including the OSCE, the International Atomic Energy Organisation and OPEC. He was also Director of the European

Commission's External Service. He recalls Horst G. Krenzler as Director-General for External Relations in the early 1990s as a very fair senior official with balanced judgement, and as a reliable support. In the third stage of his life, Christian has devoted himself to the task of communicating the importance of Europe in a changing world to a wider public. He is the author of the book *Europe for Us: Why We Need Europe*. Christian graduated from the Technical University Darmstadt as Diplom-Wirtschaftsingenieur.

Arancha González is Executive Director of the International Trade Centre (ITC). She has extensive knowledge about international trade and economics, coupled with broad experience in trade and development matters in the public and private sectors, as well as in management at multilateral organisations. Before joining ITC, Arancha served as Chief of Staff to World Trade Organization (WTO) Director-General Pascal Lamy from 2005 to 2013. During her tenure at the WTO, she played an active role in launching the WTO's Aid for Trade initiative and served as Mr Lamy's representative at the G-20. Prior to working at the WTO, Arancha held several positions at the European Commission, conducting negotiations of trade agreements and assisting developing countries in trade-development efforts. Between 2002 and 2004, she was the European Union spokeswoman for trade and adviser to the European Union Trade Commissioner. She joined the Commission in 1996 serving under the leadership of Horst G. Krenzler, then Director-General for External Relations. Arancha began her career in the private sector advising companies on trade, competition and state-aid matters. She served as an associate at Bruckhaus Westrick Stegemann, a major German law firm, in Brussels. Arancha holds a degree in law from the University of Navarra and a postgraduate degree in European Law from the University of Carlos III, Madrid.

Christoph Herrmann (editor) is Professor of Constitutional and Administrative Law, European Law, European and International Economic Law at the University of Passau, Germany. He studied law and economics at the University of Bayreuth and London. In 2002, he received his doctorate in law (Bayreuth) and in 2009 his *Habilitation* (Munich). From 2006 to 2007, Christoph was a Jean Monnet Fellow at the European University Institute, Florence. His main fields of research are European and international economic law.

Meinhard Hilf was born in Eberswalde in 1938. He undertook an apprenticeship in Hamburg between 1958 and 1960, before going on to study in Law in Geneva, Munich and Hamburg (1961–1965), and attaining the second State Exam in Law (1968). Meinhard held a position as Research Fellow Max-Planck-Institute for Public Law and International Public Law in Heidelberg from 1965 to 1980. He then became Professor of Public, European and International Public Law at Bielefeld, Hamburg, and since 2004, has been Professor at the Bucerius Law School in Hamburg.

Frank Hoffmeister holds a PhD from the University of Heidelberg (1998) and served as academic assistant at the Walter Hallstein-Institut für Europäisches Verfassungsrecht in Berlin before joining the European Commission in 2001. He worked on the Cyprus problem in DG Enlargement, specialised in EU external relations and WTO law in the Legal Service, and since 2010 has acted as Deputy Head of Cabinet of the EU Trade Commissioner De Gucht. Frank also teaches International Economic Law at the Free University of Brussels and has widely published on international and European law. In 2013, he co-authored the textbook *The Law of EU External Relations: Cases, Materials and Commentary on the EU as an International Legal Actor* (OUP) together with PJ Kuijper, J Wouters, G De Baere and T Ramopoulos. Horst Günter Krenzler and Frank Hoffmeister worked together for several years in the Expert Committee on International and European Policy of the German Liberal Party (FDP).

Roger Kampf is from Hamburg, Germany. He joined the World Trade Organization in May 2004 and works as Counsellor in the Intellectual Property Division. He is responsible for the Secretariat's work in the area of TRIPS and public health and enforcement, as well as for technical assistance in relation to intellectual property. Roger previously worked for the European Commission at its headquarters in Brussels and at the permanent representation in Geneva, where he was responsible for intellectual property issues in WTO and WIPO, as well as for government procurement, from 1998 to 2004. Prior to this, he was involved in negotiations on financial services under the GATS Agreement, and also worked as an assistant in public law and European Communities law at the University of Hamburg. Roger holds a law degree from the University of Hamburg and a degree in public administration from the École Nationale d'Administration in Paris. He has published on various aspects of EU and WTO law.

Rolf Möhler is a consultant to the WTO on agricultural trade policy, a role which he has held since 1996, when he retired as Deputy Director-General of Agriculture at the European Commission with responsibility for trade policy (1986–1996). After having studied philosophy and theology in Tübingen and Bonn, and law and economics in Munich and Bonn, he gained a PhD in law from Freiburg University; and then worked at the German Federal Ministry of Economics and at the German Ministry of Foreign Affairs in Bonn. From 1965 to 1974, he was First Counsellor at the German Permanent Representation to the European Community in Brussels, and subsequently at the German missions to GATT and to the UN in Geneva. In 1981, he became Director-General for Internal Market and Industrial Affairs at the European Commission with responsibility for trade and industrial policy, before moving to DG Agriculture as Deputy Director-General in 1986. From 1986 to 1994, he also acted as a negotiator on agriculture in the Uruguay Round trade negotiations.

Frank Montag is a senior partner with Freshfields Bruckhaus Deringer's antitrust, competition and trade group, based in the Brussels office. A member of the Cologne and Brussels bars, his practice focuses on European, German and international competition law. Frank has also extensively advised clients in the area of international trade law, including in the context of anti-dumping investigations by the European Commission and other authorities around the world. Frank had the privilege of working together with Horst G. Krenzler, who joined Freshfields as an of counsel in 1996 and advised clients on a wide range of European law and policy issues stretching across a variety of practice areas, including trade law matters.

Ernst-Ulrich Petersmann has combined an academic career at numerous universities in Germany, Switzerland, Italy and the USA with legal practice as legal advisor in the German Ministry of Economic Affairs, German representative in numerous UN and European institutions, legal counsellor in GATT, and legal consultant for the WTO, UNCTAD, the European Commission and the European Parliament. He was secretary, member or chairman of numerous GATT/WTO dispute settlement panels. From 1999 to 2014, he also chaired the International Trade Law Committee of the International Law Association. He is currently emeritus Professor of International and European Law at the European University Institute at Florence, Italy.

Christian Pitschas is an attorney-at-law based in Geneva who specialises in international economic law, in particular WTO and EU foreign trade law. He studied law in Berlin, Geneva and Athens (USA) from 1986 to 1994. From 1994 to 1997, he was a clerk with the Court of Appeals in Berlin. He started his professional career as a research assistant at the Institute for European and Public International law of the Freie Universität Berlin (1997–1999) before embarking on a career as an attorney-at-law. He worked with Freshfields Bruckhaus Deringer in Brussels and Berlin (1999–2005) and then established himself in Geneva. He lectures WTO law at the "Europa-Institut" of the University of Saarland as well as the Law School of the University of Lucerne and publishes frequently on issues of international economic law.

Hans-Joachim Prieß is a partner at Freshfields Bruckhaus Deringer LLP in Berlin, where he advises and represents clients on procurement and trade matters. He worked at the Brussels office of the firm between 1990 and 2000. He holds a doctorate in law from the University of Kiel and an LLM (Indiana).

Tibor Scharf after studies at the Universities of Oxford and Freiburg, began working as a Solicitor (England & Wales) with a London-based international law firm, before joining the European Commission's Directorate-General for Competition's Energy Unit at the end of 1998. In 2002, he moved to the Legal Service, where he has been dealing with trade defence (anti-dumping/anti-subsidy), state aid, and more recently, external relations, with a particular focus on external energy issues and EU–Russia/Central Asia relations. He regularly represents the Commission before the Court of Justice of the EU and has also appeared before the EFTA Court and the WTO (over 150 cases so far). He has widely published, including on anti-dumping.

Evelina Schulz born in 1980, studied International Relations in Wrocław (Poland), Cultural Studies in Frankfurt/Oder (Germany) and completed her education at l'Institut d'Études Politques, Sciences Po, in Paris (France) with a double degree (MA) in International Relations and Marketing. She first worked in financial marketing and banking in Paris (France). From 2006 to 2009, she worked as an assistant to German Member of the European Parliament, Vural Öger. In June 2009, she was recruited by the European Commission following an open competition, to work on Eastern Partnership-related questions within the Directorate-General for External Relations, responsible for the negotiations of the EU–Ukraine Association Agreement. In 2011, she joined the European External Action Service, serving first as Ukraine desk, before taking up the position of desk officer for relations with the United States of America in December 2013 and subsequently as of June 2014 assisting Deputy Secretary-General of the EEAS Maciej Popowski in his tasks. She has published several articles on the EU's enlargement and ENP policy.

Bruno Simma (editor) is part-time Professor of Law at the University of Michigan Law School teaching classes in Ann Arbor. From 2003 to 2012, he served as Judge to the International Court of Justice in The Hague. Bruno was Professor of International and European Community Law at the Ludwig Maximilians University Munich (1973–2003). He has been visiting professor at several European universities and lectured at the Hague Academy of International Law. From 1996 to 2002, Bruno was a member of the United Nations International Law Commission after being on the UN Committee on Economic, Social and Cultural Rights (1987–1996). He is frequently sought as arbitrator in inter-state, foreign investment, international commercial and sports disputes. Bruno holds a degree and a doctorate in law from the University of Innsbruck, Austria.

Rudolf Streinz (editor) is Professor of Public Law and European Law at the Ludwig Maximilians University Munich. He studied law, political science and history and received his doctorate in law in 1981 under supervision of Bruno Simma. In 1987, Rudolf habilitated at the University of Passau under supervision of Michael Schweitzer and was appointed Professor for Public Law, Public International Law and European Law at the University of Bayreuth, in 1989.

Milena Weidenfeller is a lawyer by training and works for the SPD parliamentary group in the German *Bundestag*. Before, she worked as civil servant in the Federal Ministry of Economic Affairs and Energy in Berlin. The area of free trade agreements and the WTO has been her responsibility since 2008.

Gabriela Wermelinger read law at the University of Bern and completed her studies in 2013 with a Master in European and International Law. She was a junior research fellow at the World Trade Institute and has been working on her PhD related to the regime of genetic resources in the law of the sea.

Gunnar Wiegand is Director for Russia, Eastern Partnership, Central Asia, Regional Cooperation and OSCE at the European External Action Service. He was also the EU's Chief Negotiator for the Association Agreements with Moldova, Georgia and Armenia, as well as the Enhanced PCA with Kazakhstan. Gunnar Wiegand holds an MA in International Relations from the Paul H. Nitze School of Advanced International Studies (SAIS) at Johns Hopkins University, Washington DC USA, and a degree in law from the University of Hamburg, Germany. He first met Horst Krenzler as a student of EC Law at the University of Bonn in 1979. In 1985, he began his career at the Institute for European–Latin-American Relations in Madrid (Spain) followed by a position as Deputy Head of Division for Europe at the Friedrich-Naumann Stiftung in Königswinter, Germany, from 1987 to 1990. Since June 1990, he has worked for EU institutions. His first post at the European Commission (Directorate-General External Relations) was that of a Desk Officer for External Aspects of German Unification, where he worked closely with the Director-General for External Relations, Horst Krenzler. From 1991 to 1993, he was Manager of Financial Services Projects at the Technical Assistance to the Newly Independent States Unit (TACIS Programme). In 1994, Gunnar Wiegand became Policy Assistant to Horst Krenzler, when he was the Director-General for External Economic Relations (1994–1997); then in 1997–1999, Deputy Head of Unit for Relations with the United States, followed by Spokesman for External Relations to Commissioner Chris Patten from 1999 to 2002. From December 2002 to 2010, he has held several management posts in the European Commission responsible for the relations with the US and Canada, Russia, for Northern Dimension and Nuclear Safety, and for Eastern Europe, Southern Caucasus and Central Asia. In 1999, Horst Krenzler and Gunnar Wiegand published an article together on EU–US relations: *EU-US Relations: More than Trade Disputes?*, European Foreign Affairs Review 4(2):153–180.

Part I
The Life and Achievements of Horst G. Krenzler

Horst G. Krenzler's Late Academic Career at the Ludwig Maximilians University Munich

Bruno Simma

If in the mid-1990s a student had looked for an exciting place to study European Community and international trade law, exciting, that is, for the quality of what was on offer, he would probably not have chosen to do so in Munich. He would have found a place in which public international law was being taught with what I think was real passion, but as to European Law, the second subject in the curriculum of the Munich Faculty of Law of which I was in charge, I fulfilled my duty of course and probably did a decent job, but I did so without the fire and excitement I felt for the former. Thus, as to what was on offer for our interested student, European Law decidedly ranked second. (Lest there be no misunderstanding, I refer to the times long before Rudolf Streinz moved from Bayreuth to Munich and Community Law thus got its own prominent faculty "representative".)

Then in 1997, Horst Krenzler entered the picture. He was introduced to me by our common friend Meinhard Hilf (who in his own career has been much more successful than I in integrating international law and Community law, also academically). From the first time we met, I found Horst not just impressive, but also representing precisely what Munich was in need of at the time: a high-ranking practitioner of European Community/Union Law able to convey his professional experience to students eager to learn how united Europe works in reality and interrelates with the rest of the world. Horst's activities during the three decades of engaging with Community Law in practice have been described in this *liber amicorum* by other friends and colleagues. At the Munich Law Faculty, due to the need felt to enrich the offerings in the field, it did not take long to arrange for a lectureship, indeed this was done by general acclaim, and Horst took up teaching what he had been responsible for developing during his 30 years in Brussels: the external relations of the European Union, its common foreign and security policy as

B. Simma (✉)
Iran-United States Claims Tribunal, The Hague, The Netherlands
e-mail: judgesimma@gmail.com

C. Herrmann et al. (eds.), *Trade Policy between Law, Diplomacy and Scholarship*, European Yearbook of International Economic Law,
DOI 10.1007/978-3-319-15690-3_1

well as international trade law. Munich students were simply taken by him, by this tall, always impeccably dressed gentleman, who was able to tell them in his quiet but crystal-clear way how Union Law really moves, because he himself had spent his professional life making it work. Horst did so without any touch of the arrogance with which important players from practice all too often condescend to transmit their knowledge to the non-illuminati. Horst combined personal modesty with intellectual sovereignty and charisma. Students and faculty alike were impressed by his commitment to teaching and the vigour with which he went about it. Thus, after a short time (considerably shorter than was the rule), his status was elevated to that of an *Honorarprofessor*, the highest rank that a person entering university teaching from the outside, as it were, is able to reach. If anybody ever deserved this, it was Horst, and I must say that he enjoyed it. And we, the academic community at the Munich Institute of International and European Law, enjoyed participating in his insights, his friendship and generosity.

The occasion at which I came to admire him most was a lecture Horst gave at the University of Michigan Law School in Ann Arbor. Horst spoke about the transatlantic controversy on genetically modified food, at a time when the debate on this topic was particularly hot and emotional, sometimes even hostile. I, too, had found myself caught in it, unable to overcome the (polite, we were after all in Ann Arbor) scepticism of colleagues and students towards the precautionary position defended by Europeans. It took Horst less than one hour of lecturing and discussion to turn the mood of his audience from overt disapproval to reflection, if not appreciation—and to provide me with a glimpse of how effective Horst must have been in the many international negotiations in which he had taken part. Europe had every reason to be grateful to Horst for what he has achieved in its service—but what I wanted to point to in this short contribution were the good reasons for academic European Law in Munich to be grateful for the ways and means by which Horst has contributed to bringing it to life.

Words of Honour in memoriam Horst Günter Krenzler (1933–2012)

Karel De Gucht

History of mankind is made by men and women. The history of European integration is made by great Europeans. Horst Günter Krenzler was amongst them. Let me explain why I think so.

From 2010 to 2014, I assumed the political responsibility for European Trade Policy. Becoming the head of a big administration was not new to me, as I previously headed the Belgian Foreign Office. But being at the helm of a big policy Directorate-General of the European Commission is different. I immediately noticed the high quality of expertise required in-house. From the case-handler to the Director-General: everybody should not only know his file by heart—he or she should also be able to convince Member States, the European Parliament and the public. In short: working in DG Trade is only possible with a great degree of knowledge, expertise and communication skills.

Such a culture cannot be created from scratch. It is growing over time. It must have been nurtured in-house. And here is where we come to Horst Günter Krenzler. When he served as Director-General in the Commission for 12 years since 1984, he was not only doing trade—during his time, he was in charge of the entire external policy of the Commission. That was probably an even more demanding job than today's double-hatted High Representative for Foreign Affairs and Vice President of the Commission for external action.

Krenzler was known to be very versatile man. His legal background allowed him to be sharp and to the point. His academic interest gave him an edge when given creative tasks, such as writing for President Delors a draft of the famous 1993 Copenhagen Criteria for the admission of new Member States in a break of the European Council meeting. His sense of duty gave younger colleagues an orientation, and his emphasis of meritocracy enabled bright talents to take on important tasks in a relatively short time after having entered the Commission.

K. De Gucht (✉)

C. Herrmann et al. (eds.), *Trade Policy between Law, Diplomacy and Scholarship*,
European Yearbook of International Economic Law,
DOI 10.1007/978-3-319-15690-3_2

Against that backdrop, I am happy to write a few words in this *Gedächtnisschrift*. When I walk in the corridors of the seventh floor of the Charlemagne Building, where the senior management of DG is located today, there are pictures of all Director-Generals and Commissioners of Trade since 1957. Sometimes you cannot be sure which function a person actually performed. Some Director-Generals had more influence over the direction of the common commercial policy than their political masters. Some Commissioners have tried to exercise their political role in a more dominant way. And sometimes, Commissioners and Director-Generals work hand-in-hand knowing that there is a division of tasks between political guidance and administrative implementation with a certain room for flexibility. When I look at the picture of Horst Günter Krenzler, I see him intuitively as the prototype of an excellent senior manager with political wisdom, whose *Lebenswerk* I pay my greatest respect to.

Horst Günter Krenzler (1933–2012): A Life for Europe

Jürgen Elvert

This brief biographical sketch of Horst Günter Krenzler's life is to a large extent relying on an interview he gave me on 20 August 2010 in his Munich apartment. This interview was part of my research related to a project on the history of the European Commission (1973–1986). Hence, this paper will largely focus on Krenzler's professional career within the European institutions and for the European Commission. The text of the interview is currently being prepared for disclosure by the Historical Archives of the European Union; it is not yet publicly available. The quotations refer to the author's copy of the interview.

Horst Günter Krenzler was born on 26 March 1933 in Wuppertal, an industrial city of the Bergisches Land east of Cologne and south of the Ruhr district. As a 10-year-old boy, he there experienced one of the first allied air raids of the Rhineland. With a distance of 67 years, Krenzler clearly remembered running through burning streets—tar being set on fire by firebombs, destroyed houses to the left and to the right, his parents' house included. Having lost nearly everything in the air raid, the Krenzler family moved to Hinterzarten to escape the war. However, even in the idyllic Black Forest the war was going on, as Freiburg increasingly was among the targets of air raids and Krenzler again witnessed the destructive power of bombs, as well as of anti-aircraft guns destroying allied bombers in the air, which then crashed nearby.

It thus can hardly surprise that Horst Günter Krenzler considered the peace-building effects as the central *raison d'être* of European integration, followed by the necessity of economic reconciliation as prerequisite for social and societal

J. Elvert (✉)
Jean-Monnet-Lehrstuhl für Europäische Geschichte, Historisches Institut, Universität zu Köln, Gronewaldstraße 2, 50931 Köln, Germany

Aarhus Institute of Advanced Studies (AIAS), Aarhus University, Høegh-Guldbergs Gade 6B, Building 1632, 8000 Aarhus C, Denmark
e-mail: juergen.elvert@uni-koeln.de

C. Herrmann et al. (eds.), *Trade Policy between Law, Diplomacy and Scholarship*, European Yearbook of International Economic Law,
DOI 10.1007/978-3-319-15690-3_3

stability as well as regaining political influence for Europe on the global stage. Growing up in the French zone of occupation, Krenzler took French as the first foreign language at school and thus gained a linguistic competence which later should become important for his professional career in the European Commission. However, he was not a born civil servant in European institutions, although international affairs interested him at an early stage. Having studied law in Freiburg, Munich and Bonn he spent his legal clerkship to a large extent abroad and visited summer courses at the London School of Economics and received practical training at the Paris Chamber of Commerce. At the same time he did a doctor's degree in International Law at the Max Planck Institute for Comparative Public Law and International Law in Heidelberg under supervision of Günther Jaenicke and Hermann Mosler and subsequently received his practising certificate at a commercial law firm in Mannheim.

As career opportunities for newcomers on the vocational field for commercial lawyers were not very promising in the mid-1960s, Krenzler decided to do the *concours* at the European Atomic Energy Community, to be put on the waiting list for jobs with the European institutions. As a commercial lawyer, Krenzler was interested in working for Commissioner Hans von der Groeben, who in the 1960s was working hard to establish new European competition law. However, he learned from Manfred Caspari, then deputy head of the von der Groeben Cabinet, that competition law was already considered a German domain in the commission. Caspari recommended to opt for international law instead, as in 1965 the negotiations of Austrian association to the EEC were conducted and many delicate legal problems had to be solved in this context.

Against this background, Horst Günter Krenzler entered the Commission as *auxiliaire* in 1965. The frame-conditions of his entry were anything but promising, as at the same time, European institutions suffered under the impact of the Empty Chair Crisis. One of its consequences was that the Commission was not able to appoint civil servants on a long-term basis; instead newcomers had to content themselves with only scantly remunerated 6-month contracts. Krenzler was not put off by this, but considered his employment by the Commission as a possibility to gain professional experience in a stimulating international environment, only to be promoted to A7 less than 2 years later, in the wake of the Luxemburg Compromise when things went back to normalcy in the European institutions. Retrospectively, Krenzler remained a supporter of Walter Hallstein's management of the Empty Chair Crisis. Even from a distance of nearly 50 years, he considered the EEC Commission's first president and his merits in institutionalising the Commission next to Jacques Delors' contributions to the European integration process. Krenzler's area of operations was attached to Commissioner Jean Rey, whom he also gave kudos as a veritable European statesman, always loyal to his staff.

Under Rey's aegis, Krenzler became member of a team of experts which had to deal with the negotiations between the EEC and the EFTA-countries and was in charge of implementing the Greek and Turkish association-treaties. Among his immediate superiors was the economist, Paolo Cecchini, who was in charge of the relations between the EEC and EFTA, later to become the author of the Cecchini Report.

Within 10 years, Horst Günter Krenzler climbed the Commission's career ladder from A7 to A4. The latter stage he reached in the Dahrendorf Cabinet, which he entered as member of cabinet only to be promoted to deputy head of cabinet a short while later. For Krenzler, this phase of his career was a very stimulating time, because Dahrendorf probably was the most intelligent and stimulating person he ever met in his life, although he strongly disagreed with the Commissioner's intergovernmental notions concerning the European *finalité politique*. Times became especially tough when Commissioner Dahrendorf anonymously published two essays in "Die ZEIT", drawing a picture of the present and future European Community, which met the approval neither of the Commission nor of the majority of Dahrendorf's staff.

In 1975, Krenzler was promoted to A3 and created the Japan Department within his directorate-general. Although in charge of the Commission's economic relations towards Japan, his competences in economic and competition law were also required on his new post, as the successful Far East export nation tried to push its way into the European market. Krenzler and his small team were in charge of negotiating new trade relations between the EC and Japan, and even convinced the strong Japanese competitor to accept certain export restrictions with regard to car exports. Besides this, the Krenzler team developed two initiatives. The Executive Training Programme was designed for young European industrialists who wanted to do business with Japan, as it provided for special information and language courses on Japanese culture and society, as well as internships in Japan. The target of Exprom, the second initiative, was to promote European business interests in Japan, and its Tokyo office soon became a hub between Japanese and European industrialists.

The expertise Krenzler had gained by running the Japanese department laid the ground for his next post, also A3-level, when he, in 1977, became head of the Commission's much larger North American department. His department's main task in these years had been to ease the strained EC–US relations which emerged out of the mutual allegation of economic protectionism, primarily in the agricultural sector.

As a leading European civil servant with solid expertise in economic and competition law, and a long history in the Commission's external relations, the next steps of Krenzler's professional career were somewhat predetermined: director for international negotiations in the industrial sector and Deputy Secretary-General of the Commission. The latter post was among the most exhausting jobs the Commission could offer in these days as part of it was to represent the Commission at COREPER as well as within the EPC-scheme (European Political Cooperation, forerunner of the Common Foreign and Security Policy). Although Krenzler himself looked back at these years with mixed feelings—being a challenging and draining job at the same time—he was very much aware that he, as a leading official of the Commission, was not only a front-ranking witness of a very important period in European integration history, but also an active designer of Europe's future shape.

Having been promoted to Deputy Secretary-General at the instigation of Étienne Davignon, he became the right hand of Émile Noël, the Commission's legendary and long-standing mastermind, director and brain. As Noël had preferred another deputy, he gave Krenzler a rather frosty welcome on the occasion of the latter's inaugural visit. However, as the newly appointed deputy secretary general had a long-standing experience in external relations and political cooperation, the two managed to overcome their differences. Noël continued to focus on community affairs, whereas Krenzler devoted himself to European political cooperation. By dealing successfully with a topic Noël obviously disliked, the new deputy slowly secured the Secretary-General's confidence. When Krenzler left this post in 1985 to become Director-General of the Commission's external relations, they parted as close friends.

In the first half of the 1980s, Horst Günter Krenzler had also closely co-operated with Jacques Delors. So his appraisal of the latter's personality and merits for the further development of European structures and institutions—the Single European Act and, of course, the Treaty of Maastricht, being the two highlights of his terms of duty—can hardly surprise. However, Krenzler, too, had left clearly visible traces. When Noël was due to retire, the German Foreign Secretary tried to persuade him to succeed Noël as secretary general of the Commission. Krenzler however was aware that this post was closely linked to that of the Commission's president and that his scope for independent action was severely limited. Therefore, he tried to ignore the signals from Bonn. However, as the Federal government was strongly interested in having a German promoted to the post of secretary general of some international or supranational institution, it was, for a while, a rather delicate situation. The deadlock was only solved at the Fontainebleau Summit of 1984, when Prime Minister Thatcher, along with her European rebate, managed to persuade the other heads of state, especially the French president, that the next secretary general of the European Commission should be British. So David Williamson succeeded Emile Noël whereas Horst Günter Krenzler became Director-General of DG 1—Foreign Relations, a post he should hold until his retirement in 1996.

His appointment to the top position of his professional career fell during a crucial phase of European history—the enacting of the Single European Act, and thus establishment of the European internal market and the preparation of the Maastricht Treaty, have to be mentioned here, as well as the Chernobyl crisis and its impact on European economy, the fall of the Iron Curtain in 1989/1990 and the subsequent establishment of economic and diplomatic relations with those former Warsaw Bloc countries opting for closer ties with the European Union. And it should also not be forgotten that he was also responsible for the third or "EFTA enlargement" of the European Union, as Austria, Finland and Sweden entered the EU in 1995. At the Copenhagen Summit of 1993, when the European Council debated the criteria for eastern enlargement, Krenzler became actively involved in policy making. In a conference break, he was requested by Jacques Delors to rapidly draft some criteria for the Central and Eastern European candidate countries: one should deal with political aspects, another with economy, a third with the *acquis communautaire* and the forth with the Union's absorption capacity. Although the Council of course modified the text which was drafted by Krenzler and his team at very short notice, the General Director of DG 1 can be taken as primary author of the Copenhagen criteria. This short anecdote may be taken as an illuminating example of how European policy making is done once in a while. And taking the conditions behind them into account it can also hardly surprise that Horst Günter Krenzler was not at all content with the way the Union managed Eastern enlargement later on.

In 1996, at the age of 63, Krenzler decided to take early retirement. The reasons for this decision were manifold. After 15 years in European top positions, he was physically worn down. Furthermore the communication between him and Commissioner Leon Brittan did not satisfy him, especially as some members of Brittan's Cabinet increasingly tried to interfere in Krenzler's areas of operation. Instead of having constant battles with a young and ambitious member of the Brittan Cabinet, who should later become Secretary General of the Commission, Krenzler decided to go back to his roots and teach international law at Munich University. Later on, he joined a large international economic law firm where he could apply his original core competences as well as his experiences gained through decades' work for the European Commission, if now in a global context.

Part II
Developments in International Trade Policy

Towards a More Balanced International Investment Law 2.0?

Marc Bungenberg

Introduction

With the entry into force of the Treaty of Lisbon,[1] the European Union (EU) has gained new competences in the area of international investment law and politics.[2] With a global economic weight equal to one quarter of global GDP and nearly half of global foreign direct investment (FDI) outflows,[3] the EU's potential in investment negotiations since the transfer of competence is readily evident. Together with the other two economic heavyweights, China and the US, it should be possible for the EU to give international investment law the necessary new face in reacting to partly reasoned critique; at the same time it is necessary to discuss the topic in a more objective way, at least in the case of publicly financed media as well as politicians.

The (new) EU competence laid down in Article 207 TFEU as part of the common commercial policy[4] includes an external treaty-making power in the field of foreign investment. The EU has the exclusive competence to negotiate

[1] Treaty of Lisbon Amending the Treaty on European Union and the Treaty Establishing the European Community, signed 13 December 2007, [2007] OJ C 306/1.

[2] See on this, for example, Bungenberg (2009), p. 195; Bungenberg (2010), p. 123.

[3] UNCTAD (2012), p. 85.

[4] Article 207(1) Consolidated version of The Treaty on the Functioning of the European Union, [2008] OJ C 115/47:

> The common commercial policy shall be based on uniform principles, particularly with regard to changes in tariff rates, the conclusion of tariff and trade agreements relating to trade in goods and services, and the commercial aspects of intellectual property, foreign direct investment, the achievement of uniformity in measures of liberalisation, export policy and measures to protect trade such as those to be taken in the event of dumping or

M. Bungenberg (✉)
Europa-Institut, Saarland University, 66041 Saarbrücken, Germany
e-mail: bungenberg@europainstitut.de

C. Herrmann et al. (eds.), *Trade Policy between Law, Diplomacy and Scholarship*, European Yearbook of International Economic Law,
DOI 10.1007/978-3-319-15690-3_4

and conclude "stand alone investment agreements"—comparable to those international investment agreements that were concluded "before" (the entry into force of the Treaty of Lisbon on 1 December 2009) by the EU Member States—as well as Free Trade Agreements (FTAs) comprising chapters on investment law. The EU is currently[5] negotiating stand-alone bilateral investment treaties (BITs) with China[6] and Myanmar,[7] as well as investment chapters as part of larger FTAs with India,[8] Japan,[9] the United States,[10] Libya,[11] Egypt, Jordan, Morocco and Tunisia,[12] Malay-

---

subsidies. The common commercial policy shall be conducted in the context of the principles and objectives of the Union's external action.

See also Bungenberg (2010), p. 123; Chaisse (2012), p. 51; Dimopoulos (2011); Hoffmeister and Ünüvar (2013), p. 57; Bungenberg (2009), p. 195; Bungenberg (2011), p. 116; Bungenberg (2011), p. 133; Bungenberg et al. (2011); Bungenberg and Herrmann (2013); Bungenberg and Reinisch (2014); Burgstaller (2009), p. 181; Calamita (2012), p. 301.

[5] The Overview of FTA and other Trade Negotiations of the Commission shows the current state of negotiations of international agreements currently negotiated by the EU, available at http://trade.ec.europa.eu/doclib/docs/2006/december/tradoc_118238.pdf.

[6] European Commission, Press Release, MEMO/13/913 of 18 October 2013, EU Investment Negotiations with China and ASEAN, available at http://europa.eu/rapid/press-release_MEMO-13-913_en.htm; European Commission, Press Release, IP/14/33 of 20 January 2014, EU and China Begin Investment Talks, available at http://europa.eu/rapid/press-release_IP-14-33_en.htm.

[7] European Commission, Press Release, IP/14/285 of 20 March 2014, EU and Myanmar/Burma to Negotiate an Investment Protection Agreement, available at http://europa.eu/rapid/press-release_IP-14-285_en.htm.

[8] European Commission, Memo, The EU's Bilateral Investment Agreements—Where Are We?, MEMO/13/915 of 18 October 2013, p. 3, available at http://europa.eu/rapid/press-release_MEMO-13-915_en.htm; see also http://ec.europa.eu/trade/policy/countries-and-regions/countries/india/.

[9] European Commission, Memo, A Free Trade Agreement between the EU and Japan, MEMO/13/283 of 25 March 2013, available at http://europa.eu/rapid/press-release_MEMO-13-283_en.htm; European Commission, Memo, First Round of EU–Japan Trade Talks A Success, MEMO/13/348 of 19 April 2013, available at http://europa.eu/rapid/press-release_MEMO-13-348_en.htm.

[10] European Commission, Press Release, IP/13/224 of 12 March 2013, European Commission Fires Starting Gun for EU–US Trade Talks, available at http://europa.eu/rapid/press-release_IP-13-224_en.htm; European Commission, Memo, European Union and United States to Launch Negotiations for a Transatlantic Trade and Investment Partnership, MEMO/13/95 of 13 February 2013, available at http://europa.eu/rapid/press-release_MEMO-13-95_en.htm; see also the Directives for the TTIP-Negotiation http://data.consilium.europa.eu/doc/document/ST-11103-2013-DCL-1/en/pdf.

[11] See http://ec.europa.eu/trade/policy/countries-and-regions/countries/libya/.

[12] See European Commission, Press Release, IP/11/1545 of 14 December 2011, EU Agrees to Start Trade Negotiations with Egypt, Jordan, Morocco and Tunisia, available at http://europa.eu/rapid/press-release_IP-11-1545_en.htm; see also for Morocco European Commission, Press Release, Joint Press Statement on the EU–Morocco Negotiations of 9 July 2014, available at http://trade.ec.europa.eu/doclib/press/index.cfm?id=1120&title=Joint-press-statement-on-the-EU-Morocco-negotiations.

sia,[13] Vietnam[14] and Thailand.[15] Negotiations with Canada[16] and Singapore[17] have already been successfully concluded. After the current system of international investment law, as well as the recent inclusion of investment law in broader FTAs, have faced strong criticism from different sides, as will be summarized in the next section, the EU as a new actor in the area of shaping international investment policy and politics seems to take an innovative approach to international investment law with the clear intention of promoting a more balanced system in conformity with an international rule of law. This contribution will discuss these developments before concluding with a brief outlook on the future of international investment law and the role of the European Union in this development.

Criticisms in Regard to the Current System and Opportunity for a Restart

The current approach in regard to international investment law is "under fire". Not only is the legal basis of international investment law fragmented with more than 3,200 International Investment Agreements (IIAs),[18] out of which EU Member States have concluded some 1,500, but it is also seen as an unbalanced and overly investor-friendly system. Some of the criticisms are that multinational enterprises as investors can initiate claims against sovereign states in front of international investment tribunals. On these, biased arbitrators would generally proliferate: one day, they would act as counsel, and the next preside over a tribunal. It is argued that the tribunals, even though deciding over public interests and the conformity of national law as well as other public measures with international investment

[13] European Commission, Press Release, EU and Malaysia Launch Negotiations for Free Trade Agreement of 5 October 2010, available at http://trade.ec.europa.eu/doclib/docs/2010/october/tradoc_146696.pdf.

[14] European Commission, Press Release, IP/12/689 of June 2012, EU and Vietnam Negotiations for a Comprehensive Free Trade Agreement, available at http://europa.eu/rapid/press-release_IP-12-689_en.htm.

[15] European Commission, Press Release, EU and Thailand Conclude Second Round of Negotiations for a Comprehensive Free Trade Agreement of 20 September 2013, available at http://trade.ec.europa.eu/doclib/docs/2013/september/tradoc_151780.pdf; Consolidated CETA Text, published on 26 September 2014, available at http://trade.ec.europa.eu/doclib/docs/2014/september/tradoc_152806.pdf.

[16] European Commission, Press Release, IP/13/972 of 18 October 2013, EU and Canada Conclude Negotiations on Trade Deal, available at http://europa.eu/rapid/press-release_IP-13-972_en.htm.

[17] European Commission, Press Release, IP/12/1380 of 16 December 2012, EU and Singapore Agree on Landmark Trade Deal, available at http://europa.eu/rapid/press-release_IP-12-1380_en.htm; European Commission, Press Release, IP/13/849 of 20 September 2013, EU and Singapore Present Text of the Comprehensive Free Trade Agreement, available at http://europa.eu/rapid/press-release_IP-13-849_en.htm.

[18] UNCTAD (2014), p. 114.

protection standards laid down in international investment agreements, do not have any democratic legitimisation. Furthermore, these protection standards would be too broad and would leave too much discretion to the arbitrators. Indeed, IIAs concluded by EU Member States in particular rarely foresee exception clauses or the right to regulate, and thus because of the aforementioned standards that are very favourable to investors, such IIAs would limit sovereign states in their (sovereign) right to regulate. Especially in investor-state dispute settlement (ISDS), a lack of transparency would exist, as well as no appellate system and no coherence in the jurisprudence of arbitral tribunals. Most of these points have been discussed throughout the past decade, but now with various negotiations under way receive new attention. From an economic point of view, it is discussed if international investment agreements do matter and attract foreign investments or are irrelevant and are thus questioned in their entirety.[19]

The aim of this contribution is not to discuss the above mentioned criticisms in detail, but to show that now is the time for a restart in international investment law and politics. It is not only to be noted that EU Member States are not allowed to negotiate or conclude new BITs any more, but with the EU as a new actor in this *matière* of investment protection, it is reacting both to existing deficits, and to partly or wholly unfounded criticism.

Possibility of a "Restart": The EU as a New Actor in International Investment Politics

The criticisms in regard to the currently existing system of international investment law exist irrespective of the EU having stepped on the "scene" of international investment politics. Nevertheless, the "new" constitutional mandate of the external economic relations of the EU more or less force especially the European Commission to react to existing critique when shaping the EU approach in this field of international economic law. Not only has the Lisbon Treaty transferred the competences in the area of foreign direct investments from the EU Member States to the EU itself as an exclusive competence[20] now being part of the Common Commercial Policy in Article 207 Treaty on the Functioning of the EU (TFEU),[21] but at the same

[19] See, for example, Hallward-Driemeier (2003), p. 21, available at http://elibrary.worldbank.org/doi/pdf/10.1596/1813-9450-3121; Tobin and Rose-Ackermann (2005), p. 22, available at http://ssrn.com/abstract=557121; Neumayer and Spess (2005), pp. 1567 (1568), available at http://eprints.lse.ac.uk/627/1/World_Dev_%28BITs%29.pdf.

[20] See Article 3 TFEU.

[21] The CCP is extended explicitly to:

> . . . the conclusion of . . . trade agreements relating to trade in . . . services, and the commercial aspects of intellectual property, foreign direct investment, the achievement of uniformity in measures of liberalization, export policy and measures to protect trade such as those to be taken in the event of dumping or subsidies.

time the European Parliament has the power to "control" all measures taken and agreements negotiated and to be concluded in this area,[22] as well as linking the exercise of all competences to the widely discussed Article 21 Treaty on the European Union (TEU).[23] These modifications led to a change of paradigm in the European external relations in general as well as in EU investment law in specific.

The European Parliament today is an important actor in the field of EU external relations. The Lisbon Treaty significantly strengthened the role of the European Parliament[24]: it now has to give its parliamentary consent in *de facto* almost all cases of new agreements. The Commission is legally obliged to provide the European Parliament with information on the conduct of the negotiations, and to report regularly to the Parliament's International Trade Committee (INTA). To exercise an influence on important trade negotiations, INTA has developed a practice of drafting reports on its own initiative, indicating its priorities during the negotiations.[25] The Parliament regularly announces *inter alia* that it will give its consent only to agreements containing a human rights clause, and calls on the Commission to include far-reaching social and environmental clauses and standards in bilateral and regional trade agreements. Soon after the entry into force of the Lisbon Treaty, in February 2010, the European Parliament decided not to give its consent to the conclusion of the Agreement on the processing and transfer of financial messaging data from the EU to the United States for purposes of the Terrorist Finance Tracking Program.[26] Another example for this is the EU–China BIT negotiations, in relation to which the European Parliament adopted a long "wish-list" with topics it wants to be covered by the agreement, ranging from the inclusion of the so-called Santiago Principles on sovereign wealth funds, and the insertion of more Corporate Social Responsibility and Labour Rights, to broader promotion of sustainable development and environmental protection.[27] This wish list also stresses the explicit requirement that the CCP shall serve the principles and objectives of the EU's external action: support for democracy and the rule of law as well as the promotion of sustainable development.

---

[22] See Krajewski (2013), p. 67; Bungenberg (2015).

[23] See on this, for example, Vedder (2013), p. 115.

[24] On the absence of Parliament in the formal process of concluding trade agreements before the Lisbon Treaty, see Quintin (1975), p. 211; Maresceau (1993), pp. 3 (9); Flaesch-Mougin (1993), p. 383; Bosse-Platière (2002), p. 527.

[25] Devuyst (2013), pp. 259 (303); Passos and Marquardt (2007), pp. 875 (904).

[26] European Parliament, Legislative Resolution of 11 February 2010 on the proposal for a Council decision on the conclusion of the Agreement between the European Union and the United States of America on the processing and transfer of Financial Messaging Data from the European Union to the United States for purposes of the Terrorist Finance Tracking Program (05305/1/2010 REV 1 C7-0004/2010 2009/0190(NLE)), [2010] OJ C 341/100; Passos (2010), pp. 269 (285–286); Passos (2011/2013), pp. 49 (52–53), available at http://www.asser.nl/upload/documents/772011_51358CLEER%20WP%202011-3%20-%20KOUTRAKOS.pdf.

[27] European Parliament, Resolution of 9 October 2013 on the EU–China negotiations for a bilateral investment agreement (2013/2674(RSP)), available at http://www.europarl.europa.eu/sides/getDoc.do?pubRef=-//EP//TEXT+TA+P7-TA-2013-0411+0+DOC+XML+V0//EN.

A new conjunction of the CCP with other political objectives of the EU, such as environmental protection and human rights, thus politicises EU investment and trade policy as this is brought under the same external action heading as other elements of EU external policy, and is therefore to be conducted within the context of the framework of the general principles and objectives of the EU's external action.[28] The broadly drafted principles and objectives of Article 21 TEU include support for democracy, the rule of law and human rights, along with more specific aims such as sustainable economic, environmental and social development, as well as good global governance and improvement of the sustainable management of global resources. Taken together, it is this increased role of the European Parliament connected with the politicisation of the entire common commercial policy which constitutes a great potential impact of the Lisbon Treaty on the new EU international investment policy.[29] In its Resolution of 6 April 2011, the European Parliament has thus emphasised that as a result of the transfer of FDI competence, the future European investment policy must meet "the EU's broader economic interests and external policy objectives."[30] It has further called on the Commission to protect the contracting parties' right to regulate[31] and to include social and environmental clauses[32] as well as a reference to the OECD Guidelines for Multinational Enterprises[33] and a provision on corporate social responsibility.[34] Thus, it is the intention of the European Parliament to use international investment agreements as a tool to promote non-economic objectives, too.

[28] Article 205 TFEU explicitly states that the CCP "shall be guided by the principles, pursue the objectives and be conducted in accordance with the general provisions" laid down in Article 21 TEU.

[29] See on this, for example, Devuyst (2013), pp. 259 (299).

[30] European Parliament, Resolution of 6 April 2011 on the future European international investment policy (2010/2203(INI)), para. 1, available at http://www.europarl.europa.eu/sides/getDoc.do?pubRef=-//EP//TEXT+TA+P7-TA-2011-0141+0+DOC+XML+V0//EN.

[31] European Parliament, Resolution of 6 April 2011 on the future European international investment policy (2010/2203(INI)), paras. 23-26, available at http://www.europarl.europa.eu/sides/getDoc.do?pubRef=-//EP//TEXT+TA+P7-TA-2011-0141+0+DOC+XML+V0//EN.

[32] European Parliament, Resolution of 6 April 2011 on the future European international investment policy (2010/2203(INI)), paras. 27-30, available at http://www.europarl.europa.eu/sides/getDoc.do?pubRef=-//EP//TEXT+TA+P7-TA-2011-0141+0+DOC+XML+V0//EN.

[33] European Parliament, Resolution of 6 April 2011 on the future European international investment policy (2010/2203(INI)), para. 27, available at http://www.europarl.europa.eu/sides/getDoc.do?pubRef=-//EP//TEXT+TA+P7-TA-2011-0141+0+DOC+XML+V0//EN.

[34] European Parliament, Resolution of 6 April 2011 on the future European international investment policy (2010/2203(INI)), para. 28, available at http://www.europarl.europa.eu/sides/getDoc.do?pubRef=-//EP//TEXT+TA+P7-TA-2011-0141+0+DOC+XML+V0//EN.

Reaction I: A More Transparent Approach by Public Hearings?

One of the biggest issues of the past decade has been the stronger engagement of civil society in the globalisation discussion in general, as well as in the conclusion of international agreements specifically.[35] In regard to the latter aspect, it at first seemed that only the multilateral negotiations of, for example, the WTO drew public attention, especially from NGOs such as Attac and others, whereas bilateral agreements (differently than the negotiation of the Multilateral Agreement on Investment (MAI) in the nineties) in the areas of trade or investment were rarely discussed at all outside the directly affected industries. The FTA with South-Korea did not get any attention during negotiations, and the Comprehensive Economic and Trade Agreement (CETA) with Canada was only discovered as a "hot issue" when negotiations were already more or less concluded.

Unlike earlier negotiation of FTAs, the Transatlantic Trade and Investment Partnership (TTIP) with the USA received maximum attention from the media and opposing civil society groups, which led to strange reactions of the German Minister for Economic Affairs and Energy and the German *Bundesrat*,[36] even at already an early stage in negotiations. The Ministry for Economic Affairs and Energy not only set up a TTIP Advisory Council, which is lacking any know-how in regard to international investment law in particular, as well as international economics in general, but also openly opposed an ISDS mechanism in the TTIP, arguing that such a mechanism is not necessary between countries following the rule of law, such as the EU or the US. This might be seen as a violation of Article 4 paragraph 3 TEU, which stipulates the responsibility of the EU Member States to support the EU during the negotiation of international agreements[37]—even more so after having given a mandate to the Commission that also comprises negotiations of an ISDS mechanism.[38] In Germany, the *Bundesrat* also discussed the TTIP negotiations, and adopted a resolution which opposed investment arbitration in the treaty and favoured legal recourse in the national state courts, stating that "[o]n this point,

[35] See, for example, Bund für Umwelt- und Naturschutz Deutschland e.V. (BUND), Wem nützt das transatlantische Freihandelsabkommen (TTIP)?, available at http://www.bund.net/themen_und_projekte/landwirtschaft/zukunft/freihandelsabkommen/; see also attac, http://www.attac.de/ttip.

[36] See Deutscher Bundesrat, Entschließung des Bundesrates anlässlich des öffentlichen Konsultationsverfahrens der Europäischen Kommission über die Modalitäten eines Investitionsschutzabkommens mit Investor-Staat-Schiedsgerichtsverfahren im Rahmen der Verhandlungen über eine Transatlantische Handels- und Investitionspartnerschaft zwischen der EU und den USA, BR-Drs. 295/14, 2 July 2014.

[37] See on this especially Schwichtenberg (2013).

[38] See, for example, the Canada-mandate, available at http://www.s2bnetwork.org/themes/eu-investment-policy/eu-documents/text-of-the-mandates.html.

the *Bundesrat* views itself as being in line with the opinion of the Federal Government."[39]

The European Commission itself reacted to the increasing public pressure—especially in regard to including ISDS in the TTIP—by suspending negotiations on this issue and initiating a public hearing[40]:

> The European Commission is consulting the public in the EU on a possible approach to investment protection and ISDS in the TTIP. The proposed approach contains a series of innovative elements that the EU proposes using as the basis for the TTIP negotiations. The key issue on which we are consulting is whether the EU's proposed approach for TTIP achieves the right balance between protecting investors and safeguarding the EU's right and ability to regulate in the public interest.

Thus, even though the title of the public consultation seems to indicate that the focus is on ISDS, in reality almost the entire breadth of international investment law is opened up for discussion and statements by the Commission. Furthermore, it can be remarked that most questions are also addressed in the investment chapter of the CETA with Canada that is given as a reference in the consultation.

Reaction II: The New EU Approach

To evaluate the new EU approach, it is important to summarise briefly the current situation that some EU Member States are trying to preserve, irrespective of the criticisms mentioned above,[41] before analysing the first publicly available text's indication of the new EU investment policy approach.

Different IIA Approaches in the Past

In, for example, German and Dutch IIAs, so-called "Gold Standards" are used: clear standards of investor protection with short wording and no or only few exemptions.[42] These rather short agreements—approximately 12 articles on 5–7 pages in total—in general mention neither sustainable development nor protection of human rights and the environment. Also they foresee only limited transparency of the

---

[39] See more at: http://www.disputeresolutiongermany.com/2014/07/upper-chamber-of-german-parliament-against-investment-arbitration-in-useu-ttip/#sthash.yh65pHOO.dpuf.

[40] European Commission, Online Public Consultation on Investment Protection and Investor-to-state Dispute Settlement (ISDS) in the Transatlantic Trade and Investment Partnership Agreement (TTIP), http://trade.ec.europa.eu/consultations/index.cfm?consul_id=179.

[41] See in this regard Braun (2011), p. 95; Lavranos (2013), p. 2, available at http://ssrn.com/abstract=2226979.

[42] See on the German Model BIT, for example, Dolzer and Kim (2013), p. 289, and on the more "European Approach" Gaffney (2015), § 11.

entire ISDS system and contain no provisions on market access. Due to the former distribution of competences between the European Community and its Member States, FTAs concluded by the EC did not include chapters investment protection, but on market access of investments,[43] the latter chapters being based on the so-called EU investment platform ("EU Minimum Platform on Investment").[44]

Agreements concluded by the US or Canada ("North American approach") differ from this European approach in various ways. North American agreements, or chapters of broader FTAs (US as well as Canadian FTAs include chapters on investment protection), foresee articles on pre-establishment as well as on post-establishment protection standards, and also cover the question of market access.[45] Furthermore, these agreements contain very detailed provisions with explanations and limitations of the material scope of application of certain standards in the agreements, and are often more than 30 pages long. Just like the BITs concluded by Member States of the European Union, they also foresee ISDS.

Content and Crucial Issues of Future EU IIAs

As Karel de Gucht pointed out in the Parliamentary Hearings in January 2010 before being appointed Commissioner for Trade, "[i]nvestment is a completely new competence for DG Trade. It is a very important enlargement of its competences as it is, of course, part of the trade scenario." Thus, the Commission has, since the entry into force of the Lisbon Treaty and together with the European Parliament, worked intensively on shaping this new EU policy. In July 2010, the Commission adopted a Policy Communication, entitled "Towards a Comprehensive European

[43] See, for example, the Free Trade Agreement between the European Union and its Member States, of the one part, and the Republic of Korea, of the other part, signed on 6 October 2010, provisionally applied since 1 July 2011, [2011] OJ L 127/6; the Agreement establishing an association between the European Community and its Member States, of the one part, and the Republic of Chile, of the other part, signed on 18 November 2002 (entry into force 1 February 2003), [2002] OJ L 352/1; the Economic Partnership Agreement between the CARIFORUM States, of the one part, and the European Community and its Member States, of the other part, signed 15 October 2008 (10 December 2009 by Haiti; entry into force: applied provisionally from 29 December 2008), [2008] OJ L 289I/1.

[44] The leaked document of a preliminary document on which the minimum platform on investment was based is available at http://www.iisd.org/pdf/2006/itn_ecom.pdf; see on the minimum platform for example Maydell (2007), p. 73; Klamert and Maydell (2008), pp. 493 (511 et seq.); for the revisited version of the Minimum Platform on Investment, see Council Document 7242/09, Limited, of 6 March 2009.

[45] See on this, for example, Newcombe (2015), § 12.

International Investment Policy".[46] Other important official documents are the Council Conclusions of 25 October 2010[47] and the European Parliament's Resolution of 6 April 2011,[48] as well as a "blueprint" adopted together with the US setting up standards of international investment law for the twenty-first century.[49] The first examples of a possible wording of EU investments chapters can be found in the different leaked texts of the CETA between the EU and Canada.[50] In the following section, examples for the positive and dynamic evolution of international investment law are given; it should be noted that this can only be a brief selection of crucial issues and is by no means exhaustive. The discussion here follows the general layout of international investment agreements (objectives, scope, standards and dispute settlement), but then also touches upon the newer topic of including "other issues".

Objectives

In the different published documents as well as in the leaked but not officially published mandates, the objectives for future EU international investment agreements were enumerated as *inter alia*: the maximisation of protection for European investors, the promotion of European standards of protection, the maximisation of Europe's attractiveness as a destination for foreign investments, the establishment of a level playing field for different economic actors and the promotion of non-economic objectives.

[46] European Commission, Communication, Towards a Comprehensive European International Investment Policy, COM(2010)343 final of 7 July 2010, p. 4, available at http://trade.ec.europa.eu/doclib/docs/2011/may/tradoc_147884.pdf.

[47] Council of the European Union, Conclusions on a Comprehensive European International Investment Policy, 3041st Foreign Affairs Council Meeting, Luxembourg, 25 October 2010, available at http://www.consilium.europa.eu/uedocs/cms_data/docs/pressdata/EN/foraff/117328.pdf.

[48] European Parliament, Resolution of 6 April 2011 on the future European international investment policy (2010/2203(INI)), available at http://www.europarl.europa.eu/sides/getDoc.do?pubRef=-//EP//TEXT+TA+P7-TA-2011-0141+0+DOC+XML+V0//EN.

[49] European Commission, Press Release, IP/12/356 of 10 April 2012, EU and US Adopt Blueprint for Open and Stable Investment Climates, available at http://europa.eu/rapid/press-release_IP-12-356_en.htm?locale=en.

[50] On the negotiations with Canada see Lévesque (2013), p. 121; see also Council Negotiating Directives (Canada, India and Singapore), 12 September 2011, available at http://www.bilaterals.org/?eu-negotiating-mandates-on&lang=en as well as at http://www.s2bnetwork.org/%20themes/eu-investment-policy/eu-documents/text-of-the-mandates.html.

Scope of Application and Market Access

The determination of the scope of application in future EU IIAs seems more or less to build upon the approach taken by different Member States of the EU, but at the same time include concrete answers to widely discussed problems.[51] The definition of investment follows the asset-based approach, treaty shopping via shell companies will be broadly excluded, and in cases of double nationality of natural persons, the principle of effective nationality applies ("dominant and effective nationality"). Sovereign wealth funds as well as State Owned Enterprises (SOEs) will be given specific attention by most likely implementing transparency obligations for those investors, who show a specific connection to governmental actions. In particular, state-owned enterprises receive financial support from the state and are therefore placed in a position of competitive advantage compared to other investors, including local enterprises, and can create "disadvantageous economic conditions".[52] It is noteworthy that in the Statement of the European Union and the United States on Shared Principles for International Investment of April 2012, the EU has agreed that "the European Union and the United States support the work of the Organisation for Economic Co-operation and Development (OECD) in the area of 'competitive neutrality', which focuses on the importance of state-owned entities and private commercial enterprises being subject to the same external environment and competing on a level playing field in a given market".[53] It remains to be seen if these ideas, found especially in the CETA draft text, will provide sufficient answers to existing problems, as well as to problems arising out of most likely more involvement of state entities in international investments.

As has been spelled out in the TTIP negotiating directives, in regard to investment "...[t]he aim is to achieve the highest levels of liberalisation and investment protection that both sides have negotiated to date in other trade deals." The opening up of domestic markets to foreign investors is one of the main purposes of trade and investment agreements, nevertheless this is not foreseen in the existing 1,500 EU Member States BITs, unlike in US or Canadian investment law approaches.[54] This opening of markets can be a very general one by only excluding specific named sectors from general liberalisation (negative list approach), or open up domestic markets by indicating the types and volume of investment that should be permitted

---

[51] See on this Bungenberg (2014), p. 402; Shan and Zhang (2014), p. 422.

[52] Vadi (2013), p. 709.

[53] Statement of the European Union and the United States on Shared Principles for International Investment, 10 April 2012, available at http://trade.ec.europa.eu/doclib/docs/2012/april/tradoc_149338.pdf.

[54] See e.g., Article 3(1) Canadian Model FIPA 2004 ("Each Party shall accord to investors of the other Party treatment no less favourable than that it accords, in like circumstances, to its own investors with respect to the establishment, acquisition, expansion, management, conduct, operation and sale or other disposition of investments in its territory."), available at http://italaw.com/documents/Canadian2004-FIPA-model-en.pdf.

by the other contracting party/parties (positive list approach).[55] This latter approach was also followed by the European Community in some of its later trade agreements based on the aforementioned investment platform in the pre-Lisbon era, when its common commercial policy powers did not include an express FDI competence and could arguably have been extended only to the trade-like aspects of access to foreign markets.[56]

The draft CETA text shows that it is primarily the Canadian approach that was pursued; the national treatment obligation also extends to "establishment, acquisition (and possibly expansion) of investments",[57] and furthermore, the draft CETA text contains a provision on market access in the form of prohibitions of specific limitations to foreign investors,[58] coupled with a prohibition of performance requirements.[59] Lately, even China has agreed to negotiate on market access with the United States on the basis of the US 2012 Model BIT; the EU will be asking for comparable treatment in the China-EU negotiations as a specific expression of regulatory competition.[60] A built-in agenda comparable to the GATS with a positive-list approach on market access[61] would be a solution for the negotiations with China on a stand-alone BIT, if agreement on a negative list is not possible between the negotiating parties.

[55] See on the different options Shan and Zhang (2014), p. 422.

[56] See e.g., the provisions on "commercial presence" of Article 65 et seq. of the Economic Partnership Agreement between the CARIFORUM States, of the one part, and the European Community and its Member States, of the other part, signed 15 October 2008 (10 December 2009 by Haiti; entry into force: applied provisionally from 29 December 2008), [2008] OJ L 289I/1, as well as Section C of Chapter 7 of the Free Trade Agreement between the European Union and its Member States, of the one part, and the Republic of Korea, of the other part, signed on 6 October 2010, provisionally applied since 1 July 2011, [2011] OJ L 127/6, which provides for MFN treatment and specific market access commitments and national treatment in separate schedules; see also Dimopoulos (2011), pp. 52–53; also Shan and Zhang (2014), p. 422.

[57] CETA Investment Text, published on 26 September 2014, Article X.7 National Treatment, available at http://trade.ec.europa.eu/doclib/docs/2014/september/tradoc_152806.pdf.

[58] CETA Investment Text, published on 26 September 2014, Article X.4: Market Access, available at http://trade.ec.europa.eu/doclib/docs/2014/september/tradoc_152806.pdf.

[59] CETA Investment Text, published on 26 September 2014, Article X.5: Performance Requirements, available at http://trade.ec.europa.eu/doclib/docs/2014/september/tradoc_152806.pdf.

[60] See European Parliament, Resolution of 9 October 2013 on the EU–China negotiations for a bilateral investment agreement (2013/2674(RSP)), available at http://www.europarl.europa.eu/sides/getDoc.do?pubRef=-//EP//TEXT+TA+P7-TA-2013-0411+0+DOC+XML+V0//EN.

[61] See on this GATS approach, for example, Ohler (2007), pp. 373 (399); see on the positive list approach also Low and Mattoo (2000), p. 449.

Standards of Treatment

The negotiating mandates for the agreements with the US,[62] Canada, India and Singapore[63] specify that:

> the negotiations shall aim to include in particular but not exclusively the following standards of treatment and rules: a) fair and equitable treatment, including a prohibition of unreasonable, arbitrary or discriminatory measures, b) unqualified national treatment c) unqualified most-favoured nation treatment, d) protection against direct and indirect expropriation, including the right to prompt, adequate and effective compensation e) full protection and security of investors and investments, f) other effective protection provisions, such as 'umbrella clause' g) free transfer of funds of capital and payments by investors as well as h) rules concerning subrogation.

The negotiating directives are a loose template and they are, at the same time, the outcome of a commonly agreed position, a compromise text, presented by the Council, which generally favours Member State positions.[64] The general negotiation directives were concretised by the Commission, also influenced by the European Parliament.[65] In a way, the Member States might never have expected this, at least not those who wanted to keep up their "gold standard approach".

A further important negotiating directive is that the right to regulate and sustainable development should be recognised as "overarching objectives of future agreements". A policy shift that first took shape in North America, namely with the adoption of the 2004 Model BITs of Canada and the United States, already leads to the adoption of more balanced investment treaties deferential to public policy considerations.[66] In this light, EU Member State BITs are generally older generation BITs, one-sidedly focused on investment protection and largely silent where the public interest is concerned.[67] However, the Commission has accepted this paradigm shift that can now be found in the formulation of especially the fair and equitable treatment standard, as well as the expropriation standard.

---

62 Available at http://data.consilium.europa.eu/doc/document/ST-11103-2013-DCL-1/en/pdf.

63 Available at http://www.s2bnetwork.org/fileadmin/dateien/downloads/EU-TTIP-Mandate-from-bfmtv-June17-2013.pdf.

64 Reinisch (2014), available at http://ssrn.com/abstract=2236192.

65 European Parliament, Resolution of 6 April 2011 on the future European international investment policy (2010/2203(INI)), paras. 23-26, available at http://www.europarl.europa.eu/sides/getDoc.do?pubRef=-//EP//TEXT+TA+P7-TA-2011-0141+0+DOC+XML+V0//EN.

66 Titi (2013), available at http://ccsi.columbia.edu/files/2014/01/FDI_86.pdf; see also Juillard (2004), p. 669.

67 Titi (2013), available at http://ccsi.columbia.edu/files/2014/01/FDI_86.pdf.

In particular with regard to the intention to preserve the host State's right to regulate in order to meet legitimate public policy objectives, the Commission stated:

> Future EU agreements will provide a detailed set of provisions giving guidance to arbitrators on how to decide whether or not a government measure constitutes indirect expropriation. In particular, when the state is protecting the public interest in a non-discriminatory way, the right of the state to regulate should prevail over the economic impact of those measures on the investor.[68]

This is done, for example, in the CETA text via an Annex pointing out that a high threshold of "substantial interference" with the right to use, enjoy and dispose of the investment has to be proven, and that arbitral tribunals do have to conduct a "balancing" exercise on a case by case basis.[69] All in all, the new EU approach contains language inspired by the police powers doctrine, trying to ensure that *bona fide* regulation in the public interest should not be considered expropriation;[70] the Commission followed the demand of the European Parliament[71] to find a "clear and fair balance between public welfare objectives and private interests" in defining indirect expropriation.[72]

Also the fair and equitable treatment (FET) standard will be faced with significant changes. For a long time, this has been the most dynamic, almost "catch all" standard. In the CETA draft, the FET standard is given an explicit substantive content.[73] The EU approach includes case law of arbitral tribunals and the legal

---

[68] European Commission, Fact Sheet, Investment Protection and Investor-to-State Dispute Settlement in EU Agreements, November 2013, p. 2, available at http://trade.ec.europa.eu/doclib/docs/2013/november/tradoc_151916.pdf.

[69] See also Hoffmeister and Alexandru (2014), p. 379.

[70] Draft CETA Investment Text, 21 November 2013, Annex: Expropriation:

> For greater certainty, except in the rare circumstance where the impact of the measure or series of measures is so severe in light of its purpose that it appears manifestly excessive, non-discriminatory measures by a Party that are designed and applied to protect legitimate public welfare objectives, such as health, safety and the environment, do not constitute indirect expropriations.

Available at http://www.tradejustice.ca/wp-content/uploads/2013/08/CETA-Draft-Investment-Text-Nov21-2013-203b-13.pdf.

[71] European Parliament, Resolution of 6 April 2011 on the future European international investment policy (2010/2203(INI)), para. 19 (calling for "protection against direct and indirect expropriation, giving a definition that establishes a clear and fair balance between public welfare objectives and private interests."), available at http://www.europarl.europa.eu/sides/getDoc.do?pubRef=-//EP//TEXT+TA+P7-TA-2011-0141+0+DOC+XML+V0//EN.

[72] Reinisch (2014), p. 679.

[73] See also Hoffmeister and Alexandru (2014), p. 379.

traditions of the EU and its Member States.[74] As is pointed out in literature, the new FET wording seems to underline the intention of the Commission to "reaffirm the right of the Parties to regulate to pursue legitimate public policy objectives" and to "set out precisely what elements are covered and thus prohibited" by FET in EU investment agreements.[75]

Also the most favoured nation principle now has received specific attention in the ongoing negotiations. It is most likely that it will expressly exclude ISDS[76] as a direct response to the *Maffezini* case.[77] This clarification is welcome from the perspective of predictability and certainty and will help avoid unnecessary litigation.[78] An umbrella clause might not be included in the new EU agreements, at least not the one with Canada, as Canada has avoided including this standard in its IIAs. Thus, this might change with other negotiating partners,[79] for example, China, Japan or South Korea, as those countries also included an umbrella clause in their trilateral agreement of 2012,[80] and it may be different again with the US, which

---

[74] Consolidated CETA Text, published on 26 September 2014, available at http://trade.ec.europa.eu/doclib/docs/2014/september/tradoc_152806.pdf. Article X.9(2):

> [E]ach Party shall accord in its territory to investors and to covered investments of the other Party fair and equitable treatment" is accompanied by a paragraph defining a breach of the FET obligation as a measure or series of measures constitut[ing]:
>
> a. Denial of justice in criminal, civil or administrative proceedings;
> b. Fundamental breach of due process, including a fundamental breach of transparency, in judicial and administrative proceedings.
> c. Manifest arbitrariness;
> d. Targeted discrimination on manifestly wrongful grounds, such as gender, race or religious belief;
> e. Abusive treatment of investors, such as coercion, duress and harassment; or

a breach of any further elements of the fair and equitable treatment obligation adopted by the Parties in accordance with paragraph 4 of this Article.

[75] European Commission, Fact Sheet, Investment Protection and Investor-to-State Dispute Settlement in EU agreements, November 2013, pp. 2, 7 et seq., available at http://trade.ec.europa.eu/doclib/docs/2013/november/tradoc_151916.pdf.

[76] Consolidated CETA Text, published on 26 September 2014, available at http://trade.ec.europa.eu/doclib/docs/2014/september/tradoc_152806.pdf. Article X.8: Most-Favoured-Nation Treatment ("4. For greater certainty, the 'treatment' referred to in Paragraph 1 and 2 does not include investor-to-state dispute settlement procedures provided for in other international investment treaties and other trade agreements.").

[77] *Emilio Agustín Maffezini v Spain*, ICSID Case No. ARB/97/7, Decision on Jurisdiction, 25 January 2000, available at http://www.italaw.com/sites/default/files/case-documents/ita0479.pdf.

[78] Reinisch (2014), p. 679.

[79] See also Hoffmeister and Alexandru (2014), p. 379.

[80] See article 5 par. 2 of the Agreement among the Government of Japan, the Government of the Republic of Korea and the Government of the People's Republic of China for the Promotion, Facilitation and Protection of Investment, signed 13 May 2012 (not yet in force), available at http://www.mofa.go.jp/mofaj/press/release/24/5/pdfs/0513_01_02.pdf.

does not have such a far-reaching concept of including contract obligations as, for example, the EU Member States.[81]

Investor-State Dispute Settlement

All EU institutions that have so far expressed an opinion on the future EU international investment policy have clearly indicated that EU investment agreements need to provide an effective ISDS system.[82] For example, the Commission has pointed out, that ISDS is "such an established feature of investment agreements that its absence would in fact discourage investors and make a host economy less attractive than others".[83] The Council has emphasised that EU investment policy should support the objective of the Union to remain "the world's leading destination and source of investment"[84] and increase legal security for EU investors abroad,[85] further expressly stressing, as mentioned above in the analysis of the Council's "Conclusions", "the need for an effective investor-to-state dispute settlement mechanism".[86] The European Parliament has dedicated five paragraphs to invest-

---

[81] European Commission, Communication, Towards a Comprehensive European International Investment Policy, COM(2010)343 final of 7 July 2010, available at http://trade.ec.europa.eu/doclib/docs/2011/may/tradoc_147884.pdf; European Parliament, Resolution of 6 April 2011 on the future European international investment policy (2010/2203(INI)), available at http://www.europarl.europa.eu/sides/getDoc.do?pubRef=-//EP//TEXT+TA+P7-TA-2011-0141+0+DOC+XML+V0//EN.

[82] European Commission, Communication, Towards a Comprehensive European International Investment Policy, COM(2010)343 final of 7 July 2010, pp. 9–10, available at http://trade.ec.europa.eu/doclib/docs/2011/may/tradoc_147884.pdf, Council of the EU, Conclusions on a comprehensive European international investment policy, 3041st Foreign Affairs Council Meeting, Luxembourg, 25 October 2010, para. 18, available at http://www.consilium.europa.eu/uedocs/cms_data/docs/pressdata/EN/foraff/117328.pdf, European Parliament, Resolution of 6 April 2011 on the future European international investment policy (2010/2203(INI)), paras. 31-35, available at http://www.europarl.europa.eu/sides/getDoc.do?pubRef=-//EP//TEXT+TA+P7-TA-2011-0141+0+DOC+XML+V0//EN.

[83] European Commission, Communication, Towards a Comprehensive European International Investment Policy, COM(2010)343 final of 7 July 2010, p. 10, available at http://trade.ec.europa.eu/doclib/docs/2011/may/tradoc_147884.pdf.

[84] Council of the EU, Conclusions on a comprehensive European international investment policy, 3041st Foreign Affairs Council Meeting, Luxembourg, 25 October 2010, Recital 6, available at http://www.consilium.europa.eu/uedocs/cms_data/docs/pressdata/EN/foraff/117328.pdf.

[85] Council of the EU, Conclusions on a comprehensive European international investment policy, 3041st Foreign Affairs Council Meeting, Luxembourg, 25 October 2010, Recital 8, available at http://www.consilium.europa.eu/uedocs/cms_data/docs/pressdata/EN/foraff/117328.pdf.

[86] Council of the EU, Conclusions on a comprehensive European international investment policy, 3041st Foreign Affairs Council Meeting, Luxembourg, 25 October 2010, Recital 18, 14, available at http://www.consilium.europa.eu/uedocs/cms_data/docs/pressdata/EN/foraff/117328.pdf.

ment dispute settlement in its Resolution of 6 April 2011.[87] On the other hand, it has to be noted that some governments, such as the Australian government[88] and now also the German Government, are turning away from ISDS, even though as already mentioned, the unanimously adopted Council mandates for negotiations with Canada, India, Singapore and the US clearly foresee this mechanism.

In regard to ISDS, it is important to highlight that the EU is for the time being precluded from offering ICSID arbitration in its future agreements, since the EU may not accede to the ICSID Convention, open only to States members of the World Bank or party to the Statute of the International Court of Justice.[89] At this stage, UNCITRAL arbitration remains the most immediately available option. While the EU is not a member of UNCITRAL and currently it may only participate in UNCITRAL work as an observer,[90] UNCITRAL rules do not limit their applicability to nationals of states which are UNCITRAL members,[91] in other words "the EU is entitled to use the Rules of Arbitration in its investment agreements if it so wishes".[92] Other potential arbitration fora would be, *inter alia*, the Permanent Court of Justice (PCA), the International Court of Arbitration of the International Chamber of Commerce (ICC), or the Arbitration Institute of the Stockholm Chamber of Commerce (SCC). There is little doubt that an effective dispute resolution mechanism will be achieved.

In suggesting the design of the ISDS mechanism, the European Commission's Communication "Towards a Comprehensive European International Investment Policy", suggests that the EU should build on Member State practices and aim for a state-of-the-art dispute settlement system, and identifies a number of key challenges.[93] One of the most topical issues in international economic law, transparency, has been the focus of recent debate in various fora,[94] including famously in the context of UNCITRAL, whose Working Group II agreed to higher levels of

---

[87] European Parliament, Resolution of 6 April 2011 on the future European international investment policy (2010/2203(INI)), paras. 31-35, available at http://www.europarl.europa.eu/sides/getDoc.do?pubRef=-//EP//TEXT+TA+P7-TA-2011-0141+0+DOC+XML+V0//EN.

[88] See Australian Government, Department of Foreign Affairs and Trade, Gillard Government Trade Policy Statement: Trading our Way to More Jobs and Prosperity, April 2011, p. 14, available at http://www.acci.asn.au/getattachment/b9d3cfae-fc0c-4c2a-a3df-3f58228daf6d/Gillard-Government-Trade-Policy-Statement.aspx; Kurtz (2012), p. 33; Nottage (2011), available at http://ssrn.com/abstract=1860505.

[89] Article 67 ICSID Convention; see on this, for example, Burgstaller (2014), p. 551.

[90] Burgstaller (2014), p. 551.

[91] E.g. see UNCITRAL and Private Disputes/Litigation on UNCITRAL's site: http://www.uncitral.org/uncitral/en/uncitral_texts/arbitration_faq.html.

[92] Hoffmeister and Ünüvar (2013), pp. 57 (78).

[93] European Commission, Communication, Towards a Comprehensive European International Investment Policy, COM(2010)343 final of 7 July 2010, p. 10, available at http://trade.ec.europa.eu/doclib/docs/2011/may/tradoc_147884.pdf.

[94] See, for example, Doha Work Programme—Decision Adopted by the General Council on 1 August 2004, WTO-Doc. WT/L/579; Ismail (2004), p. 377; Zoellner (2009); Titi (2015), § 78, including bibliography.

transparency in disputes on the basis of future investment agreements.[95] On transparency of ISDS in particular, the Commission Communication notes that:

> [i]n line with the EU's approach in the WTO, the EU should ensure that investor-state dispute settlement is conducted in a transparent manner (including requests for arbitration, submissions, open hearings, amicus curiae briefs and publication of awards).[96]

The issue has also been taken up by the European Parliament in its Resolution of 6 April 2011, which clearly states that changes to the present dispute settlement system are necessary in order to achieve greater transparency,[97] and in the negotiating directive authorising the opening of investment negotiations on the EU–US TTIP.[98]

Transparency is mostly seen as a means of promoting the credibility and legitimacy of the international economic law system,[99] although a conflict is possible between calls for a more open and transparent system and the need to protect confidential commercial and governmental information. In international investment law, transparency is understood *inter alia* as an obligation of host states to publish all legal rules affecting investors in general and, where the settlement of disputes is concerned, to conduct open proceedings and to publish arbitral awards.[100] Although it is argued in some quarters that reforms with more transparency in the entire process of dispute settlement may be contrary to the interests of investors,[101] the publication of arbitral awards is a precondition for the development of consistent case law and for inducing a modicum of legal certainty.

Furthermore in regard to more consistency[102] and predictability in interpretations, the use of quasi-permanent arbitrators (as in the EU's FTA practice) and/or

[95] See UNCITRAL, Report of Working Group II (Arbitration and Conciliation) on the work of its 58th session (New York, 4-8 February 2013), A/CN.9/765; see further United Nations General Assembly, Settlement of commercial disputes: preparation of a legal standard on transparency in treaty-based investor-State arbitration, A/CN.9/WG.II/WP.176; United Nations Commission on International Trade Law Working Group II (Arbitration and Conciliation), 58th session, New York, 4–8 February 2013; See also Bungenberg and Titi (2013), p. 425.

[96] European Commission, Communication, Towards a Comprehensive European International Investment Policy, COM(2010)343 final of 7 July 2010, p. 10, available at http://trade.ec.europa.eu/doclib/docs/2011/may/tradoc_147884.pdf.

[97] European Parliament, Resolution of 6 April 2011 on the future European international investment policy (2010/2203(INI)), para. 31, available at http://www.europarl.europa.eu/sides/getDoc.do?pubRef=-//EP//TEXT+TA+P7-TA-2011-0141+0+DOC+XML+V0//EN.

[98] See above 'The EU's first negotiating directives for investment chapters in comprehensive free trade agreements'. See also below.

[99] See Titi (2015), § 78.

[100] Knahr and Reinisch (2007), pp. 97 (110); see further Titi (2015), § 78, including bibliography.

[101] Knahr and Reinisch (2007), pp. 97 (111); Berger (1992), pp. 5 (19).

[102] See in this regard the *CME and Lauder v Czech Republic* awards that are among the most cited examples of the problems discussed here; in two simultaneous arbitrations dealing with the same facts—one conducted under the Netherlands-Czech BIT and the other one under the US-Czech BIT—one tribunal dismissed the claim and another tribunal awarded USD 353 million to the investor; see *CME v Czech Republic*, UNCITRAL (1976), 13 September 2001, Partial Award,

appellate mechanisms, where there is a likelihood of many claims under a particular agreement, are currently considered.[103] The TTIP negotiating directive likewise states that "[c]onsideration should be given to the possibility of creating an appellate mechanism applicable to investor-to-state dispute settlement under the Agreement."[104] A comparison with trade law is particularly revealing. In contrast with investment law, trade law provides a system for the settlement of international trade disputes between its members within the WTO. This system is governed by the Dispute Settlement Understanding (DSU) and applied by the WTO Dispute Settlement Body (DSB). The DSU offers a single dispute resolution system that is applicable to all WTO agreements. The creation of an appellate system in international investment law has been discussed at length,[105] and some of the new US international investment agreements and the US Model BIT foresee the possibility of negotiating a bilateral appellate body.[106]

Inclusion of Human Rights, Sustainable Development and the Right to Regulate in EU IIAs

The European Parliament proceeds to include additional considerations on the insertion of social and environmental standards in the new treaties, for example, obligations relating to the promotion of social standards, sustainable development,

pp. 109 et seq., available at http://www.italaw.com/sites/default/files/case-documents/ita0178.pdf; *Lauder v Czech Republic*, UNCITRAL (1976), 3 September 2001, Final Award, pp. 35 et seq., available at http://www.italaw.com/sites/default/files/case-documents/ita0451.pdf.

[103] European Commission, Communication, Towards a Comprehensive European International Investment Policy, COM(2010)343 final of 7 July 2010, p. 10, available at http://trade.ec.europa.eu/doclib/docs/2011/may/tradoc_147884.pdf; see on this also Tams (2014), p. 585; Calamita (2014), p. 645.

[104] Council of the European Union, Directives for the negotiation on the Transatlantic Trade and Investment Partnership between the European Union and the United States of America, of 17 June 2013, para. 23, available at http://data.consilium.europa.eu/doc/document/ST-11103-2013-DCL-1/en/pdf.

[105] See, for example, Sauvant (2008); Tams (2006).

[106] Article 28(10) US Model BIT 2012, available athttp://www.state.gov/documents/organization/188371.pdf; see also the investment chapters of the United States—Chile Free Trade Agreement, signed 6 June 2003 (entry into force: 1 January 2004), available at http://www.ustr.gov/sites/default/files/uploads/agreements/fta/chile/asset_upload_file535_3989.pdf; United States—Singapore Free Trade Agreement, signed 6 May 2003 (entry into force: 1 January 2004), available at http://www.ustr.gov/sites/default/files/uploads/agreements/fta/singapore/asset_upload_file708_4036.pdf; United States—Morocco Free Trade Agreement, signed 15 June 2004 (entry into force: 1 January 2006), available at http://www.ustr.gov/sites/default/files/uploads/agreements/fta/morocco/asset_upload_file118_3819.pdf.

human rights, good governance, etc.[107] In particular, the Parliament reiterates that future EU investment policy must promote "investment which is sustainable, respects the environment" and "encourages good quality working conditions"[108] and suggests the inclusion of a reference to the updated OECD Guidelines for Multinational Enterprises[109] and a corporate social responsibility clause.[110] The Parliament further:

> [w]elcomes the fact that a number of BITs currently have a clause which prevents the watering-down of social and environmental legislation in order to attract investment and calls on the Commission to consider the inclusion of such a clause in its future agreements.[111]

Therefore, the protection the environment and the promotion of sustainable development must not encourage investment by lowering domestic environmental or social standards or "legislation aimed at protecting and promoting cultural diversity".[112] Also from the point of view of EU constitutional obligations, according to the general principles and objectives enumerated in Article 21 TEU, IIAs must also be seen as a means of promoting the objectives enumerated in that article "in the world". As Commissioner Karel de Gucht has pointed out in his presentation and interview before the European Parliament in January 2010:

> Free trade must be a tool to generate prosperity, stability and development. . . . When part of a wider set of measures, it is a potent lever promoting European values abroad, like sustainable development and human rights. .... The EU must lead by example.

---

[107] European Parliament, Resolution of 6 April 2011 on the future European international investment policy (2010/2203(INI)), paras. 27-30, available at http://www.europarl.europa.eu/sides/getDoc.do?pubRef=-//EP//TEXT+TA+P7-TA-2011-0141+0+DOC+XML+V0//EN.

[108] European Parliament, Resolution of 6 April 2011 on the future European international investment policy (2010/2203(INI)), para. 27, available at http://www.europarl.europa.eu/sides/getDoc.do?pubRef=-//EP//TEXT+TA+P7-TA-2011-0141+0+DOC+XML+V0//EN.

[109] European Parliament, Resolution of 6 April 2011 on the future European international investment policy (2010/2203(INI)), para. 27, available at http://www.europarl.europa.eu/sides/getDoc.do?pubRef=-//EP//TEXT+TA+P7-TA-2011-0141+0+DOC+XML+V0//EN.

[110] European Parliament, Resolution of 6 April 2011 on the future European international investment policy (2010/2203(INI)), para. 28, available at http://www.europarl.europa.eu/sides/getDoc.do?pubRef=-//EP//TEXT+TA+P7-TA-2011-0141+0+DOC+XML+V0//EN.

[111] European Parliament, Resolution of 6 April 2011 on the future European international investment policy (2010/2203(INI)), para. 30, available at http://www.europarl.europa.eu/sides/getDoc.do?pubRef=-//EP//TEXT+TA+P7-TA-2011-0141+0+DOC+XML+V0//EN.

[112] Council of the European Union, Directives for the negotiation on the Transatlantic Trade and Investment Partnership between the European Union and the United States of America of 17 June 2013, para. 8, available at http://www.s2bnetwork.org/fileadmin/dateien/downloads/EU-TTIP-Mandate-from-bfmtv-June17-2013.pdf.

Conclusion

International investment law proves to be one of the most dynamic fields of international economic law and reflects current developments of economic law in general. The "ands" are included, the sovereign right to regulate is more or less accepted, and there is more detailed wording on the standards. The approach is one towards an international investment law "2.0"—more balanced and innovative. Especially the discussion and negotiation of the evolution of investment relations between the EU, China and the US will not only affect the relationship between the three most important global economic players, but also shape international investment law and politics for the next decade at least. The outcome of these negotiations—between the EU and the United States on the Transatlantic Trade and Investment Partnership, between again the EU and China on a stand-alone BIT, between the US and China on a stand-alone BIT, and the multilateral Trans-Pacific Partnership (TPP) Agreement—are likely to set the stage for the conclusions of subsequent treaties with or between other partners.

In this regard, it is most evident that in a regulatory competition, especially between the economic superpowers of the EU, China and the US, the EU cannot afford to leave the negotiating floor and abdicate the shaping of future international investment law to the other players due to false information and one-sided public pressure.

References

Berger KP (1992) The International Arbitrators' Application of Precedents. J Int Arbitr 9:4

Bosse-Platière (2002) Le Parlement européen et les relations extérieures de la Communauté européenne après le Traité de Nice. Revue Trimestrielle De Droit Européen 38:527

Braun TR (2011) For a complementary European investment protection. In: Bungenberg M, Hindelang S, Griebel J (eds) European yearbook of international economic law, special issue: international investment law and EU law, p 95

Bungenberg M (2009) Außenbeziehungen und Außenhandelspolitik. EuR Beiheft 1:195

Bungenberg M (2010) Going global? The EU common commercial policy after Lisbon. In: Herrmann C, Terhechte JP (eds) European yearbook of international economic law, p 123

Bungenberg M (2011) Internationaler Investitionsschutz im Wettbewerb der Systeme. KSzW, p 116

Bungenberg M (2011) The politics of the European Union's investment treaty making. In: Broude T, Busch ML, Porges A (eds) The politics of international economic law, p 133

Bungenberg M (2014) The scope of application of EU (model) investment agreements. In: Bungenberg M, Reinisch A (eds) The anatomy of the (invisible) EU model BIT. JWIT Special Issue, p 402

Bungenberg (2015) Article 218. In: von der Groeben H, Schwarze J, Hatje A (eds) Europäisches Unionsrecht, 7th edn

Bungenberg M, Herrmann C (eds) (2013) Common commercial policy after Lisbon

Bungenberg M, Reinisch A (eds) (2014) The anatomy of the (invisible) EU model BIT. JWIT Special Issue

Bungenberg M, Titi C (2013) Developments in international investment law. In: Herrmann C, Krajewski M, Terhechte JP (eds) European yearbook of international economic law 2014, p 425

Bungenberg M, Griebel J, Hindelang S (eds) (2011) European yearbook of international economic law. Special issue: international investment law and EU law

Burgstaller M (2009) European law and investment treaties. J Int Arbitr 26:181
Burgstaller M (2014) Dispute settlement in EU international investment agreements with third states: three salient problems. In: Bungenberg M, Reinisch A (eds) The anatomy of the (invisible) EU model BIT. JWIT Special Issue, p 551
Calamita NJ (2012) The making of Europe's international investment policy: uncertain first steps. Leg Issues Econ Integrat 39:301
Calamita NJ (2014) Dispute settlement transparency in Europe's evolving investment treaty policy. In: Bungenberg M, Reinisch A (eds) The anatomy of the (invisible) EU model BIT. JWIT Special Issue, p 645
Chaisse J (2012) Promises and pitfalls of the European Union policy on foreign investment – how will the new EU competence on FDI affect the emerging global regime? J Int Econ Law 15:51
Devuyst Y (2013) European Union law and practice in the negotiation and conclusion of international trade agreements. J Int Business Law 12
Dimopoulos A (2011) EU foreign investment law
Dolzer R, Kim Y-I (2013) Germany. In: Brown C (ed) Commentaries on selected model investment treaties, p 289
Flaesch-Mougin C (1993) Le Traité de Maastricht et les compétences externes de la Communauté européenne. Cahiers De Droit Européen 29:383
Gaffney J (2015) European bilateral approaches. In: Bungenberg M, Griebel J, Hobe S, Reinisch A (eds) International investment law
Hallward-Driemeier M (2003) Do bilateral investment treaties attract FDI? Only a bit...and they could bite. World Bank Research Paper No. 3121, p 21
Hoffmeister F, Alexandru G (2014) A first glimpse of light on the emerging invisible EU model BIT. In: Bungenberg M, Reinisch A (eds) The anatomy of the (invisible) EU model BIT. JWIT Special Issue, p 379
Hoffmeister F, Ünüvar G (2013) From BITS and pieces towards European investment agreements. In: Bungenberg M, Reinisch A, Tietje C (eds) EU and investment agreements: open questions and remaining challenges
Ismail F (2004) A development perspective on the WTO July 2004 general council decision. J Int Econ Law 8:377
Juillard P (2004) Le nouveau modèle américain de traité bilatéral sur l'encouragement et la protection réciproques des investissements. Annuaire français de droit international 50:669
Klamert M, Maydell N (2008) Lost in exclusivity: implied non-exclusive external competences in community law. Eur Foreign Aff Rev 13:493
Knahr C, Reinisch A (2007) Transparency versus confidentiality in international investment arbitration – the Biwater Gauff compromise. Law Pract Int Courts Tribunals 6:97
Krajewski M (2013) New functions and new powers for the European Parliament: assessing the changes of the common commercial policy from the perspective of democratic legitimacy. In: Bungenberg M, Herrmann C (eds) Common commercial policy after Lisbon, p 67
Kurtz J (2012) Australia's rejection of investor-state arbitration: causation, omission and implication. ICSID Rev 27(1):33
Lavranos N (2013) In defence of member states' BITs gold standard: the regulation 1219/2012 establishing a transitional regime for existing extra-EU BITs – a member state's perspective. In: EU, investment treaties, and investment treaty arbitration – current developments and challenges. TDM 10:2
Lévesque C (2013) The challenges of 'marrying' investment liberalisation and protection in the Canada-EU CETA. In: Bungenberg M, Reinisch A, Tietje C (eds) EU and investment agreements: open questions and remaining challenges, p 121
Low P, Mattoo A (2000) Is there a better way? Alternative approaches to liberalization under the GATS. In: Sauvé P, Stern RM (eds) GATS 2000: new directions in service trade liberalization, p 449
Maresceau M (1993) The concept "common commercial policy" and the difficult road to Maastricht. In: Maresceau M (ed) The European community's commercial policy after 1992: the legal dimension, p 3 (9)

Maydell N (2007) The European community's minimum platform on investment or the Trojan horse of investment competence. In: Reinisch A, Knahr C (eds) International investment law in context, p 73
Neumayer E, Spess L (2005) Do bilateral investment treaties increase foreign direct investment to developing countries? World Dev 33:1567 (1568)
Newcombe A (2015) IIAs in the Americas. In: Bungenberg M, Griebel J, Hobe S, Reinisch A (eds) International investment law
Nottage L (2011) The rise and possible fall of investor-state-arbitration in Asia: a skeptic's view of Australia's "Gillard government trade policy statement". Sydney Law School Research Paper 11/32
Ohler C (2007) Handel mit Dienstleistungen. In: Herrmann C, Weiß W, Ohler C (eds) Welthandelsrecht, p 373 (399)
Passos R (2010) Mixed agreements from the perspective of the European Parliament. In: Hillion C, Koutrakos P (eds) Mixed agreements revisited: the EU and its member states in the world, p 269 (285–286)
Passos R (2011) The European Union's external relations a year after Lisbon: a first evaluation from the European Parliament. In: Koutrakos P (ed) The European Union's external relations a year after Lisbon. CLEER Working Papers 2011/3, p 49 (52–53)
Passos R, Marquardt S (2007) International agreements – competences, procedures and judicial control. In: Amato G, Bribosia H, de Witte B (eds) Genesis and destiny of the European Constitution, p 875 (904)
Quintin M (1975) Participation de l'Assemblée parlementaire européenne au déroulement de la procédure de négociation des accords commerciaux. Revue Trimestrielle De Droit Européen 11:211
Reinisch A (2014) Putting the pieces together: an EU model BIT? In: Bungenberg M, Reinisch A (eds) The anatomy of the (invisible) EU model BIT. JWIT Special Issue, p 679
Reinisch A (2014) The EU on the investment path – Quo Vadis Europe? The future of EU BITs and other investment agreements
Sauvant KP (2008) Appeals mechanism in international investment disputes
Schwichtenberg K (2013) Die Kooperationsverpflichtung der Mitgliedstaaten der Europäischen Union bei Abschluss und Anwendung gemischter Verträge
Shan W, Zhang S (2014) Market access provisions in the potential EU model BIT: towards a "Global BIT 2.0"? In: Bungenberg M, Reinisch A (eds) The anatomy of the (invisible) EU model BIT. JWIT Special Issue, p 422
Tams C (2006) An appealing option? The debate about an ICSID appellate structure. Essays Transnational Econ Law 57
Tams C (2014) Procedural aspects of investor-state dispute settlement: the emergence of an European approach. In: Bungenberg M, Reinisch A (eds) The anatomy of the (invisible) EU model BIT. JWIT Special Issue, p 585
Titi C (2013) EU investment agreements and the search for a new balance: a paradigm shift from Laissez-faire liberalism toward embedded liberalism? Columbia FDI Perspectives 86
Titi C (2015) International investment law and good governance. In: Bungenberg M, Griebel J, Hobe S, Reinisch A (eds) International investment law
Tobin J, Rose-Ackermann S (2005) Foreign direct investment and the business environment in developing countries: the impact of bilateral investment treaties. Yale Law & Economics Research Paper No. 293, p 22
UNCTAD, World Investment Report 2012, p 85
UNCTAD, World Investment Report 2014, p 114
Vadi V (2013) Converging divergences: the rise of Chinese outward foreign investment and its implications for international (investment) law. In: Sauvant KP (ed) Yearbook on international investment law & policy 2011–2012, p 709
Vedder C (2013) Linkage of the common commercial policy to the general objectives for the Union's external action. In: Bungenberg M, Herrmann C (eds) Common commercial policy after Lisbon, p 115
Zoellner CS (2009) Das Transparenzprinzip im Internationalen Wirtschaftsrecht

"*Transleakancy*"

Christoph Herrmann

Introduction

In an unprecedented move, the Council of the European Union, on 9 October 2014 decided to officially publish the directives for the negotiations of the Trans-Atlantic Trade and Investment Partnership (TTIP).[1] The document was not new to the interested public, though. The German version had already found its way into the limelight of trade policy through a website entitled www.ttip-leak.eu—run by a Green Member of the European Parliament (MEP). Other language versions may have been available elsewhere and earlier—you never know.

When I met Horst G. Krenzler for the first time in 2003, the internet was already a more or less established research tool for lawyers. However, that confidential trade and investment negotiation or dispute settlement documents could be "leaked", i.e. published unofficially online, was beyond my imagination at that time—or what I remember in that regard. WikiLeaks was only set up in 2006[2] and its initial focus was on other matters than trade and investment policy.

Over the years, I had the privilege to meet Horst several times and he shared a tiny bit of his vast experience and insights on trade policy with me. We never touched upon the topic of transparency in trade negotiations nor on today's increasing flow of "leaked" negotiation mandates, draft agreements, WTO panel reports or similar sources. Yet, I am pretty sure that Horst would have been very surprised about the violations of confidentiality regulations which occur every time a document is leaked—especially when committed by Members of the European Parliament.

[1] Available at http://data.consilium.europa.eu/doc/document/ST-11103-2013-DCL-1/en/pdf.

[2] http://en.wikipedia.org/wiki/WikiLeaks.

C. Herrmann (✉)
University of Passau, Innstraße 39, 94032 Passau, Germany
e-mail: christoph.herrmann@uni-passau.de

C. Herrmann et al. (eds.), *Trade Policy between Law, Diplomacy and Scholarship*,
European Yearbook of International Economic Law,
DOI 10.1007/978-3-319-15690-3_5

At the same time, he would have understood the change in the character of international economic law which drives the demand for this kind of documents. Trade and investment negotiations and disputes are perceived to be more about legislation, i.e. the setting of rules, than mere tit-for-tat bargaining. Trade and investment nowadays touch upon non-economic concerns, sometimes constitutionally protected, and attract the interest of the wider public, which in particular in the EU is increasingly opposed to free-trade and investment protection alike. The failure of the Anti-counterfeiting Trade Agreement (ACTA)[3] in the European Parliament (EP) and the recent citizens' initiative against TTIP[4] are just two examples in kind.

In the present contribution, we will take a very brief look at the two main legal principles colliding in trade and investment negotiations and dispute settlement: confidentiality and secrecy on the one hand, and transparency on the other hand. We will argue that the current "balance" between the two may best be described as "*transleakancy*"—a word obviously yet unknown to the world[5]—i.e. a quasi-transparency via leaked documents only. After a brief look at the principle of transparency in international economic law and at the legal provisions governing confidentiality of as well as access to trade and investment documents in the EU and major international treaties, we will try to sketch some characteristics of "*transleakancy*" as a specific status between secrecy and transparency in the conclusions.

Transparency as a Legal Requirement in International Economic Law

The claims for more transparency in international economic law are manifold, even though it sometimes remains opaque what kind of transparency is actually being asked for. In its widest possible meaning, transparency could be understood to mean that absolutely everything that happens must be happening under public scrutiny, i.e. the widest possible dissemination of all available information about what is going on—online. One can easily see that NGO activists of the facebook generation may understand transparency in this sense. From this perspective, secrecy has a negative connotation: disguised illegitimate influence of unknown actors and betrayal of the wider public. However, less intensive and extensive forms of

[3] See European Commission, Proposal for a Council Decision on the conclusion of the Anti-Counterfeiting Trade Agreement between the European Union and its Member States, Australia, Canada, Japan, the Republic of Korea, the United Mexican States, the Kingdom of Morocco, New Zealand, the Republic of Singapore, the Swiss Confederation and the United States of America, COM/2011/0380 final of 24 June 2011.

[4] See the European Commission's rejection of the citizens' initiative "Stop TTIP" at http://ec.europa.eu/citizens-initiative/public/initiatives/non-registered/details/2041?lg=en.

[5] At least, a Google search of "*transleakancy*" did not produce any results when conducted (for the last time) on 28 October 2014.

transparency are equally easily imaginable: dissemination of relevant information to relevant actors, namely national legislatures and other decision-makers.

Diplomacy has traditionally not worked in a very transparent way.[6] Despite the claim by US President Woodrow Wilson as early as 1918, in the first of his 14 points, to abolish all forms of secret diplomacy, no rule of public international law categorically prohibits secret negotiations between governments. Only once agreements have been concluded, they shall be registered with the United Nations Treaty office (Art. 102 (1) UNCh). However, the non-compliance with that provision does not render the non-registered Treaty null and void, but only non-invokable before UN organs, including the International Court of Justice (Art. 102 (2) UNCh).

Since 2006, the WTO Transparency Mechanism for Regional Trade Agreements[7] goes a lot further by demanding that WTO members make an "early announcement" of any negotiations envisaged to lead to a RTA.[8] Of course, this obligation is limited to the fact of the start of negotiation as such and does not require any Government to make public its strategy, objectives, red lines or any other information that may endanger the success of the negotiations. With a view to negotiations in the WTO itself, the picture is quite different. Over the last 20 years and in particular after the Ministerial Conferences in Singapore (1996) and Seattle (1999) the WTO has developed an impressive practice of internal and external transparency and has largely—but not entirely—abandoned the old "Green Room" practices.[9] As a rule, WTO documents are made public online and even restricted documents will normally be de-restricted after 2 months only.[10] On the basis of Art. V:2 WTO Agreement and the 1996 Guidelines for arrangements and relations with Non-Governmental Organizations,[11] the WTO Secretariat informs NGOs and consults with them extensively; however, due to reservations on the part of WTO members, NGOs cannot be formally involved in WTO decision-making.[12]

Similarly, there is no general rule under public international law that obliges sovereign States to publish their domestic legislation, in particular not in a foreign language. Again, WTO law is an exception: Art. X of the GATT requires that Members publish "promptly" any laws, regulations, judicial decisions and administrative rulings of general application pertaining to practically all aspects of external trade law. Other WTO provisions contain similar obligations.[13] The

---

[6] See Davérède, Negotiations, Secret, in: MPEPIL online.

[7] WT/L/671, 18 December 2006, available at http://www.wto.org/english/tratop_e/region_e/trans_mecha_e.htm.

[8] E.g., the EU and the US made the early announcement for TTIP under the Transparency mechanism on 8 July 2013, see http://rtais.wto.org/UI/PublicEARTAList.aspx.

[9] See Perez-Esteve (2012).

[10] See WTO, Procedures for the Circulation and Derestriction of WTO Documents, Decision of 14 May 2002, WT/L/452.

[11] WTO, Guidelines for arrangements on relations with Non-Governmental Organizations, Decision adopted by the General Council on 18 July 1996, WT/L/162.

[12] See Perez-Esteve (2012), pp. 10 et seq.

[13] See Perez-Esteve (2012), pp. 4 et seq.; and Zoellner (2006), p. 579 (590).

external trade laws of WTO members are, furthermore, subject to the Trade Policy Review Mechanism (TPRM) including a factual presentation and extensive Q&A.[14] However, the purpose of this kind of transparency is not to enhance the *legitimacy* of WTO Members' trade laws and regulations. Its function is merely to enable other Members to monitor their compliance with WTO law and to enable economic actors to take notice of them in order to make rational business choices. Accordingly, the WTO online glossary refers to transparency as "[d]egree to which trade policies and practices, and the process by which they are established, are open and predictable".[15] Ultimately, transparency is designed to foster efficient resource allocation—not more but also not less.[16]

With regard to dispute settlement within the WTO, things have changed a lot in the last years. The WTO dispute settlement system, despite limiting formal party status to WTO members, has opened up to NGOs and the wider public in several ways: they may be involved in the drafting of parties' submissions, submit amicus curiae briefs on their own initiative or may be heard as experts. Beginning in 2005, hearings of panels, the Appellate Body or arbitration panels have occasionally been opened to the public. Written submissions are either made public by the parties to the dispute themselves or they have to provide written summaries (Art. 18.2 DSU). Panel and Apellate Body reports are made public once they have been translated into the three official languages of the WTO.[17]

In the investment field, transparency is also making progress, albeit—lacking a multilateral forum and body of law—more slowly than in the WTO. As the impact of investment agreements on domestic policy choices is even more apparent and arguably more considerable than that of the WTO legal framework, this has been increasingly criticised, together with other aspects of Investor-State Dispute Settlement (ISDS).

The negotiation of bilateral investment treaties does not have to be made public prior to registration with the United Nations Treaty Office. However, increasingly, international trade agreements contain investment chapters, so that the WTO early announcement obligations also catch the investment part. Consequently, the global availability of BITs depends on voluntary registration or notification of agreements by the contracting parties of such agreements.[18] With regard to ISDS, external transparency beyond the publication of the mere existence of a dispute depends on the applicable *lex fori* and arbitration rules on the one hand, and on the approach of the parties to a dispute on the other hand. Under the ICSID arbitration rules, written

[14] See recent moves for reform of the TPRM, Chaisse and Matsuhita (2013), p. 9.

[15] See http://www.wto.org/english/thewto_e/glossary_e/transparency_e.htm.

[16] See however, Bungenberg (2015), in this volume, p. 32: "Transparency is mostly seen as a means of promoting the credibility and legitimacy of the international economic law system".

[17] Perez-Esteve (2012), pp. 22 et seq.

[18] See http://unctad.org/en/pages/DIAE/International%20Investment%20Agreements%20(IIA)/IIA-Tools.aspx. UNCTAD provides the most comprehensive BIT database of the world, but explicitly points out that it is based on voluntary information by its members.

submissions by non-disputing third parties may be allowed, hearings may be opened to the public (if no party objects) and awards may be published by the Centre, but only with the consent of the parties.[19] Parties are of course free to publish documents on their own initiative. Under UNCITRAL arbitration rules, transparency was considered to be slightly weaker,[20] but for future agreements, the Convention on transparency for investor-state dispute settlement[21] should improve the situation significantly. Under the new rules, most documents in the proceedings would have to be made public as a matter of principle. The 2014 draft EU–Canada trade and investment agreement (CETA)[22] already refers to these rules.[23]

Confidentiality of Trade and Investment Documents: The EU Legal Framework

Transparency is one of the key principles on which the EU is based. According to Article 10(3) Treaty on European Union (TEU), every citizen shall have the right to participate in the democratic life of the Union and decisions shall be taken as openly and as closely as possible to the citizen (see also Art. 1(2) TEU). Under Art. 11 TEU, the institutions not only shall give citizens and representative associations the opportunity to make known and publicly exchange their views in all areas of Union action (para. 1), but also maintain an open, transparent and regular dialogue with representative associations and civil society (para. 2). Furthermore, the institutions shall carry out broad consultations with parties concerned in order to ensure that the Union's actions are coherent and transparent.

These general principles translate into a right of access to Union documents, laid down in Art. 15 (3) of the Treaty on the Functioning of the European Union (TFEU) and reiterated in Art. 42 of the EU Charter of Fundamental Rights. However, this right is subject to principles and conditions determined by EU legislation, namely Regulation 1049/2001,[24] which contains significant exceptions to the right of access in its Art. 4, for public interest reasons as well as privacy and integrity of business secrets.

[19] See Delaney (2008); Sackmann (2012), pp. 43 et seq.

[20] Sackmann (2012), pp. 63 et seq.

[21] UNCITRAL Arbitration Rules (as revised in 2010, with new Art. 1, para. 4, as adopted in 2013) and UNCITRAL Rules on Transparency in Treaty-based Investor-State Arbitration, Resolution adopted by the General Assembly on 16 December 2013, available at http://www.uncitral.org/pdf/english/texts/arbitration/arb-rules-2013/UNCITRAL-Arbitration-Rules-2013-e.pdf.

[22] Available at http://trade.ec.europa.eu/doclib/docs/2014/september/tradoc_152806.pdf.

[23] See Article X.33: Transparency of Proceedings of the CETA draft.

[24] Regulation (EC) No 1049/2001 of the European Parliament and of the Council of 30 May 2001 regarding public access to European Parliament, Council and Commission documents, [2001] OJ L 145/43.

On the other hand, the confidentiality of EU documents is protected by security rules of procedures of the different institutions, e.g. the Commission Decision of 29 November 2001 amending its internal Rules of Procedure,[25] the Council Decision of 23 September 2013 on the security rules for protecting EU classified information,[26] the Bureau of the European Parliament Decision concerning the rules governing the treatment of confidential information by the European Parliament[27] and the Agreement between the Member States of the European Union, meeting within the Council, regarding the protection of classified information exchanged in the interests of the European Union.[28]

The EU Commission, which is the lead negotiator for the EU side in trade negotiations (see Art. 207(3) TFEU), besides informing the Trade Policy Committee and the EP regularly, is navigating between these legal rules. On the one hand, a legitimate interest of the wider public in the actual negotiations is understandable and dissemination of information is indispensable for public backing (or at least absence of public resistance) of a trade agreement. On the other hand, the publication of negotiated texts which are not yet agreed may very well compromise the success of the negotiations. However, recently, the practice of the Commission has increasingly developed towards more transparency than in the past and has stepped up communication on it: in spring 2014, the Commission held an online consultation on the hotly debated topic of ISDS in EU trade and investment agreements and later in 2014 it lobbied the Member States to make the TTIP negotiation directives—which had already been leaked—public. After every round of the TTIP negotiations, the Commission publishes an update on the state of the negotiations. Shortly after negotiations are concluded, the agreed texts become available on the Commission's website (e.g. in the case of the EU–Singapore agreement). The Commission even published a factsheet dedicated to "Transparency in EU trade negotiations".[29] Yet, its communication strategy itself was leaked again. What is not officially available, though, are drafts of the negotiated texts on the different aspects of the agreements. Yet, they are still often "publicly" available, which brings us to the next part: leakage.

[25] Commission Decision (2001/844/EC, ECSC, Euratom) of 29 November 2001 amending its internal Rules of Procedure, [2001] OJ L 317/1.

[26] Council Decision (2013/488/EU) of 23 September 2013 on the security rules for protecting EU classified information, [2013] OJ L 274/1.

[27] European Parliament, Decision of the Bureau of the European Parliament of 6 June 2011 concerning the rules governing the treatment of confidential information by the European Parliament, [2011] OJ C 190/2.

[28] Agreement between the Member States of the European Union, meeting within the Council, regarding the protection of classified information exchanged in the interests of the European Union, [2011] OJ C 202/13.

[29] See also the Commission's latest move towards transparency under the auspices of new Trade Commissioner Cecilia Malmström: European Commission, Press release of 19 November 2014, Commission to Further Boost TTIP Transparency, available at http://trade.ec.europa.eu/doclib/press/index.cfm?id=1201

Leaked Documents in the Global Trade and Investment System: Some Observations

It is hard to give a full account of trade and investment documents which found their way into the public light despite whatever classification they may have had. To mention just a few: the draft TPP IP chapter was leaked on WikiLeaks,[30] the EU TTIP mandate was leaked at www.ttip-leak.eu by an MEP, drafts of parts of the EU–Canada CETA agreement were repeatedly leaked on different websites and the ultimate text was leaked by a German public TV station[31] some weeks before its public release.[32] Some websites are dedicated to leaking trade documents exclusively.[33]

Some observations are warranted in that regard. First, we are permanently confronted with the problem of authenticity. There is no way of knowing whether the leaked text is authentic or made-up. Secondly, you can hardly know whether the seemingly authentic text is still on the table or whether it represents a status of negotiations already abandoned. Thirdly, it is often difficult to know whether the text represents a particular view on the negotiations (e.g. of one of the parties) or whether it is consensual. Fourthly, we regularly do not know why the document has been leaked and which interests are pursued by doing so. We may easily become exploited by the leaker for his or her vested interests. Lastly (and I am sure there is more to observe), it is difficult to keep track of all the leaks which pop up here and there. Most scholars will already have attended conferences in recent times where the speakers mentioned certain leaked texts which they claimed to possess and the audience started searching them on the spot with their laptops or iPads. With regard to a level discussion field, leaked documents sometimes create more problems than they solve.[34]

Of course, leakage increases rather than reduces transparency of trade negotiations, even though sometimes in a weird, confusing and—it must be said—illegal way. All these problems could be avoided if all the texts were made public by the negotiating parties and I personally believe that practice is headed that way anyway. Negotiations which are nowadays more akin to regulatory law-making than tit-for-tat tariff cuts certainly deserve a more open treatment than they presently receive. Yet, the transparency they deserve will not be created by leaked documents, but by official publication only! What leakage creates is not transparency, it is

---

[30] See https://wikileaks.org/tpp/.

[31] See http://www.tagesschau.de/wirtschaft/ceta-101.html.

[32] See http://trade.ec.europa.eu/doclib/docs/2014/september/tradoc_152806.pdf.

[33] See http://www.bilaterals.org/?-texts-of-agreements-&lang=en.

[34] The case of the ill-informed if not deliberately misleading award-winning newspaper article "Die Macht des Geldes", Die Zeit, No. 10, 27 February 2014, p. 15 is an impressive example of these problems, cf. Griebel (2014); see however on the chance to discuss legal issues based on leaked documents: Streinz (2015), in this volume, pp. 274 et seq. (discussing *inter alia* whether the TTIP falls under the EU's exclusive or shared competence).

transleakancy: a situation in which we all seem to know more than we are publicly allowed to know, but still less than the full truth which we are interested in and believe to have a right to know and care about. In January 2015, the EU Commission has now also begun to publish selected negotiation offers for TTIP - another move towards more transparency. Further such moves will certainly follow.

References

Bungenberg M (2015) Towards a more balanced international investment law 2.0? In: Herrmann C, Simma B, Streinz R (eds) Trade policy between law, diplomacy and scholarship: Liber amicorum in memoriam Horst G. Krenzler. Springer, Heidelberg, pp. 15–37

Chaisse J, Matsuhita M (2013) Maintaining the WTO's supremacy in the international trade order: a proposal to refine and revise the role of the trade policy review mechanism. J Int Econ Law 16(1):9

Delaney J (2008) Chapter 19. Procedural transparency. In: Muchlinski P, Ortino F, Schreuer C (eds) The Oxford handbook of international investment law

Griebel J (2014) Im Namen der Wahrheit? – Kritische Anmerkungen zu der mit Otto-Brenner-Preis geehrten Berichterstattung zu TTIP und CETA, available at http://www.verfassungsblog.de/im-namen-der-wahrheit-kritische-anmerkungen-zu-der-mit-otto-brenner-preis-geehrten-berichterstattung-zu-ttip-und-ceta/

Perez-Esteve M, WTO rules and practices for transparency and engagement with civil society organizations. WTO Staff Working Paper ERSD-2012-14, 18 September 2012, available at http://www.wto.org/english/res_e/reser_e/ersd201214_e.htm

Sackmann JC (2012) Transparenz im völkerrechtlichen Investitionsschiedsverfahren

Streinz R (2015) Disputes on TTIP – does the agreement need the consent of the German Parliament. In: Herrmann C, Simma B, Streinz R (eds) Trade policy between law, diplomacy and scholarship: Liber amicorum in memoriam Horst G. Krenzler. Springer, Heidelberg, pp. 271–295

Zoellner CS (2006) Transparency: an analysis of an evolving fundamental principle in international economic law. Mich J Int Law 27:579 (590)

Multilateral Trade Policy Is Back

Knut Brünjes and Milena Weidenfeller

Introduction

The then 159 members of the World Trade Organization (WTO) agreed to the so-called "Bali Package" after intense negotiations at the Ninth Ministerial Conference in Bali, Indonesia. One of the key points was the new Agreement on Trade Facilitation. It eliminates many of the bureaucratic hurdles and difficulties surrounding the trade in goods, and creates standardised framework conditions for customs procedures. This is good news for all enterprises involved in international trade and should be implemented, as foreseen in Bali, in due course.

An Historic Step

The hard-earned agreement in Bali is an historic step. For the first time since the founding of the WTO on 1 January 1995, which was based on the former General Agreement on Tariffs and Trade (GATT) 1947, an understanding on a new multilateral agreement was reached in Bali in December 2013. This agreement on the facilitation of trade is enormously important for commercial practice. The political signal that the WTO has sent to the world with this agreement is no less important.

The length and progress, intensity and results of the negations in the run-up to and during the conference show how difficult it has become to reach agreements in

K. Brünjes (✉)
BMWi, VA, Berlin 10115, Germany
e-mail: knut.bruenjes@bmwi.bund.de

M. Weidenfeller
SPD Parliamentary Group, Berlin 12161, Germany
e-mail: milena.weidenfeller@spdfraktion.de

C. Herrmann et al. (eds.), *Trade Policy between Law, Diplomacy and Scholarship*,
European Yearbook of International Economic Law,
DOI 10.1007/978-3-319-15690-3_6

the multilateral system of the WTO, which now has 160 members. The agreements are difficult to achieve and implementing the results will take place to some extent using transitional periods to make the transition easier for weaker developing countries. In the worst case scenario, the agreements reached in Bali could also be taken hostage for completely unrelated policy reasons.

The main goals for the ongoing Doha world trade round—the integration of developing countries into the world market, the comprehensive opening of markets for industrial and agricultural goods as well as for services at the multilateral level, and the evolution of the rules based system of world trade—has received a strong impulse from the current agreement. The Ministerial Conference in Bali confirmed the Doha Development Agenda (DDA) and praised the decisions made at the conference as important milestones on the path to completion of the Doha Round. It instructed the Trade Negotiations Committee (TNC) to prepare a clearly defined work schedule for the remaining DDA topics within the next 12 months.

A Look Back: From GATT to WTO

After World War II, several international organisations and institutions were formed to shape global economy and finances. The World Bank and the International Monetary Fund were founded at the Bretton Woods Conference in 1944.

In the area of trade, the GATT was established in 1947 to determine the trade principles for the planned International Trade Organization (ITO). Because the US Congress failed to ratify the ITO charter, the GATT's already negotiated tariff concessions were provisionally established and tariff reductions based on these principles were negotiated in some successive trade rounds.

The so-called "single undertaking" emerged as an important principle of trade rounds. One round only comes to an end once an agreement has been reached in all areas ("nothing is agreed until everything is agreed"). Only in this way is it possible to achieve a horizontal balancing of interests in all areas of negotiation at trade rounds. In total, there were eight GATT trade rounds; the Doha Round is the first WTO trade round.

Founding of the WTO

The World Trade Organisation, headquartered in Geneva, was founded after the conclusion of the last successful trade round, the so-called "Uruguay Round", in 1995. As part of the Uruguay Round, the text of the original GATT treaty was expanded using numerous supplementary agreements on agriculture, technical barriers to trade, sanitary and phytosanitary measures, rules of origin, etc. The scope of the WTO extends far beyond the trade in goods, because it also includes trade in services[1] and the protection of intellectual property rights[2] and as the crown jewel of WTO, the dispute settlement system.[3]

Trade in services under GATS differs from trade in goods under GATT, because each WTO Member is free to decide which obligations it wants to assume and which not.

TRIPS however is not a means for opening the market, but regulates the cross-border exchange of intellectual property rights (IPR) and sets international minimum standards for the protection of IPR. WTO members are at liberty to provide more extensive protection, if they so choose. Like the other WTO commitments, TRIPS provisions are binding on all WTO Members.

All WTO Members approved the agreements according to the above-mentioned principle of "single undertaking." The level of commitment and various transition periods were tailored according to the level of development of each WTO Member.

Principles of the WTO

WTO Members set the rules of world trade by consensus. Their goal is worldwide trade without customs duties, and free from other barriers, based on two fundamental principles of non-discrimination, which are reflected in all WTO agreements.

The first is the "most favoured nation" principle (MFN). If a WTO Member allows another Member a commercial benefit, it must concede this benefit to all other WTO Members. Important exceptions are bilateral and regional free trade agreements.

The second is the so-called "national treatment" principle, which means that imported goods are treated exactly the same as those produced in the Member's own country.

Development of the WTO

In recent years, some structures have fundamentally changed. This includes the growing number of Members who exhibit a strong heterogeneity. After China, Russia was the last large country to have been admitted. In addition to these, even the poorest developing countries, most recently Yemen, are benefiting from

---

[1] See the General Agreement on Trade in Services (GATS), Annex 1B WTO Agreement.

[2] See the Agreement on Trade-Related Aspects of Intellectual Property Rights (TRIPS), Annex 1C WTO Agreement.

[3] See the Understanding on Rules and Procedures Governing the Settlement of Disputes (DSU), Annex 2 WTO Agreement.

membership. As a consequence, there is a stronger involvement by developing countries in the WTO's decision-making processes. For this reason, the WTO can be seen as an almost universal organisation, which incorporates more than 90 % of world trade.

The WTO Dispute Settlement Mechanism

The WTO is equipped with the Dispute Settlement Body (DSB), an efficient enforcement mechanism able to impose sanctions with which all WTO Members have to comply. In contrast, the former GATT dispute settlement mechanism could rarely resolve trade disputes, because all decisions had to be unanimous.

In the WTO, the newly created DSB framework has corrected this vulnerability. It provides for an initial consultation period between disputant Members. Afterwards, the panel phase starts automatically after 60 days if the conflict could not be resolved bilaterally. Furthermore, the panel's decisions will now be automatically adopted, except when they are unanimously rejected (principle of negative consensus).

In addition to this, Art. 17 DSU created the Appellate Body to provide an appeals process for the DSB.

Currently, the DSB is overloaded and the length of the proceedings, due to their great complexity, is seen as a problem. The system is not suited to resolve essentially political controversies (e.g. the Airbus/Boeing subsidy dispute), nor to partial agreement on items, which have to be resolved within the framework of general trade round negotiations (e.g. cotton subsidies).

WTO: In Need of Reform?

After the failure of the WTO Ministerial Conferences in Seattle and Cancun, demands for institutional reforms became louder. The WTO has been accused of having a "democracy deficit" since its inception. The fact is the WTO rules increasingly affect sensitive areas, which interfere deeply with the states' sovereignty. These include functions such as consumer and environmental protection and the protection of human and animal health.

In the WTO, Members negotiate with each other. The WTO is only the platform and solicitor. Contracts are drawn up before the WTO Secretariat and then ratified by the legislatures in each country. Like in other international fora, parliaments are not directly involved in the negotiations. To mitigate this deficiency, the proposal has been made to set up an advisory board for national parliaments at the WTO, a sort of consultation committee. Parliamentarians from the Inter-Parliamentary Union (IPU) and the European Parliament are dealing with this question. They formed the "Parliamentary Conference on the WTO" in 2001. It meets once a year with the aim of complementing multilateral negotiations with a parliamentary dimension.

There is often criticism of the consensus principle that underlies the decisions made by the WTO. It makes an agreement between the 160 Members very difficult. Every Member has a vote so it could theoretically use its veto and block decisions that are against the will of the majority of the Members. At the Ministerial Conference in Cancun in 2003, it became clear how hard it could be to reach an agreement by consensus. Various proposals were discussed, but they were discarded in the end.

After the conclusion of the Doha Round and in the context of a WTO reform, it will be necessary to find new formats of negotiation beyond the traditional world trade rounds. In this context, there will also be a discussion on a further differentiation of developing countries, which represent more than two thirds of WTO membership. In particular, the classification and role of the large emerging economies in world trade must be reconsidered. Given the strong increase of South–South trade, the previous North–South conflicts are of less interest today to many developing countries.

Challenges for the WTO: Increasing Regionalisation

The increasing number of preferential trade agreements (better known as Free Trade Agreements, FTAs) will be assessed differently.

The expert report by former GATT and WTO Director-General Peter Sutherland[4] once described them as the biggest threat to the WTO. They are politically controversial because they allow some WTO Members to receive benefits that other Members do not. Thus, the principle of most favoured nation, one of the biggest advantages of the WTO, is being undermined by such agreements, even if done so by legal means. Meanwhile, the most-favoured-nation status is more and more the exception than the rule.

Furthermore, such regional agreements often overlap so that it may lead to non-compatible rules in some instances (e.g. on the rules of origin).

In the most recent FTAs, however, other topics are in the foreground. These go beyond the aspects regulated by the framework of the WTO (so-called "WTO-Plus") and, motivated by a growing internationalisation of value-added chains, represent more of a deepening of existing integration. The WTO+ agreements deal with rules on competition policy, investment protection, transfers of capital and regulatory cooperation.

Given the great prevalence of bilateral trade agreements, the central question should be whether bilateral or multilateral integration is preferable, or whether bilateral integration on its own is harmful. What is more important, is to what extent

[4] Director-General during the transition period from GATT to WTO, 1993–1995.

and under what conditions a bilateral agreement is compatible with multilateral integration and how coherence with FTAs can be guaranteed by the WTO rules. This certainly raises starting points for synergies between multilateral and bilateral integration. Thus, bilaterally agreed liberalisations could be used increasingly as a model for multilateral cooperation on the basis of "best practice" analyses.

Political Aspects of Regional Trade Agreements

It is still controversial whether bilateral agreements can actually serve as a model for multilateral agreements or rather, within the meaning of Bhagwati's "spaghetti bowl",[5] a network of regulations interferes with transparency in international trade and therefore has the effect of increasing complexity.

Thus, there are still considerable coherence problems between multilateral and bilateral integration at the legal level. Regional agreements in the form of customs unions and free trade areas are fundamentally privileged according to GATT and GATS, as long as a more restrictive regime is not built up against third countries. The requirements are relatively vague. For example, "substantially all the trade" (GATT) or "substantially all discrimination" (GATS) will have to be dismantled within the RTAs in order for the RTA to fall outside the scope of the MFN principle.

The transparency mechanism provided for in the WTO to monitor these objectives is only a partial success, despite some progress in recent years. Even though coherence has been improved by the substantiation and tightening of rules, the acceptance of the mechanism among Members is not without reservation.

Commercial Aspects of Regional Trade Agreements

Also from an economic perspective, bilateral agreements can only be the second best solution compared to multilateral agreements, because the trade diversion caused by preferential agreements (discrimination effect) can diminish the efficiency benefits from the international division of labour. However, that is countered by trade creation (efficiency effect), which grows out of intensified trade within the integrated area. A rule of thumb states that the efficiency effect is smaller compared to the discrimination effect, depending on how small the partner countries' share of world trade is and how small the proportion of internal trade to the partner's total trade is. Conversely, the discrimination effects are minimised if the trading partners were to trade with each other even without an agreement. Taking into account that preferential agreements often extend beyond pure trade topics, additional positive

[5] Bhagwati (1995).

effects on institutional efficiency are possible, particularly with North–South RTAs (albeit from a regulatory perspective, it is not desirable to regulate non-economic aspects of trade agreements). Furthermore, regional agreements are easier to negotiate due to the smaller number of members, and disputes can be resolved more effectively, because the agreement provides better monitoring and enforcement capabilities.

From the German perspective, the highest increases in prosperity are expected by a closer cooperation of the EU with regions where the German economy will increase exports in the near future. Countries of particular interest for cooperation are the most dynamic economies in the process of industrialising, which, therefore, have a demand (especially ASEAN countries) for high-quality capital goods and the associated services from Germany (service, support; in mechanical engineering: 30 % of export). Most of them maintain high tariffs and effective non-tariff barriers to trade.

Objectives of the Doha Round

The ninth round of trade negotiations was launched—significantly influenced by the events on September 11—in November 2001 in Doha, Qatar. As a concession to developing countries at the start of a new round, an emphasis was placed on better integration of developing countries into the world trade system. This was made clear in the Doha Development Agenda (DDA).

The mandate for negotiations at the Doha round was comprehensively worded—assuming that by taking on a very wide spectrum of a total of 21 topics, the necessary balance among the strongly diverging interests of the WTO members could be achieved: fewer customs duties; more access to the market for agriculture, industrial products and services; reduction in subsidies; protection of intellectual property; fairer access to medication; rules for geographical indications, for investment, and for competition; more transparency in public procurement; trade facilitation; better disciplines for anti-dumping and protection measures; new rules for regional agreements; reform of the dispute settlement mechanism; trade and the environment; trade and technology transfer—the motto was "you name it – it's in." A new fund for expanding capacity for developing countries (DDA Global Trust Funds) and increased trade-related development assistance (Aid for Trade) was put over this compendium of heterogeneous negotiation topics.

Added to this was the above-described principle of the single undertaking, which states that agreements on partial results should only apply if an overall agreement on all issues is reached. This should allow for the necessary balance of interests beyond the limits of individual negotiation chapters.

Soon, it became apparent that requirements for the negotiations had to be scaled back. In 2003, this led to some of the new negotiation areas, known as the "Singapore issues", being dropped such as trade and investment, public procurement, and trade and competition. Only the topic of trade facilitation remained, which has now the chance of being completed successfully in the near future.

The concentration on the traditional issues of market access for industrial and agricultural products, as well as services, proved to be expedient when the subsequent negotiations were at least able to be taken so far forward that an informal ministerial meeting was convened in 2008 with the aim of concluding negotiations on a "modalities package". However, an agreement in 2008 ultimately failed, because no compromise between the main rivals, the USA and India, could be achieved in the highly contentious area of market access for agricultural products.

Since 2008, the potential for conflict within the WTO on market access for agricultural products has decreased, because a significant increase in demand in agricultural markets has contributed to the reduction of duties and domestic support measures. However conversely, the potential for conflict in the area of industrial goods trade has grown within the WTO. This is particularly due to the fact that the willingness of some emerging countries towards market opening was subordinate to the desire to build up and to protect domestic production by means of national industrialisation strategies. This was usually associated with "local content" requirements, which are inconsistent with WTO law in principle. Intensive attempts using different approaches were made in an effort to bring together negotiation positions in the area of market access for industrial goods. These remained unsuccessful in the follow-up to the informal ministerial meeting in 2008.

Subsequently, to achieve further progress at the Doha negotiations, the principle of the "single undertaking" had to be effectually dismissed. After the Eighth WTO Ministerial Conference in late 2011, an effort has been made to continue negotiations on a few of the attractive categories of the Doha Round, especially those of interest to developing countries, with the aim of an agreement at the Ninth Ministerial Conference. Due to the anticipated win–win situation, it is especially important to come to an agreement on trade facilitation—a simple, but effective set of rules for the global economy, which should lead to greater trade reliability and predictability. This was paramount in preparing for the Ninth WTO Ministerial Conference, because a reduction in bureaucracy for customs clearance will benefit all WTO Members in principle.

Studies show that developing countries would benefit even more than industrialised countries. This seems logical since the biggest hindrances and delays for the cross-border movement of goods are outdated or even completely missing infrastructure and a high susceptibility to corruption.

Charges for Customs Clearance

Various international studies (e.g. OECD, World Bank, CEPII) have shown that through the comprehensive easing of customs, savings in industrialised countries could amount to about 10 % of total trading costs and could even be up to 16 % in developing countries.

An OECD country requires on average five customs documents and 10 days for one container to clear customs. The costs for this amount to €735. In contrast to this, an African country usually requires twice as many customs documents, up to 35 days for customs clearance and even up to 44 days for imports. The average cost amounts to up to €1,500 per container. That is almost double the corresponding costs in OECD countries.

Especially in less developed countries, simpler and more standardised customs documents could already reduce expenses on goods by about 3 %. In some of these countries, more than 5 % of gross domestic product must be spent on customs clearance. This considerable amount is in return lost in company revenue. Reasons for costly processing are often due to insufficiently trained personnel and tariff structures in need of improvement or inefficient processing practices.

Nonetheless, it became apparent that many developing countries define trade facilitation as an interest of developed countries and, therefore, they want it to be treated as compensation in further negotiation topics. These were some of the known demands: Improvements in market access for developing countries and the least developed countries (LDCs), where the agricultural sector in turn was of particular importance. Since October 2012, the issue of food security, on India's insistence, eventually developed into a major point of contention and in the end almost caused the Bali package to fail.

All Agreements of the Ninth WTO Ministerial Conference at a Glance

In Bali, the WTO reached understandings on ten points, which were negotiated in the framework of the Doha Round. At a glance, these are:

I. The understanding on an agreement on trade facilitation
II. Understandings in the interests of the developing countries on:

1. A monitoring mechanism to test and improve the rules and regulations of the WTO on the special and preferential treatment of developing countries (monitoring mechanism);
2. A procedure for the implementation of so-called services waivers, which allow preferential treatment of LDCs on market access for services, like that of the generalised GATT preference system for the goods trade, which has been in place since the early 1970s;

3. Guidelines to simplify the rules of origin for preferential market access for LDCs, making for better use of LCDs' existing capacities in the granting of preferences;
4. A political declaration on establishing comprehensive duty-free and quota-free market access for products from LDCs to the markets of industrialised states and emerging countries, which are in a position to do so. The EU already granted this a long time ago for all products except arms (Everything But Arms, EBA); as well as
5. An understanding on the further reduction of customs duties and internal support measures for cotton, which until now made it more difficult for cotton-producing developing countries to access the market.

III. Decisions made by the Ministerial Conference in Bali for the area of agricultural negotiations within the framework of the Doha Round:

1. An agreement on tariff quota management for agricultural goods to improve the transparency in quota allocation by using predictable processes, so that the granted import quotas on zero tariffs or lower tariffs can be better utilised;
2. A political declaration on the commitment to the further reduction of export subsidies;
3. An implementation of an interim mechanism for the issue of public storage of agricultural goods to ensure food security for poorer sections of the population; as well as.
4. A recognition of general services programmes related to land reform and rural livelihood security to promote rural development and poverty alleviation.

The Drama of the Negotiations Before, During and After the Conference

After the Eighth WTO Ministerial Conference in December 2011, the negotiations on the Bali Package initially developed along the question of which issues might come under consideration for early partial results of the Doha Round. The common view of all WTO Members was that an agreement on trade facilitation should be an essential element of the package, but with different prospects and understanding of the intended content. This meant that the negotiations on trade facilitation, which were previously relatively constructive and quick, were now not making any progress. In addition, it was foreseeable that questions of market access for the agricultural sector would be raised by developing countries over the course of 2012. The coordination processes within the various WTO groupings have proven difficult, because it has long been unclear what concrete demands would be brought to the negotiating table.

Brazil finally put forward a proposal, the first country to do so in spring 2012, for more transparency for tariff rate quotas for agricultural products. It was tailored in such a way—against the backdrop of the candidacy of Brazil's Robert Azevêdo for the position of WTO Director-General—that the proposal in principle was met with broad acceptance. Only later did the topic become explosive between the US and China, because the proposal only set out commitments for industrialised countries and spared emerging countries, which are still listed as developing countries in the WTO's categories. In October 2012, a proposal was presented by the G33 developing countries group on India's initiative that resulted in a change to the WTO Agreement on Agriculture. The aim of this was to allow the purchase of agricultural goods at subsidised prices for large-scale storage, in order to ensure food security for poorer populations. In addition, the demand for a reduction on agricultural export subsidies was raised again by the G20 group of agricultural exporting countries in the WTO. Even before the Bali conference, the same confrontation lines were drawn as back in 2008, which had already once prevented a successful outcome at the Doha negotiations.

In the first half of 2013, there was hardly any substantial progress made on bringing the differing positions together. The crucial turning point came in September 2013, as Roberto Azevêdo took office as the new WTO Director-General. He was able to succeed by fundamentally changing the negotiation approach, which scarcely seemed possible: Up until then, the Doha negotiations had been characterised by the fact that smaller groups of key players met with each other. He undertook the—quite risky—attempt to hold negotiations on the proposals' texts while involving all then 159 WTO Members at the same time. Azevêdo was thus able to drive numerous outstanding issues forward and to bring them to a conclusion, and vote, by 25 November 2013. That, along with his tireless additional mediation efforts during the Ministerial Conference itself, can only be seen as a phenomenal success, which deserves the greatest respect. Azevêdo has found compromises for more than a hundred questions in the text of the agreement on trade facilitation during marathon sessions with the entire WTO membership. He has ironed out the disagreements between the USA and China over customs quotas and has subsequently persuaded India to compromise on the question of the storage of subsidised agricultural goods.

The success at the Geneva negotiations was already torn out from under Azevêdo's feet, even before the conference began, by India. At the last minute, the Indian government returned back to their maximum demand regardless of the negotiations reached in Geneva, which was to be permanently, not only temporarily, freed from the obligations set out in the WTO agriculture treaty on subsidised warehousing. This was not a viable option for many other WTO Members, especially for India's neighbouring countries, which were—quite understandably—afraid that their markets would be flooded with surpluses from Indian warehouses.

Thus, at the beginning of the Ministerial Conference, it was completely unclear which turn the negotiations would take. The prospects for an agreement depended on India's stance. Negotiations on the last questions for the agreement on trade facilitation were still open, but did not make sense without any prospect of an agreement with India on warehousing. Everything seemed to depend on how Indian Trade Minister Sharma would position himself in Bali. He announced his position on the second day of the conference. It was a hard stance, declaring that food security is non-negotiable for India. This message was primarily directed to his home constituency, where elections were taking place. It was obviously not primarily about finding the right balance at the WTO multilateral negotiations on a Bali package, but rather addressing Indian voters at home.

During the night of 5 and 6 December, DG Azevêdo eventually succeeded again, along with the USA and the Conference's host country, Indonesia, in finding the basis for a solution that could be consolidated to such an extent that a compromise was within reach during the course of the day on 6 December. The solution, quite unexpectedly, created a new rift between Cuba and the USA, because of the USA's embargo of Cuba. This necessitated another long night of negotiations in Bali, before a final understanding on the Bali Package could be officially agreed to on Saturday, 7 December, one day after the conference was planned to end.

At present, India, supported by some African and Latin American countries, has reopened the debate and put the Bali results on Trade Facilitation into question. In doing so, India is guided by its own internal agricultural subsidies, consciously ignoring the benefits, Trade Facilitation would have especially for developing countries. In addition, India unnecessarily opened a North-South controversy at a moment when the multilateral system needs support and unity. A failure of Trade Facilitation could put the Doha Development Agenda at risk and could mean a further erosion of the rules-based system. Small and vulnerable countries would suffer more than the main trading nations. In the end, disharmony at multilateral level would harm the interests of all nations instead of fostering trade, development, jobs, income and technology transfer.

Categorising the Results and Further Perspectives

The multilateral trading system is the central framework for world trade. It joins together industrialised and developed countries and emerging economies, as well as the least developed countries, under a set of rules, and it contains the principles of most favoured nation and non-discrimination, which create equal rights for all parties involved.

The WTO has a binding, functional and much used dispute settlement mechanism, and a system for monitoring the trade policies of its Members. In this way, it is far ahead of other international organisations.

However, in recent years, these important features have been pushed into the background, because the Doha Round still has not come to a close after more than 13 years.

With the understanding on the Bali Package, and particularly an agreement on trade facilitation, the WTO showed strong signs of life. It demonstrated that even negotiating new multilateral trade rules within the WTO framework can be completed successfully.

The agreement in Bali has an historic dimension, because in times of growing global networks of supply and value-added chains, world trade in the twenty-first century needs timely multilateral solutions more urgently than ever.

Even if the full implementation of the agreements made in Bali on trade facilitation is still uncertain, the result could be a giant leap forward for trade practice. Significant time and cost savings could be expected in North–South trade. South–South trade would benefit even more from systematic implementation, because the main hurdles for customs clearance are in developing countries.

The Ninth WTO Ministerial Conference has paved the way for continuance of the Doha negotiations step by step and preserved the possibility of full completion. The outcome of the Bali negotiations shows that even with 160 Members, the WTO is capable of making new, far-reaching decisions. However, the course of the negotiations also shows that this takes a lot of time and is becoming increasingly difficult.

At the same time, the trend for more bilateral and plurilateral agreements is expected to continue. This does not have to be seen as a disadvantage: If such agreements comply with the requirements of WTO law, and therefore create more trade liberalisation, they can be building blocks on the way to a later multilateralisation of their results.

Bilateral initiatives, as well as plurilateral negotiations, can act as a catalyst for greater flexibility and willingness to compromise on multilateral negotiations. In particular, the opening of bilateral negotiations on a free trade agreement between the EU and the USA (TTIP) has sent a wakeup call around the world and could also have a healing effect on the multilateral negotiations in Geneva. It aims at covering new ground in the area of regulatory cooperation and in drafting a modern chapter on sustainable trade. Through TTIP, issues of labour standards will be touched upon in the same way as questions of major environmental conventions. And last but not least, the trading partners will try to shape an ambitious but balanced chapter on investment protection, an area previously covered by many individual treaties of the respective Member States of the EU. Political debate on the level of protection for investments on the one hand, and the appropriate policy space or "right to regulate", continue to accompany the public debate in Germany even more heatedly than many trade topics before. It is not yet clear which will be the way forward of the main trading zones in the world on this topic, but the effort should be worthwhile.

Reference

Bhagwati JN (1995) US trade policy: the infatuation with FTAs. In: Bhagwati JN, Krueger AO (eds) The dangerous drift to preferential trade agreements, American Enterprise Institute for Public Policy Research, Washington, DC

Multilateralism as a Basis for Global Governance

Christian D Falkowski

The European Union and the Normative Multilateralism

The advent of the era of globalisation has increased considerably the call for global governance. The growing interdependence of states has underlined the need for common global actions, be it in the domain of economy, fight against poverty, climate change, energy or security against terrorism. Traditional power politics in the pursuit of narrowly defined national interests cannot keep up to meet future challenges. Strong regional and global institutions as well as transnational actors are universally regarded as the cornerstone of a future multipolar world order moving towards global governance and political interaction—a departure from state-centric understandings of world politics.

Closely linked to the emergence of global governance is the concept of multilateralism. Multilateralism is, however, not synonymous with "global governance". Rather, multilateralism refers to a particular principle, a specific way to tackle global issues. Multilateralism stands for a way of behaviour between states and/or institutions. International political stability is to be achieved through the involvement of all the parties concerned and on the basis of jointly elaborated solutions to problems.

Multilateralism can be considered as the basis, essential for making global governance really work, and effective in addressing global challenges. The classic definition of multilateralism means the handling of transnational problems by three or more parties concerned on the basis of mutually agreed general principles of conduct. An important aspect of this "idea of standards" is that the "codes of conduct" take precedence over individual interests of the parties involved. By moving from

C.D. Falkowski (✉)
Former EU Ambassador, Member of the Board of Asko Europa Stiftung Saarbrücken,
Am Alten Berg 36, 64342 Seeheim-Jugenheim, Germany
e-mail: cdfalkowski@t-online.de

C. Herrmann et al. (eds.), *Trade Policy between Law, Diplomacy and Scholarship*,
European Yearbook of International Economic Law,
DOI 10.1007/978-3-319-15690-3_7

limited interest-based behaviour towards more generally accepted principles, a growing confidence between the parties should evolve gradually.

The confidence of smaller states in the willingness of the more powerful ones to fully respect commonly agreed principles and standards is the essential aspect of the concept of multilateralism. In other words, the parties expect that the larger and more powerful states are willing to adhere to binding agreements indeed, accepting credible investigations and procedures to adjudicate any disagreements on the implementation of its multilateral commitments.

The importance of multilateralism to the European Union is obvious. Multilateralism is, so to speak, the organisational principle of European integration, or: European integration is a particular form of multilateralism. Multilateralism forms part of the European identity. As the building principle of European policy, multilateralism is based on the historical experience of Europe. The great European wars of modern times were mostly triggered by striving for hegemony, and have generally been terminated with the victory of the counter-power coalition.

American history and political awareness is significantly different. The United States have pursued with success a hegemonic policy in different periods of their history. From the beginnings of continental expansion to its present global power position, the "long march of the American Empire"[1] has been considered, apart from a few exceptions such as the Vietnam War, as a success of hegemonic and imperial policy. This experience nourishes the "myths of imperial policy"[2] and shapes until today the American view of history.

And because the positive experience with hegemonic policy is linked to a universalism of values progressing in the course of time, the American Empire feels itself justified by the idea that its policy is in the general interest of mankind. The US has also been in the position to enforce its global interests by appropriate means. The global control of digital data streams by the US for their own intelligence purposes is the latest example of successful power politics of the imperial republic.

However, the approach of the Union, determined by Europe's experience of repeated failures of imperial policy (also of the colonial policy) and by the success of its "politics of an integrative balance of power",[3] is to pursue a policy of cooperative balance towards other countries, with the result that in particular the anti-imperial policy of the so-called old Europe has beneficial effects, and it has increased the diplomatic room for manoeuvre and the influence of the EU in the world. The recent success in the negotiations with Iran over its nuclear programme has been achieved along these lines, supported by the negotiating skills of the Union representative. Another example is the Union's approach to resolve the Ukrainian crisis through negotiations and not by force.

---

[1] Kurth (2002), pp. 403–408.

[2] Snyder (2003), pp. 29–38.

[3] Link (2006), pp. 24–30.

US critics such as Robert Kagan consider multilateralism as a "weapon of the weak".[4] Those who are in favour of multilateralism simply lack the power to enforce their concepts of how to go about global problems. No wonder that it is favoured by the smaller states. And the interest of Europe to promote global multilateralism is exactly a consequence of Europe's "powerlessness". As long as the global economy and policy are determined by interests and not by norms and common standards, multilateralism will have hardly any chance. This is quite obvious in the failure of the Doha Trade Round, the insufficient results of UN climate conferences or the persistent blockage of the long-overdue reform of the UN Security Council.

Emerging countries appear rather cautious towards multilateralism, as in their view, it is dominated mainly by Western interests and Western norms, and does not sufficiently include concepts of non-OECD countries. However, many of those states are indeed too weak to use the "weapon of the weak" by themselves. Multilateralism is far more than the interaction of a group of States. In a more limited sense, almost all international initiatives could be considered as multilateral. Multilateralism as a political concept is closely linked to legitimacy and has three basic aspects:

Firstly, multilateralism signifies the obligation to work with international institutions in their *modus operandi*. That means first and foremost to work within the UN framework, but it also requires working and sharing tasks with other regional organisations, especially with NATO, the Council of Europe, the OSCE and with various regional organisations in Africa (AU), in Asia (ASEAN) and Latin America (OAS). The collaboration with these organisations does, however, not suggest that they are regarded as sacrosanct. The commitment to effective multilateralism is also a commitment to undertake necessary reforms of international organisations.

Secondly, multilateralism is also the commitment to shared norms and rules, and to solve problems and crises through rules and cooperation. The EU acting rather as a promoter of international standards than as a superpower, is less threatening for non-European States and offers a reference and starting point to round up support in multilateral fora such as the UN.

Thirdly, multilateralism means coordination and cooperation, as opposed to duplication and rivalry, i.e. the development and use of decentralised networks. An effective international policy, be it in relation to climate change, or as it is now, as regards to the financial market crisis, requires cooperation between different policy areas and fora (foreign affairs, finance, trade, development policy) and with different institutions such as the IMF, the World Bank, the G8, and the G20. Preventive and pro-active policy measures may just not be effective if they are isolated or even contradictory.

This is not very new or original, but a simple insight that only gradually asserts itself in today's politics. The EU is successful when it is united and acts with one voice; examples are the International Criminal Court (ICC) or the Kyoto Protocol,

[4] Kagan (2002).

and more recently the decisions to tackle the global economic crisis. "The more time and energy EU member states spend haggling with each other, the less time and energy they will devote to tasks farther ahead. Only if EU members aggregate their wealth and military capability will they be able to help anchor the coming transition in global power. In a world that sorely needs the EU's collective will, a divided and introverted Europe would constitute a historical setback."[5]

The US and the Interest-Based Multilateralism

The US perspective of an interest-based multilateralism is diametrically opposed to a norms-based multilateralism. In the first decade of this millennium, the EU was largely alone in calling for the implementation of multilateralism as the organising principle of global governance. The US interest in international obligations was limited at most to a few key UN organisations.

The US was, for example, not at all ready to participate in the multilateral efforts to tackle climate change. They flatly refused to enter into any obligations under an international binding treaty to limit global emissions or to agree on global emission targets. Only at the World Bank and the IMF was the US actively engaged in order to secure its influence. The US also co-operated with the World Trade Organisation, and some regional organisations received their attention as well. The obvious US unilateralism was a considerable challenge for the EU, especially as other countries such as China and India also showed little inclination to multilateralism.

The Obama administration pursues USA fundamentally pragmatic approach in US foreign policy, including multilateralism. Different organisations and events with different multilateral ideas are used for the solution of global problems. The United States entered into commitments in the sense of the traditional multilateralism in the fields of non-proliferation of nuclear weapons, security and human rights. In particular, the non-proliferation treaty is about US interests rather than the norms of multilateralism, which are obliging for international organisations such as the IAEA with its overall responsibility for monitoring compliance. The US continues to refuse to participate under international law in a global climate agreement or to ratify the statute of the International Criminal Court (ICC).

But also the US cannot ignore the world around them. As Henry Kissinger put it, "America will have to learn that world order depends on a structure that participants support because they helped bring it about."[6] However, the US will seek to coin multilateralism as its suits their interests and policy best. Multilateral organisations and forums are judged according to their instrumental value. The US can choose the way of action—whether uni-, bi- or multilateral—which is most favourable to them, and thereby favouring a particular global governance forum in different

[5] Kupchan (2012), chapter 6.

[6] Kissinger (2008).

policy fields, such as the UN, the G8, and the G20. In the words of Vice-President Joseph Biden, "we'll work in a partnership whenever we can, and alone only when we must. The threats we face have no respect for borders. No single country, no matter how powerful, can best meet these threats alone. We believe international alliances and organizations do not diminish America's power – we believe they help advance our collective security, economic interests and our values."[7]

Multilateralism vs. Bilateralism

Multilateralism has for more than half a century been the cornerstone of global trade liberalisation. Both the US and Europe have advocated free trade, in the EU up to a common trade policy with the merger of sovereign rights of Member States; and both trading powers have benefitted immensely from this policy.

Together with 12 % of the world's population, the EU and US are "covering approximately 50 % of global output, almost 30 % of world merchandise trade (including intra-EU trade, but excluding services trade), and 20 % of global foreign direct investment. The United States and the European Union are each other's primary investment and trade partners. In 2012, 63 % of US FDI went to the European Union and 44 % of FDI inflows to the United States originated from the European Union. Bilateral investment flows between the United States and European Union generated a fifth of all international merger and acquisition activity. The US accounts for 20 % of EU exports and 20 % of EU imports (excluding intra-EU trade), while the European Union accounts for 28 % of US exports and 24 % of US imports. Measured in value added terms transatlantic trade flows are even more important than when measured in gross terms. The United States receives 23 % of total EU exports and provides 21 % of EU imports on a value added basis, while the European Union accounts for 29 % of US exports and 27 % of US imports. In other words, the United States is by far the most important destination of EU value-added and the United States is by far the largest supplier of value-added in EU imports [sic.]"[8]

The EU, with a share of almost 25 % of the world gross domestic product and about 20 % of world trade is the largest exporter of goods, the biggest direct investor and the most important import market for the emerging and developing countries (55 % of all exports from these countries go to Europe, compared to only 38 % to the US and 6 % to Japan).

Globalisation has been made possible only through multilateralism, with the result of a convergence of developing with OECD countries, and the emergence of global companies. The EU has a direct influence on the development of non-OECD countries. The external economic policy of the Union is thus not only an economic

[7] Biden (2009).

[8] OECD (2013), p. 1.

instrument for the maintenance of free world trade but is also used in pursuit of its specific global political interests.

The subdivision of the value chain has significantly helped to integrate developing countries into the global economy. The global production chain allocates segments of production to different locations according to local comparative advantages, including the costs of foreign investment and trade, while intra-company trading ensures the logistics of the product through the various stages up to the market. The multilateral trade system has only made possible the globalisation of the value chain, as emphasised by Renato Ruggiero, former Director-General of the WTO:

> In the ten years to 1996, investment flows worldwide easily quadrupled, from around $60 billion to almost $300 billion per annum. In these statistics are revealed the new dialectic of globalization. The systematic reduction of trade barriers worldwide, combined with dramatic decreases in transport and communications costs, has paved the way for the emergence of a global system of production, distribution and consumption – one in which firms are increasingly free to assemble inputs from around the world and to service an equally global marketplace. This in turn has accelerated the movement of global investment, as firms learn that the best way to achieve comparative advantage in production, in sourcing, in distribution, and in technology is to establish a direct presence in foreign markets.[9]

In contrast, if trade takes place between countries in the global world through a series of bilateral agreements, all kinds of rules of rules of origin, etc. must be taken into account, i.e. the trading cost will increase with the number of respective agreements—international trade becomes more expensive. A multilateral agreement on regulatory convergence in the framework of WTO would reduce these costs. Some progress has been registered with the recent Bali trade agreement. Multilateralism and not bilateral agreements have made a decisive contribution to global prosperity, to the economic convergence of the North and South and thus to global stability and peace.

However, as soon as the United States were facing the strength of China and other BRIC countries, especially India, in multilateral trade rounds, they were starting to build up a parallel process leading to a series of bilateral agreements, allegedly to get around the stalemate of the Doha Trade Round. In bilateral agreements, it is much easier for the US to enforce their ideas of market access, investment, standards and norms from a position of strength.

Out of fear to be ousted by the US from markets secured through their bilateral agreements, the EU had no choice but to enter into this competition on trade liberalisation, so it happened when Mexico joined NAFTA in 1999. Meanwhile, the EU has concluded a number of bilateral trade agreements among others with Korea, Singapore and most recently with Canada.

Over the past 20 years, some estimated 400 bilateral free trade agreements[10] worldwide have been concluded or are under negotiation. Thus questions arise

[9] Ruggiero (1996).

[10] Defraigne (2013), p. 6.

about the role of the WTO, the liberalisation of world trade, and the principle of multilateralism, as the link between the economic and trade models of emerging countries and that of OECD countries.

A further step towards the dominance of bilateralism would be the conclusion of a US–EU transatlantic free trade agreement, known as Transatlantic Trade and Investment Partnership (TTIP). The creation of a transatlantic marketplace would change considerably the balance of power in the international trade system. This is all the more so, as it could balance out the relative loss of power of the EU and the US through a merger of trade interests, and thus set global standards for norms and standards. This would also limit the growing influence of emerging powers, such as India or China, in international trade.

> In a world where we are all connected, the transatlantic relationship remains the most important relationship we have. It is vital for the freedom, security and prosperity of both Europe and North America. The Transatlantic Trade and Investment Partnership that is now under discussion is sometimes described as an "economic NATO". Because the Transatlantic Trade and Investment Partnership can bring enormous benefits to all our nations and all our people, for generations to come. It can set a new gold standard in economic cooperation, just like NATO has long been the gold standard in security cooperation. And, just like NATO, it can be a strong pillar for a truly 'Integrated Transatlantic Community'.[11]

This quotation of a speech of NATO Secretary General Anders Fogh Rasmussen certainly reflects the US view. They are negotiating two major bilateral trade agreements in parallel: on one side in the Pacific with the Trans Pacific Partnership (TPP), that is to be a giant free trade zone. In reality, however, it will bring together countries that for security considerations seek proximity to America (against China). On the other side, the Atlantic where military security (NATO) would be combined with economic power.

In a global perspective, the US would eventually have two powerful trade instruments against the new emerging world power, China, and they could try to control China with TPP and TTIP.

> Permit me to say without being hyperbolic that there are essentially two competing models of governance in the post-Communist world. One is the transatlantic model shared by many other countries, based upon democratic governance, with free peoples, free markets, and free trade; the other is autocratic governance, state-controlled or dominated economies, and managed trade. The TTIP is an opportunity to show the world that our model of governance can produce tangible gains for our people on both sides of the Atlantic and more broadly is the best model to meet the challenges of the 21st century.[12]

Is this view expressed by Stuart E. Eizenstat, former US Ambassador the EU, the great strategy that is not so new? A block of descending powers positioned against the newcomer, trying not to share its wealth and influence. This is not the European model: the idea of "the West against the rest" which is resonating in the Washington policy is not only risky but also dangerous. The EU should design its own trade

---

[11] Rasmussen (2013).

[12] Eizenstat (2013).

strategy with emerging countries based on its own principles of multilateralism. China needs to be incorporated through multilateralism and by legal regulations in the multipolar world. The emergence of rival and soon hostile trading blocs will not serve the interests of Europe, nor meet its expectations and values; it does not serve the peace of the world. "To confront Beijing with the prospect of encirclement would risk fuelling a vicious cycle of mounting rivalry."[13]

Multilateralism and European Integration

Today, the completion of the internal market and closer cooperation in economic policy seems more urgent than ever, to match, as a counterpart, external economic and trade liberalisation. However, the European crisis management lately has hardly anything to do with a common political will of the EU, but appears to be more of an enforced coordination of separate national measures. The thereby emerging intergovernmentalism corresponds less to the concept of integration but rather to a Europe à la carte, creating different forms of participation depending on the specific national interests.

Some of the principles underpinning the EU are being put into question. Whereas the Community method is based on multilateralism, the increasing intergovernmentalism, also described as reciprocal nationalism, is basically of a bilateral nature.

> Accordingly, every state has the autonomy and the duty to regulate its own financial problems. At the same time, each nation must recognise the sovereignty of other European nations, so that all nations avoid the negative consequences of their economic policy decisions for others. This point of view is based on three principles: equality, coordinated packages of measures and mutual responsibility. A fourth principle is, in addition, the refusal to expand the EU's economic policy competence. Although this model of reciprocal nationalism may suffice for times of fine weather, in times of an impending decline of the euro, it must fail. Incompatible budgetary policies, fiscal policies, and social security and tax systems are becoming the political bomb in national and intranational arenas.[14]

In comparison to the Community method, intergovernmentalism has no coercive means or institution of proceedings like the European Court of Justice. Intergovernmentalism is block-oriented and could lead to a policy long believed as overcome, also known as Bismarck's policy of the balance of power. Such a policy could amount for the EU, so to speak, to a worst case scenario, diametrically opposed to the founding ideas of a norms-based effective multilateralism.

The EU's structural weakness is not economic but political, also because EU heavy weights like Germany are no longer fully supportive of a normative multilateralism.

---

[13] Kupchan (2012), chapter 7.

[14] Beck (2010).

> Multilateralism – the premise of German post-war politics *par excellence* – was sacrificed in a strange mixture of self-centeredness, self-importance and self-deception in the name of 'Europe' for the necessity of 'euro stability'. There is nothing wrong with representing German interests. The core of the problem is that these are misunderstood and are argued in terms of a self-confirming prophecy as a zero-sum game.[15]

The dilemma of the Economic and Monetary Union makes this very clear: a highly integrated monetary union with a single currency and central bank lacks the strength of a common economic union as the policy framework to bring together the very divergent economies of northern and southern Europe and to cushion their unavoidable economic imbalances. The so-called markets have already bluntly disclosed the growing political deficit, saved so far by a non-political institution, the European Central Bank.

Multilateralism and European Security

Effective multilateralism needs partners. For the EU, this requires in addition to stable relations with the US and Russia, strategic partners among the emerging powers, such as China and India. Fully functional international and regional organisations will gain importance as a reference point for European foreign and security policy. A policy of strengthening regional organisations must therefore be accompanied by an intensification of EU's relationship with key regional actors.

In the words of Catherine Ashton, High Representative of the EU:

> I intend to invest a lot in strengthening partnerships with what we somewhat misleadingly call the 'new powers': China, India, South Africa, Brazil, Mexico and Turkey. For too long we have seen these countries mainly through an economic prism. But it is clear that they are major political and security players too, with increasing political clout. Our mental map has to adjust — and fast. My sense is that the European response should be more generous — in making space at the top tables of global politics. Early on, when strategies are formed, not just when resources are needed for implementation.[16]

Global warming and the fight for natural resources are closely interrelated. Climate change is a threat multiplier that further exacerbates existing trends, tensions and instability. States and regions already fragile and conflict-prone can be overwhelmed. The emerging risks are not just of a humanitarian nature but also include political and security risks that affect European interests directly. Europe's security cannot be dissociated from global security. Security is to be understood in a broader sense than it was the case in times of the nation state paradigm.

Security is not restricted, but should be understood in a comprehensive and global manner, i.e. there is a relationship between all relevant factors for security issues. This approach is based on the realisation that, for example, the problem of

---

[15] Beck (2010).

[16] Ashton (2010).

poverty or minority issues are to be taken into account for the formulation of international security, as well as the non-proliferation regime or military conflict solutions. Europe must be able and willing to act in order to meet its security interests. Europe's responsibility for global security as the core of the European Security should be achieved through an international order based on effective multilateralism. "In a world of global threats, global markets and global media, our security and prosperity increasingly depend on an effective multilateral system. The development of a stronger international society, well functioning [sic.] international institutions and a rule-based international order is our objective."[17]

In a narrower regional perspective, the EU sees itself as an area of stability for its members and the neighbouring regions. The EU has a strong interest in the stabilisation of Europe and its environment. Enlargement policy today is justified mainly with the objective of promoting stability in the immediate neighbourhood. The enlargement to 28 Member States is changing the relationship with Russia, Ukraine, Moldova and Belarus, as well as with the countries bordering the Mediterranean.

The offer of EU membership has proven to be an important foreign policy tool. New EU Member States campaign for good relations with their respective neighbouring states, because they do not want to remain border states of the EU. But the dynamics of enlargement is far more driven by the urgent desire for accession of the states concerned. "The process of enlargement is determined not by EU diktat or imperial request, but rather by the unsolicited desire of these states and their internal demand for reform; and expanded is the European Union's non-hegemonic system of integration".[18]

Support for political and economic development of its neighbours is the best guarantee of peace and security for the EU. By forging closer links, termed as the European Neighbourhood Policy, the EU wants to make a decisive contribution to achieve political and economic reform with mutual advantages. For the neighbouring countries, the interest is to benefit from the achievements of the EU as a "geo-economic player", from its economic stability and from larger markets, as well as from its experience with reforms.

The Union wants to coordinate essential aspects of the foreign and security policy of the contracting parties to build a common space of freedom, security and justice. The common fight against terrorism, against the proliferation of weapons of mass destruction and the respect for international law shall secure not only the EU's borders but shall be extended to cover neighbouring states as well.

The EU's economic and political interests go well beyond its own actual area of influence. Europe is simply more affected by crises and conflicts, disturbances or blockages in international trade like the supply of raw materials than any other actor in world politics. Geopolitically, Europe is located in a region with a sensitive and

[17] Council of the European Union (2003), p. 9.

[18] Falkowski (2011), p. 113.

troubled neighbourhood, its development and policy touches immediately on the special interests of other current and potential new world powers.

Europe borders the territory of the Russian Federation to the east, from the Barents Sea in the north to the Black Sea; to the southeast, the Middle East, and to the south, the countries of North Africa. There are special political, economic and social relations, partly safety links and military presence in countries of Black Africa, Asia and Latin America, through its Member States.

The Union as a civil power is guided by the basic principles that also apply internally. The concept of Europe is based on the human rights included in the Charter of Fundamental Rights, in the Treaty of Lisbon and in the human rights clauses in bilateral agreements concluded with third countries. Member States have thus committed themselves to certain democratic and legal standards (democracy and human rights, rule of law, legalisation and economic liberalisation).

However, the EU is increasingly aware that economic progress must not always be accompanied by political progress; this is especially true as regards China. This also means that the European Union, in the face of directly relevant challenges and threats, has put its own (security) policy interests increasingly at the forefront, and thus has changed its so far rather reactive behaviour in favour of a more proactive style of external relations.

Europe sees itself increasingly confronted with challenges in the domain of foreign or security policy, or of an economic character, which would warrant a collective response. With a community-based Common Foreign and Security Policy in Europe, the coalition of 28 Member States would have a clear added value compared to the bundled external policies of the Member States.

One of the EU's prominent issues is how to ensure its economic achievements while preserving the ecological balance on Earth. The implications of the greenhouse effect are considered as potentially threatening for the stability of countries and economies in different parts of the world. Here, Europe must arrive at a common policy and defend its position against other global actors, especially the United States.

The concept of Europe as a pacifying, cooperative model generates high expectations regarding its operational capabilities and results. So far it has been able to show his strengths as a decentralised network in times of crisis, highly dependent, however, on the political skills of the respective leading statesmen.

It is about time to revise the past experience, namely, that the progress of European integration will be determined primarily by the way it is resolving difficult or even crisis situations. Such a problem-driven policy can only be reactive. The economic and financial crisis has strengthened national attitudes and weakened solidarity and trust among Member States. It cannot be excluded that in the future, intergovernmentalism could gain strength over the principle of multilateralism. An interest-based multilateralism in line with the US pattern would not do any good to the EU; Member States would have considerable difficulties to agree to a common line of policy or even action. It would be a relapse into a range of separate interest-based policies of individual Member States.

The EU is not a power in the traditional sense; it lacks the tools to act as a world power. A system, based purely on power politics driven by national interests, antagonism and confrontation would create an unfavourable environment for the EU to assert its global interests and values. It would exacerbate existing tensions in the EU and significantly weaken its importance as an international actor and its ability to safeguard its own security interests.

The informal forum of the G20 is, for the European Union, both a challenge and an opportunity to deepen their external relations and advance the concept of effective multilateralism. The G20 could open new possibilities for the transformation of the global order. The participation of the European Union as an institution in the G20 comprising global governance highlights the importance of the EU as a supranational organisation based on multilateralism and integration governed by specific standards and norms. It has also strengthened the international weight of the Union. "We are recognised as an important contributor to a better world.... For our full potential to be realised we need to be still more capable, more coherent and more active."[19]

The European Union should demonstrate the added value of effective multilateralism to other countries, namely the immense value of a global order with commonly agreed and mutually respected principles:

> If the West can help deliver to the rest of the world what it brought to itself several centuries ago – political and ideological tolerance coupled with economic dynamism – then the global turn will mark not a dark era of ideological contention and geopolitical rivalry, but one in which diversity and pluralism lay the foundation for an era of global comity.[20]

References

Ashton C (2010) Speech at the 46th Munich Security Conference, 2 February 2010. Available at http://eu-un.europa.eu/articles/en/article_9472_en.htm

Beck U (2010) Europäisch Roulette: Merkels letzte Kugel, Cicero, 26 May 2010. Available at http://www.cicero.de/berliner-republik/europ%C3%A4isch-roulette-merkels-letzte-kugel/40900

Biden JR (2009) Remarks by Vice President Biden at 45th Munich Conference on Security Policy, 7 February 2009. Available at http://www.whitehouse.gov/the-press-office/remarks-vice-president-biden-45th-munich-conference-security-policy

Council of the European Union (2003) A secure Europe in a better world: European security strategy, 12 December 2003, p 9. Available at http://www.consilium.europa.eu/uedocs/cmsUpload/78367.pdf

Council of the European Union (2008) Report on the implementation of the European security strategy: providing security in a changing world, Brussels, 11 December 2008, S407/08. Available at http://www.consilium.europa.eu/ueDocs/cms_Data/docs/pressdata/EN/reports/104630.pdf

Defraigne P (2013) From a destabilising commercial atlanticism to a strategic US–EU–China trialogue, Madariaga Paper, vol 6 (June 2013) 4, p 6. Available at http://www.madariaga.org/images/madariagapapers/06-june-2013%20-%20defraigne%20-%20from%20a%20destabilising%20commercial%20atlanticism%20to%20a%20strategic%20us-eu-china%20trialogue%20-%20madariaga%20paper.pdf

[19] Council of the European Union (2008).

[20] Kupchan (2012), chapter 7.

Eizenstat SE (2013) A new transatlantic partnership, April 2013. Available at http://esharp.eu/essay/23-a-new-transatlantic-partnership/
Falkowski CD (2011) Europe for us: why we need Europe, p 113
Kagan R (2002) Power and weakness. Policy Rev 113. Available at http://www.hoover.org/research/power-and-weakness
Kissinger H (2008) An end of hybris. The Economist, November 19
Kupchan CA (2012) No one's world
Kurth J (2002) Confronting the unipolar moment, the American empire and Islamic terrorism. Curr Hist 101:403-408
Link W (2006) Auf dem Weg zu einem neuen Europa; Herausforderungen und Antworten, pp 24–30
OECD (2013) The transatlantic trade and investment partnership: why does it matter? p 1. Available at http://www.oecd.org/trade/TTIP.pdf
Rasmussen AF (2013) Speech at the Conference "A New Era for EU-US Trade", Copenhagen, 7 October 2013. Available at http://www.nato.int/cps/en/natolive/opinions_103863.htm
Ruggiero R (1996) Managing a world of free trade and deep interdependence, WTO news, 1996 press releases, press/55. Available at http://www.wto.org/english/news_e/pres96_e/pr055_e.htm
Snyder J (2003) Imperial temptations. The National Interest 71(Spring):29–38

Trade in the XXI Century

Arancha González

Trade Era: A World of Transformation and Permanent Rebalancing

If some Rip Van Winkle[1] with a penchant for geopolitics had gone to sleep in 1989—about halfway through Horst Krenzler's tenure as the European Commission's Director-General for External Relations—he would awaken today to a startlingly different world.

While security tensions on Europe's eastern fringes might seem reassuringly familiar, he would no doubt be astonished to learn that the United States' only real rival for political and economic pre-eminence was not Japan, a reformed Soviet Union, or even the European Union, but China.

Having known a world economy dominated by the traditional industrial powers, he would be told that developing countries last year produced the majority of the world's goods and services for the first time since the nineteenth century. To his astonishment, he would notice that many of these goods and services were produced not within individual countries, but across multiple nations and even continents.

A heartening development would be the improvement in life prospects for much of humanity. Where lives free of deprivation and preventable disease once seemed achievable only for a fortunate minority, he would see that decent living standards are now within view for the majority of the world's population. Extreme poverty could be virtually eradicated within decades.

A key enabler of this extraordinary transformation has been the open global economy.

---

[1] Irving (1819).

A. González (✉)
International Trade Centre, 54-56 Rue de Montbrillant, 1202 Geneva, Switzerland
e-mail: agonzalez@intracen.org

C. Herrmann et al. (eds.), *Trade Policy between Law, Diplomacy and Scholarship*,
European Yearbook of International Economic Law,
DOI 10.1007/978-3-319-15690-3_8

As our flabbergasted Rip Van Winkle learned more about the new economic landscape, some of the changes would start to make sense. Even before his long sleep, he would have noticed how trade opening and shipping containerisation had dramatically reduced the costs of moving merchandise from one place to another. South Korea, Hong Kong, and some other East Asian countries were successfully using export markets to emulate Japan's rapid industrialisation. China, too, had been experimenting with market-oriented policies for just over a decade, with increasing success.

The continuation and spread of these two trends—the adoption of market-oriented policies; and using world markets as a source of demand, technology, and ideas—have driven the fastest growth and poverty reduction in human history.

As we look further at how the exchange of goods, services, and ideas has transformed our world—and how our evolving world has transformed the way we trade—it makes sense to look back at what has remained constant.

Trade Is as Old as Humankind

Trade is only slightly younger than civilisation itself. Not without reason did Adam Smith write that "the propensity to truck, barter and exchange one thing for another is common to all men"[2]: the archaeological record suggests that as soon as our ancestors managed to accumulate surpluses beyond subsistence needs, they sought to trade them for something that brought them greater utility or pleasure.

Ancient Mesopotamian tablets register early commercial exchanges. Nearly 5,000 years ago, the Sumerians were making bronze, which would have required them to import tin to mix with locally abundant copper. The Mediterranean basin is scattered with remnants of Greek amphorae, which bear witness to the active Bronze Age trade in precious oils, wines, and spices transported in the oval, two-handled clay storage jars. As the writer William Bernstein recounts in *A Splendid Exchange*, his tremendously entertaining history of trade and our world, intrepid Greek sailors were riding the Indian Ocean trade winds from the Red Sea to southern India and beyond more than 2,000 years ago.

Even the multi-continental value chains that have become a hallmark of modern manufacturing production are not really new. The journalist Nayan Chanda tells us that a thousand years ago, a regular triangular trade had already evolved in which African ivory was shipped to India, where skilled craftsmen carved it into jewellery that was exported through the Middle East, ultimately to adorn members of the courts of Europe.

To grasp the extent to which trade reshaped our world long before we became reliant on electronic gadgets manufactured in far-flung locations, we need look no further than our dinner plates. Horst Krenzler would surely have struggled to picture German tables without *Kartoffelsalat* or potato dumplings. Nor can we easily

---

[2] Smith (1776).

imagine Italian cuisine without tomatoes, Indian curries without chillies, English breakfasts without tea, or American food without the bread and beef combination known as a hamburger that has proven so popular around the world. Yet each of these foods was transported from one continent to another within the past 500 years.

At its best, this is what trade has always been about: enhancing our living conditions, reaching out to new frontiers, interacting with each other to establish common references about what we share and what we value.

To be sure, trade has had its dark sides as well—none darker than the slave trade, which for over two centuries in the Atlantic region was closely intertwined with commerce in sugar, rum, and other merchandise. The example of the slave trade demonstrates the importance of the terms and rules under which trade is conducted. It also underscores the fact that civil society engagement with the governments and companies that have dominated trade and trade policymaking is critical to ensure that these rules continue to reflect evolving notions of justice and human dignity.

Trade Changed the World, and the World Changed Trade

Today's open global economy is no accident. It was painstakingly rebuilt from the wreckage of the years between 1914 and 1945, and entrenched in an institutional foundation through successive rounds of multilateral trade liberalisation under the General Agreement on Tariffs and Trade. The "most-favoured nation" principle meant that trade access was not conditioned upon political considerations. Coordinated tariff reductions constrained beggar-thy-neighbour trade policies, and made it harder—though not impossible—for governments to protect influential domestic interest groups.

The multilateral trading system has been successful on a scale that its creators could not have fathomed. Global trade increased 27-fold between 1950 and 2008, three times more than the growth in global gross domestic product (GDP). The value of world trade in goods and services passed the US$22 trillion mark in 2013. Trade has become part of the fabric of economic activity. The trade to GDP ratio for the world as a whole was 60 % in 2012, up from some 25 % in the 1960s. Nearly half of world merchandise trade is in intermediate inputs, rather than in finished products.

Great Convergence in Rebalancing the World Economy

With an end of "the great divergence" with China, to use the terms of Kenneth Pomeranz,[3] explaining the reasons why industrial revolution spurred in Europe and not in Asia, East Asian countries have then sustained the highest rates of real

[3] Pomeranz (2001).

growth since the mid-1960s, which has been followed by the emergence of other new powers denominated as BRICS and now as MINTs (Mexico, Indonesia, Nigeria and Turkey). Since the mid-1960s, the average per capita incomes in the Asia region have been growing at 5 % in constant US dollars. Incomes per capita in the last 20 years have tripled, with great impact on poverty alleviation at a global level.

This has led to a new situation, where the multipolar world is not a slogan anymore but a reality in reshaping and rebalancing the influence of each nation on the global stage, and offering for the first time in human history the chance to eradicate extreme poverty at a global level.

Developing countries are trading more overall and trading more with other developing and transition economies. High-income countries have decreased steadily as export markets, as South–South commerce expands. Nearly half (45 % in 2012) of merchandise trade (exports plus imports) is between developing and transition economies. This can be explained by more trade in new markets with new products and with the support of new services.

Open Global Economy Enabled Rise of Global Value Chains

The fall in transport and communication costs has offered many opportunities to split and spread the production process across different countries as a function of their comparative advantage. This is how supply chain trade is born; having products processed and services performed in multiple countries, counting each step to add value, making it dependent on cross-border movement and even more interdependent with investment. Investment has then become a key factor to sustain trade more for transfer of knowledge and technology rather than for transfer of capital. This has led to a major shift in trade patterns, making supply chain processes associated with huge amounts of FDI the main factor for expanding networks of production, distribution and consumption throughout the world, the so-called "global value chain" phenomenon. This situation is likely to prevail, although its nature and extent may change.

Nowadays imports make up an increasing and often an indispensable share of the total value embodied in a given product, ranging from 30 to 50 % in world average and sometimes much more for small open economies that are connected to supply chain. This trend has been very well summarised as "made in the world", which is now much more than making, including designing, marketing, sharing knowledge and ideas in conceiving what the world is producing, and constantly pushing to aggregate more services to supply chains in to the "servicification" of manufacturing.

Services account for 45 % of the total value of exported goods and represent 70 %, often more, of GDP in many advanced economies. Nevertheless, only 20 % of all service production is traded, but they are everywhere in industry, agriculture or manufacturing. The capacity to blend services into processing and production is key to ensure competitiveness and diversification of trade. This is where many opportunities for poor income countries lie not only on working comparative advantage, but in looking at which services to add to supply chains, even for countries not engaged in industrial production. Capacity to ensure affordable services for the business community, such as telecommunications, transportation, financial services, accounting and legal services, will depend on ability to connect with international clients and partners, making services a key factor for competitiveness, growth and job creation.

However Many Countries Are Still Left Out

Nevertheless, between 1985 and 2012, the share of non-oil least developed countries' (LDCs) exports of goods and services fell from 1.2 to 0.9 %, while their share in world population rose from 7.5 to 9.9 %, a reflection that trade transaction costs remain much higher for low income countries than for other economies, underlining the necessity of Aid for Trade.

This can be explained by the fact that many LDCs are landlocked countries or small island developing states (SIDS), distant from big trade corridors, and their small domestic markets make their exporters less able to achieve economies of scale. But if in 2013, LDCs exports accounted for only 1 % of global trade, it is also because of inadequate infrastructure, poorly functioning trade-related institutions, and restrictive trade policies which tend to compound natural cost disadvantages.

Things can be changed with some practical reforms to facilitate trade, enhance small and medium-sized enterprises' (SME) competitiveness and enhance market access for LDC products, aiming for reduced trade costs related to import and export procedures, and increased infrastructure services at ports and cross-border posts, in particular for SMEs.

Trade in a Complex World: What Can We Expect?

We are clearly living in a multipolar world and this will continue to be the case. The new poles, i.e. those in emerging economies, are also likely to change the nature of their involvement in global markets. Increasingly, they become exporters of FDI rather than importers, the number of multinational-led firms from emerging economies in global value chains is increasing, emerging economies also play an increasingly important role in innovation.

What this probably implies is increased competition for all, high rates of innovation and a high—possibly even increased—pace of change. All segments of our economies will be affected by this: the low tech and the high tech segments; agriculture, services and manufacturing; male and female intensive activities; small, medium-sized and large firms. In order to benefit from globalisation and technological progress, economic actors will have to stand ready at any moment in time to react to change or—even better—to foresee change and be a first mover into new activities. This rapid pace of change will be beneficial for the global economy with contrasted results on the ground with losers and winners that can be different to those thought at the beginning, and we need to make sure that it will benefit the world's poorest within the post-2015 development agenda framework.

This is where the challenge remains; establishing rules for regulatory matters, on which public opinions have always diverged, that can encompass agriculture, manufacturing and services not as separate sectors but as a combination of factors that make production, trade and wealth of nations a benefit for all, even for the poorest of the globe.

Complexity in Finding the Right Frame to Deal: Multilateralism vs. Regionalism

Trade is a powerful engine for growth, but growth has to be inclusive. It has to be accompanied by domestic and regional measures aimed at ensuring its benefits are more equally distributed among citizens. As we have seen in Brazil, in Latin America and in Europe, too, growth with growing inequalities only leads to turmoil and instability.

Another thing that many do not find easy to handle is uncertainty. We have all become cruelly aware of the possibility of financial risks or climate change risks in recent years. Some northern African and Arab countries' economies are playing a high toll for geopolitical risks in the region. In Europe, the situation in Ukraine has reminded some of the risk of war, and many parallels have been drawn to the beginnings of World War I. Wise and strong leadership is required from policy makers at the national, regional and global level to contain these three types of risk (financial, climate change and geopolitical risks).

At the multilateral level, trade negotiations in the context of the Doha Round have been sluggish, albeit last year's Bali Ministerial represented an important breakthrough, notably in the area of trade facilitation. This has led to closer ties between blocks, which is not incompatible with mutual benefits at global stage amongst nations both economically and geopolitically.

In recent years, trade negotiations have been marked by a major shift towards regionalism and notably to so-called mega-regional negotiations such as the Transatlantic Trade and Investment Partnership (TTIP) or the Transpacific Partnership (TPP).

Complexity in Negotiating Concessions: The Issue of NTMs

One of the particularities of these negotiations is that they have a significant focus on non-tariff measures to trade (NTMs). In a world where tariffs are relatively low, notably because of earlier successes in multilateral trade negotiations, as well as bilateral and unilateral tariff reductions, NTMs represent an increasingly important bottleneck for trade. The costs involved in collecting information on standards and regulations in destination markets are often high. Meeting those standards or norms increases production costs and certification requirements often become very cumbersome—sometimes impossible—obstacles to surpass. And when standards and norms differ across destination markets, such costs are multiplied.

Complying with these NTMs often takes the form of fixed costs and as a result they hit small and medium-sized enterprises particularly hard. Recent firm level survey evidence collected by the International Trade Centre reveals that a large proportion of traders in Latin America are affected by NTMs, most of which are related to technical measures. For instance, over 50 % of enterprises in Peru and Uruguay and over 60 % in Paraguay reported facing such measures. Finding ways of reducing the cost of meeting NTMs can therefore have huge pay-offs in particular for SMEs. And let's remember that today's small and medium-sized enterprises could be tomorrow's multinationals.

The Agreement on Trade Facilitation reached at the WTO Ministerial in Bali aims at streamlining customs and border procedures and through that reducing the costs of these NTMs, in particular for SMEs. It is a truly innovative agreement, in that it makes commitments to implement measures conditional on financial and technical assistance being provided to developing countries, and in particular to the poorest among them. Bilateral or regional approaches to lowering the burden of NTMs could involve both components: an agreement on mutually recognising or harmonising standards or regulations, combined with technical assistance to weaker players, in particular when it comes to supporting SMEs to adjust to and comply with the agreement.

Why SMEs Are the Future of Trade

Given the estimates that more than 95 % of enterprises across the world are SMEs accounting for close to 80 % of employment, with this even greater in low income countries, focusing on SME competitiveness seems to be the sound avenue to pursue. We know that 85 % of total employment growth between 2002 and 2010 was attributable to SMEs. But we also know that in the SME ecosystem, there are many that never make it past the first year of business. There is a high mortality rate amongst start-ups. We must ensure that the survival rate improves. We also know that high-growth enterprises play a disproportionate role in job creation. SMEs are the biggest source of untapped growth potential and, by 2030, will be generating the bulk of the close to 470 million new jobs that will be required by employment-ready men and women. This is why it is excellent that the discussions on the UN post-2015 development agenda are increasingly recognising the importance of ensuring an economic growth component. The evidence clearly points to SMEs being at the heart of this growth discourse. The two major distinguishing characteristics of high-growth SMEs are their export orientation and their innovation capabilities. We must work to help survivors move up the value chain and internationalise.

Making Trade Work for Development: What Can We Do? ITC 50 and Its Role in the Post-2015 Development Agenda Debate

In 2014, the ITC celebrated its 50th anniversary. For 50 years we have worked to unlock SMEs' international competitiveness.

Fifty years later, the world of trade has changed and we are changing. Instead of purely looking at exports, we now look at trade and investment as two sides of the same coin. We now focus on value addition domestically, whether for agro-processed products, for manufactured goods and increasingly, for services. Instead of looking at products, we now look to offer solutions to SMEs that will encompass different components looking in particular to inclusiveness and sustainability. SMEs are, in and of themselves, engines for sustainable development in that they generate more than 80 % of jobs in developing countries. These jobs ensure that development progress in health, education, peace and security, and poverty reduction are well-anchored and sustained. On the other hand, the impact of SME growth goes beyond poverty reduction. SMEs also have an impact on the environment through the technologies they use and how they source products.

Environmental sustainability: we very much see it through the lens of the entrepreneur. This lens shows that the natural environment can present constraints to business development, but it can also offer huge market opportunities. For example, a recent ITC survey of agro-food exporters in Peru and Uganda found that climate change is now one of their primary competitiveness concerns due to lost productivity and unreliable supplies. These types of constraints often determine the success or failure of an SME business operation.

Women's entrepreneurship: More jobs and income reinvested in family. In developing countries, we now have eight to ten million women-owned small and medium-sized enterprises, often representing close to 40 % of total SMEs. In some of these countries these firms are growing at faster rates than those owned by men. However, women's economic empowerment must be an integral part of our agenda not only because it generates employment but because women reinvest up to 90 % of their earnings in their families and communities, linking trade to development. The kinds of inequalities described in detail today, in terms of access to and control over resources, including those needed to build productive capacities, are what we need to tackle to realise gender equality and women's economic empowerment.

Let me outline now what could be the concrete proposals on how to make trade a powerful tool to achieve goals that are currently being defined in the post-2015 Agenda.

On Trade and Agriculture

Trade in agriculture is an important facilitator for poverty reduction. With more than 70 % of LDC households living in rural settings and representing 60 % of total employment, agriculture is not only the main means of existence of the vast majority of people in poor countries. It is the present and will be the future of economic development.

The state of the rural economy is intrinsically linked to progress in agricultural productivity, lowering prices in local markets and having spill-over effects by spurring demand for non-agricultural goods and services. Empirical evidence shows that better agricultural productivity is closely linked to agro-processing and trade capacities enhancement, adding greater value into agricultural products.

This is what ITC does, working with agricultural SMEs, such as cooperatives and producer associations, to empower and raise the income of smallholder farmers, while mainstreaming environmental considerations, lowering post-harvest losses and promoting social and gender inclusiveness.

Because small and medium agro-enterprises are uniquely situated between natural sources of food supply and the dynamics of market demands, promoting small producer organisations can have enormous benefits. Firstly, in the creation of farming and non-farm rural employment, especially for women, representing between 50 to as much as 90 % of the agricultural workforce—the role of women is absolutely critical in the success of agriculture, and ITC is keen to empower the economic role of women at all stages of the supply chain.

Secondly, by the same token, economic activity is generated in the downstream areas of logistics, distribution and services, generating new skills in agriculture as well as diversification of rural economies.

Thirdly, adding value to commodities through improved services, increasing transparency and reducing transaction costs for private voluntary standards. This is how developing countries can concretely connect to global value chains through multi-stakeholder strategies.

On Trade and Industrialisation

Industrialisation is not a tool on its own, it needs to be blended with other instruments and policies for it to be fully effective. Structural transformation will require blending industrialisation with other key policies, such as education, infrastructure development, financial inclusion and innovation.

In education, progress over the last two decades has prepared Africa for the industrial phase of its growth to take-off. The percentage of sub-Saharan Africa's working age population with a secondary school education has more than quadrupled to around 40 % today from 9 % in 1975. This is similar to secondary education levels in Mexico and Turkey when they began industrialising in the 1980s. As we know, both countries are now part of the OECD. Africa has taken great steps in building human capital for a successful development. It is education and a more agile business environment, coupled with technology that is driving innovation and creativity in Africa. Just a couple of months ago, I was in Kenya and witnessed first-hand the hundreds of apps that are being developed every month.

On infrastructure development, in particular transportation and energy, I believe that much remains to be done. It is encouraging to see the focus placed by regional development banks on this key area. Finally on financial inclusion, our most recent survey of SME sentiment at the end of last year indicated that access to credit is a major impediment to SME growth and thus to industrialisation. Access to finance can be particularly difficult for SMEs that are too big for microfinance institutions, but still too small to be able to access traditional commercial bank lending. In my view, traditional banking instruments will have to be combined with more innovative sources of financing, including venture capital and social investments, to help bridge the existing gap.

On Trade, E-Business and Innovative Services

The digital economy is now one of the main factors driving global trade. Digital channels dominate and determine the nature of business transactions. Complex value chains are facilitated through the use of information flows and the question of whether an economy is investable now hinges on the notion of a receptive business climate. This not only includes ease of opening a business, trade facilitation, access to credit and available skill sets; but also the penetration of mobiles per capita, the extent of the bandwidth, the technological awareness and exposure of the potential workforce, and the capacity of the economy to innovate and be flexible with changes in technological advancement.

Business to consumer e-commerce is a smaller but increasingly powerful distribution channel (now in excess of US$1 trillion per annum) which is changing the nature of retailing in developed countries, and creating new consumer markets in developing countries. The rise of the middle class, especially in Africa, and their increasing purchasing power and quality awareness has fostered an emergence of e-commerce in the past decade that has opened up opportunities for developing countries and LDCs to better access world markets, both as providers and consumers.

The emergence of e-business presents a unique opportunity to facilitate better access for poor countries to world markets. Access to the digital economy is no longer the unique domain of business and consumers in high income countries. According to the International Telecommunication Union's latest figures, almost three billion people—40 % of the world's population—are using the internet, and close to one in three people in developing countries are online. A barrier to e-commerce is the availability of online payment solutions, which are commonly unavailable to vendors in much of Africa, for example. ITC is assisting SMEs to build a presence on the web and marketing their products and services through virtual market places, as well as helping to pioneer the use of cloud-based solutions for SMEs which would cut down on the need to make costly investments in ICT infrastructure and computing capacity.

Even in the area of logistics services, which are typically expensive and poorly adapted to the needs of small businesses in Africa, new solutions are becoming available through partnerships with some of the leading e-commerce players and transportation companies. Bypassing poor local infrastructure, African companies can use fulfilment services in developed countries to hold stock, sell and distribute from remote locations in developed countries. Internet technologies and cloud computing offer SMEs in developing countries the potential to access advanced systems at a very competitive price, assuming the availability of enough bandwidth. Online sourcing can speed the identification of potential suppliers, generate innovative alternatives and reduce prices: each a source of competitiveness that can be harnessed by SMEs in developing countries.

These are the tools of the future and will be essential in allowing SMEs to realise their growth and job creating potential in the post-2015 world. This is why we need to place SMEs and their needs at the heart of the digital agenda, place them at the heart of the XXI century information society.

Breaking Multilateral Deadlock Will Need a New Mentality

A 100 years ago, the world needed to break through physical obstacles to build canals and notably the Panama Canal that dramatically accelerated trade. Today's barriers to trade confidence seem to be bigger than oceans. We need to build new mental canals to bring more trust and more union to the global stage.

Trade as a means to reach out to new frontiers is highly symbolised by the 100 years of the Panama Canal, which was officially opened on 15 August 1914 and represents the largest engineering project ever undertaken. The shortcut greatly reduced the time for ships to travel between the Atlantic and Pacific Oceans, enabling merchant ships to avoid the lengthy and hazardous route round Cape Horn. This was not possible without high costs, firstly, in human lives, and secondly, in time with journeys back and forth. The idea was already conceived in 1534 when Charles V, Holy Roman Emperor and King of Spain, ordered a survey for a route through the Isthmus of Panama. The project was abandoned or stopped many times, and resumed just as often. 380 years later by historic circumstance, the canal linking the two biggest oceans was possible, and 100 years later in 2014, there are still important works to widen the Panama Canal in creating new traffic lines for trade.

What is at stake today is our capacity to open novel routes and expand our channels of cooperation in a new multipolar world where challenges can either be addressed globally or hit us all with unequal but general negative consequences for humanity.

And it is in this new world that the traditional values of hard work, dedication and humanity that Horst Krenzler embodied remain essential. His commitment to building a society of values based on the legacy of the European Enlightenment are a much needed anchor in today's turbulent global waters. Let us hope Horst Krenzler's life will provide an example to those of us working to ensure that trade becomes an instrument for progress and peace.

References

Irving W (1819) Rip Van Winkle and the legend of Sleepy Hollow. In: Irving W, The sketch book of Geoffrey Crayon

Pomeranz K (2001) The great divergence: China, Europe, and the making of the modern world economy

Smith A (1776) The wealth of nations, Book 1, chapter 2

Does Intellectual Property Belong to the Trade Family?

Roger Kampf

I first met Horst G. Krenzler in my former professional life as a European Commission official when he was the Director-General at the European Commission's Trade Directorate. This post was certainly made for him, as he was an excellent lawyer and a brilliant diplomat at the same time—two capacities that were and continue to be essential ingredients for making trade policy work. Later on, I worked with him in his function as the co-editor of a commentary on the EU's external trade and customs legislation.[1] This provided me with yet another opportunity to appreciate his outstanding qualities, here in the form of his academic interests and capacities.

I have chosen the old and nevertheless still interesting question as to whether intellectual property belongs to the trade family as the topic for this contribution because of the key characteristics of Horst G. Krenzler's personality, my own professional background, and, last but not least, the fact that this question was already the subject of controversial debates, including within the Commission, when he was heading DG Trade. This contribution will thus attempt to provide a short legal, academic and—hopefully also—diplomatic answer in honour of Horst G. Krenzler who was a master in all these disciplines.

The author is Counsellor in the WTO Secretariat. This contribution has been prepared strictly in a personal capacity. The views expressed are not to be attributed to the WTO, its Secretariat, or any of its Member governments.

[1] Krenzler and Herrmann (2014).

R. Kampf (✉)
World Trade Organization, Rue de Lausanne 154, 1211 Geneva, Switzerland
e-mail: roger.kampf@wto.org

C. Herrmann et al. (eds.), *Trade Policy between Law, Diplomacy and Scholarship*,
European Yearbook of International Economic Law,
DOI 10.1007/978-3-319-15690-3_9

Introduction: There Are Different Ways of Looking at the Relationship Between Intellectual Property Rights and Trade

The Agreement on Trade-Related Aspects of Intellectual Property Rights (TRIPS) forms an integral part of the set of agreements concluded when the World Trade Organization (WTO) was established as a result of the Uruguay Round negotiations in 1995. Its name leaves no doubt about the negotiators' agreement at the time that intellectual property rights (IPRs) are related to trade, hence its name, and thus belong to the WTO as the multilateral institutions administering and overviewing matters related to international trade.

This said, there are admittedly many ways of looking at and understanding the relationship between IPRs and international trade, including from the perspective of trade-related IPRs and that of IP-related trade. Some have thus sought to define this relationship in a positive way, viewing the adoption of uniform protection and enforcement standards for IPRs at international level as a necessary ingredient to foster trade in legitimate trade, or, to put it differently, to reduce trade in IPR-infringing goods.[2] There are also those views however, that have tried to shed some light on the connection from a more defensive perspective, viewing IPRs essentially as a potential barrier to legitimate trade.[3] Both these viewpoints have found their way into the WTO's TRIPS Agreement, as it takes up the potentially positive and negative linkages at the same time, namely in its Preamble, as well as in its objectives and principles.

At the same time, some voices, mainly found in the academic world and in some developing countries, are still critical about the inclusion of the TRIPS Agreement in the WTO framework altogether.[4] Either they consider that IPR protection and enforcement have literally nothing to do with trade, or they contest at least their coverage by multilateral disciplines that are administered by the WTO.

But even within the European Commission, there were views at the time when Prof. Dr. Krenzler was still heading DG Trade that questioned the appropriateness of including IPRs in trade agreements. This may, among others, explain why for a long time the free trade agreements (FTAs) concluded by the European Union (EU) only knew a very minimalist coverage of IPRs, if at all, rather than the approach taken by the US that has traditionally pursued the inclusion of a fully-fledged chapter with detailed provisions on IPRs in its FTAs.[5] This only changed since the late 1990s, when the EU began to negotiate FTAs that include a comprehensive set of substantive provisions in the field of IPRs.

[2] See, for example, Maskus and Penubarti (1995), p. 227.

[3] For an overview of the views taken see Curtis (2012), p. 8.

[4] Blyde (2006), p. 1; Stockholm Network (2012), p. 6.

[5] Kampf (2007), p. 87.

Against the background of such divergent opinions, the arguments used to support each position, theoretical and empirical evidence, as well as the way in which the link between IPRs and trade is handled in practice, in particular in the WTO and the EU, shall be reviewed in the context of the historical developments that led to the establishment of the current international framework for the protection and enforcement of IPRs. This review leads the author to conclude that the more powerful arguments plead in favour of characterising IPRs as an integral component of the international trade regime in today's globalised world, not least because both weak and strong IPRs, each in their own way, potentially have an impact on the extent to which trade takes place and the direction it takes, and are thus directly related to trade. This, in turn, confirms that the TRIPS Agreement rightly has its place among the agreements administered by the WTO.

History Shows Interesting Parallels with Today's Debate

Historically speaking, the IPR regime has known significant variations with respect to its primary functions and objectives that were admittedly not always trade-related. This may also explain why the evolution of the IPR regime has sometimes been divided into a territorial, international and global period.[6] The functions of the IP system thus range from providing an incentive to foreign workers to move to other countries to the use of the IPR regime as a protectionist tool, such as witnessed during the period of the Great Depression in the twentieth century, and finally, in the more recent past, as a means to promote trade.

At the very beginning, there was, indeed, no international framework for IPR protection, nor was there an obvious link with trade. Rather, one of the principal ideas that drove, for example, the grant of patent rights focused on the development of the local economy through the attraction of foreign skilled labour forces. Starting in the fourteenth century, IPRs would thus essentially serve the immigrant artisan to ensure exclusive exploitation of his knowledge and skills that were unknown to local artisans.[7] If at all, they were only remotely related to trade across borders in this period. This first period saw the gradual development of national frameworks for the protection of IPRs, firmly based on the principle of territoriality and not providing protection to inventors and creators beyond national borders.

Since the eighteenth century though, this changed considerably, as countries began implementing a national IP policy as part of their broader trade policy. In particular, as international trade in industrial products was growing in the second half of the nineteenth century, the link between IPRs and trade increasingly took a central role in discussions both at national and international level. This development was accompanied by a growing interest in international cooperation on IP

[6] Drahos and Smith (1999), p. 13.

[7] David (1992), pp. 9–10; Breitwieser and Foster (2012), p. 8.

matters which led, among others, to the proliferation of an important number of bilateral agreements.[8] This said, positions taken with regard to the link between IPRs and trade during this second period approached the question from radically different perspectives.[9] On the one hand, there was strong pressure to limit or abolish, for example, patent rights in order to secure free trade and competition[10] or to secure access to works created by foreign authors.[11] In other words, the proponents of this approach saw in IPRs a negative, protectionist measure that stood potentially in the way of international trade. On the other hand, others actively supported at the same time the development of an international framework for the protection and enforcement of IPRs. Their primary objective was to overcome the shortcomings and costs resulting from the territorial nature of domestic IPR regimes by providing a mechanism to inventors and creators to protect their works in other countries when those were traded across national boundaries. The advocates of this position also viewed the nascent body of IPRs governed by international treaties as almost naturally related to trade, albeit from a different, that is, positive perspective, insofar as adequate protection and enforcement of IPRs were perceived as fostering international trade.

Their efforts, based on the conviction that IPRs and trade are intimately linked to each other, as well as the above-mentioned conclusion of many bilateral agreements, were instrumental in the move towards the adoption of the first two international treaties, i.e. the Paris Convention for the Protection of Industrial Property in 1883 and the Berne Convention for the Protection of Literary and Artistic Work in 1886. Both were administered by a specialised agency, the United International Bureaux for the Protection of Intellectual Property, which was created in 1893 and, in 1967, became the World Intellectual Property Organization (WIPO). Despite the underlying link between IPRs and trade, IPRs were thus brought into an international framework that was handled in a pretty much isolated fashion for some decades and for which matters related to international trade were far from central.[12] To a large extent, they were delinked from other policy dimensions and treated as a domain that would necessarily have to be dealt with by technical experts. On the other side of the spectrum, the WTO's predecessor, the General Agreement on Tariffs and Trade (GATT) 1947 as the body in charge of liberalising and regulating international trade in goods knew only a few provisions that implicitly or explicitly related to IPRs,[13] mainly because IPRs were predominantly perceived as an

[8] Drahos and Smith (1999), p. 13.

[9] For the evolution in Germany, Switzerland and the Netherlands at that time, see Breitwieser and Foster (2012), pp. 10–11.

[10] For concrete examples, see Khan (2002), p. 29.

[11] See the illustrative description of the evolution of copyright protection in the US in the nineteenth century by Khan (2002), pp. 39–43.

[12] Curtis (2012), p. 7; Akkoyunlu (2013), p. 5.

[13] See GATT Articles III:4 (national treatment), Article IX:6 (marks of origin), XII:3(c)(iii) and XVIII:10 (in the context of balance of payment restrictions), as well as XX(d) (general exceptions).

obstacle to trade. Those provisions and the related case law under the GATT have nevertheless been taken by some already as an indicator for the link between IPRs and trade, illustrating how IPRs can impact on international trade.[14]

This rather shadowy existence of IPRs within the multilateral system only changed in the 1970s, when the US Government began establishing a much more straightforward linkage between IPRs and trade to support its call for a multilateral framework to deal with the protection and enforcement of IPRs.[15] At that time, there was growing concern about the steady increase of counterfeiting and piracy in international trade among developed countries and the perception that WIPO treaties did not provide for adequate protection standards and enforcement mechanisms. Among others, this made the US adopt "Special 301" legislation in the Omnibus Trade Act of 1988, designed to take up alleged deficiencies of IPR protection in third countries as a matter of priority in bilateral negotiations and to allow for retaliatory measures under trade statutes in case of IPR infringements.[16] But even before this, it had already led to a proposal to negotiate rules on trade in counterfeit goods as part of the Tokyo Round of multilateral trade negotiations (1973–1979) under the auspices of the then GATT. While the US and other developed countries argued that the GATT was the appropriate forum to deal with the trade-related aspects of counterfeiting and piracy, their proposed draft "Agreement on Measures to Discourage the Importation of Counterfeit Goods"[17] did not find the unanimous support of negotiators and therefore did not become part of the results of the Tokyo Round in 1979. Subsequent work in the GATT in this area, in particular that carried out by the Group of Experts on Trade in Counterfeit Goods established by the Contracting Parties in 1984, also remained inconclusive, noting, among others, the existence of diverging views as to whether the GATT was the appropriate and competent forum to take action at the international level.[18]

It was only in 1986, when trade ministers came together in Punta del Este, Uruguay, that an agreement could be reached to include a section on "trade-related aspects of IPRs, including trade in counterfeit goods" in the mandate on future trade negotiations.[19] The declared aim was to reduce the distortions and impediments to international trade, to promote effective and adequate IPR protection and to avoid that enforcement measures become barriers to legitimate trade. To do so, existing GATT provisions were to be clarified and a multilateral framework of principles,

[14] Adolf (2001), p. 49 (53).

[15] Moschini (2004), p. 5.

[16] For a detailed overview of the relevant developments in the US and the "historical institutionalism" that led to the inclusion of the TRIPS Agreement in the WTO see Sell (2010), p. 762; see also Adolf (2001), p. 49 (54).

[17] See proposal submitted by the US and the EEC, GATT Document L/4817 of 31 July 1979, as well as the revised proposal contained in GATT Document L/5382 of 18 October 1982.

[18] Report of the Group of Experts on Trade in Counterfeit Goods, GATT Document L/5878 of 9 October 1985, pp. 7–9 and 15; see also Gervais (2008), p. 8.

[19] The full text of the mandate is reproduced in GATT Document MIN.DEC of 20 September 1986, pp. 7–8.

rules and disciplines to be established. This said, in line with the controversial views already held by GATT negotiators prior to the launch of the Uruguay Round,[20] discussions in the then established negotiating group on trade-related aspects of IPRs focused in the initial phase precisely on what is also the topic of this contribution, i.e. whether and to what extent IPRs were to be considered as sufficiently trade-related so that they would be covered by the mandate. Developing countries saw the term "trade-related aspects" as only referring to trade in counterfeit goods and anti-competitive practices regarding IPRs, whereas others understood it as a broader mandate to also establish substantive rules on IPRs in general. On the occasion of the mid-term review of the Uruguay Round negotiations in April 1989, a decision in favour of a broader reading of the mandate was taken, including, in particular, the establishment of adequate standards for the protection and enforcement of trade-related IPRs.[21] Subsequent negotiations resulted in the inclusion of the TRIPS Agreement with substantive protection and enforcement standards in the results of the Uruguay Round of multilateral trade negotiations, the Final Act of which was signed at the Marrakesh Ministerial Meeting in April 1994 together with the Agreement Establishing the WTO. IPRs thus fully integrated into the trade arena when the WTO opened in 1995. In recognition of their economic importance and the steadily increasing share of services and IPRs in international trade, the new multilateral trading system administered and overviewed by the WTO was thus extended into these hitherto uncovered areas of trade.

This move back to the trade arena is, in particular, supported by rapid technological developments, the evolution of cross-border exchanges of goods, services, capital and knowledge more generally,[22] as well as the recognition of innovation and technological development as key ingredients for economic development that thus became an endogenous factor of economic growth.[23] Traditionally, trade was looked at in categories, such as products and industry sectors,[24] to expand also to services since the GATS Agreement (General Agreement on Trade in Services) became part of the WTO in 1995. This products/services/industry-based approach is still largely reflected in the way in which the WTO was conceived during the Uruguay Round negotiations. Coupled with the steady increase of global value chains[25] and the growth of corporate R&D investment in the knowledge-based industry, there is, however, also growing recognition of the importance of trade in goods and services embedding a more or less significant portion of

---

[20] UNCTAD and ICTSD (2005), p. 3.

[21] GATT Document MTN.TNC/11 of 21 April 1989, p. 21; see also Taubman et al. (2012), pp. 5–7.

[22] For a chart indicating the evolution of international trade flows of knowledge-intensive products see Verdier (2013), p. 18.

[23] Curtis (2012), pp. 4 and 6.

[24] See Sector Specific Discussions and Negotiations on Goods in the GATT and WTO, Note by the Secretariat, WTO-Document TN/MA/S/13 of 24 January 2005.

[25] The World Trade Report (2013), p. 6, estimates that almost 30 % of total trade consists of re-exports of intermediate inputs.

knowledge.[26] A 2013 report by the European Patent Office and the Office for Harmonization in the Internal Market estimated, for example, that IPR-intensive industries accounted for most of the EU's external trade, with 88 % of imports consisting of products of IPR-intensive industries, and the share of exports of such products even amounting to 90 %.[27] Hence the characterisation sometimes found in literature of both the TRIPS and GATS Agreements as the WTO's "trade in knowledge" agreements.[28] This trend towards a more knowledge-based analysis of the object of trade supports the view that IPRs are trade-related, as they typically represent the know-how and other forms of knowledge that make a physical good. As such, they have a direct bearing on market access, which is different from other issues such as labour standards, which are also described by their critics as not belonging to the WTO as the forum dealing with trade matters.

The trend to recognise IPRs as an integral part of trade is furthermore backed by the extent to which they have been covered in the more recent FTAs and which has evolved more or less in parallel with the coming into being of the TRIPS Agreement in 1995. Earlier FTAs concluded since the 1950s knew hardly, if any, IP provisions, assuming that these only had a bearing on international trade in form of an exception to liberalising such trade in line with GATT Article XX. This changed dramatically from 1997 onwards, when in particular the US, later followed by the EU and the European Free Trade Association (EFTA) pushed for the inclusion of increasingly detailed chapters regulating the protection and enforcement of IPRs in FTA negotiations with their trading partners.[29] This is not least based on the recognition that adequate IP protection can foster trade of goods and services embedding IPRs.[30] To some extent, this latest trend is now also replicated by some developing countries that sometimes seek to cover IPRs in a fairly detailed manner in their respective FTAs.[31]

Another development that established a direct link between trade instruments and IPRs outside the multilateral framework could be observed in the US where, in 1974, the amendments to the Trade and Tariffs Act had called into life "Section 301". As part of the amendments, the eligibility for the Generalized System of Preferences (GSP) that provides for unilateral trade preferences to certain goods from developing countries, was made conditional upon adequate protection of IPRs. This constituted yet another move to make IPRs an integral

---

[26] Stockholm Network (2012), pp. 12–13.

[27] European Patent Office and Office for Harmonization in the Internal Market (2013), pp. 6 and 9.

[28] Kampf (2013), p. 235 (239); Arup (2008).

[29] Seuba (2013), p. 240; Kampf (2007), p. 87; see also the WTO database on Regional Trade Agreements, available at http://rtais.wto.org.

[30] This explains why the "Directives for the negotiation on the Transatlantic Trade and Investment Partnership between the EU and the US", as adopted by the EU's Foreign Affairs Council on 14 June 2013, call for negotiations to "address areas most relevant for fostering the exchange of goods and services with IP content, with a view to supporting innovation". The Directives are available at https://www.laquadrature.net/files/TAFTA%20_%20Mandate%20_%2020130617.pdf.

[31] Valdés and McCann (2014), para. 44.

part of the US trade policy.[32] In the past, the Office of the United States Trade Representative (USTR) reviewed, for example, the status of Brazil as a GSP beneficiary country for reason of inadequate IPR protection.[33] In the case of Ukraine, GSP eligibility was even temporarily suspended for lack of adequate IP protection from 2001 to 2006 and, in 2013, Ukraine's eligibility as a GSP beneficiary was again reviewed.[34] Other WTO Members have adopted similar programmes. The EU, for example, has put in place a scheme of lower tariffs.[35] These and other such programmes are based on the so-called Enabling Clause or the "Decision on Differential and More Favourable Treatment, Reciprocity and Fuller Participation of Developing Countries", adopted under the GATT in 1979, which allows WTO Members to accord differential and more favourable treatment to developing countries.[36] Consequently, albeit constituting unilateral preferential measures, their application, including any envisaged modifications or withdrawals of GSP benefits, are governed by WTO rules, as was confirmed by the dispute between India and the EU in relation to a special arrangement under the EU's GSP scheme to combat drug production and trafficking for some selected countries that excluded India from these benefits.[37] In particular, para. 4 of the Enabling Clause thus requires notification of the planned modification or withdrawal to the other party, as well as according adequate time and opportunity to discuss any difficulties and providing support to reach a satisfactory solution. In addition, Article 19(1)(d) of the EU's Regulation No 978/2012, for example, explicitly allows for temporary withdrawal for reasons of serious and systematic unfair trading practices, provided that these practices are prohibited and actionable under the WTO Agreements and have been found as such by the competent WTO body. This usefully illustrates the potential positive side effects resulting from the inclusion of IPRs in the trade arena in the sense that it protects countries against the subjective assessment of their IPR regime by their trading partners and the subsequent adoption of unilateral measures, in this case taking the form of withdrawal of GSP benefits, without prior consultations and possibly recourse to the WTO dispute settlement mechanism in order to determine the level of TRIPS compliance.[38]

Taking the historical background provided above together with the more recent developments outside the WTO, establishing a firm link between IPRs and trade

---

[32] Sell (2010), p. 762 (773).

[33] See USTR announcement at http://www.ustr.gov/trade-topics/trade-development/preference-programs/generalized-system-preferences-gsp/gsp-documents-2.

[34] Jones (2013), p. 4.

[35] Regulation (EU) No 978/2012 of the European Parliament and of the Council of 25 October 2012 applying a scheme of generalised tariff preferences and repealing Council Regulation (EC) No 732/2008, [2012] OJ L 303/1.

[36] Decision of 28 November 1979, GATT Document L/4903.

[37] *European Communities – Conditions for the Granting of Tariff Preferences to Developing Countries*, WTO Documents WT/DS246/R of 1 December 2003 (Panel Report) and WT/DS246/AB/R of 7 April 2004 (Appellate Body Report).

[38] Jones (2013), p. 24.

through the incorporation of the TRIPS Agreement in the WTO may thus appear as a pure formality that merely confirmed a longstanding fact.

Strong Arguments for and Against a Link Between IPRs and Trade Animate the Debate

In particular, developed countries have constantly argued that IPR protection is needed to ensure that inventors and creators get adequate return for their investment in developing new technologies and bringing their creations to the market. They also see IPRs as a tool to encourage foreign direct investment and/or exports, as well as innovation and technology transfer which, in turn, would support developing countries in their efforts to build up their own technological basis and subsequently export products.[39] In addition, harmonising the standards of IP protection and enforcement would positively affect international trade insofar as transaction costs associated with such trade would be reduced.

Their interest to bring IPR standards under the GATT/WTO umbrella as part of the Uruguay Round negotiations was essentially threefold: to allow for trade-offs with other areas of negotiations and thus to achieve better outcomes in the field of IPRs, to be able to use the WTO's powerful dispute settlement mechanism, and to cover a wide range of countries in one strike, since adhering to the TRIPS Agreement was and remains a prerequisite for a country to become a WTO Member. More generally, there was also the firm belief that linking IP protection and trade would result in more effective outcomes, namely in the form of stronger protection through reliance on more powerful trade policies.[40] To support their view, the proponents argued that IPRs affected trade flows and that insufficient protection would distort trade and could act like non-tariff trade barriers. For example, firms may refrain from exporting their patent-protected goods to markets with weak IPR protection for fear of being exposed to counterfeiting and piracy. In a similar vein, trade in counterfeit and pirated goods could negatively impact on the promotion of international trade in genuine goods.[41] As this fell within the competence of the GATT, it should be mandated to address the matter.

At the same time, the international framework for the protection of IPRs, essentially composed of a set of multilateral treaties administered by WIPO, was perceived as too diverse and ineffective by the representatives of this view. From their perspective, the growing membership in some of these treaties and pressure from developing countries to weaken the international IP system made any progress

[39] Blyde (2006), p. 1. For an overview of arguments used to support the inclusion of IPRs in trade rules, see also Akkoyunlu (2013), p. 6.

[40] Sell (2010), p. 762 (771–772).

[41] For a detailed overview of the industrialised countries' arguments and principal interests, see Reichmann (1989), p. 747 (754–761).

towards further harmonisation increasingly difficult and controversial,[42] as illustrated, for example, by the failure to amend the Paris Convention in 1985. At the same time, membership in other treaties remained limited to a few countries. In addition, the absence of an effective mechanism to settle disputes in WIPO was deplored. The 1985 Report of the Group of Experts on Trade in Counterfeit Goods reflected some of this criticism. For example, concern was expressed about Article 9 of the Paris Convention since it was not binding and the determination of remedies and sanctions were left to national law. Also, the Paris Convention would not offer a proper and effective dispute settlement mechanism.[43]

On the other side of the spectrum, criticism with respect to the link between IPRs and the multilateral trading system is essentially twofold: a more radical view disputes the trade-related nature of IPRs as such, whereas a more moderate view accepts that IPRs are, at least in part, trade-related, but does not see minimum standards of protection as belonging in the WTO. Rejecting the TRIPS Agreement in today's form as part of the WTO is thus common to both views. Interestingly, this position was also taken by the copyright industry in the US in the initial phase of the Uruguay Round negotiations: although fully supportive of the view that IPRs belonged to the trade domain, it did not favour the multilateral approach because of concerns of possible trade-offs that could be made in the course of the negotiations and result in a weaker protection.[44]

The group of critics includes those who are otherwise to be counted among the advocates of free trade.[45] This is, in particular, interesting from a historical perspective, as the arguments used by representatives of this group mirror, to a large extent, the late nineteenth century debate, when many called for the abolition of patent protection as a protectionist tool that would stand in the way of free trade (see above, second section). Jagdish Bhagwati has thus constantly argued that the TRIPS Agreement does not belong to the WTO as it delays the process of liberalising trade.[46] For him, protecting IPRs "is simply a matter of royalty collection" that was forced into the WTO as a result of strong industry lobbying.[47] Similarly, others have assessed the existing standards of IPR protection and enforcement as overly restrictive, providing too high rewards to the right holders while negatively impacting on competition and innovation.[48] In their view, the TRIPS Agreement failed to recognise that the IP regime needed in developing countries to achieve their developmental and other domestic policy objectives was different from that

---

[42] Drahos and Smith (1999), p. 13; Breitwieser and Foster (2012), p. 18; Sell (2010), p. 762 (768).

[43] See the summary of views in the report of the Group of Experts on Trade in Counterfeit Goods, GATT Document L/5878 of 9 October 1985, pp. 3–4 and 7–8.

[44] Sell (2010), p. 762 (774).

[45] For an overview of arguments put forward to demonstrate the negative impact of IPRs on trade, see also Akkoyunlu (2013), p. 6.

[46] Bhagwati (2002), p. 126 (128).

[47] Bhagwati (2005); Bhagwati (1999).

[48] Drahos (2002), p. 227.

suitable for developed countries.[49] IPRs should therefore not have been included in the WTO, not least because trade negotiators were not competent for the subject matter and WIPO already existed as an international organisation to deal with IP matters that, in light of their complexity, deserved to be covered by a separate regime.[50] Consequently, the extension of the WTO's mandate to IPRs was perceived as an expansion to matters that reached far beyond a country's border and that were only tangentially trade-related at best. Therefore, they would not belong to traditional trade areas, but affected areas of vital interest to countries, such as health and food security.[51] Some went even further and classified the TRIPS Agreement as covering non-trade issues, similarly to labour and environmental standards, which would be fundamentally different from the WTO's objective of liberalising trade[52] and which would actually limit sovereign states in their right to trade, rather than making IPRs subservient to trade.[53] According to these voices, the inclusion of the TRIPS Agreement in the WTO was not a natural fit, but the result of strong industry lobbying which gained the support of policymakers in developed countries, in particular the US.[54] An imbalance was thus created in the multilateral system, as the coverage of IPRs only benefited developed countries, while developing countries faced a delay in their own technological development.[55]

Next to these critical voices are also those who hold the view that only parts of the TRIPS Agreement are trade-related, whereas other sections that are primarily aiming at setting standards and harmonising the IP regime would not belong to the WTO. This was namely the position taken by many developing countries during the Uruguay Round negotiations who voiced strong concerns about the incorporation of substantive IPR protection rules in the WTO.[56] Thus, while accepting the inclusion of provisions directed towards combating international trade in counterfeit and pirated goods, Chile rejected in the final stage of the Uruguay Round negotiations the inclusion of minimum standards of IPR protection in the WTO; rather, if at all adopted, those should be covered by a separate agreement to be administered by another international organisation, such as WIPO.[57] In a similar move, India only partially admitted that IPR protection should be dealt with as a matter of trade. Consequently, it held the view that multilateral rules under the future WTO Agreement should only apply in situations of proven trade distortion.[58] In 1991,

---

[49] Adolf (2001), p. 49 (80).

[50] Stiglitz (2005); Sell (2010), p. 762 (777, 779); Yelpaala (2012), p. 55 (113).

[51] Yelpaala (2012), p. 55.

[52] Panagariya (1999).

[53] Yelpaala (2012), p. 55 (61, 104).

[54] Sell (2010), p. 762 (763–764).

[55] Khor (1997).

[56] For a detailed overview of the developing countries' arguments and principal interests, see Reichmann (1989), p. 747 (761–766).

[57] Communication of 14 May 1990, GATT negotiating document MTN.GNG/NG11/W/72.

[58] Gervais (2008), p. 15.

the Chairman's report to the Group of Negotiations on Goods to which the composite draft text of the future TRIPS Agreement was attached, consequently took note of the fact that one approach consisted of concluding a single agreement covering the protection and enforcement standards for all IPR categories. Another approach supported by many developing countries was reported as rejecting such a comprehensive agreement. They were seeking the separation into two agreements, the first limited to provisions covering trade in counterfeit and pirated goods, to be covered by the GATT/WTO, and the second on standards and principles, to be implemented by the relevant international organisation.[59]

This position, taken by many developing countries, coincided—perhaps surprisingly—to a large extent with the approach taken by developed countries when the discussions were first initialled in the GATT. Thus, the "Agreement on Measures to Discourage the Importation of Counterfeit Goods" that had been proposed by the US and other developed countries in 1979 (see above, second section) only contained a limited number of mostly procedural provisions on IPR enforcement and suggested the establishment of a dispute settlement mechanism. At the same time, Article I.3 of the draft agreement explicitly provided that "the substantive intellectual property law of the Parties is unchanged by this Agreement".[60] In other words, the setting of minimum standards for IPR protection within the framework of the GATT had not been envisaged by the proponents at that point in time.

Until recently, the Court of Justice of the EU (CJEU) could also have been counted in the group of those who saw only parts of the TRIPS Agreement as being related to trade. First in its Opinion 1/94 which was then echoed by subsequent judgments, the Court acknowledged that the section on border measures in the TRIPS Agreement clearly belonged in the trade arena. At the same time, it considered for a long time that this would not be the case for other sections of the agreement, such as the provisions on patent protection (see below, sixth section). Others have also tried to distinguish between those TRIPS provisions that could be considered as trade-related and those for which this would not be the case. Attempts to identify the types of IPRs that could be considered as trade-related, for example, by reference to Article 7 TRIPS, concluded though that the objectives as set out in this provision are not suitable to achieve this goal.[61]

Reviewing the arguments defended by each side as briefly summarised above, the question of whether the TRIPS Agreement stands for or against liberalisation of global trade and whether, as such, it therefore belongs to the family of trade agreements administered by the WTO or not turns out to be among the most controversial issues. To answer this question, it is worthwhile to take account of the WTO's objectives more generally. As the mission statement by the former Director-General, Pascal Lamy, indicates, the organisation counts among its key

[59] Chairman's report to the Group of Negotiation on Goods, GATT negotiating document MTN.GNG/NG11/W/76 of 23 July 1990.

[60] GATT Documents L/4817 of 31 July 1979 and L/5382 of 18 October 1982.

[61] Spence (2001), p. 263.

objectives not only the reduction or elimination of barriers to trade, but also the setting of rules that govern the conduct of international trade. In a similar vein, the same statement also confirms that, for the WTO, "market opening must be accompanied by sound domestic and international policies that contribute to economic growth and development according to each member's needs and aspirations".[62] In other words, the WTO does not stand for liberalisation outside any regulatory framework. Nor does it aim at establishing a multilateral framework supportive of "wild liberalisation" that would, for example, favour free trade in counterfeit and pirated goods at the expense of trade in legitimate goods.

Quite to the opposite: as the Preamble of the TRIPS Agreement confirms, the drafters of the agreement rightly considered that the harmonious liberalisation of trade significantly relied on the promotion of a balanced set of effective and adequate standards for the protection of IPRs and for their enforcement and therefore agreed on the inclusion of the TRIPS Agreement in the WTO. The EU's common commercial policy as redefined by the Lisbon Treaty shares this vision: its objectives include the contribution to a harmonious development of global trade and the elimination of barriers to such trade (Article 206 of the Treaty on the Functioning of the EU (TFEU)). At the same time, Article 207 TFEU makes commercial aspects of IPRs part of this policy, in other words, views them as contributing to, not blocking, the achievement of the overall trade objectives.

Understood as such, the WTO's principal objective clearly speaks in favour of incorporating the TRIPS Agreement under its umbrella. Although the agreement regulates rather than liberalises trade, it nevertheless represents a milestone in the harmonious trade liberalisation that takes account of other policy objectives and, in that capacity, belongs to the WTO.

The TRIPS Agreement Links IPRs to Trade in a Manner That Is Both Offensive and Defensive

By its very name, the TRIPS Agreement obviously assumes the trade-related nature of IPRs. This is confirmed by its Preamble, as well as a number of specific provisions both in the area of substantive rights and the enforcement of IPRs. Thus, in line with the negotiating mandate of the Uruguay Round adopted in Punta del Este in 1986,[63] the Preamble of the TRIPS Agreement adopts a balanced approach to the link between IPRs and trade. On the one hand, there is the offensive interest in protecting IPRs in the course of trade. In this regard, the Preamble sees the principles, rules and disciplines established by the Agreement as a means to reduce distortions and impediments to international trade and to combat

[62] The WTO's mission statement is available at http://www.wto.org/english/thewto_e/whatis_e/wto_dg_stat_e.htm.

[63] See Taubman et al. (2012), p. 6.

international trade in counterfeit goods. On the other hand, there is the defensive interest in ensuring that enforcing IPRs is not becoming a barrier to legitimate trade, which is also recognised by the Preamble. Similarly, negotiations outside the WTO are often guided by the same motives, as was illustrated, for example, by the Preamble to the Anti-Counterfeiting Trade Agreement (ACTA) that was negotiated by a group of like-minded countries. The agreement was due to combat the proliferation of counterfeit and pirated goods through enhanced cooperation and more effective rules enforcing IPRs in order to preserve legitimate trade and the sustainable development of the world economy, while at the same time ensuring that such measures do not become barriers to legitimate trade.[64]

The substantive provisions on IPR protection and enforcement in the TRIPS Agreement that specifically address the link with trade follow the division into these two sub-categories that pursue offensive and defensive objectives. Accordingly, the first set of provisions seeks to ensure the respect of IPRs in the course of trade, including as regards the possibility to use them without being subjected to unjustified requirements, and explicitly uses the term "trade" for that purpose. Among these provisions is Article 16.1 TRIPS, according to which the trademark owner can prevent others from using, without his or her consent, in the course of trade identical or similar signs for goods or services which are identical or similar to those for which the trademark has been registered and where such use is likely to confuse consumers. Also in the field of trademarks, Article 20 TRIPS stipulates that the use of trademarks in the course of trade is not unjustifiably encumbered by special requirements. Finally, Article 69 TRIPS obliges WTO Members to cooperate and to exchange information in order to eliminate international trade in goods infringing IPRs.

The second set of provisions pursues defensive interests. It aims at ensuring that IPR protection and enforcement and related procedures do not stand in the way of legitimate trade. For example, Article 3.2 TRIPS thus provides that exceptions to WTO Members' basic obligation to guarantee national treatment to foreign right holders in relation to judicial and administrative procedures are only permitted where they are not applied in a manner that constitutes a disguised restriction to trade. Furthermore, both Articles 8.2 and 40.1 TRIPS open the door to the application of competition law in order to avoid that the abuse of IPRs or practices pertaining to IPRs unreasonably restrain trade. In the section on geographical indications, Article 24.8 TRIPS explicitly provides for the right of any person to use its name or the name of its predecessor in business in the course of trade, except where the public would be misled by such use. Last, but not least, Article 41.1 TRIPS is of significant importance in this context, as it takes up once more the underlying idea that enforcement procedures are not to be applied in a way that is blocking legitimate trade.

---

[64] See the Preamble to the ACTA, as submitted to the TRIPS Council by Australia, Canada, the EU, Korea, Japan, New Zealand, Singapore, Switzerland and the US, WTO-Document IP/C/W/563 of 17 October 2011.

This said, there are also other provisions in the TRIPS Agreement that are directly related to trade without using the term "trade" as such. For example, the section on patents refers to the act of importing in several places and thus clearly establishes a link with trade. In this regard, Article 27.1 TRIPS requires the non-discriminatory availability of patent rights regardless of whether the products are imported or locally produced. Article 28.1 TRIPS lists among the exclusive rights, the possibility to prevent third parties from importing the patent-protected product or products obtained directly from a patent-protected process without the authorisation of the right holder. It also cross-refers the right of importation to Article 6 TRIPS which has a direct link to trade, too. According to this provision, read together with the clarification provided by paragraph 5(d) of the Doha Declaration on the TRIPS Agreement and Public Health (Doha Declaration),[65] each WTO Member enjoys the freedom to determine the exhaustion regime which best meets its domestic policy objectives. Consequently, WTO Members have opted for national, regional or international exhaustion regimes. The choice impacts on the extent to which trade in goods embedding IPRs can take place: under national exhaustion, IPRs can serve to prohibit parallel imports and thus potentially function like a boundary around the national territory, whereas such parallel imports could take place in a country that has opted for international exhaustion of IPRs.

In addition, Article 31(f) TRIPS, by limiting the use of standard compulsory licences predominantly to supply the domestic market of the Member granting the licence, assumes that the non-predominant share of the production may be exported. In a similar vein, an additional flexibility, often referred to as the "Paragraph 6 System", was agreed by WTO Members back in 2003 and subsequently proposed as a permanent amendment of the TRIPS Agreement in 2005.[66] It aims at addressing the difficulty of WTO Members with insufficient manufacturing capacities to make effective use of compulsory licensing, as identified in paragraph 6 of the Doha Declaration. Under the System, WTO Members may grant special compulsory licences exclusively for the purpose of producing and exporting medicines to countries with insufficient manufacturing capacities in the pharmaceutical sector.[67] Here again, the mechanism specifically addresses a situation where exceptions to patent rights can be applied in order to make and supply the medicines needed to the importing country, so that they do not stand in the way of trading generic medicines.

Part III of the TRIPS Agreement on the enforcement of IPRs also incorporates a wide range of provisions that are directly related to trade. Thus, under Article 50.1 TRIPS, WTO Members are obliged to provide their judicial authorities with the authority to order provisional measures, including to prevent the entry into the channels of commerce of imported infringing goods immediately after customs

[65] WTO Document WT/MIN(01)/DEC/2.

[66] WTO Documents WT/L/540 and Corr. 1 and WT/L/641.

[67] For details regarding the implementation, use and functioning of the Paragraph 6 System see WHO, WIPO, and WTO (2012), pp. 177–180 and Annex II.

clearance. Similarly, the entire Section 4 is closely connected to the act of importing goods and thus to trade. It provides for mandatory border measures to be made available by WTO Members which enable the right holder to take action against the importation of allegedly counterfeit trademark or pirated copyright goods (Article 51 TRIPS). The application of such measures to suspend the importation of goods involving other infringements of IPRs and to export infringing goods remains, however, optional. The same applies to *ex officio* action (Article 58 TRIPS) and the application of border measures to imports in small quantities of a non-commercial nature (Article 60 TRIPS). In addition, Article 59 TRIPS prohibits, in principle, the re-exportation of counterfeit trademark goods in an unaltered state.

Finally, another, at first sight fairly remote, link to trade can be found in the yet to be decided question as to whether non-violation and situation complaints should apply to the TRIPS Agreement. Under Article 64.2 TRIPS, the TRIPS Council was requested to examine the scope and modalities for complaints provided for in GATT Article XXIII:1(b) and (c) and to make recommendations to the General Council by end 1999. Given the impossibility of reaching a unanimous decision on this matter, WTO Members have constantly renewed a moratorium first agreed upon at the Doha Ministerial Conference in 2001.[68] During the more than a decade-long opportunity to examine the issue, the question whether the TRIPS Agreement is a market access agreement or not figured prominently on the agenda.[69] In this regard, some delegations took the view that the TRIPS Agreement is, indeed, about market access as it aimed at reducing distortions to international trade through the establishment of minimum standards for the protection and enforcement of IPRs. Like other WTO Agreements, the TRIPS Agreements thus established conditions under which international trade was to be conducted. Others argued that the TRIPS Agreement was not principally concerned with questions of market access and provided no commitments in this respect, but also recognised that IPRs might facilitate trade and investment. In other words, both sides in this debate seem to acknowledge the close link between IPRs and trade, notwithstanding their divergent views regarding the very nature of the TRIPS Agreement as a multilateral framework that provides for market access or not.

[68] WTO Documents WT/MIN(01)/17, para. 11.1; WT/L/579, para. 1(h); WT/MIN(05)/DEC, para. 45; WT/L/783 and WT/L/842. For the most recent Decision taken at the ninth WTO Ministerial Conference held in Bali in December 2013, see WT/L/906.

[69] See the revised Summary Note on Non-Violation and Situation Complaints prepared by the WTO Secretariat in 2012, WTO Document IP/C/W/349/Rev.2, paras. 30–35.

Certain WTO Dispute Settlement Cases Have Addressed the Effect of IPR Protection and Enforcement on Trade

A number of dispute settlement cases go beyond the mere interpretation of a given TRIPS provision and extend to the implications that such interpretation may have for trade. Some of these cases have been settled while others are still pending. For the purposes of this contribution, rather than attempting to cover the entire range of relevant panel and appellate body reports, a few cases have been selected in which the relationship between IPRs and trade plays a particular role.[70] They back the view that IPRs do, indeed, directly impact on trade and that those dimensions are therefore closely linked to each other and better be dealt with under one roof, i.e. that of the WTO.

The most prominent cases which come to mind in this respect are the consultations[71] which both India and Brazil requested in 2010 with the European Union regarding generic medicines in transit.[72] The request for these consultations was motivated by a number of cases in which generic medicines, mostly manufactured in India, had been detained by EU Customs, mainly in the Netherlands, as they were transiting the Dutch territory in order to be shipped to various third country destinations.[73] While there was no infringement reported in the exporting country and in the recipient countries, Customs' action was requested by the right holders in most cases on grounds of alleged infringement of patent rights in the Netherlands. The principal measure at issue that authorised this kind of intervention by Customs in the EU was Council Regulation (EC) No 1383/2003 of 22 July 2003.[74] It went

[70] Other relevant dispute settlement cases include: *US – Section 337 of the Tariff Act of 1930 and Amendments thereto*, Report by the GATT Panel adopted on 7 November 1989, GATT Document L/6439 – 36S/345; see also the EU's request for consultations on the same subject matter in WTO Document WT/DS186/1 of 18 January 2000; *European Communities – Protection of Trademarks and Geographical Indications for Agricultural Products and Foodstuffs*, WTO Documents WT/DS174/R and WT/DS290/R of 15 March 2005; *Canada – Patent Protection of Pharmaceutical Products*, WTO Document WT/DS114/R of 17 March 2000.

[71] *European Union and a Member State – Seizure of Generic Drugs in Transit*, WTO Documents WT/DS408/1 (request for consultations by India) and WT/DS409/1 (request for consultations by Brazil).

[72] For the discussion in literature, see von Mühlendahl and Stauder (2009), p. 653; Kumar (2010), p. 506.

[73] See also the extensive discussion of the issue at the following TRIPS Council meetings: 3 March 2009, WTO Document IP/C/M/59, paras. 122–191; 8–9 June 2009, WTO Document IP/C/M/60, paras. 115–167; 27–28 October 2009, WTO Document IP/C/M/61, paras. 254–294; 2 March 2010, WTO Document IP/C/M/62, paras. 213–231.

[74] Council Regulation (EC) 1383/2003 of 22 July 2003 concerning customs action against goods suspected of infringing certain intellectual property rights and the measures to be taken against goods found to have infringed such rights, [2003] OJ L 196/7, now replaced by Regulation (EU) No 608/2013 of the European Parliament and of the Council of 12 June 2013 concerning customs enforcement of intellectual property rights and repealing Council Regulation (EC) 1383/2003, [2013] OJ L 181/15.

beyond the minimum requirements set by Article 51 TRIPS insofar as it extended the scope of border measures in the EU to cover all IPRs, including patents, and to apply to goods in transit. Both India and Brazil argued in their respective requests for consultations that the EU's Customs Regulation would be inconsistent, among others, with Article 41 TRIPS according to which enforcement procedures are to "be applied in such a manner as to avoid the creation of barriers to legitimate trade". In other words, the claimants in this case clearly saw a link between IPRs, here patents, and trade, albeit in a negative way insofar as IPRs could potentially stand in the way of trade in generic medicines. More recently, a similar debate has emerged with respect to the amendments to the Community trademark as proposed by the European Commission in 2013.[75] According to this proposal, the exclusive rights conferred on the right holder would entitle him or her under certain conditions to prevent third parties from bringing goods into the EU's customs territory irrespective of whether those are meant to be released for free circulation there. In this case, the European Parliament's (EP) rapporteur considered the proposed amendment as a potential threat to international trade[76]; ultimately, this led the EP to recommend the inclusion of additional language to ensure the smooth transit of generic medicines in compliance with the EU's international (WTO) obligations.[77] If at all needed, the question of how best to regulate IPR infringements occurring while goods are transiting a territory illustrates how important it is to address all aspects related to trade, including IPRs, in one place in order to ensure that the IPR regime is designed in a manner that fosters rather than blocks legitimate trade.

Another set of high profile cases in which the link between IPRs and trade plays a significant role relates to measures taken or envisaged by certain WTO Members requiring plain packaging of tobacco products. In no less than five WTO dispute settlement cases, the compatibility of Australia's Tobacco Plain Packaging Act and Regulations 2011, as well as of the Trademarks Amendment Act 2011 with a number of TRIPS provisions, Article 2.2 of the Agreement on Technical Barriers to Trade and Articles I and III:4 of the GATT 1994 was raised.[78] Among others, the measures taken by Australia require packages of tobacco products to be of drab

[75] Proposal for a Regulation of the European Parliament and of the Council Amending Council Regulation (EC) No 207/2009 on the Community Trademark, COM(2013) 161 final of 27 March 2013.

[76] Standeford (2014).

[77] See the EP legislative resolution adopted on 25 February 2014, available at http://www.europarl.europa.eu/sides/getDoc.do?pubRef=-//EP//TEXT+TA+P7-TA-2014-0118+0+DOC+XML+V0//EN&language=EN.

[78] *Australia – Certain Measures Concerning Trademarks and Other Plain Packaging Requirements Applicable to Tobacco Products and Packaging*, WTO Documents WT/DS434/11 of 17 August 2012 (request for the establishment of a Panel by Ukraine), WT/DS435/16 of 17 October 2012 (request for the establishment of a Panel by Honduras), WT/DS4441/15 of 14 November 2012 (request for the establishment of a Panel by the Dominican Republic); WT/DS/458/14 of 14 April 2014 (request for the establishment of a Panel by Cuba); and WT/DS/467/15 of 6 March 2014 (request for the establishment of a Panel by Indonesia).

dark brown colour, to carry graphic health warnings covering 75 % of the front surface and 90 % of the back surface of each package and to have a standardised shape; the brand, business or company name must be displayed in standard typeface and font while the display of designs and figurative features, including those forming part of trademarks and geographical indications, is prohibited. Article 20 TRIPS features among the key arguments referred to by the claimants in these cases according to whom the Australian plain packaging measures would be incompatible with this and other provisions of the TRIPS Agreement. It precludes precisely special requirements from unjustifiably encumbering the use of a trademark in the course of trade. Interestingly, this link between IPRs and trade is not only a cornerstone in the line of arguments put together by the claimants, mostly developing countries. Moreover, they construe the link here in a positive manner, in the sense that their request for adequate IPR protection is seen as being supportive of legitimate trade,[79] and not from the more defensive perspective of IPRs potentially blocking such trade, as was argued in the above cases of in-transit generic medicines and as is the more traditional view held among many developing countries (see above, second section).

Finally, an interesting issue that also demonstrates the importance of the interpretation given to IP provisions for trade is the definition of what is meant by the local working requirement in the field of patents. This question formed the object of consultations in *Brazil – Measures Affecting Patent Protection*.[80] In its request for consultations, the US argued that Article 68 of Brazil's Industrial Property Law of 14 May 1996 was inconsistent with Articles 27 and 28 TRIPS insofar as it made patents subject to compulsory licensing if the products were not manufactured locally; in other words, the mere act of importation of a patent-protected good would not satisfy the requirements under Brazil's Industrial Property Law and could result in the curtailment of exclusive patent rights. This narrow way of defining the local working requirement is by no means an exception. Indonesia, for example, in Article 17 of its Law Number 14 of 2001 Regarding Patents[81] requires the patent holder to "make products or to use the process that has been granted a Patent in Indonesia"; the patent holder can only be exempted from this obligation "if the making of the product or the use of the process is only suitable to be implemented on a regional scale". In a similar vein, the first-ever compulsory licence granted in India in March 2012 for Sorafenib, a medicine to treat kidney and liver cancer for which the German company Bayer holds the patent rights in India, was, among others, based on the ground of failure to manufacture the medicine in India. In *Natco Pharma Limited v Bayer Corporation*,[82] the Patent Controller

[79] See, for example, the statements made by Cuba at the TRIPS Council meeting of 11–12 June 2013, WTO Document IP/C/M/73/Add.1, paras. 478–479, and by the Dominican Republic at the TRIPS Council meeting of 5–6 March 2013, WTO Document IP/C/M/72, para. 12.2.

[80] WTO Document WT/DS199/1 of 8 June 2000.

[81] Full text available at WIPO Lex http://www.wipo.int/wipolex/en/text.jsp?file_id=174132.

[82] Full text of the decision is available at http://keionline.org/sites/default/files/sorafenib_nexavar_compulsory_License_12032012.pdf.

reversed the patentee's argument that importation would suffice to meet the requirements under Section 84(1) of India's Patents Act 1970 and concluded that "working in the territory of India" in this provision had to be interpreted as "manufactured to a reasonable extent in India".

In the above-mentioned case, the WTO's dispute settlement mechanism was given no opportunity to clarify the matter. Instead, the US and Brazil subsequently notified the WTO of a mutually satisfactory solution to the dispute, noting that Article 68 of Brazil's Industrial Property Law had never been used and that Brazil had committed itself to hold prior talks with the US Government should it ever envisage granting a compulsory licence on patents held by US companies on this basis.[83] There is thus no common understanding as to the exact scope of the local working requirement and its interpretation continues to be the subject of a controversial debate. The outcome of this debate significantly depends once again on the very topic of this contribution, i.e. whether or not one considers IPRs to be trade-related. Read in the context of Article 5A(2) of the Paris Convention, the view has been taken that failure by the patentee to work the patent can only mean failure to manufacture locally, rather than merely importing or selling the patent-protected product.[84] Such a narrow interpretation of the local working requirement may be justified to the extent that it is applied to a classic IP convention that establishes protection standards for IPRs in an isolated, IP-centred fashion, such as the Paris Convention. Transferring the same interpretation to an agreement that puts IPRs in a trade-related context, such as the TRIPS Agreement, would, however, appear to lead to questionable outcomes. In particular, imposing *de facto* an obligation to produce locally in order to fully enjoy the benefits of exclusive patent rights, would run counter to the trade-related nature of IPRs, as well as to the very nature of the WTO as an organisation that is designed to liberalise multilateral trade, rather than favouring local production to the detriment of such trade.

The Relationship Between IPRs and Trade Is Relevant for the Work in Other WTO Bodies

Electronic commerce is among the most prominent and fastest growing forms of modern trade. As such, it is also closely linked with the steadily increasing importance of IPR protection and enforcement since many of the products and creations offered for sale and sold on the internet are embedding IPRs. For example, trademarks can thus play an important role for consumers as source identifiers and adequate protection on the internet will facilitate access to new technologies and technology transfer. It is therefore for good reasons that the Work Programme on Electronic Commerce, adopted by the WTO General Council in 1998, instructed

[83] WTO Document WT/DS199/4 of 19 July 2001.

[84] Bodenhausen (1968), p. 71.

the TRIPS Council to examine and report on relevant IP issues arising in connection with electronic commerce, including as regards the protection and enforcement of copyright and related rights, the protection and enforcement of trademarks and new technologies and access to technology.[85] During the following years, questions related to IP and electronic commerce became a standing item on the agenda of the TRIPS Council.[86] This, in itself, can be taken as an implicit acknowledgement of the direct relationship of IPRs with trade on the internet. Since 2003, WTO Members have not shown any interest in discussing these issues in the TRIPS Council anymore. This does not, however, affect the recognition of the close link between IPRs and electronic commerce as set out above. Rather, this development can be attributed to the fact that recent discussions on electronic commerce have mostly taken place in other WTO bodies, i.e. the Committee on Trade and Development and the GATS Council. This said, the ninth WTO Ministerial Conference held in Bali in December 2013 instructed the General Council and its relevant bodies, that is including the TRIPS Council, to continue substantially invigorating the positive work under the Work Programme on Electronic Commerce and to examine the trade-related aspects of a wide range of issues in this regard.[87]

Some insights can also be drawn from the sections on intellectual property rights which constitute a regular feature of the reports produced by the WTO Secretariat in preparation for a WTO Member's periodic trade policy review. The very fact that such reports incorporate a chapter on IPRs undeniably confirms that they are considered an integral part of a country's trade policy and that this view is also accepted by the entire WTO membership. In addition, the TPR reports not only make an attempt to estimate the value of IP-relevant trade, but have occasionally also provided a definition of what such trade is understood to cover. For example, the 2013 report for Indonesia found that the country was a net importer of IPR-intensive goods in 2011, with imports of such goods amounting to USD 16.4 billion or 9.2 % of total imports, and to USD 5.8 billion of exports, which represented 2.8 % of total exports in the same year.[88] For this purpose, IPR-intensive goods were described as including the goods listed in Attachment A of the Ministerial Declaration on Trade in Information Technology Products,[89] pharmaceutical products, beverages and spirits, books and other printed media, motion picture and other developed films, as well as records, CDs, software and other recorded media.[90]

[85] See para. 4.1 of the Work Programme, WTO Document WT/L/274.

[86] For an examination of the TRIPS provisions relevant to para. 4.1 of the Work Programme, further references to discussions in the TRIPS Council and an overview of TRIPS Council documentation on electronic commerce, see the Background Note on "The Work Programme on Electronic Commerce", prepared by the WTO Secretariat, WTO Documents IP/C/W/128 of 10 February 1999 and the addendum of 15 May 2003 (IP/C/ W/128/Add.1).

[87] WTO Document WT/L/907 of 11 December 2013.

[88] WTO Document WT/TPR/S/278 of 6 March 2013, para. 3.128.

[89] WTO Document WT/MIN(96)/16.

[90] WTO Document WT/TPR/S/278, para. 3.128, footnote 74.

The Court of Justice of the European Union Has Changed Its View

How to view the link between IPRs and trade has repeatedly occupied European instances, as the answer to this question plays a decisive role in the distribution of competencies between the EU and its Member States, i.e. whether a matter falls within the EU's exclusive competence in the field of its commercial policy or whether it remained within the scope of competencies shared between the EU and its Member States. The evolution can be best traced by a closer look at the ECJ case law and the positions taken by the parties in the relevant proceedings.

Thus, in preparation for the adoption of the Marrakesh Agreement in 1994, the EU Commission had argued before the Court (ECJ) in favour of an exclusive competence of the EU to adhere to the TRIPS Agreement, as its rules were closely linked to trade in the products and services to which they applied. The ECJ accepted this view only insofar as measures to be taken by Customs at the EU's external borders were concerned. For the rest, while admitting the existence of a connection between IP and trade in goods by conferring certain exclusive rights on the owners of IPRs, the ECJ considered that these potential effects of IPRs did not specifically relate to international trade, but affected the EU's internal trade as much as, if not more than, international trade.[91] Consequently, the ECJ concluded that the TRIPS Agreement as an international instrument that primarily aimed at strengthening and harmonising the protection standards of IPRs did not generally fall within the scope of the EU's exclusive competence in relation to its common commercial policy (then Article 113 of the EC Treaty), apart from the provisions on border measures.[92] In other words, in the ECJ's view at the time, the link between IPRs and international trade as addressed by the TRIPS Agreement was there, but not strong enough to be taken into account next to the primary objective of harmonising protection standards. The ECJ therefore found that the EU and its Member States were jointly competent to conclude the TRIPS Agreement.

The ECJ's view that the TRIPS Agreement primarily aimed at strengthening and harmonising IPR protection at the global level was confirmed in subsequent judgments.[93] It also further developed the meaning of "specifically related to international trade" as referring to acts whose primary intention is to promote, facilitate or govern trade and that have direct and immediate effects on trade in the products concerned.[94] However, noting the changes introduced to the scope of the EU's common commercial policy since the entry into force of the Lisbon Treaty, which,

---

[91] ECJ, *Avis 1/94* of 15 November 1994, [1994] ECR I, 5267, para. 57.

[92] ECJ, *Avis* 1/94 of 15 November 1994, [1994] ECR I, 5267, para. 71.

[93] ECJ, C-89/99, *Schieving-Nijstad and others*, [2001] ECR I, 5874, para. 36; C-245-02, *Anheuser Busch Inc. v Budějovický Budvar, národni podnik*, [2004] ECR I, 11018, para. 65.

[94] ECJ, *Avis* 2/00, [2001] ECR I, 9713, para. 40; C-347/03, *Regione autonoma Friuli-Venezia Giulia and ERSA*, [2005] ECR I, 3785, para. 75; C-411/06, *Commission v Parliament and Council*, [2009] ECR I, 7585, para. 71.

according to Article 207(1) TFEU now also extends to the "commercial aspects of intellectual property", the ECJ reviewed its earlier jurisprudence in a landmark judgment in July 2013. While maintaining that a specific link to international trade was a prerequisite and reiterating that the TRIPS Agreement's primary objective was to strengthen and harmonise IPR protection on a worldwide scale, it concluded that the standardisation of rules under the TRIPS Agreement, although not regulating any details, aimed at liberalising international trade. Therefore, they had a specific link with international trade and, because of that link, now fell within the scope of the exclusive competence pursuant to Article 207(1) TFEU.[95] To support its view, the ECJ referred, among others, to the fact that the TRIPS Agreement was an integral part of the WTO system and, as such, fell within the scope of the WTO's dispute settlement mechanism, which allowed for cross-retaliation in areas covered by different WTO agreements. Moreover, it assumed that the drafters of Article 207 (1) TFEU must have been aware of the fact that the term "commercial aspects of intellectual property" in that provision almost literally corresponds to the title of the TRIPS Agreement.

This important change in the ECJ's jurisprudence is certainly comprehensible from the perspective of attributing an exclusive competence to the EU in the field of commercial policy, in particular against the background of the entry into force of the Lisbon Treaty and the reworded provision on the common commercial policy now found in Article 207 TFEU. This said, it is not evident at all why the specific link between the TRIPS Agreement and international trade should have become stronger merely because of this change in the distribution of competencies between the EU and its member States, nor why establishing such a specific link was needed in order to arrive at the conclusion that the EU now has exclusive competence in matters related to its commercial policy. Rather, it seems that the ECJ has finally seized the opportunity to correct what used to be a misleading assessment back in 1994 at the time of issuing Opinion 1/94, i.e. that the link between the TRIPS Agreement and international trade would only be of a remote nature.

Theoretical and Empirical Evidence Appears to Confirm the Link Between IPRs and Trade

The impact of IPR protection and enforcement on trade flows continues to be the object of various analytical studies and statistics. Looking into how trade-related IPRs are, is obviously based on the underlying assumption that there is a direct link between IPRs and trade and that it is more a matter of quantifying how strong this link is.

---

[95] ECJ, C-414/11, *Daiichi Sankyo and Sanofi-Aventis Deutschland*, 18 July 2013, not yet published, paras. 53–60.

In the first empirical study of its kind, Maskus and Penubarti established a direct link between the level of patent protection provided by a given country and the level of imports of IP-intensive goods into that country. In their view, IPRs are trade-related as the impact of different patent regimes on international trade is measurable.[96] In a similar vein, later studies have confirmed that changes in patent laws in a number of developing countries with strong imitation capacities to become TRIPS-compliant led to a significant growth of imports of high technology products from developed countries.[97] In this regard, the data on exports of pharmaceutical products from the US to India seem to back such findings, albeit emanating from a particular country- and sector-specific context. According to the WTO trade and tariff statistics,[98] these exports doubled from USD 39 million in 2000 to USD 80 million in 2005. At this point in time, India introduced full product patent protection for pharmaceutical products, taking due account of the expiry of the additional transition period of which it had availed itself under Article 65.4 TRIPS. Interestingly, during the following 5 years, exports of pharmaceutical products from the US to India rose to almost USD 200 million in 2010, to finally reach USD 225 million in 2012. Along the same lines, a study on Brazil's patent law published in 2013 noted a steady increase of the deficit in the IP trade balance since the establishment of the WTO in 1995 and, in particular, since the adoption of the Industrial Property Law No. 9.279 in 1996 and Law No. 9610 on Copyright and Neighbouring Rights in 1998.[99] According to Brazil's Ministry of Development & Industry, imports in the pharmaceutical sector, for example, have increased exponentially since then. In other words, while the impact of IPR protection and enforcement on Brazil's trade balance is reported as being substantially negative due to a significant increase of imports, as compared to a lower growth of exports, it has still resulted in much higher trade volumes all together.

Looking beyond the mere field of patents, a positive correlation between stronger IPR standards in general and complementary increases both in FDI and imports has also been reported. Based on a model for an IPR score that was specifically developed for the purpose of measuring the degree of the relationship between IPRs, FDI and imports, one study found, for example, that a 10 % increase in the IPR score would result both in a USD 1.5 billion growth of FDI and a USD 8.9 billion increase of imports, depending though on the level of industrialisation of the country concerned, in particular where high technology products are concerned.[100]

While concurring with this assumption, confirming namely the existence of important positive repercussions of higher IP protection standards on bilateral trade flows in non-fuel goods, other authors, perhaps surprisingly, did not come

---

[96] Maskus and Penubarti (1995), p. 227.

[97] Ivus (2010), p. 38; Blyde (2006), p. 6.

[98] See http://stat.wto.org/StatisticalProgram/WSDBStatProgramSeries.aspx?Language=E&subtopic=mt;ne2.

[99] Center for Strategic Studies and Debates (2013), pp. 44–49.

[100] Lesser (2001), p. 19.

to the same conclusion with respect to trade in high technology products.[101] In addition, they noted that the overall effects of stronger IP protection remained ambiguous for various reasons and vary across countries and sectors.[102] In particular, based on increased market power, companies may decide to sell fewer products or to serve the third country market through foreign direct investment or licensing of their IPRs, which, in turn, would negatively impact on trade flows.[103] Moreover, the economic impact of IPR protection would be difficult to measure in an isolated fashion, since trade in knowledge-intensive goods, for example, depended in reality on a number of other important structural factors.[104]

Looking at the evolution from the perspective of exports from countries that introduce higher standards of patent protection, evidence was also found for a positive correlation between changes to the patent regime and the growth of exports of patent-intensive goods from emerging developing countries. This was, in particular, the case when the latter have the capacity to absorb technology that is increasingly transferred into the country through trade or foreign direct investment as a result of stronger IPR protection.[105] Here again, the authors of the study considered the level of patent protection to be an important determinant for trade, noting that this link had been further strengthened since the implementation of the TRIPS Agreement.[106]

To complete the picture, it is also interesting to look at the link between IPRs and trade from a sector-specific perspective. On the occasion of the 15th anniversary of the Information Technology Agreement (ITA) in 2012, a WTO publication discussed the agreement's impact on trade, innovation and global production networks.[107] Among others, it examined the link between innovative activity, patenting and trade. In particular, it observed a significant shift towards patenting in ITA-related technologies in selected developed countries that coincided with growing trade in IT products since the entry into force of the ITA in 1997. Similarly, developing country ITA participants were reported as also witnessing an expansion of trade in such products in conjunction with higher innovative activities, in particular since the TRIPS Agreement was implemented by those countries. The report thus found a close link between the disproportionate increase of trade in IT products and the IPR regime in the countries concerned that serves to protect related innovations.[108]

---

[101] Fink and Braga (1999).

[102] Akkoyunlu (2013), pp. 1 and 7; Verdier (2013), p. 18 (20–21); Stockholm Network (2012), pp. 16–19. For an overview of studies that have examined the impact of stronger IPRs on technological progress see also World Trade Report (2013), p. 165.

[103] Moschini (2004), p. 19.

[104] Curtis (2012), p. 11.

[105] Maskus and Yang (2013), p. 34.

[106] Maskus and Yang (2013), p. 35.

[107] World Trade Organization (2012).

[108] World Trade Organization (2012), pp. 69–76.

While the preceding studies and statistics mainly focus on the effect of stronger IPRs, in particular patents, on trade, the findings of a study on "The Economic Impact of Counterfeiting and Piracy" presented by the Organisation for Economic Cooperation and Development (OECD) in 2008 approached the link between IPRs and trade from a different perspective, i.e. by looking at the potential impact of low standards of IPR protection and enforcement on trade.[109] To do so, the report examined the magnitude and effects of international trade in tangible counterfeit and pirated goods. The initial estimate was that such trade could amount to up to USD 200 billion in 2005. In an update circulated in November 2009,[110] this figure was raised to USD 250 billion in 2007, with the share of counterfeit and pirated goods in world trade increasing to 1.95 % in the same year. Among others, the report analysed the effects of counterfeiting and piracy on trade more generally, flagging the fact that the lack of data had prevented estimates on the effects of such illicit activities on trade volumes. At the same time, it saw indications according to which the structure of trade may be affected by counterfeiting and piracy, for example, by lowering the level of exports of health-sensitive products from countries that are known as important sources of counterfeit and pirated products, with a similarly negative correlation between counterfeiting and piracy and the volumes of imports on the importing country side.[111] To support these preliminary findings, reference was made to a number of empirical studies, including some of those briefly set out before, that analysed the relationship between existing IPR regimes and trade and found a positive impact of strong IPR protection on bilateral trade flows.[112] In line with these findings, the report concluded by establishing a direct link between trade in counterfeit and pirated goods and IPRs insofar as it encouraged governments and right holders to increase efforts to combat counterfeiting and piracy through measures that strengthen IP protection and by taking action to ensure appropriate enforcement of IPRs.

Empirical evidence thus seems to confirm the existence of a more or less firm and direct link between both weak and strong IPR protection and enforcement standards on the one hand and trade on the other hand.

[109] Available at http://www.oecd.org/fr/sti/ind/theeconomicimpactofcounterfeitingandpiracy.htm.

[110] Available at http://www.oecd.org/sti/ind/magnitudeofcounterfeitingandpiracyoftangibleproductsnovember2009update.htm.

[111] See OECD Document DSTI/IND(2007)9/PART1, paras. 5.9–5.14.

[112] See OECD Document DSTI/IND(2007)9/PART1, Table 5.3 and Annex 5.A3.

There Are Good Reasons to Acknowledge the Link Between IPRs and Trade

From the general point of view of policy coherence, the recognition of the trade-related nature of IPRs is an important factor for the search of the right balance between policies that provide the necessary incentives to stimulate inventions and creations through the award of private rights on the one hand, and policies that ensure access to such new products and creations by the public at large on the other hand. This link would only be very remote, if IPRs were considered in an isolated fashion, disregarding their direct relationship with trade. The historical developments set out above under the second section seem to back this view. For a long time, IP matters were almost exclusively dealt with by WIPO as a specialised agency. They thus had the status of a domain that needed to be covered by technical experts, mostly coming from national or regional IP offices, whereas the achievement of other public policy goals often only played a remote role, if any. This changed fundamentally with the entry into force of the TRIPS Agreement in 1995. As of that time, standards in the field of IPR protection and enforcement increasingly moved to the centre of a debate of an essentially multidimensional character that aims at ensuring coherence between different policy objectives. For example, in the pharmaceutical sector, patents would no longer be looked at purely from the perspective of protecting the interests of the inventor, but would also encompass questions related to the impact of their protection on trade, technology transfer and the broader public interest to achieve public health objectives, such as access to affordable medicines. In parallel, discussions would no longer be limited to a specialised agency dealing with IPRs, but would also involve other competent international organisations, such as the WTO and the World Health Organization (WHO). The intensified cooperation between the WHO, WIPO and the WTO in this particular area demonstrates the relevance of putting IPRs in the broader policy context, including by recognising their link with trade and health matters. Bringing each organisation's expertise together in a complementary fashion has resulted in a number of important contributions to worldwide capacity building. Among those achievements figures the launch of a trilateral study on "Promoting Access to Medical Technologies and Innovation" in February 2013 that addresses various policy dimensions, including IPRs, health and trade, in a holistic manner.[113]

From a European perspective, the incorporation of IPRs as an integral part of the EU's common commercial policy, first taken up by the Nice Treaty in a still somewhat ambiguous manner with regard to the exact scope of the EU's competence, and then clarified through the Lisbon Treaty, as well as the subsequent recognition of the direct link between IPRs and trade by the ECJ in its judgment of 18 July 2013[114] also have a number of significant repercussions. First and

[113] Available at http://www.wto.org/english/res_e/booksp_e/pamtiwhowipowtoweb13_e.pdf.

[114] ECJ, C-414/11, *Daiichi Sankyo and Sanofi-Aventis Deutschland*, 18 July 2013, not yet published.

foremost, acknowledging the trade-related nature of the TRIPS Agreement as a whole clearly impacts on the internal distribution of competencies and the procedures applicable in order to negotiate and conclude international agreements, as well as on the competence to interpret the provisions of the agreement. While the initial characterisation of the TRIPS Agreement as primarily aiming at harmonising IPRs and only being remotely linked to trade would make any related measure fall within the scope of Article 114 TFEU, the recognition of its direct link with trade arguably makes such measures the object of the EU's exclusive competence in commercial policy matters pursuant to Article 207 TFEU.

This, in turn, can also have a significant impact on the preservation of coherence and unity of the EU's external action. In the past, taking into account the absence of a clearly defined EU competence for IP matters, the ECJ made the response to the question as to whether national courts or the Court itself would be competent for the interpretation of the TRIPS Agreement dependent on the existence of EU law in the area of IPRs affected by the agreement. Hence, in areas where the EU had not yet legislated, the related TRIPS provisions were considered as falling outside the scope of EU law. Consequently, in those cases, the ECJ left it to the discretion of EU member States and their courts to determine the direct applicability of TRIPS provisions in national law and to interpret them.[115] The potential of this jurisprudence was to open the door towards divergent interpretations of the TRIPS Agreement by national courts which could have affected the adoption of a coherent and uniform approach in the EU's external relations. This risk has been definitely discarded by enlarging the scope of the EU's common commercial policy to encompass IPRs, based on the recognition of their direct link with trade, and the—from now on—exclusive competence of the ECJ to interpret TRIPS provisions.[116]

Moreover, it has been argued that the ECJ's exclusive jurisdiction over the TRIPS Agreement, as a consequence of the recognition of the direct link between IPRs and trade on which the exclusive EU competence in TRIPS matters is founded, could represent a milestone in furthering the harmonisation of patent law in the EU.[117] Given its competence to interpret the provisions of the TRIPS Agreement, the Court is, indeed, in a position to ensure a uniform reading of TRIPS rules in the field of patents, and thus compliance of any legislative act adopted by the EU with the standards on availability, scope and use of IPRs established by the TRIPS Agreement. In particular, the ECJ jurisdiction could help filling the gaps left by the EU legislation that created the basis for a unitary patent and the related international agreement among participating Member States that establishes a

---

[115] This was, in particular, confirmed in ECJ, C-431/05, *Merck Genéricos Produtos Farmacêuticos*, [2007] ECR I, 7001.

[116] ECJ, C-414/11, *Daiichi Sankyo and Sanofi-Aventis Deutschland*, 18 July 2013, not yet published.

[117] See Dimopoulos and Vantsiouri (2012), pp. 21–24.

Unified Patent Court.[118] Furthermore, in contrast to the future Unified Patent Court, which will be limited to consider matters related to the unitary patent, the ECJ could ultimately also assume the role of an overarching judicial authority as the application of TRIPS standards will also extend to the adjudication of patent infringement cases by national courts. Through its jurisdiction, it could thus support the development of common minimum standards applicable to the unitary patent, as well as to European patents without unitary effect granted by the European Patent Office and national patents. This, in turn, would constitute an important contribution to ensure legal certainty and to provide more comfort to the users of the patent system across the EU.

Finally, a brief look at the first ever proposed amendment to a multilateral agreement in the WTO is also enlightening here. In December 2005, WTO Members unanimously adopted the Protocol Amending the TRIPS Agreement (see above, fourth section).[119] In 2007, the EU submitted its instrument of acceptance to the WTO.[120] Among others, it stated that the acceptance of the TRIPS amendment would be binding on its member States pursuant to then Article 300(7) of the EC Treaty. Consequently, at least from the EU's perspective, no instrument of acceptance by an individual Member State has been received since then. This can only be taken as recognition of the direct connection between the proposed amendment and trade which must be assumed in order to come to the conclusion that the acceptance of the TRIPS amendment falls within the EU's exclusive competence. Taking into account the very object of the amendment, i.e. to facilitate the export of medicines to countries with insufficient manufacturing capacities in the pharmaceutical sector through the grant of special compulsory licences, the link with trade was also more than obvious in this case. However, had one nevertheless defended the position that IPRs are not or only in part trade-related, establishing an exclusive EU competence for the acceptance of the TRIPS amendment would not have been possible at all. Instead, also under EU law, acceptance by individual Member States would have been required, thus potentially further delaying the—admittedly already slow—process leading to the entry into force of the TRIPS amendment.[121]

[118] See Regulation (EU) No 1257/2012 of the European Parliament and of the Council of 17 December 2012 implementing enhanced cooperation in the area of the creation of unitary patent protection, [2012] OJ L361/1, Council Regulation (EU) No 1260/2012 of 17 December 2012 on implementing enhanced cooperation in the area of the creation of unitary patent protection with regard to the applicable translation arrangements, [2012] OJ L/361/89; and the Agreement on a Unified Patent Court (as signed by 25 Member States on 19 February 2013 and awaiting ratification by at least 13 Member States, including Germany, France and the UK, for its entry into force, see status available at http://www.consilium.europa.eu/policies/agreements/search-the-agreements-database?command=details&lang=en&aid=2013001&doclang=EN), [2013] OJ C 175/1. For a summary overview, see also the Trade Policy Review of the EU, report prepared by the WTO Secretariat, WTO Document WT/TPR/S/284 of 28 May 2013, paras. 3.259.–3.265.

[119] WTO Document WT/L/641 of 8 December 2005.

[120] Text available at http://www.wto.org/english/tratop_e/trips_e/amendment_e.htm.

[121] For the status of acceptances, see http://www.wto.org/english/tratop_e/trips_e/amendment_e.htm.

Conclusion: The Need for a Holistic Approach in One Place

The topic covered in this contribution is multifaceted and can be approached from different perspectives. For example, the discussion needs to go beyond considering whether, and possibly which, IPRs are trade-related in order to also enquire if and what are the IP-related aspects of trade. Thus, in addition to looking at the relationship between IPRs and trade in the more traditional way that essentially refers to trade in goods and services embedding IPRs, whether physical or through electronic commerce, another important link between these two dimensions takes the form of trade in IP as such. Beyond the classical way of buying, selling or licensing technology that is not embedded in intermediary or final products,[122] more recent initiatives need to be taken into account that aim at establishing platforms that allow for IPRs to be traded and thus strengthen the role of IPRs as a potentially important financial asset for companies. For example, in his Policy Address 2013, the Chief Executive of Hong Kong, China, announced the establishment of a working group on IP trading that is due to advise on the strategy to promote the development of the territory as an IP trading hub and to recommend measures to facilitate such trading.[123] The idea behind the creation of this trading platform is to support innovators and creators in capitalising the value of their respective IP portfolios by offering the necessary infrastructure that brings together sellers, buyers and intermediaries involved in IP trading in a single place. At the same time, the IP trading platform is designed to foster the development of Hong Kong, China, as a knowledge-based economy driving the exploitation and commercialisation of IPRs, and thus ultimately innovation and growth.[124] In parallel, a new financial exchange, named Intellectual Property Exchange International (IPXI), has become operational in 2013. Based in Chicago, it allows for the non-exclusive licensing and trading of IPRs as assets.[125] While the debate on whether IPRs are trade-related appears to focus primarily on the traditional link between trade in goods and services embedding IPRs, the buying, selling and transfer of IPRs on a bilateral basis or through IP trading platforms constitutes another element for which the fact that trade can take place entirely relies on the very existence of IPRs[126] and of which due account needs to be taken when discussing the relationship between these two dimensions.

---

[122] For trademark licensing and franchising, see World Intellectual Property Report (2013), pp. 62–73.

[123] Extract of the Policy Address available at http://www.policyaddress.gov.hk/2013/eng/p44.html.

[124] See Strategic Framework at http://gia.info.gov.hk/general/201311/22/P201311220572_0572_136351.pdf.

[125] For more details about the operation of the platform, see IPXI website at http://www.ipxi.com/inside-ipxi/the-exchange.html.

[126] Stockholm Network (2012), p. 15.

To the extent that a distinction between the "pure" dimension of IPRs, i.e. the side which has nothing to do with trade, and their trade dimension is still be made, it must, however, be duly recognised that the borderline between those categories of IPRs is very thin and evolving with the advent of new technologies, players and ways in which trade is taking place. Therefore, the term "trade-related aspects of IPRs" needs to be interpreted in a dynamic way that takes future developments into account. Innovations and creations nowadays play a central role in the global economy on which growth and increased productivity increasingly rely. IPRs and other intellectual assets, such as know-how, are representing an ever more important share of the intangible assets held by industries across many, if not most, manufacturing and services sectors in knowledge-based economies.[127] This, in turn, favours a steady increase of trade in knowledge products,[128] of technology transfer and of global value chains more generally and will inevitably result in all IPR aspects being related to trade in one way or another. Any attempt to decouple both dimensions therefore appears somewhat artificial. On the contrary, the need to work towards a balanced approach to IPRs within the framework of trade becomes ever more pressing with the growth of the global knowledge economy.

Recognising that both the legal framework for IPRs and the way in which IPRs are managed at institutional level are trade-related does, of course, not mean that there are not many other equally or even more important factors that directly impact on trade, rather the opposite: it is of utmost importance to bear the multidimensional character of IPRs in mind: they are trade-related, but equally also relate to other important policy dimensions, such as human rights,[129] health, environment, agriculture, research policies and related funding, the existence of a transparent and effective procurement regime, competition rules, standards, the education level and technology absorption capacity in countries, to name but a few.[130] A comprehensive assessment of the relationship between IPRs and trade will therefore only succeed where all these different dimensions and policies are taken up in a holistic and balanced manner. Among others, this includes a thorough examination of how the steps taken to respond to the "shoulds" of the TRIPS Agreement, i.e. the objectives listed in Article 7, could be further enhanced so that technological innovation and the transfer and dissemination of technology is promoted to the advantage of their producers and users and in a manner conducive to social and economic welfare while respecting a balance of rights and obligations. Rather than continuing a debate about the trade-related nature of IPRs that is unlikely to lead to any concrete outcomes, discussions should focus on how to achieve this vital

[127] For example, a 2011 study by Hassett and Shapiro, found that the value of intellectual capital, including IPRs and other intellectual assets, has increased in the US economy by almost 40 % in only 6 years. According to their estimates, it grew from between USD 5 and 5.5 trillion in 2005 to between 8.1 and 9.2 trillion in 2011.

[128] Akkoyunlu (2013), p. 1.

[129] See, for example, Drahos and Smith (1999), p. 13.

[130] Curtis (2012), p. 5.

balance between different policy dimensions that is the very basis for sound trade in the future. For this to happen, integrating IPRs in a multilateral framework like the one administered by the WTO seems to be the most appropriate way forward.

References

Adolf H (2001) Trade-related aspects of IPRs and developing countries. Develop Econ 39:1, p. 49

Akkoyunlu Ş (2013) The correlation between the level of patent protection and international trade. Swiss National Centre of Competence in Research, Working Paper, p 36

Arup C (2008) The world trade organization knowledge agreements, 2nd edn

Bhagwati J (1999) Economic freedom: prosperity and social progress. Keynote speech delivered to the conference on economic freedom and development, Tokyo, June 1999. Available at http://www.umich.edu/~websvcs/projects/mitsui-new/symp99docs/bhagwati-ef.pdf

Bhagwati J (2002) Afterword: the question of linkage. Am J Int Law 96(1):126

Bhagwati J (2005) From Seattle to Hong Kong. Foreign Affairs, December 2005 (WTO Special Edition)

Blyde JS (2006) Assessing the impact of intellectual property rights on trade flows in Latin America. INTAL-ITD Occasional Paper 34, January 2006

Bodenhausen GHC (1968) Guide to the application of the Paris convention for the protection of industrial property. United International Bureaux for the Protection of Intellectual Property

Breitwieser A, Foster N (2012) Intellectual property rights, innovation and technology transfer: a survey. Working Papers 88, The Vienna Institute for International Economic Studies

Center for Strategic Studies and Debates (2013) Brazil's patent reform: innovation towards national competitiveness. Available at http://bd.camara.gov.br/bd/bitstream/handle/bdcamara/14797/brazils_patent_reform.pdf?sequence=4

Curtis JM (2012) Intellectual property rights and international trade: an overview. Centre for International Governance Innovation Paper 3. Available at http://www.cigionline.org/publications/2012/5/intellectual-property-rights-and-international-trade-overview

David PA (1992) The evolution of intellectual property institutions and the panda's thumb, pp 9–10

Dimopoulos A, Vantsiouri P (2012) Of TRIPS and traps: the interpretative jurisdiction of the court of justice of the EU over patent law. TILEC Discussion Paper 25. Available at https://pure.uvt.nl/portal/files/1453882/2012_025.pdf

Drahos P (2002) The rights to food and health and intellectual property in the era of biogopolies. In: Bottomley S, Kinley D (eds) Commercial law and human rights, p 227

Drahos P, Smith H (1999) Universality of intellectual property rights: origins and development. In: WIPO, intellectual property and human rights, p 13. Available at http://www.wipo.int/export/sites/www/freepublications/en/intproperty/762/wipo_pub_762.pdf

European Patent Office/Office for Harmonization in the Internal Market (2013) Intellectual property rights-intensive industries: contribution to economic performance and employment in the European Union

Fink C, Braga CAP (1999) How stronger protection of intellectual property rights affects international trade flows. World Bank, Policy Research Working Papers. Available at http://elibrary.worldbank.org/doi/book/10.1596/1813-9450-2051

Gervais D (2008) The TRIPS agreement: drafting history and analysis, 3rd edn

Hassett KA, Shapiro RJ (2011) What ideas are worth: the value of intellectual capital and intangible assets in the American Economy. Available at http://www.sonecon.com/docs/studies/Value_of_Intellectual_Capital_in_American_Economy.pdf

Ivus O (2010) Do stronger patent rights raise high-tech exports to the developing world? J Int Econ 81(1):38

Jones VC (2013) Generalized system of preferences: background and renewal debate. Congressional Research Service Report for Congress, July 2013. Available at https://www.fas.org/sgp/crs/misc/RL33663.pdf
Kampf R (2007) TRIPS and FTAs: a world of preferential or detrimental relations? In: Heath C, Kamperman Sanders A (eds) Intellectual property & free trade agreements, p 87
Kampf R (2013) From data to wisdom, the contribution of intellectual property to the knowledge pyramid. In: Beldiman D (ed) Access to information and knowledge, p 235
Khan ZB (2002) Intellectual property and economic development: lessons from American and European history. Study Paper 1a, Commission on Intellectual Property Rights
Khor M (1997) The WTO and the South: implications and recent developments. Third World Network. Available at http://www.twnside.org.sg/title/pli-cn.htm
Krenzler HG, Herrmann C (2014) EU-Außenwirtschafts- und Zollrecht, May 2014
Kumar S (2010) Border enforcement of intellectual property rights against in-transit generic pharmaceuticals: an analysis of character and consistency. Eur Intellect Property Rev 32(10): 506. Available at http://ssrn.com/abstract=1383067
Lesser W (2001) The effects of TRIPS-mandated intellectual property rights on economic activities in developing countries, WIPO. Available at http://www.wipo.int/export/sites/www/about-ip/en/studies/pdf/ssa_lesser_trips.pdf
Maskus KE, Penubarti M (1995) How trade-related are intellectual property rights. J Int Econ 39(3–4):227
Maskus KE, Yang L (2013) The impacts of post-TRIPS patent reforms on the structure of exports. RIETI Discussion Paper Series 13-E-030
Moschini G (2004) Intellectual property rights and the world trade organization. In: Anania G, Bohman M, Carter C, McCalla A (eds) Agricultural policy reform and the WTO: where are we heading? Chapter 19
Panagariya A (1999) TRIPS and the WTO: an uneasy marriage. Available at: http://www.columbia.edu/~ap2231/Policy%20Papers/TRIPSWTO2.pdf
Reichmann JH (1989) Intellectual property in international trade: opportunities and risks of a GATT connection. Vanderbilt J Transnational Law 22:747. Available at http://scholarship.law.duke.edu/faculty_scholarship/453/
Sell SK (2010) The rise and rule of a trade-based strategy: historical institutionalism and the international regulation of intellectual property. Rev Int Polit Econ 17(4):762
Seuba X (2013) Intellectual property in preferential trade agreements: what treaties, what content? J World Intellect Property 16(5–6):240
Spence M (2001) Which intellectual property rights are trade-related? In: Francioni F (ed) Environment, human rights & international trade, p 263
Standeford D (2014) EU trademark reform delayed; debate includes goods-in-transit, harmonisation, intellectual property watch of 25 February 2014. Available at http://www.ip-watch.org/2014/02/25/debate-over-goods-in-transit-harmonisation-delay-eu-trademark-reform/?utm_source=post&utm_medium=email&utm_campaign=alerts
Stiglitz JE (2005) Intellectual property rights and wrongs. Available at: http://www.project-syndicate.org/commentary/intellectual-property-rights-and-wrongs
Stockholm Network (2012) Free to trade? Available at http://www.stockholm-network.org/downloads/publications/Free_to_Trade.pdf
Taubman A, Wager H, Watal J (eds) (2012) A handbook on the WTO TRIPS agreement
UNCTAD/ICTSD (2005) Resource book on TRIPS and development
Valdés R, McCann M (2014) Intellectual property provisions in regional trade agreements: revision and update. WTO staff working paper, June 2014. Available at http://www.wto.org/english/res_e/reser_e/ersd201414_e.pdf
Verdier T (2013) Smart trade. Finance Dev 50(4):18. Available at http://www.imf.org/external/pubs/ft/fandd/2013/12/verdier.htm

von Mühlendahl A, Stauder D (2009) Territorial intellectual property rights in a global economy – transit and other "free zones". MPI Studies on Intellectual Property, Competition and Tax Law 6, p 653

WHO/WIPO/WTO (2012) Promoting access to medical technologies and innovation, available at: http://www.wto.org/english/res_e/booksp_e/pamtiwhowipowtoweb13_e.pdf

World Intellectual Property Report (2013) Brands – reputation and image in the global marketplace. Available at http://www.wipo.int/export/sites/www/freepublications/en/intproperty/944/wipo_pub_944_2013.pdf

World Trade Organization (2012) 15 years of the information technology agreement. Available at http://www.wto.org/english/res_e/publications_e/ita15years_2012full_e.pdf

World Trade Report (2013) Factors shaping the future of world trade. Available at http://www.wto.org/english/res_e/booksp_e/world_trade_report13_e.pdf

Yelpaala K (2012) Quo Vadis WTO? The threat of TRIPS and the biodiversity convention to human health and food security. Boston Univ Int Law J 30(1):55. Available at http://www.bu.edu/ilj/files/2014/05/article_yelpaala.pdf

Is the WTO Agreement on Agriculture Still Up-to-Date?

Rolf Möhler

The Agreement on Agriculture

Already the Haberler Report of 1958 made the distinction between support measures that raise the internal market price above the level of world market prices that require border protection,[1] and export subsidies and measures that make consumers benefit from lower world market prices but compensate farmers for the loss of income.[2] The Agreement on Agriculture (AoA), that is one of the salient features of the Marrakesh Agreement that concluded the Uruguay Round Trade Negotiations, embraces the latter. By reducing border protection, limiting export subsidies and reducing trade-distorting support, while opening up ways of less distorting forms of support, it favours income over market price support. It broke new ground in three areas. On market access it established the principle that all import barriers had to be converted into tariffs which had to be reduced by 36 % on average (24 % for developing countries). Domestic support has been constrained. Each WTO Member had to take a commitment on the maximum level of its trade-distorting support and rules have been laid down for not or least trade-distorting support. Developing countries that had not provided trade-distorting support in the past and therefore could not bind a level of trade-distorting support (Aggregate Measurement of Support, AMS) were not allowed to exceed the *de minimis* threshold of 10 % of the value of their agricultural production. Export subsidies have been submitted to quantitative and budgetary limits. In accordance with GATT practice, the specific

[1] GATT (1958).

[2] Brink (2011), pp. 23 (24).

R. Möhler (✉)
Former Deputy Director-General for Agriculture, European Commission, Avenue Napoleon 39, 1180 Bruxelles, Belgium
e-mail: rolf.moehler@skynet.be

C. Herrmann et al. (eds.), *Trade Policy between Law, Diplomacy and Scholarship*, European Yearbook of International Economic Law,
DOI 10.1007/978-3-319-15690-3_10

commitments by Members were included in their respective schedules that contain now their tariff bindings, as in the past, along with their bindings on domestic support and export subsidies.[3]

Agricultural Trade and Policy Since the Agreement on Agriculture Was Concluded

The Agreement on Agriculture (AoA), as all the other Uruguay Round agreements, came into effect on 1 January 1995. In the following five years, world trade in agricultural products either stagnated or even receded. This was mainly due to the recession caused by the currency and financial crises in Asia in 1997 followed by the monetary crisis in Brazil and in Russia in 1998. But it was also a consequence of the new rules embodied in the AoA that put limits on exports subsidies of major exporters like the US and the EU, without giving a strong push to opening up markets. Only after 2000 did agricultural exports take off again, increasing by 9 % from 2000 to 2005 and by 9 % from 2005 to 2013.[4] This was again mainly due to economic factors, in particular to the spectacular growth of China that led to growing demand for agricultural products. But the new rules of agricultural trade, reining-in distortions, had their impact, too. China joined the WTO in 2001.

Unlike its impact on trade, the AoA had a major influence on agricultural policies. Although OECD data show that there has been little change in nominal support for producers (in Producer Support Estimates, PSE) over the last 25 years (EUR 205 billion in 1995–1997 and EUR 195 billion in 2011–2013; EUR 194 billion in 2013) the share of support in the total agricultural output (defined as farm gross receipts) declined from 30 % in 1995–1997 to between 18 % and 19 % in 2011–2013.[5] This may in part be due to rising producer prices. However, there is a major shift in the use of policy instruments away from the most trade-distorting support, i.e. market price support, to direct payments that are in many cases less distorting.[6] The OECD estimates that the most production and trade-distorting support in the OECD (defined as market price support, output based payments and payments on variable input use) fell from 22 % of gross farm receipts in 1995–1997 to 9 % in 2010–2012.[7] This trend is not limited to the OECD. If major non-OECD countries in Eastern Europe (Russia, Ukraine Kazakhstan), in Asia (China, Indonesia), in Africa (South Africa) and in Latin America (Brazil, Chile) are included the decline is still from 16 % in 1995–1997 to 11 % in 2010–2012.[8] On

[3] Articles 4, 6, 9.3 AoA.

[4] WTO (2014), p. 61.

[5] OECD (2014), p. 27; Table 2.2, p. 72.

[6] Swinnen et al. (2012), pp. 1089 (1091).

[7] OECD (2013), p. 43.

[8] OECD (2013), p. 43.

the other hand, trade-distorting support increased in emerging economies. High levels of such support remain in China, Indonesia, Russia and Turkey.[9]

A recent World Bank study that uses a comprehensive global economy-wide model and covers 82 countries and 75 agricultural products comes to similar results. On the basis of this study, Anderson points out that the Nominal Rates of Assistance (NRA) to farmers (expressed as a percentage by which government policies have raised gross returns to famers above what they would have been without government intervention) rose for high-income countries until the mid-1980s of the last century, but then declined until 2010 to a quarter of the peak rate. In developing countries, NRAs to farmers were negative until the mid-1990s when they turned slightly positive. This was mainly due to an increase in GDP per capita in developing countries that led to a shift in emphasis on farming.[10] Anderson estimates that policy reforms from the early 1980s to the mid-2000s improved global economic welfare by USD 233 billion per year and that developing countries benefited proportionately more than high-income countries. He finds that the average real price in international markets for agricultural and food products would have been 13 % lower without policy changes, and that for developing countries as a group, net farm income was 4.9 % higher than without the reforms.[11] The reforms of trade and agricultural policies cannot be attributed to the AoA alone, but it has been an essential part of the process. The impact of the AoA on agricultural policies is often played down.[12] It is therefore welcome that a recent econometric analysis came to the conclusion that the AoA has been instrumental in shifting support away from market price support towards direct income support.[13]

The Impact of the Agreement on Agriculture on Policy in the EU, the US and Japan

The Common Agricultural Policy of the EU, the US Farm Bills, and agricultural policy in Japan provide an illustration of the policy shift as it shows up in their notifications to the WTO. The measurement of support is somewhat different from the PSE of the OECD and the NRA of the World Bank. The main difference is the handling of border protection. Trade-distorting support that has to be reduced is defined by the AoA as Aggregate Measurement of Support (AMS). It covers market price support, output- and input-based payments, as well as direct payments. However, market price support is calculated as the difference between the farm gate price and a fixed reference price, not world market prices, as in the PSE and the

[9] OECD (2013), p. 46 Figure 2.3.

[10] Anderson (2013), pp. 260 et seq.

[11] Anderson (2009), pp. 51 et seq.

[12] E.g. by Blandford and Orden (2011), pp. 97 (100).

[13] Swinnen et al. (2012), pp. 1089 (1099).

NRA. In addition, PSE and NRA do not exclude *de minimis* support. Furthermore, a range of payments listed in Annex 2 AoA ("green box"), including direct payments that do not require production, are not part of the AMS. Direct payments that are part of a production-limiting programme and meet certain criteria are not subject to a reduction commitment ("blue box").

The reform of the **EU Common Agricultural Policy (CAP)** in 1992 preceded the conclusion of the Uruguay Round trade negotiations. Thus the notification on the year 1995–1996 shows the results in terms of classifications introduced by the AoA: AMS of more than EUR 50 billion, almost entirely made up of market price support, a blue box of more than EUR 20 billion housing the direct payments that compensated for the reduction of market price support, and a green box of EUR 18.8 billion.[14] By 2010–2011, the last year for which a notification is available, AMS had fallen to EUR 6.501 billion, the blue box to EUR 3.141 billion and the green box had shot up to EUR 68.051 billion.[15] This was the result of the CAP reform of 2003–2004. Direct payments were decoupled from production and transformed into Single Farm Payments to make them fit for paragraph 6 of the green box, which exempts decoupled income support to farmers from reduction commitments. In the 2014 budget of the EU, EUR 38.252 billion has been allocated to decoupled income support. The "Health Check" reform of 2008 extended the use of the Single Farm Payments to almost all sectors with only a few exceptions. The most recent CAP reform of 2013 has kept the basic structure of the Single Farm Payment, but has added enhanced environmental requirements for farms with at least 15 ha. 30 % of their entitlement is linked to specific agricultural practices beneficial to the climate and the environment. This will curb production. Besides decoupled income support, investment aid, environmental payments and regional assistance are important components of the green box. Environmental payments and regional assistance have doubled since 1995–1996, and reached EUR 7.237 billion and EUR 4.452 billion, respectively, in 2010–2011, whereas investment aid remained in most years above EUR 5 billion, rising to more than EUR 7 billion in 2010–2011, without showing a clear trend. Whether the newly enlarged possibilities to re-couple support to production will be used by Member States to a significant extent remains to be seen. Re-coupled support is likely to be notified as blue box support, as is already the case in the 2009–2010 and 2010–2011 notifications. Market price support will remain low, because of high world market prices. Therefore, AMS in 2015–2016 will be closer to the EUR 6.5 billion notified in 2010–2011 than to the estimate of EUR 10.9 billion made by Josling and Swinbank.[16] These figures are in any case well below the final bound AMS of EUR 72.244 billion for the EU-27.[17] But Josling and Swinbank are right with their

---

[14] Josling and Swinbank (2011), pp. 61 (66).

[15] EU's Notification to the WTO Committee on Agriculture, 13 February 2014, G/AG/N/EU/17, pp. 9, 12.

[16] Josling and Swinbank (2011), pp. 61 (92); Blandford and Josling (2011), pp. 69 (94) even come to EUR 18.9 billion.

[17] EU's Notification to the WTO Committee on Agriculture, 13 February 2014, G/AG/N/EU/17.

estimate of slightly below EUR 60 billion in the green box, while the blue box will not exceed EUR 2 billion, much below the estimate of EUR 4.7 billion.[18] The new Single Market Organisation does not provide for export subsidies any more, except in crisis situations.

In the **USA**, the impact of the AoA is less obvious but nevertheless significant, too. The 1996 Farm Bill replaced deficiency payments available to main crops by direct payments that were granted on the basis of 7-year production flexibility contracts. Payments were based on historical yields and acreage, not current production. Farmers were free to plant the crops they wanted with the exception of fruit and vegetables. As there was no obligation to produce, the US has notified these payments as decoupled income support of the green box (paragraph 6).[19] These payments were kept in the 2002 Farm Bill and in the 2008 Farm Bill. Unfortunately, they have not been extended by the 2014 Farm Bill. The payments started with USD 5.2 billion in 1996, increased to USD 6.5 billion in 2003 and, with the exception of 2004, were then slightly above USD 6 billon until 2009, but fell below 6 billion dollars in 2010 and 2011.[20] Support under the green box has more than doubled between 1995 and 2011, rising from USD 46 billion to USD 125,117 billion.[21] This is mainly due to the increase of domestic food aid that grew from USD 37.5 billion to USD 103,151 billion during this period.[22] Environmental payments including the Conservation Reserve Program (CRP) come third in the US green box. Being insignificant until 2001, they jumped to USD 2.5 billion in 2002 and increased to USD 4.914 billion in 2011.[23] New environmental programmes like the Environmental Quality Incentive Program and the Conservation Security Program have complemented the CRP that has been the primary environmental programme since 1985.[24] AMS in the US started with USD 6.213 billion in 1995–1996 jumping to USD 16.826 billion in 1999 and then decreasing to USD 4.653 billion in 2011, with peaks of USD 11.595 billion and USD 12.943 billion in 2004 and 2005, respectively. With market price support rather stable over the years, hovering at around USD 6 billion per year until 2008, the variations are

[18] Josling and Swinbank (2011), pp. 61 (92).

[19] In the *Cotton Case*, the Panel and Appellate Body ruled that the programme did not meet the criteria of paragraph 6 of the green box because of the ban on fruit and vegetables (Appellate Body Report, *US—Subsidies on Upland Cotton*, WT/DS267/AB/R, paras. 341-342). Although this is correct, the policy in substance meets the requirements of the green box to a large extent.

[20] Blandford and Orden (2011), pp. 97 (108); US' Notifications to the WTO Committee on Agriculture, 1 October 2012, G/AG/N/USA/89, p. 6; 29 August 2011, G/AG/N/USA/80, p. 6 and 9 January 2014 G/AG/N/USA/93, p. 6.

[21] US' Notification to the WTO Committee on Agriculture, 9 January 2014, G/AG/N/USA/93, p. 9.

[22] US' Notification to the WTO Committee on Agriculture, 9 January 2014, G/AG/N/USA/93, p. 5.

[23] Blandford and Orden (2011), pp. 97 (108); US' Notification to the WTO Committee on Agriculture, 9 January 2014, G/AG/N/USA/93, p. 7.

[24] Blandford and Orden (2011), pp. 97 (107).

due to non-exempt direct payments—mainly for corn, cotton and soybeans—when prices were low.[25] With the 2008 Farm Bill, market price support for dairy fell because of a new method to calculate support.[26] The 2008 Farm Bill also introduced the Average Crop Revenue Election Program (ACRE) that sought to stabilise farmers' revenues for a particular crop against short-term variations in price and volume of production. The programme had the potential to increase AMS,[27] but farmers did not take it up in sufficient numbers. Total support is much higher than the figures on AMS suggest, as they do not include non-products' specific *de minimis* support (i.e. support below 5 % of the value of production of US agriculture). This form of support started at USD 1.5 billion in 1995, rose to USD 7.4 billion in 1999, and then fell gradually to USD 2.2 billion in 2007, only to increase again from 2008 to 2011, when it stood at USD 9.232 billion.[28] Non-product-specific support consists mainly of crop and income insurance subsidies, which tend to increase with higher prices, as the value of production is higher. Thus in 2011, more than 95 % of non-product-specific *de minimis* support was crop and income insurance payments.[29] Blandford and Orden have made estimates on the development of support under the 2008 Farm Bill from 2009 to 2016. They estimate that green box support will climb to USD 117.5 billion, AMS will slightly increase to USD 5 billion and non-product-specific *de minimis* support will rise before falling gradually to USD 4.8 billion in 2016. Thus, the difference between notified current total AMS and the Bound Total AMS would be USD 14.1 billion in 2016.[30] With the 2014 Farm Bill, this may overstate green box support, as decoupled income support is abolished and food aid, as well as conservation programmes, are being curbed, while AMS is likely to be higher although traditional market support instruments (countercyclical payments, ACRE and dairy support programmes) have been scrapped. AMS could increase because the new support programmes provide the potential to increase support for wheat, corn and soybeans if prices decline.[31] Non-product-specific support could be significantly higher if the

[25] Blandford and Orden (2011), pp. 97 (99, 104, 118, 122 et seq.); US' Notifications to the WTO Committee on Agriculture, 12 October 2010, G/AG/N/USA/77, p. 12; 29 August 2011, G/AG/N/USA/80, p. 2.

[26] Blandford and Orden (2011), pp. 97 (130).

[27] Blandford and Orden (2011), pp. 97 (147).

[28] For 2008, see: US' Notification to the WTO Committee on Agriculture, 12 October 2010, G/AG/N/USA/77, pp. 10–11. For 2011, see: US' Notification to the WTO Committee on Agriculture, 9 January 2014, G/AG/N/USA/93, pp. 23–25.

[29] See US' Notification to the WTO Committee on Agriculture, 9 January 2014, G/AG/N/USA/93, pp. 23–25.

[30] Blandford and Orden (2011), pp. 97 (131–132).

[31] Smith (2014), pp. 5 et seq.

new crop and income insurance programmes (Supplementary Coverage Option, Stacked Income Protection Plan for Cotton) come under this category. The re-established livestock-oriented new disaster relief programme seems to be green box compatible.[32]

Japan, which imports more than 50 % of its food, has a highly protected agricultural sector, of which rice is the predominant product. Nevertheless, overall support levels sharply decreased since the AoA came into force. In the early years of implementation of the AoA (1995 to 1997), notifications of support showed a high level of AMS (between JPY 3,507 billion and JPY 3,170 billion). In 1998, the Japanese government abolished the administered price for rice which led to the disappearance of market price support for rice. AMS fell to JPY 766.3 billion in 1998.[33] The Japanese government still purchases rice on the market, but asserts that this is for food security reasons only and does not support market prices. Godo and Takahashi believe that at least in some years, purchases for food security purposes also served to support prices.[34] If this were the case, the purchases could not be counted under the green box, but come under the AMS. As the sums spent are negligible, this would not change the overall picture. Market price support for milk was abolished in 2001. After market price support for wheat and barley was also dropped, market price support remained for sugar, starch, beef and veal and silkworm cocoons.[35] Until 2007, it was mandatory for Japanese farmers to divert part of the rice fields to production of wheat, barley, potatoes, soybeans and sugar beets. Income support was provided to farmers who participated in the rice diversion programme and was notified as blue box support.[36] Through the reform of 2007, it became voluntary. The subsidies farmers received for the diversion was replaced by a new scheme that was in part decoupled income support, and therefore eligible to the green box, in part non-exempt direct payments.[37] These reforms reduced AMS further to JPY 564.8 billion in 2009, the last year for which a notification to the WTO is available.[38] Green box support is the predominant form of support to Japanese agriculture. Although it fell by around 40 % since 1995, in 2006 it was more than three times higher than AMS, but less than double in 2009.[39] The main component of the green box is support for rural infrastructure. The shrinking of expenditure for this purpose is the main explanation for the fall in green box support. Payments for producer retirement and environmental payments are two

[32] Smith (2014), p. 5.

[33] Godo and Takahashi (2011), pp. 153 (174–175).

[34] Godo and Takahashi (2011), pp. 153 (177).

[35] Godo and Takahashi (2011), pp. 153 (177).

[36] Godo and Takahashi (2011), pp. 153 (167).

[37] Godo and Takahashi (2011), pp. 153 (164–165).

[38] Japan's Notification to the WTO Committee on Agriculture, 18 August 2011, WTO G/AG/N/JPN/167, p. 23.

[39] Godo and Takahashi (2011), pp. 153 (168–169); Japan's Notification to the WTO Committee on Agriculture, 18 August 2011, WTO G/AG/N/JPN/167, pp. 24 et seq.

other significant components of the green box, although they pale in comparison to infrastructure payments. Decoupled income support for grains, potatoes, soybeans and sugar came only with the 2007 reform. After the 2009 elections, which were won by the Democratic Party of Japan, agricultural policy shifted to greater self-sufficiency in food. Rice production was encouraged by new Income Support Payments (ISP) for producers of rice, made up of a predetermined and a price contingent component.[40] The ISP for upland crops were a combination of payments on areas cultivated in the past, and output payments. This could have increased AMS to double the level reached in 2008, although Godo and Takahashi claim that the payments for rice fit the blue box, because farmers had to divert land to other production, but not for upland crops.[41] With the Liberal Democratic Party (LDP) again in power, agricultural policy seems to have shifted to making Japanese farms more competitive by increasing their size and to support multifunctional agriculture. ISP will be halved in 2014 and phased out in 2018. This should further reduce AMS, whereas support for rural development may be mainly green box support. Godo and Takahashi estimate that current AMS will be JPY 900 billion in 2015, which compares to bound AMS of almost JPY 4,000 billion.[42]

Notifications of domestic support by the EU, the US and Japan confirm the trend of shifting domestic support from its most trade-distorting form to less distorting ways of providing support. This is obvious for the EU, where since 2003–2004, the bulk of support shifted to decoupled income payments in terms of paragraph 6 of the green box. In Japan, the shift is no less dramatic, triggered by the elimination of market price support for rice, dairy, wheat and barley. In the US, too, green box support has shot up. Although the record on AMS is not satisfactory the US is broadly on track with decreasing AMS, unless the 2014 Agricultural Act reverses this trend.

The Impact of the Agreement on Agriculture on Major Emerging Economies

The data available on emerging economies that are major agricultural exporters or importers, i.e. Brazil, China and India, shows that the impact of the AoA follows a pattern somewhat different from those in major developed countries.

Before the 1990s, **Brazil**'s agricultural policy was based on guaranteed minimum prices for major crops, rural credit support and debt rescheduling.[43] Whereas market price and debt support still persist, Brazil has since developed an agrarian reform policy promoting land reform and resettlement that benefits mainly

[40] Godo and Takahashi (2011), pp. 153 (166); OECD (2013), p. 182.

[41] Godo and Takahashi (2011), pp. 153 (182).

[42] Godo and Takahashi (2011), pp. 153 (181, 184).

[43] Nassar (2011), pp. 223 (225, 229).

so-called family farmers. These policy measures are notified under "general services" in the green box.[44] USD 438.5 million was spent on this reform programme in 2010, the last year for which a notification is available. In 2010, other major components of general services were extension and advisory services (USD 799.8 million) and infrastructural services (USD 622.1 million). General services are the biggest component of the green box, followed by public stockholding for food security and domestic food aid. In the early years after 1995, overall green box support was high, only to fall off in subsequent years. Since 2005, it has increased again, and reached USD 4,906 million in 2010. Support for crop insurance and disaster relief account only for a small part of green box support. Expenditure on development programmes under Art. 6.2 AoA, which exempts investment subsidies generally available to farmers and agricultural input subsidies to low income or resource poor farmers in developing countries from the reduction commitment, have strongly increased since 2004–2005, when they stood at USD 626 million, to USD 1,651 million in 2009–2010.[45] The most important component is investment credit, on which USD 1,443.9 million were spent in 2009–2010, more than doubling from the year before.[46] Major AMS programmes are price support and equalisation premiums for maize, rice, wheat, cotton and soybeans, although in most years, support falls under the *de minimis* rule, but for one or two products. In 2008–2009, it was wheat, in 2009–2010, it was cotton.[47] Nassar wonders whether, in calculating market price support, the government should not have taken as "eligible production" the whole production instead of the volume purchased.[48] But if Nassar is right that there was a minimum price but no guarantee that the government would purchase at this price, there was no price support and the sums spent should have been notified as other non-exempt support. It is unlikely that it had changed the picture significantly. Non-product-specific support has been continuously *de minimis*. Its main component is expenditure for debt rescheduling. Overall, *de minimis* support is substantial, taking second place after green box support with USD 3,210 million in 2009–2010.[49] Nassar does not make any projections on the size of the green box in 2016, but estimates that product-specific and non-product-specific support will remain *de minimis*.[50]

[44] Nassar (2011), pp. 223 (225, 238–239); Brazil's Notification to the WTO Committee on Agriculture, 23 April 2013, G/AG/N/BRA/30.

[45] Brazil's Notification to the WTO Committee on Agriculture, 23 April 2013, G/AG/N/BRA/30, p. 8.

[46] Brazil's Notification to the WTO Committee on Agriculture, 23 April 2013, G/AG/N/BRA/30, p. 8.

[47] Nassar (2011), pp. 223 (229 et seq., 232 et seq.); Brazil's Notifications to the WTO Committee on Agriculture, 1 March 2012, G/AG/N/BRA/27, and 23 April 2013, G/AG/N/BRA/30.

[48] Nassar (2011), pp. 223 (263).

[49] Nassar (2011), pp. 223 (234); Brazil's Notification to the WTO Committee on Agriculture, 23 April 2013, G/AG/N/BRA/30, pp. 9, 14.

[50] Nassar (2011), pp. 223 (268).

In **China**, accession to the WTO precedes agricultural policy reform. Taxation of agricultural production was only abolished around 2006 and support for agriculture took off.[51] But the bulk of this support is provided as general services, i.e. support to infrastructure, training and extension services. It is therefore no surprise that almost all support is notified under the green box. From 2005 to 2008, the last year for which notifications are available, green box payments almost doubled to CNY 593 billion.[52] Although the bulk of China's support in the green box comes under general services, it includes also public stockholding for food security purposes, environmental and regional assistance programmes, as well as decoupled income support since 2004.[53] The latter increased from CNY 11.6 billion in 2004 to CNY 23.6 billion in 2008. However, it is not clear whether direct payments to grain producers are decoupled income support in conformity with paragraph 6 of the green box. Ni fails to mention that the payments are also made when no production takes place, as is essential for this provision to apply.[54] However, if these payments are counted as non-product-specific support, they remain below 8.5 % of agricultural production, the *de minimis* level that has been fixed in the accession negotiations with China. One may also doubt whether the temporary storage programmes for rice, maize, soybeans, rapeseed sugar and pork come under the public stockholding for food security purposes as laid down in paragraph 3 of the green box.[55] If not, although being substantial (CNY 57.9 billion in 2008), they would remain below the *de minimis* threshold of non-product-specific support of CNY 360.5 billion.[56] Product-specific AMS measures are subsidies for improved crop varieties and market price support for rice and wheat.[57] In 2008, as in the years before, product specific support was far below the *de minimis* thresholds for the products concerned.[58] Market price support was negative in 2008, as in the years before. However, China uses as eligible production in calculating market price support only the production purchased by its official agencies, not overall production as required by the AoA. As long as market price support is negative, this does not matter. But if the administered prices increased above the external reference price, AMS could shoot up if total production had to be multiplied by the price difference. Cheng suggests that in countries like China with a high self-consumption, a solution could be to use the marketable surplus instead

[51] Ni Hongxing (2013), p. 12; Cheng (2011), pp. 310 (321, 324).

[52] Ni Hongxing (2013), p. 23.

[53] Ni Hongxing (2013), p. 23; Cheng (2011), pp. 310 (321–322, 324); China's Notification to the WTO Committee on Agriculture, 13 October 2011, G/AG/N/CHN/21.

[54] Ni Hongxing (2013), pp. 12–13; Cheng (2011), pp. 310 (328 et seq.) expresses his doubts too.

[55] Ni Hongxing (2013), pp. 14–15.

[56] As estimated by Cheng (2011), pp. 310 (326).

[57] Ni Hongxing (2013), p. 13 also mentions the farm machinery purchase subsidy but it does not appear in China's notification. The programme could fall into the green box as investment support but in the notification it does not show up there.

[58] China's Notification to the WTO Committee on Agriculture, 13 October 2011, G/AG/N/CHN/21, pp. 8 et seq.

of overall production.[59] The comprehensive subsidies for agricultural inputs make up for the bulk of China's AMS. They increased from CNY 2.1 billion in 2005 to CNY 78.7 billion in 2008. They are notified as non-product specific *de minimis* support.[60] In the accession negotiations to the WTO, China has foregone the possibility to have recourse to development programmes in conformity with Article 6.2 AoA. China does not make use of the blue box. In his estimates of domestic support in China up to 2016, Cheng expects green box support to arrive at CNY 522 billion in that year, an amount already exceeded in 2008.[61] Non-product-specific support would come to CNY 91 billion, an amount close to the figure for 2008, but comfortably below the *de minimis* threshold of CNY 444.1 billion. But he fears China may breach the commitment to comply with the *de minimis* threshold for product-specific support if China raises the administered price above the external reference price, or extends price support to products other than wheat and rice, e.g. to cotton and soybeans. The choice of purchased instead of total production could be crucial in this context.

In **India**, agriculture is of major economic importance in terms of its contribution to GDP and to rural employment. Self-sufficiency in food is the main goal of agricultural policy, which is primarily pursued by high border protection. But domestic support is important, too. It is provided in two ways, through green box support, and development support in accordance with Article 6.2 AoA. Support under the green box is substantial and made up 40 % of total support in 2010–2011.[62] It more than tripled from USD 6.183 billion in 2004–2005 to USD 19.479 billion in 2010–2011, the last year for which notifications are available.[63] The most important component is stockholding for food security purposes, which takes about 70 % of the green box, followed by structural adjustment aid (through provision of interest subsidies and debt restructuring) and general services.[64] Payments for measures protecting the environment are minor in comparison. Support under Article 6.2 AoA is substantial. Payments almost tripled between 2004–2005 and

[59] Cheng (2011), pp. 310 (333).

[60] China's Notification to the WTO Committee on Agriculture, 13 October 2011, G/AG/N/CHN/21, pp. 22, 25.

[61] Cheng (2011), pp. 310 (340 et seq.); China's Notification to the WTO Committee on Agriculture, 13 October 2011, G/AG/N/CHN/21, p. 5.

[62] India's Notification to the WTO Committee on Agriculture, 1 October 2014, G/AG/N/IND/10 Corr. 1, p. 3, Gopinath (2011), pp. 277 (283 et seq.).

[63] India's Notification to the WTO Committee on Agriculture, 1 October 2014, G/AG/N/IND/10 Corr. 1, p. 3.

[64] India's Notification to the WTO Committee on Agriculture, 1 October 2014, G/AG/N/IND/10 Corr. 1, p. 3; Gopinath (2011), pp. 277 (283, 286).

2010–2011 from USD 10.689 billion to USD 31.610 billion, the lion's share going to input subsidies.[65] Like China, India provides these input subsidies mainly by way of subsidising provision of fertilisers, electricity and irrigation.[66] India provides market price support for some agricultural commodities, too, in particular for rice and wheat. However, in most years support was negative, as the external reference price was higher than the administered price. But this has changed recently as a result of price inflation. Already in 2007–2008, market price support for rice has turned positive while being *de minimis*.[67] Gopinath estimates that by 2015–2016 price support for wheat will also have turned positive.[68] Like Brazil and China, India has calculated market price support on the basis of purchased quantities. Gopinath estimates that on this basis market price support for rice and wheat in 2015 will be still *de minimis*, but not if total production is taken into account. Although since 1998–1999, no non-product-specific support has been notified, Gopinath believes that this form of support could amount to USD 1.654 billion in 2015/2016. But it would still be *de minimis*.[69]

In Brazil and India, green box and development support under Art. 6.2 of the AoA are the main forms of support. The green box comes first in Brazil and takes second place in India. In China, the green box is the dominant form of support, as development support is not available. In Brazil and China, *de minimis* non-product-specific support is significant, but non-existent in India. In China and India, product-specific AMS remains well below the *de minimis* level. As long as market price support remains negative, there is no risk of exceeding the limit of *de minimis* product-specific support. But if market price support becomes positive, either because of increased administrative prices or inflation, product-specific AMS for certain products could exceed *de minimis* levels and require policy adjustments. Although Brazil has an AMS commitment, it faces a similar risk for certain products.

The Agreement on Agriculture in the Doha Round

The shortcomings of the AoA were obvious already at the conclusion of the Uruguay Round trade negotiations. They can be summed up as: insufficient market access commitments in developed, as well as in developing countries; tariffication

[65] India's Notification to the WTO Committee on Agriculture, 10 September 2014, G/AG/N/IND/10, p. 5.

[66] Gopinath (2011), pp. 277 (285, 288); India's Notification to the WTO Committee on Agriculture, 10 September 2014, G/AG/N/IND/10, p. 5.

[67] India's Notification to the WTO Committee on Agriculture, 10 September 2014, G/AG/N/IND/10, pp. 16 et seq.

[68] Gopinath (2011), pp. 277 (305).

[69] Gopinath (2011), pp. 277 (290 et seq., 304 et seq.).

did not do much to lower effective protection; too much leeway for domestic support in developed countries; and the failure to ban export subsidies. Therefore, Article 20 AoA committed Members to continue negotiations on substantial and progressive reductions in support and protection. In November 2001, the Ministerial Conference in Doha called a new round of comprehensive trade negotiations (called Doha Development Agenda) that took over the agricultural negotiations begun a year before. The Doha Ministerial Declaration defined three main areas for the agricultural negotiations: substantial improvement in market access; reductions of, with a view to phasing out, all forms of export subsidies; and substantial reductions in trade-distorting support. Thus, the work programme was basically a continuation of the Uruguay Round negotiations on agriculture. The Doha Round, however, did not deliver what the AoA had promised.

One of the reasons for the breakdown of the negotiations in 2008 was the stalemate in the negotiations on agriculture. There were unbridgeable differences of approach in particular between the US and India on market access to be provided by developing countries. This stalemate overshadowed the substantial progress made in the agricultural negotiations, for in the three main areas of negotiation, there was widespread consensus on most of the issues, as the Revised Draft Modalities for Agriculture of 2008 reveal.[70]

On **market access**, a tiered formula should reduce border protection by tariffs. For developed countries, the reduction rate increases from 50 % for tariffs of 20 % and below, to 70 % for tariffs higher than 75 %. The minimum average cut is 54 %, which compares to 36 % in the Uruguay Round. Developing countries have to cut their tariffs by two-thirds of what is requested from developed countries, and the tiers start with 30 % tariff protection and go up to 130 %. Developing countries are not required to make tariff cuts that go beyond a 36 % average cut. For developed countries, the Special Safeguard Clause of Article 5 AoA has to be limited to 1 % of tariff lines and is to be phased out. Developing countries can keep the Clause, but limited to 2.5 % of tariff lines. Developed countries had asked for the possibility to designate so-called sensitive products for which the tariff reduction could be one-third, one-half or two-thirds less than required according to the formula. Near consensus was that sensitive products may cover up to 4 % of tariff lines. Developed countries that make use of this possibility have to provide increased market access of no less than 4 % of domestic consumption. Developing countries can designate one third more tariff lines as sensitive than developed countries, and they are not required to provide increased market access in exchange. But the negotiations stumbled on the exceptions. Developing countries had asked for two additional instruments: special products and a Special Safety Mechanism (SSM). No consensus was reached on these instruments, as they were susceptible to blunt the impact of the formula tariff reductions. However, the Ministerial Conference in

[70] WTO Committee on Agriculture, Walker Report, 21 April 2011, TN/AG/W/4/Rev.4, pp. 13 et seq.

Bali in December 2013 reached an Understanding on Tariff Rate Quota Administration Provisions for Agricultural Products.[71]

On **export competition**, the draft modalities ban export subsidies as from 2013, and provide for disciplines on export credits, export credit guarantees or insurance programmes, on international food aid and on agricultural exporting state trading enterprises. Export financing support shall be limited to credits with maximum repayment terms of 180 days for developed countries, as well as developing countries. Export credit guarantees, insurance and reinsurance programmes shall be self-financing, with a rolling programme of costs and losses over 4 years for developed, and 6 years for developing countries. Export subsidies by agricultural state trading enterprises, and government financing and underwriting of losses of those enterprises, shall be eliminated. These enterprises shall not have export monopoly powers any more. Some exceptions are provided for those enterprises in developing countries. The Ministerial Conference in Bali adopted a declaration that commits Members to keep the use of export subsidies and of measures with equivalent effect significantly below commitments.[72]

On **domestic support**, the Draft Modalities provide for three major steps to reduce support: the creation of a new, more encompassing category of domestic support; the Overall Trade-Distorting Domestic Support (OTDS), which includes the AMS but also *de minimis* and blue box support; the tiered reduction formulas for OTDS and AMS; and the cap on product-specific AMS levels.[73] An OTDS of more than USD 60 billion has to be reduced by 80 %, an OTDS between USD 10 and 60 billion by 70 %, and one of 10 billion or below by 55 %. In a similar way, the bound total AMS that is greater than USD 40 billion has to be reduced by 70 %, the one between USD 15 and 40 billion by 60 %, and the Total AMS equal to USD 15 billion or below by 45 %. In both cases, the EU is in the first, and the US in the second category. The product-specific AMS has to be bound on the average level of the years 1995 to 2000. A slightly different formula applies to the US. Allowances for *de minimis* support of developed countries are reduced by half from 5 % of the value of agricultural production to 2.5 % of the value of agricultural production. Blue box support would also encompass support that is not subject to a production limiting programme if it does not require production. Blue Box support is capped at 2.5 % of the value of agricultural production and has to be expressed in product-specific support that must not exceed the average value of support provided on a product-specific level in the 1995 to 2000 period. The green box will be amended as well. The most significant amendment is the ban on updating the base areas for decoupled income support and structural adjustment assistance.[74] An exceptional

---

[71] See Draft Ministerial Decision of 6 December 2013 on an Understanding on Tariff Rate Quota Administration Provisions, WT/MIN(13)/W/11.

[72] See Ministerial Declaration of 7 December 2013 on Export Competition, 11 December 2013, WT/MIN(13)/40, WT/L/915.

[73] Brink (2011), pp. 23 (40–41).

[74] Annex 2 paras. 6 and 11 AoA.

update is not precluded, however, if producer expectations and production decisions are unaffected and the uniform unitary rate per crop is not increased. Furthermore, the Ministerial Conference in Bali took a decision on the interpretation of the term "general services" of paragraph 2 of the green box.[75] In addition, the Conference decided to start negotiations on the implementation of paragraph 3 of Annex 3 of the Agreement on Agriculture (Public Stockholding for Food Security Purposes). India, supported by other developing countries, had expressed the concern that this provision could lead to AMS notifications by India exceeding its *de minimis* threshold because of inflation.[76]

Assuming that the 2008 Draft Modalities had been accepted, their implementation would be a significant update of the AoA and the ensuing commitments undertaken by Members in their schedules. In developed countries, market access would be substantially improved, export subsidies and other forms of export subsidisation would be eliminated, and bound support levels would be much closer to applied support, constraining the possibility to increase support. With relatively high producer prices prevailing, neither the EU, nor the US, nor Japan would have to change its agricultural policies in a major way.[77] However, it would be difficult if not impossible to increase market price support or non-exempt direct payments in a substantial way. According to Josling and Swinbank, in 2015–2016, the **EU** would be EUR 7 billion below its OTDS limit and EUR 11 billion below its Doha AMS limit.[78] For the **US**, Blandford and Orden come to the conclusion that on basis of the 2008 Farm Bill, OTDS and Total AMS bindings would not be exceeded but the leeway between current OTDS and AMS would be substantially reduced. Non-product-specific support would be still *de minimis*, but product-specific AMS limits for dairy and sugar could be breached.[79] The Agricultural Act of 2014 may have diminished this risk for dairy, as two support programmes have been abolished. However, the new support programmes could drive total AMS beyond its reduced limit of USD 7.64 billion. But it is unclear how the new Price Loss Coverage and Agricultural Risk Coverage payments will be notified, the leeway to use product and non-product-specific *de minimis* support being reduced.[80] In **Japan**, OTDS and AMS limits would not be a problem, but for the recently introduced Income Support

[75] See Draft Ministerial Decision of 6 December 2013 on General Services, WT/MIN(13)/W/9.

[76] See Draft Ministerial Decision of 6 December 2013 on Public Stockholding for Food Security Purposes, WT/MIN(13)/W/10. The Decision prevented Members from launching a dispute settlement procedure on this matter until a permanent solution was to be found by the 11th Ministerial Conference in 2017. End of July 2014, the new government of India withdrew its approval of the Bali Decision and blocked the implementation of the decisions taken in Bali. By Decision of 27 November 2014 of the WTO General Council, WT/GC/W688, an agreement has been reached which accelerates the procedure and clarifies that no dispute settlement procedure could be launched as long as no permanent solution has been achieved.

[77] Blandford and Josling (2011), pp. 69 (93–94).

[78] Josling and Swinbank (2011), pp. 69 (93).

[79] Blandford and Orden (2011), pp. 97 (142–143).

[80] Smith (2014), pp. 11 et seq.

Payments for rice. They could have exceeded OTDS and product-specific AMS and blue box limits,[81] but they will be phased out.

Under the 2008 Draft Modalities, **Brazil** would face tighter and additional constraints on domestic support. But Nassar assumes that neither the OTDS nor the AMS limit would be exceeded in the foreseeable future. Product-specific AMS would be *de minimis* (6.7 % of the value of production in the case of Brazil) except for wheat.[82] However, Brazil can fix the product-specific AMS level of wheat at 20 % of the value of production during the base period if it complies with its total AMS commitment.[83] In **China**, the OTDS limit is no constraint because of the large value of production that is, via *de minimis* support, an important element in calculating the OTDS. The large volume of potential of non-product-specific *de minimis* support provides considerable leeway for Chinese agricultural policy. A sensitive issue however, is product-specific AMS. If administered prices for wheat, corn and soybeans were substantially increased or extended to soybeans, support could exceed the product-specific *de minimis* limit. To use as eligible production the volume of purchased products instead of total production could be crucial.[84] As in China, in **India** the OTDS limit is not a constraint because of the huge volume of production. For the same reason, the non-product-specific *de minimis* support limit gives considerable leeway to agricultural policy. The problem is product-specific support for rice and wheat. Inflation has led to positive market price support. If total production is used as eligible production, Gopinath estimates that the product-specific AMS limit is widely exceeded. But India uses the purchased volume to calculate market price support.[85]

In times of lower prices, the 2008 Draft Modalities would provide developing countries with new possibilities to increase protection by way of using the Special Safeguard Clause, the Special Safeguard Mechanism, and Special Products that could be exempted from further tariff reduction. This could hamper the reform process triggered by the AoA.[86]

[81] Godo and Takahashi (2011), pp. 153 (184–185).

[82] Nassar (2011), pp. 223 (269 et seq.).

[83] As a Member with an AMS commitment, Brazil can make use of the flexibility in the WTO Committee on Agriculture's Walker Report, 21 April 2011, TN/AG/W/4/Rev.4, para. 27.

[84] Cheng (2011), pp. 310 (346).

[85] Gopinath (2011), pp. 277 (305–306).

[86] Anderson (2009), pp. 3 (54–55).

New Challenges

Food Security

Since the conclusion of the Uruguay Round in 1994, agricultural markets have fundamentally changed. In the run-up to the Uruguay Round and still after its conclusion, there was abundance of supply that led to very low prices. It was obvious that agricultural policies in developed countries, in particular in the EU and the US, had seriously aggravated the situation. Food security was not a major issue. The AoA was intended to reverse the situation by reducing support and by giving more leeway to market forces. By and large, the AoA has succeeded. Trade-distorting support went down. The high public stocks that overshadowed markets disappeared, and producer prices increased. But rising prices because of supply constraints put food security back on the table. Until now, food security concerns have been triggered by failing harvests because of natural disasters in a given year, not by a persistent lack of food independent of climatic disasters, although they may become more frequent. But the OECD-FAO Agricultural Outlook 2014–2023 expects declining growth rates for production of main agricultural products while demand remains firm.[87] This appears to confirm what Tangermann calls a shift from demand-constrained to supply-constrained markets for food and agricultural products.[88] The basic approach of the AoA to reduce and, where possible, to eliminate government support and let the markets work, is still valid also in times of supply constraints. Higher prices are the best incentive for famers to produce more and reduce the need for government support. De Schutter, the UN Special Rapporteur on the Right to Food, confirms that trade can play a key role in addressing food insecurity and he is right in urging countries to increase their food production, in particular of small-scale farmers.[89] The expected increase of food demand should of course push governments and international organisations to look for ways and means to improve productivity in agriculture, in particular in developing countries. Support to agricultural research is of special importance in this context. But this is not a matter for the AoA to promote. It should ensure that trade rules do not hamper those efforts. The green box exempts not only support of agricultural research from the reduction commitment, but under the heading "General services", also a wide range of measures like pest and disease control, extension and advisory services, marketing and promotion services, infrastructural services. It is welcome that the Ministerial Conference in Bali has clarified the scope of these general services by adding a number of services from the 2008 Draft Modalities to the non-exhaustive list in the green box.[90] There are more provisions in the green box, e.g. investment

[87] OECD (2014), pp. 30 et seq.

[88] Tangermann (2013), p. 11; available at http://www.ictsd.org/sites/default/files/research/AG_Policy_ok.pdf.

[89] De Schutter (2011), p. 14.

[90] See Draft Ministerial Decision of 6 December 2013 on General Services, WT/MIN(13)/W/9.

support, regional assistance, disaster relief and decoupled income support, which can help famers in developing as well as developed countries to cope with production failures. In addition, developing countries may have recourse to investment and input subsidies as foreseen by Art. 6.2 AoA. But we should not return to market management as a means to provide food security as suggested by de Schutter.[91] It may be convenient as a short-term relief, but it is no long-term solution. If trade liberalisation, as foreseen by the 2008 Draft Modalities, is liable to threaten poor farmers, a developing country may adapt its market access accordingly by exempting from tariff reductions sensitive or special products, or by applying special safeguard measures. But this may also inhibit structural reform that could increase food security in the longer term.[92] The AoA does not prevent Members from providing food assistance to people in need or from building up stocks of commodities that could be used for emergencies as long, as there is no market price support involved.[93] The 2008 Draft Modalities delete this requirement for developing countries. In the WTO, India has claimed that its public stockholding programme is in danger as inflation has led to AMS being notified in conformity with footnote 5. The Bali Ministerial Conference has agreed to negotiate a solution to this issue for traditional staple food crops in developing countries. During these negotiations, Members refrain from challenging developing countries on this provision.[94]

The AoA does not impede Members' providing **food aid** to countries in need on a regular or an emergency basis[95] but the safeguards against using food aid as a cover for subsidised food and agricultural exports are weak. In the Doha Round, broad agreement has been reached on new disciplines to prevent displacement of local production and commercial transactions by food aid. The 2008 Draft Modalities include a new article on food aid to be inserted into the AoA.[96] This article would commit Members to provide food aid untied and in fully grant form. In-kind food aid must not have adverse effects on local or regional production. Monetisation of in-kind food aid is banned, with exceptions for least developed and net food-importing countries. Special rules would apply in emergency situations, but monetisation of in-kind food aid would also be prohibited, with exceptions for least developed countries.[97]

[91] De Schutter (2011), p. 10.

[92] Häberli (2010), pp. 297 (311).

[93] AoA Annex 2 paragraph 3 with footnotes 5, and paras. 5 and 6).

[94] See Draft Ministerial Decision of 6 December 2013 on Public Stockholding for Food Security Purposes, WT/MIN(13)/W/10, para. 2.

[95] Article 10.4 AoA.

[96] WTO Committee on Agriculture, Revised Draft Modalities for Agriculture, 6 December 2008, TN/AG/W/4/Rev.4 Annex L.

[97] Häberli (2010), pp. 297 (316) claims that Annex L does not improve the situation. But his selective quotations of Annex L do not give sufficient credit to the text as a whole.

There is, however, one area where the AoA does not respond adequately to the challenges of food security: in emergency situations. In those situations, Members often have recourse to export bans, export restrictions or export taxes. WTO rules do not restrain the use of export taxes and permit export prohibitions or restrictions temporarily applied to prevent or relieve critical shortages of foodstuffs.[98] Article 12 AoA, that complements the GATT rule, is rather weak. It requires "due consideration" to be accorded to the effects on importing Members' food security, to notification and to consultation. But it only applies to quantitative restrictions[99] and provides for consultations only. The 2008 Draft Modalities would be an improvement, as they reinforce the actual obligations to notify and to consult, and provide a limit of 12, maximum 18 months for an export restricting measure. But this does not go far enough, as the time limit in no way eliminates or mitigates the disruptive effect of the measure on the overall market situation, as export restrictions in emergency cases are normally not applied for longer than 12-month periods, as the situation improves with the prospect of a new harvest. A first step should be to bring export taxes under Article 12 AoA, too.[100] Furthermore, as suggested by Tangermann, Members should be obliged, when applying export restrictions or export taxes, to allow exports up to a certain percentage of average exports of the last 3 years.[101]

Biofuels

Not so long ago hailed as a means to reduce consumption of fossil fuels, biofuels have recently run into an increasing opposition from environmentalists and food security activists. The former doubt the pretended reduction of CO^2 emissions compared to fossil fuel use, and the latter are concerned about the impact of rising food prices on the poor in developing countries. Whatever the merits of this debate are, the AoA is only involved in the margins. The specific support to biofuels comes in the form of tax credits or mandates to refiners to add a specific percentage of biofuels to fossil fuels used in the transport sector. This form of support comes

[98] Article XI:2 lit. a GATT 94.

[99] Howse and Josling (2013), p. 17 argue that Article XI:2 lit. a GATT 94 and Article 12 AoA do not exempt taxes with predominantly trade-restricting purposes but this is hardly compatible with the wording of these provisions.

[100] Häberli (2010), pp. 297 (318) agrees.

[101] Tangermann (2013), available at http://www.ictsd.org/sites/default/files/research/AG_Policy_ok.pdf; for other options to remedy the situation, see ICTDS Information Note, June 2014, on Agricultural Export Restrictions, Food Security and the WTO, pp. 7 et seq.

under the AoA as far as it provides a benefit to famers, as the producers of the basic product, i.e. sugar and maize in the case of ethanol, and rapeseed in the case of biodiesel.[102] It is difficult to deny that blending mandates and support to the producer of biofuel benefit the famers, too. However, tax credits do not come under the AoA. Benefits to farmers through higher producer prices, because of the blending mandates, are obvious but difficult to calculate, and have not been notified by Members. The fact that the AoA covers ethanol but not biodiesel is irrelevant in this context. It has been suggested to suspend tax credits and blending mandates in cases of food crises. Häberli goes even further and proposes a ban on biofuel subsidies in rich countries, at least for staple food crops.[103] Whatever the merits of such measures might be, they do not come under the AoA. Tax credits do come under the Agreement on Subsidies and Countervailing Measures (ASCM), but not the blending mandates, as they are not a "financial contribution". Tangermann suggests considering adapting the AoA in such a way as to cover all biofuel support.[104] While there may be a need for such rules, the AoA does not seem the right place to host them. The AoA is basically concerned with support aimed at farmers. Biofuel support serves primarily to reduce the use of fossil fuels. This is energy policy.

Climate Change

Climate change was not an issue when the AoA was negotiated, but it is a major issue today. There is broad consensus that climate change will bring warmer temperatures, change rainfall patterns and increase the frequency of extreme weather events. Rising sea levels will increase the risk of flooding of arable land. However, there is still uncertainty about the impact on a regional level. It is likely that the negative impact on agricultural production will be more strongly felt in tropical and subtropical areas than at higher latitudes. There are estimates that by 2050 yields of wheat in Africa will decrease by 17 % and maize by 5 %, in South Asia maize by 16 % and sorghum by 11 %.[105] But the contribution the AoA can make to the mitigation of and adaptation to climate change is limited. Among the

---

[102] Annex 3 para. 7 AoA; Blandford (2013), p. 6, available at http://e15initiative.org/wp-content/uploads/2013/08/Blandford_AG_E15_think-piece_26.08.13.pdf, denies the application of the AoA but ignores Annex 3 para. 7 AoA.

[103] Häberli (2010), pp. 297 (314).

[104] Tangermann (2013), p. 20, available at http://www.ictsd.org/sites/default/files/research/AG_Policy_ok.pdf.

[105] Wheeler and von Braun (2013), pp. 508 (510 et seq.).

broad measures under consideration, only subsidies would fit its remit. Tax measures are not covered by the AoA. Regulations come under the WTO Agreement on Technical Barriers to Trade (TBT Agreement). In its green box[106] the AoA exempts payments under environmental programmes from the reduction commitment of support. The text is drafted in such a way that most subsidies for measures reducing greenhouse gas (GHG) emissions would come under its provisions, were there not the requirement that the amount of payments shall be limited to the extra cost or loss of income involved. Blandford raises the question whether in case of sequestration activities, i.e. keeping atmospheric carbon in the ground, there is not a reason to make incentive payments, as those measures may reduce agricultural production.[107] But this is also true for other measures that reduce GHG emissions. Therefore, incentive payments should be admitted in all cases where a significant reduction of GHG emissions is achieved. This could be done by a footnote to Annex 2 paragraph 12 AoA. The green box also includes provisions that could help adaptation to climate change. It exempts expenditure on research, on training services, and on extension and advisory services from the commitment to reduce support.[108] The same is true for payments providing relief from natural disasters.[109] Structural adjustment assistance provided through investment aids and payments under regional assistance programmes could also help to adapt to climate change.[110] These provisions have not been written with the possible devastating effects of climate change in mind, but adaptation to climate change is one form of structural adjustment, and regions that are still prosperous may become disadvantaged as a result of climate change.[111]

Summary and Conclusions

Insufficient market access for agricultural products that was the result of the Uruguay Round still persists. Applied tariffs in developing countries are in many cases below bound rates but this means that market access at these rates is not reliable. Notifications by Members on domestic support mirror the findings made by Anderson, Swinnen *et al.* that domestic support has shifted in developed countries to less trade-distorting support, i.e. mainly green box support. A similar trend is apparent in emerging economies, but in these countries we also see an

[106] Annex 2 AoA para. 12.

[107] Blandford (2013), p. 5, available at http://e15initiative.org/wp-content/uploads/2013/08/Blandford_AG_E15_think-piece_26.08.13.pdf.

[108] Annex 2 AoA paras. 1a), c) and d).

[109] Annex 2 AoA para. 8.

[110] Annex 2 AoA paras. 11 and 13.

[111] Blandford (2013), p. 16, available at http://e15initiative.org/wp-content/uploads/2013/08/Blandford_AG_E15_think-piece_26.08.13.pdf.

increase in trade-distorting support via non-product-specific support that is still *de minimis*, and development programmes (Article 6.2 AoA). Product-specific support has the tendency to increase, too. Inflation can turn market price support from negative to positive. Once it has become positive, the use of eligible quantities of products becomes crucial for keeping support for a specific product below the *de minimis* cap. But even if the purchased production and not total production is chosen as eligible quantity, the *de minimis* cap appears to become an effective brake on product-specific support in most emerging economies, as they do not have an AMS commitment like Brazil. This effect will be felt under the AoA. The 2008 Draft Modalities leave it untouched. Export subsidies have disappeared in practice but rules on export credits and food aid are still insufficient.

As long as the 2008 Draft Modalities have not been accepted and implemented, the AoA is not up-to-date. If implemented, they would put a brake on any attempt to return to more trade-distorting support, but there would be little incentive to move to less trade-distorting policies. In the green box, environmental payments should be allowed to include incentives for measures reducing GHG emissions. Food security would be enhanced if efficient rules on export restrictions and taxes were enacted.

References

Anderson K (2009) Five decades of distortions to agricultural incentives. In: Anderson K (ed) Distortions to agricultural incentives: a global perspective 1955–2007

Anderson K (2013) Trade policies and global food security. In: Barrett CB (ed) Food security and sociopolitical stability

Blandford D (2013) International trade disciplines and policy measures to address climate change mitigation and adaptation in agriculture, p 6

Blandford D, Josling T (2011) The WTO agricultural modalities proposals and their impact on domestic support in the EU and the United States. In: Martin W, Mattoo A (eds) Unfinished business? The WTO's Doha Agenda

Blandford D, Orden D (2011) United States. In: Blandford D, Orden D, Josling T (eds) WTO disciplines on domestic support

Brink L (2011) The WTO disciplines on domestic support. In: Orden D, Blandford D, Josling T (eds) WTO disciplines on agricultural support

Cheng F (2011) China. In: Orden D, Blandford D, Josling T (eds) WTO disciplines on agricultural support

De Schutter O (2011) The WTO and the post-global food crisis agenda. Briefing Note 04 (November 2011), p 14

GATT (1958) Trends in international trade (The Haberler Report)

Godo Y, Takahashi D (2011) Japan. In: Orden D, Blandford D, Josling T (eds) WTO disciplines on agricultural support

Gopinath M (2011) India. In: Orden D, Blandford D, Josling T (eds) WTO disciplines on agricultural support

Häberli C (2010) Food security and WTO rules. In: Karapinar B, Häberli C (eds) Food crises and the WTO

Howse R, Josling T (2013) Agricultural export restrictions and international trade law: a way forward. International Food & Agricultural Trade Policy Council, p 17

Josling T, Swinbank A (2011) European Union. In: Orden D, Blandford D, Josling T (eds) WTO disciplines on agricultural support
Nassar A (2011) Brazil. In: Orden D, Blandford D, Josling T (eds) WTO disciplines on agricultural support
Ni Hongxing (2013) Agricultural domestic support and sustainable development in China. ICTSD Issue Paper 47, p 12
OECD Agricultural Policy Monitoring and Evaluation 2013
OECD Agricultural Policy Monitoring and Evaluation 2014
OECD (2014) FAO Agricultural Outlook 2014-1023
Smith VH (2014) The 2014 Agricultural Act: US farm policy in the context of the 1994 Marrakesh Agreement and the Doha Round. ICTSC, Issue Paper No. 52
Swinnen J, Olper A, Vandemoortele T (2012) Impact of the WTO on agricultural and food policies. The World Economy
Tangermann S (2013) Agriculture and food security group, a post-Bali food security agenda
Wheeler T, von Braun J (2013) Climate change impacts on global food security. Science 341
WTO International Trade Statistics 2014, p 61

Why Do the EU and Its Court of Justice Fail to Protect "Strict Observance of International Law" (Article 3(5) TEU) in the World Trading System and in Other Areas of Multilevel Governance of International Public Goods?

Ernst-Ulrich Petersmann

Introduction

I met Horst G. Krenzler the first time during my work as research fellow at the Max-Planck Institute for International and Comparative Public Law in the late 1970s at Heidelberg, where Krenzler campaigned for the Liberal Democratic Party in the first direct elections to the European Parliament. During our later meetings in EC institutions at Brussels where I represented Germany as legal advisor to the German Ministry of Economic Affairs, our discussions focused less on academic than on diplomatic conceptions of international trade law and policies. This contribution in honour of Krenzler begins with a short discussion of why economic and political theories of trade agreements fail to convincingly explain the reality of international trade law. It then discusses the five major legal narratives of conceptualising, designing and interpreting international trade agreements. The Lisbon Treaty differs from all other international trade agreements by its "constitutional approach" to the regulation of the EU's customs union and by its "cosmopolitan guiding principles" (in Article 21 TEU) for the EU's external policies. While the *Kadi* jurisprudence of the Court of Justice of the European Union (CJEU) and the *Solange* jurisprudence of the German Constitutional Court are successful examples of European leadership for promoting rule of law in the collective supply of international public goods (PGs) demanded by citizens, this contribution criticises the frequent disregard by political and judicial EU institutions for their legal WTO obligations to provide "security and predictability to the multilateral trading system", including individual access to justice and judicial remedies in domestic courts. The treatment of EU citizens as mere objects rather than legal subjects of

E.-U. Petersmann (✉)
European University Institute, Via dei Roccettini 9, 50014 San Domenico di Fiesole, Italy
e-mail: ulrich.petersmann@eui.eu

C. Herrmann et al. (eds.), *Trade Policy between Law, Diplomacy and Scholarship*,
European Yearbook of International Economic Law,
DOI 10.1007/978-3-319-15690-3_11

WTO trade rules illustrates a systemic failure to protect international rule of law for the benefit of EU citizens in mutually beneficial international trade, including "strict observance of international law" (Article 3(5) TEU) in conformity with the cosmopolitan legal principles prescribed by EU law (Articles 3 and 21 TEU) for the EU's external actions.

Failures of Economic Theories to Explain the Design of International Trade Agreements

According to Nobel laureate Paul Krugman, "[i]f economists ruled the world, there would be no need for a World Trade Organization. The economist's case for free trade is essentially a unilateral case: a country serves its own interests by pursuing free trade regardless of what other countries may do."[1] Economic theories justifying the different reality of reciprocal trade liberalisation in the context of trade agreements can only partially explain trade rules and institutions, for example, the legal ranking—in the General Agreement on Tariffs and Trade (GATT 1947)—of diverse trade policy instruments according to their economic efficiency so as to increase "Kaldor-Hicks efficiency", enabling governments to use the gains from trade liberalisation for compensating all domestic citizens adversely affected by import-competition and still be better off.[2] Yet, the explanations offered by economic "terms-of-trade" theories—i.e. that governments negotiate trade agreements in order to reciprocally liberalise "optimal tariffs" and protect market access commitments against "terms-of-trade" manipulation—are inconsistent with those offered by economic "commitment theories", according to which reciprocal trade liberalisation commitments are necessary on domestic policy grounds for overcoming political pressures from import-competing producers for "import protection" by enlisting political support from export industries benefitting from reciprocal trade liberalisation (e.g. in terms of additional export opportunities, importation of cheaper inputs). As explained by Ethier and Regan,[3] there is little evidence for the claims by "terms-of-trade" theories:

- that governments actually engage in systematic "terms-of-trade manipulation" exploiting "national market power";
- that they have the knowledge and political support for manipulating international prices through thousands of "optimum tariff items" aimed at improving terms-of-trade;
- that the terms-of-trade tariff revenue will always outweigh the domestic costs from import protection;

[1] Krugman (1997), p. 113.

[2] Cf. Regan (2006), p. 951; Ethier (2007), p. 605.

[3] Cf. Petersmann (1986), p. 405.

- that terms-of-trade considerations can explain all trade rules (e.g. prohibitions of trade embargoes, export subsidies, and of voluntary export restraints, the injury requirement for safeguard measures, third-party adjudication, etc.); and
- that "politically motivated trade protection" distorting domestic prices is "politically efficient" and therefore not liberalised by reciprocal trade agreements, notwithstanding the fact that trade agreements and trade negotiators tend to focus on reducing politically motivated import protection, export subsidies and voluntary export restraints and hardly ever refer to "terms-of-trade" manipulation.

My own publications have always emphasised that economic theories—for example, explaining the gains from liberal trade, from undistorted market competition, "separation of policy instruments", use of "optimal interventions" for correcting "market failures", and efficient policy instruments for addressing collective action problems in supplying "public goods"—are important for the rational design of many trade regulations.[4] Unfortunately, economists often continue to use economic models without regard to the legal context of trade policy-making. As "Pareto efficiency" (in the sense of making the government applying the trade policy measure better off and nobody else worse off) remains rare in international trade regulation, defining "efficiency" and "politically optimal tariffs" in terms of whatever policy objectives and preferences a government pursues avoids reviewing the "input legitimacy" of trade regulation, for instance in terms of democratic legitimacy, rule of law, general consumer welfare and respect for human rights. Even though such "principles of justice" are not mentioned in many functionally limited trade agreements (like WTO law), citizens and democratic parliaments increasingly insist on transparent and democratic trade policy-making for the benefit of citizens, as illustrated by the European Parliament's refusal, in 2012, to ratify the draft "Anti-Counterfeiting Trade Agreement" (ACTA) negotiated by the EU Commission without public debate[5] or, in 2014, by the French and German opposition to providing for secretive investor-state arbitration in the Transatlantic Trade and Investment Partnership (TTIP) Agreement. The political and legal goals of democratic constitutionalism to "institutionalise public reason" for the benefit of democratic people and their fundamental rights depend not only on economic, but also on political and legal justifications of trade rules, institutions and dispute settlement systems, for instance in terms of limiting abuses of political and private power and reconciling rational utility-maximisation with the common "reasonable self-interests" of citizens.[6] The unnecessary poverty of more than one billion of poor people living on USD 1 per day or less, and the widespread disregard for human rights and general consumer welfare inside many WTO Members, prompt

[4] On the need for reconciling the diverse economic and legal approaches in interpreting international economic law see my chapter IV on "Need for an Economic Analysis of International Economic Law", in: Petersmann (1991), pp. 73–94.

[5] Cf. Cremona (2014), p. 155.

[6] Cf. the Introduction to Petersmann (2012).

also economists to increasingly challenge reductionist conceptions of the utility-maximising *homo economicus* and of neglect (e.g. by advocates of "Kaldor-Hicks efficiency" focusing on potential—rather than actual—compensation of losers by winners) for equal rights and personal autonomy (e.g. in political preference aggregation sacrificing some people for the benefit of all others). "Human development approaches" emphasise that satisfaction of basic needs, "development as freedom" (e.g. to develop one's human capacities) and fulfilment of the human rights obligations of governments are morally and legally more legitimate policy goals than authoritarian governmental preference aggregation to the detriment of general consumer welfare (which would require free trade and non-discriminatory regulation of "market failures" inside and beyond states).[7]

Competing Legal Narratives of International Trade Regulation

While the "terms-of-trade explanation" of trade agreements focuses on economics, the "commitment theory" perceives politics as the main explanation for reciprocal trade liberalisation commitments. Both approaches reflect (1) power-oriented "Westphalian conceptions" focusing on reciprocal agreements among sovereign states promoting "Kaldor-Hicks efficiency". They tend to disregard that there are at least four additional, competing legal conceptions of international trade regulation proceeding from different political and legal value premises,[8] such as (2) national constitutional and democratic conceptions of multilevel economic regulation promoting accountability of international economic organisations through national parliamentary control and "global administrative law" (GAL) principles; (3) multilevel constitutional approaches to trade regulation in the EU and European Economic Area (EEA) complementing multilevel political trade governance by multilevel judicial protection of constitutional rights and human rights of citizens, for instance in the 31 EEA Member States and beyond (e.g. through the EU Association Agreement with Turkey); (4) multilevel economic regulatory approaches in regional trade agreements among constitutional democracies (e.g. NAFTA) as well as in worldwide Agreements regulating not only discriminatory trade policy instruments, but also non-discriminatory "optimal economic interventions", corrections of "market failures" as well as of "governance failures" (e.g. in the WTO Agreements on technical barriers, (phyto)sanitary regulations, trade-related intellectual property agreements, and on government procurement); and (5) cosmopolitan approaches to the regulation of transnational commercial law, investment law and regional economic integration by multilevel judicial protection of cosmopolitan rights (such as freedom of contract, property rights, freedom of

[7] Cf. Sen (2000); Nussbaum (2011).

[8] The following survey is a brief summary of Petersmann (2012), chapter I.

arbitration, access to justice) by both transnational arbitration and national courts supervising arbitration procedures at the seat of the arbitral tribunal and enforcing arbitral awards in domestic jurisdictions. The following survey of these five "legal narratives" of commercial and trade regulation focuses on their underlying "principles of justice" justifying trade law and governance on the basis of legal and political rather than merely economic principles. In my discussions with Krenzler and other trade politicians (e.g. during my work as GATT legal counsel from 1981 to 1990), my arguments for limiting power-oriented trade policies by multilevel legal and judicial protection of cosmopolitan rights of citizens—aimed at decentralising and depoliticising international trade regulation by empowering citizens to invoke and enforce in domestic courts precise and unconditional treaty guarantees ratified by parliaments for the benefit of citizens—were regularly criticised as being politically "unrealistic" and "too academic".[9] Arguably, this "political realism" of trade diplomats reflects their self-interests in avoiding legal, democratic and judicial accountability *vis-à-vis* citizens for their welfare-reducing, intergovernmental protectionism and violations of treaty obligations ratified by parliaments for the benefit of citizens. In view of the functional unity of commercial, trade, investment and intellectual property transactions in the context of global "supply chains" for "international production" and distribution of goods and services, economic actors and citizens rightly criticise why commercial, investment and intellectual property rights can be enforced by citizens in domestic courts, but trade disputes continue to be "politicised" and transformed into intergovernmental disputes and potential "trade wars" among states, as illustrated by the about 15 GATT and WTO panel, appellate and arbitral rulings against EC import restrictions for bananas from 1991 up to 2012 and the more than 50 simultaneous court proceedings inside the EU persistently ignoring, at the request of diplomats, GATT and WTO dispute settlement rulings against the EC to the detriment of EU citizens, investors and traders relying on the rule of law promises of EU law and requesting access to cheaper bananas from Latin American countries in conformity with the GATT/WTO obligations of the EU.

International Economic Law (IEL) as "Westphalian Order" Protected by Power (e.g. GATT 1947)?

National "political realism" focuses on states as main international actors in a "billiard ball model" of "international law among egoist states" driven by power politics so as to maximise national security and other "state interests". Realists claim that, as state-centred international law reflects the *status quo* distribution of power rather than "principles of justice", also "international adjudication is unable to impose effective restraints upon the struggle for power on the international

[9] Cf. Petersmann (1983), p. 397.

scene."[10] International courts can only be effective "in those spheres which do not affect the security and existence of the state".[11] "Political disputes" over the use of force and the distribution of power underlying the applicable rules of international law risk eluding judicial control and being "non-justiciable", as illustrated by the fact that the Permanent Court of International Justice (PCIJ) considered only once such an international dispute.[12] Similarly, also national courts tended to be ineffective in constraining democratic revolutions challenging power-oriented, authoritarian legal systems (e.g. in England in the seventeenth century, America and France in the eighteenth century). Colonial and intergovernmental power politics in the context of the General Agreement on Tariffs and Trade (GATT 1947, which was not ratified by the US Congress) prior to the establishment of its Legal Office in 1982/83 illustrated the IEL dimensions of "political realism". Many GATT rules and GATT dispute settlement rulings were not effectively implemented inside domestic legal systems (e.g. in the context of import restrictions on cotton and textiles from less-developed countries) if domestic interest groups and power-oriented majority politics objected to the adjustment costs resulting from trade liberalisation and trade regulation. As GATT 1947 was applied only on the basis of a "Protocol on Provisional Application" without ratification by national parliaments and subject to "grandfather clauses" protecting GATT-inconsistent national legislation, the first and second Directors-General of GATT 1947 (i.e. Wyndam White and Olivier Long)—albeit both lawyers by training—deliberately avoided establishing a GATT Office of Legal Affairs up to the 1980s. "Political realists" conceive of IEL as "international law among sovereign states" (e.g. GATT 1947) prioritising rights of governments over rights of citizens so as to enable power-oriented, "pragmatic intergovernmental management" of transnational economic relations. Even though GATT diplomacy aimed at remedying some injustices of colonial politics (e.g. by adding Part IV on "Trade and Development" to GATT 1947), trade diplomats often continue expressing the view of Thrasymachos in Plato's *Republic* that justice is merely whatever the powerful say it is. Realist conceptions of foreign power politics in a "society of states" fail to protect justice *vis-à-vis* individuals, including domestic citizens participating in the global division of labour without effective judicial remedies against violations of UN and WTO agreements ratified by national parliaments for the benefit of citizens, yet ignored by most domestic courts at the request of governments interested in limiting their legal, democratic and judicial accountability *vis-à-vis* citizens for (inter)governmental restrictions of equal liberties and human rights in the foreign policy area.[13] The military annexation of Crimea by Russia in March 2014 is a recent reminder

[10] Morgenthau (1951), p. 224.

[11] Carr (1940), p. 249.

[12] Cf. Morgenthau (1951), p. 224 (discussing the PCIJ advisory opinion on the dispute over the German-Austrian Customs Union, PCIJ Ser. A/B, No. 41).

[13] Cf. Petersmann (2012), chapters V and VI.

that transnational rule of law in EU political and economic relations with Russia remains subject to opportunist power politics by Russian rulers.

IEL as Global Administrative Law Based on National Democratic Decision-Making (e.g. the Bretton Woods and 1979 Tokyo Round Agreements)?

The foreign policies of liberal states tend to be guided in diverse ways by their domestic "principles of justice".[14] "Wilsonian liberalism" believed that, following World War I, the USA could protect international peace through promoting liberal democratic values and institutions for peaceful resolution of international disputes. But the rejection by the US Congress of US membership in the League of Nations and of US acceptance of the compulsory jurisdiction of the PCIJ illustrated that also democratic people might refuse projecting national democratic and judicial institutions onto international levels of governance in a world including non-liberal and "outlaw states". Neither under the League of Nations nor under the UN has it been possible to institute effective "world parliaments" and "world courts" with universal compulsory jurisdictions. "Democratic New Haven approaches" to US foreign policies following World War II succeeded in persuading other states to ratify the UN Charter and other agreements establishing UN specialized agencies (like the Bretton Woods institutions) on the basis of drafts prepared by the US Government, and to incorporate explicit references to "principles of justice" and "human rights and fundamental freedoms for all" into the UN Charter and other UN agreements, like UN human rights conventions and the 1969 Vienna Convention on the Law of Treaties.[15] Yet, the policy-oriented "democratic participant perspective" of the New Haven School was also invoked in order to justify US legal privileges (e.g. veto rights in UN and Bretton Woods institutions), unilateral military interventions, US refusals to participate in international PGs regimes (like compulsory jurisdiction of the ICJ, the International Criminal Court, and the Kyoto Protocol on climate change prevention), and discriminatory economic sanctions (e.g. by means of Section 301 of the US Trade Act); even though constitutional and economic liberalism requires protecting freedom of trade across frontiers and correcting market failures through non-discriminatory internal regulations in order to maximise consumer welfare, discretionary trade policy powers tend to be "captured" by protectionist interest groups also inside constitutional democracies without effective judicial protection of "equal freedoms" as "first principle of justice".[16] Rawls' proposals for a Law of Peoples justify the existing principles of UN law for the national pursuit of international justice in an international society of liberal states,

---

[14] Cf. Garcia (2013), at pp. 67 et seq.

[15] Cf. the Preamble of the VCLT.

[16] Cf. Petersmann (2012); and Garcia (2003).

non-liberal but "decent states", outlaw states, and states burdened by unfavourable conditions,[17] without proposing a theory of global justice based on cosmopolitan or communitarian principles limiting the "justice deficits" of international law. The limited "duties of international assistance" recognised in Rawls' Law of Peoples for a non-ideal "society of states" confirm that nationalist "democratic conceptions" of IEL aim at legitimising international economic regulation in terms of parliamentary ratification and control of IEL agreements (e.g. US congressional ratification of the Bretton Woods Agreements, congressional control of financial assistance by the Bretton Woods institutions, US "fast track authority" for negotiating and ratifying the 1979 Tokyo Round Trade Agreements) without effective protection of human rights, justice and international PGs across national borders. Also American GAL proposals for promoting transparent administration and legal accountability in international organisations are often based on principles of US administrative law (like the "Chevron doctrine"' on judicial restraint underlying Article 17.6 of the WTO Agreement on Anti-dumping) without evidence that such principles of US administrative law have become general principles of international law and fit the different legal context of international organisations eluding effective parliamentary control.

IEL as Multilevel Constitutional Protection of "Aggregate PGs" (e.g. European Economic Law)?

All UN member states have adopted national (big C) Constitutions (written or unwritten) that recognise the importance of international law and institutions for the collective supply of international "aggregate PGs" demanded by citizens, including functionally limited (small c) "treaty constitutions" (sic) establishing UN specialized agencies like the International Labour Organization (ILO), the World Health Organization (WHO), the Food and Agriculture Organization (FAO) and the UN Educational, Scientific and Cultural Organization (UNESCO), whose founding treaties were explicitly called "constitutions". Such functionally limited treaty constitutions constitute multilevel governance powers (the "enabling function" of constitutions); subject governments to legal and institutional restraints (the "limiting function" of constitutions); commit government policies to protecting PGs (like protection of human rights and "sustainable development") through agreed regulatory instruments (the "regulatory function" of constitutions); and legitimise law and governance by "principles of justice" (the "justificatory function" of consti tutions), such as labour rights justifying ILO law, human rights to education and democratic governance justifying UNESCO law, rights to health protection justifying WHO law, and freedom from hunger justifying FAO law. Yet, the inadequate legal, democratic and judicial accountability of governments dominating UN

[17] Cf. Rawls (1999), pp. 59 et seq.

decision-making processes entails that most UN institutions fail to protect international PGs effectively for the benefit of all citizens, like UN human rights law (HRL) and transnational rule of law for the benefit of citizens. Even though globalisation continues to transform most national PGs into international "aggregate PGs" and increases transnational interdependencies and global cooperation among citizens, communitarian and cosmopolitan conceptions of IEL have become effective only in regional free trade areas and common markets like the EU. The regional treaties establishing the EU, the EEA and the European Convention on Human Rights (ECHR) are interpreted and enforced by national and European courts as "constitutional instruments" protecting regional PGs—like the European internal market, human rights, fundamental freedoms and transnational rule of law for the benefit of citizens—for instance through "constitutional interpretations" (e.g. of "internal market freedoms", parliamentary prerogatives and judicial cooperation) guaranteeing cosmopolitan rights of citizens, democratic and judicial accountability of governments, and "evolutionary interpretations" adjusting indeterminate rules to "cosmopolitan public reason".[18]

IEL as Functionally Limited PGs Regimes Based on "Commutative Justice" (e.g. WTO Law)?

The WTO Agreement establishes multilevel, legal governance and dispute settlement systems outside the UN legal system aimed at promoting reciprocal liberalisation and regulation of a multilateral trading system based on mutually agreed "commutative justice principles",[19] like reciprocal market access commitments (e.g. GATT Articles II, XXVIII) subject to sovereign rights to protect non-economic PGs (e.g. Articles XIX-XXI GATT). Yet, similar to UN law, WTO law remains dominated by "intergovernmental decision-making" and fails to protect its treaty objectives (like "sustainable development") effectively due to inadequate regulation of "market failures", "governance failures" and of legal, democratic and judicial "accountability mechanisms". WTO dispute settlement bodies recognise that WTO law does not constitute a "self-contained regime"; treaty-based IEL systems remain embedded into general and treaty law, as illustrated by the WTO

[18] Cf. Petersmann (2013), p. 45.

[19] The Latin term "commutare" means "to exchange"; "commutative justice" refers to agreements on functionally limited "treaty principles of justice" like reciprocal market access commitments and the economic efficiency principles underlying the legal ranking of economically 'optimal trade policy instruments' in GATT/WTO law (e.g. non-discriminatory domestic regulation and subsidies rather than border discrimination; tariffs rather than non-tariff trade barriers; sanitary regulations on the basis of science-based "risk-assessments" rather than on the basis of discriminatory protectionism). Due to the absence of universally agreed criteria of just results of economic exchange, IEL provides for more dispute settlement procedures than most other areas of international law.

provisions for cooperation with other treaty regimes (e.g. IMF law) and regulatory agencies (e.g. national and non-governmental risk assessment institutions in the field of technical and sanitary regulation). Yet, even though WTO law provides for a multilevel legal and dispute settlement system protecting also individual "access to justice" in domestic courts (cf. GATT Article X and numerous other WTO provisions), many governments limit their domestic legal and judicial accountability for harmful violations of their WTO obligations by insisting that domestic courts should not apply WTO law and WTO dispute settlement rulings for the benefit of citizens. Similarly, many free trade agreements (e.g. by the USA) remain dominated by hegemonic power politics rather than liberal and constitutional "principles of justice".[20]

IEL as "Cosmopolitan Justice Regimes" (e.g. Commercial, Investment and Human Rights Law)?

Cosmopolitan conceptions of IEL[21] aim at multilevel legal and judicial protection of commercial, property and other rights of citizens and transnational rule of law protecting citizens through institutionalised networks of national and transnational courts and arbitral tribunals. Cosmopolitan legal regimes—like transnational commercial and investment law and arbitration, rights-based free trade agreements like the EEA, common market and competition law agreements of the EU, international criminal law and related adjudication—have proven to protect international PGs (like transnational rule of law, fundamental rights) more effectively than "Westphalian regimes" prioritising rights of governments over rights of citizens without effective legal, democratic and judicial accountability of governments *vis-à-vis* adversely affected citizens.[22] Similar to defining "cosmopolitan constitutionalism" by the trio of human rights, rule of law and democratic governance, transnational cosmopolitan regimes are characterised by multilevel judicial protection of individual rights, democratic governance and rule of law for the benefit of citizens, for instance through:

- cooperation between national courts and arbitral tribunals in the recognition, surveillance and enforcement of arbitral awards (e.g. pursuant to the 1958 New York Convention on Recognition and Enforcement of Foreign Arbitral Awards);

[20] Cf. Garcia (2013), e.g. pp. 260 et seq. (describing US abuses of power in NAFTA and CAFTA dispute settlement procedures as illustrating "how US trade policy is not always consistent with notions of justice", pp. 257, 324).

[21] The Greek term *κοσμοπολίτης—kosmopolites* refers to a "citizen of the world" recognising all human beings as morally equal and constituting a single world community that should avoid national prejudices.

[22] Cf. Petersmann (2012), pp. 145 et seq.

- cooperation among national and regional economic and human rights courts like the European Free Trade Area (EFTA) Court, the CJEU and the European Court of Human Rights (ECtHR);
- the arbitration and annulment procedures of the International Centre for the Settlement of Investment Disputes (ICSID) in cooperation with national courts; or
- the more than half a dozen international criminal courts complementing national criminal jurisdictions.

Multilevel cooperation among domestic and international courts in their joint enforcement of transnational legal orders can promote mutually beneficial, transnational cooperation among citizens, governmental and non-governmental actors for the collective supply of PGs (like common markets, human rights, transnational rule of law). But multilevel "judicial governance" must remain embedded into intergovernmental cooperation and transnational governance networks of regulatory agencies (like central banks, competition authorities, food safety, environmental and other regulatory agencies) subject to legal, democratic and judicial accountability mechanisms promoting legitimacy and domestic political support.[23] Justification of multilevel governance in terms of protecting cosmopolitan rights and transnational cooperation among sub-state actors (e.g. in the context of transnational "supply chains" for "international production" of goods and services like energy and food security, and cooperation among Hong Kong, Macau and Taiwan as sub-state WTO Members recreating a common market with China) can reinforce the "constitutional functions" of multilevel rules and institutions for protecting international PGs demanded by citizens.[24] It requires national, regional and worldwide tribunals to engage not only in more "judicial comity" in jointly clarifying—through "dynamic judicial interpretations" with due respect for democratic rule-clarification—the constitutional, legislative, executive and international legal limits of multilevel governance affecting fundamental rights of citizens, such as privacy rights neglected by mass surveillance of personal data by unaccountable security agencies and their private-sector partners, property rights of savers and investors affected by one-sided "economic justifications" of monetary and financial under-regulation or secretive "intergovernmental restrictions" (like unpublished "voluntary export restrictions") undermining rights of citizens and of parliaments. Multilevel judicial governance in IEL should promote mutually coherent interpretations of the "principles of justice" underlying UN, WTO, regional and national legal systems and exercise judicial deference *vis-à-vis* legitimately diverse regulations and "reasonable disagreements", for instance if—in Euro governance adjudication—economists from the European Central Bank invoke "economic demand side" justifications of using central bank powers broadly for shifting economic adjustment costs onto Eurozone countries with current account surpluses (like

[23] On this emergence of a "new disaggregated world order" and "judges constructing a global legal system" see: Slaughter (2004), pp. 65 et seq.

[24] Cf. Petersmann (2012), chapters I to IV.

Germany), and reject "economic supply side" arguments that the lack of deflationary "demand side deficits" justifies keeping economic adjustment pressures on over-indebted Eurozone economies persistently violating the EU budget, debt and economic convergence disciplines.

How to Reconcile the Diverse Economic and Legal Methodologies? The Example of EU Law and Politics

Most EU citizens remain "rationally ignorant" of the economic, legal and political complexities of intergovernmental decision-making and political compromises in EU, UN and WTO institutions. They rather evaluate the EU institutions and their multilevel economic governance in terms of the unique promises of EU law that the

> "Union is founded on the values of respect for human dignity, freedom, democracy, equality, the rule of law and respect for human rights" (Article 2 TEU), "in which decisions are taken as openly as possible and as closely as possible to the citizen" (Article 1 TEU); and
>
> "the Union's action on the international scene shall be guided by the same principles which have inspired its own creation, development and enlargement, and which it seeks to advance in the wider world: democracy, the rule of law, the universality and indivisibility of human rights and fundamental freedoms, respect for human dignity, the principles of equality and solidarity, and respect for the principles of the United Nations and international law" (Article 21 TEU).

The EU Charter of Fundamental Rights (ECFR) protects—in conformity with national and international HRL and also WTO law—comprehensive guarantees of "access to justice" for "everyone"[25] and governmental duties of justifying "[a]ny limitation on the exercise of the rights and freedoms recognised by this Charter" as being legally necessary for protecting the fundamental rights and general interests of EU citizens.[26] Hence, the EU institutions and EU Member States have to justify also their EU, UN and WTO decision-making in terms of "cosmopolitan principles of justice" that are easier to understand for citizens than intergovernmental decision-making in distant UN and WTO institutions. Also the diverse policy proposals by academics for EU, UN and WTO reforms (e.g. for EU representation in UN institutions, reforming Eurozone governance on the basis of "the principle of subsidiarity" rather than federalism, supervision of over-indebted Eurozone Member States by the "troika" of the IMF, the European Commission and the European Central Bank) should more clearly reveal and justify their value premises so that citizens can evaluate and democratically discuss the legal coherence, "financial

[25] Cf. Article 47 ECFR.

[26] Cf. Article 52(1) ECFR. On guarantees of "access to justice" in UN law, WTO law and EU law see: Francioni (2007); Cançado Trindade (2011); Petersmann (1997), pp. 194 et seq., 233 et seq.; European Union Agency for Fundamental Rights (2011). On the human right to justification: Forst (2012).

risks" and redistributive effects of, for example, EU monetary and financial regulations. My own publications proceed from the principles underlying EU citizenship and democratic governance that:

- in constitutional democracies like the EU Member States, citizens are the "democratic owners" and "principals" of all governance institutions (as "agents" with limited, delegated powers), whose legitimacy derives from respecting, protecting and fulfilling human and constitutional rights of citizens, other "principles of justice"[27] and democratic "public reason" recognised in EU law;
- as UN HRL, the WTO dispute settlement system and EU law protect individual rights of "access to justice" and to public justification of governmental restrictions of equal freedoms and require "strict observance of international law"[28] and mutually consistent interpretations, claims by EU governments to "freedom of manoeuvre"[29] to violate international UN and WTO agreements ratified by parliaments for the benefit of citizens require justification in terms of fundamental rights of EU citizens, as illustrated by the *Kadi* jurisprudence of the CJEU protecting human rights in the foreign policy area[30]; and
- conflicts of interests among EU citizens insisting on "access to justice" and EU institutions limiting their legal, democratic and judicial accountability *vis-à-vis* citizens (e.g. for welfare-reducing violations of WTO guarantees of non-discriminatory conditions of transnational competition and rule of law) require citizen-oriented public justifications which citizens—as democratic authors and addressees of legitimate law—can accept as "public reason" rather than mere intergovernmental power politics violating EU law (like disregard for more than a dozen of GATT/WTO dispute settlement rulings against the EU in the "banana dispute" from 1991 to 2012 without effective EU legal remedies of adversely affected EU citizens and EU Member States interested in complying with WTO law and avoiding legal responsibility for EU majority decisions violating international law).

[27] Cf. Article 2 TEU.

[28] Cf. Article 3 TEU.

[29] The term "freedom of manoeuvre" continues to be used by both the political EU institutions and the CJEU (e.g. in Joined cases C-120 and C-121/06 P, *FIAMM and Others v Council and Commission*, [2008] ECR I, 6513, para. 119) as the only justification for their disregard of legally binding WTO rules and WTO dispute settlement rulings.

[30] On failures by the CJEU to protect the EU law requirement of "strict observance of international law" (Article 3(5) TEU) *vis-à-vis* EU violations of UN and WTO obligations to the detriment of EU citizens, without even demanding the EU institutions to prove how violations of international treaties ratified by all parliaments inside the EU are necessary for promoting legitimate "Community interests" as defined by the Lisbon Treaty, see Petersmann (2011), p. 214.

Need for Respecting Legitimate "Methodological Pluralism"

In contrast to consequentialist economic approaches focusing on utility maximisation by the rational *homo economicus* and on his instrumental use of "rule by law" (e.g. based on "law and economics"), legal jurisprudence focuses on the reasonableness of human beings (*homo ordinans*) insisting on "principles of justice" and constitutional justifications of the legal input-legitimacy and democratic output-legitimacy of the use of legislation, administration, judicial remedies and private law by governments and citizens. Lawyers use the term legal methodology as referring to the respective conceptions of the sources and "rules of recognition" of law, the methods of interpretation, the "input legitimacy", functions and systemic nature of legal systems and of their relationships to other areas of law and politics. The necessary respect for legitimate "methodological pluralism" (e.g. in terms of competing jurisprudential conceptions of positive law, natural law and sociological conceptions of law, "monist" or "dualist" legal doctrines of the relationships between national and international legal systems) requires more comprehensive "balancing" of public and private interests in determining "public reason", "rule of law" and legitimate "Community interests" inside the EU as well as in interpreting the common "principles of justice" justifying UN, WTO and EU law.[31] Such respect argues for reconciling and integrating the five competing doctrinal approaches to IEL (as discussed above) in light of the EU law requirement to promote "cosmopolitan constitutionalism" also in the EU's external actions.[32] Hence, the EU's UN and WTO policies should use the EU's "soft power" and "normative power" more actively for exercising "cosmopolitan leadership" in multilevel governance of international PGs demanded by EU citizens by interpreting the "constitutional principles" common to UN, WTO and EU law for the benefit of citizens in order to justify EU law and governance as legitimate exercise of power. National courts and the EU Court of Justice rightly interpret EU law as a cosmopolitan legal system whose "primary rules of conduct" (e.g. the internal market law) and "secondary rules of recognition, change and adjudication" derive their legitimacy from protecting human and constitutional rights of citizens, transnational rule of law and democratic governance for the benefit of citizens.[33]

In EU external relations, public and private interests inside the EU often diverge as to how the EU law requirements of promoting "strict observance of international law"[34] and the EU's "cosmopolitan constitutional law" principles (e.g. in Article 21 TEU) should be reconciled with the fact that UN and WTO law also protect power-oriented conceptions of "sovereign equality of states" (e.g. based on factual

---

[31] On the need for respecting "methodological pluralism" in legal and democratic justifications of law, governance and "public reason" see: Petersmann (2012), p. 921.

[32] Article 21 TEU.

[33] On the characteristics of "legal systems" as a union of "primary rules of conduct" and "secondary rules of recognition, change and adjudication" see Hart (1994), chapter V.

[34] Article 3(5) TEU.

governmental control over a population in a recognised territory). Neither UN nor WTO law effectively limits "state sovereignty" by protecting the multilevel legal obligations of all UN Member States to respect "popular sovereignty" and "individual sovereignty" as recognised in UN HRL. EU law has not conferred any explicit powers on EU institutions to violate international law to the detriment of EU citizen interests in "rule of law" and a rules-based "social market economy" based on "strict observance of international law".[35] Hence, the political claims by EU institutions for "freedom of manoeuvre" to violate international treaties ratified by parliaments—without offering adversely affected citizens and EU Member States effective judicial remedies—are increasingly contested by citizens, national governments and the Court of Justice[36]; this is illustrated also by the persistent violations of the budget, debt and economic convergence disciplines of EU law[37] by most Member States of the European Monetary Union ushering in the financial, economic, social and democratic EU crises since 2008 at the expense of private savings and fundamental rights of EU citizens. Systemic disregard by EU institutions and member state governments for the rule of law requirements of EU constitutional law also risk undermining the democratic legitimacy of EU law, the fundamental rights of EU citizens, economic and social welfare and political support for EU integration.

Need for Reconciling Legal, Economic and Political Methodologies

Just as the different legal narratives of IEL reveal diverse jurisprudential and doctrinal conceptions of legal systems, also economists are confronted with methodological controversies resulting from competing value premises (e.g. regarding the relationship between governmental and private interests). "Constitutional economics" focuses on utilitarian "Pareto efficiency" in the sense of governmental duties to maximise individual preference satisfaction (methodological individualism). "Welfare utilitarianism" focuses on maximising the aggregate individual welfare levels proceeding from the assumption that promoting national welfare (e.g. in terms of gross domestic product (GDP)) will lead to higher levels of individual preference satisfaction. Yet, most economists evaluate and interpret UN and WTO agreements on the basis of "Kaldor-Hicks efficiency" focusing on government preferences justifying governmental policies if the expected social benefits exceed the expected social costs and make it possible for agents to whom benefits accrue to compensate those bearing net costs. European competition, customs union

[35] Article 3(5) TEU.

[36] On competing claims by national, EU and WTO dispute settlement bodies to define the legal limits and responsibilities of EU institutions for violations of international law, see above.

[37] Cf. Article 126 TFEU.

and internal market law and its rights-based interpretation by European courts—with due regard for "law and economics" (e.g. in competition and environmental law and policies) and also for the human rights obligations of governments to protect equal freedoms as the "first principle of justice" (Rawls) and general consumer welfare for the benefit of all citizens—illustrate the widespread recognition inside EU law and policies of the need for reconciling the diverse economic, constitutional and international legal approaches to economic regulation.[38]

"Realist" political scientists continue to view international relations as dominated by power politics requiring prioritisation of national interests (notably in national security).[39] As the EU institutions lack a common military "hard power" and are constitutionally committed to promoting "community interests" rather than state interests, political analyses of the EU's role in international politics tend to focus on the civilian "soft power" of the EU (e.g. in terms of promoting common EU and UN policy objectives through financial assistance, know-how, market access opportunities) and its "normative power" (e.g. in terms of justifying multilevel governance in terms of "cosmopolitan constitutionalism") to influence foreign policies through normative justifications and economic assistance (e.g. based on the "human rights clauses" in international agreements of the EU with more than 130 third countries) rather than through physical force.[40] Just as economic integration inside the EU has aimed at promoting also legal and political integration beyond utilitarian economic justifications, so the EU's Common Commercial Policy has also promoted political and legal policy objectives. For instance:

- The EU model of rights-based, multilevel constitutionalism has transformed the EU into the most successful "civilian power" for multilevel, democratic governance of international "aggregate public goods" (such as protection of common markets, "democratic peace" and peaceful settlement of disputes inside the EU and EEA). The EU remains the only regional organisation that has successfully realised the "4-stage sequence" of constitutional, legislative, administrative and judicial "institutionalisation of public reason" (Rawls) not only inside constitutional democracies but also on the level of regional law and institutions governing integration among 500 million EU citizens.
- The EU's multilevel human rights guarantees as codified in the EU Charter of Fundamental Rights, like the accession of the EU to the UN Convention on the Rights of Persons with Disabilities (2009) and to the ECHR,[41] continue to develop multilevel human rights guarantees in European governance far beyond those of any other international organisation.
- The EU accession and "neighbourhood policies", and the EU's accommodation of third countries (like the EFTA countries) requesting participation in the EU's

---

[38] Cf. Petersmann (1991). On the diverse "atomistic" and "socially embedded" conceptions of individuals in economics, see: Davis (2003).

[39] For a recent overview, see: Slaughter (2013), p. 613.

[40] Cf. Petersmann (2013/2014), p. 15.

[41] Cf. Article 6 TEU.

internal market without joining the supranational EU institutions, remain models for peaceful change based on respect for legitimate "constitutional pluralism" and "cosmopolitan constitutionalism" (e.g. limiting internal market regulation by fundamental rights and judicial remedies of EU citizens).

– Many regional economic institutions (like the Andean Common Market, Mercosur, the CARIFORUM-EU Economic Partnership Agreement) emulate the rules-based EU institutions (e.g. compulsory international adjudication) rather than power-oriented alternatives (like NAFTA institutions).

As the legal and democratic context of European integration remains unique, other regional or worldwide economic integration regimes are unlikely to adopt the "EU model" of multilevel economic, legal and democratic governance of transnational PGs. But the pro-EU demonstrations by democracy advocates in the Ukraine illustrate the "normative power of attraction" of EU association and accession policies empowering people to enjoy multilevel protection of fundamental rights and rule of law through transformative EU agreements. Yet, just as "in economics ... very little attention is given to the theory of the individual",[42] the diverse foreign policy approaches discussed above—such as "national political realism" focusing on states and state interests, "liberal international institutionalism" focusing on reciprocally agreed rules and institutions for intergovernmental supply of international PGs, and alternative cosmopolitan and constitutional approaches to multilevel governance of international PGs focusing on the reasonableness of individuals and on their democratic "public reason"—often proceed from diverse political conceptions of individuals, governments and of multilevel "governance" without clarifying their mutual interrelationships and "overlapping principles of justice" as recognised in UN, WTO, EU and national legal systems.[43] The disagreement as to what procedural, distributive, corrective and commutative "climate justice" and "common, but differentiated responsibilities" require in restricting greenhouse gas emissions, or the political opposition against liberalising free movements of persons in the EU (e.g. so as to restrict perceived "welfare tourism" by Romanians, Bulgarians or economic migrants from Africa), in free trade agreements with the USA (e.g. US opposition against immigration from Mexico) and under Mode 4 of the WTO's General Agreement on Trade in Services, illustrate the "constitutional value problems" underlying international economic regulation.

[42] Davis (2003), p. 1.

[43] On the diversity of theories of justice justifying IEL and their common "constitutional core principles", see Petersmann (2012), chapters I and VI.

Need for Interdisciplinary Clarification of the "Principles of Justice" Underlying IEL

The EU sets a worldwide example, as recognised by the conferral on the EU of the 2012 Nobel Peace Prize, for the practical possibility of realising the "Kantian moral imperative" of transforming intergovernmental power politics into "democratic peace" based on respect for "constitutional pluralism" as well as "cosmopolitan constitutionalism" underlying European economic law and HRL. The tensions between power-oriented and normative approaches to designing, evaluating and justifying EU external actions are reflected in many negotiations on EU participation in UN and WTO decision-making. For example, Anglo-Saxon arguments in favour of "pragmatic ad hoc solutions" for the diverse EU policy objectives in UN institutions (e.g. UN Security Council reforms, and "human rights approaches" to reforming international economic regulation as suggested by the UN High Commissioner for Human Rights) and for maximising EU values through "double memberships" of both the EU as well as of EU Member States (e.g. as two complementary sources of legitimacy and power in the FAO, WTO and in other international institutions with "double membership" of the EU and its Member States) are often challenged by warnings of "too much pragmatism" and "ad hoc policies" that can cause too many "bad precedents" exploited by vested interest groups. The contrast between, on the one side, the rights-based *Kadi* jurisprudence of the CJEU annulling EU regulations implementing UN Security Council sanctions against alleged terrorists on grounds of violations of fundamental rights[44] and, on the other side, the WTO jurisprudence of the CJEU denying rights of EU citizens as well as of EU Member States to judicial protection of EU compliance with WTO obligations and WTO dispute settlement rulings, including rights to compensation of injuries caused to EU traders by lawful trade sanctions in response to EU violations of WTO law,[45] appears likewise influenced by the diverse constitutional traditions of interpreting constitutionalism as "constitutional contracts" among institutions (e.g. the "Bill of Rights" enacted by the British Parliament in 1689 and accepted by the new King as a "constitutional limitation" so as to uphold the nation's "ancient rights and liberties") rather than as "social contracts among equal citizens" establishing governments with constitutionally limited powers deriving their legitimacy from protecting fundamental rights of citizens (e.g. following the American and French human rights revolutions of the eighteenth century). EU law

[44] Cf. ECJ, C-402/05 P and C-415/05 P, *Kadi and Al Barakaat Foundation v Council and Commission*, [2008] ECR I, 6351; Joined Cases C-584/10 P, C-593/10 P and C-595/10 P, *Commission and Others v Kadi*, Judgment of 18 July 2013, not yet reported, para. 131; see the discussion of this jurisprudence below.

[45] Cf. Thies (2013).

defines constitutional democracy in terms of constitutional rights of citizens rather than in terms of English traditions of "parliamentary freedom to regulate", and protects also "the freedom to conduct a business in accordance with Union law".[46] Hence, Anglo-Saxon arguments against judicial protection of EU "market freedoms" and other fundamental rights in the external trade relations of the EU's customs union[47] are difficult to reconcile with the comprehensive EU guarantees of fundamental rights and transnational rule of law. As EU law does not confer powers on the EU to violate international treaties ratified by parliaments for the benefit of citizens, persistent EU violations of GATT/WTO obligations and of related GATT/WTO dispute settlement rulings require a higher burden of justification as being necessary for protecting legitimate EU community interests than "political question theories" inside national constitutional democracies like the USA, especially if such EU violations of the "rule of law" undermine consumer welfare, non-discriminatory conditions of competition and equal rights of EU citizens and redistribute "protection rents" to powerful interest groups.[48] In view of the comprehensive EU guarantees (e.g. in Article 47 ECFR) of individual rights to effective judicial protection and remedies in the EU, the CJEU's reluctance to comply with legal binding judgments of other international courts (including WTO Appellate Body rulings against the EU), and the Court's unconvincing claims that the "nature and structure" of the WTO Agreement as well as of the UN Convention on the Law of the Sea (UNCLOS) exclude rights of EU citizens and of EU Member States to invoke and enforce clear and precise WTO or UNCLOS treaty obligations in domestic and European courts, raise similar questions of justice and justification of EU violations of international law without adequate legal and judicial remedies for adversely affected EU citizens.[49]

Modern brain research and constitutional philosophy emphasise the need for reviewing the spontaneous "fast thinking" of rational egoists guided by "basic instincts", traditions and value preferences by more reasonable "slow thinking" of responsible citizens.[50] Similarly, harmful "external effects" caused by utility-maximising pursuit of self-interests by rational economic and political actors must remain constitutionally restrained by "checks and balances" (e.g. legal, democratic and judicial accountability mechanisms) protecting the reasonable common

[46] Article 16 EU Charter of Fundamental Rights.

[47] cf. Article 28 TFEU and Article XXIV GATT.

[48] Cf. Petersmann (2014), p. 187.

[49] Cf. below and Pernice (2013), pp. 381, 589.

[50] On the distinction—as two dialectic thinking processes characteristic of human rationality—of "unconscious, intuitive fast thinking" from "conscious slow thinking" based on deductive reasoning double-checking the cognitive biases of human instincts and intuition, see Kahneman (2011). Modern theories of justice emphasise similarly the dynamic and dialectic nature of constitutional democracies depending on a "four-stage sequence" (cf. Rawls 1972, pp. 195 et seq.) of transforming agreed "principles of justice" into constitutional and legislative rules and their administrative and judicial enforcement subject to democratic accountability mechanisms and judicial remedies of citizens.

interests and constitutional rights of citizens adversely affected by "rational egoism", majority politics and non-inclusive "intergovernmentalism" driven by public and private utility maximisation. The more globalisation transforms national PGs into transnational "aggregate PGs" (like human rights, rule of law, democratic governance, and mutually beneficial monetary, trading, environmental and security systems) that national legal systems can protect only in close cooperation with international law and institutions, the more multilevel governance problems must be resolved in conformity with transnational rule of law protecting the common core of "human rights and fundamental freedoms for all"[51] recognised in UN, WTO, EU and national legal systems, with due respect for legitimate "constitutional pluralism", "subsidiarity principles" and "duties to protect" sovereign rights of peoples and individuals to regulate their diverse private and public, national, transnational and international "contexts of justice" in legitimately diverse ways (e.g. by protecting higher standards of human rights at local, national and regional levels of governance than in UN institutions).[52] Just as the American and French human rights advocates in the "democratic revolutions" of the eighteenth century had good reasons to interpret constitutionalism as "social contracts" among citizens on "principles of justice" (e.g. as pronounced in the 1776 US Declaration of Independence rejecting British feudal and colonial disregard for human rights, and the 1789 French Declaration on the Rights of Man and the Citizen also rejecting colonial slave trade and other feudal human rights violations), EU citizens have good reasons in the twenty-first century to prioritise their constitutional rights and the emerging, multilevel "human rights constitution" over the limited, delegated powers of all governance agents and the "regulatory capture" of intergovernmental decision-making in UN and WTO institutions without effective protection of PGs demanded by citizens.[53]

[51] Cf. Article 1 UN Charter.

[52] On the need for protecting private and public supply of PGs demanded by citizens through "cosmopolitan constitutionalism" recognising citizens as authors and addressees of constitutional rights (e.g. rights of access to justice and to public justification of governmental restrictions of equal liberties and social rights) that need to be progressively institutionalised (e.g. through constitutional, legislative, administrative and also international law-making, adjudication, "participatory" and "deliberative democracy") in response to the "public reason" of citizens as "agents of justice" see Petersmann (2011), p. 9.

[53] On the emerging "human rights constitution" see: Petersmann (2006), p. 29.

Why Does the EU Fail to Protect Transnational Rule of Law in Multilevel WTO Governance Through "Consistent Interpretations" and "Judicial Comity"?

The universal recognition by all UN member states of human rights, including rights to democratic governance based on participatory, representative and deliberative democracy, has entailed increasing recognition of the need for rule of law in national and international legal systems for multilevel governance of transnational aggregate PGs demanded by citizens; for, democratic self-government of citizens remains an illusion if democratically adopted Constitutions, legislation and international agreements approved by parliaments for the benefit of citizens are not respected, and complied with, by the legislative, executive and judicial branches of governments. Multilevel governance systems for the collective supply of functionally limited international PGs—e.g. through UN, WTO and EU law and policies promoting mutually beneficial monetary, trading, development, environmental, communication and legal systems for a global division of labour—cannot operate effectively and legitimately without respect for democratic self-determination, rule of law, access to justice and corresponding duties of states and autonomous customs territories (like the EU, Hong Kong, Macau and Taiwan as independent WTO Members) to protect human rights. All legal systems of "primary rules of conduct" and "secondary rules of recognition, change and adjudication"[54] require clarification and progressive development through legislation, administration, impartial dispute settlement and adjudication that citizens can recognise and support as democratically legitimate. Hence, the UN Charter and the WTO Agreement—similarly to the Lisbon Treaty—constitute, limit and regulate legislative, administrative and judicial powers and justify their legitimate use by duties to protect human rights (e.g. Articles 1, 55 and 56 UN Charter), "raising standards of living, ensuring full employment and a large and equally growing volume of real income and effective demand", and "the optimal use of the world's resources in accordance with the objective of sustainable development".[55]

Rule of Law as a Constitutional Principle of EU Law and Guiding Principle for the EU's External Actions

Due to the universal recognition of human rights, most constitutional democracies, European courts, other regional organisations and also the UN now acknowledge

[54] Cf. Hart (1994), chapter V.

[55] Preamble of the WTO Agreement. For a discussion of the different kinds of public goods—like 'best shot PGs' (like a medical invention), "weakest link PGs" (like nuclear non-proliferation), and "aggregate PGs" (like democratic peace)—and their diverse "production strategies" see: Barret (2007); Petersmann (2012).

the difference between power-based "rule by law" and constitutionally limited "rule of law", the latter deriving its legitimacy from protection of human rights, democratic governance and other principles of justice.[56] Since the 1986 judgment by the CJEU in *Les Verts v Parliament*[57] and the explicit confirmation by EU Member States of "their attachment to the principles of liberty, democracy and respect for human rights and fundamental freedoms for all and of the rule of law" in European Union treaties (e.g. in the Preamble of the 1992 Maastricht Treaty, Article 6 of the 1997 Amsterdam Treaty, Article 2 of the 2007 Lisbon TEU), the "rule of law" has become recognised as a constitutional principle limiting all EU powers.[58] Article 21 of the Lisbon TEU prescribes respect for human rights, democracy and rule of law also as guiding principles for the external policies of the EU. Yet, the normative impact of EU "rule of law policies" and actions at the international level and their effectiveness have remained limited, for instance in the EU enlargement and neighbourhood policies, the EU's foreign and security policies, and the EU's commercial, financial and development policies *vis-à-vis* third countries.[59] The EU, like the Council of Europe[60] and more recently also UN institutions, constantly links the rule of law to the principles of human rights and democratic government as interconnected and interdependent principles of law.[61] Yet, even though the *Kadi* jurisprudence of the CJEU has transposed the *Solange* jurisprudence (e.g. by the German Constitutional Court and the European Court of Human Rights) to the EU implementation of UN Security Council sanctions in order to protect human rights and rule of law as "essential elements" of EU law and of the human rights conditionality of many EU agreements (e.g. the Cotonou Agreement), the political EU institutions and also European courts persistently disregard rule of law as a WTO legal and dispute settlement principle.

The European Kadi and Solange Jurisprudence as Models for Multilevel Judicial Protection of Transnational Rule of Law

Article 47 ECFR protects the right to an effective remedy and to a fair trial as a cosmopolitan right of "everyone", including alleged foreign terrorists. The four *Kadi* judgments of the General Court and CJEU since 2005 relate to EU regulations implementing UN Security Council sanctions adopted under Article 41 UN Charter

---

[56] Cf. Petersmann (2012), chapter V. On "thin" and "thick" theories of rule of law see: Zürn et al. (2012).

[57] ECJ, C-294/83, *Les Verts v Parliament*, [1986] ECR, 1365.

[58] Cf. Pech (2010), p. 359.

[59] Cf. the detailed study by Pech (2012/2013).

[60] Cf. Article 3 of the Statute of the Council of Europe.

[61] Cf. Pech (2012/2013), pp. 30 et seq.

vis-à-vis Mr Kadi and other alleged terrorists in response to the terrorist attacks of 11 September 2001. The Security Council had identified Mr Kadi (a wealthy citizen of Saudi-Arabia) as a possible supporter of Al-Qaida and had ordered the freezing of his assets. In the first judgment of 2005 on Mr Kadi's legal challenge of the EU regulation implementing the Security Council sanctions, the General Court refused to fully review the EU regulation in view of the judicial immunity of the Security Council sanctions; the Court only reviewed whether the Security Council had violated fundamental rights of Mr Kadi protected by *jus cogens* and did not find such infringements. On appeal, the CJEU fully reviewed the lawfulness of the EU implementing regulation on the ground that all EU legal acts must remain consistent with the fundamental rights protected by EU law, even in case of implementation of UN Security Council sanctions; the Court also found—without pronouncing on the legality of the UN Security Council measures—that the EU implementing regulation had violated the claimant's fundamental right to be informed of the grounds for his subjection to sanctions, his right to be heard, his access to effective judicial review, and the right to protection of property.[62]

As the EU Commission and Council decided to maintain the sanctions, Mr Kadi appealed to the General Court once again. In its judgment of 2010, the General Court annulled the contested EU sanctions *vis-à-vis* Mr Kadi on the ground of infringements by the EU institutions of the rights of the defence, the right to respect for property and the principle of proportionality, and also of the right of Mr Kadi to effective judicial review. In its judgment of 18 July 2013, the CJEU rejected the appeal and concluded that effective "judicial review is indispensable to ensure a fair balance between the maintenance of international peace and security and the protection of the fundamental rights and freedoms of the person concerned, those being shared values of the UN and the European Union".[63] The judgment mentions a number of improvements in the UN Security Council procedures for delisting and *ex officio* re-examination of sanctions at UN level (such as the creation, in 2009, of the office of an independent Ombudsperson processing requests to be delisted from the UN sanctions list). Yet, the CJEU concurred with a previous finding of the ECtHR that these procedural improvements do not guarantee the listed persons effective judicial protection.[64] The *Kadi* judgment may be construed in conformity with the *Solange* jurisprudence of the German Constitutional Court as well as of the ECtHR to the effect that "as long as" (which means "solange" in German) the higher level of law (i.e. UN law in the *Kadi* cases, EU law in the *Solange* jurisprudence of the German Constitutional Court) does not guarantee equivalent protection of fundamental rights, the courts at lower levels of multilevel legal and

[62] Cf. ECJ, C-402/05 P and C-415/05 P, *Kadi and Al Barakaat Foundation v Council and Commission*, [2008] ECR I, 6351; Joined Cases C-584/10 P, C-593/10 P and C-595/10 P, *Commission and Others v Kadi*, Judgment of 18 July 2013, not yet reported, para. 131.

[63] ECJ, Joined Cases C-584/10P, C-593/10P and C-595/10P, *Commission and Others v Kadi*, Judgment of 18 July 2013, not yet reported, para. 131.

[64] ECJ, Joined Cases C-584/10P, C-593/10P and C-595/10P, *Commission and Others v Kadi*, Judgment of 18 July 2013, not yet reported, para. 133.

judicial systems must guarantee such fundamental rights. Just as the German Constitutional Court and the ECtHR refrained from exercising their jurisdiction "as long as" the CJEU protects fundamental rights in ways equivalent to the constitutional protection under German constitutional law and the ECHR respectively, the CJEU might limit its judicial review of EU measures implementing UN Security Council sanctions once UN law offers equivalent procedural and substantive legal protection of individual rights of the defence, property rights and effective judicial protection.[65] Both the *Kadi* and the *Solange* jurisprudence suggest that, as UN and regional human rights conventions leave states "margins of appreciation" for implementing and protecting higher standards of human rights in their national legal systems, multilevel legal regulation and judicial protection of civil, political, economic, social and cultural rights must be based on mutually consistent interpretations and "judicial comity" (e.g. regarding the local remedies rule in HRL), "subsidiarity" and "loyal cooperation" among the different levels of governance, with due respect for the sovereign rights of states to guarantee higher levels of constitutional protection at national levels than at international levels of governance.[66] Yet, international trade and investment law differ from HRL by the fact that WTO law and bilateral investment treaties (BIT) often protect *higher standards* of economic freedoms, property rights, non-discrimination and transnational rule of law than those in *national* trade and investment legislation permitting discriminatory border discrimination against foreign goods, services and investments.

The EU Should Exercise Leadership for Interpreting Also the Multilevel WTO Legal and Dispute Settlement System for the Benefit of Citizens

The more globalisation transforms national PGs demanded by citizens (like open markets promoting consumer welfare) into international "aggregate PGs" that national constitutions can protect only together with international law and multilevel governance institutions, the more important multilevel guarantees of cosmopolitan rights and of "access to justice" and judicial remedies protecting transnational rule of law for the benefit of citizens become. For instance:

- Some national constitutions have responded to systemic foreign policy failures by providing for broad legal and judicial remedies whenever "rights are violated by public authority".[67]

[65] Cf. Kokott and Sobotta (2012), p. 1015.

[66] On the different judicial methodologies applied by the CJEU, the EFTA Court and the ECtHR (e.g. regarding national "margins of appreciation") see: Petersmann (2013), p. 45.

[67] Cf. Article 19(4) German Basic Law.

- All EU and EEA Member States protect international commercial and investment law as cosmopolitan legal systems offering effective legal and judicial remedies to traders, producers, investors and consumers based on judicial protection of cosmopolitan rights (e.g. freedom of contract, private property rights, freedom of arbitration, individual rights to effective judicial remedies) and cooperation among national courts and transnational arbitral tribunals in protecting transnational rule of law.
- Some free trade agreements concluded by the EU (such as the EEA Agreement with EFTA states) are explicitly committed to facilitating "access to justice", "rule of law" and "rights to an effective remedy and to a fair trial" by providing for the establishment of independent courts (like the EFTA Court) protecting judicial remedies of states and non-governmental actors.
- The GATT and the WTO Agreements include a large number of requirements to make available judicial, arbitral or administrative tribunals and independent review procedures not only at international governance levels among WTO Members, but also in domestic legal systems in the field of GATT,[68] the WTO Anti-dumping Agreement,[69] the WTO Agreement on Customs Valuation,[70] the Agreement on Pre-shipment Inspection,[71] the Agreement on Subsidies and Countervailing Measures,[72] the General Agreement on Trade in Services,[73] the Agreement on Trade-Related Intellectual Property Rights[74] and the Agreement on Government Procurement.[75]
- In international investment law, the legal guarantees of access to justice at national and international levels (e.g. in the ICJ) have become supplemented by about 3,000 bi- and plurilateral treaty guarantees of individual access to transnational arbitration protecting private and public rights in cooperation with national courts at the seat of arbitration and at the place of the judicial enforcement of arbitral awards.
- Some environmental conventions—like the 1998 Aarhus Convention on Access to Information, Public Participation in Decision-Making and Access to Justice in Environmental Matters—protect individual "access to a review procedure before a court of law or another independent and impartial body established by law"[76] in transnational environmental regulation.
- UN and regional human rights covenants (e.g. Article 34 ECHR, and the Optional Protocol to the UN Covenant on Economic, Social and Cultural Rights)

---

[68] Cf. Article X GATT.

[69] Cf. Article 13 Anti-dumping Agreement.

[70] Cf. Article 11 Agreement on Customs Valuation.

[71] Cf. Article 4 Agreement on Pre-shipment Inspection.

[72] Cf. Article 23 Agreement on Subsidies and Countervailing Measures.

[73] Cf. Article VI GATS.

[74] Cf. Articles 41-50, 59 TRIPS.

[75] Cf. Article XX Agreement on Government Procurement.

[76] Article 9 Aarhus Convention.

increasingly extend protection of individual access to legal and (quasi)judicial remedies in case of violation of economic and social rights beyond national courts subject to prior exhaustion of local remedies.

Arguably, the constitutional and human rights obligations of the EU and EU Member States and their reciprocal duties of cooperation in areas of shared competences (like international "mixed agreements" concluded by both the EU and its Member States) constitutionally limit the role of the CJEU as:

- "gatekeeper" regarding the entry and effect of international law into the EU legal system, as well as
- "judicial protector" of the autonomy of the EU legal order and of its "rule of law system" protecting access to justice and other fundamental rights of citizens.

The Court's acceptance of other multilateral dispute settlement systems if they enlarge the powers of the CJEU[77] contrasts with the Court's reluctance to interpret EU law in conformity with the jurisprudence of international courts other than the EFTA Court and the ECtHR; the rare references by the CJEU to judgments of other international courts make clear that the CJEU acknowledges only in theory, but not in practice that judgments of other international courts (like the WTO Appellate Body) may have legally binding effects also for the CJEU.[78] Since the 1972 *International Fruit Company* cases,[79] the GATT/WTO jurisprudence of the CJEU continues to be characterised by biased interpretations of GATT/WTO legal and dispute settlement obligations aimed at limiting the legal and judicial accountability of EU institutions for their violations of GATT/WTO obligations ratified by parliaments for the benefit of EU citizens, by denying both citizens and EU Member States rights to invoke and enforce the EU's GATT/WTO obligations in national and EU courts, for instance on the grounds:

- that GATT/WTO rules are not sufficiently "precise and unconditional"—notwithstanding the fact that many GATT/WTO prohibitions of tariffs and non-tariff trade barriers and trade discrimination are more precise and unconditional than the often vague EU customs union rules based on GATT/WTO law;
- that lack of "reciprocity" by other GATT/WTO Members prevents "direct applicability" of GATT/WTO rules inside the EU—notwithstanding the Court's more convincing jurisprudence that lack of reciprocity in domestic judicial

[77] Cf. Opinion 1/00 on the establishment of a European Common Aviation Area and the "Discussion Document" adopted by the CJEU on 5 May 2010 suggesting to provide—in the negotiations on EU accession to the ECHR—for an explicit rule prohibiting the ECtHR to decide on applications against the EU without first allowing the CJEU to examine those complaints in the light of the EU's HRL, cf. Lock, Walking on a Tightrope: The Draft ECHR Accession Agreement and the Autonomy of the EU Legal Order, CMLR 48 (2011), pp. 1025.

[78] Cf. Kuijper (2013), p. 589 and Bronckers (2007), p. 601.

[79] ECJ, Joined Cases C-21-24/72, International Fruit Company v Produktschap voor Groenten en Fruit, [1972] ECR, 1219.

enforcement of free trade area rules is no impediment to their direct applicability in EU courts;

- that the existence of "safeguard clauses" require denying "direct applicability" of GATT/WTO obligations in European courts even if such safeguard clauses have not been invoked by EU institutions;
- that the "structure and objectives" of GATT/WTO law exclude the application of GATT/WTO rules in European courts—notwithstanding the explicit GATT/WTO guarantees of individual access to justice in domestic courts and arbitration procedures and the WTO requirement of ensuring the conformity of domestic "laws, regulations and administrative procedures with [the] obligations as provided in the annexed Agreements"[80]; or
- that the WTO/DSU provision[81] mentioning the possibility of avoiding lawful trade retaliation in response to EU non-compliance with WTO obligations through mutually agreed compensation prevents the CJEU from applying legally binding WTO dispute settlement rulings on the illegality of EU trade measures and their obligatory termination after the "reasonable period of time" determined through WTO dispute settlement rulings.[82]

The deliberate misinformation by the EU Commission of the CJEU regarding GATT jurisprudence (e.g. in the *Dürbeck case*, where the GATT panel finding against the EC was not yet publicly available) and the longstanding disregard by the CJEU for the EU's WTO obligations (e.g. of "prompt compliance with recommendations or rulings of the DSB" requiring termination of illegal measures[83]) suggests that the GATT/WTO jurisprudence of the CJEU pursues institutional self-interests of EU institutions (e.g. avoidance of judicial accountability of the political EU institutions *vis-à-vis* the "violation victims" and "retaliation victims" of WTO-inconsistent EU measures, judicial autonomy of the CJEU *vis-à-vis* other international courts) without adequate regard to the reasonable interests of EU citizens in "strict observance of international law".[84] If the CJEU exceptionally refers to WTO dispute settlement rulings, it is to bolster its own interpretations of trade and intellectual property rules (e.g. of TRIPS provisions) rather than to review the legality of EU measures.[85] Following some 15 GATT/WTO dispute settlement panel, Appellate Body and arbitration awards since 1991 against the illegal EU import restrictions on bananas, the agreement of 8 November 2012 between the EU

[80] Article XVI:4 WTO Agreement.

[81] Article 22 Dispute Settlement Understanding (DSU).

[82] For a detailed discussion of the legally unconvincing GATT/WTO jurisprudence of the CJEU, see: Petersmann (2011), p. 214; and Thies (2013).

[83] Cf. Articles 21.1 DSU. See generally Articles 21-23 DSU.

[84] Article 3(5) TEU.

[85] Cf. ECJ, C-245/02, *Anheuser-Busch*, [2004] ECR I, 11018, para. 49.

and ten Latin American countries on the final settlement of this longest-running series of trade disputes in the history of the multilateral trading system[86] reminds EU citizens of how rent-seeking economic lobbies also inside the EU—including the EU's few banana trading companies—may be powerful enough to lobby the political EU institutions to persistently violate the "rule of law" principles of EU and GATT/WTO law to the detriment of EU consumers, whose annual "protection costs" from these illegal import restrictions were estimated to be the equivalent of an illegal tax amounting to several billion euros per year for the benefit of a handful of EU trading companies importing bananas from (former) colonies of a few EU Member States.

The Multilevel WTO Trading and Legal System Should Be Protected as a Global PG Rather than as a "Westphalian Arena" for Intergovernmental Power Politics

As many benefits (e.g. in terms of legal security, access to the best markets for goods and services demanded by consumers) of the WTO trading and legal system are open to all countries and "non-exhaustible", academics and policy makers increasingly analyse the world trading system from the perspective of "PGs theories" in order to better understand the functional unity of the local, national, regional and international components of the world trading system, its "collective action problems" and the need for reconciling "overlapping PGs" (e.g. through increasing cooperation among the WTO and UN institutions in order to avoid "regime collisions" through a "Geneva consensus").[87] WTO law justifies this conception of the WTO as an "aggregate PG" in view of the WTO provisions:

- recognising the "systemic nature" and "basic principles" underlying WTO rules[88];
- emphasising that "the dispute settlement system of the WTO is a central element in providing security and predictability to the multilateral trading system"[89];
- mandating the WTO dispute settlement bodies "to preserve the rights and obligations of Members under the covered agreements, and to clarify the

[86] Cf. WTO press release of 8 November 2012 on "Historic Signing Ends 20 years of EU-Latin American Banana Dispute", available at www.wto.org/english/news_e/news12_e/disp_08nov12_e.htm.

[87] See, e.g., the contributions by the former WTO Director-General, Lamy, and the former President of the European Parliament, Borell, as well as by numerous academics, to Petersmann (2012).

[88] Cf. the Preamble to the WTO Agreement: "determined to preserve the basic principles ... underlying this multilateral trading system".

[89] Article 3.2 DSU.

existing provisions of those agreements in accordance with customary rules of interpretation of public international law"[90];

- requiring "each Member [to] ensure the conformity of its laws, regulations and administrative procedures with its obligations" under WTO law,[91] and excluding "reservations ... in respect of any provision of this Agreement"[92];
- prescribing legal protection of individual access to justice also in domestic legal systems inside WTO Members, for instance in the field of GATT,[93] the WTO Anti-dumping Agreement,[94] the WTO Agreement on Customs Valuation,[95] the Agreement on Pre-shipment Inspection,[96] the Agreement on Subsidies and Countervailing Measures,[97] the General Agreement on Trade in Services,[98] the Agreement on Trade-Related Intellectual Property Rights[99] and the Agreement on Government Procurement[100];
- providing for institutionalised review of free trade and customs union agreements (e.g. pursuant to Article XXIV GATT and Article V GATS), other plurilateral trade agreements (e.g. pursuant to Articles II:3, III:1 and X:9 WTO Agreement) and domestic trade policies (e.g. pursuant to Article III:4 WTO Agreement); and
- promoting "greater coherence in global economic policy-making"[101] and related policy areas (e.g. as required by the 1994 Ministerial Decision on "Trade and Environment") in view of the interdependencies between the monetary, financial, trade, environmental and related legal systems as "overlapping aggregate PGs".

The customary law requirements of interpreting treaties in conformity with "any relevant rules of international law applicable in the relations between the parties", as codified in Article 31(3)(c) VCLT, and of settling "disputes concerning treaties, like other international disputes, ...in conformity with the principles of justice and international law" as "embodied in the Charter of the United Nations", including "universal respect for, and observance of, human rights and fundamental freedoms for all", as recalled in the Preamble of the VCLT, likewise call for "consistent interpretations" of "overlapping PGs regimes". Whereas WTO institutions

90 Article 3.2 DSU.
91 Article XVI:4 WTO Agreement.
92 Article XVI:5 WTO Agreement.
93 Cf. Article X GATT.
94 Cf. Article 13 Anti-dumping Agreement.
95 Cf. Article 11 Agreement on Customs Valuation.
96 Cf. Article 4 Agreement on Pre-shipment Inspection.
97 Cf. Article 23 Agreement on Subsidies and Countervailing Measures.
98 Cf. Article VI GATS.
99 Cf. Articles 41-50, 59 TRIPS.
100 Cf. Article XX Agreement on Government Procurement.
101 Article III:5 WTO Agreement.

increasingly cooperate with other international organisations (like the IMF, the World Bank, WIPO and the WHO) so as to "limit the likelihood of a clash of regimes"[102] (e.g. by promoting financial "aid for trade" and mutually consistent "balancing" of economic and non-economic rights), domestic courts in the EU and USA disregard—at the request of trade politicians and vested interests—the "consistent interpretation" requirements of national, regional and WTO legal systems. The CJEU has recognised that citizens may rely upon, and derive rights from, treaty and customary international law rules, but in practice refuses to construe EU law in conformity with WTO obligations and WTO dispute settlement rulings for the benefit of EU citizens.[103] As constitutional democracies protect national PGs by constitutional approaches and justify legal protection of freedom of trade among domestic citizens in terms of "principles of justice" (like "equal freedoms" as "first principle of justice" in terms of Kantian and Rawlsian constitutionalism): Why do citizens, parliaments, "courts of justice" and governments so often shun their democratic responsibilities for interpreting WTO rules—and protecting welfare-enhancing freedoms of trade beyond state borders—in conformity with "principles of justice" like the human rights guarantees of access to justice and rule of law? Are WTO diplomats justified in pursuing "sustainable development" as an explicit treaty objective of the WTO without any reference in WTO rules to general consumer welfare, democratic governance and human rights which, according to the UN resolutions on the "right to development", are the moral and legal justification for designing international economic law and institutions?[104] Is it justifiable that, at the request of trade politicians (notably from the USA), anti-dumping and other trade remedies disputes continue to be exempted from the general remit of the WTO Legal Affairs Division handling all other WTO disputes? Why do most domestic courts, at the request of trade politicians, not participate in "providing security and predictability to the multilateral trading system"[105] through "consistent interpretations" of domestic trade laws in conformity with WTO obligations and "judicial comity" *vis-à-vis* WTO dispute settlement rulings, so as to hold governments accountable to adversely affected citizens for welfare-reducing abuses of trade policy powers in violation of WTO agreements ratified by parliaments for the benefit of citizens? From a "PGs" perspective, the constitutional experience of all democracies that "rule of law" is a precondition for democratic supply of national public goods, is even more important for transnational "aggregate public goods"

[102] Cf. WTO (2013), p. 15. A recent illustration is the joint study by the WHO et al. (2013), notwithstanding its explicit disclaimer that it does not purport to present any authoritative legal interpretations of WTO rules that remain the exclusive authority of the WTO Ministerial Conference and the WTO General Council (cf. Article IX:2 WTO Agreement).

[103] For a detailed discussion, see: Kuijper (2013), p. 589.

[104] Cf. Tietje (2014), p. 543.

[105] Article 3 DSU.

like the WTO agreements ratified by parliaments so as to provide "security and predictability to the multilateral trading system"[106] for the benefit of citizens. As long as trade rules continue to be distorted by power politics, their lack of fairness and legitimacy is bound to undermine also their economic efficiency, transnational rule of law and democratic support by reasonable citizens.[107]

Arguably, the "consistent interpretation" requirements of national and international legal systems also imply "judicial comity" requirements whenever national and international "overlapping jurisdictions" are confronted with essentially the same disputes over legal interpretations, and "judicial administration of justice" requires or justifies mutually coherent decisions. The WTO Appellate Body report on *Brazil—Retreaded tyres* defined some of the legal conditions under which judicial regard to previous national and regional dispute settlement rulings on related trade disputes may be justifiable.[108] WTO jurisprudence also confirms that jurisdictional overlaps between WTO and regional dispute settlement procedures may entail competing jurisdictions for "double breaches" of both WTO and regional trade rules and "double exercises" of such jurisdictions unless an "exclusive forum clause" may justify judicial deference by one jurisdiction in favour of the other.[109] Dispute settlement proceedings outside the WTO increasingly refer to WTO rules and WTO dispute settlement jurisprudence (e.g. as evidence for factual determinations, procedural aspects, general principles of international law, the rules on treaty interpretation, and substantive rules).[110] Also the design of dispute settlement procedures in regional trade agreements is increasingly influenced by the quasi-judicial model of the WTO dispute settlement system and jurisprudence, notwithstanding the fact that—apart from the regional dispute settlement institutions in the European Union and the European Economic Area (i.e. the CJEU and the EFTA Court), as well as in a few Latin-American economic integration regimes (like MERCOSUR, the Andean Community, the CACM and CARICOM)—the actual use of many other regional economic dispute settlement procedures

---

[106] Article 3 DSU.

[107] Cf. Garcia (2013), criticising US attitudes of "regulating my market at home, and deregulating markets abroad in order to facilitate exploitation of other markets internationally", as well as US power politics in NAFTA and CAFTA dispute settlement procedures (pp. 260 et seq.).

[108] WTO DS332/AB/R adopted on 17 December 2007 (the Appellate Body held that the national and MERCOSUR court decisions authorising imports of used tyres resulted in the import ban being applied in a discriminatory manner as Brazil had not invoked the environmental justifications in the national and MERCOSUR court proceedings that Brazil had invoked in the WTO dispute settlement proceedings).

[109] In the *Mexico—Soft Drinks* dispute, the WTO Appellate Body noted explicitly that NAFTA's exclusive forum clause had not been exercised (cf. WTO DS308/AB/R, para. 54). On the problems of justifying a WTO panel decision declining jurisdiction in favour of an "exclusive jurisdiction" agreed among WTO Members in a regional trade agreement, see: Marceau and Wyatt (2010), p. 67. For a complete overview of GATT/WTO jurisprudence involving regional trade agreements, see: de Mestral (2013), p. 777.

[110] For the identification of 150 references in international dispute settlement proceedings outside the WTO to WTO rules and dispute settlement procedures, see: Marceau et al. (2013), p. 481.

remains limited, for instance due to the preference of countries (e.g. in NAFTA) to submit their disputes to the WTO.[111] Yet, at the request of governments interested in limiting their own legal and judicial accountability *vis-à-vis* domestic citizens for injury caused by illegal trade restrictions, domestic courts in many WTO Members continue to disregard WTO obligations, WTO dispute settlement rulings and transnational rule of law for the benefit of citizens. Overcoming this "legal fragmentation" of global "aggregate public goods" (like a mutually beneficial world trading system, and judicial protection of transnational rule of law for the benefit of citizens) requires limiting abuses of the "executive dominance" in multilevel governance of international public goods. Even though neither "consistent interpretations" nor "judicial comity" may require compliance with intergovernmental "rule by law", judicial protection of transnational "rule of law" for the benefit of citizens—including "providing security and predictability to the multilateral trading system"[112]—requires judicial consideration of the impact of relevant international legal obligations and related dispute settlement rulings on the "administration of justice" in related disputes in other jurisdictions.

The "Structural Biases" of Functionally Limited Regimes on "Overlapping PGs" Require a "Geneva Consensus" on Mutually Coherent Interpretations

Transnational rule of law is also of crucial importance for reconciling reciprocal market access commitments enabling a welfare-increasing, global division of labour with non-economic PGs regimes limiting the sovereign rights of WTO Members by "duties to protect" non-economic PGs as regulated in UN law (like human rights, "sustainable development" and GAL principles underlying the law of UN specialized agencies). Even though the UN specialized agencies and the WTO are based on separate treaty regimes, they protect functionally limited "aggregate PGs" that interact (e.g. monetary, trade and environmental regimes) and must be construed coherently in order to protect "overlapping PGs" effectively, as illustrated by the increasing cooperation of the WTO with ever more UN specialized agencies.[113] The "general exceptions" in WTO Agreements use indeterminate legal terms (like "public order", "public health") that depend on procedures and institutions clarifying "incomplete agreements" in conformity with the UN legal obli-

[111] Cf. Chase et al. (2013).

[112] Article 3 DSU.

[113] Cf. Pitaraki (2014).

gations of WTO Members (e.g. the health and tobacco control regulations of the WHO, the food aid regulations of the FAO) and the legal obligations of each WTO Member to "ensure the conformity of its laws, regulations and administrative procedures with its obligations" under the treaties concerned.[114] The "dispute settlement system of the WTO"[115] and EU law recognise the systemic character of their respective dispute settlement systems and the need for interpreting international treaties—as required by the customary rules of treaty interpretation codified in the VCLT—"in conformity with the principles of justice and international law", including "human rights and fundamental freedoms for all".[116] National, regional and worldwide tribunals emphasise that this "integration principle" of international treaty interpretation requires mutually "consistent interpretations" of overlapping legal obligations of governments and "judicial comity" among courts of justice in "overlapping jurisdictions" so as to administer justice in their common task of impartial dispute settlement aimed at protecting transnational rule of law for the benefit of citizens, for instance by "providing security and predictability to the multilateral trading system".[117] WTO law—similarly to UN human rights law and EU law—provides for legal and judicial remedies not only at intergovernmental levels; it also protects individual access to justice in domestic legal systems, for instance in the field of GATT,[118] the WTO Anti-dumping Agreement,[119] the WTO Agreement on Customs Valuation,[120] the Agreement on Pre-shipment Inspection,[121] the Agreement on Subsidies and Countervailing Measures,[122] the General Agreement on Trade in Services,[123] the Agreement on Trade-Related Intellectual Property Rights[124] and the Agreement on Government Procurement.[125] As multilevel governance and adjudication derive their democratic legitimacy from protecting human and constitutional rights of citizens, national and international dispute settlement bodies must cooperate in their common task of promoting mutually consistent interpretations and transnational rule of law for the benefit of

[114] Cf. Article XVI:4 WTO Agreement.

[115] Article 3 DSU.

[116] Preamble and Article 31 VCLT.

[117] Article 3 DSU.

[118] Cf. Article X GATT.

[119] Cf. Article 13 Anti-dumping Agreement.

[120] Cf. Article 11 Agreement on Customs Valuation.

[121] Cf. Article 4 Agreement on Pre-shipment Inspection.

[122] Cf. Article 23 Agreement on Subsidies and Countervailing Measures.

[123] Cf. Article VI GATS.

[124] Cf. Articles 41-50, 59 TRIPS.

[125] Cf. Article XX Agreement on Government Procurement. Cf. Petersmann (1997), pp. 194 et seq., 233 et seq.

citizens cooperating in the collective supply of international PGs and in promoting the mutual legal coherence of fragmented legal regimes.[126] Whereas the "Washington consensus" focused one-sidedly on the complementary efforts by the Bretton Woods institutions to promote monetary and financial stability and liberal trade and payments regimes, the "Geneva consensus" emphasises the systemic need to protect also the mutual coherence of WTO law with the law of all other UN specialized agencies promoting and regulating interdependent PGs for the benefit of citizens: even though "trade opening is essential for achieving growth and development, the benefits resulting from open trade depend on the quality of policies in other areas"[127] as regulated through multilevel HRL, monetary, financial, health, environmental law and other fields of international law.

Multilevel legal and judicial protection of cosmopolitan legal and social rights in international HRL, commercial, investment, criminal law and in many regional free trade and customs union agreements based on GATT Article XXIV proceed from "individualist conceptions of constitutionalism" based on mutual respect for "human dignity" and "reason and conscience"[128] of human beings as universal foundations of cosmopolitan rights. EU constitutional lawyers rightly interpret also the Lisbon Treaty mandate for the EU external relations policies (e.g. Articles 3, 21 TEU) in terms of "cosmopolitan constitutionalism", for instance recognising citizens as authors and addressees of constitutional democracies entitled to protection of human rights and transnational rule of law also beyond nation states. Diplomats claiming "foreign policy discretion" often fail to convincingly respond to constitutional and human rights arguments that legal, democratic and judicial accountability mechanisms holding "Westphalian intergovernmentalism" accountable to citizens will contribute to "institutionalising public reason" beneficial for all (e.g. also protecting diplomats against undue interest group pressures). The "executive dominance" in the legal interpretation by diplomats of the five competing paradigms of foreign policies and IEL (as discussed above) and of multilevel governance of international "aggregate PGs" (like the horizontally and vertically interdependent monetary, trading, investment, environmental, human rights and rule of law systems) is increasingly challenged by civil society, democratic parliaments and courts of justice in order to limit the intergovernmental disregard for human rights, rule of law and consumer welfare (which are not explicitly mentioned

[126] Legal duties of judicial cooperation among national and international courts are increasingly recognised beyond national, regional and functional legal systems (like human rights and economic integration law, international commercial, investment and criminal law), for instance in case of "overlapping jurisdictions" among international courts (e.g. in the *Mox Plant* dispute submitted to arbitration under the OSPAR environmental convention, the dispute settlement procedures of the UN Law of the Sea Convention and of EU law; in the *Brazil—Retreaded Tyres* dispute submitted to both MERCOSUR arbitration and WTO dispute settlement proceedings); cf. Petersmann (2012), chapter VIII.

[127] Cf. Lamy (2013).

[128] Article 1 Universal Declaration of Human Rights (UDHR).

in WTO law) and the obvious governance failures in collective protection of international PGs.

Conclusion: HRL and EU Law Require Promoting Cosmopolitan IEL

The more all UN member states accept human rights obligations under the UN Charter, under UN human rights conventions and general international law as codified in UN, regional and national HRL (like the UN Convention on the Rights of the Child ratified by more than 190 states), the more principles of procedural, distributive, corrective and commutative justice must be construed in conformity with HRL. Many UN human rights instruments confirm that "[a]ll human rights are universal, indivisible and interdependent and interrelated"; "it is the duty of States, regardless of their political, economic and cultural systems, to promote and protect all human rights and fundamental freedoms."[129] Yet, HRL has never been effectively institutionalised in UN law and worldwide institutions dominated by power-oriented "Westphalian intergovernmentalism" based on "sovereign equality of states" protecting non-democratic rulers against democratic and judicial accountability (e.g. due to lack of jurisdiction of international courts, veto powers of non-democratic governments blocking UN Security Council responses to human rights violations abroad). Human rights are also neither mentioned nor effectively protected in WTO law and adjudication. As most national legal systems of UN member states focus one-sidedly on protecting civil and political rights (e.g. in US constitutional law and practices) or economic rights (e.g. in communist countries like China) without comprehensive protection of the "indivisibility" and "interdependence" of civil, political, economic, social and cultural rights as required by UN HRL, also the EU has so far refrained from invoking human rights in WTO negotiations and WTO adjudication in spite of the EU's insistence on including human rights clauses into all its other trade agreements.

Need for Interpreting IEL in Conformity with HRL

The incorporation of "inalienable" human rights into positive national and international legal systems confirms the "dual nature" of modern international law,

[129] Vienna Declaration and Programme of Action adopted at the UN World Conference on Human Rights by more than 170 states on 25 June 1993 (A/CONF.157/24, para. 5). This "universal, indivisible, interrelated, interdependent and mutually reinforcing" nature of human rights was reaffirmed by all UN member states in numerous human rights instruments such as UN Resolution 63/116 of 10 December 2008 on the "60th anniversary of the Universal Declaration of Human Rights" (UN Doc A/RES/63/116 of 26 February 2009).

as illustrated also by the customary law requirements of interpreting international treaties and settling international disputes "in conformity with the principles of justice" and the human rights obligations of states, as recalled in the Vienna Convention on the Law of Treaties[130] as well as in other UN agreements.[131] UN law does not limit the "sources of law" and "rules of recognition" to "international conventions. . .recognised by states".[132] The additional sources of international law and their legal interpretation—like "(b) international custom, as evidence of a general practice accepted as law; (c) the general principles of law recognised by civilized nations; (d). . .judicial decisions and the teachings of the most highly qualified publicists of the various nations, as subsidiary means for the determination of the rules of law"[133]—may depend no less on recognition by citizens, civil society, parliaments, courts of justice and HRL than on claims by diplomats that they control the *opinio juris sive necessitatis* as traditional gate-keepers of "Westphalian international law among states". It was due to the multilevel guarantees of civil, political, economic, social and cultural rights and their multilevel judicial protection by the CJEU, the European Free Trade Area Court, the ECtHR and by national courts in the 31 EEA Member States that EU law, EEA law and European HRL were transformed from "international treaties among states" into cosmopolitan "constitutional legal orders" protecting cosmopolitan rights and "European public goods" (like transnational rule of law) for the benefit of citizens.

The constitutional commitments of EU law, EEA law and European institutions to multilevel, legal and judicial protection of civil, political, economic, social and cultural human rights and fundamental freedoms (like the EU's "internal market freedoms"), the EU accession to regional and UN human rights conventions, the EU's insistence on including "human rights clauses" into international agreements with third states, and the EU's willingness to forego such agreements if third countries (e.g. Australia and New Zealand) objected to "human rights clauses", illustrate a unique European leadership for protecting the "indivisibility" of human rights as required by European and UN HRL. Inside the EU and the EEA, HRL has empowered citizens and citizen-driven transformation of "Westphalian international law" through transnational participatory, parliamentary and "deliberative democracy" and judicial protection of cosmopolitan rights and remedies limiting abuses of public and private power. The innovative elaboration of the EU Charter of Fundamental Rights by a "European Convention"—composed not only of representatives of governments but also of civil society, national parliaments and the

[130] Cf. Preamble and Article 31 VCLT.

[131] For example, Article 1 UN Charter.

[132] Article 38(1)(a) Statute of the International Court of Justice (ICJ Statute).

[133] Article 38(1) ICJ Statute.

European Parliament—entailed a new multilevel system of "dignity rights",[134] "freedoms",[135] "equality rights",[136] "solidarity rights",[137] "citizens' rights"[138] and other guarantees of "justice".[139] This multilevel constitutional protection of fundamental rights in Europe—in conformity with the Convention rights protected by the ECHR[140]—has developed HRL far beyond the traditional categories used in UN human rights conventions. Just as national constitutional courts insist on reviewing whether EU acts remain consistent with the limited powers and constitutional restraints of the EU, the *Kadi* jurisprudence of the CJEU refuses to apply EU acts violating the fundamental rights guarantees of EU law, even if they implement UN Security Council "smart sanctions".[141] The judicial remedies offered by the human rights jurisprudence of European courts in the field of IEL are also in stark contrast to the jurisprudence of most other regional economic courts outside Europe, as illustrated by Zimbabwe's refusal to comply with the 2008 judgment of the Southern African Development (SADC) Tribunal against Zimbabwe's illegal expropriations of white farmers and the subsequent dissolution of the SADC Tribunal by SADC governments.[142] Regrettably, in the external trade relations of the EU, the explicit exclusion (e.g. in EU decisions implementing the recent free trade agreements with Korea and Latin-American countries) of rights of citizens to invoke EU trade agreements in domestic courts reveals power politics also by EU trade politicians interested in excluding legal and judicial accountability *vis-à-vis* citizens for welfare-reducing violations of international trade agreements.

EU Leadership for Promoting "Human Rights Coherence" of WTO Law?

Human rights cannot be effective—also in IEL—unless they are "institutionalised" throughout the legal and political system and constitute "public reason". Yet,

---

[134] Chapter I EU Charter of Fundamental Rights (ECFR).

[135] Chapter II ECFR.

[136] Chapter III ECFR.

[137] Chapter IV ECFR.

[138] Chapter V ECFR.

[139] Chapter VI ECFR.

[140] Cf. Articles 52,53 ECFR.

[141] Cf. ECJ, C-402/05 P and C-415/05 P, *Kadi and Al Barakaat Foundation v Council and Commission*, [2008] ECR I, 6351; Joined Cases C-584/10 P, C-593/10 P and C-595/10 P, *Commission and Others v Kadi*, Judgment of 18 July 2013, not yet reported, para. 131: and Petersmann (2014), p. 187.

[142] Cf. Ruppel (2012), p. 141.

"public reason" beyond a national "democratic demos" cannot be left to government executives or their trade diplomats[143]; it can be progressively established only by following the "democratic principles" of EU law[144] for promoting participatory, representative and deliberative democratic self-government, "cosmopolitan constitutionalism", impartial clarification of transnational "principles of justice" (including procedural, distributive, corrective, commutative justice and equity principles) and multilevel judicial protection of cosmopolitan rights in multilevel political, judicial and cosmopolitan governance of "aggregate PGs" beyond state borders. Even though governments have no legitimate powers to exempt international organisations from the constraints of HRL, the law of the Bretton Woods institutions, WTO law and many regional economic organisations mention neither human rights nor other constitutional restraints of intergovernmental power politics. Hence, even though citizens are "agents of justice" whose human rights and democratic consent condition the legitimacy of law and governance, citizens continue to be treated by UN and WTO law as mere objects without effective legal and judicial remedies against intergovernmental power politics. The "human rights clauses" in EU law and in economic EU agreements with more than 130 third states acknowledge that IEL must remain "constitutionally embedded" and protect cosmopolitan rights of producers, traders, investors and consumers participating in the global division of labour. IEL regimes with cosmopolitan rights—for example, in the EU, EEA, NAFTA, investment, intellectual property, commercial law and arbitration agreements—have proven to protect consumer welfare and rule of law more effectively for the benefit of citizens than "Westphalian IEL regimes" prioritising rights and interests of governments over those of citizens (e.g. by failing to protect legal, democratic and judicial remedies of citizens against corrupt rulers).[145] European economic and human rights courts, commercial and investor-state arbitral tribunals, and national courts recognise ever more internal market rights, property rights, human, labour and other cosmopolitan rights of citizens participating in the international division of labour. The admission of *amicus curiae* briefs in order to take into account third party interests affected by economic disputes, the "judicial balancing" between legal market access commitments and exception clauses (e.g. GATT Article XX) reserving sovereign rights and duties to protect non-economic values (like human rights), and the judicial interpretation of economic provisions (e.g. on technical regulations, sanitary standards, intellectual property rights) in the light of other treaty provisions protecting non-economic public interests (like protection of public health pursuant to Article 8 TRIPS) are justifiable also by the customary law requirements of interpreting treaties and settling disputes "in conformity with principles of justice" and other "relevant rules of international law applicable in the relations between the parties" (Article 31(3)(c) VCLT). Human rights are essential for protecting "access to justice",

[143] Cf. Lomba (2014), p. 97.

[144] For example, Articles 9-12 TEU.

[145] Cf. Petersmann (2013) 2, p. 47.

due process of law, democratic and judicial "balancing" of public and private rights and interests affected by economic regulation. As none of the UN human rights conventions provide for effective judicial remedies, some human rights advocates argue that economic agreements offering material benefits for compliance with human rights, changing the "cost-benefit calculations" of human rights violators, and setting incentives for "participatory democracy" may be more important for promoting human rights and satisfying basic needs than pushing more countries to ratify UN human rights conventions.[146]

Why is it then that WTO dispute settlement bodies have so far never referred to the human rights obligations of all WTO Members as relevant context for interpreting WTO rules and justifying trade restrictions which WTO Members adopted in order to protect non-economic public goods like human health and human rights? Why has the EU never invoked human rights arguments in WTO dispute settlement proceedings (e.g. in order to justify the EU import restrictions on seal products and harmful asbestos) in spite of the fact that UN human rights bodies long since emphasise the need for a "human rights approach" to interpreting WTO law, and also the former EU Commissioner and WTO Director-General, Pascal Lamy, has acknowledged in numerous speeches the legal relevance of HRL for WTO rules, trade policies and for the "Geneva consensus" necessary for protecting the mutual coherence of UN and WTO law?[147] Why does the EU Commission favour investor-state arbitration in the proposed Transatlantic Trade and Investment Partnership Agreement even though many citizens and some EU Member States (like France and Germany) rightly argue that domestic courts could offer more constitutionally justified judicial remedies provided domestic judges would respect international legal obligations of the EU rather than ignore WTO law at the request of EU trade politicians?

The human rights clauses in the EU's international trade agreements have both "domestic" as well as "foreign policy functions", i.e. to prevent violations of law by EU institutions (e.g. by justifying suspension of treaty benefits in response to human rights violations abroad) and to promote "human rights coherence" in multilevel governance institutions and in foreign jurisdictions of EU trading partners. Due to the multilevel, constitutional and judicial limitations of governance powers of EU Member States and EU institutions by multilevel human rights and judicial remedies, "negative human rights coherence"—in the sense of absence of contradictions between EU trade rules and human rights—is essentially secured;

---

[146] Cf. Hafner-Burton (2009).

[147] Cf. Lamy (2013).

national and European judgments establishing violations of the EU's human rights obligations in the implementation of EU agreements remain rare.[148] "Positive human rights coherence"—in the sense of mutual synergies among HRL and IEL—remains, however, a permanent challenge, as illustrated by the large number of WTO dispute settlement rulings against illegal, welfare-reducing EU trade restrictions violating WTO law to the detriment of EU citizens and the EU requirements of "strict observance of international law".[149] The WTO Appellate Body ruling against the EU's "drugs arrangements" conditioning preferential tariffs to less developed countries on their combat against the production and trafficking of narcotics[150] prompted the EU to adopt new "GSP+ arrangements" offering additional tariff preferences to "vulnerable" less developed countries accepting and monitoring 16 human rights and ILO conventions and 7 out of 11 additional "good governance" conventions[151]; this explicit "human rights conditionality" of certain GSP preferences illustrates that legal linkages of human rights and EU trade regulations may also be challenged in WTO dispute settlement proceedings. Regrettably, the treaty commitments to "respect for democratic principles and human rights" in the "new generation" of EU "deep and comprehensive free trade agreements"[152] have not prevented the political EU institutions from adopting EU rules preventing EU citizens from challenging EU violations of these free trade rules in domestic courts, in line with the long-standing policy of EU institutions to prevent citizens from holding EU institutions legally and judicially accountable in European courts for their violations of WTO rules as established in dozens of GATT/WTO dispute settlement rulings against the EU.[153]

---

[148] See ECJ, C-402/05 P and C-415/05 P, *Kadi and Al Barakaat Foundation v Council and Commission*, [2008] ECR I, 6351; Joined Cases C-584/10 P, C-593/10 P and C-595/10 P, *Commission and Others v Kadi*, Judgment of 18 July 2013, not yet reported, para. 131; and ECtHR, *Saadi v Italy*, Appl. No. 37201/06, Judgment of 28 February 2008, in which the ECtHR decided that the deportation by Italy of a Tunisian citizen to Tunisia would breach Article 3 ECHR and could not be justified by a presumption that Tunisia would respect its human rights obligations as confirmed in the human rights clause of the EU-Tunisia association agreement.

[149] Article 3(5) TEU.

[150] WTO Appellate Body Report, *EC-Tariff Preferences*, WT/DS246/AB/R, adopted 20 April 2004.

[151] Cf. Article 9 of Council Regulation 980/2005 of 27 June 2005 applying a scheme for generalised tariff preferences, OJ L 169/1.

[152] For example, in Article 1 of the EU-Korea Framework Agreement, 2010.

[153] Cf. Petersmann (2011), p 214.

Can Human Rights "Run Like a Silver Thread" Through EU Foreign Policies Without "Strict Observance of International Law" (Article 3(5) TEU)?

The EU strategies for promoting human rights coherence of the EU's international agreements—mainly based on the three tools of "human rights clauses", "human rights dialogues" and "human rights assistance"—have been of limited effectiveness.[154] Since the 1948 Universal Declaration of Human Rights, UN human rights instruments emphasise "that human rights should be protected by the rule of law".[155] As national parliaments have not delegated powers to the EU institutions to violate international law, EU law emphasises the constitutional limitation of all EU policies by "rule of law" and "strict observance of international law".[156] In her speech of 16 June 2010, the EU High Representative for Foreign Affairs, C. Ashton, confirmed to the European Parliament that "human rights, democracy and rule of law … will run like a silver thread" through the EU's foreign policies. Yet, following some 15 GATT/WTO dispute settlement panel, Appellate Body and arbitration awards since 1991 against the illegal EU import restrictions on bananas, the agreement of 8 November 2012 between the EU and ten Latin American countries on the final settlement of this longest-running series of trade disputes in the history of the multilateral trading system[157] reminds citizens of how rent-seeking economic lobbies also inside the EU—including the EU's few banana trading companies—may be powerful enough to lobby the political EU institutions to persistently violate the "rule of law" principles of EU and GATT/WTO law to the detriment of EU consumers, whose annual "protection costs" from these illegal import restrictions were estimated to be the equivalent of an illegal tax amounting to several billion euros per year. The persistent refusal of EU politicians to grant EU citizens legal and judicial remedies against EU violations of international trade rules, even if the "reasonable period" for implementing legally binding WTO dispute settlement rulings has expired, confirms the legal experience from the Eurozone crisis that "rule of law" inside the EU risks not being stronger than in a "banana republic". The persistent violations—by more than 20 out of the 28 EU Member States—of the agreed EU legal disciplines for fiscal, debt and economic convergence policies[158] contributed to debt defaults (i.e. violations of contract law) necessitating bailouts of ever more over-indebted EU Member States (like Greece, Portugal, Ireland, Spain and Cyprus), as well as of bankrupt banks, at the expense of European taxpayers, thereby undermining also rule of law, protection of human

[154] Cf. Petersmann (2013/2014), p. 15; and Golabek (2013), chapter 6.3.

[155] Preamble, UDHR.

[156] Articles 2, 3 and 21 TEU.

[157] Cf. WTO press release of 8 November 2012 on "Historic Signing Ends 20 years of EU-Latin American Banana Dispute", available at www.wto.org/english/news_e/news12_e/disp_08nov12_e.htm.

[158] Cf. Article 126 TFEU.

rights (e.g. in Greece) and the legitimacy of European governance. As illegal economic and trade restrictions have economic effects similar to illegal taxes on EU citizens and redistribute "protection rents" in illegal ways, the lack of effective judicial remedies of EU citizens against welfare-reducing EU violations of world trade rules and financial disciplines confirms the EU's neglect of "rule of law" for the benefit of citizens. The CJEU—rather than fulfilling its constitutional mandate of ensuring "that the law is observed",[159] including international treaty obligations as integral part of the Community legal system—has endorsed the legally unfounded claims of the political EU institutions to have "freedom of manoeuver"[160] to violate UN and WTO law without explaining how, for example, EU non-compliance with WTO dispute settlement rulings can serve legitimate "Community interests".

Inside states, extending human rights of "access to justice" to economic policies may remain within the discretion of democratic lawmakers. In international organisations based on limited delegation of powers and "rule of law", citizens and national parliaments have good reasons to insist on "strict observance of international law"[161] and more comprehensive judicial remedies—as guaranteed by Article 47 ECFR—in order to protect transnational rule of law for the benefit of citizens. For, the more globalisation transforms national PGs into transnational "aggregate PGs", the more the welfare of citizens depends on cosmopolitan rights protecting the responsibility of citizens for securing rule of law, including "strict observance of international law" as required by the Lisbon Treaty. As long as non-inclusive intergovernmentalism prevails in the EU's external relations over the protection of rights of citizens and democratic "accountability mechanisms",[162] human rights and rule of law for the benefit of citizens remain at risk also inside the

[159] Article 19 TEU.

[160] As stated above, the term "freedom of manoeuvre" continues to be used by both the political EU institutions and the CJEU (e.g. in Joined cases C-120 and C-121/06 P, *FIAMM and Others v Council and Commission*, [2008] ECR I, 6513, para. 119) as the only justification for their disregard of legally binding WTO rules and WTO dispute settlement rulings. Since the 1972 *International Fruit Company Case* (ECJ, Joined Cases C-21-24/72, [1972] ECR, 1219), the justifications submitted by the EU Commission to the CJEU for denying citizens' and EU Member States' rights to invoke and enforce the EU's GATT/WTO obligations—e.g. that GATT/WTO rules are less "precise and unconditional" than EU rules; that "reciprocity" and "safeguard clauses" require denying "direct applicability" of GATT/WTO obligations in European courts; or that WTO law accepts compensation and sanctions as alternative "options of compliance" with WTO obligations—continue to be obviously inconsistent with GATT/WTO law and reflect bureaucratic self-interests of EU politicians to avoid accountability for arbitrary violations of international legal obligations *vis-à-vis* EU citizens. Sadly, the CJEU's endorsement of such "political question doctrines" seems to be likewise influenced by judicial self-interests in limiting the influence of international courts (e.g. WTO jurisprudence) on the CJEU and avoiding conflicts with the political EU institutions. In its recent case law, the CJEU has similarly refrained from applying UN conventions (like the UN Convention on the Law of the Sea, the ICAO Chicago Convention) as legal standards for reviewing the lawfulness of EU acts.

[161] Article 3 TEU.

[162] Cf. UN High Commissioner for Human Rights (2013).

EU, as explained by Immanuel Kant already more than 200 years ago: "the problem of establishing a perfect civil constitution is subordinate to the problem of a law-governed external relationship with other states and cannot be solved unless the latter is also solved".[163] The EU should lead by example in interpreting mutually beneficial trade agreements not only in terms of rights and obligations of governments, but as protecting also cosmopolitan rights and judicial remedies for the benefit of citizens. Arguably, Article 21 TEU requires such "cosmopolitan leadership" for protecting human rights and rule of law also in the EU's external relations as a matter of justice rather than of bureaucratic benevolence.

References

Barret S (2007) Why cooperate? The incentive to supply global public goods

Bronckers M (2007) The relationship of the EC courts with other international tribunals: non-committal, respectful or submissive. Common Market Law Rev 44

Cançado Trindade AA (2011) The access of individuals to international justice

Carr EH (1940) The twenty-years crisis 1919–1939

Chase C, Yanovich A, Crawford J-A, Ugaz P (2013) Mapping of dispute settlement mechanisms in regional trade agreements – innovative or variations on a theme?

Cremona M (2014) International regulatory policy and democratic accountability: the EU and the ACTA. In: Cremona M, Hilpold P, Lavranos N, Schneider S, Ziegler A (eds) Reflections on the constitutionalisation of international economic law. Liber Amicorum for Ernst-Ulrich Petersmann

Davis JB (2003) The theory of the individual in economics. Identity and value

de Mestral ACM (2013) Dispute settlement under the WTO and under regional trade agreements: an uneasy relationship. J Int Econ Law 16:4

Ethier WJ (2007) The theory of trade policy and trade agreements: a critique. Eur J Polit Econ 23:3

European Union Agency for Fundamental Rights (2011) Access to justice in Europe: an overview of challenges and opportunities

Forst R (2012) The right to justification. Elements of a constructivist theory of justice

Francioni F (ed) (2007) Access to justice as a human right

Garcia FJ (2003) Trade, inequality and justice: toward a liberal theory of just trade

Garcia FJ (2013) Global justice and international economic law. Three takes

Golabek M (2013) "Weaving a silver thread". Human rights coherence in EU foreign affairs and counter-terrorism

Hafner-Burton EM (2009) Forced to be good: why trade agreements boost human rights

Hart HLA (1994) The concept of law

Kahneman D (2011) Thinking, fast and slow

Kant I (1991) Idea for a universal history with a cosmopolitan purpose. In: Reiss H (ed) Political writings

Kokott J, Sobotta C (2012) The Kadi case – constitutional core values and international law – finding the balance? Eur J Int Law 23

Krugman P (1997) What should trade negotiators negotiate about? J Econ Lit 35:1

Kuijper PJ (2013) "It shall contribute to ... the strict observance and development of international law". The role of the court of justice. In: Rosas A, Levits E, Bot Y (eds) The court of justice and the construction of Europe: analyses and perspectives on sixty years of case-law

[163] Cf. Kant (1991), p. 47.

Lamy P (2013) The Geneva consensus. Making trade work for all
Lomba P (2014) Constructing a "We": collective agency and the EU. In: Cremona M, Hilpold P, Lavranos N, Schneider SS, Ziegler AR (eds) Reflections on the constitutionalisation of international economic law. Liber Amicorum for Ernst-Ulrich Petersmann
Marceau G, Wyatt J (2010) Dispute settlement regimes intermingled: regional trade agreement and the WTO. J Int Dispute Settlement 1:1
Marceau G, Izaguerri A, Lanovoy V (2013) The WTO's influence on other dispute settlement mechanisms: a lighthouse in the storm of fragmentation. J World Trade 47
Morgenthau H (1951) Politics among nations. The struggle for power and peace
Nussbaum MC (2011) Creating capabilities. The human development approach
Pech L (2010) A union founded on the rule of law: meaning and reality of the rule of law as a constitutional principle of EU law. In: European constitutional law review
Pech L (2012/2013) Rule of law as a guiding principle of the EU's external actions. CLEER Working Paper 2012/2013
Pernice I (2013) The right to effective judicial protection and remedies in the EU. In: Rosas A, Levits E, Bot Y (eds) The court of justice and the construction of Europe: analyses and perspectives on sixty years of case-law
Petersmann EU (1983) Application of GATT by the court of justice of the European communities. Common Market Law Rev 20
Petersmann E-U (1986) Trade policy as a constitutional problem. On the "Domestic Policy Functions" of international trade rules. Aussenwirtschaft 41
Petersmann E-U (1991) Constitutional functions and constitutional problems of international economic law
Petersmann E-U (1997) The GATT/WTO dispute settlement system
Petersmann E-U (2006) Human rights, markets and economic welfare: constitutional functions of the emerging UN human rights constitution. In: Abbott F, Breining C, Cottier T (eds) International trade and human rights
Petersmann E-U (2011) International economic law in the 21st century: need for stronger "Democratic Ownership" and cosmopolitan reforms. In: Czapliński W et al (eds) XXXI Polish yearbook of international law
Petersmann E-U (2011) Can the EU's disregard for "Strict Observance of International Law" (Article 3 TEU) be constitutionally justified? In: Bronckers M, Hauspiel V, Quick R (eds) Liber Amicorum for J. Bourgeois
Petersmann E-U (2012) JIEL debate: methodological pluralism and its critics in international economic law research. J Int Econ Law 15
Petersmann E-U (2012) International economic law in the 21st century. Constitutional pluralism and multilevel governance of interdependent public goods
Petersmann E-U (ed) (2012) Multilevel governance of interdependent public goods. Theories, rules and institutions for the central policy challenge in the 21st century. EUI Working Paper RSCAS 2012/23
Petersmann E-U (2013) Multilevel judicial governance in European and international economic law. In: Besson S, Ziegler A (eds) Le juge en droit européen et international
Petersmann E-U (2013) Human rights require "Cosmopolitan Constitutionalism" and cosmopolitan law for democratic governance of public goods. Contemp Read Law Soc Justice 5:2
Petersmann E-U (2013/2014) Integrating human rights into EU trade relations – the EU as a global role model? In: Takacs T, Ott A, Dimopoulos A (eds) Linking trade and non-commercial interests: the EU as a global role model? CLEER Working Paper 2013/2014
Petersmann E-U (2014) Multilevel judicial protection of "Access to Justice" and the EU's duty to contribute 'to the strict observance and development of international law'. In: Avbelj M, Fontanelli F, Martinico G (eds) Kadi on trial. A multifaceted analysis of the Kadi trial
Pitaraki A (2014) Institutional linkages: WTO-IMF, World Bank, WIPO, WHO. A global administrative law approach as a means for supplying public goods
Rawls J (1972) A theory of justice

Rawls J (1999) Law of peoples
Regan DH (2006) What are trade agreements for? Two conflicting stories told by economists, with a lesson for lawyers. J Int Econ Law 9:4
Ruppel OC (2012) The case of Mike Campbell and the dissolution of the SADC tribunal. In: Madolo N (ed) International economic law. The voices of Africa
Sen A (2000) Development as freedom
Slaughter A (2004) A new world order
Slaughter A-M (2013) International law and international relations theory: twenty years later. In: Dunoff JL, Pollack MA (eds) Interdisciplinary perspectives on international law and international relations. The state of the art
Thies A (2013) International trade disputes and EU liability
Tietje C (2014) The right to development within the international economic legal order. In: Cremona M, Hilpold P, Lavranos N, Schneider SS, Ziegler AR (eds) Reflections on the constitutionalisation of international economic law. Liber Amicorum for Ernst-Ulrich Petersmann
UN High Commissioner for Human Rights (2013) Who will be accountable? Human rights and the post-2015 development agenda
WTO (2013) World Trade Report 2013: factors shaping the future of world trade
WHO, WIPO and WTO on Promoting Access to Medical Technologies and Innovation, 2013
Zürn M, Nollkaemper A, Peerenboom R (eds) (2012) Rule of law dynamics in an era of international and transnational governance

Part III
Transatlantic Trade Relations

The EU/US Transatlantic Relationship: The Indispensable Partnership

Günter Burghardt

Introduction

HGK (as Horst Günter Krenzler used to be referred to in the fashion of Commission in-house acronyms) had been a personal friend and close colleague during our largely parallel careers of almost four decades with the European Commission, and the EU/US transatlantic relationship, from trade to foreign policy, has continuously been at the top end of our respective priorities and agendas.

When I first joined the Commission as a trainee in May 1968, I was assigned to a small desk placed inside HGK's office, which he already shared with two other officials, altogether in charge of implementing the EC's Association Agreements with Greece and Turkey, an administrative unit in the Commission's External Relations Directorate-General, at the historic, however overpopulated, "Avenue de la Joyeuse Entrée", close to the offices President Hallstein had left a year ago. HGK was my early mentor. Our paths crossed again many times from my joining the Commission as a permanent official in 1970 until HGK's retirement in 1996.

When I succeeded HGK as the Commission's Political Director under President Jacques Delors in 1987, he became the Director-General of the DG External Affairs under successively Commissioners Willy De Clercq, Frans Andriessen and Sir Leon Brittan. And when I took charge in 1993, as Director-General for External Political Relations (DG IA), HGK continued at the helm of the traditional external economic and trade relations DG I, from the third Delors Commission (1993/1994) to his retirement in 1996 under the Santer Commission, with DG IA under the responsibility of Commissioner Hans van den Broek and DG I under Sir Leon Brittan. During all those years, we both were part of the Commission President's team for European Council meetings, bilateral summits with third countries,

G. Burghardt (✉)
Vossenlaan 12, 3080 Tervuren, Belgium
e-mail: burghardt-byl@skynet.be

C. Herrmann et al. (eds.), *Trade Policy between Law, Diplomacy and Scholarship*, European Yearbook of International Economic Law,
DOI 10.1007/978-3-319-15690-3_12

including with the US, and multilateral summits, such as the G7/G8. I am grateful for the opportunity to contribute to HGK's legacy with a few thoughts on the transatlantic relationship, the theme of one of our major, if not the most important, common foreign policy endeavours we had the privilege to embark upon side by side. Later on, while I served as the EC's Ambassador to the US from November 1999 till the end of President Bush Junior's first term in December 2004, HGK and his wife Nina were our visitors at the European Commission's Kalorama Residence in Washington DC.

The "Indispensable Partnership"[1]

Any assessment of the European Union's external relations would be incomplete without paying tribute to the vital partnership between the EU and the US, the oldest and strategically most important chapter of the EU's gradually evolving external policies. European integration and the EU/US relationship are like the two sides of one medal: As the late President Walter Hallstein formulated it, "America is a child of Europe",[2] and Einstein stated at Princeton "America and Europe are family". Those "sound bites" not only describe the close historical and cultural roots between the "old" and the "new" world, but the US also stood at the cradle of the very beginnings of Europe's post-World War II unification process. Hallstein was a regular visitor to Washington. His Clayton lectures at the Fletcher School of Law and Diplomacy, and his many speeches, were an early contribution to the understanding by the Washington constituencies of the transformative process in Europe, and his conversations with President Kennedy, in particular in April 1962,[3] had inspired the latter to deliver his visionary speech on 4 July Independence Day in Philadelphia with the twin proposal of a "transatlantic partnership of equals" and a "Declaration of Interdependence" between the "New World" and the "New Europe", should the European Agenda successfully materialise.

Earlier on, Jean Monnet, the first President of the European Coal and Steel Community's (ECSC) High Authority, had closely cooperated with the Truman and Eisenhower Administrations, based on their common experience in Washington during World War II, and benefitted from active US support from his first day in

[1] The term emerged in my conversations with former Secretary of State Albright during my posting in Washington to mirror President Clinton's characterisation of "America, the indispensable nation", and to counter the Bush (Junior) doctrine of unipolarism and US exceptionalism.

[2] Hallstein (1969), p. 238.

[3] Hallstein had met first with President Kennedy at the White House in May 1961. The Commission's Washington Delegation has kept a full documentation of his pronouncements. On November 17, 2001, I directed our Press service to issue a news release on his 100th birthday. John Tuthill, the US Ambassador to the Community from 1962 to 1966 had contributed an article with his personal recollection for our Europe magazine's May–June 1982 edition.

office in August 1952. George Ball, an American lawyer and Undersecretary of State during the Kennedy Administration, had an office at the French *Commissariat au Plan* advising Monnet on the ECSC Treaty negotiations.[4] One of Monnet's immediate aims after taking office was to obtain international recognition of the new Community as an independent player in the world. The US obliged when Secretary Dean Acheson,[5] in the last year of the Truman Administration, on August 11, 1952, the day after Monnet's inaugural ceremony, sent a diplomatic note assuring the ECSC "strong support… The US will now deal with the Community on coal and steel matters." And 3 months later, at the start of the Eisenhower Administration, Secretary Dulles nominated David Bruce[6] as the first US Ambassador to the ECSC[7] and followed up with an official visit to Monnet's Headquarters in Luxemburg on February 8, 1953.[8] Dulles informed Monnet, who was planning an informal trip to Washington that Eisenhower proposed to turn this into an official visit. On 3 June 1953, Monnet was housed like a Head of State at Blair House, the Presidential Guest House, and was welcomed as the representative of the new Europe.[9]

The "Big Picture"

Since those early beginnings the EU–US relationship has remained the most powerful, the most comprehensive and the strategically most important relationship in the world, despite the rise of new power centres on other continents.[10]

Most powerful: The EU and the US combine roughly half of the global GDP, with around 17 trillion USD each. They stand for some 40 % of world trade in goods and even more in services. They hold 80 % of the global capital markets. They are each other's main trading partner and source, as much as recipient, of foreign direct

[4] Ball describes his intimate relationship with Jean Monnet and his involvement "as a private American lawyer" with the Schuman Plan negotiations in his memoirs: *The Past has another Pattern*, 1982, pp. 69–99.

[5] Acheson's memoirs, *Present at the Creation*, 1969, are an invaluable source of information about the US role as a deeply committed "midwife" during the early stages of European integration.

[6] Bruce was a top professional diplomat with a distinguished career, having been posted as Ambassador to Paris, London and Bonn.

[7] Monnet reciprocated by opening a liaison office in Washington in 1954 which over the decades evolved into a fully-fledged EU Commission Delegation with diplomatic status conferred in 1972 by an act of Congress, headed by an Ambassador accredited to the US President since 1990, and formally becoming the EU Delegation as part of the EEAS with the entry into force of the Lisbon Treaty on 1 December 2009.

[8] Duchêne (1994), p. 236.

[9] Duchêne (1994), p. 244.

[10] For a periodic update on economic facts and figures see the annual Survey on the Transatlantic Economy by Daniel Hamilton and Joseph Quinlan from the SAIS Johns Hopkins Center for Transatlantic Relations, Washington DC.

investment. And since the introduction of euro notes and coins on January 1, 2002, the by now 18 member states of the Eurozone with a combined GDP of around USD 13 trillion share the second most important world currency in terms of global foreign reserves, international bond issues and money market demand.[11]

Most comprehensive: There is scarcely an issue that does not involve the transatlantic relationship—from Afghanistan to Ukraine; from WTO to counter-terrorism; from aircraft to data privacy; from bananas to GMOs—the EU and the US are involved bilaterally, regionally or globally.[12]

Strategically most important: Europe matters to America and America matters to Europe because of major converging concerns, largely compatible values and overlapping interests. "When we quarrel we make headlines, when we work together, we make progress."[13]

Trade Policy: An Early Backbone of the Overall EU/US Relationship—From the Torquay to the Kennedy Round

Although the ECSC Treaty had not formally mandated the High Authority to conduct trade negotiations in the areas of its sectoral responsibilities for coal and steel, its successful start and the prospect of wider economic integration among the Six after the failure to ratify the European Defence Community Treaty in the French Assembly on 30 August 1954 created an early dynamic on both sides of the Atlantic to engage in successive rounds of multilateral trade negotiations within the General Agreement on Tariffs and Trade (GATT). For the US, although supportive of the political process in Europe, this was a means to participate in its economic benefits, while Monnet and Hallstein were anxious to mitigate the effects of liberalisation within the Six on the UK, notably after De Gaulle's veto suspending accession negotiations in January 1963.

Until the end of the 1960s, transatlantic trade liberalisation was essentially pursued within the multilateral setting of the General Agreement on Tariffs and Trade. Regular rounds of multilateral negotiations inside GATT mirrored important stages in European economic integration: the 1950 to 1951 Torquay Round coincided with German accession to GATT and the negotiation and ratification of the ECSC Treaty; the 1955 to 1956 Geneva Round was driven by the decision of the Six at the Messina conference to start negotiations leading to the EEC and Euratom

[11] Burghardt (2005), pp. 23 et seq.

[12] During my term in Washington, absent an overall transatlantic treaty relationship, the close to 100 members of our Delegation were involved in the management of about 50 individual agreements of all kind, from trade to competition policies, from product regulatory to standard issues, from research to justice and home affairs.

[13] Secretary of State Colin Powell during the EU/US Ministerial meeting at the Department of State on 18 December 2002.

Treaties; and the 1960 to 1962 Dillon Round accompanied the first stage of the implementation of the customs union within the EEC. Those three rounds centred on important tariff reductions among, at the time, around 40 GATT member states. Immediately after the crisis triggered by De Gaulle's veto against UK membership, Hallstein, in a speech at New York's Columbia University on 8 March 1963, responded to the US Trade Expansion Act with the proposition to reenergise the transatlantic partnership by preparing what later became known as the "Kennedy Round", which lasted from 1964 to 1967 and brought together an enlarged GATT membership of more than 60 countries. The EEC participated as such, and the Commission signed the Final Act on behalf of the Community. In addition to further tariff cuts, negotiations entered into new territory, covering non-tariff barriers and trade in agriculture.

From the 1969 EC Summit in The Hague to "1992": The Completion of the EC's Internal Market

The December 1969 Summit meeting at The Hague marked the successful end of the transitional period under the European Economic Community Treaty with the completion of the EC's Customs Union, reopened the process leading to the January 1973 enlargement from six to nine members, including the UK, Denmark and Ireland and agreed on first steps on cooperation in the area of foreign policy. Thus, Europe "graduated" into a fuller player able to propel the transatlantic partnership into higher orbit in terms of both process and substance, at a time when the relationship had reached a low point because of, *inter alia*, US President Nixon's unilateral decision in August 1971 to end the direct convertibility of the US Dollar to gold, a decision that greatly complicated the on-going preparations of a new multilateral round of trade negotiations. Robert Schaetzel, the retiring US Ambassador to the EC, described the overall situation as "a dialogue of the deaf across the Atlantic".[14]

When, in January 1973, Sir Christopher Soames joined the Ortoli Commission (1973–1977) as Vice President in charge of external relations, his reputation and personal authority provided a further boost to the Community's international role.[15] Relations with the US hugely benefitted from his tenure, bilaterally and globally, on process and on substance.

[14] Fortune Magazine, November 1972, pp. 148–154.

[15] I had moved from the Legal Service to DG I, the External Relations Directorate-General, in 1972, and remember the arrival in 1973 of a first class wave of UK colleagues at all levels, including my new Director Leslie Fielding, under whom I became the desk officer for the US and Canada, and Sir Christopher's team of personal advisors under Chef de Cabinet David Hannay. Edmond Wellenstein, Director-General of DG I, who had started his career as Deputy Secretary-General of the High Authority with Jean Monnet and Max Kohnstamm, was one of the most gifted Commission officials I had the privilege to work under.

Soames from the outset succeeded in increasing the level and substance of regular consultations between the Commission and the US Administration, which had begun in 1970 under the "Dahrendorf/Samuels formula".[16] Under Soames' leadership other Commissioners would accept to join the team, such as Haferkamp (Economy and Finance), Gundelach (Internal Market), Lardinois (Agriculture), Cheysson (Less Developed Countries (LDCs) and Simonet (Energy). The US responded by fielding a team at Undersecretary level of the corresponding government departments, as well as from the White House, such as the Office of the United States Trade Representative (USTR) and the Chairman of the Council of Economic Advisors. As a result, the substance of the "High Level Consultations" as they were henceforth called covered the whole range of policies gradually being implemented at Community level.

Energy was a case in point. Following the first energy crisis in 1973, US Secretary of State Henry Kissinger had invited the Commission, the EC Member States and other industrialised countries at foreign minister level for a 3-day crisis meeting in February 1974 at the State Department, only to become extremely frustrated by quarrels over competences among the Europeans.[17] Similarly, the Nixon/Kissinger "Year of Europe" initiative failed in 1974 because the "Nine" were unable to agree on a joint response within the intergovernmental context of "European Political Cooperation",[18] while the Commission moved on to intensify the dialogue in its areas of community competence.

Concerning trade, Soames reached a crucial agreement with US Treasury Secretary Shultz at the September 1973 GATT conference in Tokyo on the launch of what became known as the Tokyo Round (1973–1979).[19] Bilaterally, disputes on non-tariff barriers,[20] agriculture, the EC's Mediterranean policy and its relations with the African, Caribbean and Pacific Group of States (ACP), as well as the EC regime of generalised preferences were among the recurring agenda items.

---

[16] Ralf Dahrendorf was the member in charge of External Relations and Trade in the Malfatti/Mansholt Commission (helped, incidentally, by Horst Krenzler as his deputy chef de cabinet) and Samuels was the US Undersecretary for Economic Affairs in the Department of State. Meetings took place twice a year, alternatively in Brussels and in Washington.

[17] As the secretary of the Commission delegation to the conference, I witnessed the endless coordination meetings of the "Nine", while Kissinger restlessly waited for an EC common position to emerge in order to resume the plenary session. Cf. Kissinger's detailed account in his memoirs *Years of Upheaval*, 1982, pp. 896–925.

[18] "Europe had responded to the Year of Europe initiative with a procedure in which those who talked with us were not empowered to negotiate while those who could have negotiated with us no longer had the authority to talk." Kissinger, *Years of Upheaval*, 1982, p. 189.

[19] Next to the interaction between monetary and trade policy, protectionism in agricultural policies on both sides of the Atlantic, the role of developing countries, and anti-dumping and subsidy rules had been other key issues on the mandate (called the "Global Undertaking") for the round.

[20] 20 % of EC industrial exports were subject to US quantitative restrictions, as compared with 4 % of EC imports from the US. As another example, my first dossier as a desk officer was to deal with the ban of US exports to the EC of ferrous scrap, a commodity essential to the steel industry.

From 1977 to 1980, Commission President Roy Jenkins continued raising the Commission's external profile, both as a partner in the EC's relationship with the US and globally. Jenkins took office simultaneously with the start of US President Carter's term. Carter sent Vice President Mondale on an early European tour, which Mondale started off with a visit to the Commission in January 1977, and invited Jenkins for a first visit to the White House in April. While the discussions with Mondale in Brussels centred on European fears of US protectionism, which threatened to increase an already sizeable EC trade deficit with the US, Jenkins secured President Carter's commitment for a strong role of the US in the on-going round of multilateral trade negotiations (MTN) in Geneva. Carter was the first US President to visit the Commission Headquarters in Brussels in January 1978. The biannual high-level consultations between the Commission, led by Vice-President Wilhelm Haferkamp, and the US Administration became a regular and broader exercise, and the "Tokyo Round" was successfully concluded in November 1979 with more than 100 countries around the table.[21] As to the Commission's global role, President Jenkins managed to become part of the privileged circle of world leaders, which had started off in Rambouillet in 1975 and became known as the yearly World Economic Summit. He first joined the third such meeting in July 1978 at London, mainly in order to introduce the discussions on the state of play at the MTN.[22] Jenkins had to endure a staunch fight with France's President Giscard d'Estaing to obtain a place at the table for the Commission to represent the European Community at an "Economic" conference.[23] Later on, the Commission became an officially invited full member of the G7, as from the fourth meeting at Bonn in 1979.

The 1981 to 1984 Commission under President Gaston Thorn coincided with the first term of the Reagan Administration. Despite President Reagan's liberal philosophy, US protectionism took the upper hand against the background of a sputtering world economy and growing US trade deficits. US anti-dumping and anti-subsidy action against steel and agricultural imports from the EC and the Russia pipeline dispute are cases in point, and required increased conflict management. In 1981, President Thorn visited Washington and US Secretary of State Haig travelled to Brussels twice in the company of his colleagues from Commerce, Baldridge, Agriculture, Block, and USTR, Brock, for meetings with their Commission counterparts Haferkamp, Davignon and Gundelach (replaced by Dalsager after

---

[21] A great deal of merit at the working level has to be attributed to the team led by Roy Denman, the newly appointed Director-General for External Relations coming from a London Board of Trade background, and his excellent and tireless efforts with Bob Strauss, the US chief negotiator, whom I was able to closely witness as Denman's personal assistant.

[22] Jenkins owed this invitation to President Carter's support. Carter was on the record as considering "US cooperation with the EC as an essential feature in the international effort to strengthen the world economy, to build a more open and orderly trading system, to develop a constructive policy towards meeting the needs of the developing countries and improving stability in other parts of the world." Press memo of the US Mission to the EC, 19 April 1977.

[23] Roy Jenkins discusses the episode in his *European Diary 1977–1981*, 1989, pp. 22, 74–77, 95–100.

Gundelach's passing away in office in 1981). When Secretary Shultz took over from Haig in 1982, he agreed with Thorn to bolster the traditional biannual consultations at sub-cabinet level by adding an annual cabinet level meeting with the Commission at the Berlaymont in December each year to coincide with the NATO ministerial meeting in Brussels. On the foreign policy front, the transatlantic climate deteriorated as a consequence of the June 1980 Venice Declaration of the European Council on the situation in the Middle East ("land for peace"), in addition to policy differences in relations with the Soviet Union. While France resisted regular meetings at ministerial level in the framework of European Political Cooperation (EPC) because of fear of US interference with EPC decision-making, and the Commission, for its part, wanting to avoid duplication of contacts, the European Council agreed in March 1982 to hold regular, at least once during each Presidency, Political Directors Troika (former, present and incoming Council Presidencies) meetings at the level, on the US side, of the Assistant Secretary for Europe at the State Department.[24]

At the end of the Thorn Commission, a host of unfinished transatlantic business remained on the table. Multilaterally, the remainder of the GATT work programme (such as on quantitative restrictions and trade in agriculture) had started to merge into the preparations for a new round of talks. The EC position since the London Economic Summit was to be ready to join in preparatory work, without in principle to be able to agree to the formal launching of such a round, in the absence of agreement of subject matters and without having secured the support of LDCs. More generally, multilateral trade issues were increasingly dealt with in informal meetings of trade ministers in the run-up to the Bonn G7 Summit, as well as within OECD, partly because of certain disillusionment with the operations of the GATT system and the perceived need for further measures to "roll back" protectionism.

Bilateral relations with the US had become an area of intense activity, across the board of a growing number of policies, hand in hand with the process of deepening of the EC's economic union and its enlargement negotiations with Spain and Portugal, after Greece had joined in 1981. The Reagan Administration had become known for "tough noises" on trade policy and major bilateral issues could blow up overnight, such as the unilateral restrictions imposed on EC exports of pipes and tubes and the October 1984 US Trade and Tariff Act, a piece of protectionist legislation by the US Congress. On process, at the end of 1984, the Commission could look back with some satisfaction to having established a pretty efficient crisis management system with the US Administration, hinging principally on the—since 1981 regular—December Ministerial conference between a team of US Ministers led by Secretary Shultz and a corresponding team of Members of the Commission.

[24] It was understood that the Commission participated in the Troika meetings to ensure coordination with Community matters. The Commission representative was the Deputy Secretary-General, also in charge of participating in COREPER (the Council Committee of Member States' Permanent Representatives), having an overall view of Commission activities. Horst Krenzler assumed this role until the summer of 1987.

The transition from the Thorn to the first Delors Commission was marked by two somewhat humoristic anecdotes not entirely uncharacteristic of the general atmosphere of transatlantic relationship as explained above. When Secretary Shultz arrived for his last meeting with the Thorn Commission at the Berlaymont in December 1984 and the two Delegations were seated around the table in the Commission's meeting room on the 13th floor, he pointedly pulled a banana out of his briefcase and laid it squarely on the table in front of him. His gesture was an unusual protest against a recent speech by Roy Denman, the Commission's Ambassador in Washington at the time, and of course a greatly embarrassed participant of the gathering, in which he had compared the US with a "Banana Republic", because of the US protests against preferential imports of bananas into the EU from the associated ACP countries to the detriment of American trading companies. Even more embarrassing was a second incident, when Shultz, after Thorn's opening remarks, asked whether it was true that Jacques Delors, the incoming Commission President, had made a speech in Paris the day before, in which he was quoted by the press to have said that Americans had a revolver in one hand and a bible in the other.[25]

During the decade (1985–1994) of Jacques Delors' Commission Presidency, the European Communities evolved into a fully-fledged European Union with the internal market almost completed; the institutional system reinforced through the Single European Act and the Maastricht Treaty setting up the European Union; Economic and Monetary Union with a common currency, the euro, well on its way; enlargement from 10 to 15 members with a European Economic Area around the EU successfully completed; a pre-accession process with the new democracies in Central and Eastern Europe and the Mediterranean launched and a normalisation with Russia and the former Soviet republics achieved with the help of Gorbachev and Yeltsin. Internationally, the EU/US relationship was the key factor to make all this possible, with 9/11, the fall of the Berlin wall on 9 November 1989, the historic turning point, and the November 1990 Paris Conference, transforming CSCE into OSCE, the symbolic event of the consolidation of the Greater Europe.

1985 was a difficult starting point. Internally, Delors needed to turn europessimism ("I want my money back" policies) into a new dynamism. The way to achieve this was the early announcement, in his programme speech to the European Parliament in January, of the "1992" programme to complete the internal market; the conclusion in March of the enlargement negotiations with Spain and Portugal, which had dragged on for 6 years; and an institutional reform via an Intergovernmental Conference leading to the Single European Act (SEA) launched in June and completed in December. All this went not unnoticed on the other side of the

[25] As I was seated on the chair behind Thorn, which is normally reserved for the Chef de cabinet of the President (I had instead been asked to attend as Delors' incoming deputy chef and diplomatic advisor), Thorn turned around to me and requested that I immediately got in touch with Delors in Paris to verify the accuracy of the press story. I duly left the room and got on the phone. The quote had been correct and I discreetly confirmed with Thorn. To everybody's great relief, the meeting had resumed in the meantime in the usual businesslike mode.

Atlantic, although increasingly virulent protectionist initiatives by the US Congress, partly vetoed by President Reagan, and unilateral trade policy measures enacted by the Administration prompted Commissioner Willy De Clercq to visit with Commerce Secretary Baldridge and USTR Brock in Washington in March.

Delors concluded, although unenthusiastically, that an early visit by himself to the US, including a meeting with President Reagan in the Oval Office, a week before his first G7 Summit in Bonn in early May with the US President and other world leaders in attendance, was an indispensable move to connect his ambitious European with the transatlantic and global agendas.[26] From 23 to 27 April 1985, Delors visited New York, Washington and Northern California. In New York, Delors met with the world of finance and had dinner with George Ball to revisit the past and take advice on how to deal with the present.[27] In California, Delors spent one day in and around Silicon Valley on technology issues (meeting with the CEOs of Hewlett Packard and Intel, and visiting their manufacturing facilities, Stanford University and the Bay Area International Business Forum) and the following day on a whirlwind tour round some of the key sectors of Californian agriculture, such as almonds, citrus, wine and dairy.[28] The Washington leg, however, was to be the crucially important "*plat de résistance*" of the visit with a fully packed 48-hour schedule. Our US interlocutors regarded the visit with a mixture of interest and apprehension. This arose partly from Delors' reputation as a rigorous former French minister of finance,[29] and partly from the above mentioned press reports of remarks he had made in Paris in December 1984 at which Secretary Shultz had taken offence. These fears were effectively laid to rest by the speech Delors gave at the National Press Club, by the reasoned line he took in discussions with the Administration and Congress, and, above all, by the unexpectedly warm atmosphere and friendly exchange at the Oval Office meeting.

[26] Preparation and participation of the visit fell on me as his foreign policy advisor. We opted for a fuller programme, around and, of course, beyond the strategically important meeting at the White House, in order to reach out to main decision-makers and to underline Delors' interest in getting an idea of the other America "beyond the Belt Way". At my modest level, I was looking forward to my first handshake with a US President in the holy grail of the Oval Office (it so happened that I was the official representative of the European Commission at the state act and funeral service for President Reagan at Washington Cathedral on 6 June 2004, in my capacity as the EU Commission's Ambassador in the US). Hundreds of pages of briefing papers from the Commission services and our Washington Delegation, reflecting the density of transatlantic relations and great number of bilateral disputes, had to be condensed into operational speaking notes and well-intended "background" advice on how to handle US interlocutors.

[27] Ball (1982), pp. 69–99.

[28] A gesture much appreciated by both President Reagan and Secretary Shultz given their Californian backgrounds and the pressure on them by their constituencies on the Hill and within a business community heavily dependent on exports to Europe.

[29] In that capacity Delors had, in the company of President Mitterrand, paid host to President Reagan at the June 1984 40th anniversary commemorations of the Allied landing at the beaches of Normandy.

On Tuesday morning, 23 April, President Delors, in the company of Roy Denman, the Commission's Head of Delegation in the US, and me, arrived at the North West Gate of the White House. We were greeted by Secretary Shultz and the Chief of Protocol, Selwa Roosevelt, a granddaughter of the former President. Delors signed the guest book in the Roosevelt room before being escorted to the Oval Office for the joint "public" photo opportunity with Reagan open to the accredited White House press corps, followed by the "private" meeting. Reagan and Delors sat down in the traditional two chairs next to each other in front of the chimney, while Denman and myself, assigned to the sofa on Delors' side, found ourselves outnumbered, on the opposite side, by a long row of Reagan's advisors including Vice President G. H. W. Bush, Secretary Shultz, Chief of Staff Don Regan, US Ambassador to the EC Middendorf, US G7 Sherpa Wallis and a bunch of additional note-takers. While the meeting was slated for 10 min as a largely ceremonial occasion, President Reagan extended it himself to half an hour, waving away anxious aides. Delors thanked for the invitation and welcome and recalled Reagan's visit to Normandy in June 1984 and the latter's deep moral and emotional involvement. Reagan appreciated Delors' good, solid style and his timely visit shortly before the Bonn Economic Summit, which, he hoped, would conclude in favour of new multilateral trade talks to start in 1986. Delors said Europe was back on track and laid out his agenda, the creation of a common market of 320 million consumers, the accession of Spain and Portugal as the consecration of the return of these two countries to democracy, and the expectation of the Milan European Council in June to take decisions leading towards political union. The Bonn Summit should promote trade, financial and monetary matters, without the Commission being able, at this stage, to commit to a date for the opening of a new round. He stressed the need for Japan to open up its market and to internationalise the Yen. Reagan agreed and expected Nakasone, a courageous friend, to show leadership. Delors raised European preoccupations about steel exports to the US. Both Kohl and Mitterrand were likely to raise this issue in Bonn if a solution were not found before. Reagan said he had asked Commerce Secretary Baldridge to "find a solution right now", which in turn triggered an intervention by Don Regan about US preoccupations with the EC's common agricultural policy. Discussions then took a more philosophical tone, with Reagan showing sympathy for Delors' analysis of agriculture in Europe, in particular the survival of small farmers, as a problem of society. To obvious signs of unease on his bench, Reagan concurred that agriculture was not there only "to produce big money". The meeting ended in a relaxed atmosphere and was later described by Shultz at the lunch he offered for Delors at the State Department as "a very good one".

Delors' ensuing presentation, entitled "Europe should not be written off", was well received by a packed National Press Club. At his 3-hour meeting and lunch with Secretary Shultz, he was cross-examined in some detail on his attitude to international monetary reform. He was listened to with increasing respect and was able to dispel US suspicion that his insistence on the interaction between monetary and trade policy was an excuse to delay the trade round. With Baldridge he courteously but firmly declined an—insufficient—offer to settle the steel issue.

On the Hill he met with key members of the Senate Finance Committee and had breakfast with the House Ways and Means Committee. Meetings with Secretary of Agriculture Block and the Federal Reserve Chairman Paul Volcker completed Delors' DC tour. As a particular sign of grace, Secretary Shultz attended the dinner hosted by Denman at the Commission residence. Shultz's habit was not to dine out often, and never before had an acting US Secretary of State attended a dinner at our residence. Shultz and Delors struck up a friendly relationship.

All in all, this "opening set" in support of the EC's transatlantic agenda had been timely and successful, although it would not prevent some US circles suspecting Delors' programme of completing the internal market by 1992 would create "Fortress Europe". More importantly, the visit had inaugurated a climate of confidence and constructive cooperation between Delors and the successive Reagan, Bush and Clinton Presidencies.

The remaining term of the first Delors Commission, coinciding with President Reagan's second term, continued to require constant trade policy crisis management bilaterally, despite the successful opening, on 20 September 1986 at Punta del Este, of what would become known as the "Uruguay Round" of multilateral trade negotiations. Negotiations were to include new subject matters, such as trade in services, intellectual property rights and investment rules, in addition to traditional items. Evolving hand in hand with the ongoing completion of the EC's 1992 internal market programme, the Round would lead to replacing GATT with the World Trade Organisation (WTO) in 1995. Although the negotiating mandate required "standstill" and "roll back" as to bilateral trade restrictions not in conformity with existing GATT rules during the process of the Round, the US side added new transatlantic irritants, such as Airbus and hormones, to the long list of issues under review. The 1988 US "Omnibus Trade and Competitiveness Act" or "Trade Bill" enacted by Congress ultimately provided the US President with formal negotiating authority at the Uruguay Round. In December 1988 at the last of the annual Delors/Shultz ministerial meetings at the Berlaymont, in that configuration, both sides were able to look back at a legacy somewhat suboptimal on results while excellent on personal chemistry.[30]

In addition to the consultations with the Commission becoming more "political", the signature on 28 February 1986 of the Single European Act (SEA) and its entering into force on 1 July 1987 provided an opportunity for a major step in

---

[30] As from December 1986, Delors had introduced the habit of preceding the plenary meeting with restricted bilateral discussions in his office, separately with Secretary Shultz and Treasury Secretary Baker. With Shultz issues discussed included the evolution of East/West relations and the Reagan/Gorbachev summits, as well as relations with Turkey, against the background of traditionally strong US backing for progress in EC/Turkey membership talks. With Baker, Delors exchanged views on the G5 Finance Ministers meetings, from which the Commission was excluded at the time. Shultz used to warmly thank Delors in a personal letter after the meeting, stressing the highly useful exercise notably of the informal part of the discussions "unfortunately complicated by our trade relations". Shultz called the US and the EC the "center of gravity of the Free World".

strengthening the dialogue with the US in the area of European Political Cooperation (EPC).[31] Consistency between the external relations of the Communities and—intergovernmental—EPC policies was to be ensured by the Member State holding the rotating Council Presidency and the Commission. To this effect the Commission was "fully associated with the proceedings of Political Cooperation".[32] This, of course, included the organisation of the transatlantic relationship in all its aspects. During 1986, consultations between US Secretary Shultz and the Netherland's Foreign Minister (and later Commissioner) Hans van den Broek under Dutch Presidency, continued under UK Presidency by Geoffrey Howe, led to agreement reached by EC foreign ministers at their informal meeting at Brockett Hall, with the participation of Jacques Delors, on a set of procedures,[33] later on confirmed by Shultz.

From "Eleven Nine" (November 9, 1989)[34]: "Europe Whole and Free"—To the EC–US Transatlantic Declaration (TAD)

Already during Reagan's second term, Vice President Bush had opened another channel of communication when he called on President Delors on 27 June 1985. With policy developments in the Soviet Union and the countries in Central and Eastern Europe gaining traction, the Vice President used to stop over in Brussels for meetings with NATO Secretary General Lord Carrington and Delors to discuss his visits to EC Member States and Eastern capitals, such as Warsaw and Moscow. These informal encounters would prove particularly valuable during Bush's own Presidency (1989–1992), coinciding with the second Delors Commission, when a new chapter in the transatlantic relationship started around the fall of the Berlin wall on 9 November 1989.

[31] Art. 30 SEA for the first time institutionalised EPC within a single treaty, alongside the provisions that were needed in order to strengthen the legal base relating to Community competences for completing internal market legislation.

[32] Art. 30(3)(c) SEA.

[33] Semiannual visits to the US by the foreign minister holding the Council Presidency; meetings of the Political Director Troika with the Assistant Secretary for Europe at the State Department; and regular contacts between the diplomatic missions of the "Twelve" and the US Administration in Washington; with Commission participation at all levels. Political Director Troika meetings had occasionally already been held in Washington since 1983 with Assistant Secretary Burt and Ridgeway. Foreign minister level meetings had started to take place in the margins of the September UNGA sessions in New York.

[34] A term I suggested during my time in Washington, as it conveniently contrasted with what became known as "Nine Eleven", 11 September 2001, the terrorist attacks on New York and Washington. While "Eleven Nine" was the symbolic event leading to the most productive phase of transatlantic interaction under the "first Bush" or "Bush 41", "Eleven Nine" and its aftermath symbolise the most divisive period of the "Second Bush" or "Bush 43", the 43rd President of the United States.

President Bush made the opening set in his speech at Boston University on 21 May 1989, with French President Mitterrand at his side, who was on a state visit to the US.[35]

On 30 May, Bush and Secretary Baker travelled to Brussels for meetings with NATO and the Commission (Delors/Andriessen). Upon his invitation, Delors responded with a visit to the White House for lunch with Bush, meetings with Baker and the House and Senate leaderships on 14 June 1989.[36] Only 4 weeks later, Bush and Delors met again with the other G7 leaders at the July "*Sommet de l'Arche*" in Paris, coinciding with the bicentenary of the French revolution. On his way to Paris, Bush had visited Warsaw and Budapest to arrive at the G7 dinner with a heightened sense of urgency concerning necessary support for what would be called later the "new democracies" of Central and Eastern Europe. Bush joined forces with Chancellor Kohl of Germany and Canadian Prime Minister Mulroney to convince a reluctant Mitterrand and a more than sceptical UK Prime Minister Thatcher that, in the absence of any other suitable body, the European Commission should be tasked with the coordination of a massive financial assistance programme. In a way, the subsequent EU pre-accession and later accession process leading to the EU's May 2004 eastern enlargement had its early roots at the memorable G7 dinner on 14 July 1989 at the Hotel de la Marine overlooking Place de la Concorde, surrounded by the gorgeous festivities so ably orchestrated by Mitterrand's Sherpa Jacques Attali.[37]

So, the ingredients of the menu were on the table when the political earthquake in Europe, the fall of the Berlin wall, accelerated the process and prompted action on improving the institutional mechanisms of transatlantic consultation and cooperation. What was remarkable was the deep familiarity, knowledge about and

[35] "A New Century holds the promise of a united Europe...already moving toward greater economic integration, with the ambitious goal of a single European market in 1992...There has been an historical ambivalence on the part of some Americans toward a more united Europe...This Administration is of one mind. We believe a strong, united Europe means a strong America... The United States welcomes the emergence of Europe as a partner in world leadership. We are ready to develop with the European Community and its member states new mechanisms of consultation and cooperation on political and global issues...to putting an end to the division of Europe."

[36] Bush and Baker had fielded a strong team to proceed with putting ambitions into practice, including with respect to the ever longer "laundry list" of trade and other economic issues. On the US side the co-leaders were Under Secretary for Economic Affairs Robert Zoellick, Commission Director-General Krenzler's opposite number, while Robert Kimmit, Under Secretary for Political Affairs, who had already worked with Baker at the Treasury, was my Political Director counterpart. The EC Troika met twice with the US in 1989, under Spanish and under French Presidency, with a broad foreign and security policy agenda. The Washington October 25/26 session of the Political Directors Troika was presided over on the US side, for the first time, at Under Secretary level by Bob Kimmit who brought in a number of Assistant Secretaries in charge of key dossiers, and added meetings with key members of the House and the Senate, as well as with the Pentagon.

[37] Delors' Sherpa Pascal Lamy and I missed part of the fun exchanging little notes with Delors at the dinner table next door and having to explain to an understandably worried Frans Andriessen that new tasks had just been put on his shoulders for which resources had yet to be found.

appreciation by the US leadership of the role assumed by Europe's institutions, including the Commission, in those historic moments.

On 4 December 1989, President Bush stopped over in Brussels on his way back to Washington from a key bilateral summit with President Gorbachev in Malta to debrief NATO partners at an impromptu summit meeting. In a remarkable gesture, Bush had asked for an informal meeting with Delors before the NATO meeting. That meeting took place in the early morning in Stuivenberg Castle at the northern periphery of Brussels. Bush was accompanied by Baker, US Ambassador to the EU Niles, Chief of staff Sununu and National Security Advisor Scowcroft. Vice-President Andriessen, the two chef de cabinets Lamy and Wijnmalen, HGK and I assisted on Delors' side. The meeting lasted for over an hour and confidentiality had been agreed on both sides. Reviewing my four pages of notes taken from the discussion, I can report, however, President Bush's worries about what he had heard from Gorbachev about the depressing state of the Soviet economy. The US and Europe needed to encourage every action by the Soviet Union which would move the latter closer to market economy, including by offering observer status with GATT and considering granting MFN status. Andriessen described the agreement reached between the EC and the USSR. The EC was ready to open its market, but there was a problem of Soviet Union competitiveness. When Delors asked whether Gorbachev had again referred to his "Common European House" concept, Bush replied that Gorbachev had maintained his defensive attitude stating that "walls must not be moved", which had to be understood as a substitute for warning against unwelcome dynamics, in particular in the direction of the Baltic States, while on the issue of the inner-German border he had restated that "history will judge what happens". Bush expressed hope that European integration would not slow down after the events in Berlin. Baker asked whether the Commission detected any change in German resolve to move fully towards European unity. Delors replied that if Chancellor Kohl would not agree to Economic and Monetary Union (EMU) at the forthcoming December European Council meeting in Strasburg, this would indeed be a very bad sign. It was agreed to go into more detail at the annual Commission meeting with Baker on 15 December right after the Strasburg European Council.

At the end of that same day, Delors received a handwritten letter by Bush with the US President's speaking notes for his afternoon intervention at the NATO Summit attached. In his remarks "on the Future of Europe", Bush had set out the architecture of what henceforth became known as his "Europe Whole and Free" concept, based on four principles, three organisations and two processes, to allow for German unification and the consolidation of the Greater Europe, with strong US involvement at all levels. The four principles were the right for self-determination; respect for existing borders, subject to freely and voluntarily agreed changes; German unification within the context of European integration and of the NATO Alliance; and a massive coordinated effort of economic and financial support for the new democracies in Central and Eastern Europe. Three organisations and two processes were key to frame the collective effort: the European Community reinforced through a process of increased integration, together with its role, as agreed at the Paris G7 meeting, to coordinate economic assistance for the new democracies within a G24 group of donor countries; NATO, to be tasked with "New Missions" to promote greater freedom in the East; the Commission on Security and Cooperation in Europe (CSCE) to play a greater role in the future of Europe with its political and economic "baskets", supporting human rights, free elections, allowing the reconciliation of the two principles of self-determination and the respect of borders, and helping the Soviet Union to develop its economy.

It fell on Secretary Baker to publicly present this comprehensive concept, capturing what amounted to a peaceful revolutionary momentum in Europe's post-World War II history, in his memorable speech in Berlin, on 12 December.[38] Again, the US–EC interaction was presented as a key element in the new architecture.[39]

Against this background, the Brussels EC/US ministerial meeting on 15 December 1989, in addition to its traditional trade and economic agenda items, responded to the foregoing events with new ideas on the organisational aspects of transatlantic interaction. Secretary Baker delivered prepared remarks following up on President Bush's pronouncements less than a fortnight ago, and the meeting concluded, unusually, with a "Joint Declaration". Baker, again, stressed the vital role the EC has to play in an era of extraordinary times for Europe. He quoted US statements in support of European integration from Bush back to Eisenhower. This process must go on economically, to keep the Uruguay Round moving forward, with combined EC and US leadership, and politically, in shaping, together, the transformations in Eastern Europe. Baker went on with a long paragraph on the future organisation of EC/US consultations: "Because we are firmly convinced that the EC will provide a cornerstone for the New Europe, we think it is sensible to explore a closer US-EC linkage." This linkage should combine "the rich network of ties with the nations of the Community" with "working more closely with the Community institutions the Twelve create." Baker went on to say that he did not have "a preconceived model of transatlantic cooperation with the EC". Both sides should "begin a dialogue" with the aim to bring together exchanges on foreign policy within EPC with the broad range of our economic relationship "in parallel with Europe's efforts to achieve a common internal market by 1992". He was anxious not to be seen interfering with the EC's own institutional evolution and ended with Bush's *leitmotiv*: "By working more closely together, the US and the EC

---

[38] Baker (1989).

[39] "As Europe moves toward its goal of a common internal market, and as its institutions for political and security cooperation evolve, the link between the US and the EC will become even more important. We want our transatlantic cooperation to keep pace with European integration and with institutional reform. To this end, we propose that the US and the EC work together to achieve, whether in treaty or some other form, a significantly strengthened set of institutional and consultative links. . . ."

can contribute to the architecture of a New Europe, a Europe whole and free." The Joint Declaration captured the gist of this statement.[40]

Early in 1990, the Commission embarked on a thorough stocktaking on both the substance and the options for procedural arrangements to strengthen the EC/US dialogue in response to the changing environment.[41] While the US were perfectly able to interact with the Europeans in NATO and the CSCE,[42] it was well understood that the US were looking for ways to keep track with the fast-evolving EC agenda,[43] and that this was a legitimate objective to be accommodated in the interest of both sides. On the European side, the problem was to accommodate the evolving nature of the integration process, which seemed to argue against rigid transatlantic treaty commitments. On substance, issues of community competence, from trade to common economic policies, were well dealt with by the Commission at ministerial level, extended in 1990 to two sessions, in February in Washington, and in December in Brussels, as well as by individual Commissioners with their US counterparts.[44] However, the US was aiming to move towards dialogue with a single European partner, presenting the EC and its Member States, the "Twelve", with the problem of "globalising" matters of community and intergovernmental nature, and drawing into the exercise, as a more permanent feature, the Presidency of the EC Council. At the occasion of a visit to the White House on 27 February 1990 of Irish Prime Minister Haughey, under Irish Council Presidency, President Bush understandably took the view that modalities on the European side were for the Europeans to decide. After a meeting between Presidents Bush and Delors at the White House on 24 April 1990, a first set of arrangements took shape with

[40] "The Commission of the European Communities and the United States consider it opportune, at this juncture, to reaffirm the importance they attach to EC-US relations and to declare their intent to strengthen further their relationship... Representatives of the EC Commission and the United States will meet early in 1990 to examine ways of strengthening coordination in the growing number of areas of common interest. Our goal is to assure the continued vitality of transatlantic ties at a time of accelerating European integration."

[41] This exercise took place under the authority of President Delors and Commissioner Andriessen, with, at service level, HGK in the lead on community and me on EPC matters.

[42] In the CSCE framework, transatlantic coordination took place in NATO format on security and human rights issues. This had, however, proved increasingly inadequate with the CSCE's second, the economic, basket.

[43] This had, to some degree, already been the case with the aborted 1973 "Year of Europe" initiative, at the time perceived by some EC Member States as Kissinger's attempt to "gate crash" the EC through obtaining a place at the EC table. The Nine, therefore, had replied with a "European identity" statement, adopted at their Summit meeting on 14 December 1973 at Copenhagen, insisting on the EC as "*une identité distincte et originale*". US participation in the Community's own decision making would remain an unacceptable proposition.

[44] As of July 1990, the list of current and potential EC–US agreements and contacts had reached an impressive number of around 60, in areas such as agriculture and fisheries, science and technology, the environment, transport, telecommunications and competition policies. While agreements on individual trade items and on standards and certification issues were at the centre of Commission competence, some of the new areas reached into a "grey zone" of mixed responsibility with Member States.

agreement on combined Presidency of the European Council/ President of the Commission/ President of the United States meetings once every semester, to start under the incoming Italian Presidency[45]; an additional meeting each year between the US Secretary of State, the twelve foreign ministers and the Commission[46]; and increased EPC contacts in Troika format at working level. Furthermore, the June 1990 Dublin European Council agreed in principle that EC/US cooperation "could take the form of a joint transatlantic declaration".

Negotiations on the Transatlantic Declaration on EC–US Relations (TAD)[47] were conducted during the second half of 1990[48] and the text was agreed on November 23, 1990 in the margins of the CSCE Summit at the Centre Kléber in Paris, after final drafting sessions in the margins of the conference between EC Political Directors and US Deputy Secretary Zoellick. It saw the light at a place and at a moment coinciding with the signing of the "Charter of Paris for a New Europe",[49] which transformed CSCE, a "Conference" into OSCE, an "Organisation", thus reinforcing another pillar of the Bush "Europe whole and free" concept. The TAD, in its introductory preamble, puts the "Year of Europe" squabbles behind it by stressing a "partnership on an equal footing" and noting the EC's "own identity". There follow chapters on "Common Goals", on "Principles of US-EC Partnership", on broad areas of "Cooperation", from economic to cultural policies, and on "Trans-national Challenges". While security issues, such as the fight against terrorism and the proliferation of weapons of mass destruction were covered, military security was excluded at the explicit request of the US. Although the US had actively supported the European Defence Community Treaty in the early 1950s, their position henceforth was that issues of military security were matters to be discussed in NATO. This was perfectly in line with Art. 30 paragraph 6 of the Single European Act (SEA), which limited cooperation among the Twelve to "political and economic aspects of security". However, the Europeans were only

[45] The first meeting in this format took place on 13 November 1990 in Washington between President Bush, the PM of Italy Andreotti and Commission President Delors.

[46] The meeting was additional to the annual dinner, since September 1987, with the US Secretary of State in the margins of the September UN General Assembly in New York. The new format was practised for the first time on 3 May 1990 after a NATO ministerial meeting in Brussels.

[47] Available at http://eeas.europa.eu/us/docs/trans_declaration_90_en.pdf.

[48] Contacts to that effect were pursued, among others, in the margins of the G7 Summit in Houston, Texas, from 9 to 11 July 1990. As Houston was President Bush's hometown, he did not spare any efforts to display typical local Texan habits like horseshoe throwing, and to create a particularly warm and informal atmosphere for the talks at Rice University. Moreover, the EC-led G24 assistance programme could show an excellent start: since the Paris G7 Summit a year ago, a total of close to 25 billion ECU in grants and loans had been collected, of which 78 % by the EC and its member states, and 7 % by the US, a "burden-sharing" more than favorable for the Europeans.

[49] The Charta was signed by 34 Heads of State or Government, including Chancellor Kohl for the freshly united Germany, as well as on behalf of the EC by Commission President Jacques Delors and the Italian Foreign Minister Dini in charge of the Council Presidency, available at http://www.osce.org/mc/39516?download=true.

a month away from the opening of an intergovernmental conference (IGC) to negotiate a political union treaty next to the IGC on Economic and Monetary Union.[50] Political union was intended to include an element of common defence through the Western European Union (WEU). The US position risked therefore to be out-dated because of the process of European integration moving forward. Had TAD acquired "treaty" quality, instead of a "declaration", the EC's future margin of manoeuvre might have been even more limited.[51] Finally, the "Institutional Framework for Consultation" at the end of the TAD text codified the procedural arrangements agreed earlier on, namely biannual consultations at the level of the three presidents (US, EC Council Presidency and European Commission) as well as of foreign ministers (12+1+1), while adding another element of flexibility at foreign minister level by including meetings between the US Secretary of State and the EC Foreign Ministers Troika. Biannual consultations between the EC Commission and the US government at cabinet level were maintained. The already existing contacts between the European Parliament and the US Congress were encouraged. An evolutionary clause was included to allow future institutional developments to be duly reflected.[52]

EC/US dialogue during 1991 and 1992, the first years under the TAD, took place against the background of the EC's internal treaty negotiations on EMU and political union, concluded at the European Council meeting on 10 December and signed on 7 February 1992 in Maastricht. On the international front, the US and the EC stood firmly together in the first Gulf War and its aftermath, contrary to deep disagreements in relation to the second war against Iraq under Bush "43". The TAD's institutional arrangements were used intensely, with additional ad-hoc meetings in various formats.

Three summit meetings took place in 1991: PM Santer of Luxemburg and President Delors with President Bush on 4 April in Washington; Dutch PM Lubbers and Delors, joined by Foreign Minister van den Broek and Commissioner Andriessen with Bush and Baker in the margins of the G7 Summit in London on 16 July; and the Lubbers/Delors/Bush Summit on 9 November in The Hague. At foreign minister level, international crisis management required utmost flexibility

---

[50] Both conferences were opened immediately after the European Council meeting in Rome, on 14–15 December 1990.

[51] A particularly undiplomatic expression of the US position was the Dobbins/Bartholomew memorandum in the spring of 1991, addressed to the EU Member States members of NATO, assembled at the IGC negotiations presided over by the Netherland's Foreign Minister (and later European Commissioner), Hans van den Broek, at Noordwijk. That demarche was a robust outside interference with the aim of hardening the stand of those Member States who already took minimalist positions towards the Common Security and Defence provisions of the Maastricht Treaty.

[52] It is interesting to note that this first ever codified institutional framework of the TAD has broadly survived over the many years, while, on substance, a long list of transatlantic initiatives has gradually emerged through the sequence of EU presidencies and Commission as well as US initiatives leading up to today's Transatlantic Trade and Investment Partnership (TTIP) negotiations, which formally started in the Summer of 2013.

and produced about ten meetings by Baker with either the EC Troika, including Commissioner Andriessen, or, in a smaller setting, with successively the Luxemburg and then Netherlands Presidency Foreign Ministers Poos and van den Broek, together with Andriessen, in Washington, Luxemburg, The Hague and Geneva; and the 12+1+1 dinner in the margins of UNGA in New York. There was considerable travel across the Atlantic in both directions by individual members of the Commission and US cabinet ministers, as well as by members of the European Parliament and the US Congress.

In 1992, under Portuguese and UK Council presidencies, the frequency of meetings continued according to the TAD schedule, including Summits between Bush, PM Cavaco Silva and Delors on 22 April in Washington, and on 18 December with UK PM Major as the host. Dialogue on Community matters was supported by sub-cabinet level meetings under the leadership, on the European side, by the Commission's Director-General for External Relations and, on foreign policy matters, by the Political Directors' Troika, with the participation of the Commission's Political Director, and at the level of an increasing number of EPC working groups, including, as the newest addition, on justice and home affairs. A central agenda item at the December Delors/Baker ministerial meeting, to which Baker arrived on his return from Moscow, was EC/US coordination of support to the Commonwealth of Independent States (CIS), the independent successor states of the former Soviet Union, as well as the organisation of delivery of food aid, including to the cities of Moscow and St. Petersburg.

From TAD to NTA, the New Transatlantic Agenda of 1995

The—unexpected and abrupt—end of the Bush Administration after the victory of Bill Clinton at the November 1992 US presidential elections, a young and fairly unknown former Governor of Arkansas, confronted the Europeans with a changing America after 12 years of Republican administrations. President Clinton had made it clear that the key to his foreign and security policy was a strong domestic economy. He had secured election on a platform of change and renewal. This raised questions about what this meant in terms of US priorities in economic and foreign policies, against the background, it had to be admitted, of a mixed record on the European side as well. While the EC had largely achieved its 1992 programme of completing the internal market, signed, on 2 May 1992, a European Economic Area Agreement with EFTA countries and entered into a first generation of Europe Agreements with Central and Eastern European countries, the ratification of the Maastricht Treaty (MT) had been slowed down considerably by the negative result of the first Danish referendum on 2 June 1992. After the close outcome of a referendum in France on 20 September and an agreement on modified conditions for Denmark at the European Council meeting on 12 December 1992, a second referendum was held with a positive result on 18 May 1993. This removed the obstacle for a late ratification in the UK and the MT finally entered into force on

1 November 1993, to allow for introducing the new mechanisms of the EU's Common Foreign and Security Policy (CFSP).

Another "hangover" was the protracted Uruguay Round multilateral trade negotiations. Roughly 2 months before the early November US presidential elections, Delors had received a personal telegram from President Bush, dated 7 September 1992. Bush expressed understanding that Delors could not push the negotiations at "this delicate moment", ahead of the French referendum on the MT Treaty. "My thoughts are with you at this important time." He added, however, that the Administration stood ready for early resumption thereafter "leading to a rapid breakthrough and conclusion of the Round this year". Somehow anticipating defeat, the message expresses Bush's political credo: "I believe strongly in the process of European integration. European unity is good for Europe, good for the United States and good for the Atlantic Community. This is a conviction shared by American Administrations since the Second World War, and I believe it will remain a tenet of American foreign policy." As far as Clinton was concerned, his focus on the economy was a good omen for general support of the Uruguay Round, and for a fresh attempt to get bilateral trade policy conflicts under control.

In January 1993, Delors started his third term as Commission President, this time for a limited period of 2 years, in order for him to preside over the running in of the Maastricht Treaty and to allow his successor to start the first 5-yearly mandate of the Commission under the new institutional arrangements of the MT in January 1995, to coincide with the electoral cycle of the European Parliament, due for renewal in the summer of 1994. Because of his relatively short time in office, Delors set out for an early fact-finding tour to Washington from 17 to 19 March 1993. His visit with President Clinton and Vice President Gore in the White House on 18 March, literally marching over the boxes still unpacked, produced a remarkably spontaneous meeting of minds. Both, Clinton and Gore, laid out a programme of the largest social and economic reforms ever established in the US, and they shared with Delors a vivid interest in global issues. Clinton was aware of the US economy's increasing dependency, after the relative self-sufficiency of the past, and of the transatlantic marketplace representing the lion's share of the global economy. The financing of his domestic program presupposed a high degree of burden sharing, notably with Europe, to manage the international agenda. Clinton, much like Delors, was a son of the lower class and had succeeded through his own determination. He was more concerned with content than with the status symbols coming with his office. He agreed with Delors on the imperative to coordinate the US and the EC growth initiatives, including macroeconomic and monetary policies, bilaterally and with Japan in the G7 process. Concerning foreign policy, Clinton had chosen mature and experienced advisors,[53] many from the Carter Administration.

[53] In choosing Warren Christopher (67) as Secretary of State, Clinton had chosen experience over flair, openly displaying dislike for large meetings, such as the 12+1+1 EU/US foreign ministers formula of the TAD. His deputy, Clifton Wharton (66), was a prominent Afro-American with a development policy background. Russian-speaking Madeleine Albright's post as Ambassador to the UN carried cabinet status.

As to Clinton's foreign policy priorities, Delors had been well-briefed with respect to initial US misgivings with the EC.[54] The Administration was ready for shared leadership with the EC, including the envisaged WEU/EU caucus on security under the MT, provided that immovable positions would not be taken by the EC "before full consultation" with the US had taken place. The EC crisis management in the former Yugoslavia was judged highly inefficient because of disunity among EC Member States about how to deal with Serb heavy weapons, while maintaining an arms embargo against all parties. There was fierce criticism with the announcement on 2 February of the EC's support for the Vance/Owen plan without prior consultation of the US. The same had been true with the EC's recognition of Croat and Slovenian independence. On this and other policy issues, Political Directors were tasked to prepare for the next EC/US Summit meeting with Danish PM Nyrup Rasmussen and Delors on 7 May 1993 in Washington.[55] Interestingly, Delors introduced a public speech in Washington right after the visit in the White House as follows:

> President Clinton called for leadership as a new global economy unfolds before our eyes. He invited us to face this new challenge and to respond to it in a positive way. The wind of change, fuelled by an enthusiastic and dynamic young President of the United States is now crossing the Atlantic. I am convinced that it will add a new dimension to transatlantic relations.

Meanwhile in Brussels, the General Affairs Council of 8 March 1993, had decided that part of the foreign ministers informal ("Gymnich" style) meeting on 24/25 April at the Hindsgavl Castle in Denmark would deal with relations with the US. Ministers should focus on content, as the TAD did not need to be revisited on mechanics. Political Directors were invited to contribute. The Commission saw this as a welcome opportunity for another systematic stocktaking, and submitted a comprehensive policy paper to the Council.[56] The communication updated facts and figures with respect to transatlantic economic interdependence and burden-sharing, two of the priority themes of the Clinton Administration. It covered at great length the mixed record in the area of bilateral trade,[57] with the US legal system

---

[54] Delors had dispatched me ahead of the Oval Office meeting to take soundings on 17 March with Peter Tarnoff, the Under Secretary for Political Affairs and my Political Director counterpart in the State Department, and his team, as well as with Jenone Walker and Tony Wayne at the National Security Council (NSC).

[55] Clinton sent Delors an elaborate "thank you" letter on 24 April, also to report about his summit with Russian President Yeltsin and his subsequent talks with Japan's PM Miyazawa on burden-sharing regarding financial help for Russia ahead of the June G7 meeting in Tokyo.

[56] Communication on Relations between the Community and the United States, SEC(93) 538 final of 6 April 1993. The document was prepared under the joint authority of Sir Leon Brittan, in the third Delors Commission in charge of "External economic affairs and trade policy" (with DG I under HGK), and Commissioner Hans van den Broek, in charge of "External relations and enlargement" (with DG IA under myself in the process to being set up to support the Commission's role under the MT).

[57] "While the vast majority of EC-US bilateral trade flows is largely trouble free, EC-US relations are still adversely affected by some profound divergences of view and a number of serious bilateral trade conflicts in areas such as steel, telecommunications and Government Procurement".

giving domestic legislation, such as the Trade Act of 1988, primacy over international trade law. It requested the US to refrain from such unilateral action and to adhere to internationally agreed dispute settlement procedures. It lauded the quality of bilateral dialogue, having led to cooperative solutions such as on Airbus, and to a breakthrough on agriculture, and to the signature of new agreements such as on competition policy, energy and financial services. It called for an early warning system, in order to detect and to resolve trade issues before they would develop into political problems. It stated that wide gaps remained in the Uruguay Round negotiations and it ended with a long "to do list".

Against the background of the informal discussions of EU foreign ministers at Hindsgavl Castle, the PM of Denmark, Rasmussen, and President Delors agreed with US President Clinton at a Summit in Washington on 7 May 1993 to revisit the substantive part of the TAD with a view of adapting its content to the changed circumstances. Joint work was set in motion under the watch of foreign ministers during the remainder of 1993 by the Danish and Belgian presidencies, together with Commissioner van den Broek, in the course of four meetings with Secretary Christopher, as well as by Commissioner Brittan in numerous encounters with USTR Mickey Kantor. While the latter had their hands full with the management of a long list of bilateral trade policy issues, including the negotiation of a memorandum on public procurement, as well as with bringing the Uruguay Round to a conclusion,[58] foreign policy priorities focussed on the ongoing war in the former Yugoslavia, economic support for Russia and the other members of the CIS, and the Middle East peace process. Furthermore, a first set of "joint actions" and "common positions" on a variety of international issues were agreed by the EU Council at the end of 1993 under Art. J of the MT,[59] with the effect of considerably enlarging the scope of transatlantic consultations at the level of Political Directors and of EPC working groups.

1994, the last year of the Delors decennium, and 1995, the first year of the Santer Commission, were marked by intense work on the New Transatlantic Agenda (NTA), formally agreed at an EU/US Summit meeting in Madrid, on 3 December 1995.

The state of play was reviewed at the two summits in 1994: on 11 January, with President Clinton, the PM of Greece, Papandreou, and Delors; and on 12 June in Berlin, with Chancellor Kohl and Delors on the EU side. President Clinton made four trips to Europe during this year, and supported the effort in key addresses at Brussels' Hotel de Ville on 9 January[60] and at the French Assembly in Paris on

[58] The Final Act was signed in Marrakesh (Morocco) on 15 April 1994. The World Trade Organization (WTO), successor to GATT, started operations on 1 January 1995.

[59] Art. J establishing CFSP and, in particular, Art. J.3 TEU the notion of joint actions.

[60] "My Administration supports European Union, and Europe's development of stronger institutions ... The fall of the Soviet empire and Western Europe's integration are the two greatest advances for peace in the last half of the 20th century."

9 June.[61] Richard Holbrooke, the then Assistant Secretary of State for European Affairs, our US counterpart in Political Directors' Troika meetings and architect of the 1995 Bosnia Peace Accord negotiated at a US Air force base in Dayton, Ohio, underpinned Clinton's concept with a thorough article in the March/April edition of Foreign Affairs.[62]

At the start of the Santer Commission in 1995, the arrangements at working level referred to above continued, with the difference that Santer had allocated foreign relations portfolios among four commissioners, with each being in charge of a mix of geographic and thematic responsibilities.[63] On the US side, continuity of work had been assured with the appointment by President Clinton, as from early 1993, of Stu Eizenstat, the US Ambassador to the EU, as the point person in charge of coordinating US input out of Brussels into NTA discussions.[64] However, reflections were still in flux as to the format of a new transatlantic agreement at the time of the EU/US Summit on 15 June in Washington between Presidents Clinton, Chirac and Santer. President Santer articulated this in a public speech at the Willard Hotel ahead of the White House meeting.[65] As a consequence, the summit participants agreed on the need to set up a "Senior Level Group (SLG)" with the task to sort out bits and pieces and to come up with a coherent proposal. The SLG convened for a first meeting in Washington on 24 July hosted by Under Secretary Tarnoff at the Department of State, and preceded, on the same day and place, by a foreign ministers meeting. While Vice-President Brittan participated at the ministerial level for the Commission, Director-General Krenzler led the Commission team at the SLG. The Commission went into both meetings well prepared on substance. Immediately after the 15 June EU/US Summit, the Commission had agreed on a comprehensive policy paper in the form of a communication to the Council entitled

---

[61] "We want Europe to be strong. That is why America supports Europe's own steps toward greater unity – the European Union, the WEU, and the development of a greater European defense identity. We now must pursue a shared strategy that depends upon integrating the entire continent through three sets of bonds, security cooperation, market economics and democracy."

[62] Holbrooke (1995), p. 38.

[63] Van den Broek: Foreign Policy (EPC) and Europe; Brittan: Trade and North America; Marin: Mediterranean Policy, Latin America and the Middle East; Matutes: ACP and development policies. DG I under Brittan and DG IA under van den Broek remained in charge of together coordinating the transatlantic relationship under all aspects.

[64] Eizenstat was a former key member of the Carter White House staff. After his stint in Brussels from 1993 to 1996, he occupied senior positions at Commerce and Treasury in DC. I remember his first call on me in early 1993, after his introductory visits with Commissioners van den Broek and Brittan. He looked at me and said: "You have been longer in this business than me. Can you tell me what we can do better?" A hard worker, he took careful notes and went into great detail. We share sincere friendship ever since.

[65] "You are all aware of the increasingly active debate that has started on both sides of the Atlantic on whether we should aim for a more formalized relationship in the future to replace the Transatlantic Declaration. Various options are being looked at – an 'economic cooperation agreement', an 'economic space arrangement', a TAFTA, Transatlantic Free Trade area, an EU-NAFTA Agreement or a fully fledged Transatlantic Treaty taking political and security matters on board." (Sic.)

"Europe and the US: The Way Forward".[66] The paper included an inventory of "components of a new relationship" covering security, foreign policy, economic and trade, as well as various stakeholder dialogues. Ambassador Eizenstat, who participated in both the ministerial level and the SLG meetings on the US side, introduced a similar range of areas and underlined the importance of moving from consultation to common action. Ministers agreed with this *leitmotiv* and charged the SLG to proceed on this basis. The SLG met again in September in Washington and in October in Madrid and agreed on a draft political statement entitled "The New Transatlantic Agenda", accompanied by an EU/US "Action Plan". Both documents were agreed at the EU/US Summit in Madrid on 3 December, ahead of the Madrid European Council meeting.

The coincidence of a landmark agreement in transatlantic relations with the EU's Madrid European Council meeting on 15 and 16 December 1995 was yet another illustration of both processes moving forward hand in hand and providing mutually reinforcing momentum. The EU had embarked on a new phase in its widening and deepening processes. Austria, Finland and Sweden had just joined to bring the EU's membership from 12 to 15 and agreement had been reached on a timetable for the start of accession negotiations with the new democracies in Central and Eastern Europe, as well as with Cyprus and Malta. The EU had embarked on a far-reaching road map entitled "Agenda 2000", including an agreement to enter the third and final phase of Economic and Monetary Union with the introduction of the single currency, the euro, on 1 January 1999[67]; to revisit major common policies, such as agriculture and structural reforms, in prolongation of the successful completion of Delors' Internal Market agenda; and on the EU's multiannual budgetary framework for 2000–2006.

Against this background the NTA's objective was, in the logic of the TAD's evolutionary clause, to move from consultation to common action, including "all aspects" of security and defence policies, for which the MT, in Art. J.4, provided the legal base on the EU side. Until today, the NTA constitutes the most elaborate and comprehensive constitutional basis for the EU/US transatlantic relationship. On procedure, it has left in place the organisational framework of the TAD, with the understanding that levels and periodicity of meetings must be result-oriented and handled flexibly. The one addition was to maintain the SLG,[68] which had so successfully supported the NTA negotiating process. Henceforth the Senior Level Group would meet regularly, twice a year, at the under secretaries of state for political and for economic affairs level on the US side, and the two Commission

[66] Commission of the European Communities, Communication COM(95) 411 final of 26 July 1995.

[67] During my term in Washington, we celebrated with our American friends the introduction of euro notes and coins at a New Year's party in our Delegation on 31 December 2001, as well as on Schuman Day, 9 May 2002, at the premises of the Federal Reserve upon invitation by Chairman Greenspan.

[68] "We have entrusted the Senior Level Group to oversee work on this Agenda and particularly the priority actions we have identified." The New Transatlantic Agenda, p. 6, available at http://eeas.europa.eu/us/docs/new_transatlantic_agenda_en.pdf.

Director-Generals for External Relations[69] and their opposite numbers in the Council Presidency country on the EU side, with both the US Ambassador to the EU and the Commission's Ambassador to the US in attendance. With the help of modern communication technology, meetings could be called as necessary by conference call and video conference. Biannual summits[70] were reduced to one regular meeting a year after the June 2001 summit in Göteborg, in the first year of the Bush "43" Administration,[71] with special meetings as required.[72] After the entry into force of the EU's Lisbon Treaty in December 2009, which created the function of a permanent EU Council President, there was some flux concerning the continuity of summit meetings. The first "regular" EU/US summit under the new Lisbon formula with US President Obama took place in the margins of a NATO summit on 20 September 2010 in Lisbon, with EU Council President van Rompuy and Commission President Barroso, followed by the 11 November 2011 summit in the same composition in Washington. There were no meetings scheduled in either 2012 or 2013, until the most recent Summit held in Brussels on 26 March 2014.[73] Henceforth, summits will normally alternate between Washington and Brussels.

On content, the NTA, in a language reflecting the spirit of joint responsibility, sets out a "Framework of Action" with four main chapters: (I) Promoting Peace And Stability, Democracy And Development Around The World; (II) Responding To Global Challenges; (III) Contributing To The Expansion Of World Trade And Closer Economic Relations, notably by creating a New Transatlantic Marketplace

[69] After HGK's retirement Hans Beseler had taken over at DG I, while I remained in charge of DG IA before moving to Washington in January 2000.

[70] "We will use our regular Summits to measure progress and to update our priorities." The New Transatlantic Agenda, p. 6, available at http://eeas.europa.eu/us/docs/new_transatlantic_agenda_en.pdf.

[71] President Bush had been faced with sharp criticism from the 16 members of the European Council (the 15 Heads of State or Government and Commission President Prodi), whom he had met collectively at the invitation by Sweden's PM Persson, because of his Administration's early disavowal of a number of international agreements, including the "Kyoto Protocol" on climate change and the International Criminal Court Treaty. At a subsequent lunch with EU Heads of Mission in Washington, Condoleezza Rice, the President's National Security Advisor, told us how much the President had disliked the "Göteborg bashing".

[72] This was already the case immediately after the September 11, 2001 attacks on New York and Washington, when Commission President Romano Prodi and the Belgian PM Verhofstadt were dispatched by the European Council to visit President Bush in the Oval Office on 27 September. The EU's representatives expressed unreserved solidarity and proposed starting work on a common anti-terrorism agenda. President Bush readily replied that "this challenge to the entire world provides us with a new opportunity to work together". Sadly, that opportunity was not fully grasped because of his ill-conceived and divisive "war on terror" agenda.

[73] Critical comments went like: "Obama has no appetite for EU/US summits." A more down to earth explanation by Washington insiders is that he was against meetings for the sake of photo opportunities and insists that meetings should be held if something important needs to be decided. Clearly, with the Spring 2014 crisis over Russia and Ukraine and because of the need to maintain the momentum in the Transatlantic Trade and Investment Partnership (TTIP) negotiations between the US and the EU, that need had become self-evident.

at the bilateral level; and (IV) Building Bridges Across The Atlantic. The latter goal includes five stakeholder "dialogues", a Transatlantic Business Dialogue (TABD), a Transatlantic Environmental Dialogue (TAED), a Transatlantic Consumer Dialogue (TACD), a Transatlantic Labour Dialogue (TALD) and, last but not least, a Transatlantic Legislators Dialogue (TLD) among members of Congress and the European Parliament. A joint EU–US Action Plan was attached to the body of the NTA text outlining immediate objectives within the four chapters.

From the NTA to Today's TTIP Negotiations

This chapter briefly stretches across the second Clinton and the two Bush "43" into the on-going Obama Administrations. Developments broadly fall into three parts: the first marked by the initial implementation of the NTA, the second by "Nine Eleven, 2001" and its aftermath, and the third by the run-up to TTIP.

During the remainder of the Clinton years until the end of 2000, coinciding with the Santer Commission (1995–1999) and the first year of the Prodi Commission in 2000, work routinely focussed on the Joint EU–US Action Plan which comprised some 150 specific action points ranging from reducing barriers to transatlantic trade and investment, to promoting links between colleges and universities. As to the dialogues, there was a forceful start of TABD under the co-chairmanship of a European and a US CEO of major companies for respectively an annual term. TABD was launched at Seville, in the margins of the Madrid transatlantic summit in December 1995. The other stakeholder dialogues were equally active, although at less systematic intervals. Increasingly important became the legislators' dialogue, with meetings between the delegation of the European Parliament for relations with the US Congress and their congressional counterparts developing ever-broader agendas hand in hand with the substance of the meetings at government level. It has to be said, however, that the meetings in Washington were better attended and more substantial, as it proved difficult to convince members of Congress to spare time for transatlantic travel. In the context of the NTA, the filling of the notion of a New Transatlantic Partnership was a particular challenge for successive EU presidencies, who in turn tried to leave their mark on the issue. The EU/US SLG took a strong lead in coordinating the broad menu of economic and political aspects of the NTA. It sent regular reports to the bilateral EU/US summit meetings.[74] This work

[74] An inventory of the SLG reports to the EU/US summits on 13 May (Clinton/PM of Italy Prodi/Santer) and 16 December 1996 (Clinton/PM of Ireland Bruton/Santer), both in Washington; on 28 May (Clinton/PM of the Netherlands Kok/Santer) in The Hague and 5 December 1997 (Clinton/PM of Luxemburg Juncker/Santer) in Washington; and on 18 May 1998 (Clinton/PM of the UK Blair/Santer) in London can be found in Transatlantic Policy Network, Toward Transatlantic Partnership: Cooperation Project Report, the Transatlantic Policy Network, 1998, available at http://www.tpnonline.org/WP/wp-content/uploads/2013/09/Toward_Transatlantic_Partnership_Cooperation_Project.pdf.

underpinned the launch, at the 18 May 1998 EU/US summit in London, of two Declarations, one filling in the concept of Transatlantic Economic Partnership with the dual objective to reduce many of the remaining barriers to the free flow of commerce and to ease the conduct business across the Atlantic; and one on Transatlantic Partnership on Political Cooperation, focussing on coordination to fight terrorism and on economic sanctions policies, as well as on burden-sharing, notably in the former Yugoslavia,[75] and in supporting democracy and market economy in Central and Eastern Europe.[76] Furthermore, the London summit agreed on an "Understanding with Respect to Disciplines for the Strengthening of Investment Protection", and on informal understandings with respect to US sanctions legislation such as "Helms-Burton"[77] directed against Cuba and "ILSA",[78] dealing with Iran and Libya.

The next step forward within the NTA occurred at the EU/US summit in Bonn on 21 June 1999, back-to-back with the 18 to 20 June G8 meeting in Cologne. The Bonn Declaration committed both sides to a "full and equal partnership in economic, political and security affairs", outlining how the EU and the US wanted to shape their relationship over the next decade and ahead into the next century.[79] Again, this upbeat rhetoric needs to be measured against the background of EU and US developments. On the EU side, the Amsterdam Treaty, signed on 2 October 1997, had entered into force on 1 May 1999, strengthening the "S" in Common Foreign and Security Policy (CFSP), and preparing the EU for the landmark enlargement with the new democracies of Central and Eastern Europe, together with other achievements under the "Agenda 2000", such as the entry into the final phase of EMU with the switch to the single currency, the euro. Another robust US engagement in Europe had brought the Second Balkan War on Kosovo to a successful end, when we greeted with relief the return of Martti Ahtisaari[80] from Belgrade to the Cologne Gürzenich, the venue of the G8 meeting, with the news that Milošević had yielded to the West's demands. Three years into President Clinton's second term, US Secretary Madeleine Albright, who had taken over from Warren Christopher, had developed a "Triple Crown" concept, based on NATO, the EU–US and the OSCE, in the good old tradition of the creative Bush/Baker times.[81] This

[75] The Commission had taken the lead, together with the World Bank, of the post-Dayton Bosnia donor conferences.

[76] The 28 May 1997 EU/US summit at The Hague had issued a Statement on "Assistance to Central and Eastern Europe and the independent states of the Former Soviet Union".

[77] Official name: Cuban Liberty and Democratic Solidarity (Libertad) Act 1996, available at http://www.treasury.gov/resource-center/sanctions/Documents/libertad.pdf.

[78] Iran and Libya Sanctions Act 1996, renamed the Iraq Sanctions Act on 30 September 2006, available at http://www.house.gov/legcoun/Comps/Iran%20Sanctions%20Act%20Of%201996.pdf.

[79] It is indeed remarkable, in hindsight, how this language would contrast with US policies post "Nine Eleven", less than 2 years later!

[80] President of Finland and UN Special Envoy for Kosovo.

[81] Albright had developed a close relationship with Commissioner van den Broek since the time of her Ambassadorship at the UN in New York during the first Clinton term.

initiative had been spelled out by Albright's Assistant Secretary of State for European Affairs, Marc Grossman,[82] as a way of using the three transatlantic summits during 1999, NATO, OSCE and EU–US, to give new impetus within the three "legs", security, foreign policy and economy, of the concept. Grossman states that the US had taken the lead in enlarging and revitalising NATO and in building a new, broader relationship with the EU. He explains that the US was now "ready to make the next logical step" in defining a vision for a Euro-Atlantic Partnership for the twenty-first century.

All in all, towards the end of the Clinton Administration, the EU–US relationship based on the EU's policy aspirations and achievements and on a functioning transatlantic partnership, had become more intertwined and interdependent. The years since the end of the Cold War—when the "glue" of common threats supposedly loosened the transatlantic bonds—actually marked the most intense period of transatlantic cooperation ever. The economic relationship had become a stabiliser of the overall relationship. Particularly in the areas of trade and investment, regulatory cooperation and competition policies, EU–US interaction had reached an unprecedented level of intensity. In a nutshell, it became widely recognized by the Administration, legislators and the business community that the transatlantic economy constituted the most globalised part of the global economy. Perhaps, due to this solid foundation, both partners were better prepared to withstand the rocky times ahead, when the Nine Eleven 2001 earthquake unexpectedly hit hard, and led the Bush "43" Administration to embark on an ill-conceived, unilateral and divisive, instead of unifying, "war on terror" agenda.

A dramatic change of direction in the transatlantic relationship marked the start of President George W. Bush's first term in early 2001.[83] As mentioned above, tensions had already started during the first months preceding "Nine Eleven". However, the unprecedented terrorist attacks on the United States mainland on 11 September profoundly affected America's sense of invulnerability and security at home.[84] While, after the spontaneous visit with President Bush at the White House of the Belgian PM Guy Verhofstadt in his capacity of European Council President, together with Commission President Romano Prodi, transatlantic

[82] Remarks on "The Future of the US-Europe Relationship", speech delivered to the Houston World Affairs Council, 1 October 1998.

[83] For a more "on the record" assessment of the most divisive years in the overall EU–US relationship from 2001 to 2005, coinciding with my term as the European Commission's Ambassador in Washington, see my presentation at the College of Europe in Bruges: Burghardt (2006).

[84] I was able to witness the impact at close range in Washington DC. In the early morning of 11 September, I was briefing the members of the European Parliament's delegation for relations with the US Congress in the press room of the Commission Delegation premises on 2100 M Street when news came in about a plane having hit the north tower of New York's World Trade Center. We decided to switch on the TV screen and followed "live" the day's incredible events, including the plane crash into the Pentagon building a few miles away from our meeting room. Our meeting later that day with Congressional counterparts in an almost deserted Capitol Hill, after having crossed a ghost downtown filled with police cars and army vehicles, was a deeply moving experience. In this hour of tragedy "we were all Americans".

cooperation in the area of justice and home affairs became a topical issue,[85] the US-led "war on terror" quickly divided the international community and drove a wedge right through the European Union membership. After a short period of international unity in relation to the need for military operations in Afghanistan, the US engaged in a policy of unilaterally determining the agenda, preferring recourse to ad-hoc "coalitions of the willing" over partnerships of equals, with the invasion of Iraq, based on false assumptions, at the centre of profound disagreements.

In retrospect, the polarising "you are either with us or against us" Bush doctrine was an offspring of the traditional neoconservative foreign policy school, based on factors such as overreliance on the military superiority of the world's sole hyper power, with a defence budget equal to all other countries' defence budgets combined; a missionary zeal of America, the chosen country, called by history and divine providence to defend freedom and democracy, God's gift to mankind; an oversimplified distinction between right and wrong, good and evil; and a refusal to let "others" have a say in determining America's course of action. Patterns like Secretary of Defence Rumsfeld's distinction between the "old" and the "new" Europe; Bob Kagan's "America is from Mars, Europe is from Venus"; or John Bolton's disdain for a UN system at which he was supposed to represent his country, were illustrations of a mind-set adverse to a privileged partnership with an, admittedly, more complex European Union organisation.

The EU, for reasons of its own shortcomings, proved unable to respond collectively as a union.[86] Its members split into those who decided to follow, most outspokenly the UK (Blair), Spain (Aznar), Italy (Berlusconi), as well as most candidate countries from Central and Eastern Europe (hence, Rumsfeld's enthusiasm for "new Europe"), and those who advocated a more comprehensive and internationally legitimised approach, led by Chancellor Schröder of Germany and France's President Chirac, to what Europe used to call "fight against terrorism" as opposed to "war on terror". As a consequence, for much of 2002 and 2003, the general tenor in the US–EU relationship remained uneasy and combative. This did not prevent, however, the conclusion of important agreements on homeland security and counter-terrorism matters, and continuity in the economic relationship. At the 2 May 2002 Bush/Aznar/Prodi summit meeting in Washington, both sides agreed on a Positive Economic Agenda (PEA),[87] in the context of NTA, including

[85] On the EU side, the Amsterdam Treaty had reinforced the legal base for common action in Justice and Home Affairs; a long neglected "third pillar". The excellent cooperation between Commissioner Vitorino and the EU Council counter-terrorism coordinator de Vries on the EU side, Attorney General Ashcroft at the Department of Justice and Homeland Security Secretary Tom Rich on the US side, became a success story under the NTA.

[86] Javier Solana, the EU's foreign policy chief, explained in an International Herald Tribune article dated 12 August 2006, that in the absence of EU common positions, he had no choice but to practice the art of making himself invisible.

[87] Available at http://trade.ec.europa.eu/doclib/docs/2006/june/tradoc_114066.pdf.

Guidelines on Regulatory Cooperation and Transparency[88] and a Financial Markets Regulatory Dialogue.[89]

During 2004, a presidential election year in the US with another very close outcome in favour of Bush, some of the rifts began to settle. Foreign policy had uncharacteristically dominated the presidential campaign in a country deeply divided. After a period of patriotic conformism and almost zero tolerance with respect to criticising a President "Commander in Chief" at war, critical voices took issue with the course of US foreign policy and its increasingly negative effects on America's public image. The case was made for America to reach out to its partners, and notably to the EU, after the Eurozone had been consolidated with the introduction of euro notes and coins in 2002, and after the Treaty of Nice, in effect since February 2003, had brought necessary institutional reform to allow enlargement negotiations with eight candidate member states from Central and Eastern Europe plus Cyprus and Malta to be successfully completed. The neoconservative agenda of pre-emption and pre-eminence, of "the mission determining the coalition" had obviously met with limits of military, financial and moral overstretch.

On the EU side, lessons had to be learned as well. It had become evident that no single Member State on its own was able to ultimately influence the Washington decision-making process, and that collective engagement with enhanced capabilities could make a difference. Moreover, putting aside past differences over the invasion of Iraq had to make room for the need to address together post-Saddam Iraq as part of the problems of the wider Middle East, a region closer to Europe than to the US. The triple G8, EU/US, and NATO summit meetings in June 2004 displayed a new sense of realism, with a quite substantive set of seven policy declarations at the EU–US meeting at Dromoland Castle in Shannon, Ireland on 26 June 2004.[90]

The coincidence in transatlantic changeovers in November 2004 (after the June European Parliament elections for the first time in 25 EU Member States)—the start of the Barroso Commission on 1 November, coinciding with the re-election of President Bush for a second term on 2 November—created an opening for reassessing the state of the transatlantic relationship, all the more since Barroso had earned Bush's gratitude, when he, in his capacity as PM of Portugal, had hosted a last minute so-called "Atlantic Summit" meeting on 16 March 2003 on the Azores with Bush, Blair, and Aznar. The meeting had produced a joint statement on "A Vision for Iraq and the Iraqi People"[91] right before the beginning of the US-led invasion on 20 March.

[88] Available at http://ec.europa.eu/enterprise/policies/international/files/guidelines3_en.pdf.

[89] See http://ec.europa.eu/internal_market/finances/global/index_en.htm.

[90] The G8 Summit under US President Bush's chairmanship from 7 to 10 June in Sea Island, Georgia (with the participation of Chirac, Schröder, Blair, Berlusconi, Koizumi, Martin, Putin and Commission President Prodi together with Irish PM Ahern), the NATO Summit in Istanbul, Turkey, and the annual EU/US Summit under Irish Council Presidency in Ireland.

[91] Available at http://www.monde-diplomatique.fr/cahier/irak/a9939.

A first strong gesture was the visit by President Bush to the EU Headquarters in Brussels on 22 February 2005, starting with a meeting with the Commission, and followed by a summit with all 25 EU Heads of State or Government. The meeting reaffirmed joint commitment to transatlantic partnership, "irreplaceable and vital", and discussed common challenges, including the Middle East, Iraq, Iran, the Balkans and Russia, global economic and environmental issues. Four months later, the June 2005 Summit in Washington, in addition to joint declarations on the promotion of democracy, the Middle East, UN reform, counter-terrorism, non-proliferation and Africa, launched a "EU-US Initiative to Enhance Transatlantic Economic Integration and Growth"[92] and agreed to set up a "High Level Regulatory Co-Operation Forum".[93] On 18 October 2005, Commission President Barroso's invitation to the White House, the first individual visit by a Commission President outside the NTA routine since many years, completed the list of conciliatory gestures. Discussions focussed on the WTO Doha Round, transatlantic economic issues and, again, Bush's pet subject matter, the promotion of democracy around the world. All in all, 2005 had changed the rhetoric, ended polarisation and put the NTA back on track.

Two years later, at the Washington summit meeting on 30 April 2007, upon an initiative by the German Chancellor, Angela Merkel, a "Framework for Advancing Transatlantic Integration between the EU and the US"[94] was signed by President Bush, Chancellor Merkel and Commission President Barroso, which in its section IV established a "Transatlantic Economic Council (TEC)". This fresh transatlantic initiative had been initiated during Germany's Council Presidency in order to ensure that the "sudden death" of the EU's draft Constitutional Treaty following the negative referenda in France and the Netherlands on, respectively, 29 May and 1 June 2005, would not adversely affect transatlantic dynamism. Pressure in favour of a "Transatlantic Partnership Agreement" had also mounted at the European Parliament.[95] Work under the TEC was led by a cabinet level official from the US President's Executive Office, putting the White House in charge of coordinating the relevant US government departments, and by the Commissioner for Trade on the EU side.

---

[92] Available at http://www.europarl.europa.eu/document/activities/cont/201004/20100427ATT73625/20100427ATT73625EN.pdf.

[93] The Forum was launched at ministerial level on 30 November 2005, hosted by the EU side, with the participation of relevant commissioners, Member States' ministers representing three successive Council presidencies, and a US team led by the Secretary of Commerce. A second meeting in Washington on 9 November 2006 followed up on the 26 June Vienna Summit which had agreed on a "Roadmap for EU/US Regulatory Cooperation". The ministerial meeting was co-chaired by US Secretaries of Commerce, Gutierrez, and of Energy, Bodman, with Commission Vice-President Verheugen and the Finnish minister for trade on the EU side.

[94] Available at http://trade.ec.europa.eu/doclib/docs/2007/may/tradoc_134654.pdf.

[95] Reports by MEPs Elmar Brok of 8 May 2006, A6-0173/2006, and Erika Mann of 20 April 2006, A6-0131/2006.

After the entry into force on 1 December 2009 of the EU's Lisbon Treaty, which had rescued the essential elements of the failed Constitutional Treaty, and as a result of the TEC's report to the 29 November 2011 Washington summit,[96] work during the first term of the Obama Administration (2009–2012), coinciding with the second Barroso Commission, and the appointment of Van Rompuy as the first permanent President of the European Council, a Joint US–EU Statement[97] was released in the margins of a G20 meeting at Los Cabos, Mexico, on 19 June 2012, by the three Presidents (Obama, Van Rompuy and Barroso). The statement urged a "High Level Working Group on Jobs and Growth (HLWG)", which had submitted an interim report to leaders, to prepare a mandate for negotiations of "an ambitious and comprehensive market opening arrangement".

The re-election of President Obama in November 2012 led to an acceleration of events immediately after his inauguration for a second term on 21 January 2013. In a scenario well-orchestrated on both sides, the HLWG, co-chaired by USTR Ron Kirk and by the EU Commissioner for Trade Karel De Gucht, submitted its "Final Report on Jobs and Growth" on 11 February 2013. The report concludes with a recommendation "that the US and the EU launch negotiations on a comprehensive, ambitious agreement that addresses a broad range of bilateral trade and investment issues, including regulatory issues, and contributes to the development of global rules."[98] The next day, on 12 February, in his traditional "State of the Union" address to the US Congress, President Obama included the following sentence: "And tonight, I am announcing that we will launch talks on a comprehensive Transatlantic Trade and Investment Partnership with the European Union." Again, one day later on 13 February, the three Presidents, Obama, Van Rompuy and Barroso, in a joint declaration, pledged to "initiate the internal procedures necessary to launch negotiations on a Transatlantic Trade and Investment Partnership (TTIP)".[99] Finally, at the first meeting, on 14 February, between the newly appointed US Secretary of State Kerry with the EU High Representative and Commission Vice-President Ashton, herself a former European trade commissioner, Kerry remarked that this major transatlantic initiative was to "rebalance" the recent new US focus on Asia with the negotiation of a "Transpacific Partnership (TPP)".

Today,[100] after some six decades of EU/US interaction since the early Monnet years, the transatlantic relationship is based on an immense "acquis" of policy

[96] This meeting also established a similar body, next to TEC, the "Transatlantic Energy Council".

[97] European Commission, Press Release MEMO/12/462 of 19 June 2012, Joint Statement by U.S. President Obama, European Commission President Barroso and European Council President Van Rompuy, available at http://europa.eu/rapid/press-release_MEMO-12-462_en.htm.

[98] The final report is available at http://trade.ec.europa.eu/doclib/docs/2013/february/tradoc_150519.pdf.

[99] Henceforth, "TTIP" will have to be remembered as a novel abbreviation in the transatlantic dictionary of acronyms.

[100] This manuscript was completed on 18 March 2014, shortly before US President Obama's visit to Brussels for an EU/US summit meeting on 26 March 2004.

statements, legal texts and organisational decisions. While TAD, NTA, SLG, TABD, PEA, TEC and HLWG stand for attempts to bring various strands of the relationship under a common roof, no single overarching Treaty had so far been a realistic option. The sheer weight, and its effects on the global scene, of the world's two major economic powerhouses entering into an overall bilateral, and institutionalised, relationship was traditionally considered a negative factor, in particular for the pursuit of multilateral trade negotiations. However, with the lapse of the WTO Doha Round, opened as far back as 2001, and against the background of new powerful actors emerging around the globe, the case for a historic economic agreement has become more compelling now. Since the formal opening of TTIP negotiations in July 2013, broad stakeholder consultations, four negotiating rounds at official level and two assessments by the chief negotiators on both sides, it is still too early to speculate on the outcome. And if, over the next 2 years or so, negotiations can be concluded, provided, among others, the US President will obtain fast track authority, ratification will not be an easy task, notably with the US Congress, famously known for its record in this respect.[101]

References

Baker JA (1989) A new Europe, a new Atlanticism: architecture for a new era. Address to the Berlin Press Club, 12 December 1989

Ball G (1982) The past has another pattern, pp 69–99

Burghardt G (2005) Successes and challenges for the euro. In: Posen A (ed) The euro at five: ready for a global role. Institute for International Economics, Special report 18, pp 23 et seq

Burghardt G (2006) The European Union's transatlantic relationship. CoE's EU Diplomacy Papers, p 2. Available at https://www.coleurope.eu/system/files_force/research-paper/edp_2-2006_burghardt.pdf?download=1

Duchêne F (1994) Jean Monnet: the first statesman of interdependence

Hallstein W (1969) Der unvollendete Bundesstaat, p 238

Holbrooke R (1995) America, a European Power. Foreign Affairs 74(2):38. Available at http://www.foreignaffairs.com/articles/50770/richard-holbrooke/america-a-european-power

[101] The manuscript was completed on March 18, 2004 (because of the developments re TTIP since than).

Transatlantic Disputes on Non-tariff Barriers to Trade: From Asbestos to the EU Fuel Quality Directive

Hans-Joachim Prieß and Katrin Arend

Introduction

Americans and Europeans "make different risk assessments."[1]

With that statement at the 1999 Stanford European Forum, Horst G. Krenzler touched the very heart of a long row of disputes between the US, the EU, and Canada in the WTO legal framework, which concerned so-called non-tariff barriers to trade. These transatlantic disputes have affected many different areas of core domestic policy and regulation, such as public health or the environment, as past WTO cases, e.g. *EC – Asbestos*,[2] *EC – Hormones*[3] and *US – Continued Suspension*[4] indicate.

Today, we are about to see the development towards another dispute between Canada and the EU arising from the Directive 2009/30/EC[5] (*Fuel Quality Directive*) and its implementing measures. Like in other disputes on non-tariff barriers to

[1] Horst G. Krenzler, speech given at the meeting of the Stanford's European Forum on 29 September 1999.

[2] *European Communities – Measures Affecting Asbestos and Products Containing Asbestos* WT/DS135.

[3] *European Communities – Measures Concerning Meat and Meat Products (Hormones)*, WT/DS26.

[4] *United States – Continued Suspension of Obligations in the EC – Hormones Dispute*, WT/DS320.

[5] Directive 2009/30/EC of the European Parliament and of the Council of 23 April 2009, amending Directive 98/70/EC as regards the specification of petrol, diesel and gas-oil and introducing a mechanism to monitor and reduce greenhouse gas emissions and amending Council Directive 1999/32/EC as regards the specification of fuel used by inland waterway vessels and repealing Directive 93/12/EEC, [2009] OJ L 140/88.

H.-J. Prieß (✉) • K. Arend
Freshfields Bruckhaus Deringer LLP, 10785 Berlin, Germany
e-mail: hans-joachim.priess@freshfields.com; katrin.arend@freshfields.com

C. Herrmann et al. (eds.), *Trade Policy between Law, Diplomacy and Scholarship*,
European Yearbook of International Economic Law,
DOI 10.1007/978-3-319-15690-3_13

trade, the WTO Members concerned disagree on the risks which goods that are about to be put on the market pose to a certain public policy objective. This differing evaluation leads to a different level of precaution, which, in turn, translates into different requirements and standards these goods have to fulfil before being put on the market. In trade relations between WTO Members, different standards may have the effect of market access requirements. They disfavour the industries of those WTO Members where lower standards apply and this has (at least) the effect of restricting trade.

Unlike many other WTO Members, the countries on both sides of the Atlantic are quite ready to challenge their differing risk assessments before the WTO adjudicating bodies, if these have a negative impact on their export figures. As a result, transatlantic disputes have markedly shaped the understanding of the WTO rules regulating non-tariff barriers to trade. Given the ever increasing significance of the global fuel market, it would not surprise, if we were to see a dispute on the legality of the Fuel Quality Directive under WTO law in near future. Before turning to the most important transatlantic non-tariff barrier disputes and the WTO consistency of the Fuel Quality Directive in further detail, we will shortly describe the concept of non-tariff barriers and the relevant rules delimiting the WTO Member's freedom to impose them.

Non-tariff Barriers to Trade

Unsurprisingly, non-tariff barriers to trade (NTB) can best be explained in relation to tariffs. Tariffs are customs duties and taxes imposed upon importation (clearance for free circulation) or as an internal measure in order to generate state revenues and, at the same time, obtain a competitive advantage for the domestic industry.[6] Together with a system of preferences based on rules of origin, they can also be used to give an advantage to products imported from one country over those of another. The costs of these policies are typically borne by the consumer who must pay more for foreign products. Despite the—at times—complicated tariff nomenclature and rules of origin, overall tariffs are transparent and straightforward.

By contrast, NTBs consist of virtually any measure having a trade restrictive effect other than a tariff. Due to their enormous variety and the manifold historical and domestic policy reasons underlying them, it is impossible to establish a precise positive definition,[7] or even to state the exact number of NTBs.[8] They comprise *inter alia* bans, permissions or licences, technical or administrative standards and labelling requirements.[9] Various attempts have been made to classify at least

[6] C.f. also Fraser (2012), p. 1033.

[7] See Stoll and Schorkopf (2006), p. 111.

[8] Tietje (1998), pp. 31 et seq.

[9] Echols (1996), p. 191; see also Heese (2012).

certain groups of NTBs according to their type, function or particular effect.[10] Most importantly, it should be noted that NTBs may be primarily directed at restricting trade and, in this respect therefore, may follow policies similar to tariffs, such as quantitative restrictions, import prohibitions, import licences or monetary support of domestic companies. Likewise, it is possible for NTBs to have a non-trade objective which (only) incidentally causes trade restrictions. These may take the form of national differences regarding scale units, divergent requirements of labelling or administrative standards. Technical standards[11] and sanitary and phytosanitary measures[12] are also typically considered to fall within this category.[13] The non-trade objective pursued may well be—and often is—a legitimate public policy. Compliance with such public policy produces transaction costs, which are typically borne by the suppliers.

The huge variety and the number of different purposes make it difficult to detect and, also, to assess NTBs. They are regulated in several international trade agreements within the WTO legal framework, most notably the General Agreement on Tariffs and Trade (GATT), the Agreement on Technical Barriers to Trade (TBT Agreement) and the Agreement on the Application of Sanitary and Phytosanitary Measures (SPS Agreement). However, as a result of the dual nature of NTBs, which serve legitimate public policies on the one hand, and restrict trade on the other, the applicable rules circumscribing and delimiting the WTO Members' freedom to impose NTBs are necessarily sketchy. Together with the importance which WTO Members attach to defend their public policy choices, this setting provides much scope for dispute. In addition, the relative economic significance of NTBs *vis-à-vis* tariffs has strongly increased.[14] NTBs may soon, if not already, be considered to have replaced tariffs as the standard form of protectionism.[15] So too the number of NTB-related disputes will rise.

Against this background, scrutinising a particular NTB under the applicable WTO provisions is an exercise which is becoming ever more frequent and also difficult. Hitherto, the most controversial and extensive disputes within the context of NTBs had resulted from disagreements between the EU, the US, and Canada. Disputes between these WTO Members, such as, *inter alia*, *EC – Asbestos*, *EC – Biotech*,[16] *US – Continued Suspension* and the *EC – Hormones* case have shaped the current understanding of the WTO rules on NTBs. *EC – Asbestos* in particular

[10] See particularly Tietje (1998), pp. 30 et seq.; see also Stoll and Schorkopf (2006), pp. 130 and 139.

[11] See *inter alia* Jessen (2010), p. 381 (382 et seq.).

[12] See Echols (1996), p. 191.

[13] See Fraser (2012), p. 1033 (1034 et seq.).

[14] Ahn (2002), p. 85 (86); Santana and Jackson (2012), p. 462; Tietje (1998), p. 33.

[15] Tietje (1998), p. 34 refers to different studies according to which, already in the 1980s, about 40 % of the overall trade was affected by NTBs.

[16] *European Communities – Measures Affecting the Approval and Marketing of Biotech Products*, WT/DS291-293.

has strongly influenced the interpretation of the TBT Agreement,[17] while *EC – Hormones* did so in relation to the SPS Agreement.[18] On that basis, they are considered to be among the most high-profile[19] cases in WTO dispute settlement.[20] Before looking at some of these disputes in more detail, we will outline the relevant WTO provisions regulating NTBs.

WTO Provisions Regulating Non-tariff Barriers to Trade

WTO provisions applicable to NTBs generally accept the Members' legitimate interests to regulate their internal (trade-related) matters according to their own discretion.[21] At the same time, however, regulations implementing these legitimate interests must follow certain rules, in particular the principle of non-discrimination. These rules are primarily contained in the GATT, the TBT Agreement and the SPS Agreement.

GATT

The core legal principles laid down in the GATT are still considered to be the crucial legal benchmark for NTBs.[22] They comprise the prohibition of quantitative restrictions pursuant to Article XI GATT and the principle of non-discrimination contained in Article I:1 GATT (the most-favoured nation obligation) and Article III:4 GATT (national treatment obligation). Contrary to the absolute prohibition of quantitative restrictions, the principle of non-discrimination establishes only a relative standard of protection. It prohibits discriminatory treatment of third countries' imported products *vis-à-vis* foreign and domestic "like" products. Accordingly, the principle applies only in relation to "like" products. In practice, it is often crucial to the legality of a trade restrictive measure whether there exists a like product to which the most-favoured nation or the national treatment obligations can apply. In terms of a precise definition of likeness, the WTO texts provide no guidance. However, the WTO adjudicating bodies, i.e. the panels and the Appellate Body have established four criteria for assessing the likeness of products: (1) the properties, nature and quality of the products; (2) the end use of the products;

[17] Jessen (2010), p. 381 (392).

[18] Sharma (2002), p. 1 (2); Gehring (2010), p. 396 (406, para. 28).

[19] For the term "high-profile" cases, see Kaienburg (2010), pp. 35 et seq.

[20] Echols (1996), p. 191 (195, 207 and 208).

[21] See Fraser (2012), p. 1033 (1035).

[22] Santana and Jackson (2012), p. 462 (471).

(3) consumers' tastes and habits in respect of the products; and (4) the tariff classification of the products.[23]

Even where a NTB discriminates between like products or imposes quantitative restrictions, this does not mean that the NTB is incompatible with the GATT. Article XX GATT entitles WTO Members to pursue certain policies which have a trade-restrictive effect, provided that they are "not applied in a manner which would constitute a means of arbitrary or unjustifiable discrimination".[24] In the context of NTBs, WTO Members most often rely on Article XX(b) and (g) GATT, according to which measures may be upheld that are necessary to protect human, animal or plant life or health or that relate to the conservation of exhaustible natural resources, respectively.[25] The existing case law shows that the standard which NTBs must meet in order to fall within the scope of these justifications is rather high and only rarely met.

TBT Agreement

The TBT Agreement supplements the GATT provisions with regard to technical regulations, standards and conformity assessment procedures.[26] A technical regulation is defined as a document stipulating product characteristics or their related processes and production methods (PPMs), compliance with which is mandatory.[27] In terms of its principal structure, the TBT Agreement is similar to the GATT. Article 2.1 of the TBT Agreement contains the most-favoured nation and the national treatment obligations, while the subsequent provisions entitle WTO Members to enact technical regulations implementing their public policies, provided that such technical regulations are not prepared, adopted, or applied in a manner that creates unnecessary obstacles to international trade. Furthermore, the restraint of trade caused by a technical regulation shall not exceed the extent reasonably necessary to achieve the legitimate objective pursued, such as the protection of human health or safety, animal or plant life or health, or the environment.[28] In addition, WTO Members are required to carry out an assessment of the risks that are likely to result if the legitimate objectives were not achieved.[29] In that respect, the TBT Agreement builds on Article XX GATT and provides to some extent more

[23] Sacerdoti and Castren (2011), p. 65, para. 14, with reference to Appellate Body Report, *European Communities – Measures Affecting Asbestos and Products Containing Asbestos*, WT/DS135/AB/R, para. 91, and *Japan – Taxes on Alcoholic Beverages*, WT/DS8, 10, 11/AB/R.

[24] *Chapeau* of Article XX GATT.

[25] Stoll and Strack (2011), pp. 498 et seq., paras. 1, 4).

[26] Ahn (2002), p. 85 (89).

[27] Cf. Herrmann (2007), p. 215 (240 et seq., para. 549).

[28] Article 2.2 TBT Agreement.

[29] Tamiotti (2007), p. 220, para. 24.

precise rules than the latter.[30] However, the exact relationship between the TBT Agreement and the GATT is not clear.[31] In *Korea – Dairy*, the Appellate Body held that the WTO Agreement is a "Single Undertaking" and therefore "all WTO obligations are generally cumulative and Members must comply with all of them simultaneously".[32] In *EC – Asbestos*, it held that "the TBT Agreement imposes obligations on Members that seem to be *different* from, and *additional* to, the obligations imposed on Members under the GATT".[33] *EC – Sardines* confirms this approach. In this case, the Appellate Body made it clear that while "two agreements [can] apply simultaneously [. . .] a panel should normally consider the more specific agreement before the more general agreement".[34]

SPS Agreement

The SPS Agreement contains specific regulations regarding sanitary and phytosanitary measures (SPS measures), which are measures to protect life or health of animal, plant or human from pertinent SPS risks.[35] Unlike the GATT or TBT Agreement, the SPS Agreement does not impose a non-discrimination obligation based on like products. Instead, it requires the WTO Members to abstain from discrimination where "identical or similar conditions" exist.[36] Yet, the SPS Agreement permits discrimination even in this case, provided that the SPS measure is necessary to protect human, animal or plant life or health and is based on scientific principles and evidence.[37] Particularly the latter requirement has the effect that the SPS Agreement is narrower than the TBT Agreement[38] since subjective, non-scientific factors, e.g. cultural/moral preferences or consumer tastes, do not suffice as a justification for trade restrictive measures.[39] Once the requirements of the SPS Agreement are met, the SPS measure shall be presumed to

---

[30] Stoll and Schorkopf (2006), p. 133, paras. 394 et seq.

[31] The preamble of the TBT Agreement reads "further the objectives of GATT", while there is no explicit reference to Article XX GATT.

[32] Appellate Body Report, *Korea – Definitive Safeguard Measure on Imports of Certain Dairy Products*, WT/DS98/AB/R, paras. 74 and 41; Koebele (2007), p. 183, para. 3.

[33] Appellate Body Report, *European Communities – Measures Affecting Asbestos and Products Containing Asbestos*, WT/DS135/AB/R, para. 80 (emphasis in the original).

[34] Appellate Body Report, *European Communities – Trade Description of Sardines*, WT/DS231/AB/R, paras. 7.15 et seq.; see also Stoll and Schorkopf (2006), p. 137, para. 412.

[35] Ahn (2002), p. 85 (87).

[36] Article 2.3 SPS Agreement.

[37] Prieß and Pitschas (2000), p. 519 (543).

[38] See also Rigod (2013), p. 503; Gehring (2010), p. 396 (402, para. 14 and p. 399, para. 6).

[39] Seibert-Fohr (2007), p. 400, para. 22; for "scientific principles" see also Echols (1996), p. 191 (198).

be in accordance with the GATT, especially the provisions of Article XX (b) GATT.[40]

The relationship between the SPS and the TBT Agreement is specified in Article 1.5 of the latter. In accordance with this provision, the TBT Agreement shall not apply to SPS measures. Accordingly, where an SPS measure has been identified, it is exclusively subject to the SPS Agreement, if even it has been implemented in the form of a technical regulation.[41]

Dispute Settlement

NTB cases may be resolved by reference to either the SPS/TBT Committees or the dispute settlement body (DSB).[42] While the former play a more important role in dispute prevention, the DSB is involved when the disputants require that their case be decided by a neutral panel or the Appellate Body. The procedural rules are set forth in the WTO Dispute Settlement Understanding (DSU). The decisions of the panels and the Appellate Body carry a strong precedential value, which is why they remain highly relevant today. Particularly, with regard to NTBs, panel and Appellate Body decisions provide a more precise understanding of the legal requirements to be satisfied under the covered agreements. As a result, WTO Members frequently refer to these decisions in order to support their own position. In the following, we will look at the often cited *EC – Asbestos* and the *EC – Hormones* cases and how they have shaped the legal requirements to be fulfilled by NTBs.

EC – Asbestos

The *EC – Asbestos*[43] case between the European Communities (EC) and Canada[44] arose from a French decree prohibiting the production, marketing, importation and exportation of asbestos and all goods containing asbestos for public health reasons.[45] In 1998, Canada (the world's second largest asbestos manufacturer at that time)[46] requested consultations with the EC maintaining that the French decree was

[40] Article 2.4 SPS Agreement.

[41] Ahn (2002), p. 85 (88).

[42] See Fraser (2012), p. 1033.

[43] *European Communities – Measures Affecting Asbestos and Products Containing Asbestos*, Appellate Body Report, WT/DS135/AB/R.

[44] The US acted as a third party to the dispute.

[45] Appellate Body Report, *European Communities – Measures Affecting Asbestos and Products Containing Asbestos*, WT/DS135/AB/R, paras. 1 et seq.

[46] Neumann (2015), p. 130.

in violation of Articles 2 and 5 SPS Agreement, Article 2 TBT Agreement and Articles III, XI and XIII GATT.[47] The Panel concluded that the French decree was inconsistent with the national treatment obligation laid down in Article III:4 GATT.[48] The Panel then examined whether the EC could rightly invoke Article XX(b) GATT as a justification for its asbestos ban. In this respect, Canada and the EC essentially disagreed on whether a certain asbestos product posed a human health risk.[49] According to the Panel this was a matter of sufficient scientific evidence. In the particular case, the Panel found that the EC had established a *prima facie* case of a human health risk and that Canada had not presented sufficient evidence to rebut this finding.[50] Because there was no alternative measure available to the EC which could fulfil the human health protection objective, the Panel considered the asbestos ban to be justified under Article XX(b) GATT.[51] With regard to the TBT Agreement, the Panel held that it did not apply to the asbestos ban but to the exceptions of that ban, because only the latter constituted a technical regulation.[52] However, since Canada did not challenge these exceptions, the Panel did not examine them.

On appeal, the Appellate Body held that the ban by the French decree was a "technical regulation", as defined in Annex 1.1 of the TBT Agreement, and thus covered by the TBT Agreement.[53] It did not, however, make any more substantive findings because of the insufficiency of the facts.[54] With regard to the GATT, the Appellate Body reversed the Panel's finding that the products were "like" and the measures therefore inconsistent with Article III:4 GATT.[55] According to the Appellate Body, Canada failed to show that a competitive relationship[56] between the products and the like products existed.[57] Finally, the Appellate Body confirmed

---

[47] *European Communities – Measures Affecting Asbestos and Products Containing Asbestos*, Panel Report, WT/DS135/R, paras. 1.1 and 1.2.

[48] Panel Report, *European Communities – Measures Affecting Asbestos and Products Containing Asbestos*, WT/DS135/R, pp. 429–431, paras. 8.144 et seq.

[49] Prieß and Pitschas (2000), p. 519 (537 et seq.).

[50] Panel Report, *European Communities – Measures Affecting Asbestos and Products Containing Asbestos*, WT/DS135/R, p. 446, para. 8.194.

[51] Panel Report, *European Communities – Measures Affecting Asbestos and Products Containing Asbestos*, WT/DS135/R, p. 446, para. 8.222.

[52] Panel Report, *European Communities – Measures Affecting Asbestos and Products Containing Asbestos*, WT/DS135/R, p. 413, para. 8.72.

[53] Appellate Body Report, *European Communities – Measures Affecting Asbestos and Products Containing Asbestos*, WT/DS135/AB/R, pp. 23 et seq. (29, paras. 76–77).

[54] See the case analysis by Pauwelyn (2002), p. 63 (66).

[55] Appellate Body Report, *European Communities – Measures Affecting Asbestos and Products Containing Asbestos*, WT/DS135/AB/R, pp. 31 et seq. (48 and 50, paras. 126, 131 and 132).

[56] Appellate Body Report, European Communities – Measures Affecting Asbestos and Products Containing Asbestos, WT/DS135/AB/R, paras. 97–99, 126.

[57] Appellate Body Report, European Communities – Measures Affecting Asbestos and Products Containing Asbestos, WT/DS135/AB/R, pp. 52 et seq., paras. 139 and 141.

the Panel's view that in any case the ban was justified under Article XX (b) GATT, because it "protect[ed] human life or health" and "no reasonably alternative measure" existed.[58] Especially, a "controlled use" would not be a conceivable alternative.[59]

EC – Hormones

EC – Hormones—a dispute between the EC, the US and Canada—concerned an EC prohibition of the sale and import of beef to which certain kinds of natural or synthetic hormones had been administered for growth purposes. As a result, US farmers suffered extensive export shortfalls. The US successfully challenged the measures as being inconsistent with, *inter alia*, the SPS Agreement.

With regard to the requirements for a justification of an SPS measure, the Appellate Body emphasised that the right of a WTO Member to define its appropriate level of protection is not absolute and must be backed by a substantive scientific justification when exceeding international standards of protection.[60] Accordingly, the WTO Members do not enjoy unfettered discretion when deciding on their level of SPS protection.[61] Instead, a "rational relationship" between the measure and the empirical risk assessment conducted by the WTO Member concerned must exist.[62] Against this background, the EC could not defend its hormones ban before the Panel and the Appellate Body. It was not based on any risk assessment as prescribed by Article 5.1 SPS Agreement, nor did it conform to international standards as laid down in Article 3.1 SPS Agreement. After the decision of the Appellate Body, the EC refused to implement the decision.[63] New disputes arose on the state of implementation of the decision and retaliatory measures imposed to enforce implementation.[64]

---

[58] Appellate Body Report, European Communities – Measures Affecting Asbestos and Products Containing Asbestos, WT/DS135/AB/R, pp. 57 et seq. (63, para. 175).

[59] Appellate Body Report, European Communities – Measures Affecting Asbestos and Products Containing Asbestos, WT/DS135/AB/R, p. 63, paras. 173–174.

[60] Appellate Body Report, European Communities – Measures Concerning Meat and Meat Products (Hormones), WT/DS26/AB/R, paras. 163–173.

[61] Prieß and Pitschas (2000), p. 519 (542 et seq.).

[62] Appellate Body Report, European Communities – Measures Concerning Meat and Meat Products (Hormones), WT/DS26/AB/R, para. 193.

[63] Gehring (2010), pp. 406 et seq.

[64] *United States – Continued Suspension of Obligations in the EC – Hormones Dispute*, WT/DS320 and *Canada – Continued Suspension of Obligations in the EC – Hormones Dispute*, WT/DS321.

Results for a Justification of NTBs

EC – Asbestos and *EC – Hormones* are but the very top of a long list of transatlantic disputes on NTBs. Overall this case law on NTBs gives rise to two major observations. First, it is very difficult to meet the standard required for a justification of NTBs under the GATT, the SPS or the TBT Agreement. The only instance where an NTB fully complied with WTO law was *EC – Asbestos*, where it was obvious that there existed no alternative measure to the introduction of an import ban on asbestos. The Appellate Body held, that "France could not reasonably be expected to employ any alternative measure if that measure would involve a continuation of the very risk that the Decree seeks to 'halt'. Such an alternative measure would, in effect, prevent France from achieving its chosen level of health protection."[65]

Second, the case law illustrates that a risk assessment and reliable scientific evidence of an actual positive effect of the NTB is absolutely key to its justification under WTO law. All parties concerned, the EU, the US, and Canada have already learned that poor evidence, an overly narrow assessment of the risks, and lack of even-handedness of the NTB in view of the general standard of protection within the regulating Member puts the WTO consistency of an NTB at risk. Thus, it is important to prepare the introduction of a new NTB very carefully in order to avoid the unnecessary and unpleasant exercise of redrafting an NTB according to the rulings of a WTO panel.

A New NTB on the Horizon: EU Fuel Quality Directive

When adopted in June 2009, the Fuel Quality Directive was intended to introduce "a new element in the legislation that sets as an objective the reduction of the greenhouse gas intensity of energy supplied for use in road vehicles and non-road mobile machinery."[66] To this end, Article 7a(2) of the Fuel Quality Directive requires fuel suppliers to reduce life cycle greenhouse gas emissions of the fuels

---

[65] Appellate Body Report, *European Communities – Measures Affecting Asbestos and Products Containing Asbestos*, WT/DS135/AB/R, para. 174.

[66] Directive 2009/30/EC of the European Parliament and of the Council of 23 April 2009 amending Directive 98/70/EC as regards the specification of petrol, diesel and gas-oil and introducing a mechanism to monitor and reduce greenhouse gas emissions and amending Council Directive 1999/32/EC as regards the specification of fuel used by inland waterway vessels and repealing Directive 93/12/EEC, [2009] OJ L 140/88 (Directive 2009/30/EC on fuel quality), Consultation paper on the measures necessary for the implementation of Article 7a(5), available at http://ec.europa.eu/environment/air/transport/pdf/art7a.pdf.

and energy supplied by up to 10 % by 31 December 2020, compared with a fuel baseline standard of 2010.[67] However, for the Fuel Quality Directive to be implemented, a calculation methodology[68] for the determination of the life cycle greenhouse gas emissions from fossil fuels[69] and the baseline standard need to be established. It is on the basis of such fuel value and baseline standard that suppliers calculate the type and amount of fuel which they are entitled to import and release into free circulation in order to meet the emission target set by the Fuel Quality Directive.

Although the Fuel Quality Directive has been in force for 5 years, an implementing measure setting forth the fuel value is yet to be adopted. In essence, two calculation methods for determining the fuel value exist. One could either measure the *actual* greenhouse gas emissions or rely on *default values* that are assigned to each type of fuel according to its feedstock. Eventually, in its draft implementing measure, the Fuel Quality Committee (Committee) chose the latter option of employing default values.[70] However, when deciding on its own draft implementing measure in February 2012, the Committee expressed neither a favourable nor an unfavourable view on the chosen methodology.[71] This means that the draft implementing measure, which had been forwarded to the EU Parliament and the Council for adoption, can more easily be rejected.[72]

Currently, the Commission is preparing a new proposal for an implementation measure and, in this respect, has undertaken a new impact assessment. Although the impact assessment was completed in June 2013, its results have not yet been published at time of writing. Indeed, it is expected that the results will be disclosed along with the new Commission proposal in summer 2014. In view of the Commission's note on EU 2030 climate targets, it is appears likely that the Commission will not much change its default value methodology.[73]

Impact on the Canadian Fuel Industry

Canada harshly criticises the Fuel Quality Directive as being inconsistent with WTO law. This is no surprise. The EU is one of the largest net importers of fuels

[67] See Recital 9 of Directive 2009/30/EC on fuel quality.

[68] See also Recital 8 of Directive 2009/30/EC on fuel quality.

[69] Article 7a(5) Directive 2009/30/EC on fuel quality.

[70] Ducharme (2012).

[71] Cf. Voting sheet, V019449/01; the meeting's summary record, S019725/01.

[72] Cf. Article 5a(4) of the Second Comitology Decision, Council Decision (2006/512/EC) of 17 July 2006 amending Decision 1999/468/EC laying down the procedures for the exercise of implementing powers conferred on the Commission, [2006] OJ L 200/11; for a more detailed description of the further procedure compare Ducharme (2012).

[73] European Commission, COM(2014) 15 final of 22 January 2014, A Policy Framework for Climate and Energy in the Period from 2020 to 2030.

and Canada will belong to the most affected fuel suppliers. While most of the fuels imported into the EU still originate in South America, Russia or the Middle East, Canada has an increasing interest in the EU market. This increasing interest arose from a policy change towards certain alternative exploitation methods (e.g. fracking) in the US. As a result, the US has become more independent from Canadian supplies and Canadian suppliers started to export more fuel to the EU.

Irrespective of their particular origin, the fuels currently imported by the EU are in many respects similar, as are the purposes for which the fuels are essentially used. The one major difference between fuels from Russia or the Middle East and fuels from Canada is the way in which they are produced. Most fuels are processed by using conventional crude oil. By contrast, Canadian suppliers use tar sand as a feedstock for their fuels. In the Fuel Quality Directive, fuels from tar sands are referred to as so-called "unconventional" fuels. Compared to conventional fuels, their production at the upstream level is in general more energy intensive.[74]

The EU framework on fuel quality ties in these different processes and production methods. It imposes requirements on fuel suppliers according to the energy-intensity of the particular process and production method. That way, the EU framework particularly induces fuel suppliers to switch to conventional fuels in order to meet the emission targets set out by the EU. On the basis of the latest known Commission proposal, the exact mechanism causing this switch would be the above-mentioned "default value". Depending on its exact value, it can be expected that it will influence the decision of the fuel supplier whether or not to import a particular fuel in order to meet the emission targets.

Because fuels from Canadian tar sands are very likely to receive a poor value compared to conventional fuels, the Canadian government together with oil companies interested in tar sands have strongly opposed the Fuel Quality Directive.[75] Canadian Natural Resources Minister, Joe Oliver, made clear that the Canadian government considers the proposed European calculations an unfair discrimination against Canada's tar sands, their foundation being significantly erroneous in methodology and data,[76] and that it is prepared to escalate the case to the WTO dispute settlement body.[77] So far, the EU Commission has rejected these findings as "inadequate".[78]

[74] Ducharme (2012).

[75] See Carrington (2012) and Paris (2012).

[76] Canadian Press (2013).

[77] Paris (2013).

[78] Carrington (2013).

Compatibility of the EU Fuel Quality Directive with WTO Law

These developments give rise to the question whether or not the Fuel Quality Directive, and in particular the proposed calculation method for the default value, comply with WTO law. As outlined above, the WTO legal framework generally prohibits any governmental influence on the traders' market behaviour insofar as it constitutes an unjustifiable discrimination or burden on trade. Nonetheless, at the same time, the WTO considers certain environment- and conservation-related measures to be justifiable. In view of the foregoing, the most relevant questions that need to be taken into account when assessing the compatibility of the Fuel Quality Directive under WTO law are whether the fuel quality requirements constitute a discriminatory measure or restriction of trade within the meaning of the GATT; whether they need to be considered as a technical regulation within the TBT Agreement and whether the EU may invoke a justification for introducing fuel quality requirements.

Non-discrimination Obligation Under the GATT

Whether or not the fuel quality requirements can be considered a discriminatory measure under the GATT is assessed in a three-step approach. Firstly, the GATT must be applicable to the calculation of the fuel's default value. Secondly, there must exist a like product in relation to the Canadian fuels. Finally, Canadian fuels must be treated less favourably than the like product in respect of, *inter alia*, their import, sale, or distribution.

It seems to be quite clear that fuels are subject to the disciplines of GATT and that a poor default value for unconventional fuels based on their energy intensive production is likely to affect its purchase by the EU fuel suppliers *vis-à-vis* conventional fuels. Therefore, the default value, together with the emission target, may conceivably affect the import within the meaning of Article I:1 GATT. However, for a discrimination to exist, the measure must concern "like" products, as defined by panels and the Appellate Body. Thus, the determinant under WTO law is whether Canadian producers can convincingly argue that life cycle emissions of fuels derived from tar sands are comparable to those of fuels obtained from heavy oils of other origins with better grades. At the downstream level, the fuels appear to be alike in terms of their properties, uses and other criteria developed by the WTO adjudicating bodies. When taking a closer look at the feedstock/upstream level however, tar sands (bitumen) and crude oil differ in their physical properties and their tariff classification. In fact, bitumen is described as a precursor to synthetic crude oil (SCO): it needs further treatment (i.e. energy and hydrogen) to produce synthetic crude oil from it.[79] So, at this level, the fuels might not be considered like products. However, since the Fuel Quality Directive and the Commission proposal

[79] Ducharme (2012).

place the requirements for fuel suppliers at the product level rather than at the feedstock level, there is a considerable chance that a WTO panel will lay greater emphasis on the fuels' similarities at the downstream level and consider conventional and unconventional fuels to be like products. On that basis, a violation of the non-discrimination obligation under Article I:1 GATT can be argued convincingly.

Furthermore, the EU rules on the default value read together with the emission targets may also be considered to be a measure affecting imports of unconventional fuels within the meaning of Article XI GATT. Contrary to discriminatory measures, a border measure is prohibited irrespective of the existence of a like product. Accordingly, if the default value of the unconventional fuels is set at a level which effectively precludes EU fuels suppliers from importing these fuels in accordance with their obligation to meet the emission target, the EU rules will qualify as an import restriction.

Technical Regulation Under the TBT Agreement

The EU regime could also be challenged as a technical regulation under the TBT Agreement. There are several grounds which support a finding that the EU regime on fuels amounts to a technical regulation, i.e. a stipulation of product characteristics or their related processes and production methods (PPMs), compliance with which is mandatory[80]: First of all, (1) the EU regime classifies fuels according to their life cycle greenhouse gas emissions and, therefore, applies to an identifiable group of products (the identified fuels). Further, (2) it lays down process and production methods (PPMs) related to the fuels. Along with the implementation proposal, the Fuel Quality Directive would prescribe the way in which fuels must be produced in order to be accorded a favourable default value. Finally (3), the EU regime on fuels is mandatory, i.e. it obligatorily applies to all fuels imported into the EU and to EU fuel suppliers.

Provided that the EU regime on fuels constitutes a technical regulation, it comes within the TBT Agreement's scope of application and may be in violation of the non-discrimination principle contained in Article 2.1 TBT Agreement. Under Articles I:1 and III:4 GATT alike, a violation of the Article 2.1 TBT Agreement requires discriminatory treatment and the likeness of the examined products. In this respect, the aforementioned principles apply with the result that there is a considerable likelihood that the calculation of the default values together with the emission targets infringe Article 2.1 TBT Agreement.

[80] Cf. Herrmann (2007), p. 215 (240 et seq., para. 549).

Environment- and Conservation-Related Justifications

Even if the fuel quality requirements amount to a (discriminatory) measure under GATT or the TBT Agreement, the EU might still be able to rely on exceptions under the corresponding agreement in order to justify its measure. Under the TBT Agreement, the EU may invoke Article 2.2, which is framed along the lines of Article XX GATT stipulating general exceptions from the non-discrimination obligations. Both agreements recognise the WTO Members' right to follow their own environmental policy within the boundaries set by the relevant provisions. Due to the provisions' parallel construction and in order to avoid repetition, the following part will assess a potential EU environment- and conservation-related justification only under the heading of Article XX GATT.

Possible exceptions under Article XX GATT that the EU may rely on are the environment-related justification pursuant to Article XX(b) GATT and the conservation-related justification contained in Article XX(g) GATT. In order to successfully invoke Article XX(b) GATT, the EU would have to show that the system under the Fuel Quality Directive and the Commission proposal on the calculation of the fuel value is necessary for the purpose of achieving the EU's environmental policy objectives. Such assessment of necessity will include a weighing of all factors involved, such as (1) the contribution made by the measure to the enforcement of the law or regulation at issue, (2) the importance of the interests or values protected by the measure, or (3) the impact of the law or regulation on imports or exports. Article XX(g) GATT on the other hand requires that the measure be *primarily aimed* at the conservation of exhaustible natural resources. This does not presuppose identical treatment of imports, but rather even-handedness in the imposition of restrictions in the name of conservation. Some serious doubts have been voiced in this respect because the values set for so-called conventional fuels are based on calculations that do not take into account the flaring and venting which occurs in the extraction processes in e.g. the Middle East. The broadly interpreted concept of "exhaustible natural resources" includes living and non-living resources, as well as clean air. Whichever exception the EU intends to rely on, it also needs to consider the "Chapeau" clause of Article XX GATT, containing the principles of *non-discrimination* and *least trade-restrictive measure*.

On the whole, the existing case law on NTBs has shown that the threshold for legitimately adopting environmentally motivated trade-restrictive measures is rather high. In the past, only *EC – Asbestos* can serve as a transatlantic NTB precedent where the Panel and the Appellate Body found that the measure protected human life or health and that "no reasonably available alternative measure" existed. Case law on environment-related measures other than NTBs confirms this observation. Members either failed to take into account the different conditions that would apply in the exporting countries or they failed to enter into negotiations with the exporting countries pursuing bilateral or multilateral agreements to the same end (*US – Shrimp/Turtle*).[81] Furthermore, in *US – Gasoline*,[82] the US failed to apply a less trade-restrictive alternative measure. In this case, the Panel found that the measure in question—a policy to reduce air pollution resulting from the consumption of gasoline—was not "necessary" under Article XX(b) GATT, whereby it established that it is the necessity of the discriminatory aspect of the measure, not the necessity of the policy goal, that is to be examined.[83]

Ultimately, the success of a defence by the EU under Article XX GATT will largely depend on three main aspects. Firstly, the precise effect of the measure on the domestic *vis-à-vis* foreign fuel production (even-handedness),[84] secondly, the scientific evidence supporting the effectiveness of the measure (necessity test), and thirdly, whether the determination of an "actual" instead of a "default value" of the particular fuel is a feasible alternative measure.

Conclusions

In previous disputes, both Canada and the EU have lost WTO dispute settlement proceedings because they failed to justify their claim or measure sufficiently. In *EC – Hormones*, the EC could not provide sufficient scientific evidence supporting the measure. In *EC – Asbestos*, however, Canada lost the dispute, because it failed in its obligation to demonstrate the inconsistency of the measures—and France was able to provide sufficient evidence to support the European measure.

With regard to the current issue, it can be concluded that the EU Fuel Quality Directive likely falls within the scope of the WTO framework as a discriminatory measure and a technical regulation. WTO law, however, allows for exceptions for the protection of the environment, even though the threshold of these exceptions is rather high. Whether the EU fuel quality regime is able to meet this threshold will depend on the questionable even-handedness of the measure, its scientific support and the available alternative measures. With regard to prior disputes and according to present knowledge, it will be difficult for the EU to fulfil these criteria and—perhaps—convince the WTO bodies. In order to overcome the challenges of a possible WTO dispute, the EU would be well advised to seriously reflect on how to justify its environment-related fuel quality measures. At least at this juncture, it appears to be doubtful that the EU will be successful in a WTO case.

[81] Appellate Body Report, United States – Import Prohibition of Certain Shrimp and Shrimp Products, WT/DS58/AB/R.

[82] Appellate Body Report, United States – Standards for Reformulated and Conventional Gasoline, WT/DS2/AB/R.

[83] Panel Report, United States – Standards for Reformulated and Conventional Gasoline, WT/DS2/R, para. 6.22.

[84] For the application of the principle of even-handedness under the TBT Agreement, see Mavroidis (2013), p. 509 (513).

Acknowledgement The authors thank Greta-Josefin Harnisch and Justus Bartelt for their assistance. The remaining errors are entirely those of the authors. The opinions expressed in this article are the authors' own and do not represent those of Freshfields Bruckhaus Deringer LLP.

References

Ahn D (2002) Comparative analysis of the SPS and the TBT agreements. Int Trade Law Regul 8(3):85

Canadian Press, Canada-EU oil sands battle continues with new report. Huffington Post, 13 November 2013. Available at http://www.huffingtonpost.ca/2013/11/13/canada-eu-oil-sands_n_4267666.html

Carrington D (2012) Canada threatens trade war with EU over tar sands. The Guardian, 20 February 2012. Available at http://gu.com/p/35gkf

Carrington D (2013) Europe "stigmatising" Canada by labelling tar sands oil highly polluting. The Guardian, 19 November 2013. Available at http://gu.com/p/3kga7

Ducharme M (2012) The European fuel quality directive: will it stay or will it go? 12 March 2012. Available at http://ablawg.ca/2012/03/12/the-european-fuel-quality-directive-will-it-stay-or-will-it-go/

Echols M (1996) Sanitary and phytosanitary measures. In: Stewart T (ed) The World Trade Organization, p 191

Fraser V (2012) Horizontal mechanism proposal for the resolution of non-tariff barrier disputes at the WTO: an analysis. J Int Econ Law 15(4):1033

Gehring MW (2010) Gesundheitspolizeiliche und pflanzenschutzrechtliche Maßnahmen (SPS). In: Hilf, Oeter (eds) WTO-Recht, 2nd edn

Heese M (2012) Protektionismus. In: Bergmann JM (ed) Handlexikon der Europäischen Union, 4th edn

Herrmann C (2007) Inländergleichbehandlung, innerstaatliche Regulierung und technische Handelshemmnisse. In: Herrmann C, Weiß W, Ohler C (eds) Welthandelsrecht, 2nd edn, p 215

Jessen H (2010) Technische Handelshemmnisse (TBT). In: Hilf M, Oeter S (eds) WTO-Recht, 2nd edn, p 381

Kaienburg N (2010) Compliance in High Profile-Fällen der WTO, pp 35 et seq

Koebele M (2007) Article 1 TBT agreement. In: Wolfrum R, Stoll P-T, Seibert-Fohr A (eds) WTO – technical barriers and SPS measures, p 183

Mavroidis PC (2013) Driftin' too far from shore – why the test for compliance with the TBT agreement by the WTO appellate body is wrong, and what should the AB have done instead. World Trade Rev 12(3):509

Neumann J (2015) In: Pitschas C, Neumann J, Herrmann C (eds) WTO-Recht in Fällen, 2nd edn, p 130

Paris M (2012) EU delays "anti-oilsands" fuel quality directive decision. CBC Radio Canada, 20 April 2012. Available at http://www.cbc.ca/news/politics/eu-delays-anti-oilsands-fuel-quality-directive-decision-1.1178297

Paris M (2013) Ottawa adds detail to fight against fuel quality directive. CBS Radio Canada, 13 November 2013. Available at http://www.cbc.ca/news/politics/ottawa-adds-detail-to-fight-against-fuel-quality-directive-1.2424171

Pauwelyn J (2002) Cross-agreement complaints before the appellate body: a case study of the EC-Asbestos dispute. World Trade Rev 1(1):63

Prieß HJ, Pitschas C (2000) Protection of public health and the role of the precautionary principle under WTO law. Fordham Int Law J 24(1–2):519

Rigod B (2013) The purpose of the WTO agreement on the application of sanitary and phytosanitary measures (SPS). Eur J Int Law 503

Sacerdoti G, Castren K (2011) Article I GATT. In: Wolfrum R, Stoll P-T, Hestermeyer H (eds) WTO – trade in goods, p 65

Santana R, Jackson L (2012) Identifying non-tariff barriers: evolution of multilateral instruments and evidence from the disputes (1948–2011). World Trade Rev 11(3):462

Seibert-Fohr A (2007) Article 2 SPS agreement. In: Wolfrum R, Stoll P-T, Seibert-Fohr A (eds) WTO – technical barriers and SPS measures, p 400

Sharma R (2002) WTO beware: the newest global non-tariff barriers. Int Trade Law Regul 8(1):1

Stoll P-T, Schorkopf F (2006) World economic order. World Trade Law

Stoll P-T, Strack L (2011) Article XX(b) GATT. In: Wolfrum R, Stoll P-T, Hestermeyer HP (eds) WTO – trade in goods, pp 498 et seq

Tamiotti L (2007) Article 2 TBT agreement. In: Wolfrum R, Stoll P-T, Seibert-Fohr A (eds) WTO – technical barriers and SPS measures, p 220

Tietje C (1998) Normative Grundstrukturen der Behandlung nichttarifärer Handelshemmnisse in der WTO/GATT-Rechtsordnung

Transatlantic Trade and Investment Partnership Agreement and the Development of International Standards

Christian Pitschas

Introduction

Horst Günter Krenzler conducted and steered trade negotiations on behalf of the EU for a long time. After his resignation from the European Commission, he continued to be closely involved in matters concerning the Union's common commercial (trade) policy, both as a professional and academic, until his untimely death. There is no doubt that he would have been intrigued by the ongoing attempt of the EU and the US to build a more integrated "transatlantic marketplace"[1] by concluding a transatlantic free-trade agreement (FTA). With this in mind, the following observations will address the current negotiations between these two global (trade) players and focus specifically on the regulatory aspects of these negotiations.[2]

[1] Statement by then EU Trade Commissioner Karel De Gucht on the Transatlantic Trade and Investment Partnership (TTIP) ahead of the second round of negotiations, European Commission, Press Release, MEMO-13-835 of 30 September 2013, p. 1, available at http://europa.eu/rapid/press-release_MEMO-13-835_en.htm?locale=EN.

[2] In its announcement of launching trade negotiations with the US, the European Commission stressed that TTIP "will aim to go beyond the classic approach of removing tariffs and opening markets on investment, services and public procurement. In addition, it will focus on aligning rules and technical product standards which currently form the most important barrier to transatlantic trade". Further, the European Commission pointed out that "the most significant trade barrier is not the tariff paid at the customs, but so-called 'behind-the-border' obstacles to trade". European Commission (2013d), pp. 1–2, available at http://trade.ec.europa.eu/doclib/press/index.cfm?id=869. The EU's chief negotiator, Garcia Bercero, stated at the end of the latest negotiating round in July 2014 that the regulatory agenda "is considered to be the most economically significant part of TTIP and what makes TTIP different from the other trade agreements",

C. Pitschas (✉)
Bernzen Sonntag Rechtsanwälte, Rue de l'Arquebuse 10, 1204 Geneva, Switzerland
e-mail: pitschas@msbh.de

C. Herrmann et al. (eds.), *Trade Policy between Law, Diplomacy and Scholarship*,
European Yearbook of International Economic Law,
DOI 10.1007/978-3-319-15690-3_14

Early 2013, the EU and the US announced their intention to start negotiating a bilateral FTA dubbed the "Transatlantic Trade and Investment Partnership" (TTIP).[3] The name does not seem to be coincidental: It indicates that the negotiations regarding the conclusion of a Trans-Pacific Partnership (TPP), currently conducted by a number of Pacific countries including the US, form a backdrop to the negotiations between the EU and the US. For the EU, therefore, the TTIP negotiations are also an attempt to prevent being side-lined, in political and economic terms, by those other plurilateral trade negotiations. For the US, the TTIP negotiations serve at least two goals: first, to put pressure on their Pacific partners to agree on an ambitious trade deal as a means of avoiding to fall behind in the "race" with the EU; second, to place the US in the middle of two "major" trading regions with—politically close—third countries,[4] thereby also trying to keep the People's Republic of China in check as regards trade matters.[5] Moreover, the lack of progress in the Doha Round[6] is a prime motive for both the EU and the US in seeking to conclude an FTA.[7] Most recently, Russia's annexation of Crimea, which has thrown the relationship of Western democracies with Russia into disarray, provided another strong geopolitical impetus to the TTIP negotiations.[8]

EU-US trade—latest round of talks on transatlantic trade pact ends in Brussels, 18 July 2014, available at http://trade.ec.europa.eu/doclib/press/index.cfm?id=1132.

[3] European Union and United States to launch negotiations for a Transatlantic Trade and Investment Partnership, 13 February 2013, pp. 1–2, available at http://trade.ec.europa.eu/doclib/press/index.cfm?id=869. The Council adopted a decision on the negotiating directives for the Commission on 14 June 2013, see European Commission (2013e), available at http://europa.eu/rapid/press-release_MEMO-13-564_en.htm.

[4] Biden (2014), p. 9 ("The two agreements now in the works would place the US at the centre of two vast trading regions").

[5] See the comments by Stevens (2013), p. 9, and Donnan (2014a), p. 2.

[6] In spite of the modest success of the ninth WTO Ministerial Conference held in Bali in December 2013, which agreed on a Trade Facilitation Agreement and certain measures in the areas of agriculture as well as special and differential treatment of LDCs (see the overview on the WTO website, available at http://www.wto.org/english/thewto_e/minist_e/mc9_e/balipackage_e.htm; as well as Brünjes and Weidenfeller (2015), in this volume, p. 47), the core elements of the Doha-Round—market access in agriculture, non-agricultural goods and services—still awaits its conclusion (see the statement of WTO Director-General Azevêdo to the General Council on 14 March 2014, available at http://www.wto.org/english/news_e/news14_e/gc_rpt_14mar14_e.htm). The inability of WTO Members to adopt the protocol on the application of the Trade Facilitation Agreement has cast a new shadow on their willingness to revive the dormant Doha-Round and even threatens the proper functioning of the multilateral trading system, according to WTO Director-General Azevêdo, see his statement at the informal meeting of the Trade Negotiations Committee on 31 July 2014, available at http://www.wto.org/english/news_e/news14_e/tnc_infstat_31jul14_e.htm.

[7] Then EU Trade Commissioner De Gucht stressed that "good multilateral rules on these kind of issues take a lot more time to achieve, if at all, because they are complicated. Working bilaterally within the TTIP to begin with is therefore much easier than working with the 159 members of the WTO", What We Need to Make TTIP Work, p. 3, available at http://europa.eu/rapid/press-release_SPEECH-14-357_en.htm.

[8] ICTSD (2014), p. 11; Kafsack (2014b).

Prior to announcing the start of the TTIP negotiations, both sides had set up a so-called "High-Level Working Group on Jobs and Growth" whose task consisted of identifying policies and measures that could spur the transatlantic trade and investment relationship. After intensive deliberations, this Working Group issued a final report which recommended negotiations on "a comprehensive, ambitious agreement that addresses a broad range of bilateral trade and investment issues, including regulatory issues, and contributes to the development of global rules".[9] In particular, the economic gains that could be potentially reaped from a transatlantic FTA are estimated to be significant: A study commissioned by the European Commission estimates that an FTA between the EU and the US, once fully implemented, would increase the EU GDP by 0.4 % (or EUR 120 billion per annum) and the US GDP by 0.5 % (or EUR 95 billion per annum) as a result of expanded bilateral trade between the EU and the US.[10] In their efforts to explain to the civil society why they have entered into these negotiations, both sides allude persistently to these potential economic benefits. Much of these welfare aspects, namely as much as 80 %,[11] would stem from the reduction of non-tariff barriers to trade (NTBs) or "behind the border policies" given that the average tariff rates of the EU and US are already rather low.[12]

Against this backdrop, it is not surprising that the TTIP negotiations pursue the goal of aligning the respective norms, standards and technical regulations of both parties and, more broadly, their approach to regulatory action so as to minimise the impact on cross-border trade.[13] At the same time, the TTIP agenda

[9] High-Level Working Group on Jobs and Growth (2013), p. 6.

[10] European Commission (2013c), pp. 6–7. See also MEMO/13/211 of 13 February 2013, available at http://europa.eu/rapid/press-release_MEMO-13-211_en.htm.

[11] European Commission (2013c), p. 6. In its communication "Global Europe: Competing in the World", the European Commission had already emphasised that "the economic gains from tackling non-traditional, behind-the-border barriers are potentially significant in the EU and US", p. 10 (2006). In the same vein, the Commission's communication "Trade, Growth and World Affairs" states with respect to the trade relationship with the US that "the biggest remaining obstacles lie in the divergence of standards and regulations across the Atlantic, even though we have very similar regulatory aims", p. 11 (2010b). See also ECORYS (2009), for an overview of NTBs in various sectors of economic activity and the possible effects of their reduction.

[12] On average, EU tariffs amount to 5.2 % and US tariffs amount to 3.5 % (see European Union and United States to launch negotiations for a Transatlantic Trade and Investment Partnership, 13 February 2013, p. 2, available at http://trade.ec.europa.eu/doclib/press/index.cfm?id=869. Interestingly, the final report of the High-Level Working Group on Jobs and Growth notes that "both sides should consider options for the treatment of the most sensitive products", p. 3, available at http://trade.ec.europa.eu/doclib/docs/2013/february/tradoc_150519.pdf, which means presumably that the planned removal of customs duties will not cover 100 % of bilateral trade.

[13] "The goal of this trade deal is to reduce unnecessary costs and delays for companies, while maintaining high levels of health, safety, consumer and environmental protection", see European Union and United States to launch negotiations for a Transatlantic Trade and Investment Partnership, 13 February 2013, p. 2, available at http://trade.ec.europa.eu/doclib/press/index.cfm?id=869. In his press statement following the political stocktaking meeting with USTR Froman,

of "regulatory coherence" stirs a public debate within the EU and US about the ensuing consequences for consumers; there is widespread concern that this regulatory agenda will trigger a race to the bottom and thus lead to a lowering of standards (in a broad, non-technical sense), thereby creating risks for consumers' health and safety, the environment or other policy areas.[14] Then EU Trade Commissioner De Gucht sought to assuage these concerns by insisting that no European standard relating to the areas of health, environment and food would be lowered as a result of TTIP.[15]

In this context, it is worth recalling that this is not the first time the EU negotiates an FTA containing specific disciplines on NTBs. The FTA with South Korea, for instance, sets forth (sector-specific) commitments relating to the elimination and reduction of NTBs, in particular as regards consumer electronics, motor vehicles, pharmaceuticals and chemicals.[16] In a similar manner, the FTA negotiated with Singapore also includes (sector-specific) disciplines on NTBs, especially as regards electronics, motor vehicles, pharmaceuticals and equipment to generate renewable energy.[17] The focus on NTBs and regulatory barriers to trade in FTA negotiations corresponds to the Union's strategy of pursuing deep and comprehensive trade agreements that dismantle NTBs and establish a more systematic regulatory cooperation with major third countries.[18]

EU Trade Commissioner De Gucht stressed: "What we aim to achieve in TTIP is that these regulatory agencies coordinate more closely with each other" (Statement/14/12, 18 February 2014, p. 2; available at http://europa.eu/rapid/press-release_STATEMENT-14-12_en.htm?locale=EN. See also European Commission (2014), p. 1, available at http://trade.ec.europa.eu/doclib/docs/2014/may/tradoc_152462.pdf.

[14] See Financial Times (2013b), p. 2; Financial Times (2014a), p. 6; Financial Times (2014b); Donnan (2014b), p. 3; Kafsack (2014a), p. 9; Caldwell (2014), p. 9. A similar concern is voiced with respect to the TTIP chapter on investment protection, in particular as regards its investor-state arbitration provisions, in that firms from the other party would avail themselves of the investor-state arbitration mechanism against regulatory measures, e.g. in the environmental area, that may have a negative impact on their businesses, see F.A.Z. (2013), p. 19; ICTSD (2014), p. 11.

[15] De Gucht (2014c); see also European Commission (2014), p. 5, available at http://europa.eu/rapid/press-release_STATEMENT-14-12_en.htm?locale=EN.

[16] European Commission (2010), pp. 1 and 3–5: The EU–South Korea FTA is "the first of the new generation of FTAs launched in 2007 as part of the 'Global Europe' initiative" and "the most comprehensive free trade agreement ever negotiated by the EU" (p. 1). The Commission stated that the EU–South Korea FTA "will inform our approach for further FTAs under negotiation", (2012), p. 12, available at http://trade.ec.europa.eu/doclib/docs/2012/july/tradoc_149807.pdf.

[17] European Commission (2013a), pp. 4–6. Contrary to the EU–South Korea FTA, the FTA with Singapore has not entered into force yet; European Commission (2013b), p. 4.

[18] European Commission (2013c), pp. 4–5, and 7; see also European Commission, pp. 5–6, available at http://ec.europa.eu/commission_2010-2014/president/news/archives/2013/02/pdf/20130205_2_en.pdf and De Gucht (2014a), p. 2.

What would set the TTIP apart is, of course, its scale and scope, since the EU and US stand for roughly one third of global trade flows.[19] Inevitably, therefore, these negotiations attract a lot of attention from third parties due to the effect that a TTIP would have on their trade relations with the EU and the US.[20] Indeed, the EU and the US are cognisant of the impact on third countries but claim that such impact would be benign in nature due to positive (direct and indirect) spill-over effects.[21] They argue that the envisaged alignment of the EU's and the US' regulatory regimes would reduce compliance costs of companies in third countries that export to the EU or the US and provide an incentive to third countries to move towards any new common standard created in the framework of TTIP.[22]

In fact, the negotiating parties envisage that "there may be areas in which the development of common or technically equivalent standards could be considered".[23] In turn, it is suggested that such common standards "are more likely to be followed around the world"[24] and hence stand "a good chance of becoming international standards".[25] It appears that this latter aspect is very present in the negotiators' minds: Their public announcements proclaim that both sides could set the benchmark for developing global standards.[26] In his welcoming remarks prior to

[19] European Union and United States to Launch Negotiations for a Transatlantic Trade and Investment Partnership, 13 February 2013, p. 1, available at http://trade.ec.europa.eu/doclib/press/index.cfm?id=869. Together, the EU and US account for 46 % of world GDP, see European Commission (2013c), p. 10.

[20] See The Economist (2013), p. 39; Le Temps (2014), p. 8.

[21] European Commission (2013c), pp. 10–11. In contrast, a study conducted by the Ifo-Institute on behalf of the Bertelsmann-Stiftung finds that TTIP would have negative effects on third countries, see Financial Times (2013a).

[22] European Commission (2013c), p. 11. See also De Gucht (2014b), pp. 4–5 ("many of the regulatory barriers we remove will not only benefit European and American companies but also exporters from developing countries").

[23] European Commission, p. 5, available at http://trade.ec.europa.eu/doclib/docs/2013/july/tradoc_151627.pdf.

[24] European Commission, p. 2, available at http://trade.ec.europa.eu/doclib/docs/2013/july/tradoc_151605.pdf. As was candidly pointed out by De Gucht, "many of the technical solutions will be able to be applied more widely, especially as they will already be operating in 40% of the world economy" (2014b), p. 5. De Gucht reiterated this stance in a speech in Berlin on 5 May 2014: "And if the agreement covers 40% of the world economy, that will be a basis for future work with a wider set of partners", What We Need to Make TTIP Work, p. 3, available at http://europa.eu/rapid/press-release_SPEECH-14-357_en.htm.

[25] De Gucht (2013), p. 6. In a recent speech in Paris, De Gucht pointed out that "the third way people would benefit from regulatory cooperation is because whatever we do together would provide an excellent basis for future global efforts towards regulatory coherence". The Future of TTIP – The Benefits and How to Achieve them, 10 April 2014, p. 5, available at http://europa.eu/rapid/press-release_SPEECH-14-314_en.htm.

[26] European Commission, Press Release at the occasion of the conclusion of the third round of negotiations, 20 December 2013. De Gucht stressed that common approaches of the EU and the US "may shape regulation around the world, including in countries like Brazil, India, China and Russia, where today standards are typically much lower than in the US and the EU", (2014c),

the first stocktaking meeting with United States Trade Representative (USTR) Froman in February 2014, Commissioner De Gucht stated openly: "What we are trying to do is [...] work together to make sure that we can continue to play a leading role in world markets about norms and standard setting – not in a 'closed shop' manner, but in an open way".[27]

Given that the regulatory alignment sought under the TTIP should ostensibly serve also as a vehicle for (contributing to) the development of international standards, this "standard setting" for the international community is further examined below along the following lines: firstly, the main components of the envisaged regulatory chapter of the TTIP and their perceived potential to contribute to international standard setting are identified; secondly, the approach to international standard setting under the TTIP is compared to the understanding of this process in relevant WTO Agreements; and finally, some concluding remarks are offered.

Regulatory Chapter of the TTIP

Main Elements and Instruments

The "regulatory part" of the TTIP negotiations is composed of five elements: (a) sanitary and phytosanitary measures, (b) technical barriers to trade, (c) annexes for specific goods and services sectors, (d) cross-cutting disciplines on regulatory coherence and transparency regarding goods and services, and (e) a framework for regulatory cooperation.[28] Although these elements differ in scope, as some are sectoral and some are horizontal in nature, they share two overarching aims: first, to make—both existing and future—regulations more *compatible*; and second, to promote increased *cooperation* between the regulatory bodies of both sides.[29] Regulatory compatibility and cooperation are intertwined because the

---

pp. 6–7. See also European Commission (2014), p. 3, available at http://trade.ec.europa.eu/doclib/docs/2014/may/tradoc_152462.pdf.

[27] European Commission, Statement/14/11, 17 February 2014, p. 1. In a similar vein Karel De Gucht: "This means that TTIP will be an important way for us to shape regulations, norms, including on investment, and ultimately values that govern economic exchange worldwide", (2014a), p. 2.

[28] European Commission 11 February 2013, p. 4, available at http://trade.ec.europa.eu/doclib/docs/2013/february/tradoc_150519.pdf.

[29] European Commission, pp. 3–4, available at http://trade.ec.europa.eu/doclib/docs/2013/july/tradoc_151605.pdf; European Commission, p. 3, available at http://trade.ec.europa.eu/doclib/docs/2013/july/tradoc_151622.pdf. See also De Gucht (2013), pp. 4–5; De Gucht (2014d), p. 3. The EU's chief negotiator, Garcia Bercero, underlined at the end of the latest negotiating round that "enhanced regulatory cooperation is essential if the EU and the US wish to play a leading role in the development of international regulations and standards based on the highest levels of protection". EU–US trade—latest round of talks on transatlantic trade pact ends in Brussels, 18 July 2014, available at http://trade.ec.europa.eu/doclib/press/index.cfm?id=1132.

compatibility of regulations will ultimately bear fruit only if the competent regulatory bodies, which are responsible for applying and enforcing those regulations, are willing to cooperate with one another.[30]

In order to achieve regulatory compatibility and cooperation, the aforementioned elements have to rely on certain instruments. In this respect, the final report of the High-Level Working Group on Jobs and Growth referred to "early consultations on significant regulations, use of impact assessments, periodic review of existing regulatory measures, and application of good regulatory practices" as well as "regulatory harmonization, equivalence, or mutual recognition, where appropriate".[31] It should be noted in this context that some of these instruments form part of a broader set of regulatory policies and practices that were identified by the OECD Regulatory Policy Committee and recommended to OECD members with a view to improving regulatory quality,[32] including the promotion of regulatory coherence through coordination mechanisms between the supranational, national and sub-national levels of government.[33]

Irrespective of their distinct characteristics, the various elements and instruments of TTIP's regulatory chapter are first and foremost intended to foster regulatory compatibility and cooperation in the *bilateral* trade relationship between the EU and the US. This raises the question of how the bilateral process of regulatory alignment between the EU and the US is supposed to bring about *international* standards.

Potential Contribution to International Standard Setting

Three patterns of how the regulatory agenda of the TTIP could potentially contribute to international standard setting are discernible at this stage of the negotiations: (1) cooperation of the parties' regulatory bodies in international standardisation organisations[34]; (2) use of international standards as a basis for regulatory action[35];

[30] It has been pointed out that the early identification of potential regulatory friction is a key part of regulatory cooperation and an effective regulatory cooperation should operate as a means of pre-empting trade concerns, WTO (2014), p. 32.

[31] High-Level Working Group on Jobs and Growth (2013), p. 4. On the use of harmonisation, equivalence and mutual recognition in bilateral and regional FTAs as a means to achieve regulatory coherence as well as the differences in the approaches pursued by the US and the EU see Lesser (2007), paras. 27 et seq., paras. 43–44, and 51–53; see also WTO (2011b), pp. 140–141.

[32] OECD (2012), available http://www.oecd.org/governance/regulatory-policy/49990817.pdf.

[33] OECD (2012), available http://www.oecd.org/governance/regulatory-policy/49990817.pdf, p. 5, I.10.

[34] European Commission, p. 5, available at http://trade.ec.europa.eu/doclib/docs/2013/july/tradoc_151627.pdf; European Commission (2014), p. 1, available at http://trade.ec.europa.eu/doclib/docs/2014/may/tradoc_152462.pdf.

[35] European Commission, p. 2, available at http://trade.ec.europa.eu/doclib/docs/2013/july/tradoc_151622.pdf.

and (3) unilateral adoption by third countries of newly created transatlantic standards.[36] The manner and extent to which these patterns would or could contribute to the development of international standards differs considerably.

The first pattern—cooperation of the EU and US regulatory bodies within international standardisation organisations—seems to be the most obvious and possibly most promising way to contribute to the making of international standards. The responsibility of devising relevant international standards lies with the international standardising organisation concerned. Any international standard adopted by such organisations will have benefitted, in principle, from input received from all of their members. By cooperating and coordinating their input into the process of developing a relevant international standard within an international standardisation organisation, the EU and the US will be more influential in the standard setting process than if they acted on their own, especially if they pursued different or even divergent objectives instead. This type of "coalition building" is a natural phenomenon occurring within any international organisation that seeks to establish a common denominator for its membership.[37] It is also a sign for members' willingness to engage in the collaborative effort of the organisation's members to find such common denominator which will then form the basis for an international standard.

In contrast, the second pattern—the use of existing international standards as a basis for regulatory action—will only have an *indirect* effect on international standards. This behaviour does not contribute *per se* to the development of international standards since it relies on an existing standard as a foundation for subsequent regulatory action.[38] Nonetheless, this kind of behaviour is meaningful in relation to international standards in two respects: First, it confirms that the international standard concerned is sufficiently appropriate and effective so as to serve as a relevant basis for regulatory action at the national level; second, it fulfils the core purpose of the international standard in constituting a common benchmark for regulatory action at the domestic level of all members of the organisation that has set the standard in question.[39]

The third pattern—the expectation that third countries would unilaterally adopt transatlantic standards created under the TTIP—appears to be the most sensitive and possibly most controversial one since it seeks to exploit the dominant position of the transatlantic trade relationship within global trade. The first pattern consists

---

[36] European Commission (2013c), p. 10.

[37] It has been stated that the "development of international standards is, by definition, a form of multilateral cooperation", WTO (2012a), p. 179.

[38] See OECD (2012), p. 12, I.12, available http://www.oecd.org/governance/regulatory-policy/49990817.pdf, recommending to "give consideration to all relevant international standards".

[39] It must be noted, though, that the linkage between regulatory action and international standards is often very difficult to establish because of a lack of transparency, i.e. there is a lack of information that would allow to identify, for a given sector, whether and to which extent international standards form the basis for regulatory action, see Fliess et al. (2010), paras. 74–75, and 76 et seq. As regards services, the problem is compounded by the fact that international standards are much less prevalent as compared to goods, WTO (2012a), p. 185.

of multilateral action through participation in the international standard setting process. While the second pattern consists of unilateral action, this unilateral action is rooted in a multilateral outcome, i.e. an existing international standard previously adopted by an international standardising organisation, and may induce widespread reliance on the international standard in question for regulatory action at the national level. In contrast, the third pattern bears no (direct) relationship to plurilateral or multilateral discussions and efforts regarding the setting of international standards since this pattern implies that no relevant international standard yet exists or, conversely, an existing international standard will be deemed not to be relevant, appropriate or effective for the pursuit of the regulatory goal in question. Thus, the third pattern relies simply on the fact that the EU and US stand for roughly one third of global trade and that this, in and of itself, would provide third countries with an "incentive to move towards any new transatlantic standards that the TTIP creates".[40] Although this so-called "indirect spill-over effect" may well materialise, as a *factual* matter, it appears somewhat difficult to reconcile this policy stance with the understanding that international standards should result from a collaborative effort of the membership of a relevant international standardisation organisation provided that one exists and is active in the area in question.

The aforementioned patterns will be contrasted below with pertinent WTO rules that relate to international standards.

International Standards and WTO Law

Several WTO Agreements refer, in one way or the other, to international standards. In light of the abovementioned elements of the regulatory chapter of the TTIP, three WTO Agreements are particularly relevant: as regards trade in goods, the Agreement on Technical Barriers to Trade (TBT Agreement) and the Agreement on the Application of Sanitary and Phytosanitary Measures, and as regards trade in services, the General Agreement on Trade in Services (GATS). The following considerations differentiate between trade in goods, on the one hand, and trade in services, on the other, because of their distinct characteristics and the different rules that apply under the said Agreements; the focus here is on the TBT Agreement and the GATS, respectively.

Before turning to these two multilateral trade agreements in more detail, though, it is noted that these agreements serve in the present context as the most important examples of multilaterally agreed "benchmarks" for the three regulatory patterns regarding international standard setting which are currently contemplated in the TTIP negotiations. What is of interest here is the question how the common intention of the EU and the US to proceed with respect to international standard setting compares to the multilateral "benchmarks" established by the TBT

[40] European Commission (2013c), p. 10.

Agreement and the GATS. As WTO Members, the EU and the US have to adhere to their obligations under those agreements. Neither Article XXIV GATT 1994 nor Article V GATS allow them to "opt out" from those obligations. For one thing, both provisions provide for exceptions from (non-discrimination) obligations under the GATT or GATS as regards the *internal* (*inter se*) trade between or among the parties to an FTA.[41] When it comes to the contribution of FTA parties to the standard setting at the international level, though, said exceptions do not apply because in this instance their internal (*inter se*) trade relationship is not a stake. For another, Article XXIV GATT 1994 is *ipso iure* inapplicable to obligations under the TBT Agreement[42] whereas the two GATS provisions which are relevant in the present context—Articles VI and VII GATS—do not come under the scope of Article V GATS.[43]

Trade in Goods and Technical Barriers to Trade

The preamble of the TBT Agreement recognises the important contribution that international standards can make to improving the efficiency of production, facilitating the conduct of international trade and enabling a technology transfer to developing countries. It is not surprising, therefore, that the preamble encourages the development of international standards in order to promote the harmonisation of technical regulations.[44]

Article 2 of the TBT Agreement concerning the preparation, adoption and application of technical regulations by central governmental bodies[45] imposes

[41] Notwithstanding the fact that both provisions also set out requirements regarding the impact of an FTA on the trade with other WTO Members not parties to the FTA in question.

[42] The Appellate Body observed that "the *TBT Agreement* does not contain among its provisions a general exceptions clause. This may be contrasted with the GATT 1994, which contains a general exceptions clause in Article XX." Appellate Body report, *US – Clove Cigarettes*, WT/DS406/AB/R, par. 101. Referring to this ruling, the Appellate Body later stated that "Article XX of the GATT 1994 has been found by the Appellate Body not to be available to justify a breach of the Agreement on Technical Barriers to Trade (TBT Agreement).", Appellate Body report, *China – Rare Earths*, WT/DS431/AB/R, WT/DS432/AB/R, WT/DS433/AB/R, para. 5.56. The same conclusion applies, *mutatis mutandis*, to Article XXIV GATT 1994.

[43] Article V GATS allows the conclusion of economic integration agreements by WTO Members if two conditions are met: such agreements must have substantial sectoral coverage and provide for the absence or elimination of substantially all discrimination, in the sense of Article XVII. However, Articles VI and VII GATS relate to domestic regulation and recognition which are both distinct from national treatment in the sense of Article XVII GATS. See also Marchetti and Mavroidis (2012), pp. 426–427, who argue that recognition is not necessary for the establishment of a PTA.

[44] In this way, international standards can play a crucial role in the process of achieving regulatory alignment on a global scale, Wijkströma and McDaniels (2013), para. 2.1.

[45] The provisions of the TBT Agreement regarding central government bodies apply to the EU, as per the explanatory note to paragraph 6 of Annex 1 to the TBT Agreement.

two obligations on WTO Members with respect to international standards which are particularly relevant in the present context: (1) to base national technical regulations on relevant international standards,[46] and (2) to participate in the preparation of international standards by appropriate international standardising bodies.[47] Before turning to these obligations in some more detail, it is important to apprehend how the TBT Agreement understands the notion of "international standard" as this has an impact on the contours of the aforementioned obligations.

International Standard Within the Meaning of the TBT Agreement

Annex 1 to the TBT Agreement (Annex 1) sets out the terms and their definitions for purposes of the TBT Agreement. The definitions of the terms "standard" and "international body or system" seem to be particularly relevant as regards the meaning of international standard in the framework of the TBT Agreement since there is no explicit definition of the terms "international standard" or "international standardisation organisation/body".

The definition of "standard" reads as follows: "Document approved by a recognized body, that provides, for common and repeated use, rules, guidelines or characteristics for products or related processes and production methods, with which compliance is not mandatory. It may also include or deal exclusively with terminology, symbols, packaging, marking or labelling requirements as they apply to a product, process or production method." The explanatory note to this definition states in relevant part: "For the purpose of this Agreement standards are defined as voluntary and technical regulations as mandatory documents. Standards prepared by the international standardization community are based on consensus. This Agreement covers also documents that are not based on consensus." Moreover, the definition of the term "international body or system" reads as follows: "Body or system whose membership is open to the relevant bodies of at least all Members." The aforementioned definitions of the terms "standard", including the explanatory note, as well as "international body or system", when read together, may serve to understand the meaning of "international standard" in the context of the TBT Agreement.

Moreover, the introductory part of Annex 1 refers to the definitions used in the sixth edition of the "ISO/IEC Guide 2: 1991, General Terms and Their Definitions Concerning Standardization and Related Activities" (Guide). The latter definitions have the same meaning under the TBT Agreement when used in that agreement provided that they do not conflict with the definitions spelled out by Annex 1.[48] The Guide defines "international standard" as a "standard that is adopted by an international standardizing/standards organization and made available to the public".

---

[46] Article 2.4 TBT Agreement.

[47] Article 2.6 TBT Agreement.

[48] Appellate Body, *US – Tuna II (Mexico)*, WT/DS381/AB/R, para. 354.

Further, the Guide defines "standards body" as a "standardizing body recognized at national, regional or international level, that has as a principal function, by virtue of its statutes, the preparation, approval or adoption of standards that are made available to the public".

Based on the aforementioned definitions, the Appellate Body arrived at the conclusion that a "standard has to be adopted by an 'international standardizing *body*'" in order to constitute an international standard in the sense of the TBT Agreement.[49] In turn, an international standardizing body is a "body that has recognized activities in standardization and whose membership is open to the relevant bodies of at least all Members".[50] As regards the element of "recognized activities in standardization", the Appellate Body held that "evidence of recognition by WTO Members as well as recognition by national standardization bodies would be relevant".[51] As regards the element of "openness", the Appellate Body noted that "a body will be open if membership to the body is not restricted. It will not be open if membership is *a priori* limited to the relevant bodies of only some WTO Members".[52]

In this respect, the Appellate Body also had recourse to the TBT Committee Decision on Principles for the Development of International Standards, Guides and Recommendations with Relation to Articles 2, 5, and Annex 3 of the Agreement[53] which it considered to constitute a subsequent agreement within the meaning of Article 31(3)(a) of the 1969 Vienna Convention on the Law of Treaties.[54] This decision was adopted with a view to guiding WTO Members in the development of international standards by setting out six principles which relate to transparency, openness, impartiality and consensus, effectiveness and relevance, coherence and development.[55] Relying on the principle of openness, as set out by said TBT Committee decision, the Appellate Body took the view that "in order for a standardizing body to be considered 'international' for the purposes of the *TBT Agreement*, it is not sufficient for the body to be open, or have been open, at a particular point in time. Rather, the body must be open 'at every stage of standards development'".[56] Further, a standardising body "must be open 'on a non-discriminatory basis'".[57]

---

[49] Appellate Body, *US – Tuna II (Mexico)*, WT/DS381/AB/R, para. 356 (emphasis in the original).

[50] Appellate Body, *US – Tuna II (Mexico)*, WT/DS381/AB/R, para. 359.

[51] Appellate Body, *US – Tuna II (Mexico)*, WT/DS381/AB/R, para. 363.

[52] Appellate Body, *US – Tuna II (Mexico)*, WT/DS381/AB/R, para. 364.

[53] G/TBT/1/Rev. 11 of 16 December 2013.

[54] Appellate Body, *US – Tuna II (Mexico)*, WT/DS381/AB/R, para. 372.

[55] The observance of these principles has been a prominent feature in the discussions of WTO Members within the TBT Committee. Following the last triennial review of the TBT Agreement by the TBT Committee, it is likely that WTO Members will focus on how standardising bodies implement these six principles in their standard-setting practice, Wijkström and McDaniels (2013), para. 3.16.

[56] Appellate Body, *US – Tuna II (Mexico)*, WT/DS381/AB/R, para. 374.

[57] Appellate Body, *US – Tuna II (Mexico)*, WT/DS381/AB/R, para. 375.

The foregoing observations lead to a preliminary conclusion with respect to the development of standards under the TTIP: Any such standard would not constitute an *international* standard in the sense of the TBT Agreement because the TTIP will not constitute an international standardising body within the meaning of that agreement. In particular, the TTIP will not be open on a non-discriminatory basis since membership to the TTIP will *a priori* be limited to the EU and US. That being said, standards developed by the EU and the US in the TTIP framework could serve as a template for the development of international standards by international standardising bodies if the EU and the US work together in such bodies to this end, as envisaged by the first pattern of TTIP's regulatory agenda.

International Standards as a Basis for Technical Regulations

Having clarified the meaning of international standard under the TBT Agreement, the obligation imposed by Article 2.4 TBT Agreement can now be addressed. This provision reads:

> Where technical regulations are required and relevant international standards exist or their completion is imminent, Members shall use them, or the relevant parts of them, as a basis for their technical regulations except when such international standards or relevant parts would be an ineffective or inappropriate means for the fulfilment of the legitimate objectives pursued, for instance because of fundamental climatic or geographical factors or fundamental technological problems.

This provision mandates WTO Members to use international standards as a basis for their technical regulations but subjects this obligation to certain conditions.[58] The words "as a basis" circumscribe the link that has to exist between a relevant international standard and a technical regulation: it has to be "a very strong and very close relationship".[59] For this to be the case, the international standard has to be the "principal constituent or fundamental principle for the purpose of enacting the technical regulation".[60]

The said obligation is qualified in several respects, however. To start with, the obligation only applies if an international standard exists or its completion is imminent. This condition is self-explanatory.

Next, an international standard has to be (at least partially) relevant for the technical regulation in question. This condition is closely linked to the aforementioned obligation of using international standards as a basis for technical regulations since an international standard cannot be the principal constituent of a

[58] By codifying scientific and technical knowledge developed at the global level, the use of international standards in technical regulations may help to generate economies of scale and production efficiencies, reduce transaction costs and facilitate international trade, thereby contributing to regulatory convergence, see WTO (2014), p. 22.

[59] Appellate Body, *EC – Sardines*, WT/DS231/AB/R, para. 245.

[60] Appellate Body, *EC – Sardines*, WT/DS231/AB/R, paras. 243–244.

technical regulation unless it is *relevant* for that technical regulation. For this to be the case, the international standard must somehow matter or be material to the substantive (i.e. scientific and/or technical) content of the technical regulation in question. As per the definition in Annex 1, a technical regulation lays down product characteristics or their related processes and production methods in a mandatory manner. It may also include or deal exclusively with terminology, symbols, packaging, marking or labelling requirements as they apply to a product, process or production method. Accordingly, the international standard in question has to "bear upon, relate to, or be pertinent to"[61] (one of) the elements (i.e. product characteristics, terminology, labelling etc.) that are laid down, included or dealt with by the technical regulation in question so as to be relevant for that technical regulation. Put differently, a comparison between the international standard and the technical regulation has to show that their respective (scientific and/or technical) subject matters overlap, at least partially.

Finally, WTO Members may refrain from resorting to a relevant international standard if it were an ineffective or inappropriate means for the fulfilment of the legitimate objective pursued by the technical regulation in question. Clearly, the adjectives "ineffective" and "inappropriate" refer to distinct situations, as is also reflected by the examples referred to in Article 2.4 TBT Agreement.[62] Conceptually, effectiveness has to do to with the *results* of the means employed while appropriateness pertains to the *nature* of the means employed.[63] Accordingly, an international standard is an ineffective means if it is not capable of achieving the legitimate objectives pursued by the technical regulation, and an inappropriate means if it is not suitable for accomplishing the legitimate objectives pursued by the technical regulation at stake.[64] It follows that both the effectiveness and the appropriateness (or suitability) of an international standard have to be determined in relation to the legitimate objective(s) pursued, and the level of protection sought, by the technical regulation in question.[65] The determination of the effectiveness and the appropriateness (or suitability) of international standards involves inevitably an element of discretion given that WTO Members may pursue different policy objectives with distinct levels of protection due to divergent national preferences and circumstances.[66] Depending on the preferences and circumstances involved, an international standard may thus be deemed by some WTO Members to be an ineffective or inappropriate means for achieving a particular legitimate objective

[61] Appellate Body, *EC – Sardines*, WT/DS231/AB/R, paras. 229–232.

[62] By way of example, Article 2.4 TBT Agreement mentions three situations where an international standard could be ineffective or inappropriate, namely because of fundamental climatic or geographical factors or fundamental technological problems. These examples provide an indication as to the meaning of "ineffective" and "inappropriate", respectively.

[63] Appellate Body, *EC – Sardines*, WT/DS231/AB/R, para. 285.

[64] Appellate Body, *EC – Sardines*, WT/DS231/AB/R, para. 288.

[65] Appellate Body, *EC – Sardines*, WT/DS231/AB/R, para. 287.

[66] WTO (2014), p. 21.

or the desired level of protection,[67] irrespective of the fact that international standards should not give preference to the characteristics or requirements of specific countries or regions when different needs or interests exist in other countries or regions.[68]

The second pattern discerned in the regulatory agenda pursued by the TTIP negotiations correlates to the requirement set forth by Article 2.4 TBT Agreement since this pattern contemplates to rely on international standards as a basis for regulatory action at the domestic level. In order to give full meaning to Article 2.4 TBT Agreement, TTIP parties would have to adopt the following approach under the said pattern: first, they would have to determine whether there are or will be in the near future any (at least partially) relevant international standards in relation to an envisaged technical regulation; second, they would have to establish whether the identified international standard would be both an effective and appropriate means to achieve the legitimate objectives, and the desired level of protection, that the envisaged technical regulation is intended to pursue.

The suggested approach would be important not only so as to abide by the obligation set out by Article 2.4 TBT Agreement. Additionally, said approach would have the benefit that TTIP parties could avail themselves of the presumption provided for by Article 2.5 TBT Agreement. Pursuant to this provision, a technical regulation that is "prepared, adopted or applied for one of the legitimate objectives explicitly mentioned in paragraph 2, and is in accordance with relevant international standards [...] shall be rebuttably presumed not to create an unnecessary obstacle to international trade".[69] However, the presumption only arises if a technical regulation meets two conditions: first, it seeks to achieve a legitimate objective listed *explicitly* in Article 2.2 TBT Agreement[70] and, second, it is in conformity with the international standard in question. This "conformity" requirement is linked to the obligation that WTO Members must use relevant international standards as a basis for their technical obligations. The latter requirement would not be met if a technical regulation and the international standard concerned contradicted each other or if a technical regulation was based on only some (as opposed to all) of the relevant parts of the international standard concerned.[71] Even if a technical regu-

---

[67] See Wijkström and McDaniels (2013), para. 2.5.

[68] WTO (2013), para. 10 (principle of effectiveness and relevance).

[69] Article 2.2 TBT Agreement mentions explicitly, albeit only by way of example, a number of legitimate objectives: national security requirements, the prevention of deceptive practices, protection of human health or safety, animal or plant life or health, or the environment.

[70] The presumption does not arise if the legitimate objective pursued by the technical regulation in question is not "explicitly" mentioned in Article 2.2 TBT Agreement in spite of the fact that policy objectives other than those listed explicitly in Article 2.2 TBT Agreement may be legitimate in terms of that provision, see Appellate Body report, *US – Tuna II (Mexico)*, WT/DS381/AB/R, para. 313; *US – COOL*, WT/DS384/AB/R, WT/DS386/AB/R, para. 370.

[71] Appellate Body, *EC – Sardines*, WT/DS231/AB/R, paras. 248 and 250.

lation is in accordance with relevant international standards, though, the presumption is only *rebuttable* in nature.[72] Yet in order to rebut a presumption arising under Article 2.5 TBT Agreement, it would have to be demonstrated that a technical regulation is more trade-restrictive than necessary to fulfil a legitimate objective, in terms of Article 2.2 TBT Agreement.[73]

Participation in the Preparation of International Standards

The obligation to use relevant, effective and appropriate international standards as a basis for technical regulations is complemented by the requirement set forth by Article 2.6 TBT Agreement. Pursuant to this provision, WTO Members have to "play a full part, within the limits of their resources, in the preparation by appropriate international standardizing bodies of international standards for products for which they either have adopted, or expect to adopt, technical regulations". The introductory part of this provision highlights the rationale underlying this obligation, namely to harmonise technical regulations on as wide a basis as possible. The participation of as many WTO Members as possible in standard setting activities of international standardising bodies will mean that the international standards will be apt to become benchmarks for future technical regulations,[74] thereby contributing to regulatory convergence.[75] The said rationale is related to the abovementioned obligation to use relevant, appropriate and effective international standards as a basis for technical regulations since the harmonisation sought by international standards would not be realised if WTO Members could simply neglect such standards.

The obligation to play a full part in the preparation of international standards by appropriate international standardising bodies is mitigated by a condition of a *factual* nature, namely the limits of WTO Members' resources, in terms of human, financial and technical resources. This condition takes into account that developing countries, especially the least-developed among them, have only (very) limited (or even no) resources at their disposal. The participation of WTO Members in the preparation of international standards may thus range from full to partial to no participation at all, depending on the resources available to them to this end.[76]

Notwithstanding the said resource limitation, the obligation to participate in standard setting activities of international standardising bodies applies if the

[72] Appellate Body report, *US – Tuna II (Mexico)*, WT/DS381/AB/R, para. 348.

[73] On Article 2.2 TBT Agreement and its conditions see the Appellate Body reports, *US – Tuna II (Mexico)*, WT/DS381/AB/R, paras. 311–323, and *US – COOL*, WT/DS384/AB/R, WT/DS386/AB/R, paras. 369–379.

[74] Wijkström and McDaniels (2013), para. 2.2.

[75] WTO (2014), p. 22.

[76] This state of affairs may create a risk of capture or bias in international standard setting activities, Wijkström and McDaniels (2013), para. 4.4.

standard setting activity relates to a *product* for which WTO Members have already adopted technical regulations, or expect to do so. For the obligation to apply, it is thus sufficient that technical regulations adopted by WTO Members pertain to the same products as the international standards being prepared by the appropriate international standardising bodies. In other words, the nexus between technical regulations of WTO Members and nascent international standards is created by the products that are covered by both the technical regulations and the nascent international standards. This shows the interaction between Article 2.6 and Article 2.4 of the TBT Agreement: the former is concerned with the situation where international standards have not yet come into existence, whereas the latter addresses the situation where international standards already exist, or their completion is imminent.

The first pattern identified in the regulatory agenda of TTIP corresponds to the aforementioned obligation. The caveat relating to the limits of WTO Members' resources is irrelevant for the TTIP parties. Consequently, they are duty-bound to participate fully in the preparation by appropriate international standardising bodies of international standards for products for which they will have adopted technical regulations, or expect to do so. The intention of the TTIP parties to cooperate in international standardising bodies does not contradict said duty. To the contrary, the rationale underlying that duty, namely to harmonise technical regulations on as wide a basis as possible, lends support to WTO Members willing to cooperate within international standardising bodies and coordinate their participation in the standard setting activities of such bodies since such behaviour is conducive to the development of international standards by the bodies concerned.

This leads to the third pattern perceived in the regulatory agenda of the TTIP, namely the expectation that standards developed by the TTIP parties would be adopted by third countries in order to gain a better access to the transatlantic market for their goods. Even if this expectation became reality, it would not mean that the EU and the US could disregard their obligation under Article 2.6 TBT Agreement. If they adopt, or expect to adopt, technical regulations in the TTIP framework for products for which international standards are being prepared by the appropriate international standardising bodies, they have to play a full part in the preparation of those standards, even if they could advocate that their transatlantic standards should provide a blueprint for the international standards to be prepared.

Trade in Services and International Standards

In contrast to the preamble of the TBT Agreement, the GATS' preamble does not mention international standards and their relevance for (the regulation of) international trade in services. Rather, the GATS' preamble refers to the right of WTO Members to regulate, and introduce new regulations, on the supply of services within their territories in order to meet national policy objectives. The short hand reference of the GATS for this particular right of WTO Members is "domestic regulation".

Domestic regulation is subject to certain disciplines set forth by Article VI GATS most of which only apply to services sectors in which WTO Members have undertaken specific commitments on market access and/or national treatment.[77] One of these disciplines is concerned with the *application* of licensing and qualification requirements and procedures as well as technical standards by WTO Members and makes reference to international standards applied by WTO Members.[78] The authorisation, licensing or certification of (domestic and foreign) service suppliers is governed by domestic standards or criteria. Accordingly, the *recognition* of education or experience obtained, requirements met, or licences or certifications granted in a particular country plays a crucial role in determining whether these domestic standards or criteria are met. In this respect, Article VII GATS calls on WTO Members to contribute to the establishment and adoption of common international standards by relevant intergovernmental and non-governmental organisations.[79]

The requirements under Articles VI and VII GATS relating to international standards, including the understanding of this notion in the GATS context, and their import for the regulatory patterns identified in the TTIP context are explored in the following.

International Standards for Trade in Services

The definitions set out by Article XXVIII GATS for purposes of this agreement comprise neither a definition of the term "international standard" nor a definition of the notion "technical standard". In the area of services, a standard may be understood to mean a document that provides for criteria or rules that specify the characteristics of a service and/or the manner in which a service is performed.[80] Performance-related standards serve ultimately the aim to improve the quality of a service and assist service suppliers in meeting regulatory requirements, for instance pertaining to public health, safety and the environment.[81] Given that the quality of a service is inextricably linked to the competence of the supplier, standards often lay down qualification criteria to be met by service suppliers.[82]

[77] GATS' disciplines that hinge on specific commitments are commonly referred to as "conditional" obligations. The counterpart is disciplines that apply irrespective of specific commitments which are commonly referred to as "unconditional" obligations; see Adlung and Mattoo (2007), p. 63 (66).

[78] Article VI.5(b) GATS.

[79] Article VII.5 GATS.

[80] WTO (2012b), para. 20.

[81] WTO (2012b), para. 38.

[82] WTO (2012b), para. 30.

A standard is international in nature if it has been developed by an international body or organisation.[83] It is interesting to note that Articles VI.5(b) and VII.5 GATS use a somewhat different language in this respect: Article VI.5(b) GATS refers to "international standards of relevant international organizations"; the latter term is defined as "international bodies whose membership is open to the relevant bodies of at least all Members of the WTO".[84] By way of analogy to the principle of openness applicable in the context of the TBT Agreement, it may be argued that an international body in the aforementioned sense has to be open at every stage of its standardisation activity on a non-discriminatory basis.[85] In contrast, Article VII.5 GATS refers to "relevant intergovernmental and non-governmental organizations" as regards the establishment and adoption of international standards. Despite the difference in wording, it is submitted that the meaning is the same as in the case of Article VI.5(b) GATS. As Article VII.5 GATS is concerned with *multilaterally* agreed criteria for recognition as well as the development of *international* standards in this respect, the intergovernmental and non-governmental organisations also must have an international character. Accordingly, they constitute international organisations of either an intergovernmental or a non-governmental nature, as the case may be. Furthermore, it is irrelevant that Article VII.5 GATS differentiates between intergovernmental and non-governmental organisations whereas Article VI.5(b) GATS simply refers to international organisations. This is because international standardising activities are carried out by both non-governmental and intergovernmental bodies of an international nature.[86] In view thereof, it has to be assumed that Article VI.5(b) GATS also extends to international bodies of a non-governmental nature; otherwise, a large part of international standardisation activities would be excluded from its scope of application.

For (technical) standards to fall within the scope of the GATS, they have to meet the conditions of Article I.1 GATS.[87] This provision states that the GATS "applies to measures by Members affecting trade in services". While a technical standard adopted by a WTO Member, as envisaged by Article VI.4 GATS, constitutes a measure within the meaning of Article I.1 GATS,[88] international standards do not because of their *international* nature, i.e. they cannot be attributed to WTO Members unless a Member has transposed an international standard into its domestic law.[89] Yet this does not mean that international standards do not come within the

[83] WTO (2012b), para. 44. See also WTO (2012a), p. 185.

[84] Footnote 3 to Article VI.5(b) GATS. This definition is identical to the definition of the notion "international body or system" in para. 4 of Annex 1 to the TBT Agreement.

[85] See above on the principle of openness in the context of the TBT Agreement and the conclusions derived by the Appellate Body on the basis of this principle.

[86] WTO (2012b), paras. 49–50.

[87] WTO (2012b), para. 26.

[88] A measure means any measure by a Member, whether in the form of a law, regulation, procedure, decision, administrative action, or any other form, pursuant to Article XXVIII (a) GATS.

[89] WTO (2012b), para. 15.

scope of the GATS since Articles VI.5(b) and VII.5 GATS confer on international standards a specific function in relation to (certain) regulatory measures by WTO Members affecting trade in services. Therefore, international standards are relevant to the regulatory measures by WTO Members addressed by Articles VI.5(b) and VII.5 GATS and thus fall under its scope in this regard.

In light of the above considerations, it may be preliminarily concluded that any standard developed by the EU and the US within the TTIP framework would not amount to an *international* standard in the sense of the GATS: TTIP is not an international (intergovernmental) organisation for purposes of the GATS, in particular its Articles VI.5(b) and VII.5, given that membership in the TTIP is *a priori* limited to the EU and the US. This conclusion does not prevent the EU and the US from cooperating and coordinating their work in international standardising bodies with a view to contributing to the development of (truly) international standards, possibly by taking pertinent transatlantic standards as a reference point, as envisaged by the first pattern of the regulatory agenda under discussion in the TTIP negotiations.

Application of International Standards in Relation to Regulatory Measures

Pending the outcome of the negotiations of WTO Members regarding disciplines for the domestic regulation of services trade,[90] Art. VI.5(a) GATS imposes a *stand-still* obligation on WTO Members regarding the application of certain regulatory measures by mandating, *inter alia*, that such measures not be applied in a manner that could not reasonably have been expected at the time the specific commitments were made.[91] In determining whether a WTO Member complies with this stand-still obligation, "account shall be taken of international standards of relevant international organizations applied by that Member", pursuant to Article VI.5(b) GATS.

Article VI.5(b) GATS refers to international standards applied by a WTO Member but does not require WTO Members to make use of international standards in relation to the regulatory measures covered by this provision.[92] This implies that WTO Members enjoy discretion as regards the application of international standards. However, should they choose to apply international standards, this has to be taken into account in determining whether the WTO Member in question complies with the stand-still obligation set forth by Article VI.5(a) GATS. In other words, the application of international standards is not determinative of whether the WTO

[90] On the state of play in these negotiations see the WTO (2011a), available at http://docsonline.wto.org/imrd/directdoc.asp?DDFDocuments/t/s/wpdr/w45.doc.

[91] Nicolaïdis and Trachtman (2000), p. 259; Trachtman (2003), p. 67.

[92] Krajewski (2003), p. 152.

Member in question complies with the stand-still obligation but it may be said to weigh in favour of a finding that the latter obligation is being complied with.[93] This presupposes, of course, that the international standards applied by the WTO Member in question are relevant to the (application of the) regulatory measure at issue. This would be the case if the international standards concerned specify criteria or rules that are "incorporated" in the licensing or qualification requirements or the technical standards whose application is at stake.

Article VI.5(b) GATS has an impact on the second pattern of the regulatory agenda of the TTIP negotiations, i.e. the use of international standards as a basis for regulatory action. To the extent that the TTIP parties agree on new regulatory measures in the sense of Article VI.5(a) GATS and base them on relevant international standards, this would have to be taken into account as a positive factor in determining whether the regulatory measures concerned are in conformity with the stand-still obligation imposed by Article VI.5(a) GATS.

Developing International Standards for Recognition

Article VII.1 GATS provides that WTO Members "may recognize the education or experience obtained, requirements met, or licences or certifications granted in a particular country", thereby leaving it entirely to WTO Members whether they wish to provide such recognition.[94] If WTO Members proceed in this regard, recognition "should be based on multilaterally agreed criteria".[95] Again, no obligation is imposed on WTO Members.[96] However, Article VII.5 GATS directs WTO Members to work in cooperation with relevant intergovernmental and non-governmental organisations "towards the establishment and adoption of common international standards and criteria for recognition and common international standards for the practice of relevant services trades and professions". Hence, this is an obligation to engage in the process of international standardising activity but the obligation only arises "in appropriate cases".[97] WTO Members thus enjoy a certain degree of discretion in this respect.

Article VII.5 GATS differentiates two types of international standards: on the one hand, international standards for recognition, and on the other, international standards for the practice of relevant services trade and professions.[98] Both types of international standards have to be "common". Given that international standards, by definition, represent a common understanding of a particular characteristic or process shared by those involved in the standardisation process, the word

[93] This does not amount to a (rebuttable) presumption, see WTO (1999), para. 35.

[94] Marchetti and Mavroidis (2012), p. 415 (421).

[95] Article VII.5, first sentence, GATS.

[96] Marchetti and Mavroidis (2012), p. 415 (422).

[97] Krajewski (2008), para. 12.

[98] Krajewski (2008), para. 12.

"common" must mean something different in order for it not to be redundant. Arguably, by qualifying international standards as common, Article VII.5 GATS seeks to avoid a situation where *divergent* international standards for recognition or the practice of services trade and professions would emerge, depending on the international body involved in the standardising activity. Article VII.5 GATS thus requires WTO Members to strive for consistency in the international standardising process relevant to recognition and the practice of services trades and professions.

International standards for recognition would be standards that specify criteria for the recognition of the education or experience obtained, requirements met, licenses or certifications granted in a particular country.[99] Since each services sector has its own specificities,[100] the criteria for recognition have to be different for each sector so as to reflect its specificities. While each services sector has a number of common characteristics, the practices in a given sector may nonetheless differ from country to country. This is why Article VII.5 GATS also refers to international standards for the *practice* of relevant services trades and professions. Such standards would specify criteria for the manner in which the services concerned would have to be performed.[101]

The aforementioned requirement under Article VII.5 GATS impacts on the first pattern of the regulatory agenda contemplated by the TTIP parties whereby they intend to cooperate within international standardising bodies. As per the said requirement, the TTIP parties would have to cooperate with relevant international bodies with a view to establishing and adopting international standards of the abovementioned types, although this obligation would arise in appropriate cases only. In assessing whether a given situation constitutes an appropriate case within the meaning of Article VII.5 GATS, the TTIP parties would enjoy some discretion. The fact that the TTIP parties envisage to coordinate their standpoints within relevant international bodies would not run counter the aforementioned obligation; rather, it would further the objective of developing international standards.

Conclusions

A "regulatory agenda" is at the core of the TTIP negotiations. This regulatory agenda focuses on the ways and means to make the regulation of economic activity on both sides of the Atlantic more compatible, including through an increased cooperation between their respective regulatory bodies. The underlying idea is that this sort of regulatory convergence offers by far the highest potential for raising the economic welfare of both the EU and the US. However, the negotiating parties' vision goes beyond creating a transatlantic marketplace based on an aligned

---

[99] Krajewski (2008), para. 12.

[100] WTO (2012b), para. 86(e).

[101] WTO (2012b), para. 86(c).

regulatory framework. Rather, they also seek to make an impact on the global level by influencing the international standard setting through the creation of transatlantic standards as an inherent part of their regulatory alignment.

As regards the latter aspect, three patterns are discernible at this stage of the TTIP negotiations: The first pattern would consist of an increased cooperation of the TTIP parties' regulatory bodies within international standardising bodies. The second pattern would involve the use of international standards as basis for regulatory action within the TTIP framework. While these two patterns relate, directly or indirectly, to the international standardising process, the third pattern is of an entirely different nature. This last pattern is characterised by the expectation of the TTIP parties that third countries would adhere to, or even adopt, the transatlantic standards developed within the TTIP framework, thereby *de facto* elevating these standards to the status of international standards. The expectation embodied by this last pattern is worrisome as it displays a willingness of the EU and the US to rely on their economic power in shaping international trading relationships beyond the TTIP.

When comparing the aforementioned patterns with relevant rules of the TBT Agreement (with respect to goods trade) and the GATS (with respect to services trade), it becomes clear that the pertinent rules of these two multilateral trade agreements of the WTO concerning international standards are somewhat different. However, the starting point under both agreements is the same: A standard is *de iure* international in nature only if it has been developed by an international standardising body which requires the openness of the body in question to the relevant bodies of at least all WTO Members on a non-discriminatory basis. It follows that any standard developed within the TTIP framework will not constitute an international standard for purposes of either the TBT Agreement or the GATS because TTIP is *a priori* limited to the EU and the US. This has a clear implication for the aforementioned third pattern: Even if transatlantic standards were followed by third countries, this would not somehow transform these standards into international standards in the sense of the TBT Agreement or the GATS. For this to be the case, transatlantic standards would have to go through the "vetting" process undertaken by international standardising bodies.

Next, both the TBT Agreement and the GATS impose on WTO Members an obligation to participate in the work of international standardising bodies although both agreements condition this obligation somewhat. These conditions have different implications: The TBT Agreement makes a reservation as regards the limits of WTO Members' resources which is, however, irrelevant to the EU and the US. Accordingly, the EU and the US are required to participate in the standardising activity of appropriate international standardising bodies for products for which they will adopt technical regulations, or intend to do so, within the TTIP framework. Their expectation that transatlantic standards would be followed by third countries will not relieve them of this legal duty. TTIP parties will remain free, of course, to present their transatlantic standards as blueprints for international standards to be developed by the appropriate international standardising bodies. The situation is less clear cut under the GATS. In principle, the same legal duty as under the TBT Agreement applies here but it is mitigated since it arises "in appropriate cases" only, thereby leaving a margin of discretion to WTO Members. Moreover, the scope of the obligation under the GATS is more limited than its counterpart under the TBT Agreement. This is because it is concerned with the development of international standards for recognition and the practice of relevant services trades and professions; the obligation thus does not cover the whole realm of international standardising activities for services trade.

Further, both the TBT Agreement and the GATS confer a role on international standards in the domestic regulatory sphere but in rather distinct ways. The TBT Agreement mandates WTO Members to base their technical regulations on relevant international standards unless the latter were ineffective or inappropriate in achieving the (legitimate) policy objectives pursued or the level of protection sought. The second pattern under the envisaged regulatory agenda of TTIP correlates to said requirement although TTIP parties retain some discretion in determining whether existing international standards are relevant, effective and appropriate. In marked contrast to the TBT Agreement, the GATS does not oblige WTO Members to base their domestic regulatory measures addressed by Article VI GATS (namely licensing and qualification requirements and procedures as well as technical standards) on international standards. But if they do, they stand a better chance of being considered in compliance with the disciplines under Article VI.5(a) GATS.

The foregoing observations show that the first and second pattern contemplated by the EU and the US in the TTIP negotiations as regards the future participation of their regulatory bodies in the process of standard setting by international standardising bodies as well as the use of international standards as a basis for their future regulations of both goods and services correspond to requirements set forth by the TBT Agreement and the GATS, respectively. In contrast, the third pattern envisaged under the prospective regulatory agenda of TTIP appears to undermine the requirements of those two multilateral trade agreements. Admittedly, WTO Members retain some discretion in deciding whether international standards are relevant, effective and appropriate (in the case of the TBT Agreement) or whether it is appropriate to contribute to the standard setting work of relevant international standardising bodies (in the case of the GATS). Nonetheless, in the first instance, the EU and the US ought to undertake good faith efforts in achieving truly international solutions for regulatory issues before forging ahead on a unilateral basis in the expectation that their economic weight will "persuade" third countries to follow suit. Consequently, the third pattern should remain a measure of last resort.

References

Adlung R, Mattoo A (2007) The GATS. In: Mattoo A, Stern RM, Zanini G (eds) A handbook of international trade in services, p 63

Biden J (2014) We cannot afford to stand on the sidelines of trade. Financial Times, 28 February 2014, p 9

Brünjes W (2015) Multilateral trade policy is back. In: Herrmann C, Simma B, Streinz R (eds) Trade policy between law, diplomacy and scholarship: Liber amicorum in memoriam Horst G. Krenzler. Springer, Heidelberg, pp. 47–59

Caldwell C (2014) Popular sentiment is hardening against free trade. Financial Times, 1/2 March 2014, p 9

De Gucht K (2013) Transatlantic trade and investment partnership (TTIP) – solving the regulatory puzzle. The Aspen Institute Prague Annual Conference, 10 October 2013. Available at http://trade.ec.europa.eu/doclib/docs/2013/october/tradoc_151822.pdf

De Gucht K (2014a) EU trade policy as a means to influence globalization. Humboldt-Universität zu Berlin, 22 May 2014, p 2. Available at http://trade.ec.europa.eu/doclib/docs/2014/may/tradoc_152514.pdf

De Gucht K (2014b) Stronger foundations for Europe's economic future. Copenhagen, 19 February 2014, pp 4–5. Available at http://europa.eu/rapid/press-release_SPEECH-14-141_en.htm

De Gucht K (2014c) The transatlantic trade and investment partnership: where do we stand on the hottest topics in the current debate? Lecture and discussion at Atlantikbrücke, Düsseldorf, 22 January 2014. Available at http://europa.eu/rapid/press-release_SPEECH-14-52_en.htm

De Gucht K (2014d) The transatlantic trade and investment partnership: the real debate. European Affairs Committee of the *Bundesrat*, 22 May 2014, p 3

Donnan S (2014a) China craves invitation to join global trade club. Financial Times, 3 April 2014, p 2

Donnan S (2014b) France offers trade embrace as European objections grow. Financial Times, 17 February 2014, p 3

ECORYS (2009) Non-tariff measures in EU-US trade and investment – an economic analysis. Final report, 11 December 2009. Available at http://trade.ec.europa.eu/doclib/docs/2009/december/tradoc_145613.pdf

European Commission, Trade: A Key Source of Growth and Jobs for the EU

European Commission, EU-US Transatlantic Trade and Investment Partnership. Technical Barriers to Trade. Initial EU position paper

European Commission, Transatlantic Trade and Investment Partnership. The Regulatory Part

European Commission, EU-US Transatlantic Trade and Investment Partnership. Trade Cross-Cutting Disciplines and Institutional Provisions. Initial EU position paper

European Commission (2006) Global Europe: Competing in the World, COM(2006) 567 final of 4 October 2006

European Commission (2010) EU-South Korea free trade agreement: a quick reading guide (October 2010a), pp 1, 3–5. Available at http://trade.ec.europa.eu/doclib/docs/2009/october/tradoc_145203.pdf

European Commission (2010b) Trade, Growth and World Affairs, COM(2010) 612 final of 9 November 2010

European Commission (2012) Commission Staff Working Document, External Sources of Growth (18 July 2012)

European Commission (2013a) An informal overview over the content of the EU-Singapore FTA (20 September 2013), pp 4–6. Available at http://trade.ec.europa.eu/doclib/docs/2013/september/tradoc_151723.pdf

European Commission (2013b) The EU's bilateral trade and investment agreements – where are we? MEMO/13/1080 of 3 December 2013, p 4. Available at http://europa.eu/rapid/pressrelease_MEMO-13-1080_en.htm

European Commission (2013c) Transatlantic trade and investment partnership: the economic analysis explained, September 2013. Available at http://trade.ec.europa.eu/doclib/docs/2013/september/tradoc_151787.pdf

European Commission (2013d) European Union and United States to Launch Negotiations for a Transatlantic Trade and Investment Partnership, 13 February 2013

European Commission (2013e) Press Release, MEMO-13-564 of 14 June 2013, Member States Endorse EU–US Trade and Investment Negotiations
European Commission (2014) The transatlantic trade and investment partnership (TTIP): TTIP explained, 8 May 2014
F.A.Z. (2013) Industrie und EU gehen auf Freihandelskritiker zu, 7 March 2013, p 19
Financial Times (2013a) Trade deal would benefit US most, study finds, 17 June 2013
Financial Times (2013b) Trade pact prompts fear of lower standards, 14 October 2013, p 2
Financial Times (2014a) Time to advance on transatlantic trade, 17 February 2014, p 6
Financial Times (2014b) Public cast doubt on EU-US trade deal, 10 April 2014
Fliess B, Gonzales F, Kim J, Schonfeld R (2010) The use of international standards in technical regulation. OECD Trade Policy Papers No. 102, paras. 74–75, 76 et seq
High-level working group on jobs and growth. Final report, 11 February 2013. Available at http://trade.ec.europa.eu/doclib/docs/2013/february/tradoc_150519.pdf
ICTSD (2014) Leaders call for strong EU-US trade deal as Ukraine crisis deepens. Bridges Weekly Trade News Digest 18:11. Available at http://www.ictsd.org/bridges-news/bridges/news/leaders-call-for-strong-eu-us-trade-deal-as-ukraine-crisis-deepens
Kafsack VH (2014a) In den Krallen des Chlorhuhns, F.A.Z., 20 February 2014, p 9
Kafsack VH (2014b) Ukraine-Krise beflügelt Freihandels-Gespräche, FAZ, 23 March 2014. Available at http://www.faz.net/-gqg-7nn3r
Krajewski M (2003) National regulation and trade liberalization in services, p 152
Krajewski M (2008) Article VII GATS. In: Wolfrum R, Stoll P-T, Feinäugle C (eds) WTO – trade in services, para. 12
Lesser C (2007) Do bilateral and regional approaches for reducing technical barriers to trade converge towards the multilateral trading system? OECD Trade Policy Working Paper No. 58
Le Temps (2014) L'agriculture suisse retient son souffle, 22 April 2014, p 8
Marchetti JA, Mavroidis PC (2012) I now recognize you (and only you) as equal: an anatomy of (mutual) recognition agreements in the GATS. In: Lianos I, Odudu O (eds) Regulating trade in services in the EU and the WTO
Nicolaïdis K, Trachtman JP (2000) From policed regulation to managed recognition in GATS. In: Sauvé P, Stern RM (eds) GATS 2000, p 259
OECD (2012), Recommendation of the Council on Regulatory Policy and Governance
Stevens P (2013) Trade trumps missiles in today's global power plays. Financial Times, 22 November 2013, p 9
The Economist (2013) A transatlantic tipping-point, 27 April 2013, p 39. Available at http://econ.st/12K5fFz
Trachtman JP (2003) Lessons for the GATS from existing WTO rules on domestic regulation. In: Matttoo A, Sauvé P (eds) Domestic regulation & services trade liberalization, p 67
Wijkström E, McDaniels D (2013) International standards and the WTO TBT agreement: improving governance for regulatory alignment. WTO Staff Working Paper ERSD-2013-06. Available at http://www.wto.org/english/res_e/reser_e/ersd201306_e.pdf
WTO (1999) Article VI:4 of the GATS, Disciplines on Domestic Regulation Applicable to all Services, Note by the Secretariat (S/C/W/96 of 1 March 1999)
WTO (2011a) Chairman's Progress Report, Disciplines on Domestic Regulation Pursuant to GATS Article VI:4 (S/WPDR/W/45 of 14 April 2011)
WTO (2011b) World Trade Report
WTO (2012a) World Trade Report
WTO (2012b) Technical Standards in Services, Note by the Secretariat (S/WPDR/W/49 of 13 September 2012)
WTO (2013) TBT Committee decision, G/TBT/1/Rev. 11 of 16 December 2013
WTO (2014) The WTO agreements series: technical barriers to trade, 2nd edn

Disputes on TTIP: Does the Agreement Need the Consent of the German Parliament?

Rudolf Streinz

The TTIP Under Critical Review

The Start of the TTIP Negotiations

In February, 2013 US President Barack Obama and EU Commission President José Manuel Barroso announced that talks between the United States and the European Union would take place to negotiate an agreement on the Transatlantic Trade and Investment Partnership (TTIP) to create a Transatlantic Free Trade Area (TAFTA). In March 2013, the EU Commission sent to the Council of the EU a recommendation for a Council Decision authorising the opening of negotiations on a comprehensive trade and investment agreement, called the TTIP, between the EU and the USA.[1] On 14 June 2013, the Council (Foreign Affairs, Trade) unanimously approved a mandate to the Commission for the negotiation of such an agreement.[2] On the occasion of that same meeting, the representatives of the governments of the Member States meeting within the Council[3] further mandated the European

[1] Document COM(2013) 136 final (EU RESTRICTED).

[2] See Press Release of the Council of the European Union of 14 June 2013, 10919/13, available at http://www.consilium.europa.eu/uedocs/cms_data/docs/pressdata/EN/foraff/137485.pdf. The mandate is contained in EU-Document No 7398/13—LIMITE. The directives for the negotiations of the Transatlantic Trade and Investment Partnership between the European Union and the United States of America were officially published by the Council at last on 9 October 2014, available at http://data.consilium.europa.eu/doc/document/ST-11103-2013-DCL-1/en/pdf.

[3] That forum needs to be distinguished from the Council as an organ of the European Union (Article 13 TEU), cf. Streinz (2012), paras. 371 et seq.

R. Streinz (✉)
Ludwig Maximilians University Munich, 80539 Munich, Germany
e-mail: streinz.pers@jura.uni-muenchen.de

C. Herrmann et al. (eds.), *Trade Policy between Law, Diplomacy and Scholarship*,
European Yearbook of International Economic Law,
DOI 10.1007/978-3-319-15690-3_15

Commission to negotiate on behalf of the Member States in areas that have remained within the exclusive competence of the Member States in order to allow for a comprehensive trade and investment agreement.[4] This demonstrates that the planned comprehensive agreement is designed to include matters for which the competences have not been conferred upon the European Union (neither as exclusive nor as shared competences) but remain with the Member States in accordance with the principle of conferral (Article 5 paras. 1 and 2, Article 4 para. 1 TEU). The inclusion of these matters entails a so-called mixed agreement between the US on one side and the EU and its Member States on the other side (see below). Additionally, the Council (Foreign Affairs, Trade) adopted directives for the negotiations on the comprehensive TTIP.[5] These directives contain instructions concerning the nature and scope of the agreement, its preamble and general principles, objectives, market access (trade in goods, trade in services and establishment, investment protection, "including areas of mixed competence, such as portfolio investment, property and expropriation aspects",[6] public procurement), regulatory issues and non-tariff barriers, including sanitary and phytosanitary measures (SPS),[7] rules on intellectual property rights, trade and sustainable development, customs and trade facilitation, existing sectoral trade agreements (e.g. on trade in wine), trade and competition, trade-related energy and raw materials, trade-related aspects of small and medium-sized enterprises, capital movement and payments, transparency, the inclusion of other areas of law, if mutually desired, institutional framework and final provisions.

The Problem of "Transparency" of the Negotiations

The information contained in that document has been classified RESTREINT UE/EU RESTRICTED which means that its "unauthorised disclosure could be

---

[4] EU-Document No 7399/13—LIMITE.

[5] Council of the European Union, 17 June 2013, Document No 11103/13 RESTREINT UE/EU RESTRICTED: Directives for the negotiation on the Transatlantic Trade and Investment Partnership between the European Union and the United States of America, available at http://data.consilium.europa.eu/doc/document/ST-11103-2013-DCL-1/en/pdf. The US point of view is published in a press release of the Office of the United States Trade Representative of March 2014, U.S. Objectives, U.S. Benefits in the Transatlantic Trade and Investment Partnership: A Detailed View, available at http://www.ustr.gov/about-us/press-office/press-releases/2014/March/US-Objectives-US-Benefits-In-the-TTIP-a-Detailed-View.

[6] Council of the European Union, 17 June 2013, Document No 11103/13 RESTREINT UE/EU RESTRICTED: Directives for the negotiation on the Transatlantic Trade and Investment Partnership between the European Union and the United States of America, para. 22, available at http://data.consilium.europa.eu/doc/document/ST-11103-2013-DCL-1/en/pdf.

[7] Council of the European Union, 17 June 2013, Document No 11103/13 RESTREINT UE/EU RESTRICTED: Directives for the negotiation on the Transatlantic Trade and Investment Partnership between the European Union and the United States of America, para. 25, available at http://data.consilium.europa.eu/doc/document/ST-11103-2013-DCL-1/en/pdf.

disadvantageous to the interests of the European Union or of one or more of its Member States".[8] Therefore, all addressees were "requested to handle this document with the particular care required by the Council's Security Rules for documents classified RESTREINT UE/EU RESTRICTED". Although there can be legitimate reasons to keep the specific content of an agreement or the negotiating directives secret,[9] the Council has to provide "a clear and coherent statement of reasons concerning its refusal to disclose those parts of a requested document".[10] The EU Commission was blamed for negotiating in secret without informing the public and also without providing sufficient information to the European Parliament and national parliaments. The Commission, however, refers to the negotiating mandate, agreed unanimously by all EU Member States. It points out that TTIP is no exception in the area of trade policy. Much rather, it is supposed to be a matter of course that the EU is represented at the negotiating table by the European Commission which works according to guidelines agreed by the EU Member States.[11] They specify the EU's red lines and what the Commission can and cannot discuss.[12] The Commission emphasises that the Council, which consists of representatives of the Member States' governments, and the European Parliament are also regularly involved in the negotiating process. It further claims that there have been more than

---

[8] Council Decision (2001/264/EC) of 19 March 2001 adopting the Council's security regulations, [2001] OJ L 101/1.

[9] See Antwort der Bundesregierung auf die Kleine Anfrage der Abgeordneten Klaus Ernst u.a. und der Fraktion DIE LINKE (Response of the German Federal Government to the Brief Parliamentary Enquiries by Members of Parliament Klaus Ernst and others and the parliamentary group THE LEFT) of 28 January 2014, Bundestags-Drucksache 18/351, p. 5, No. 14, available in German at http://dipbt.bundestag.de/dip21/btd/18/003/1800351.pdf. Problematic in this regard was the refusal of the US delegation to allow the Commission to deliver the former's negotiation papers to the EU Member States.

[10] General Court, T-529/09, *Sophie in't Veld v Council* of the European Union, Judgement of 4 May 2012, paras. 120 and 121–125: application of a Member of the European Parliament for annulment of the Council's decision of 29 October 2009 refusing full access to Document No 11897/09 of 9 July 2009 containing an opinion of the Council's Legal Service entitled "Recommendation from the Commission to the Council to authorise the opening of negotiations between the European Union and the United States of America for an international agreement to make available to the United States Treasury Department financial messaging data to prevent and combat terrorism and terrorist financing" (Document No 11897/09), based on Article 4 para. 1 lit. a and para. 2 Regulation (EC) No 1049/2001 of the European Parliament and of the Council of 30 May 2001 regarding public access to European Parliament, Council and Commission documents, [2001] OJ L 145/43.

[11] See Article 207 para. 3, Article 218 paras. 2–4 TFEU.

[12] See European Commission (2014c), p. 2. Concerning "red lines" see e.g. the Directives of negotiation, Council of the European Union, 17 June 2013, Document No 11103/13 RESTREINT UE/EU RESTRICTED: Directives for the negotiation on the Transatlantic Trade and Investment Partnership between the European Union and the United States of America, para. 8 ("promoting high levels of protection for the environment, labour and consumers, consistent with the EU acquis and Member States' legislation"), para. 9 (exclusion of "provisions that would risk prejudicing the Union's or its Member States' cultural and linguistic diversity"), available at http://data.consilium.europa.eu/doc/document/ST-11103-2013-DCL-1/en/pdf.

45 meetings with the Member States, also at ministerial level, more than 65 important TTIP documents have been sent to the European Parliament and over 80 parliamentary questions have been answered.[13] The Commission published reports on each of the six rounds of negotiation talks conducted by the Commission and the US Trade Representative (USTR) since July 2013 which were also presented to the national parliaments, e.g. the German *Bundestag*.[14] The Commission launched a public consultation.[15] EU Trade Commissioner Karel de Gucht published a press statement following the stocktaking meeting with USTR Michael Froman on the TTIP and emphasised that the European Parliament, whose consent is necessary,[16] would "not in the end approve a trade deal that undermines our European values or the social standards we have built over so many years" and he would not approve such a deal either.[17] Moreover, the Commission published the state of play of TTIP negotiations ahead of the sixth round of talks.[18] This is why the Commission takes the position that the TTIP negotiations are the most transparent trade negotiations ever. But neither the directives nor the EU basis for the negotiating text were officially published.[19] However, a copy of the directives of 14 June 2013 was leaked. So was—in March 2014—a copy of the EU negotiating text of 3 July

---

[13] European Commission (2014b), pp. 3 et seq.

[14] See Rathke (2014), 3.1 with further references concerning the Reports of the European Commission on the first three rounds of negotiations (cf. e.g. Commission, EU papers discussed with the US during the third round of negotiations (16–20 December 2013), 6 March 2014) and the information of the German *Bundestag* (e.g. Referat PE 4, EU-Verbindungsbüro, Bericht aus Brüssel 03/2014, available at http://www.no-ttip.de/Material/Kompetenzen.pdf); Bericht des Bundesministeriums für Wirtschaft und Energie über die Ergebnisse der dritten TTIP-Verhandlungsrunde, 16.–20. Dezember 2013, Washington 12. Februar 2014, BReg-Dok 57/2014. See also the answer of the German Federal Government, Bundestags-Drucksache 18/351, p. 5, No. 14, available at http://dipbt.bundestag.de/dip21/btd/18/003/1800351.pdf.

[15] European Commission (2014c).

(1) Consulting and updating the public. (2) Conferring with governments and MEPs. (3) Getting advice from outside experts. (4) Hearing from other interest groups.

[16] See Article 218 para. 6 lit. a(v) TFEU: The TTIP is based on Article 207 TFEU whose para. 2 requires that the European Parliament and the Council act by means of regulations in accordance with the ordinary legislative procedure (Article 294 TFEU). See Nettesheim and Duvigneau (2012), paras. 46 and 48; Weiß (2014), p. 515 (520, para. 6).

[17] European Commission (2014a), p. 2.

[18] European Commission, State of Play of TTIP negotiations after the 6th Round, 29 July 2014, available at http://trade.ec.europa.eu/doclib/docs/2014/july/tradoc_152699.pdf.

[19] On 21 January 2014, EU Trade Commissioner Karel de Gucht (on 1 November 2014, Cecilia Malmström took office as EU Trade Commissioner) promised "to publish a proposed text for the investment part of the talks which will include sections on investment protector and on investor-to-state dispute settlement, or ISDS", available at http://trade.ec.europa.eu/doclib/press/index.cfm?id=1015&title=Commission-to-consult-European-public-on-provisions-in-EU-US-trade-deal-on-investment-and-investor-state-dispute-settlement. But in its publication IP/14/92 of 27 March 2014, available at http://europa.eu/rapid/press-release_IP-14-292_de.htm, the Commission only cited examples of the text of the Comprehensive Economic and Trade Agreement between the EU and Canada (CETA). See the critical assessment by Krajewski (2014), p. 2.

2013 on trade in services, investment, and e-commerce[20] and—in May 2014—a copy of the initial EU position on raw materials and energy. Therefore, the discussion can now be based on texts and not only on speculations or even assertions which in some cases have no factual background.[21]

Critical Points of TTIP

Not only NGOs but also academics like Martti Koskenniemi[22] or Noam Chomsky[23] and national parliaments of the Member States have criticised the lack of transparency and the secrecy of the negotiations. EU Trade Commissioner Karel de Gucht responded by emphasising that the Commission had regularly consulted a broad range of civil society organisations in writing and in person, including one meeting with 350 participants from trade unions, NGOs and business.[24] The question is, however, whether these consultations had a real influence on the point of view of the EU Commission and hence on the negotiations.

The alleged boosting effect of TTIP on the economy is highly disputed—and probably not really predictable. As to the content of TTIP, the main critics from NGOs, trade unions and consumer groups refer to the fear of lower standards concerning products, especially foodstuffs,[25] but also social and environmental standards, workers' protection and consumer rights. This effect is not necessarily the result of harmonisation but may be one of the consequences of mutual recognition. Critics say that the lowering of standards would mostly benefit large businesses. But there are also examples of small and medium-sized enterprises (SMEs) profiting enormously.[26] A very critical point is the planned investor protection through the inclusion of an investor-to-state dispute settlement (ISDS).

---

[20] Document TRADE B1, B2/asc/2557028, available at http://keionline.org/sites/default/files/eu-kommission-position-in-den.pdf. See DIE ZEIT (2014). See also the website of the GREEN PARTY http://www.ttip-leak.eu/.

[21] Concerning disinformation by NGOs see Greive (2014), p. 4. See however on the reliability of leaked documents, Herrmann (2015), in this volume, p. 45.

[22] Konttinen (2013); in English at http://www.helsinkitimes.fi/finland/finland-news/domestic/8717-professor-finland-s-legislative-power-may-be-in-jeopardy.html.

[23] Durham University Lecture, 22 May 2014, available at http://www.youtube.com/watch?v=wJtfWZGxnGI.

[24] De Gucht (2013). See also Parker/Alemanno (2014), p. 8: "Overall, both sides offer the key element of transparency and public participation, but they do so to differing degrees at different stages in the process. Clearly, the EU legislative drafting process is more transparent, rigorous and inclusive of stakeholders in the formative stages of legislation".

[25] Serious critical points are the use of Genetically Modified Organisms (GMOs) or hormone-treated beef, but there also odd questions being asked such as those relating to "chlorine-soaked-chickens". Concerning the negotiation positions of the EU see Kraus (2015), p. 19 (20 et seq.).

[26] See, e.g., Greive (2014), p. 1: Benefit to the Remscheid based SME "Hodura" (different norms concerning toys).

Critics fear that especially environmental standards could be affected if not the courts of the State where the investment takes place but arbitral tribunals such as those administered by the International Centre for Settlement of Investment Disputes (ICSID) will be competent to decide.[27] Furthermore, the exclusion of national courts is deemed to run counter to the principles of national sovereignty and democracy.[28] The argument of the EU Commission,[29] that US companies already have the right to take an EU government to court under existing ISDS-rules like the Energy Charter,[30] is ambiguous: On the one hand the problems of the Vattenfall case[31] support the arguments of the critics; on the other hand TTIP provides a chance to learn from past shortcomings and introduce improved rules of arbitration, especially setting out a clear-cut scope of application.[32]

---

[27] The German Federal Government, too, has a very restrictive view on this topic, see Antwort der Bundesregierung auf die Kleine Anfrage der Fraktion der SPD (Response of the Federal Government to the Brief Parliamentary Enquiry by the parliamentary group of the Social Democratic Party) of 24 September 2013, Bundestags-Drucksache 17/14787, p. 2, No. 2, available at http://dipbt.bundestag.de/doc/btd/17/147/1714787.pdf.

[28] See, e.g., Eberhardt (2013), p. 29.

[29] European Commission (2014c), pp. 3 et seq.

[30] Energy Charter Treaty (ECT). The USA is not a party of this Treaty. There was only a lawsuit initiated by a UK subsidiary of the US-based AES Summit Generation Ltd. v. Hungary, ICSID Case No. ARB/01/4. The Case Yukos Universal Ltd. v. Russian Federation is particularly interesting. Despite Russia's termination of the provisional application of the ECT it is (until 19 October 2029) under an obligation to afford the investment protection provisions pursuant to part III of the ECT.

[31] There are two cases: 1. Vattenfall AB, Vattenfall Europe AG, Vattenfall Europe Generation AG & Co. KG (Sweden) v. Federal Republic of Germany, ICSID Case No. ARB/09/6. Subject matter: Construction of a coal-fired power plant and environmental protection measures (expropriation), EUR 1.4 billion. Settled by agreement among the parties embodied in an award by consent dated 11 March 2011. 2. Vattenfall AB (Sweden) et al. v. Germany, ICSID Case No. ARB/12/12. Subject matter: Nuclear power plant, EUR 700 million. The case is pending. See Antwort der Bundesregierung auf die Kleine Anfrage der Fraktion BÜNDNIS 90/DIE GRÜNEN (Response of the German Federal Government to the Brief Parliamentary Enquiry of the parliamentary group ALLIANCE 90/THE GREEN PARTY), Bundestags-Drucksache 18/2451 of 01 September 2014, available in German at http://dipbt.bundestag.de/doc/btd/18/024/1802451.pdf.

[32] Concerning the problems of ISDS see Krajewski (2014), p. 2. and on possibilities for reform Bungenberg (2015), in this volume, p. 15. The protection of investors by BITs (Bilateral Investment Treaties) was the subject matter of a seminar for students specialising in International and European Public Law at the Ludwig Maximilians University Munich (LMU). I was gratefully pleased that my colleagues and distinguished experts Horst Günter Krenzler, Bruno Simma and Christoph Herrmann discussed the relevant problems (e.g. cloudy terminology like "fair and equitable"; need for approval by the European Parliament for further EU agreements) with the very impressed students. Thanks to the co-operation with Horst Günter Krenzler, Christoph Herrmann (then my research assistant and now my colleague at the Faculty of Law at the University of Passau) and I had the opportunity to present special seminars on World Trade questions with a practical background. Horst Günter Krenzler also contributed to conferences of the LMU, see e.g. Krenzler and Pitschas (2006), p. 11.

In its resolution of 14 May 2013,[33] the European Parliament welcomed the negotiations on TTIP in principle,[34] but mentioned some sensitive issues where the position of the EU ought to be steady as a rock. Thus, it considered it "essential for the EU and its Member States to maintain the possibility of preserving and developing their cultural and audiovisual policies, and to do so in the context of their existing laws, standards and agreements" and called, therefore, "for the exclusion of cultural and audiovisual services, including those provided online, to be clearly stated in the negotiating mandate".[35] The agreement should include strong protection of precisely and clearly defined areas of intellectual property rights (IPRs), including geographical indications[36] and should guarantee full respect for EU fundamental rights standards, especially a high level of protection of personal data.[37] The European Parliament emphasised the sensitivity of certain fields of negotiation, such as the agricultural sector, where perceptions of Genetically Modified Organisms (GMOs), cloning and consumer health tend to diverge between the US and the EU. Nevertheless, it saw "an opportunity in enhanced cooperation in agriculture trade, and stresses the importance of an ambitious and balanced outcome in this field. But the agreement must not undermine the fundamental values of either side, for example the precautionary principle in the EU."[38]

---

[33] European Parliament, Resolution on EU Trade and Investment Negotiations with the United States of America, 2013/2558(RSP), Document B7-0187/2013, available at http://www.europarl.europa.eu/oeil/popups/ficheprocedure.do?lang=en&reference=2013/2558%28RSP%29.

[34] European Parliament, Resolution on EU Trade and Investment Negotiations with the United States of America, 2013/2558(RSP), Document B7-0187/2013, paras. 4–8 (in general) and paras. 8–10 (concerning the negotiating mandate), available at http://www.europarl.europa.eu/oeil/popups/ficheprocedure.do?lang=en&reference=2013/2558%28RSP%29.

[35] European Parliament, Resolution on EU Trade and Investment Negotiations with the United States of America, 2013/2558(RSP), Document B7-0187/2013, para. 11, available at http://www.europarl.europa.eu/oeil/popups/ficheprocedure.do?lang=en&reference=2013/2558%28RSP%29.

[36] European Parliament, Resolution on EU Trade and Investment Negotiations with the United States of America, 2013/2558(RSP), Document B7-0187/2013, para. 12, available at http://www.europarl.europa.eu/oeil/popups/ficheprocedure.do?lang=en&reference=2013/2558%28RSP%29.

[37] European Parliament, Resolution on EU Trade and Investment Negotiations with the United States of America, 2013/2558(RSP), Document B7-0187/2013, para. 13, available at http://www.europarl.europa.eu/oeil/popups/ficheprocedure.do?lang=en&reference=2013/2558%28RSP%29. This point became very important (and an argument against conducting negotiations on TTIP at all) after the discovery of the NSA scandal.

[38] European Parliament, Resolution on EU trade and investment negotiations with the United States of America, 2013/2558(RSP), Document B7-0187/2013, para. 17, available at http://www.europarl.europa.eu/oeil/popups/ficheprocedure.do?lang=en&reference=2013/2558%28RSP%29. This principle is expressly laid down in Article 7 of Regulation (EC) 178/2002 (so called basic regulation on foodstuffs, [2002] OJ L 31/1). See Streinz (2009), p. 53. But this is a general principle of EU law (see Streinz 1998, p. 413 [418 et seq.] and is relevant in all cases of risk assessment, e.g. concerning the matter of environmental protection, cf. ECJ, C-473/98, *Kemikalieinspektionen v Toolex Alpha*, [2000] ECR I, 5702, paras. 38 et seq., para. 45. For different points of view between the EU and the US see Mavroidis (2003), p. 233.

It stressed that financial services must be included.[39] The Parliament "reminds the Commission of its obligation to keep Parliament immediately and fully informed at all stages of the negotiations (before and after the negotiating rounds)".[40] This obligation is enshrined in Article 218 para. 10 TFEU. But Parliament furthermore "recalls the need for proactive outreach and continuous and transparent engagement by the Commission with a wide range of stakeholders, including business, environmental, agricultural, consumer, labour and other representatives, throughout the negotiation process, in order to ensure fact-based discussions, build trust in the negotiations, obtain proportionate input from various sides, and foster public support by taking stakeholders' concerns into consideration". It "encourages all stakeholders to actively participate and to put forward initiatives and information relevant to the negotiations". Members of the national parliaments like the Members of the German *Bundestag* can be very important "other representatives", at least if their formal consent is necessary for the entry into force of TTIP. The European Parliament is aware of this aspect, having in mind its own role. It "recalls that Parliament will be asked to give its consent to the future TTIP agreement, as stipulated by the Treaty on the Functioning of the European Union, and that its positions should therefore be duly taken into account at all stages".[41]

TTIP is also debated critically and with diverging points of view in national parliaments.[42] In the German *Bundestag* the parliamentary groups of the opposition

[39] European Parliament, Resolution on EU Trade and Investment Negotiations with the United States of America, 2013/2558(RSP), Document B7-0187/2013, para. 18, available at http://www.europarl.europa.eu/oeil/popups/ficheprocedure.do?lang=en&reference=2013/2558%28RSP%29.

[40] European Parliament, Resolution on EU trade and investment negotiations with the United States of America, 2013/2558(RSP), Document B7-0187/2013, para. 23, available at http://www.europarl.europa.eu/oeil/popups/ficheprocedure.do?lang=en&reference=2013/2558%28RSP%29.

[41] European Parliament, Resolution on EU trade and investment negotiations with the United States of America (2013/2558(RSP)). Document B7-0187/2013, para. 25, available at http://www.europarl.europa.eu/oeil/popups/ficheprocedure.do?lang=en&reference=2013/2558%28RSP%29. The obligation to obtain the consent of the European Parliament is embodied in Article 218 para. 6 subpara. 2 lit. a(v) TFEU.

[42] The UK parliament, e.g., had a Panel Discussion on the potential impact of TTIP on specific sectors in the UK on 14 July 2014.

parties BÜNDNIS 90/DIE GRÜNEN (ALLIANCE 90/GREEN PARTY) and DIE LINKE (THE LEFT) and some of their MPs submitted parliamentary questions[43] and initiated very intensive inquiry proceedings[44] dealing with a lot of sensitive issues and critical points of TTIP and the respective positions of the Federal Government which is formed by a coalition of the Christian Democrats (CDU), the Christian Social Union (CSU) and the Social Democrats (SPD).[45] There were

[43] See e.g. the Responses of the Federal Government to: Kleine Anfrage der Abgeordneten Beate Walter-Rosenheimer u.a. und der Fraktion BÜNDNIS 90/DIE GRÜNEN (Brief Parliamentary Enquiry by MP Beate Walter-Rosenheimer and others and the parliamentary group ALLIANCE 90/GREEN PARTY) of 5 June 2013, Bundestags-Drucksache 17/13735: "Planung und Verhandlung einer transatlantischen Handels- und Investitionspartnerschaft", available at http://dipbt.bundestag.de/doc/btd/17/137/1713735.pdf; Kleine Anfrage der Abgeordneten Katharina Dröge u.a. und der Fraktion BÜNDNIS 90/DIE GRÜNEN (Brief Parliamentary Enquiry of MP Katharina Dröge and others and the parliamentary group ALLIANCE 90/GREEN PARTY) of 11 March 2014, Bundestags-Drucksache 18/828: "Position der Bundesregierung zum weiteren Verlauf der Verhandlungen zum Transatlantic Trade and Investment Partnership und den ökonomischen Auswirkungen", available at http://dipbt.bundestag.de/doc/btd/18/008/1800828.pdf; Kleine Anfrage der Abgeordneten Katharina Dröge etc. und der Fraktion BÜNDNIS 90/DIE GRÜNEN of 21 March 2014, Bundestags-Drucksache 18/919: "Erfahrungen, Bedeutung und zukünftiger Umgang mit Klauseln zu Investor-Staat-Schiedsgerichtsverfahren als Teil von bilateralen Handelsabkommen", available at http://dipbt.bundestag.de/doc/btd/18/009/1800919.pdf; at last Kleine Anfrage der Abgeordneten Katharina Dröge u.a. und der Fraktion BÜNDNIS 90/DIE GRÜNEN of 18 August 2014, Bundestags-Drucksache 18/2371 (not yet answered), available at http://dipbt.bundestag.de/doc/btd/18/023/1802371.pdf; Kleine Anfrage der Abgeordneten Dr. Petra Sitte u.a. und der Fraktion DIE LINKE (Brief Parliamentary Enquiry by MP Dr. Petra Sitte and others and the parliamentary group THE LEFT) of 11 September 2013, Bundestags-Drucksache 17/14734: "Das geplante Freihandelsabkommen TTIP/TAFTA zwischen den USA und der Europäischen Union und seine Auswirkungen auf die Bereiche Kultur, Landwirtschaft, Bildung, Wissenschaft und Datenschutz", available at http://dipbt.bundestag.de/doc/btd/17/147/1714734.pdf; Kleine Anfrage der Abgeordneten Klaus Ernst u.a. und der Fraktion DIE LINKE (Brief Parliamentary Enquiry by MP Klaus Ernst and others and the parliamentary group THE LEFT) of 28 January 2014, Bundestags-Drucksache 18/258: "Verhandlungen zum EU-USA-Freihandelsabkommen", available at http://dipbt.bundestag.de/doc/btd/18/002/1800258.pdf.

[44] See Große Anfrage der Abgeordneten Klaus Ernst u.a. und der Fraktion DIE LINKE (Parliamentary Enquiry by MP Klaus Ernst and others and the parliamentary group THE LEFT) of 30 January 2014, Bundestags-Drucksache 18/432: "Soziale, ökologische, ökonomische und politische Effekte des EU-USA Freihandelsabkommens", available at http://dipbt.bundestag.de/doc/btd/18/002/1800258.pdf.

[45] From January to September the German Federal Government replied to about 25 written questions of MPs or parliamentary groups on TTIP. During the 17th legislative period the Federal government was based on CDU/CSU and FDP (The Liberals). Then, the Social Democrats as opposition party asked by Kleine Anfrage der Fraktion der SPD (Brief Parliamentary Enquiry by the parliamentary group of the SPD) of 24 September 2013, Bundestags-Drucksache 17/14787: "Transatlantische Handels- und Investment-Partnerschaft", available at http://dipbt.bundestag.de/doc/btd/17/147/1714787.pdf.

even demands to stop[46] or to suspend[47] the negotiations. TTIP was debated in special forums of the Parliament.[48] Some "no goes" were formulated or at least discussed.[49] The *Bundesrat* (chamber of the German *Länder*), too, debated TTIP.[50] Both legislative organs of Germany think that TTIP should be concluded as a mixed agreement which needs to be ratified by the Federal Republic of Germany with their consent.[51] The academic advice service of the *Bundestag* published an expert opinion endorsing this stance.[52] The same view was taken by both Houses of Parliament in the UK,[53] by the governments of France[54] and Austria[55] and by the chairs of the relevant committees in the national parliaments of the Netherlands, Austria (both *Nationalrat* and *Bundesrat*), Belgium, the Czech Republic (both

[46] See Antrag der Abgeordneten Thomas Nord u.a. und der Fraktion die Linke (Motion by MP Thomas Nord and others and the parliamentary group THE LEFT) of 8 April 2014, Bundestags-Drucksache 18/1093: "Die Verhandlungen zum EU-USA-Freihandelsabkommen TTIP stoppen", available at http://dipbt.bundestag.de/doc/btd/18/010/1801093.pdf.

[47] See Entschließungsantrag der Fraktion BÜNDNIS 90/DIE GRÜNEN (Motion to decide a resolution by the parliamentary group ALLIANCE 90/GREEN PARTY) of 18 November 2013, Bundestags-Drucksache 18/65, "zu der verabredeten Debatte zu den Abhöraktivitäten der NSA und den Auswirkungen auf Deutschlands transatlantische Beziehungen", available at http://dipbt.bundestag.de/doc/btd/18/000/1800065.pdf.

[48] See Deutscher Bundestag, PuK 2 – Parlamentskorrespondenz: TTIP: Abgeordnete für mehr Transparenz. Ausschuss für Umwelt, Naturschutz, Bau und Reaktorsicherheit – 19.02.2014; Forderung nach Klausel für Kultur im TTIP. Ausschuss für Kultur und Medien – 04.06.2014; Chancen und Risiken von TTIP. Parlamentarischer Beirat für nachhaltige Entwicklung, 3 July 2014.

[49] Especially exclusion of ISDS, no lower standards in social and environmental questions and concerning foodstuffs, exclusion of cultural questions.

[50] Decision of the *Bundesrat* of 11 July 2014 (924th session): Lack of transparency of the negotiations on TTIP; critical point of view concerning ISDS. There were also inquiries to the Governments of the *Länder* by Members and parliamentary groups of the parliaments of the German Federal States (*Länder*), see e.g. Große Anfrage von Abgeordneten der Bremischen Bürgerschaft und der Fraktion BÜNDNIS 90/DIE GRÜNEN an den Senat der Freien und Hansestadt Bremen (Enquiry of MPs of the parliament of Bremen to the Senate—the Government of Bremen as a Federal State of Germany), Drucksachen 18/1078 und 18/1187.

[51] See Antwort der Bundesregierung auf die Kleine Anfrage der Abgeordneten Katharina Dröge u.a. und der Fraktion BÜNDNIS 90/DIE GRÜNEN (Brief Parliamentary Enquiry by MP Katharian Dröge and others and the parliamentary group ALLIANCE 90/GREEN PARTY) of 10 April 2014, Bundestags-Drucksache 18/1118, pp. 2 et seq., available at http://dipbt.bundestag.de/doc/btd/18/011/1801118.pdf.

[52] Rathke (2014).

[53] See House of Lords, European Union Committee, 14th Report of Session 2013–2014, The Transatlantic Trade and Investment Partnership, p. 54, para. 173; House of Commons, The Transatlantic Trade and Investment Partnership (TTIP), Standard Note SN/EP/6688 (Wepp), 3 October 2014, p. 10. See also below.

[54] See the response of Mme Nicole Bricq, ministre du commerce extérieur to the parliamentary questions of MP Mme Maréchal-Le Pen, JO 2014, p. 1267.

[55] Schriftliche Information gemäß § 6 EU-InfoG zu Pkt. 2 der Tagesordnung des EU-Ausschusses des Bundesrates (written information of the Austrian Federal Government to the *Bundesrat*) of 14 May 2014, p. 2.

Chamber of Deputies and Senate), France, Germany, Hungary, Ireland, Latvia, Luxembourg, Malta, Poland (both *Sejm* and Senate), Portugal, Slovakia and Slovenia.[56] However, the opinion of the EU Commission seems to differ.[57] Former EU Trade Commissioner Karel de Gucht wanted to submit the issue to the Court of Justice of the European Union if the EU's exclusive competence continues to be contested.[58] On 30 October 2014, De Gucht's second to last day in office, the Commission eventually requested a Court of Justice Opinion on the competence to sign and ratify the Free Trade Agreement with Singapore.[59] Therefore the question whether TTIP needs the consent of the national parliaments of the EU Member States and in Germany the consent of the *Bundestag*—or even the consent of the *Bundesrat*, too—has become relevant in practice.

---

[56] See Tweede Kamer der Staten-General, Letter to EU Commissioner for Trade Karel De Gucht in the framework of the political dialogue: the role of national parliaments in free trade agreements of 25 June 2014: "The chairs of relevant committees in national parliaments who are signatories to this letter believe that free trade agreements should be considered as mixed agreements, since they contain provisions that concern policy areas which were within the competences of the member states. For CETA as well as TTIP (as well as can be foreseen at this stage), this is the case for certain elements of policy areas such as services, transport and investor protection". The chairs added a further argument which seems to express that TTIP should be ratified by the national parliaments in any case: "In view of the important role national parliaments have in the democratic decision making process of the EU, we feel that it is of great importance that trade agreements such as CETA and TTIP are ratified by the national parliaments. Therefore, we ask you to consider comprehensive trade agreements such as TTIP and CETA as mixed agreements".

[57] So the impression of the German Federal Government, see Bundestags-Drucksache 18/1118, p. 3, No. 7.

[58] See European Commission, Karel De Gucht, SPEECH/14/406 to European Affairs Committee of the *Bundesrat*, Berlin, 22 May 2014, The Transatlantic Trade and Investment Partnership: The Real Debate, pp. 4 et seq., available at http://europa.eu/rapid/press-release_SPEECH-14-406_en.htm. The EU Commission could ask the ECJ for its opinion according to Article 218 para 11 TFEU, see Antwort der Bundesregierung auf die Kleine Anfrage der Abgeordneten Klaus Ernst u.a. und der Fraktion DIE LINKE (Response of the German Federal Government to the Brief Parliamentary Enquiries by Members of Parliament Klaus Ernst and others and the parliamentary group THE LEFT) of 28 January 2014 (No. 211), available at http://dipbt.bundestag.de/dip21/btd/18/003/1800351.pdf. See, however, European Commission (2014b), p. 6: "Depending on policy areas covered in the final agreement the 28 national parliaments of the EU's Member States might also have to approve the deal". In his speech to the German *Bundesrat,* SPEECH/14/406, Berlin, 22 May 2014, The Transatlantic Trade and Investment Partnership: The Real Debate, available at http://europa.eu/rapid/press-release_SPEECH-14-406_en.htm, Karel De Gucht also said that having in mind the wide scope of the negotiations TTIP may probably ("wahrscheinlich") become a mixed agreement with the consequence that national parliaments and also the *Bundesrat* must be included in the decision ("dass nationale Parlamente und Verfassungsorgane wie der Bundesrat über TTIP mitentscheiden werden").

[59] European Commission, Press Release, IP/14/1235 of 30 October 2014, Singapore: The Commission to Request a Court of Justice Opinion on the Trade Deal, available at http://trade.ec.europa.eu/doclib/press/index.cfm?id=1185.

Different Starting Points for the Need of Control by National Parliaments Over EU Agreements

Overview

The starting point for the need of control by national parliaments over EU agreements and the extent of the influence of the parliaments depends upon the question whether the European Union has exclusive competence to conclude the treaty or not. The competence to conclude the treaty depends upon the content of the agreement. National parliaments have the biggest influence if a mixed agreement is necessary to conclude the treaty with the intended content as this would require the approval of national parliaments. Therefore, the EU Commission is eager to avoid a mixed agreement. But this leads to the problem that some topics must be excluded. Some legal aspects may be doubtful and this is the reason why EU trade commissioner Karel de Gucht wanted to ask the European Court of Justice to issue an advisory opinion in accordance with Article 218 para. 11 TFEU. If the Union has exclusive competence the influence of national parliaments is restricted to the control of the German representatives in the European institutions. Real representatives of the Member State Germany are the Federal Chancellor as Head of Government (Article 65 Basic Law) in the European Council (Article 15 para. 2 TEU) and the Federal Minister acting in the Council (Art. 16 para. 2 TFEU: "representative of each Member State at ministerial level"). This control is based on national law (see below), but ever since the entry into force of the Treaty of Lisbon, it is expressly not only accepted but "welcomed" by EU law.[60] The German members of the European Parliament, however, are independent. The influence of the national parliament, the *Bundestag*, is limited to informal consultations. The "German" member of the EU Commission is part of an institution which shall be "completely independent". For this reason the members of the Commission "shall neither seek nor take instructions from any Government or other institution, body, office or entity" (Article 17 para. 3 subpara. 3 TEU), including the national parliament. This is why even informal consultations have to be restricted to the competent Commissioner.[61]

The extent of the influence on the national representatives in the Council depends on the question whether the decision on TTIP can be based on a qualified majority or whether the Council shall act unanimously. In the latter case the national parliament can instruct the representative in the EU institution to veto upon TTIP. Whether this instruction is legally binding is a question of national law; but the national regulation has to be in accordance with European Union law (see below).

---

[60] See Article 10 para. 2 subpara. 2, Article 12 TEU.

[61] See, e.g., the consultations between Karel De Gucht and the German *Bundesrat*, SPEECH/14/406, Berlin, 22 May 2014, The Transatlantic Trade and Investment Partnership: The Real Debate, available at http://europa.eu/rapid/press-release_SPEECH-14-406_en.htm.

The Requirement of Approval for a Mixed Agreement

The Qualification of TTIP: Is It a Mixed Agreement?

TTIP must be concluded as a mixed agreement if it touches on subject matters which fall outside the competence of the European Union and therefore remain within the competence of the Member States.[62] But a mixed agreement will also be used in a case where competence over the subject matter of the agreement is shared between the Member States and the EU (concurrent competence),[63] even if there is no legal requirement for this.[64] Thus, a mixed agreement is only excluded if all of its subject matters are within the exclusive competence of the Union according to Article 2 para. 1, Article 3 TFEU. As long as the content of the agreement is not conclusively determined, the question whether TTIP must be a mixed agreement can only be answered on the basis of the information published during the ongoing negotiations.[65] But there is a tendency that it shall be concluded as a mixed agreement—if it will be concluded at all.[66]

The Treaty of Lisbon, in order to abolish the lack of clarity resulting from the Nice Treaty amendments,[67] significantly expanded the exclusive external competences of the EU concerning the common commercial policy (CCP).[68] Transport however remains outside the CCP[69] and is a shared competence[70] which is likely to mean that trade agreements containing significant provisions on transport will continue to be mixed agreements.[71] Furthermore, agreements that cover other

[62] Principle of conferral, Art. 5 para. 1 TEU; Art. 4 para. 1 TEU.

[63] Craig and de Búrca (2011), p. 334. Concerning the shared competences see Art. 2 para. 2 and Art. 4 TFEU.

[64] Hartley (2010), p. 174.

[65] On timings and process of TTIP negotiations see House of Commons, The Transatlantic Trade and Investment Partnership (TTIP), Standard Note SN/EP/6688 (Wepp), 3 October 2014, pp. 3 et seq.

[66] Former EU Trade Commissioner Karel De Gucht said that there was a danger that the TTIP would never be agreed because a lack of political leadership had reduced the chances of an agreement by 2015 and that afterwards there could be further delays because of the US presidential election, Financial Times, Time Is Running out for US–Europe Trade Deal, 26 September 2014.

[67] See Herrmann and Streinz (2014), p. 587 (612 et seq., § 11 paras. 41 and 43) with further references. ECJ (Grand Chamber), *Opinion 1/08, GATS – Schedules of specific commitments – Common transport policy*, [2009] ECR I, 11129.

[68] See Art. 207 para. 1 TFEU.

[69] Art. 207 para. 5 TFEU. Cf. Hahn (2011), para. 45; Dashwood et al. (2011), p. 948. This exemption was included according to a mandate of the European Council, see Herrmann and Streinz (2014), p. 587 (613, § 11 para. 44); Weiß (2011), para. 53. See however Bungenberg (2010b), p. 123 (132).

[70] Art. 4 para 2 lit. g TFEU.

[71] Craig and de Búrca (2011), p. 322.

policies outside the scope of the CCP still call for mixed agreements.[72] This especially concerns competition law beyond the functioning of the internal market,[73] where the EU has no exclusive EU competence, and trade deals extending to fields for which the EU has no internal harmonisation competence, such as health, culture, occupation, social policy, industry, environment and consumer protection.[74]

With regard to TTIP the following subject matters could require a mixed agreement or at least lead to a mixed agreement according to the current practice: transport services (even though the mandate does not specifically mention them the final treaty may be extended to this area), competition law beyond the functioning of the internal market (insofar as the mandate urges the Commission to include competition rules on cartels, mergers and state aid),[75] mutual recognition, harmonisation and better cooperation between regulating entities to eliminate non-tariff trade barriers[76] (insofar as shared competences or even competences of the Member States are touched, e.g. certain standards in the field of employment).[77] However, provisions concerning the mutual recognition or even harmonisation of certain standards may be considered as falling predominantly within the competence for the CCP so that Article 207 TFEU provides an exclusive legal basis.[78] Foreign direct investment is expressly mentioned in Article 207 para. 1 TFEU and is thus within the exclusive competence of the EU. But it is controversial whether this field also includes portfolio investment[79] which is mentioned expressly in the

---

[72] Cf. Bungenberg (2010b), p. 123 (133). See e.g. the Free Trade Agreement between the European Union and its Member States, of the one part, and the Republic of Korea, of the other part of 15 October 2009, [2011] OJ L 127/1.

[73] Only this aspect is covered by the exclusive competence of the EU, see Art. 3 para. 1 lit. b TFEU; Weiß (2011), paras. 52 et seq.

[74] Harmonisation according to Art. 114 TFEU applies for the achievement of the internal market (Art. 26 TFEU) which falls under the shared competence, Art. 4 para. 2 lit. a TFEU as well as social policy (ibid. lit. b), environment (ibid. lit. e), consumer protection (ibid. lit. f) and energy (ibid. lit. i). Concerning health protection harmonisation of the laws and regulations of the Member States is expressly excluded (Art. 168 para. 5 TFEU).

[75] See No. 36 of the mandate, available at http://data.consilium.europa.eu/doc/document/ST-11103-2013-DCL-1/en/pdf.

[76] See No. 25 of the mandate, available at http://data.consilium.europa.eu/doc/document/ST-11103-2013-DCL-1/en/pdf.

[77] See Art. 149 para. 3, Art. 153 para. 2 lit.a TFEU: exclusion of harmonisation; Art. 153 para. 5 TFEU: complete exclusion of the competence of the EU. No. 32 of the mandate, available at http://data.consilium.europa.eu/doc/document/ST-11103-2013-DCL-1/en/pdf, mentions the inclusion of "mechanisms to support the promotion of decent work through effective domestic implementation of International Labour Organization (ILO) core labour standards".

[78] Cf. Weiß (2011), paras. 76 et seq. for the different opinions on the meaning of Art. 207 para. 6 TFEU.

[79] See Weiß (2011), paras. 40 and 44. For shared competence e.g. Dimopulos (2011), pp. 104 et seq.; Bungenberg (2001), p. 29 (40 et seq.).

mandate as an area of "mixed competence".[80] The legal service of the Council,[81] the governments of the Member States and the majority of academics[82] consider that investor-to-state dispute settlement (ISDS)[83] can only be included by a mixed agreement. However, due to mounting political opposition[84] in this regard, it remains to be seen whether this part of the mandate can be realised at all.

The classification of TTIP and the legal necessity of a mixed agreement may remain disputed. But in the end, "mixity" is the result of a political choice.[85] Sixteen chairs of EU committees of national parliaments have urged Trade Commissioner De Gucht to ensure that TTIP will be concluded as a mixed agreement. This point of view is shared at least by the majority—if not by all—of the Member States. Even EU Trade Commissioner De Gucht stated that he considered it "very likely" that the treaty will be a mixed agreement (see above). If the ECJ should really be seized with the matter it is doubtful whether it will decide the question in favour of an exclusive competence of the EU because it has been quite careful in its decisions on this topic. The Court has ruled that none of the possible difficulties which may arise from the nature of mixed agreements will provide a reason for altering the classification of the competence, or for arguing that it should be exclusive.[86] Thus, from the perspective of the EU TTIP will be concluded as a mixed agreement—if it will be concluded at all.

Extent of the Approval Required from the EU and the Member States

A mixed agreement needs to be concluded by both the European Union and (in most cases)[87] all 28 Member States. Being an important treaty, TTIP will be concluded in

---

[80] See No. 22 of the mandate, available at http://data.consilium.europa.eu/doc/document/ST-11103-2013-DCL-1/en/pdf.

[81] Opinion of the Legal Service of the Council, Council Doc. 17144/12 of 30 November 2012.

[82] See Dimopulos (2011), pp. 190 et seq. See however e.g. Bungenberg (2010a), p. 81 (88 et seq.). An added problem: the ICSID Convention is only open to states that are parties of the ICSID Convention and it is doubtful whether it will be opened for the EU; see Reinisch (2011), p. 43 (53) with further references.

[83] See No. 23 of the mandate, available at http://data.consilium.europa.eu/doc/document/ST-11103-2013-DCL-1/en/pdf.

[84] Even the EU Commission is considering renouncing ISDS, cf. EU erwägt Verzicht auf Schiedsgerichte bei TTIP, Die ZEIT, 23 October 2013, available at http://www.zeit.de/wirtschaft/2014-10/ttip-eu-kommission-schiedsgerichtsverfahren.

[85] Dashwood et al. (2011), p. 939.

[86] Craig and de Búrca (2011), p. 335; Müller-Ibold (2012), Vorb. Art. 206–207, paras. 12 et seq. See e.g. ECJ (Grand Chamber), *Opinion 1/08, GATS – Schedules of specific commitments – Common transport policy*, [2009] ECR I, 11129, para. 127.

[87] For exemptions concerning territorially limited regimes like the Convention on the protection of the Alps (Alpine Convention), Council Decision 96/191/EC of 26 February 1996, [1996] OJ L 61/31 (EU and Austria, France, Germany, Italy, Slovenia/Switzerland. Liechtenstein, Monaco), see Kumin and Bittner (2012), p. 75 (82).

a two-step procedure: The negotiations end with the signing of the treaty. After that, the treaty is handed to the competent authorities of the EU and of the Member States whose approval is necessary for the ratification of the treaty. The necessary voting majority in the Council depends on the content of the treaty. This leads to different effects concerning the influence of the Member States and probably the influence of the national parliaments.[88]

Conclusion and Ratification by the European Union

For the conclusion of an agreement in the framework of the CCP, the Council shall act by a qualified majority.[89] But if the agreement includes provisions "in the fields of trade in services, commercial aspects of intellectual property" and in "foreign direct investment", unanimity of the Council is necessary if these provisions require unanimity for the adoption of internal rules on these subjects.[90] The Council shall also act unanimously for the conclusion of agreements "in the field of trade in cultural and audiovisual services, where these agreements risk prejudicing the Union's cultural and linguistic diversity" and "in the field of trade in social, education and health services, where these agreements risk seriously disturbing the national organisation of such services and prejudicing the responsibility of Member States to deliver them".[91] According to the mandate, TTIP "shall not contain provisions that would risk prejudicing the Union's or its Member States' cultural linguistic diversity, namely in the cultural sector nor limit the Union and its Member States from maintaining existing policies and measures in support of the cultural sector given its special status within the EU and the Member States".[92] Audiovisual services are explicitly excluded from the chapter on trade in services and establishment.[93] Other aspects of TTIP, e.g. intellectual property rights[94] or

[88] Cf. Art. 10 para. 2 subpara. 2 TEU.

[89] Art. 207 para, 4 subpara. 1 TFEU.

[90] Art 207 para. 4 subpara. 2 TFEU. But after the Treaty of Lisbon most of the relevant articles do not require unanimity, see Hahn (2011), para. 118: Only Art. 65 para. 3 and 4 TFEU. Concerning Art. 118 TFEU, however, the establishment of language arrangements (which are a necessary element for European intellectual property rights) requires the Council to act unanimously (Art. 118 para. 2 TFEU). Therefore, the rule of Art. 118 para. 1 TFEU (majority voting of the Council in the framework of the ordinary legislative procedure) has no effect in practice. See Stieper (2011), para. 27; Pernice and Hindelang (2010), p. 407 (412); Streinz (2013), p. 892 (894).

[91] Art. 207 para. 4 subpara. 3 TFEU.

[92] See No. 9 of the mandate, available at http://data.consilium.europa.eu/doc/document/ST-11103-2013-DCL-1/en/pdf.

[93] See No. 21 of the mandate, available at http://data.consilium.europa.eu/doc/document/ST-11103-2013-DCL-1/en/pdf.

[94] See No. 28 et seq. of the mandate, available at http://data.consilium.europa.eu/doc/document/ST-11103-2013-DCL-1/en/pdf.

foreign direct investment,[95] require the Council to act unanimously. The Council, on a proposal by the negotiator, shall adopt a decision authorising the signing[96] and the conclusion of the agreement.[97] The Council shall adopt the decision to conclude the agreement only after obtaining the consent of the European Parliament because TTIP covers fields to which the ordinary legislative procedure[98] applies.[99] After the adoption of the treaty by the organs of the Union it will be ratified by the Council according to international law.[100]

Conclusion and Ratification by the Member States

The Member States become parties of a mixed agreement in their own right. Therefore, the separate conclusion and ratification by each Member State is required. To ensure the complete implementation of the treaty, i.e. those parts which fall under the competence of the EU as well as the parts which fall within the competence of the Member States, and to demonstrate the uniform representation of the European Union (and its Member States) in international law, mixed agreements ought possibly to enter into force simultaneously for the EU and all of its Member States.[101] Therefore, the EU will ratify the treaty only after its ratification by all Member States.[102] The principle of loyalty (Article 4 para. 3 TEU) may urge the Member States to conclude and to ratify the treaty if the Council, on a proposal by the Commission, has decided that the participation of the EU is in the interest of the European Union.[103] But in principle there is no such obligation.[104]

---

[95] See No. 22 et seq. of the mandate, available at http://data.consilium.europa.eu/doc/document/ST-11103-2013-DCL-1/en/pdf.

[96] Art. 207 para. 3, Art. 218 para. 5 TFEU.

[97] Art. 207 para. 3, Art. 218 para. 6 TFEU.

[98] Art. 289 para. 1, Art. 294 TFEU.

[99] Art. 207 para. 3, Art. 218 para. 6 lit. a(v), Art. 207 para. 2 TFEU. See Lorenzmeier (2011), para. 49; Müller-Ibold (2012), Art. 207 AEUV para. 75. Concerning the intensive participation of the European Parliament in CCP agreements like TTIP see Nettesheim and Duvigneau (2012), AEUV paras. 46 et seq.

[100] See Schmalenbach (2011), para. 7.

[101] See Müller-Ibold (2012), Art. 216, para. 15.

[102] See Rosas (2000), p. 200 (207 et seq.); Eeckhout (2004), pp. 218 et seq.

[103] See Kumin and Bittner (2012), p. 75 (83) with reference to Recitals 8 to 10 of Council Decision (2004/294/EC) of 8 March 2004, [2004] OJ L 97/53 (concerning liability in the field of nuclear energy).

[104] Rathke (2014), 5.2, available at http://www.no-ttip.de/Material/Kompetenzen.pdf. See to this question Neframi (2002), p. 193 (198 et seq.). Concerning Member States' duty to cooperate when exercising their retained powers see Hillion (2010), pp. 106 et seq. concerning the risk of delay or even blockade see Sattler (2007), pp. 139 et seq.

Insofar as the agreement could be concluded by the Union alone, the Member States are, however, obliged to secure the implementation of these obligations.[105] If there is no express differentiation between the provisions concerning competences of the EU and those remaining exclusive competences of the Member States,[106] according to international law, the agreement as a whole forms an "integral part" of Union law[107] and is binding upon the Union as well as its Member States.[108] The ECJ is competent to interpret mixed agreements as a whole.[109]

If a mixed agreement demands the ratification by all parties and a Member State does not ratify the treaty, those parts of the agreement which fall within the exclusive competence of the EU can be preliminarily applicable.[110] If the content of the agreement falls within the exclusive competence of the EU or the shared competence between the EU and its Member States, the Union is responsible for the treaty as a whole. In this case the ratification by all Member States is not necessary. Only if parts of the agreement fall under the remaining exclusive competence of the Member States,[111] their ratifications are peremptorily required.[112]

Required Approval of the German *Bundestag*

If TTIP will take the shape of a mixed agreement, the ratification of the treaty by the German Federal President[113] will require the approval of the *Bundestag* as legislative organ.[114] The consent must take the shape of a federal law. Keeping in mind its importance, there is no question that TTIP regulates the political relations of the Federation. Furthermore, TTIP relates to subjects of federal legislation because its

[105] See ECJ, C-12/86, *Demirel v Stadt Schwäbisch Gmünd*, [1987] ECR I, 3719, para. 11; ECJ, *Opinion 1/94*, *WTO/GATS/TRIPS*, [1994] ECR I, 5267, para. 108; ECJ, C-459/03, *Commission v Ireland (Mox Plant)*, [2006] ECR I, 4635, para. 85. See Kaiser (2009), pp. 53 et seq.

[106] For the declaration of the division of competences by declarations to mixed agreements to prove transparency against third parties see Kumin and Bittner (2012), p. 75 (80).

[107] See ECJ, C-12/86, *Demirel v Stadt Schwäbisch Gmünd*, [1987] ECR I, 3719, para. 7; ECJ, C-459/03, *Commission v Ireland (Mox Plant)*, [2006] ECR I, 4635, para. 82.

[108] See ECJ, C-12/86, *Demirel v Stadt Schwäbisch Gmünd*, [1987] ECR I, 3719, para. 9; ECJ, *Opinion 1/94*, *WTO/GATS/TRIPS*, [1994] ECR I, 5267, para. 108.

[109] See ECJ, C-12/86, *Demirel v Stadt Schwäbisch Gmünd*, [1987] ECR I, 3719, paras. 10, 12; ECJ, C-53/96, *Hermès International v FHT Marketing Choice*, [1998] ECR I, 3606, paras. 22 et seq.

[110] See e.g. Recital 5 of the Council Decision 2004/368/EC of 30 March 2004 concerning the provisional application of the Agreement on the participation of the Czech Republic etc. in the European Economic Area and the provisional application of four related agreements, [2004] OJ L 130/1.

[111] See Art. 5 para. 1, Art. 4 para. 1 TEU, Art. 207 para. 6 TFEU.

[112] See Kaiser (2009), p. 83.

[113] See Art. 59 para. 1 sentence 2 Basic Law. See Streinz (2014), Art. 59, para. 9.

[114] Art. 77 para. 1 sentence 1 Basic Law.

content must be implemented by federal acts.[115] But the *Bundestag* will only be able to vote *en bloc* in favour or against the treaty, amendments concerning the treaty itself are excluded.[116] Therefore, the *Bundestag* must try to influence the content of the treaty at an earlier stage.

Influence of the German Bundestag on the German Representatives in EU Institutions

Basis in German Law

According to Article 23 para. 2 Basic Law (BL)[117] the *Bundestag* shall participate in matters concerning the European Union. The Federal Government shall keep the *Bundestag* informed, comprehensively and at the earliest possible time. Before participating in legislative acts of the EU the Federal Government shall provide the *Bundestag* with an opportunity to state its position and shall take this position into account during the negotiations.[118] The details are regulated by the Act on Cooperation between the Federal Government and the German Bundestag in Matters Concerning the European Union.[119] This Act determines the notification principles (Section 3) and the projects of the European Union within the meaning of this Act (Section 5). Therefore the duty to inform the *Bundestag* and to secure the participation of the parliament in European matters[120] includes not only negotiating mandates for the European Commission to engage in negotiations on international agreements of the EU but also items for discussion, initiatives, negotiating mandates and negotiation guidelines for the European Commission in the framework of the common commercial policy.[121] The *Bundestag* must be informed as early as possible, i.e. at the beginning of the treaty negotiations.[122] But the participation is

[115] Art. 59 para. 2 Basic Law. Cf. Streinz (2014), Art. 59, para. 32.

[116] Article 82 para. 2 Rule of Procedure of the Bundestag. See Streinz (2014), Art. 59, para. 51. Concerning the role of national parliaments in external relations see Bollrath (2008), pp. 175 et seq.

[117] Basic Law for the Federal Republic of Germany; Grundgesetz für die Bundesrepublik Deutschland (GG); translation by Tomuschat/Curry.

[118] Art. 23 para. 3 sentence 1 and 2 Basic Law.

[119] Gesetz über die Zusammenarbeit von Bundesregierung und Deutschem Bundestag in Angelegenheiten der Europäischen Union (EUZBBG) of 4 July 2013, Federal Law Gazette (BGBl.) 2013 I, p. 2170, based on Art. 23 para. 3 sentence 3 Basic Law. This law terminates the same law of 12 March 1993 (BGBl. I, p. 311), strengthening the role of the *Bundestag*.

[120] See Section 3: The notification shall be comprehensive, as early as possible and continuous and shall cover, in particular, the Federal Government's decision-making process, the preparation and course of discussions within the institutions of the EU.

[121] Section 5 para. 1 No. 5 and 6.

[122] See Koch (2011), p. 316, para. 20.

also continuous because the relevant projects of the EU include proposals for legislative acts of the EU,[123] and agreements like TTIP must be concluded and ratified by legislative acts. Before participating in projects, especially as a member of the Council in its legislative functions,[124] the Federal Government shall give the *Bundestag* the opportunity to deliver an opinion. The Federal Government shall use this opinion as a basis for its negotiations. If the main interests expressed in the decision of the *Bundestag* do not hold sway, the Federal Government shall invoke the requirement of prior parliamentary approval in the negotiations. Before a final decision, the Federal Government shall endeavour to reach agreement with the *Bundestag*. But this shall not prejudice the right of the Federal Government, in awareness of the *Bundestag*'s opinion, to take divergent decisions for good reasons of foreign and integration policy. In this case the Federal Government does, however, have to account for its motives—if requested by one quarter of the Members of the *Bundestag*—in a plenary debate.[125]

Conformity with EU Law

This legal situation in Germany must be, and is indeed, in conformity with EU law. The aforementioned rules concretize Article 10 para. 2 subpara. 2 TEU which demands that the representatives of the Member States in the Council be "democratically accountable" to their national parliaments. Moreover, national parliaments are invited to "contribute actively to the good functioning of the Union".[126] But such contribution must not lead to a blockade of the law making process in the Council.[127] Therefore, the national provisions must be an appropriate compromise between the necessary influence of the national parliament and the necessary margin of negotiations for the representative of the Member State in the Council. The German solution ensures the fulfilment of this obligation.[128]

Different Effect According to the Voting Procedure Which Is Required by EU Law

The amount of influence the German Bundestag has depends on the voting procedure which is required by EU law concerning CCP agreements (see above). If unanimity in the Council is required, the instruction of the German representative in the Council may urge him to veto the decision on the agreement if no acceptable

[123] Section 5 para. 1 No. 4.

[124] See Art. 16 para 2 and para. 1 TEU.

[125] Section 8 paras. 1, 2, 4 and 5.

[126] Art. 12 lit. a TEU.

[127] Cf. Art. 4 para. 3 TEU.

[128] See Streinz (2014), Art. 23, para. 114.

compromise can be reached. In the case of majority voting it may be easier for the German representative to justify his approval to the agreement. He could take the position that he avoided being outvoted by granting some concessions not foreseen in the parliamentary debate.

Inclusion of the German *Bundesrat*?

Required Approval of the Bundesrat

If TTIP is a mixed agreement and needs to be ratified in Germany, the treaty requires the consent or participation in the form of a federal law, of the bodies responsible in such a case for the enactment of federal law.[129] Not only the *Bundestag* but also the *Bundesrat*[130] is "responsible" for the enactment of federal law. The *Bundestag* shall submit the law to the *Bundesrat* which can at least object to a bill adopted by the *Bundestag*. But this objection may be overruled by the *Bundestag*.[131] If the content of TTIP touches matters which would require the consent of the *Bundesrat* were it a national law, the act of consent to the treaty requires the consent (and not only the "participation") of the *Bundesrat*, too. The areas of legislation in which the consent of the *Bundesrat* is required for a bill to become law must be named as such in the Basic Law. One such area is state liability,[132] which the TTIP would affect if a comprehensive dispute settlement regime is included in the treaty.

Influence of the Bundesrat on the German Representatives in EU Institutions

Not only the *Bundestag*, but also the *Bundesrat* must be informed by the Federal Government in matters concerning the European Union.[133] In a different form and to a different extent, in comparison to the *Bundestag*,[134] it shall participate in the decision-making process of the Federation, especially the representation of Germany in the Council as legislative organ of the EU,[135] insofar as it would have been competent to do so in a comparable domestic matter, or insofar as the subject falls

[129] Art. 59 para. 2 sentence 1 Basic Law.

[130] See Art. 50, Art. 77 Basic Law.

[131] See Art. 77 paras. 3 and 4 Basic Law.

[132] Art. 74 para. 1 No. 25 in conjunction with Art. 74 para. 2 Basic Law.

[133] Art. 23 para. 2 Basic Law.

[134] See Streinz (2014), Art. 23, paras. 118 et seq.

[135] See Art. 16 paras. 2 and 1 TEU.

within the domestic competence of the *Länder*.[136] The German *Länder* participate in matters concerning the European Union through the *Bundesrat*.[137] The rules for this participation of the Bundesrat and the *Länder* are comprised in Article 23 paras. 4 to 6 and, in greater detail, in the Act on Cooperation between the Federation and the *Länder* in Matters Concerning the European Union.[138] Relevant areas touched by TTIP may be certain professional rules in the context of liberalisation of the service sector which fall under the competence of the *Länder*[139] and rules concerning the cultural sector.[140]

Conclusion

The German parliament has at least some influence on the negotiations of TTIP via its control over the German representative in the Council. The German government has to inform the *Bundestag* as well as the *Bundesrat*. The *Bundestag* and in certain cases also the *Bundesrat* have the opportunity to deliver an opinion which shall form the basis of the German position in the Council. But the opinion of the parliament is not strictly binding. The government may take divergent decisions for good reasons of foreign and integration policy. But in this case it has to state the reasons for its deviation. The impact of this control depends upon the requested voting procedure in the Council. The *Bundestag* can veto TTIP if it is concluded as a mixed agreement. In this case the agreement requires not only the ratification by the Member State Germany but according to German constitutional law the consent of the *Bundestag*, in certain cases also the consent of the *Bundesrat*. Whether TTIP needs to be concluded as a mixed agreement depends upon its content and remains controversial. But probably it will be concluded by the EU as a mixed agreement at least for political reasons.[141] Some provisions which are mentioned in the mandate, especially whether a comprehensive dispute settlement regime should be established at all or at least only with significant changes of the current practice, are highly disputed. But the question remains whether the US will be amenable to the mounting European misgivings and, if so, what trade-offs it would demand.

---

[136] Art. 23 para. 4 Basic Law.

[137] Art. 23 para. 2, Art. 50 Basic Law.

[138] Gesetz über die Zusammenarbeit zwischen Bund und Ländern in Angelegenheiten der Europäischen Union (EUZBLG) of 12 March 1993 (BGBl. 1993 I, p. 313), amended by Act of 22 September 2009 (BGBl. I, p. 3031).

[139] See Antwort der Bundesregierung auf die Kleine Anfrage der Fraktion BÜNDNIS 90/DIE GRÜNEN (Response of the Federal Government to the Brief Parliamentary Enquiry by the parliamentary group ALLIANCE 90/GREEN PARTY) of 10 April 2014, Bundestags-Drucksache 18/1118, p. 2.

[140] Cf. the different points of views on "TTIP and Culture" of the EU and the US, paper of the European Commission of 16 July 2014.

[141] Concerning this aspect in general see Maresceau (2010), p. 16.

Therefore it is doubtful whether TTIP will be concluded at all—not only the EU but also the US could lose interest in the project.[142] Yet if TTIP should fail, this may have consequences for bilateral agreements in commercial policy in general and especially for the common commercial policy of the European Union.

References

Bollrath L (2008) Die Vertragsschlusskompetenz der Europäischen Gemeinschaften auf dem Gebiet der Gemeinsamen Handelspolitik, pp 175 et seq

Bungenberg M (2001) The division of competences between the EU and its member states in the area of investment politics. In: Bungenberg M, Griebel J, Hindelang S (eds) International investment and EU law, p 29

Bungenberg M (2010a) Die Kompetenzverteilung zwischen EU und Mitgliedstaaten "nach Lissabon". In: Bungenberg M, Griebel J, Hindelang S (eds) Internationaler Investitionsschutz und Europarecht, p 81

Bungenberg M (2010b) Going global? The EU common commercial policy after Lisbon. In: Herrmann C, Terhechte JP (eds) European yearbook of international economic law, p 123

Bungenberg M (2015) Towards a more balanced international investment law 2.0. In: Herrmann C, Simma B, Streinz R (eds) Trade policy between law, diplomacy and scholarship: Liber amicorum in memoriam Horst G. Krenzler. Springer, Heidelberg, pp. 15–37

Craig P, de Búrca G (2011) EU law. Text, cases and materials, 5th edn

Dashwood AA et al (2011) Wyatt and Dashwood's European Union Law, 6th edn

De Gucht K (2013) You're wrong, George Monbiot – there is nothing secret about this EU trade deal. The Guardian, 18 December 2013. Available at http://gu.com/p/3ya2k

DIE ZEIT, Grüne leaken Geheimdokument zum Freihandelsabkommen, 7 March 2014. Available at http://www.zeit.de/wirtschaft/2014-03/freihandelsabkommen-ttip-eu-usa

Dimopulos A (2011) EU foreign investment law

Eberhardt P (2013) Konzerne versus Staaten: Mit Schiedsgerichten gegen die Demokratie, Blätter für deutsche und internationale Politik, p 29

Eeckhout P (2004) External relations of the European Union. Legal and constitutional foundations, pp 218 et seq

European Commission (2014a) Statement/14/12, "Stepping up a Gear", 18 February 2014, p 2. Available at http://europa.eu/rapid/press-release_STATEMENT-14-12_en.htm

European Commission (2014b) The transatlantic trade and investment partnership (TTIP). TTIP explained, 8 May 2014. Available at http://trade.ec.europa.eu/doclib/docs/2014/may/tradoc_152462.pdf

European Commission (2014c) Towards an EU-US trade deal. Making trade work for you, 28 March 2014. Available at http://trade.ec.europa.eu/doclib/docs/2014/march/tradoc_152276.pdf

Greive M (2014) Tod eines Handelsabkommens, Welt am Sonntag, 22 July 2014, p 4. Available at http://www.welt.de/130348973

Hahn M (2011) Art. 207 AEUV. In: Calliess C, Ruffert M, EUV/AEUV-Kommentar, 4th edn

Hartley TC (2010) The foundations of European Union Law, 7th edn, p 174

Herrmann (2015) Transleakancy. In: Herrmann C, Simma B, Streinz R (eds) Trade policy between law, diplomacy and scholarship: Liber amicorum in memoriam Horst G. Krenzler. Springer, Heidelberg, pp. 39–46

[142] Concerning the legislative and regulatory process of the US see Parker and Alemanno (2014).

Herrmann C, Streinz T (2014) Die EU als Mitglied der WTO. In: von Arnauld A (ed) Europäische Außenbeziehungen, EnzEuR, vol 10, p 587
Hillion C (2010) Mixity and coherence in EU external relations: the significance of the "duty of cooperation". In: Hillion C, Koutrakos P (eds) Mixed agreements revisited. The EU and its member states in the world, pp 106 et seq
Kaiser F (2009) Gemischte Abkommen im Lichte bundesstaatlicher Erfahrungen
Koch A (2011) In: von Arnauld A, Hufeld U (eds) Systematischer Kommentar zu den Lissabon-Begleitgesetzen, p 316 para. 20
Konttinen J (2013) Professori: Suomen valta säätää lakeja voi vaarantua, Helsingin Sanomat, 15 December 2013. Available in Finnish at http://www.hs.fi/sunnuntai/a1386995885773
Krajewski M (2014) Zu Investitionsschutz und Investor-Staat-Streitbeilegung im Transatlantischen Handels- und Investitionspartnerschaftsabkommen (TTIP), Kurzgutachten für die Bundestagsfraktion BÜNDNIS 90/DIE GRÜNEN, 1 May 2014, p 2
Kraus M (2015) Die Transatlantische Handels- und Investitionspartnerschaft (TTIP) – Bedeutung für den Lebensmittelhandel, Behr's Jahrbuch für die Lebensmittelwirtschaft 2015, p 19
Krenzler HG, Pitschas C (2006) Die Gemeinsame Handelspolitik im Verfassungsvertrag – ein Schritt in die richtige Richtung. In: Herrmann C, Krenzler HG, Streinz R (eds) Die Außenwirtschaftspolitik der Europäischen Union nach dem Verfassungsvertrag, p 11
Kumin A, Bittner P (2012) Die "gemischten" Abkommen zwischen der Europäischen Union und ihren Mitgliedstaaten einerseits und dritten Völkerrechtssubjekten andererseits, EuR-Beiheft 2, p 75
Lorenzmeier S (2011) Art. 218 AEUV para. 49. In: Grabitz E, Hilf M, Nettesheim M (eds) Das Recht der Europäischen Union. Kommentar
Maresceau M (2010) A typology of mixed bilateral agreements. In: Hillion C, Koutrakos P (eds) Mixed agreements revisited. The EU and its member states in the world, p 16
Mavroidis P (2003) The trade disputes concerning health policy between EC and US. In: Petersmann E-U, Pollack MA (eds) Transatlantic economic disputes. The EU, the US, and the WTO, p 233
Müller-Ibold T (2012) In: Lenz CO, Borchardt K-D (eds) EU-Verträge. Kommentar, 6th edn
Neframi E (2002) International responsibility of the European community and of the member states under mixed agreements. In: Cannizzaro E (ed) The European Union as an actor in international relations, p 193
Nettesheim M, Duvigneau JL (2012) Art. 207. In: Streinz R (ed) EUV/AEUV-Kommentar, 2nd edn
Parker R, Alemanno A (2014) Towards effective regulatory cooperation under TTIP: a comparative overview of the EU and US legislative and regulatory systems, p 8. Available at http://ec.europa.eu/trade/policy/in-focus/ttip/resources/
Pernice I, Hindelang S (2010) Potenziale europäischer Politik nach Lissabon – Europapolitische Perspektiven für Deutschland, seine Institutionen, seine Wirtschaft und seine Bürger, EuZW, p 407
Rathke H (2014) Fragen zur Zuständigkeitsverteilung zwischen EU und Mitgliedstaaten sowie zur Ratifikation des Abkommens über eine Transatlantische Handels- und Investitionspartnerschaft, Ausarbeitung des Wissenschaftlichen Dienstes des Deutschen Bundestags (PE 6 – 3000 – 49)
Reinisch A (2011) The division of powers between the EU and its member states "after Lisbon". In: Bungenberg M, Griebel J, Hindelang S (eds) International investment and EU law, p 43
Rosas A (2000) The European Union and mixed agreements. In: Dashwood AA, Hillion C (eds) The general law of EC external relations, p 200
Sattler S (2007) Gemischte Abkommen und gemischte Mitgliedschaften der EG und ihrer Mitgliedstaaten, pp 139 et seq
Schmalenbach K (2011) Art. 218 AEUV para. 7. In: Calliess C, Ruffert M (eds) EUV/AEUV-Kommentar, 4th edn
Stieper M (2011) Art. 118 AEUV para. 27. In: Grabitz E, Hilf M, Nettesheim M (eds) Das Recht der Europäischen Union. Kommentar

Streinz R (1998) The precautionary principle in food law. Eur Food Law Rev 8:413
Streinz R (2009) Risk decisions in cases of persisting scientific uncertainty: the precautionary principle in European food law. In: Woodman G, Klippel D (eds) Risk and the law, p 53
Streinz R (2012) Europarecht, 9th edn, paras. 371 et seq
Streinz R (2013) Die Verstärkte Zusammenarbeit: Eine realistische Form abgestufter Integration, JuS, p 892
Streinz R (2014) In: Sachs M (ed) Grundgesetz. Kommentar, 7th edn
Weiß W (2011) Art. 207 AEUV. In: Grabitz E, Hilf M, Nettesheim M (eds) Das Recht der Europäischen Union. Kommentar
Weiß W (2014) Vertragliche Handelspolitik der EU. In: von Arnauld A (ed) Europäische Außenbeziehungen, EnzEuR, vol 10, p 515

Part IV
EU External Relations

Towards a New Neighbourhood Policy of the European Union

Thomas Cottier and Gabriela Wermelinger

Four Circles of European Integration

Horst Krenzler was one of the towering architects of the European Economic Area (EEA) Agreement. When, at the end of the 1980s, the European Communities focused on internal deepening and integration, the EEA offered European Free Trade Association (EFTA) countries wider participation in the internal market, while staying outside in terms of European Union (EU) membership—for the time being. The EEA Agreement was construed to be a comfortable waiting room for EFTA members postponed in joining the Union.[1] For the first time, an association agreement developed a sophisticated institutional architecture going beyond mixed committees and entailing rules on monitoring and judicial dispute settlement. Austria, Finland and Sweden subsequently joined the Union in 1995, while Norway, Iceland and Liechtenstein opted to stay with the EEA. Switzerland, in a landmark referendum in December 1992, failed to join the EEA and subsequently embarked on a complicated trail of bilateral agreements. This effort eventually, and by 2004, largely substituted for the EEA, albeit not in an identical manner and with substantial differences, in particular in terms of institutional design.

The rejection of the EEA at the Swiss ballot came as a strong disappointment to the EU and EFTA Members, as Switzerland had placed a strong emphasis on

[1] Agreement on the European Economic Area, 2 May 1992, [1994] OJ L 1/3. For an overview of the basic features of the EEA Agreement, see http://www.efta.int/eea/eea-agreement/eea-basic-features. For a history of the EFTA and the EEA, see Fenger et al. (2012), pp. 15 et seq. (for EFTA) and pp. 53 et seq. (for EEA). For an in depth analysis of the EEA Agreement, see Norberg et al. (1993).

T. Cottier (✉) • G. Wermelinger
Department of Economic Law IEW, World Trade Institute, University of Bern, Hallerstrasse 6, 3012 Berne, Switzerland
e-mail: thomas.cottier@wti.org; gabriela_wermelinger@hotmail.com

C. Herrmann et al. (eds.), *Trade Policy between Law, Diplomacy and Scholarship*,
European Yearbook of International Economic Law,
DOI 10.1007/978-3-319-15690-3_16

negotiating an appropriate institutional framework for the EEA. The agreement broke new ground. A two-pillar model was implemented upon renegotiation, following a critical review by the European Court of Justice (ECJ).[2] The model installed the EFTA Court and the EFTA surveillance authority (ESA).[3] The European Court of Justice assumes responsibility for complaints of one of the Parties originating from unresolved disputes in the EEA council (an avenue never used). More importantly, the Commission and the Court are responsible for monitoring the implementation of the EEA Agreement within Member States of the Union. *Vice versa*, and in parallel, oversight and adjudication of cases arising in EFTA countries are submitted to the ESA[4] and the EFTA Court[5] established under

---

[2] The Commission requested the Opinion of the Court of Justice on the compatibility of the EEA Agreement with the EEC Treaty with regard to the system of judicial supervision. The first opinion was the Opinion of the Court of 14 December 1991, ECJ, *Avis 1/91*, [1991] ECR I, 6079. The Court issued a negative Opinion. As a consequence, the system of judicial supervision was renegotiated. For further details of the Opinion's statement, see Eeckhout (2011), pp. 312 et seq. Upon renegotiation and the replacement of the EEA Court with an EFTA Court composed of judges from EFTA countries with a more limited jurisdiction, the Court issued a positive Opinion, i.e. the Opinion of the Court of 10 April 1992, *Avis 1/92*, [1992] ECR I, 2821.

[3] Art. 108 of the EEA Agreement reads:

> The EFTA States shall establish an independent surveillance authority (EFTA Surveillance Authority) as well as procedures similar to those existing in the Community including procedures for ensuring the fulfilment of obligations under this Agreement and for control of the legality of acts of the EFTA Surveillance Authority regarding competition.
> The EFTA States shall establish a court of justice (EFTA Court).
> The EFTA Court shall, in accordance with a separate agreement between the EFTA States, with regard to the application of this Agreement be competent, in particular, for:
>
> (a) actions concerning the surveillance procedure regarding the EFTA States;
> (b) appeals concerning decisions in the field of competition taken by the EFTA Surveillance Authority;
> (c) the settlement of disputes between two or more EFTA States.

[4] Article 109 paragraph 1 of the EEA Agreement. The competences of the ESA are laid down in Article 5 of the Agreement between the EFTA States on the Establishment of a Surveillance Authority and a Court of Justice. The main task of the ESA is to ensure the correct implementation and application of EEA rules by the EFTA/EEA States. With regard to surveillance, ESA plays a role for the EEA/EFTA States that is comparable to that of the European Commission *vis-à-vis* the EU Member States under Article 258 TEU (ex-Article 226 of the EC Treaty). For a detailed account in French and German, see the materials prepared by the Swiss Government in 1992, Botschaft zur Genehmigung des Abkommens über den Europäischen Wirtschaftsraum, BBl 1992 IV 33, pp. 502 et seq.

[5] For the competences of the EFTA Court, see Articles 27 et seq. of the Agreement between the EFTA States on the Establishment of a Surveillance Authority and a Court of Justice, in particular Articles 36 and 37. Essentially, the jurisdiction of the EFTA Court corresponds to the jurisdiction of the ECJ. The Court's work consists mostly of infringement actions brought by the ESA against an EFTA State, and nullity actions concerning decisions taken by the ESA with regard to competition law and state aid law matters. It further renders references for preliminary ruling on the interpretation of EEA law by national courts of EFTA States. See e.g. Baudenbacher

the EFTA Court Agreement.[6] Both avenues became important in securing the rule of law and in the implementation of the Agreement in relation to Norway, Iceland and Liechtenstein, and the EU Members, and *vice versa*. They both provide for preliminary rulings and thus open the system not only to complaints by the Commission and the ESA, but also to private actors and thus domestic courts. The EEA is thus subject to the main driving forces of integration by law in the European realm. In deploying their functions, the Commission and the EFTA Surveillance Authority developed close cooperation. The European Court of Justice and the EFTA Court engaged in a judicial dialogue. While the EFTA court was frequently inspired by precedents of the ECJ, the latter also has been regularly informed by judgments of the EFTA Court.[7] While legal developments relating to the internal market are led by the European Court of Justice, the two courts engaged in what may properly be called a judicial dialogue in the European context.[8]

The two-pillar approach, thanks to the farsightedness of Horst Krenzler and his colleagues, developed into a successful model for what today may be called the third circle of European integration—the EEA—next to the Monetary Union and the internal market of Member States, which constitute the first and second circles of European integration. The EEA amounts to the closest form of what one would expect to be at the heart of the neighbourhood policy of the European Union.

---

et al. (2005); and the Swiss Government's Botschaft zur Genehmigung des Abkommens über den Europäischen Wirtschaftsraum, BBl 1992 IV 33, pp. 510 et seq.

[6] Agreement between the EFTA States on the Establishment of a Surveillance Authority and a Court of Justice of 31 December 1994, [1994] OJ L 344/1. This Agreement has been adjusted by a Protocol signed in Brussels on 17 March 1993 ("Surveillance and Court Adjusting Protocol") and by the Agreement Adjusting certain Agreements between the EFTA States signed in Brussels on 29 December 1994 ("Adjusting Agreement").

[7] The European Court of Justice followed the EFTA Court in several opinions and judgments. A non-exhaustive selection of judgments includes, for example, Case T-115/94, *Opel Austria v Council*, [1997] ECR II, 39, para. 61, citing para. 40 of Case E-1/94, *Restamark*, [1994] EFTA Ct. Rep. 15; Case T-13/99, *Pfizer v Council*, [2002] ECR II, 3305, para. 115, citing paras. 1 and 2 of Case E-3/00, *ESA v Norway*, [2000/2001] EFTA Ct. Rep. 73; Case C-345/05, *Commission v Portugal*, [2006] ECR I, 10633, para. 40, citing Case E-1/03 *ESA v Iceland*, [2003] EFTA Ct. Rep. 143 via C-471/04, *Keller*, [2004]; Case C-522/04, *Commission v Belgium*, [2007] ECR I, 5701, para. 44, citing Case E-1/03, *ESA v Iceland*, [2003] EFTA Ct. Rep. 143; Case T-401/08, *Säveltäjäin Tekijänoikeustoimisto Teosto Ry*, [2013] not yet published, para. 91, citing para. 90 of Case E-15/10, *Posten Norge*, [2012] EFTA Ct. Rep. 246; Case T-392/08, *AEPI*, [2013] not yet published, para. 81, citing para. 90 of Case E-15/10, *Posten Norge*, [2012] EFTA Ct. Rep. 246; Case T-410/08, *GEMA*, [2013] not yet published, para. 72, citing para. 90 of Case E-15/10, *Posten Norge*, [2012] EFTA Ct. Rep. 246; Case C-49/11, *Content Services*, [2012] not yet published, para. 45, citing Case E-4/09, *Inconsult Anstalt*, [2009/2010] EFTA Ct. Rep. 86; Case T-70/99, *Alpharma v Council*, [2002] ECR II, 3495, para. 136, citing Case E-3/00, *ESA v Norway*, [2000/2001] EFTA Ct. Rep. 73; Case C-140/97, *Rechberger*, [1999] ECR I, 3499, para. 39, citing Case E-9/97, *Sveinbjörnsdóttir*, [1998] EFTA Ct Rep. 95.

[8] The ECJ and EFTA dialogue thus forms part of the wider dialogue among courts in Europe; see Dialog über die Grenzen: Symposium zum 75. Geburtstag von Jörg Paul Müller, 41 EuGRZ 1 (2014) 1–5, in particular the paper by Hertig Randall, Der grundrechtliche Dialog der Gerichte in Europa, p. 5.

Norway, Iceland and Liechtenstein, in subsequent years, benefitted from legal stability and security in their relations to the Union. Switzerland, on the other hand, until the present day, has not found an appropriate institutional framework beyond traditional modes of mixed committees. It goes without saying that the model based upon the 1972 EFTA EEC Free Trade Agreements no longer is able to live up to the legal and dynamic complexities of the *acquis communautaire* retained in bilateral agreements for both parties. Today, new agreements will depend on finding an appropriate framework for what may be called the fourth circle of integration, following the EEA Agreement as the third circle of European integration.[9]

The fourth circle of integration thus entails states with which the Union has entered a special and close economic relationship under association agreements without, however, fully applying the EEA Agreement thereto. This circle entails Switzerland, but also other countries in Europe not being members of the EU or the EEA. We think of the European microstates located within Member States, in particular Andorra, San Marino, Monaco and Vatican City. Moreover, we think of neighbouring countries to the East, in particular Ukraine, Belarus, Moldova, Georgia, and the States within the Mediterranean, in particular Morocco, Tunisia, Libya, Egypt, Israel, Palestine and Syria, Albania, Serbia, Bosnia Herzegovina and Kosovo. As there are no defined geographical boundaries of Europe and European neighbourhood, developments may incorporate further states into the neighbourhood policy, in particular Turkey and possibly Russia and the customs unions with Belarus and Kazakhstan. The fourth circle of integration will vary over time, demarcating these relations from trade and free trade agreements with countries of other continents and the Members of the WTO, in what could be called a fifth and sixth circle of integration—no longer European in nature.

The fourth circle cannot be defined *ex ante* and for good, but should be able to be dealt with under Article 8 of the Treaty on European Union (TEU). We briefly review the current European Neighbourhood Policy (ENP) under this provision, and ask to what extent it could be combined with EFTA–EEA structures in defining a new and more comprehensive Neighbourhood Policy of the European Union, encompassing all the current and potential countries belonging to the fourth circle of integration.

[9] Cottier (2013b), p. 67 (78).

The European Neighbourhood Policy in Light of Article 8 TEU

Background

The fall and collapse of the Soviet Union and empire, and the fall of the Berlin wall, amounted to a major challenge for European integration. At the time, a diverse landscape of newly independent states in wider Europe and ever-changing borders and neighbours, of post-communist countries, still fragile political systems, frequent corruption and organised crime, low living standards, and low human rights standards contrasted with stable democratic states with high living standards. This spectrum required a neighbourhood policy which was able to pay due respect to diverging levels of political and social economic development, and able to offer a range of different perspectives on further integration. Threats to security caused by regional conflicts, terrorism, organised crime, environmental hazards or potential state failures facilitated an increasing and common interest in creating stability and security outside the first two circles of integration (the Monetary Union and the internal market) and the EEA Agreement with EFTA States.[10] The European Neighbourhood Policy is based on the structure of partnership and cooperation agreements.[11] It was particularly developed as a result of the enlargement of the EU to Central and Eastern European and two Mediterranean states in 2004, resulting in new borders and new neighbours.[12] It was enacted to politically and economically deepen the relationship between neighbours to the Union outside the first three circles of European integration. The European Neighbourhood, in practice however, not only includes immediate neighbours but also embraces the neighbours of the neighbours.

The EU's main interest in the policy lies in securing peace, security and a friendly environment of shared values and prosperity along its borders.[13] This is particularly important with regard to the limited absorption capacity of the EU. The new ENP therefore seeks to create an area of prosperity, stability and security for the enlarged EU and its neighbours.[14]

---

[10] Cottier (2013b), p. 67 (78).

[11] Commission of the European Communities, Communication from the Commission to the Council and the European Parliament, Wider Europe – Neighbourhood: A New Framework for Relations with our Eastern and Southern Neighbours, COM (2003) 104 final of 11 March 2003.

[12] Geiger (2010), pp. 51–52, para. 2; Bender-Säbelkampf (2012), pp. 22–28, paras. 3–5.

[13] Bender-Säbelkampf (2012), pp. 22–28, para. 15; Commission of the European Communities, European Neighbourhood Policy: Strategy Paper, COM (2004) 373 final of 12 May 2004.

[14] For more information, see Streinz (2012), pp. 82–85, paras. 3–6.

An Open Normative Framework

The European Neighbourhood Policy was constitutionalised in Article 8 TEU by the Lisbon Treaty, thus providing the legal basis for a special relationship between the EU and its neighbours. Relations of the EU to neighbouring countries greatly vary and reflect a philosophy of variable geometry which, to a much lesser extent, can also be found within the EU.[15] Yet, not all of these relations are framed under the Neighbourhood Policy of Article 8 TEU, despite its broadly worded text:

> Article 8 of the TEU
>
> The Union shall develop a special relationship with neighbouring countries, aiming to establish an area of prosperity and good neighbourliness, founded on the values of the Union and characterised by close and peaceful relations based on cooperation.
>
> For the purposes of paragraph 1, the Union may conclude specific agreements with the countries concerned. These agreements may contain reciprocal rights and obligations as well as the possibility of undertaking activities jointly. Their implementation shall be the subject of periodic consultation.

The wording is based on Article 217 of the Treaty on the Functioning of the European Union, dealing with the relationship between the EU and neighbouring countries through association agreements.[16] Paragraph 1[17] of Article 8 TEU describes the goal of the ENP, while paragraph 2[18] lists the instruments of the ENP. The exact procedural requirements, however, remain undefined in the provision and disputed.

Article 8 addresses a close and special relationship between the EU and neighbouring countries, yet without perspective of immediate or medium-term membership. It entails the principles of differentiation and conditionality. A privileged relationship is envisaged to build upon a commitment to share the values of the Union and to deepen political alliance and economic integration. It is thus conditioned to a legal, social, economic and political approximation of neighbours to EU law and values as outlined in Article 2 of the TEU. The ENP partner states are offered an incentive of developing the opportunity to be given full market access, including its four freedoms (free movement of goods, services, persons and capital), and to receive short-term financial assistance and visa facilitations. Thus, the ENP aims at offering an incentive to access the internal market mainly in exchange for efforts towards more stability and security, democracy, the rule of law, respect for human rights and a market-oriented economy conditioned by sharing common

[15] For further information on the developments within the Union, see the Final Report of the Future of Europe Group of the Foreign Ministers of Austria, Belgium, Denmark, France, Italy, Germany, Luxembourg, the Netherlands, Poland, Portugal and Spain, 17 September 2012, available at http://www.statewatch.org/news/2012/sep/eu-future-of-europe-report.pdf.

[16] Article 217 TFEU states: "The Union may conclude with one or more third countries or international organisations agreements establishing an association involving reciprocal rights and obligations, common action and special procedure."

[17] See Streinz (2012), pp. 82–85.

[18] For further information on the instruments, see Streinz (2012), pp. 82–85.

interests and the Union's values. The ENP emphasises the need to further strengthen existing regional and sub-regional cooperation and to develop new cooperation agreements. In order to achieve these goals individual Action Plans are developed and sub-committees established to monitor the progress made. Progress is tracked in progress reports.[19]

The wording of Article 8 of the TEU, as outlined above, implies a proximity in terms of substance, yet the terms Neighbourhood and Europe remain largely undefined. From an historical context, one would expect that relations with Switzerland or a number of European microstates fully surrounded by territories of the Member States would be at the heart of neighbourhood policy of the Union enshrined in Article 8 TEU. Instead, The ENP was specifically created in 2003 to particularly distinguish between an enlargement of the Union and special relations with neighbours without a membership opportunity in the near future as the defining feature.[20] Neither EFTA-Members (Norway, Iceland or Liechtenstein, nor Switzerland)[21] nor microstates like Andorra, San Marino and the Vatican were considered to be part of the neighbourhood policies conducted under the provision of Article 8 TEU.[22] The same holds true for Switzerland. Instead, the provision was applied to depict relations with a wider circle of countries in the wider neighbourhood, in particular to the East, but also within the Mediterranean basin.[23] Before joining the EU in 2004[24] and 2007,[25] the new Member States leading to the enlargement to 27, belonged to this group. Today, it entails actual and potential relations with Ukraine, Moldova, Belarus, Serbia and Kosovo, Albania, Georgia, Armenia, Azerbaijan and Bosnia-Herzegovina, as well as Algeria, Egypt, Israel, Jordan, Syria, Palestine, Lebanon, Libya, Tunisia and Morocco. Relations with these countries operate under a wide range of different agreements and institutional arrangements. The agreements all are based upon the precepts of EU law, extending those beyond borders, but continue to vary in accordance with different economic constellations and needs in place. They show comparable

---

[19] For more information on Action Plans, see Schmalenbach (2011), pp. 162–168; for general information, see Commission of the European Communities, Communication from the Commission to the Council and the European Parliament, Wider Europe – Neighbourhood: A New Framework for Relations with our Eastern and Southern Neighbours, COM (2003) 104 final of 11 March 2003, p. 16.

[20] Commission of the European Communities, Proposal for a Regulation laying down general provisions establishing a European Neighbourhood and Partnership Instrument, COM (2004) 628 final of 29 September 2004, p. 2.

[21] This is mainly due to the high levels of integration including participation in the Schengen Agreement, see Kellerhals and Uebe (2012), pp. 143–147.

[22] See Cottier (2014a), p. 141 (142); Geiger (2010), pp. 51–52, paras. 3 et seq.; Bender-Säbelkampf (2012), pp. 22–28, para. 10; Bitterlich (2012), pp. 63–65, para. 2.

[23] Commission of the European Communities, Communication from the Commission: European Neighbourhood Policy: Strategy Paper, COM (2004) 373 final of 12 May 2004.

[24] The enlargement to the East and the Mediterranean entailed the following countries: Cyprus, Czech Republic, Estonia, Hungary, Latvia, Lithuania, Malta, Poland, Slovakia and Slovenia.

[25] In 2007 Romania and Bulgaria followed suit.

institutional arrangements in terms of monitoring and further developing the agreements by means of joint bodies. Dispute settlement often is modelled after the WTO dispute settlement mechanism,[26] providing for *ad hoc* panels, but stopping short of permanent institutions, let alone courts and the instrument of preliminary rulings.

Since neighbourhood policy under Article 8 TEU does not include the third and fourth circles of integration, but is rather limited to a wider and further range of relations in a greatly varying manner, it does not come as a surprise that Article 8 has remained without much guidance and normative influence. EFTA countries cannot rely upon it in shaping special relations with the EU, and other countries cannot extract particular guarantees. They remain largely exposed to the vagaries of foreign policy. The difference for the rest of the world, shaped on the basis of other agreements, such as Economic Partnership Agreements or proper Free Trade Agreements is difficult to tell. It is difficult to distinguish the level of integration in the fifth and sixth circles from that which existed prior to neighbourhood policies, and from neighbourhood-independent WTO rights and obligations under GATT,[27] GATS,[28] TRIPS,[29] and related special agreements and understandings, respectively.[30]

Diversity and the Quest for a Common Architecture

European neighbours of the Union, of course, hardly fit into a single framework. Their levels of legal, social and economic development greatly varies. It entails rich countries, such as Norway and Switzerland. It entails microstates, developing countries and a wide range of different political systems.[31] Such diversity does not allow for single and uniform rules, but requires a hybrid system of flexibility and differentiation. It is thus not conceivable to simply extend the rights and obligations under the EEA Agreement to all neighbouring countries. It could not match the needs and possibilities of these relationships, except in a few cases. Diversity calls for continued differentiation in treaty relations in terms of substantive rights and obligations, albeit they all are informed by values and principles

[26] See, for example, the EU–Ukraine Association Agreement: Commission of the European Communities, EU–Ukraine Association Agreement. "Guide to the Association Agreement", p. 5, available at http://eeas.europa.eu/images/top_stories/140912_eu-ukraine-associatin-agreement-quick_guide.pdf; see also, World Trade Organization, Political & Quasi-Adjudicative Dispute Settlement Models in European Union Free Trade Agreements. Is the quasi-adjudicative model a trend or is it just another model?, Staff Working Paper ERSD-2006-09, pp. 12–22.

[27] General Agreement on Tariffs and Trade.

[28] General Agreement on Trade in Services.

[29] Agreement on Trade-Related Aspects of Intellectual Property Rights.

[30] World Trade Organization (2008); See generally, Cottier and Oesch (2005); van der Bossche and Zdoug (2013).

[31] See Cottier (2014a), p. 141 (144).

inherent to European Union law as envisaged by Article 8 TEU. Yet, diversity does not exclude a common framework for neighbouring countries in terms of surveillance and dispute resolution. Different levels of development call for diverging rights and obligations on substance. However, they do not call for differentiation in terms of legal protection and dispute settlement. In fact, sovereign equality of States offers an argument to develop common structures, securing equal rights of legal protection, both for States and individuals in relations among such countries, and with the European Union. The terms "neighbourhood" and "special relations" of Article 8 TEU should thus be interpreted broadly. It should equally be applied to EFTA countries and microstates.[32]

It is submitted, for such reasons, that the institutional structure developed for the EEA could equally provide the institutional foundation for relations with the neighbours of the Union. Article 8 TEU provides the basis for policies seeking to develop a joint and comprehensive framework of mutual surveillance and dispute settlement within wider Europe. Each of the countries would bring their own treaty rights and obligations to the table commensurate to levels of social and economic development. But they would all share a common architecture, modelled upon the institutions of the EEA enshrined in EFTA. All the neighbouring countries would be subject to the system of two pillars and courts and the division of labour developed for the EEA. The Commission and the European Court of Justice remain responsible for monitoring and implementing all these diverging agreements by Member States of the Union, as they are already today. Surveillance and judicial control on the part of neighbours, however, would be effected by the ESA and the EFTA Court, allowing both for complaints by other States, the ESA and individuals in preliminary rulings.

The system sketched here of course implies that neighbouring countries of the Union would join EFTA and thus establish among themselves a common treaty regime focusing on the institutional design. European neighbours and the EU would develop an institutional framework agreement incorporating the ESA and the EFTA Court, as well as the Commission and the European Courts. Multilateral agreements would establish the foundations for neighbourly relations outside the Union, but *with* the Union, agreements would be modelled after the institutional provisions of the EEA Agreement. This model agreement would, however, not include substantive provisions, rights and obligations, which continue to pertain to existing and diverse agreements between neighbours and the EU, and among neighbours of the EU. This may entail free trade under the EFTA Convention, but need not. Relations among these neighbouring countries may also continue to be based upon WTO law, while relations to the EU are subject to preferential trade and the institutional agreement operating under EFTA structures. The architecture thus combines a

[32] Also in favour of a broader interpretation: Hanf (2012), p. 109 and Maresceau (2008), p. 305; the narrow approach is mainly a political decision by ENP partners. However, Declaration No. 3 on Article 8 of the Treaty on European Union, [2010] OJ C 83/337, also shows that Article 8 TEU can be applied to further countries not included in the current ENP practice under this provision. See also, van Elsuwege and Petrov (2011), p. 688 (701–702).

core of common institutions among non-members, while leaving the substance of the agreements individualised and under a concept of variable geometry. The point is to create common institutions linking neighbouring countries to the EU on common ground. Next to the first three circles of integration (monetary union, internal market, European Economic Area) the fourth circle of integration will thus be constituted on the basis of common institutions and individualised treaty obligations in association and bilateral agreements with the Union. It differs from the fifth circle based upon Free Trade Agreements with countries outside of Europe, such as Korea, or Economic Partnership Agreements, such as the agreement with Caribbean States, and finally, the sixth circle of WTO law.

Squaring an Institutional Framework for the Fourth Circle of Integration

Two models are conceivable for the fourth circle of European integration and thus for the European neighbourhood policy.

Model 1: Extension of EEA Institutions to Present and Future Members of the EFTA

Firstly, the framework could continue to be placed with the existing European Free Trade Association and thus extending the present EEA institutions to all present and future members of the EFTA. The model implies that relations among neighbouring countries are at least subject to the EFTA Convention and thus a free trade agreement. For example, Switzerland and Norway will be linked by the EFTA Convention. In relations to the EU, Norway will operate under EEA rules while Swiss–EU relations continue to be based upon a series of bilateral agreements.[33] Inherently, this will leave a number of countries outside the framework at the outset, as sufficient interests to engage in a free trade in goods and services beyond WTO levels may not yet be present and only evolve over time. The model thus develops gradually building enlarged EFTA membership. Neighbouring countries of the EU would seek to join EFTA adhering to the EFTA Convention and thus contributing to a wider free trade zone next to the European Union based upon the monetary union and the internal market. EFTA, again, will develop into the major partner of the EU in the European realm. It will regain its historical role, which it has largely lost, due to increasing integration of its former Members into the European Union. The model is suitable in particular to integrate the European microstates and gradually expand to other neighbouring countries in Europe and

[33] See Cottier (2014b), pp. 585–587.

North Africa. The EU would encourage countries to join the EFTA platform, and EFTA Members would carefully assess whether the time is ripe for acceding to the EFTA Convention and membership status. In some way, the model resembles the European Court on Human Rights, linking both procedural and substantive standards. While procedural rules are uniform, the substantive rights and obligations reflect diversity.[34]

Model 2: European Neighbouring Country Framework Agreement (NCFA)

Secondly, it is conceivable to extract the EFTA institutions and place them in what could be called the European Neighbouring Country Framework Agreement (NCFA). This agreement entails all neighbouring states, together with the EU. Existing institutions designed for the EEA Agreement are transformed into institutions of wider jurisdiction.[35] The Agreement establishes a joint surveillance authority and a court identical to the EFTA Court. Likewise, EU Member States are subject to this surveillance and jurisdiction in their relations with these countries. The multilateral Framework Agreement continues the operation of the EFTA court under a different heading, comprising all non-EU European countries willing to join. The agreement is limited to institutional provisions while substantive rights and obligations with the EU and with other European countries remain subject to individual treaty relations. Differently than the first option, members under this system are not necessarily members of the EFTA Convention. The Agreement, short of providing for a minimum FTA like EFTA, is open to a wider range of countries with diverging interests. For example, relations between Egypt and the EU will be based upon an association agreement while those to other countries in the region may be based upon preferential trade agreements or WTO law. The EU and other Members of the NCFA encourage countries seeking relations under Article 8 TEU to join the Framework Agreement and to support its institutions. In some way, the model resembles Membership to the Statute of the International Court of Justice, which is not linked to particular substantive provisions but provides a procedural framework to address disputes among States.

[34] See Cottier (2013a), p. 43 (46–47); Cottier (2014a).

[35] Also in favour of a framework agreement: Wüger and Scarpelli (2006), p. 287 (319 et seq).

Conclusion: Towards Greater Coherence in a New Neighbourhood Policy

Since the EU is moving to a closer Union with a strong focus on domestic affairs, a clearer separation between domestic and foreign affairs, between relations within the first and second circle of integration, and special relations under the third and fourth circles of integration, as well as between the Union and the fifth and sixth circle of integration outside of European integration, needs to be drawn. Relations between the EU and its European neighbourhood, and the EU and the world at large need to be distinguished. As European integration is characterised by variable geometry, tailor-made solutions are needed in relations with neighbours; a single regime with different levels of social and economic development and different historical and constitutional settings is not suitable. Thus, Article 8 TEU explicitly allows for preferential and special relations on the basis of the principle of differentiation. However, notwithstanding the flexible approach of special relations between the EU and its neighbours, a common institutional framework must be provided to ensure coherency and stability.

It may be objected that the institutions presented in the preceding paragraph are not suitable to assess a wide range of different treaty obligations, albeit they may have a common core founded in the common law of European integration. Yet, it is the most natural business of courts to hear and assess cases on the basis of diverging rights and obligations. Courts and judges are accustomed to apply a wide range of sources of law. The International Court of Justice is the prime example in point. Jurisdiction is not limited to a specific set of agreements. They are not inherently limited to a particular set of rules, such as WTO law, EU law or EEA law. Except where relations continue to be exclusively based upon WTO law, surveillance and dispute resolution may thus be placed in the hands of the joint multilateral authorities under the extended EFTA pillar or the Framework Agreement. It will provide the framework to gradually build the foundations of a common European law based upon shared principles but diverging positive rules encompassing the entire European neighbourhood.

This is not the time and place to sketch out the legal architecture of extending the EFTA court to other members of EFTA in dealing with their mutual relations and those with the EU. Nor is it the time and place to draft a European Framework Agreement. The paper simply seeks to introduce the basic idea of extending the successful two-pillar model to a wider neighbourhood and to make this the common core of a new neighbourhood policy under Article 8 TEU. It would seem that this should be in the interest of the EU. As in the early 1990s when deepening came before enlargement, the EU of 28 again has limited capacities to absorb new members. Moreover, a number of States, such as Norway and Switzerland, continue to see their advantages outside the Union for the time being. Enlarging EFTA or creating a new Framework entailing these countries should bring about a better burden-sharing among the EU and EFTA countries in building Europe with its different cycles of integration in a coherent and mutually supportive manner.

We wonder what Horst Krenzler might have said to these ideas. We learn from him and his colleagues that each generation has to engage in creative solutions to impending problems of European integration. The EEA institutional model which he crafted and negotiated on behalf of the EU remains an inspiring, creative and encouraging example in the process of building Europe in unity and diversity alike.

References

Baudenbacher C, Tresselt P, Örlygsson T (eds) (2005) The EFTA court: ten years on

Bender-Säbelkampf A (2012) Art. 8. In: Mayer H, Stöger K (eds) Kommentar zu EUV und AEUV: Unter Berücksichtigung der österreichischen Judikatur und Literatur, pp 22–28

Bitterlich J (2012) Art. 8 EUV. In: Lenz C-O, Borchardt K-D (eds) EUV-Verträge Kommentar: EUV – AEUV – GRCh, 6th edn, pp 63–65

Cottier T (2013a) EFTA free trade agreements: past, present and future. EFTA Bulletin, p 43

Cottier T (2013b) The perspective from outside: squaring the 4th circle of European integration. In: Pichler J, Balthasar A (eds) The report on the future of Europe – striking the balance between "unity" and "diversity"? Proceedings of the Conference on European Democracy 2013, Schriften zur Rechtspolitik 36, p 67

Cottier T (2014a) Die Schweiz und Europa: Herausforderungen im Vierten Kreis der Integration. In: Neuhaus H (ed) Europa zu Beginn des 21. Jahrhunderts: Atzelsberger Gespräche 2013, FAU Forschungen Reihe A, Geisteswissenschaften, Band 1, p 141

Cottier T (2014b) Für eine Anbindung an bestehende EFTA Strukturen. In: Cottier T et al (eds) Die Rechtsbeziehungen der Schweiz und der Europäischen Union, pp 585–587

Cottier T, Oesch M (2005) International trade regulation: law and policy in the WTO, the European Union and Switzerland

Eeckhout P (ed) (2011) EU external relations law, 2nd edn, pp 312 et seq

Fenger N, Sánchez Rydelski M, van Stiphout T (2012) European Free Trade Association (EFTA) and European Economic Area (EEA), pp 15 et seq. (for EFTA) and pp 53 et seq. (for EEA)

Geiger R (2010) Art. 8. In: Geiger R, Khan D-E, Kotzur M (eds) EUV, AEUV: Vertrag über die Europäische Union und Vertrag über die Arbeitsweise der Europäischen Union: Kommentar, 5th edn, pp 51–52

Hanf D (2012) The ENP in the light of the new "neighbourhood clause" (Article 8 TEU). In: Lannon E (ed) The European Neighbourhood Policy's Challenges. College of Europe Studies/ Cahiers du Collège d'Europe No. 14, p 109

Kellerhals A, Uebe W (2012) Artikel 8 (Nachbarschaftspolitik). In: Schwarze J (ed) EU-Kommentar, 3rd edn, pp 143–147

Maresceau M (2008) The relations between the EU and Andorra, San Marino and Monaco. In: Dashwood A, Maresceau M (eds) Law and practice of EU external relations. Salient features of a changing landscape, p 305

Norberg S et al (1993) The European Economic Area, EEA law: a commentary on the EEA agreement

Schmalenbach K (2011) Art. 8 EUV. In: Calliess C, Ruffert M (eds) EUV AEUV Kommentar, 4th edn, pp 162–168

Streinz R (2012) Art. 8 EUV. In: Streinz R (ed) EUV/AEUV – Vertrag über die Europäische Union und Vertrag über die Arbeitsweise der Europäischen Union, 2nd edn, pp 82–85

van der Bossche P, Zdoug W (2013) The law and policy of the world trade organization, 3rd edn

van Elsuwege P, Petrov R (2011) Article 8 TEU: towards a new generation of agreements with the neighbouring countries of the European Union? 30 Eur Law Rev 5:688
World Trade Organization (2008) The legal texts, the results of the Uruguay round of multilateral trade negotiations, 14th edn
Wüger D, Scarpelli S (2006) Die vernachlässigten institutionellen Aspekte der Bilateralen Verträge und die Aushandlung eines Rahmenvertrags. In: Epiney A, Egbuna-Joss A, Wyssling M (eds) SJE Schweizerisches Jahrbuch für Europarecht 2005/2006, p 287

The EEA in Perspective

Franz Blankart

The European Union and the Normative Multilateralism

Following the dramatic events of two world wars, the European Union (EU) was designed as a project for peace. In this respect, it has proved successful. It is, indeed, thanks to the EU and NATO that my generation and the generations that followed were never mobilised. Today's situation is something that could only have been dreamt of by the generation of my father, who was born in 1895: these men lived through two world wars while in their prime. However, if Switzerland had been invaded during the last two wars, it would have become a founding member of the EU, the UN and NATO. As is frequently the case, people who find themselves in a fortunate position often forget their good fortune.

Since Switzerland was not involved in the Second World War, it regarded the EU, the UN and NATO as peace agreements or *pacta inter alios facta*—believing either rightly or wrongly that its own armed neutrality had saved it from two worlds wars. Consequently, Switzerland took the view that it had no reason to join with former warring nations in defining a new world order. The attitude adopted by Switzerland contains some truth—and possibly also an element of myth.

Switzerland has closely observed the building of Europe—never entirely ruling out the possibly of accession—but seeking first to find a *middle* way between isolation and membership. This reflected the fact that the European Economic Community was regarded by the USSR as an economic arm of NATO in Europe—creating problems in terms of neutrality. The Swiss Federal Council had nevertheless always wanted to see the establishment of a strong and united community, this for security reasons. Furthermore, it believed that only a strong

F. Blankart (✉)
Graduate Institute of International Studies, 1142 Geneva, Switzerland
e-mail: f.blankart@bluewin.ch

C. Herrmann et al. (eds.), *Trade Policy between Law, Diplomacy and Scholarship*, European Yearbook of International Economic Law,
DOI 10.1007/978-3-319-15690-3_17

community is capable of negotiating and making concessions. Consequently, the Swiss Federal Council did not, in any way, hope that the building of the European Economic Community would fail.

It was with this in mind that the then Federal Councillors Max Petitpierre, Hans Schaffner and Friedrich Traugott Wahlen, State Secretary Paul Jolles, Ambassador Pierre Languetin and their successors defined Switzerland's policy on Europe. It consisted firstly of the founding of EFTA,[1] then the Free Trade Agreement of 1972,[2] and then the second generation treaties of 1973–1986,[3] leading to the European Economic Area (EEA)[4] and the Bilateral Agreements I[5] and II.[6] It should be mentioned in passing that Switzerland had concluded dozens of treaties with the EU before EEA membership was rejected.[7]

What is the EEA? The Free Trade Agreement of 1972[8] allows for the free cross-border movement of industrial goods between the two parties to the agreement, provided the goods originated in the territory of those two parties. As a result, it is possible to send a medicine from Switzerland to a member country without being subject to customs duties or quantitative restrictions. However, free trade is not the same as free commercialisation. To achieve this, it is necessary for an EU Member State to recognize—on a reciprocal basis—the Swiss procedures for the registration of that medicine. The same principle applies to the professions: A Swiss doctor can automatically cross the border to go for dinner in an EU-country but is not permitted to open a surgery there in order to sell his expertise. For this to be possible, it is necessary to have a harmonised system or the mutual recognition of medical qualifications. This is the aim of the internal market and the EEA.

In other words: in terms of the four freedoms—free movement of goods, services, persons (freedom of establishment) and capital—Union citizens and the

---

[1] EFTA Convention, Stockholm, 4 January 1960, subsequently revised by the Vaduz Convention, 21 June 2001.

[2] [1972] OJ L 300/189.

[3] See, for example, the Agreement between the European Economic Community, the Swiss Confederation and the Republic of Austria on the widening of the scope of the regulation concerning Community transit, 17 May 1977, [1977] OJ L 142/3.

[4] Agreement on the European Economic Area, 2 May 1992, [1994] OJ L 1/3.

[5] The "Bilateral Agreements I" framework includes seven agreements of 1999 concerning: free movement of persons, [2002] OJ L 144/6; technical barriers to trade, [2002] OJ L 114/369; public procurement markets, [2002] OJ L 114/430; agriculture, [2002] OJ L 114/132; research, [2002] OJ L 114/468; civil aviation, [2002] OJ L 114/73; and overland transport, [2002] OJ L 114/91.

[6] The "Bilateral Agreements II" framework includes nine agreements of 2004 concerning: Schengen/Dublin, [2008] OJ L 53/52; taxation of saving, [2004] OJ L 385/30; processed agricultural products, [2005] OJ L 23/19; MEDIA programme, [2006] OJ L 90/23; environment, [2006] OJ L 90/37; statistics, [2006] OJ L 90/2; combatting fraud, [2009] OJ L 46/8; pensions, available at http://www.europa.admin.ch/dokumentation/00438/00464/00645/index.html?lang=en.

[7] For a complete list of Swiss–EU treaties, see EU Treaties Office Database: Switzerland, available at http://ec.europa.eu/world/agreements/searchByCountryAndContinent.do?countryId=3820&countryName=Switzerland.

[8] [1972] OJ L 300/189.

Swiss would have equal rights in the EU market and the Swiss market. This would be the aim of the EEA. It would represent the continuation and the successful implementation of the Free Trade Agreement.

The rejection of EEA membership on 6 December 1992[9] cost us dearly. I could cite numerous examples of this—from the lack of growth during the 1990s and the Swissair debacle to the noise pollution caused by aircraft flying over Zurich, to name but a few. Because the Swiss public barely reads the texts presented to it before casting its votes, it prefers to succumb to emotion—and everyone knows that emotion is not a good basis for objective decision-making. Furthermore, the Swiss public has a short memory. The EEA, which was 20 years ahead of its time, is today no longer known by people, now that it has reappeared in the public debate.

The *main* responsibility for the rejection of EEA membership did not, incidentally, lie with Swiss National Councillor Christoph Blocher but with the Swiss Federal Council. Following the final round of negotiations, it announced to the Swiss public—at 3.00 a.m. (!) while abroad (!) and from the press room of the European Commission in Luxembourg (!)—that going forward, Switzerland's policy on Europe would be focused on accession to the EU.[10] Since then, the nation has been divided. Most of the people who were responsible for that decision are either deceased or have long since retired from politics.

Instead of taking up the idea of EEA membership again and putting it to a second public vote in Switzerland 2 years later, the Swiss Federal Council decided to pursue the bilateral approach that was to prove effective in the 1970s and 1980s. In other words: the Swiss Federal Council wanted Switzerland to be able to participate in the internal market through the Bilateral Agreements. This option is, in itself, justifiable provided the negotiators don't regard it as a precursor to EU membership. When you see the way in which Switzerland's national highways and the Gotthard Tunnel have been opened up to the EU without Switzerland gaining anything in return, however, you start to ask questions... The slogan "Membership as a strategic goal" was an unpleasant blend of the end and the means—as is so often the case in Switzerland—and was therefore a non-starter. In the end, the Swiss public finally accepted the Bilateral Agreements I and II—and did so with a combination of misgivings and economic hope.

The Bilateral Agreements are—to a large extent—chapters of the EEA Agreement (with the exception of the Schengen/Dublin Agreement, for example, or the accord on combating customs fraud). However, by returning to these chapters, the negotiators left aside the *institutional* provisions of the EEA Agreement because they were working on the assumption that Switzerland would become a member of the EU before the end of the century. Now that Switzerland has substantial access to the internal market (except in the case of services and part of the freedom of establishment) without being a member of either the EEA or the EU, the EU is

[9] Blocher (2002), p. 3.

[10] Switzerland applied for EC membership on 20 May 1992: Vahl and Grolimund (2006), p. 10.

calling for an institutional set-up that is equivalent to that of the EEA.[11] The EU expects all those that want to operate in its territory to play by the rules. This is the condition that will apply to *all* future agreements governing access to the internal market. The EU has clearly stated and restated that without a solution to this problem, *there will be no more bilateral agreements governing market access*.[12] This point needs to be considered.

Why? Internal market law is always evolving. It is amended very rapidly in response to the needs that arise as the market develops, as is EEA law. In other words: internal market law—i.e. Union law—is an "internal law between states" and is therefore flexible. In contrast, the Bilateral Agreements are derived from public international law and are therefore static. Each amendment that is made to them is subject to ratification or approval processes. The Swiss Federal Council is trying to find a bilateral solution to this problem. However, those people who experienced the EEA negotiations first hand know that there are a limited number of options.

In a letter dated 16 June 2012,[13] the President of the Swiss Confederation submitted Switzerland's proposals on the subject of institutions to the then President of the European Commission, José Manuel Barroso (who happens to have been one of my students). Like any negotiator, I analysed these proposals from the perspective of the European Commission and compared them with what has previously been said about this subject over the past 4 years. In doing so, I arrived at the conclusion that the European Commission is unlikely to approve them.

And what about these rules?

- The resumption of the development of EU legislation relating to the internal market;
- Surveillance to ensure that these rules are applied;
- Dispute settlement, arbitrage and the interpretation of internal market rules.

Let's consider these three points.

[11] See European Parliament, Joint Parliamentary Committee on the European Economic Area, Report on the future of the EEA and the EU's relations with the small-sized countries and Switzerland, 30 May 2013, pp. 2, 9 et seq., available at http://www.europarl.europa.eu/document/activities/cont/201305/20130531ATT67141/20130531ATT67141EN.pdf.

[12] See for example Council of the European Union, Conclusions on EU relations with EFTA countries, 8 January 2013, pp. 10 et seq., available at http://data.consilium.europa.eu/doc/document/ST-5101-2013-INIT/en/pdf.

[13] See https://www.news.admin.ch/dokumentation/00002/00015/index.html?lang=en&msg-id=44974.

The Resumption of the Development of EU Legislation Relating to the Internal Market

The history of negotiations between Switzerland and the EU concerning market access can be seen as a quest—a quest to enable Switzerland to participate in the preparation of Union legal acts. It is effectively during this preparatory phase that common premises can be established that will serve as the basis of equivalent legal provisions that can subsequently be mutually recognised or harmonised by them. By being party to this decision-shaping, it is possible for Switzerland to reduce the extent to which Union legislation is reinstated "unilaterally" and to consequently reduce its loss of sovereignty. To express it another way: if Union law that Switzerland contributed to formulate is reinstated, this does not constitute a loss of Swiss sovereignty. However, only members of the EEA can be involved in formulating Union law.

The visionary negotiator of the Free Trade Agreement of 1972, Paul Jolles, had already identified this problem back in 1970. It was for this reason that he intentionally refrained from proposing a system of *joint decision-making* and, instead, recommended that Switzerland should be involved in the preparation of Community provisions ("*decision-shaping*").[14] This premise, which was his legacy to his successors, is not simply a matter of rhetoric. On the contrary: this premise was fully integrated into the Agreement on Thermonuclear Fusion and Plasma Physics of 14 September 1978,[15] the Agreement on the International Occasional Carriage of Passengers by Coach and Bus of 26 May 1982[16] and the Insurance Agreement of 10 October 1989,[17] as well as having been *largely* integrated into the EEA Agreement[18] and in the Schengen/Dublin Agreement.[19]

The Swiss Federal Council has acknowledged that future bilateral agreements should be based on the Union acquis—i.e. the existing body of EU law—which represents a major concession. During the conclusion of a bilateral agreement, the acquis would therefore be taken over directly in the form of a specific provision on this subject. What will happen, however, if the EU amends the acquis following the ratification of the agreement? According to the Swiss Federal Council, a subsequent amendment of this nature would not automatically have to be adopted by Switzerland.

Clear rules were defined in the EEA Agreement[20] to address this problem: Swiss experts would be invited by the European Commission to participate in formulating

[14] Schwok (2010), p. 99 (106).

[15] [1978] OJ L 242/2.

[16] [1982] OJ L 230/39.

[17] [1991] OJ L 205/3.

[18] [1994] OJ L 1/3.

[19] [2008] OJ L 53/52.

[20] [1994] OJ L 1/3.

a legislative proposal, which is then subject to a process whereby the contracting partners are kept constantly informed and are consulted on this matter.

This is the solution that the Swiss Federal Council would like to reinstate for future bilateral agreements. If, after following this procedure, opinions are still divided on the subject, the Federal Council has stated that the Joint Committee would be assigned responsibility for the problem. Since this Joint Committee is a diplomatic body that only reaches unanimous decisions, the bilateral agreement would be suspended in the event of any disagreement and—as a last resort—would be retracted. In other words, the Swiss Federal Council is proposing a solution that is identical to the EEA Agreement—which would be a good solution. However, it is uncertain whether the EU will accept it.

The Surveillance of the Application of Internal Market Rules

During the negotiation of the EEA Agreement, one Community demand became of key importance: the homogeneity of internal market law. This meant that it was necessary to apply internal market law in an identical manner in all EU member states, and consequently also in all EFTA states that are members of the EEA. The rules had to be applied in the same way in each EEA state.

This principle of homogeneity—which is not customary in a federal state such as Switzerland—was intended to ensure legal certainty. During the negotiations of the EEA Agreement, we finally accepted this legacy of the French Revolution. Hence, it is not surprising that this request has resurfaced in the context of the bilateral agreements and that the solution should be supranational. A country, according to the opinion of the Commission,[21] cannot monitor itself.

However, the Swiss Federal Council does not want a supranational approach. It would therefore ensure that monitoring was carried out by a body designated by the Swiss Parliament. This body would operate in the same manner as the EFTA Surveillance Authority within the EEA but would be of a purely national nature. Having listened to President Barroso, I doubt whether this solution would be accepted by the Council of the EU and the European Parliament.

[21] See, for example, European Parliament, Joint Parliamentary Committee on the European Economic Area, Report on the future of the EEA and the EU's relations with the small-sized countries and Switzerland, 30 May 2013, p. 4, available at http://www.europarl.europa.eu/document/activities/cont/201305/20130531ATT67141/20130531ATT67141EN.pdf.

Dispute Settlement, Arbitrage and Interpretation of Internal Market Rules

The same problem applies with regard to the judicial authorities. The Swiss Federal Council is trying to avoid a supranational judicial authority. It proposes a body comprising a special chamber of the Swiss Federal Court. A body of this nature could perhaps resolve differences and provide arbitrage. For the interpretation of internal market rules, it would be essential, however, for the Court of Justice of the European Union to accept another court at its side. This will not be the case. One need only read the opinions on this subject.

I would therefore be astonished if this solution were to be accepted by the EU. This is because within the geographical area covered by the agreements, Switzerland has to respect the same material and institutional rules as EU Member States as well as EFTA states that are members of the EEA—which goes without saying. The opening-up of the market makes it necessary for these rules—both material and institutional—to be applicable in Switzerland in a non-discriminatory manner. This is the way in which Switzerland would respect the premise of homogeneity.

In other words: the EU does not want to open up its market if Switzerland does not do the same for Union and Swiss participants in Switzerland in accordance with material and institutional Union rules. The Swiss Confederation must therefore return to the supranational provisions of the EEA Agreement. France, for example, must agree to have its conduct in the internal market supervised by supranational bodies—the European Commission and the Court of Justice of the EU—and Norway must also agree to the same monitoring being performed by two supranational bodies of the EEA—the EFTA Surveillance Authority and the EFTA Court of Justice. I really don't see why an exception would be made in the case of Switzerland.

The Swiss Federal Council is effectively seeking to construct a bilateral EEA, i.e. an alliance that would pave the way for new standards for Switzerland alone, and it is trying to appoint a Swiss supervisory authority as well as an authority—which would ultimately be Swiss—to address judicial problems. The question of whether the Swiss Federal Council will succeed in building a bilateral and non-supranational EEA remains largely unanswered.

The fact of the matter is that the Swiss Federal Council's institutional proposal, which was submitted to the then President of the European Commission José Manuel Barroso in June 2012, is largely based on the EEA Agreement—with the matter of supranationality being the sole exception. This is apparently the reason why the Swiss Federal Council is avoiding the EEA option. It is, nevertheless, astonishing, given that the Swiss Federal Council accepted the supranational nature of the bodies of the EEA without hesitation 22 years ago and then even went on to accept the European Court as the judicial authority in the Bilateral Agreement on

Civil Aviation[22] several years later. This was in fact the first case where Switzerland had accepted the authority of foreign judges! Furthermore, Switzerland accepted the authority of a supranational court for the judgment of human rights violations in Europe[23] and a supranational court to address disputes within the WTO.[24]

We have to work on the assumption that the European Council and the European Court will not accept national surveillance and national judicial authorities.

I have reached the following conclusions:

If the EU insists on the homogeneity of Union law and the law of the bilateral agreements, and if this homogeneity is monitored by a supranational body, then the bilateral agreements—in the form defined by the Swiss Federal Council—have no future. The only options that are left are therefore to join the EU, to renounce other bilateral agreements or to become a member of the EEA. Since EU membership is not a realistic possibility for my generation or the one that follows it, the only possible courses of action that remain are to renounce other bilateral agreements or to become a member of the EEA. The renunciation of future bilateral agreements will come at a high price, since each directive governing market access places EU and EEA member states on an equal footing—meaning that Switzerland is automatically discriminated against. For our country—which does over CHF 1 billion of trade with the EU every business day—a solution of this nature is simply untenable.

Consequently, there is only one solution: an EEA Agreement adapted to the present situation, 22 years after it was rejected.

References

Blocher C (2002) Ten years after rejecting the EEA agreement: a current assessment and outlook, p 3, December 2002. Available at http://www.blocher.ch/uploads/media/ewr_en.pdf

Schwok R (2010) Specificities of Switzerland's relations with EFTA and the EEA. In: Bryn K, Einarsson G (eds) EFTA 1960–2010: elements of 50 years of European history, p 99 (106)

Vahl M, Grolimund N (2006) Integration without membership: Switzerland's bilateral agreements with the European Union, p 10

[22] For example, ECJ, C-547/10 P, *Switzerland v European Commission*, Judgement of 7 March 2013, not yet published.

[23] Protocol No. 2 to the European Convention on Human Rights.

[24] Art. 1.1 Understanding on Rules and Procedures Governing the Settlement of Disputes.

The EU and Its Eastern Partnership: Political Association and Economic Integration in a Rough Neighbourhood

Gunnar Wiegand and Evelina Schulz

Introduction: The Eastern Partnership Post-Vilnius Agenda

Following some turbulent months in EU–Ukraine relations, the Association Agreement between Ukraine and the EU was signed in Brussels at the European Council on 27 June 2014, together with the agreements with Moldova and Georgia.[1]

This historic event reversed the decision taken on 21 November 2013, by the previous Ukrainian government to suspend[2] the signature of the already long initialled Association Agreement, including its Deep and Comprehensive Free

The views and opinions expressed in this article are those of the authors.

[1] See statement by President Van Rompuy at the occasion of the signing ceremony, EUCO 137/14, Presse 375, PR PCE 126 of 27 June 2014, available at http://www.consilium.europa.eu/uedocs/cms_data/docs/pressdata/en/ec/143415.pdf; and European Commission, Press Release, MEMO/14/430 of 23 June 2014, The EU's Association Agreements with Georgia, the Republic of Moldova and Ukraine, available at http://europa.eu/rapid/press-release_MEMO-14-430_en.htm.

[2] On 21 November 2013, the Ukrainian government adopted a resolution on suspension of the preparation process to conclude the Association Agreement with the EU. See statement by Ukrainian Department of Information and Communication of the Secretariat of the CMU, 21 November 2013, available at http://www.kmu.gov.ua/control/en/publish/article?art_id=246866213.

G. Wiegand (✉)
European External Action Service, Office SCHU 05/340, Rond Point Schumann 9A, 1046 Brussels, Belgium
e-mail: gunnar.wiegand@eeas.europa.eu

E. Schulz (✉)
European External Action Service, Office JOYE 02/448, Rond Point Schumann 9A, 1046 Brussels, Belgium
e-mail: evelina.schulz@eeas.europa.eu

C. Herrmann et al. (eds.), *Trade Policy between Law, Diplomacy and Scholarship*, European Yearbook of International Economic Law,
DOI 10.1007/978-3-319-15690-3_18

Trade Area (AA/DCFTA).[3] The political parts of the Association Agreement with Ukraine were signed in a first step at an Extraordinary EU–Ukraine Summit on 21 March 2014,[4] the same day Russia formally annexed Crimea, and exactly 4 months after the suspension decision.

On 16 September 2014, the EU–Ukraine AA/DCFTA was ratified by Ukraine. The European Parliament gave simultaneously its consent on the Agreement.[5] This important step was preceded by a meeting on 12 September 2014 between EU Trade Commissioner De Gucht, Minister of Foreign Affairs of Ukraine Klimkin and Minister of Economic Development of the Russian Federation Ulyukayev and resulted in a Joint Ministerial Statement[6] on the implementation of the EU–Ukraine Association Agreement/DCFTA. The Ministers agreed to delay until 31 December 2015 the provisional application of the DCFTA while continuing autonomous trade measures of the EU to the benefit of Ukraine during this period.[7] This unprecedented step was the result of trilateral consultations on the impact of the EU–Ukraine DCFTA on Russia. It paved the way for ratification of the Agreement while avoiding the withdrawal of Russian trade preferences to Ukraine under the CIS-

---

[3] Two years earlier, in 2012, the chief negotiators of the EU and Ukraine had already initialled the text of the AA, which included provisions on the establishment of a DCFTA as an integral part. See European Commission, Press Release, MEMO/12/238 of 30 March 2012, available at http://europa.eu/rapid/press-release_MEMO-12-238_en.htm. The remaining DCFTA parts were initialled on 19 July 2012.

[4] The signature by the EU's 28 Heads of States and Governments, Presidents Van Rompuy and Barroso and Ukrainian Prime Minister Yatsenyuk applied in a first step only to political provisions of the Agreement: the Preamble, Article 1 and Titles I, II, and VII. See text of the "Final Act", available at http://eeas.europa.eu/delegations/ukraine/documents/association_agreement/final_act_text_en.pdf. See also the statement by President Van Rompuy at the occasion of the signing ceremony, EUCO 68/14, Presse 176, PR PCE 61, 21 March 2014, available at http://www.consilium.europa.eu/uedocs/cms_Data/docs/pressdata/en/ec/141733.pdf and the details in the agreements database: http://www.consilium.europa.eu/policies/agreements/search-the-agreements-database?command=details&lang=en&aid=2013005&doclang=EN; see Council Decision (2014/295/EU) of 17 March 2014 on the signing, on behalf of the European Union, and provisional application of the Association Agreement between the European Union and the European Atomic Energy Community and their Member States, of the one part, and Ukraine, of the other part, as regards the Preamble, Article 1, and Titles I, II and VII thereof; and European Council, Conclusions, EUCO 7/14, CO EUR 2, CONCL 1, 20/21 March 2014, pp. 12–14. See also text of the Agreement in [2014] OJ L 161/3-2137.

[5] See Law of Ukraine N1678-VII and see text adopted by the European Parliament P8_TA(2014)0014.

[6] See European Commission, Press Release, STATEMENT 14/276 of 12 September 2014, Joint Ministerial Statement on the Implementation of the EU–Ukraine AA/DCFTA, available at http://europa.eu/rapid/press-release_STATEMENT-14-276_en.htm.

[7] See Joint statement of the Council and the Commission on the EU–Ukraine Association Agreement, 29 September 2014, available at http://www.consilium.europa.eu/uedocs/cms_Data/docs/pressdata/EN/foraff/144955.pdf. See also Council of the European Union, Press Release of 29 September 2014, ST 13634/14 PRESSE 485, EU–Ukraine Association Agreement to start applying in two stages, available at http://www.consilium.europa.eu/uedocs/cms_Data/docs/pressdata/EN/foraff/144957.pdf.

FTA. The threats of countermeasures have been repeated as recently as in December 2014 by Russian Federation Prime Minister Medvedev in an article published in Nezavisimaya Gazeta.[8]

Since August 2013, Ukraine had been subject to unprecedented Russian customs control at the Ukraine-Russian borders. This, combined with significant other subsequent Russian pressures, led then President Yanukovych and Prime Minister Azarov to state that the economic impact of the AA/DCFTA was of such magnitude that its related costs—notably with regard to the alleged adverse impact on Ukrainian exports to Russia—had to be carefully studied and significant compensation had to be agreed. Within this context, then President Yanukovych reached a deal with Russian President Putin providing for a significant reduction of the Russian gas price (from USD 410 to USD 268.5 per 1,000 m^3) and a USD 15 billion loan over 18 months to prevent Ukraine from economic collapse.[9]

During the 4 months between suspension and actual signature of the AA, dramatic events unfolded in Ukraine. Massive demonstrations of hundreds of thousands of Ukrainians, outraged by the turnaround of their leadership in view of association with the EU developed into a permanent protest. "Euromaidan" was established on Kiev's Independence Square and attempts of violent suppression by the authorities led to more far reaching demands, including the resignation of the President. Ukraine saw the worst violent clash in its history with more than 100 deaths and hundreds of injured, kidnapped and disappeared persons.

EU efforts to mediate between government and opposition, carried out by then High Representative/Vice President Catherine Ashton and Commissioner Štefan Füle in a series of missions to Kiev, culminated in a deal brokered by the Foreign Ministers of France, Germany and Poland on 21 February 2014.[10]

The following day, on 22 February, Yanukovych abandoned his functions as President, allowing a new governmental formation, voted in by a constitutional

---

[8] See article by Russian PM Medvedev published on 15 December 2014 in Nezavisimaya Gazeta, Дмитрий Медведев, Россия и Украина: жизнь по новым правилам, available at http://www.ng.ru/ideas/2014-12-15/1_medvedev.html.

[9] This deal materialised shortly after the Eastern Partnership Summit in Vilnius. Following a meeting of the Russian–Ukrainian Interstate Commission on 17 December 2013, President Putin said at a news conference: "[K]nowing the difficulties the Ukrainian economy is facing, difficulties that I think are largely due to the global financial and economic crisis, in the aim of supporting Ukraine's budget, the Russian Government has decided to invest USD 15 billion in reserves from the Russian National Wealth Fund in Ukrainian government securities", see http://eng.kremlin.ru/transcripts/6421.

[10] The deal was accompanied by a joint press statement in which the three foreign ministers of France, Germany and Poland welcomed "the signing of the agreement on the Settlement of the crisis in Ukraine, commend[ed] the parties for their courage and commitment to the agreement and call[ed] for an immediate end to all violence and confrontation in Ukraine", see press release, 21 February 2014, available at http://www.auswaertiges-amt.de/DE/Infoservice/Presse/Meldungen/2014/140221-UKR.html. The text of the deal is available at the webpage of the German Foreign Ministry http://www.auswaertiges-amt.de/cae/servlet/contentblob/671350/publicationFile/190051/140221-UKR_Erklaerung.pdf.

majority of 371 votes, with significant parts of Yanukovych's Party of Regions supporting the new government. One of the first steps taken by the new government was to reverse the decision of AA suspension and to urge the EU to move ahead with signature of the AA as soon as possible.[11]

The agreement was signed 1 month later, on 21 March 2014, the same day Russia formally annexed Crimea.[12] The annexation, preceded by an illegal referendum on 16 March, a fully-fledged military assault on Crimea violating Ukraine's territorial integrity, independence and sovereignty, led to the worst crisis in Russia's relations with the EU and the US in decades. The annexation was also condemned by a wide majority of countries around the globe, as evidenced by the vote on the United Nations General Assembly Resolution N. 11493 of 27 March 2014 on the "Territorial Integrity of Ukraine" which was adopted with 100 delegations voting in favour, eleven against and 58 abstentions.[13]

The turbulences in Ukraine did not remain limited to Crimea, but expanded into the Eastern and Southern parts of Ukraine, at the border with Russia. On 11 May 2014, in many towns of the self-proclaimed *Donetsk and Lugansk People's Republics* referenda on the status of the *Oblasts* took place. These referenda sought to legitimise the establishment of the separatist "republics", with the support of illegally armed militia. The results of the referenda were not recognised by any government, including those of Ukraine, the United States, the Member States of the European Union,[14] and even Russia. The following months of "hybrid warfare"

[11] The new Ukrainian government under Arseniy Yatseniuk declared on 6 March 2014 its readiness to sign the Association Agreement, see statement by Ukrainian Department of Information and Communication of the Secretariat of the CMU, 6 March 2014, available at http://www.kmu.gov.ua/control/en/publish/article?art_id=247082343&cat_id=244314975.

[12] On 21 March 2014, during the 349th extraordinary session of the Federation Council of the Federal Assembly of the Russian Federation, Foreign Minister Sergey Lavrov presented two documents for consideration: a draft Federal Law "On Ratification of the Agreement between the Russian Federation and the Republic of Crimea on acceptance of the Republic of Crimea into the Russian Federation and the creation of new constituent entities of the Russian Federation" and the draft Federal Constitutional Law "On acceptance of the Republic of Crimea into the Russian Federation and the creation of new constituent entities of the Russian Federation – the Republic of Crimea and the Federal City of Sevastopol". The approval of these two documents formalised the reunification of Crimea and the Russian Federation, creating two new constituent entities of the Federation, see http://www.mid.ru/brp_4.nsf/0/1EB0F5937A80B6B444257CA500519090 and http://council.gov.ru/press-center/photo/27743/.

[13] On 27 March 2014, the 68th UN General Assembly affirmed its commitment to Ukraine's sovereignty, political independence, unity and territorial integrity within its internationally recognised borders, underscoring the invalidity of the 16 March referendum held in autonomous Crimea. The Assembly adopted a resolution titled "Territorial Integrity of Ukraine" (A/RES/68/262), calling on States, international organisations and specialized agencies not to recognise any change in the status of Crimea or the Black Sea port city of Sevastopol, and to refrain from actions or dealings that might be interpreted as such. See press release GA/11493, 27 March 2014, available at http://www.un.org/News/Press/docs/2014/ga11493.doc.htm.

[14] See remarks by former High Representative Catherine Ashton at the press conference following the Foreign Affairs Council on 12 May 2014, "The European Union will not recognise any

by separatists with the support of Russia[15] and the "Anti-Terror Operation" of Ukrainian armed forces and security services led to many victims, significant displacements and resulted in massive humanitarian needs.[16]

Considering the origins and motivations of the EU's Eastern Partnership policy (EaP) as well as the actual content of the EU's Association Agreements with its Eastern partners and their economic impact on Russia, it is clear that all of these developments were unintended consequences.

The Eastern Partnership Summit that took place on 28–29 November 2013 in Vilnius between the EU and six Eastern neighbouring states[17] was meant to be a turning point in the EU's relations with its Eastern neighbours. The success of the EaP policy was seen by many as a yardstick for measuring the EU's foreign policy impact and transformative powers in its eastern neighbourhood, with an association beneath the threshold of enlargement.

The non-signature of the Ukraine Association Agreement was not the only setback that the Vilnius Summit had to face. In September 2013, just a few months prior to Vilnius, Armenia announced that it would not move further with negotiations on its AA with the EU. As a consequence, the planned initialling ceremony of three AAs in the end only included two: Georgia and Moldova. Moreover, the progress on AA negotiations with Azerbaijan was disappointing and had stalled, due to some conceptual and political differences between the two Parties already in early 2013.

Only history will show whether the Vilnius Summit with the dramatic subsequent events in Ukraine was indeed a turning point towards a positive or a negative direction from an EU foreign policy perspective.

In a positive scenario, this Summit and the following months will be seen as the moment when "the point of no return" was reached by three EaP countries (Georgia, Moldova and Ukraine). Countries accept political association and economic integration with the EU as a decisive tool for domestic transformation and modernisation on the same values basis as the EU, strengthening the rule of law, fighting corruption and applying a vast number of EU norms and standards and thus creating a level playing field for domestic and foreign economic operators. Vilnius might

---

illegitimate and illegal 'referenda'"; available at http://www.eeas.europa.eu/statements/docs/2014/140512_02_en.pdf.

[15] In response to the illegal annexation and deliberate destabilisation of a neighbouring sovereign country, the EU imposed restrictive measures against the Russian Federation. See special coverage of the EU newsroom on "EU sanctions against Russia over Ukraine crisis", available at http://europa.eu/newsroom/highlights/special-coverage/eu_sanctions/index_en.htm. See also Background Note on "EU restrictive measures in view of the situation in Eastern Ukraine and the illegal annexation of Crimea", Council of the European Union, 29 July 2014, available at http://www.consilium.europa.eu/uedocs/cms_data/docs/pressdata/EN/foraff/144159.pdf.

[16] At the time of writing, an estimated number of up to 4,000 victims have reportedly been killed. The number of internally displaced people from the Donbass region and Crimea is estimated at around 5,001,157 by the Ukrainian National Coordination Council for IDP.

[17] Republic of Armenia, Republic of Azerbaijan, Belarus, Georgia, Republic of Moldova and Ukraine (further on referred to as "Armenia", "Azerbaijan", "Moldova").

also be assessed as a first of many interim steps[18] towards an eventual accession of Moldova, Ukraine and Georgia to the EU.[19]

In a negative scenario, the transformative impact of the EaP initiative will be limited and the countries would ultimately not live up to their commitments and thus not qualify for any further steps on the path towards fulfilling their aspirations. One of the reasons could be the lack of capacity to implement the ambitious reforms foreseen in the association with the EU: systemic rigidities, vested interests and rampant corruption could prevent the necessary political, legal and institutional reforms, hampering economic liberalisation in having real impact. Another negative scenario could be the lack of political will, resulting either from external political, military and economic pressure or from internal domestic opposition capable of changing course and abandoning the intended association with the EU in the short-term and the integration of these countries into the EU in the long-term.

In either scenario, a close look at the Association Agreements with EaP partners is necessary in order to analyse and assess their impact and what would be required to optimise it. Before doing so, an overview of the preceding policy context will help to place this new wave of agreements within the wider context of the EU's foreign policy projection in its neighbourhood. Finally, a critical analysis will be provided which focuses on the possibility of finding a compatible solution between the two paths of EU integration and Customs Union membership to overcome the dilemma for EaP countries: how to live up to an ambitious political association and economic integration process with the EU while taking account of their political and economic domestic situations and not undermining their socio-economic, historical and political links with Russia.

From Partnership to Association: Genesis of the Eastern Partnership

Newly Independent States and Their Cooperation Partnership with the EU

The new Association Agreements (AA) with the Eastern Partnership countries are supposed to replace the Partnership and Cooperation Agreements (PCA) which the EU had negotiated in the early 1990s with each of the successor states of the Soviet Union. In 1994 the PCAs with Ukraine, Russia and Moldova were signed and 2 years later Georgia, Armenia and Azerbaijan followed suit. Even though the PCA

---

[18] See Devrim and Schulz (2009b).

[19] See Foreign Affairs Council conclusions of 10 February 2014 on Eastern Partnership: "The Council expresses its conviction that this Agreement does not constitute the final goal in EU-Ukraine cooperation", http://www.consilium.europa.eu/uedocs/cms_data/docs/pressdata/EN/foraff/140960.pdf.

with Belarus was also signed in 1995, it has so far never been ratified, since Member States and the European Parliament raised concerns with regard to the human rights situation in Belarus. Due to the rather long ratification procedures of the EU, the PCAs entered into force only a couple of years after signing between 1997 and 1999[20] with the Russia PCA having been the first.[21]

These PCAs were designed as comprehensive agreements, governing the entirety of the EU's relations with the "countries of the Former Soviet Union", a term often used in the 1990s. The PCAs helped to normalise and develop relations across many fields with newly independent states, of which none had any relations with the EU before. The aim of these agreements was to strengthen the democratic and economic development of the partner countries through cooperation in some selected policy areas and a suitable framework for political dialogue. The partnerships aimed to provide a basis for cooperation in legislative, economic, social, financial, scientific, civil, technological and cultural fields. The PCAs with Ukraine, Russia and Moldova also provided already the prospect of setting up in the future free trade areas.[22] The idea was to accompany the transition of the partner countries to a market economy[23] and to encourage trade and investment.

The PCAs, however, did not reflect the new competences in many key policy areas that the EU had been entrusted (for example, in Common Foreign and Security Policy, Home and Justice) nor did they contain a dynamic agenda facilitating political and institutional reforms and much closer economic and sectoral cooperation. Furthermore, although the Agreements established the so-called "Cooperation Councils" responsible for supervising the implementation of the PCAs, the monitoring capacities of these institutional bodies remained limited. Thus, the emphasis in the PCAs was laid on "cooperation" between partners with a rather loose form of commitment and a lack of real enforcement obligation as well as dispute settlement.

[20] See PCA with Ukraine, Council and Commission Decision (98/149/EC, ECSC, Euratom) of 26 January 1998, [1998] OJ L 49/1; PCA with Moldova, Council and Commission Decision (98/401/EC, ECSC, Euratom) of 28 May 1998, [1998] OJ L 181/1; PCA with Georgia, Council and Commission Decision (1999/515/EC, ECSC, Euratom) of 31 May 1999, [1999] OJ L 205/1; PCA with Armenia, Council and Commission Decision (1999/602/EC, ECSC, Euratom) of 31 May 1999, [1999] OJ L 239/1; PCA with Azerbaijan, Council and Commission Decision (1999/614/EC, ECSC, Euratom) of 31 May 1999, [1999] OJ L 246/1.

[21] See PCA with the Russian Federation, Council and Commission Decision (97/800/ECSC, EC, Euratom) of 30 October 1997, [1997] OJ L 327/1.

[22] See for Ukraine OJ L 49, Volume 41, 19.02.1998, p. 3 (Arts. 4 and 10). See for Moldova OJ L 181/3 (Arts. 4 and 10). See for Russia OJ L 327/3 (Arts. 1, 3 and 10).

[23] The EU recognised formally Ukraine with a market economy status in 2005 whereas Russia received this recognition 3 years earlier in 2002.

The EU's Neighbourhood Policy for Its New Neighbours in the East

Ten years after the signature of these PCAs, the geographic scope of the EU changed dramatically, affecting also the geopolitics of the European continent. After the two enlargements of 2004 and 2007,[24] the EU found itself suddenly in a situation where it shared direct borders not only with Belarus, Ukraine, Moldova and Russia, but the new Member States bordering the Black Sea also linked the EU to the countries in the South Caucasus.

Shortly before the major enlargement to the East became a reality, then President of the European Commission Romano Prodi coined the key terms for a new European neighbourhood policy (ENP) by stating that the countries around the EU, from Morocco and the Mediterranean, to the Black Sea and to Russia and Ukraine, should form an "arc of stability" and "a ring of friends" with the ability to participate in the various EU policies and programmes ("everything but institutions").[25]

Russia and the ENP

Russia was supposed to be part of the ENP. The European Commission made this explicit by sending then Enlargement Commissioner Günther Verheugen[26] to Moscow in October 2003. Verheugen underlined that "Russian participation in our neighbourhood policy forms an obvious and integral part of such an approach".[27] But Russia declined the EU's invitation to take part in the ENP. Instead, the "Common Spaces" for EU–Russia cooperation were established at the EU–Russia Summit in November 2003.[28]

There are various attempts to explain Russia's refusal to be part of the ENP. One is that Russia has special and strategic relations with the EU, notably in terms of trade and energy relations, which differ substantially from the other 16 ENP countries.[29] One can assume that Russia did not want to be monitored/measured

---

[24] With the major enlargement to the East in 2004, eight of the ten new Member States were Central and Eastern European countries. In 2007 Romania and Bulgaria joined the EU.

[25] Prodi (2001, 2002).

[26] Commissioner Verheugen had been entrusted with the preparations for the EU's new neighbourhood policy—an area added in the next Commission to Benita Ferrero Waldner's External Relations and ENP portfolio. See http://ec.europa.eu/archives/commission_1999_2004/verheugen/index_en.htm as well as http://ec.europa.eu/archives/commission_2004-2009/ferrero-waldner/index_en.htm.

[27] Speech of Verheugen (2003).

[28] Joint Statement of the 12th EU–Russia Summit, Rome, 6 November 2003, 13990/03, Presse 313.

[29] Of the 16 ENP countries, 12 are currently fully participating as partners in the ENP, having agreed on ENP Action Plans: Armenia, Azerbaijan, Egypt, Georgia, Israel, Jordan, Lebanon,

by the EU through the so called ENP Action Plans which set out the partner country's agenda for political and economic reforms and also provide the EU's instrument to monitor and assess progress in implementation on a yearly basis in so-called ENP progress reports.[30] Another reason is that Russia did not want to become "object" of an EU policy, as the approach towards Moldova or Morocco was perceived, but rather be "subject" on the basis of equality and reciprocity at a level of a strategic partner. This is reflected in the four Common Spaces and the related detailed Roadmaps of action, adopted at the EU–Russia Summit in May 2005.[31] A new impetus for EU–Russia relations was also intended with the launch of negotiations of a "New Agreement" in 2008[32] which was meant to replace the 1994 PCA and to provide for a strengthened legal basis and legally binding commitments covering all main areas of EU–Russia relations. To complement the negotiation and building on results achieved under the Common Spaces approach so far, in 2010 the Partnership for Modernisation was launched,[33] serving as a flexible framework for promoting reform, enhancing growth and raising competitiveness.

In sum, while there had been one policy of the EU towards its Eastern continental neighbours following the demise of the Soviet Union in the 1990s, the first decade of the 2000s saw an increased deviation between EU–Russian relations on the one side and a specific policy towards Eastern neighbours on the other side.

The *finalité* of the ENP: Aims and Objectives

The ENP signalled a growing awareness that the EU needed to protect its interests in its new neighbourhood by promoting political stability and economic prosperity, contributing to new business opportunities and preventing instability which may

---

Moldova, Morocco, Palestine, Tunisia and Ukraine. Algeria is currently negotiating an ENP action plan and Belarus, Libya and Syria remain outside most of the structures of ENP. See http://eeas.europa.eu/enp/index_en.htm.

[30] Once a year, the European External Action Service and the European Commission publish reports assessing the progress made towards the objectives of the Action Plans and their successor documents, the Association Agendas. See http://eeas.europa.eu/enp/documents/progress-reports/index_en.htm.

[31] 15th EU–Russia Summit, Moscow, 10 May 2005, Road Maps, 8799/05 ADD 1, Presse 110, 11 May 2005. The four Road Maps are: Road Map for the Common Economic Space; Road Map for the Common Space of Freedom, Security and Justice; Road Map for the Common Space of External Security; and Road Map for the Common Space of Research and Education, including Cultural Aspects, available at https://www.consilium.europa.eu/uedocs/cmsUpload/84815.pdf.

[32] Joint statement of the EU–Russia Summit on the launch of negotiations for a new EU–Russia agreement, Khanty-Mansiysk, 27 June 2008, 11214/08, Presse 192, available at http://www.consilium.europa.eu/ueDocs/cms_Data/docs/pressData/en/er/101524.pdf.

[33] Joint Statement on the Partnership for Modernisation, 25th EU–Russia Summit, Rostov-on-Don, 31 May–1 June 2010, 10546/10, Presse 154, available at http://www.consilium.europa.eu/uedocs/cms_Data/docs/pressdata/en/er/114747.pdf.

lead to new large-scale migratory flows. At the same time this new approach represented the recognition that ever new rounds of enlargements were politically and financially unfeasible, notably since domestic political support in a significant number of Member States was lacking, often referred to as the so-called "enlargement fatigue".[34] Thus, the ENP did not attempt to address the perennial issue of possible future membership, but left it simply open for Member States as well as neighbouring countries to interpret the "*finalité*" of the ENP according to national interests.

The ENP had been created in anticipation of the 2004 enlargement round, in order to provide a framework for the EU's relations with its new neighbours. The dual policies of enlargement and ENP were conceptualised as distinct EU strategies and the clear differentiation between the two became at the same time more ambiguous.[35] The ENP provided the opportunity to develop privileged political and economic relations with a degree of integration going beyond normal cooperation with third countries, but stopping short of enlargement. Bilateral Action Plans are intended to anchor reforms and bring the countries closer to the EU ("approximation"). Specific annual Country Progress Reports[36] on the implementation of the Action Plans as well as a specific financial instrument, the European Neighbourhood Partnership Instrument,[37] with multi-annual country strategies are key instruments to support these objectives.

The emphasis of the ENP was on new forms of cooperation and related financial assistance. New contractual commitments to anchor the new neighbouring countries closer to the EU were already envisaged. Given that the Mediterranean neighbours of the EU already had Euro-Mediterranean Association Agreements (except Syria and Libya), the possibility of obtaining new contractual commitments was most relevant for the eastern neighbours. Subsequently, the European Commission proposed a negotiation mandate for a new agreement with Ukraine in September 2006. This mandate was given by the Council only some 4 months

[34] Devrim and Schulz (2009a).

[35] This policy was first conceptualised in the Commission's communication, Wider Europe—Neighbourhood: A New Framework for Relations with our Eastern and Southern Neighbours, adopted in March 2003, COM(2003) 104 final of 11 March 2003. See for a detailed analysis of the ENP in comparison to enlargement: Devrim and Schulz (2009a), pp. 4–7.

[36] See the last series of country progress reports, European Commission, Press Release, IP/14/315 of 27 March 2014, Neighbourhood at the Crossroads—Taking Stock of a Year of Challenges, available at http://europa.eu/rapid/press-release_IP-14-315_en.htm.

[37] In the period 2007–2013, the ENPI provided financial assistance with a total volume of nearly EUR 12 billion in grants. For the period 2014–2020, the ENPI will be succeeded by a new European Neighbourhood Instrument (ENI) with a budget of around EUR 15.4 billion. The ENI will strengthen some of the key features of the ENPI, notably greater differentiation between countries based on progress with reforms and new mechanisms to support an incentive based approach (often referred to as "more for more"). See also Regulation (EU) No 232/2014 of the European Parliament and the Council of 11 March 2014 establishing a European Neighbourhood Instrument, OJ L 77/27.

later and the negotiations started in March 2007.[38] In February 2008, following Ukraine's accession to the World Trade Organization, the EU and Ukraine also launched negotiations on a Free Trade Area, later upgraded and called a Deep and Comprehensive Free Trade Area,[39] as a core element of the new agreement.

A Need for Differentiation Within the ENP: The Eastern Dimension

In 2008, the EU's relations with its neighbours were driven by the national interest of some Member States. After the re-launch of its relations to the South with the establishment of the "Union pour la Mediterranée" under French Presidency in 2008, a new initiative for the East followed: the Eastern Partnership (EaP). The Partnership aimed to intensify the EU's relations with its three eastern European (Belarus, Moldova, and Ukraine) and three south-eastern neighbours (Armenia, Azerbaijan and Georgia) in the South Caucasus.

With the establishment of the ENP, the EU had hoped to avoid the creation of new dividing lines between the new eastern EU Member States and their closest neighbours. In this regard, the EaP was a deepening of that approach.

Eastern Partnership: From a Polish–Swedish Proposal to an EU Policy

Following a debate by the European Council in March 2008 on the need to strengthen the eastern dimension of the ENP, Poland and Sweden put forward a proposal to launch an Eastern Partnership in May 2008.[40] In line with the European Council Conclusions of June 2008, the European Commission was supposed to establish the modalities for the EaP with a dedicated communication in spring 2009.[41] However, the Russian military action against Georgia in August 2008

---

[38] The Council adopted the mandate on 22 January 2007. See Council of the EU, 2776th Council meeting, General Affairs and External Relations, Brussels, 22 January 2007, 5463/07, Presse 7.

[39] Traditionally, standard FTAs foresee mutual opening of markets for goods and services. The reason that the EaP agreement refer to "*Deep and Comprehensive*" areas is that they would go much further. "*Deep*" relates to the extensive coverage of non-tariff barriers in many sectors aiming at eliminating "behind the border" obstacles to trade, thus partially opening/extending the EU internal market to a third country. "*Comprehensive*" relates to the scope of the agreement since it covers an unprecedented wide array of trade-related issues (such as IPRs, procurement and competition). See, for example, http://eeas.europa.eu/delegations/georgia/documents/eu_georgia/dcfta2012_01_en.pdf.

[40] See press release of the 2870th Council meeting, General Affairs and External Relations, Brussels, 26–27 May 2008, 9868/08, Presse 141, p. 24, available at http://europa.eu/rapid/press-release_PRES-08-141_en.htm.

[41] See Presidency Conclusions, European Council, Brussels, 19/20 June 2008, 11018/1/08 REV 1, 17 July 2008.

accelerated this process and the Commission brought forward its Communication on the EaP to December 2008.[42]

This Communication supported the aspirations of the eastern neighbours for closer ties with the EU, basing the EU's commitment on strict conditionality—especially regarding progress made by partner countries in the areas of human rights, democracy and the rule of law. The Commission underlined that the EU's ambitions for the relationship would depend on the extent to which these European values are respected and implemented in each country. This approach was emphasised later as the "more for more" principle of the Eastern Partnership which was spelled out more precisely in the ENP-Review in May 2011.[43] The EU proposed also more intensive day-to-day support for its partners' reform efforts through a new Comprehensive Institution Building programme. In addition, as mentioned above, the Commission called to upgrade the contractual relations with the partner countries by launching a new generation of Association Agreements. It also proposed a network of Free Trade Areas that could lead in the longer term to the establishment of a Neighbourhood Economic Community. Other objectives included progressive visa liberalisation for partner countries' citizens, deeper cooperation to enhance mutual energy security and support for economic and social policies to reduce disparities within and across borders.

The New Agreement for Ukraine Sets the Precedent

Similarly, following on from the Georgia crisis, the leaders of the EU and Ukraine agreed at the EU–Ukraine Summit in Paris in September 2008[44] that the PCA should be succeeded by an Association Agreement in line with Article 217 of the TFEU. Consequently, the New Agreement with Ukraine which was already under negotiation was renamed an "Association Agreement" (AA). Ukraine therefore became the frontrunner but also a test case for the EU's new approach of shaping its relations with its Eastern neighbours.

The negotiations on the AA with Ukraine, a document of considerable length exceeding 2,000 pages,[45] were going to take no less than 5 years. This process

[42] Communication from the Commission to the European Parliament and the Council, Eastern Partnership, COM(2008) 823 final of 3 December 2008; Council of the European Union, Extraordinary European Council, 11 and 12 December 2008, Presidency Conclusions, Brussels, 17271/1/08, REV 1, 13 February 2009.

[43] See Joint Communication by the High Representative of the European Union for Foreign Affairs and Security Policy and the European Commission, A New Response to a Changing Neighbourhood., Brussels, COM(2011) 303 of 25 May 2011.

[44] See Joint Declaration on the EU–Ukraine Association Agreement, Council of the European Union, EU–Ukraine Summit, Paris, 9 September 2008, 12812/08, Presse 247, available at http://www.consilium.europa.eu/ueDocs/cms_Data/docs/pressData/en/er/102633.pdf.

[45] The text of the EU–Ukraine Association Agreement is published in the *Official Journal of the European Union*, [2014] OJ L 161/3-2137.

responded also to a strong wish by the Ukrainian side to significantly upgrade its relations with the EU in the wake of the eastward enlargements of 2004 and 2007. This approach was also strongly favoured by the new Ukrainian leadership of President Yushchenko and Prime Minister Tymoshenko, who had come to power in January 2005, following the "Orange Revolution".[46] Backed by large popular support in favour of European integration, the Ukrainian leadership's main aim with the AA was to obtain the promise of a European perspective for Ukraine. Ukrainian leaders characterised the negotiations with the EU as an effective mechanism of EU integration, arguing in favour of an approach of realism.[47] Thus, the Ukrainian negotiators' aim was to prepare for an agreement which was as similar to, and ambitious as possible in terms of scope and in terms of political ambition/vocation as the Europe Agreements with Central European countries or the Stabilisation and Association Agreements with the countries of the Western Balkans. It was considered that such an approach would prepare the way to move to the next political step: EU accession negotiations. This difference of long-term ambition was never solved but left explicitly open, due to the EU's Member States' division over that question.

The EU's negotiators but also the relevant Eastern Partners followed the Ukraine negotiation precedent and, as of 2010, the negotiations on Association Agreements with Moldova, Georgia, Armenia and Azerbaijan[48] started.

EaP Multilateral

The Eastern Partnership Association Agreements constitute the core instrument of the bilateral track. The EU's EaP policy also includes a dynamic multilateral track. This track with its biannual summit meetings,[49] its multitude of ministerial level

[46] See also Woerhel (2014), p. 1.

[47] See interview with Hryhoriy Nemyria, former Deputy Prime Minister of Ukraine (2007–2010), "We chose a realistic path to EU integration", Euractiv, 30 July 2009, available at http://www.euractiv.com/foreign-affairs/ukraine-deputy-pm-chose-realistic-path-eu-integration/article-184534.

[48] European External Action Service, first joint progress report negotiations on the EU–Republic of Moldova Association Agreement, Chisinau, 8 June 2010, available at http://eeas.europa.eu/moldova/docs/2010_06_aa_joint_progress_report1.pdf; European Commission, Press Release, IP/10/955 of 15 July 2010, EU Launches Negotiations on Association Agreements with Armenia, Azerbaijan and Georgia, available at http://europa.eu/rapid/press-release_IP-10-955_en.htm. The texts of the Moldova and Georgia Association Agreements were published in the *Official Journal of the European Union*, see for Moldova [2014] OJ L 260/4-738 and for Georgia [2014] OJ L 261/4-743.

[49] The biannual Eastern Partnership summits involve Heads of States or Governments of the 28 EU Member States and the EaP partner countries, as well as on the EU side the President of the European Council and the President of the Commission. The annual meetings of Ministers of Foreign Affairs in Brussels review progress and provide more detailed political guidance for the policy. In addition, the EaP also provides for regular informal gatherings in different sectoral ministerial configurations, taking place in the Eastern Partnership region.

meetings, as well as its four thematic platforms[50] and related expert panels, and five high profile flagship initiatives,[51] promotes the exchange of best practices between EaP partner countries and the EU Member States. This includes also a very active and visible Eastern Partnership Civil Society Forum with six national platforms, providing significant policy input.[52] In addition, interested third countries such as the US, Russia, Japan, Canada, Norway, and Switzerland meet twice annually in the so-called EaP Information and Coordination Group. Furthermore, regular coordination meetings at senior level with International Financial Institutions provide a solid political and coordination framework for the development of individual relations at bilateral level. The multilateral track is an inclusive process, since all six EaP partner countries fully participate in all activities, with no exception.[53]

Political Association and Economic Integration: In Concrete Terms

The EU's Association Agreements (AA) with the Eastern Partnership countries are designed to constitute a new stage in the development of the contractual relations between both sides. They represent pioneering documents based on political association and economic integration between the EU and its eastern partners, with the highest degree of mutual commitments. The AAs present a shared commitment to close and lasting relationships, based on common values. Thus, the AAs are a concrete way to foster a dynamic relationship between the EU and its eastern partners, focusing on support to core reforms, on economic recovery and growth, governance and sector cooperation. They envisage ambitious cooperation on home and justice affairs, including a perspective for visa-free travel. The AA also offers gradual integration with the EU Internal Market by setting up Deep and Comprehensive Free Trade Areas (DCFTAs). These go further than classic free trade areas, since they foresee the approximation to relevant EU norms and standards in return

[50] The four thematic platforms focus on (1) Democracy, good governance and stability; (2) Economic integration and convergence with EU policies; (3) Energy security and transport; and (4) Contacts between people.

[51] The EaP flagship initiatives are designed to give additional momentum, concrete substance and more visibility to the EaP policy. They seek to mobilise multi-donor support, funding from different International Financial Institutions and investment from the private sector. See http://eeas.europa.eu/eastern/initiatives/index_en.htm.

[52] In its 2008 EaP Communication (COM(2008) 823 final), the European Commission proposed "to support the further development of Civil Society Organisations (CSOs)" and, in particular, "to establish an Eastern Partnership Civil Society Forum (CSF) to promote contacts among CSOs and facilitate their dialogue with public authorities", p. 14. See also concept paper developed by the European Commission, available at http://eap-csf.eu/assets/files/Documents/EaPCSFconceptpaper29jan2012final_eng.pdf.

[53] For further information on the EaP multilateral track see http://eeas.europa.eu/eastern/faq/index_en.htm#13 and http://eeas.europa.eu/eastern/index_en.htm.

for large-scale market access, while providing a strong binding framework to ban all arbitrary trade-restrictive measures, including export duties and quantitative export restrictions. The AAs also constitute a reform agenda for the EaP countries, based around a comprehensive programme of approximation of EaP's legislation to EU norms and standards in a great number of sectoral cooperation areas. In short, the Agreements are unprecedented in their breadth (number of areas covered) and depth (detail of commitments and timelines), leaving the way open for further progressive developments by neither explicitly referring to nor formally excluding an EU membership prospect.

Political Association

The Agreements establish an "association" between the EU and the Eastern Partnership country, moving from the previous "cooperation partnership" to a new level of political ambition. With the exception of the EEA countries (Norway, Iceland and Liechtenstein) and Western Balkan candidate countries, the EU has never negotiated such comprehensive and far reaching agreements, notably with regard to partial opening of the EU's Internal Market to participation by a third country, but also with regard to the partners' commitments to approximate to the EU acquis.

Values and Principles of Associated Partners

In order to live up to the ambition of this political project of association with the EU, the Agreements put a strong emphasis on values and include an important list of general principles to which both Parties ought to be bound, such as respect for democratic principles, human rights and fundamental freedoms as defined in relevant international instruments; respect for the rule of law; respect for sovereignty and territorial integrity, inviolability and independence and countering the proliferation of weapons of mass destruction, related materials and means of delivery. The Agreements also underline the principles of free market economy, good governance, the fight against corruption, transnational organised crime and terrorism, the promotion of sustainable development and effective multilateralism.

The inclusion of a specific set of "essential elements" in the Agreements underlines the significance of this new "political association", since the violation of one of these essential elements by one of the Parties could give rise to specific measures under the Agreement, including the suspension of (trade) rights and obligations. These elements are respect for democratic principles, human rights and fundamental freedoms as defined in relevant international instruments; respect for the rule of law; and countering the proliferation of weapons of mass destruction, related materials and means of delivery. In the specific case of Ukraine, the promotion of respect for the principles of sovereignty and territorial integrity, inviolability and independence also constitute essential elements of the Association Agreement.

Level and Dimension of Association in the Area of Foreign Policy

The "political association" is further underpinned by the enhancement of cooperation in foreign and security policy. The Agreements set out the aims of a strengthened political dialogue—going beyond the ambition of the PCAs and reflecting the EU's new foreign policy instruments—by promoting gradual convergence on foreign and security matters with the aim of the EaP countries' ever deeper involvement in the EU security area. The Agreements establish a number of fora for the conduct of political dialogue, and provide an innovation also for dialogue and cooperation on domestic reform, based on the common principles set out by the Parties. There are also provisions for intensified dialogue on foreign and security policy, including Common Security and Defence Policy (CSDP), for the promotion of peace and international justice by ratifying and implementing the Rome Statute of the International Criminal Court (ICC), and for joint efforts in relation to regional stability, conflict prevention, crisis management,[54] military and technological cooperation, anti-terrorism, anti-proliferation, disarmament and arms control.

Justice, Security and Mobility

In the field of justice, freedom and security, the Agreements pay particular attention to the rule of law, human rights and fundamental freedoms which guide cooperation between the EU and eastern partners in this area. The reinforcement of judicial institutions and practices is also part of the cooperation. The AAs set out the framework for cooperation on migration, asylum and border management, on personal data protection, money laundering and terrorism financing and on anti-drugs policy. This cooperation provides for movement of persons, visa facilitation and readmission and gradual steps towards a visa-free regime[55] in due course,

[54] Framework Agreements for participation in EU crisis management operations have been signed with three EaP countries: with Ukraine in 2005, with Moldova in 2012, and with Georgia in 2013. Ukraine, for example, participated in the EU led CSDP mission by sending its frigate Hetman Sagaidachniy to join the EU Naval Force ATALANTA. The frigate carried out counter-piracy patrols in the Gulf of Aden and Western Indian Ocean. Georgia expressed interest to contribute to the EUFOR RCA operation with one company-sized unit. Moldova for its turn expressed interest to contribute to the EU military operation in the Central African Republic; however, due to the deteriorating security situation in the region, Moldova has withdrawn its proposal.

[55] The enhanced mobility of citizens is one of the core objectives of the EaP. In parallel to the AA process, the EU carries out Visa Liberalisation Dialogues with interested EaP countries. The main tools are the Visa Liberalisation Action Plans, so called VLAPs, which are tailor-made for each partner country and structured around four blocks concerning: (1) document security, including biometrics; (2) integrated border management, migration management, asylum; (3) public order and security; and (4) external relations and fundamental rights. See European Commission, Press Release, IP/13/1085 of 15 November 2013, Commission Assesses the Implementation of VLAPs by Moldova, Ukraine and Georgia. Furthermore, the EU has already concluded visa facilitation

provided that relevant conditions for well-managed and secure mobility are in place. The AAs commit both sides to further develop their judicial cooperation in civil and criminal matters.

Economic Integration

Economic Integration Through a Wide Range of Sector Cooperation

The Association Agreement strengthens significantly—in comparison to the PCA—sector level cooperation between the EU and the partner country in more than 30 policy areas, such as: energy, transport, environment protection, industrial and small and medium enterprise cooperation, social development and protection, equal rights, consumer protection, education, training and youth, as well as cultural cooperation. These sectors correspond to the different areas of the EU acquis and reflect the magnitude of EU policies. They are inspired by the "35 Accession chapters" which are being negotiated with each candidate country within the enlargement context. Similarly to the accession process in the enlargement context, the chapters correspond to the areas in which reforms are needed so as to prepare for economic integration, or—with regard to selective DCFTA aspects—to prepare for the participation in some parts of the EU's Internal Market.

In all of the aforementioned areas, enhanced cooperation starts on the basis of current frameworks, both bilateral and multilateral, with the aim of more systematic dialogue and exchange of information and good practice, supporting core reforms, economic recovery, growth as well as good governance.

Deep and Comprehensive Free Trade Area (DCFTA)

The most important innovation within the AA is the Deep and Comprehensive Free Trade Area which goes beyond a traditional FTA and offers gradual integration with the EU's Internal Market. As a medium and long-term objective, it is intended to base trade between the EU and EaP countries largely on the same conditions as between EU Member States.

The DCFTA foresees the tackling of non-tariff barriers to trade, since the EaP country is asked to align over time its norms and standards with those of the EU in key areas of the Internal Market, notably technical norms and standards for

---

agreements (VFAs) with Armenia, Moldova, Georgia and Ukraine. The VFAs with EaP partner countries entered into force in 2013–2014: 1 January 2014 (Armenia), 1 July 2013 (amended VFA for Moldova and Ukraine) and 1 March 2013 (Georgia). Based on these VFAs, both EU and non-EU citizens benefit from simplified procedures for issuing visas. An overview on the existing VFA process is available at http://ec.europa.eu/dgs/home-affairs/what-we-do/policies/borders-and-visas/visa-policy/index_en.htm.

industrial goods, sanitary and phytosanitary standards for agricultural goods, customs cooperation, services, intellectual property rights, public procurement and competition, thus leading successively to ever greater and far reaching market access.

In terms of eliminating technical barriers to trade, the partner country will progressively adapt its technical regulations and standards to those of the EU. To this end, the DCFTA commits both Parties to negotiate an Agreement on Conformity Assessment and Acceptance of Industrial Products to ensure that in specific sectors, the partner country's legislation and market surveillance systems are in line with those of the EU. As regards trade in animals, plants and their products the DCFTA provides for the alignment of sanitary and phytosanitary (SPS) and animal welfare legislation with the EU's and the setting up of a rapid consultation mechanism to resolve SPS-related trade disruptance, including a specific early warning system for veterinary and phyto-sanitary emergencies. Part of the DCFTA is also a Protocol on mutual administrative assistance in customs matters which provides a stronger legal framework for efforts to ensure the correct application of customs legislation and the fight against infringement.

The DCFTA provides for national treatment and most favoured nation treatment of companies, subject to limited reservations, and the possibility to access the EU's Internal Market in the fields of financial, telecommunications, postal and courier, and international maritime services—if and when the EaP country has fully and effectively implemented the EU acquis in these fields. Provisions on Intellectual Property Rights (IPRs), designs (including unregistered ones), and patents which complement and update the WTO TRIPS Agreement and include provisions for the enforcement of IPRs based on the EU's internal rules are also part of the DCFTA. In addition, a high level of protection for EU and partner countries' agricultural Geographical Indications constitutes an integral part of the DCFTA,[56] not only those relating to wines and spirits, but also any new products added to the list of protected GIs through regular consultations.

The DFCTA also constitutes an unprecedented example in terms of integration of the public procurement markets, in allowing possible access of EaP countries to the EU Public Procurement Market—once the EaP country has adopted the current EU public procurement acquis. As a result, EaP country suppliers and service providers will have mutual market access to the public procurement markets, with the exception made for the defence sector. By aligning its competition law and enforcement practice to that of the EU acquis, EaP state-controlled enterprises

[56] For Moldova and Georgia the GI Agreements which already entered into force in April 2013 and in April 2012 respectively constitute an integral part of the AA/DCFTA. See Council Decision (2013/7/EU) of 3 December 2012 on the conclusion of the Agreement between the European Union and the Republic of Moldova on the protection of geographical indications of agricultural products and foodstuffs, [2013] OJ L 10/1 as well as Council Decision (2012/164/EU) of 14 February 2012 on the conclusion of the Agreement between the European Union and Georgia on protection of geographical indications of agricultural products and foodstuffs; [2012] OJ L 93/1.

will be subject to the same provisions as EU Member States, ensuring that no discrimination by monopolies will be allowed. The section on subsidies is particularly significant in so far as it contains a commitment on behalf of the EaP country to adopt a domestic system of state aid control similar to that which exists in the EU and to establish an operationally independent authority entrusted with the control of state aid.

On trade-related energy issues, the DCFTA introduces binding provisions on pricing, including via the prohibition of dual pricing, on transit of energy products with a view to ensuring the security of supply, and on non-discriminatory treatment of energy-related investments. The DCFTA also provides for commitments on the enforcement of multilateral labour and environmental standards, along with a commitment to refrain from waiving or derogating from such standards in a manner that affects trade or investment between the parties.

Finally, another key innovation within the DCFTA is the introduction of a binding bilateral dispute settlement system. Effective settlement procedures based on the model of the WTO Dispute Settlement Understanding will provide for swift resolution of trade disputes, including by allowing the affected party to impose proportionate sanctions, with faster procedures for urgent energy disputes. Specific provisions on transparency and dialogue with civil society and stakeholders have also been agreed.

The AA Methodology of Economic Integration

Key to the DCFTA but also to the sector-level cooperation is a comprehensive menu of regulatory approximation set out in the Annexes to the Agreements. The Annexes include specific schedules for the transposition and implementation of selected parts of the EU acquis by the Eastern Partnership country. The AA/DCFTA binds the EaP countries to approximate to existing EU legislation, following a period of transition which varies from between 2 and 15 years and depends on the sector as well as on the specific country.

The methodology which was designed for the new generation of Association Agreements is the gradual and dynamic approximation of EaP countries' legislation to EU legislation, norms and standards. The *gradual* character of this approximation has two dimensions, on the one hand it is the approximation over time, implying a step-by-step gradual rapprochement of the partner country's set of rules and legislation to the existing EU's legislation. On the other hand, a *differentiated* approximation is foreseen, meaning that only a selected part of for example the environment or agriculture EU acquis is reflected in the Annexes. This is mostly a result of negotiations, reflecting the political and economic relevance both sides have attached to the policy area. The selection is however also a reflection of the degree of the partner countries administrative, financial and institutional capacity to commit to the approximation to EU legislation in a specific area.

The Annexes are in principle subject to updates, in order to take into account the evolution of EU law (legislation, policies and principles). This evolution is conceptualised by the term "dynamic approximation", implying that the EaP countries will not only approximate their legislation to the current but also to possible future EU legislation. This is of particular importance in terms of partner countries' EU Internal Market access as they are required to automatically and constantly align their legislation with the EU acquis. The updates of the Annexes within the sectoral parts of the AA, which are not market-access related, are not subject to automatic alignment but to future approval of both Parties via the institutional bodies established under the AAs. Hence the timely and full approximation to the EU acquis is of particular importance for the areas where in principle the partner country could be granted EU Internal Market access. The latter is the case for the public procurement market as well as for financial, telecommunications, postal and courier, and international maritime services. Although the fulfilment of the approximation commitment of the sectoral Annexes is irrelevant for the granting of market access, it is crucial for ensuring the country's economic integration with the EU.

Taking into account of the fact that once EU Internal Market access is granted, there is a need to monitor the partner countries' progress in keeping up-to-date with regulatory developments in the EU, specific institutions were established under the Agreements and financial resources made available.

New Institutions and Resources

The AAs include an updated institutional framework encompassing cooperation and dialogue fora from ministerial[57] down to the level of technical subcommittees. A specific decision-making role is foreseen for an Association Council and by delegation also for an Association Committee, which may also meet in a specific trade-configuration. The monitoring mechanism, partly inspired by the enlargement screening mechanism, allows the Association Council and/or Committee to evaluate the partner countries' adaptation of national legislation to EU legislation as well as the functioning of the relevant administrative and institutional infrastructures. The result of the monitoring process will eventually lead to the EU's unilateral decision to grant the EaP country market access in areas specified in the AAs. In addition, the AAs also provide for other monitoring fora such as a Parliamentary Association Committee or a Civil Society Platform, representing inter alia civil society, non-governmental organisations as well as social partners, trade-unions and employers.

[57] In the case of Ukraine also regular summit-level meetings are foreseen.

EU's Financial Assistance

The AA negotiations were not a stand-alone exercise: EU assistance to Eastern Partnership countries is linked with the reform agenda as it emerges from the result of negotiations. The Comprehensive Institution Building Programme (CIB)[58] was particularly important in this regard, since it was designed to help partner countries strengthen the capacities of key institutions involved in preparing, negotiating and implementing the new AAs. Furthermore, the CIB supported the creation of the DCFTAs and the management of enhanced mobility opportunities in a secure environment. For the period 2014–2020, a new financial instrument, the European Neighbourhood Instrument (ENI),[59] will support countries in the EU's neighbourhood with a budget of around EUR 15.4 billion. During this period, Ukraine will benefit from approximately EUR 1.4 billion, starting with around EUR 355 million in 2014 and followed by a yearly amount of EUR 130 million for the years 2015–2020. Moldova and Georgia will each benefit from between EUR 335 and EUR 410 million in the years 2014 and 2017.

EaP Association Agendas

In support of the Association Agreement process, specific Association Agendas for the EaP countries were developed. These Agendas replace the ENP Action Plans and are designed to prepare and facilitate the implementation and entry into force of the Association Agreements. They are political implementation tools, spelling out concrete reform steps and related support. They set out the partner country's agenda for political and economic reforms, with short and medium-term priorities of 3–5 years, while reflecting the country's needs and capacities. The Ukraine Association Agenda was the first to be agreed back in 2009 and was subsequently updated in

[58] The total amount for the CIB counted EUR 167 million from the ENPI budget in the period from 2011 to 2013. The overall CIB allocation was divided among five EaP countries: Armenia (EUR 33 million), Azerbaijan (EUR 19 million), Georgia (EUR 31 million), Moldova (EUR 41 million), and Ukraine (EUR 43 million). Belarus did not participate in the CIB. For the CIB, see http://www.eeas.europa.eu/eastern/docs/eap_vademecum_en.pdf as well as http://eeas.europa.eu/eastern/docs/2011_eap_implementation_en.pdf and for the country specific Annual Action Programmes see http://ec.europa.eu/europeaid/funding/funding-instruments-programming/annual-action-programmes_en.

[59] The ENI will build on and strengthen some of the key features of the ENPI, notably greater differentiation between countries based on progress with reforms, and two new mechanisms to support an incentive-based approach (often referred to as "more for more"). These are: (1) an umbrella programme of 10 % of the ENI budget to be allocated to better performing countries; and (2) the ability to vary bilateral allocations up or down within a range. See http://eeas.europa.eu/enp/how-is-it-financed/index_en.htm.

2011 and 2013.[60] The Association Agendas for Moldova and Georgia were adopted on 26 June 2014,[61] just 1 day before the historic signature of the Association Agreements.

The Prospects and Potential of EaP AA/DCFTAs

As outlined above, the EU has never before opened up its Internal Market to participation by a third country to the degree it has offered to the EaP countries. This unprecedented and unique offer was on the one hand motivated by the need to bridge the gap between membership and partnership, and on the other hand by the pursuance of new market opportunities in the partners' mutual economic interests in new markets and regions. This is built on the European Commission's important expertise in the gradual expansion of its Internal Market rules, either through means of the enlargement instrument or by cooperating with countries of the European Economic Area. This ambitious offer was only made possible since the partners in the East also realised that EU membership realistically, if at all, would only be possible with a long-term perspective, and only following the integration of the Western Balkan countries in the EU. Hence, partner countries have made extensive commitments to align with the EU acquis. In return for effective and measurable implementation and enforcement of the acquis, the EU offered gradual access to its Internal Market, which in the mid- to long-term would stimulate economic growth, notably through enhanced trade and investment.[62]

With the acceptance of this approach EaP partner countries followed reluctantly the EU's logic: first creating "more Europe inside" their countries, thus creating different conditions for possible future decision-making, with the EU avoiding any explicit reference to the membership question, which remains thus open. It seems that the Eastern partner countries were able to apply a realistic approach to integration and preferred to pocket what was politically on offer in terms of association with the EU, rather than overstretch the then EU-27 Member States' willingness to cooperate politically and economically.

In May 2011, the European Commission made a major attempt to get a firmer commitment towards a possible long-term perspective of EU membership for Eastern partners based on successful implementation of AA related commitments.

---

[60] The EU–Ukraine Association Agenda was adopted by the EU–Ukraine Cooperation Council on 23 November 2009 and entered into effect on 24 November 2009, see http://eeas.europa.eu/ukraine/docs/eu_ukr_ass_agenda_24jun2013.pdf.

[61] See European Union External Action Service, Press Releases of 26 June 2014, 140626/04, available at http://eeas.europa.eu/statements/docs/2014/140626_04_en.pdf and 140626/05 http://www.eeas.europa.eu/statements/docs/2014/140626_05_en.pdf.

[62] See, for example, Langbein (2009), p. 1; Radeke (2012).

The ENP review communication made an explicit reference[63] to Article 49 TFEU,[64] which is broadly known as the article providing for a membership perspective. However, this never became official EU policy nor was it an EU negotiation position in the AA process, given the reluctance of a significant number of Member States to go that far.[65]

In perspective, the Eastern partner's closer economic integration with the EU through the AA/DCFTA represents a powerful stimulant to the country's economic growth. The AA will create business and investment opportunities in both the EU and EaP. By moving beyond simple MFN treatment, covering preferential trade in goods, services and agricultural products, the DCFTA will promote real economic modernisation and integration with the EU. Higher standards of products with resulting innovation gains, better market choices and consumer protection for citizens, and above all, the Eastern partners' capacity to compete effectively in international markets should be the result of this process. Cooperation chapters of the AA will help the partner countries address supply-side constraints, and are linked together with the DCFTA parts of the AA to capacity building measures and financial assistance. The AA is therefore designed to provide a focus for cooperation, and will form the core of the countries' domestic reform and modernisation agenda.

[63] In its ENP review of 2011, the Commission set out: "Some EaP countries attach great importance to their European identity and the development of closer relations with the EU enjoys strong public support. The values on which the European Union is built – namely freedom, democracy, respect for human rights and fundamental freedoms, and the rule of law – are also at the heart of the process of political association and economic integration which the Eastern Partnership offers. These are the same values that are enshrined in article 2 of the European Union Treaty and on which articles 8 and 49 are based", COM(2011) 303, p. 14; see also Arts. 2, 8 and 49 TFEU.

[64] Article 49 TFEU states "Any European State which respects the values referred to in Article 2 and is committed to promoting them may apply to become a member of the Union. The European Parliament and national Parliaments shall be notified of this application. The applicant State shall address its application to the Council, which shall act unanimously after consulting the Commission and after receiving the consent of the European Parliament, which shall act by a majority of its component members. The conditions of eligibility agreed upon by the European Council shall be taken into account."

[65] While welcoming the Commission's ENP review, the European Council did not take up the references to Article 49 TFEU with regard to Eastern partners, see Council conclusions on the ENP, 3101st Foreign Affairs Council meeting, Luxembourg, 20 June 2011, available at http://www.consilium.europa.eu/uedocs/cms_Data/docs/pressdata/EN/foraff/122917.pdf.

Critical Analysis: What Happened to the Eastern Partnership?

The Eastern Partnership policy comprises a multitude of initiatives with a dedicated multilateral dimension. However, the perceived impact of the AA/DCFTAs as the core instruments in advancing the goals of the Eastern Partnership with the most committed and ambitious three partner countries has been—notably since the Vilnius Summit—at the centre of public and political attention. After years of negotiation and subsequent initialling, the signature of these agreements has created exaggerated fears and ambitions.

At no time has the EU's external attraction as normative power been seen as more promising by some and more threatening by others.[66] The time this asset could be seen as merely "soft power" appears to be over. At the same time, the right of independent European states to make sovereign choices[67] in taking over EU norms has never been challenged since the end of the Cold War. The opposition of Russia to the Eastern Partnership policy has been driven by geopolitical and strategic considerations, while its opposition is voiced with regard to the economic integration ambitions of some of our common neighbours.

The Russian Factor

The Vilnius Summit did suddenly catapult the Eastern Partnership to the forefront of attention with regard to the EU's foreign policy. Although the EU's policy towards Russia was not formally part of the Vilnius Summit agenda, German Chancellor Angela Merkel rightly underlined during the official dinner that "at the table, there is another invisible guest". It became clear from this moment on that the EU's Eastern Partnership policy would need to consider the Russian factor more explicitly, and cater for Russia's sensitivities better to make the EaP successful.

---

[66] See, for example, Speck (2014).

[67] Former Commission President Barosso set out in the 2013 State of the Union speech "Today, countries like Ukraine are more than ever seeking closer ties to the European Union, attracted by our economic and social model. We cannot turn our back on them. We cannot accept any attempts to limit these countries [sic.] own sovereign choices. Free will and free consent need to be respected. These are also the principles that lie at the basis of our Eastern Partnership, which we want to take forward at our summit in Vilnius", European Commission, SPEECH/13/684 of 11 September 2013, State of the Union Address 2013, available at http://europa.eu/rapid/press-release_SPEECH-13-684_en.htm. See also Joint statement by the President of the European Commission José Manuel Barroso and the President of the European Council Herman Van Rompuy on Ukraine, European Commission, MEMO/13/1052 of 25 November 2013: "the European Union will not force Ukraine, or any other partner, to choose between the European Union or any other regional entity.", available at http://europa.eu/rapid/press-release_MEMO-13-1052_en.htm.

The EU's soft power, with its long-term impact leading to transformation of whole societies, promoting fundamental freedoms and the rule of law as well as functioning market economies, has been seriously challenged by Russia's hard power with its short-term impact, using coercion and providing significant energy price incentives and financial support. But the reverse is also true. The new context created by the sudden reverses in Ukrainian politics with regard to its relations with both the EU and Russia have generated an unprecedented public interest in EU foreign policy and re-awakened fears of a new era of Cold War rivalries on the European continent. If the AA/DCFTAs are really the cause for such fears, then they are grossly exaggerated, since they are not designed to lead to new dividing lines on this continent, but to promote additional economic opportunities without severing traditional ties.

The Eurasian Project

Seen from the Russian perspective, the AA/DCFTAs represented an obstacle to the potential success of Russia's Customs Union which was announced on 9 June 2009 by then Prime Minister Putin,[68] and is supposed to become Russia's most important foreign policy project. In addition, the perception in Russia of having lost its hegemony over its traditional Cold War sphere of influence, notably in Central Europe and the Baltic countries is an important factor to take into account.[69] Russians often recall the alleged broken promise to former Soviet leader Mikhail Gorbachov at the time of German reunification: that NATO would not enlarge eastwards.[70] Since 1990, 12 rounds of NATO enlargement have taken place.

This perceived encroachment in Russia's traditional sphere of influence, with the former Soviet republics being considered as "near abroad",[71] had been clearly limited to NATO expansion, which constitutes a deep red line for Russia. In 2004, Vladimir Putin reiterated a negative view of NATO expansion, but explicitly

[68] For a detailed analysis of the origins and objective of the Russia's Eurasian integration project, see: Wisniewska (2013).

[69] See, for example, Karaganov (2014); or Lukyanov (2014).

[70] See interview with then President Dmitry Medvedev in *Spiegel* of 9 November 2009. Medvedev indicated that that when the Berlin Wall came down, it had "not been possible to redefine Russia's place in Europe. After the disappearance of the Warsaw Pact, we were hoping for a higher degree of integration. But what have we received? None of the things that we were assured, namely that NATO would not expand endlessly eastwards and our interests would be continuously taken into consideration. NATO remains a military bloc whose missiles are pointed towards Russian territory. By contrast, we would like to see a new European security order." Available at http://www.spiegel.de/international/world/spiegel-interview-with-russian-president-dmitry-medvedev-oil-and-gas-is-our-drug-a-660114.html.

[71] The term "common neighbourhood", consistently used by the EU in its dealings and negotiations with Russia, has never been accepted by the Russian side.

identified the enlargement of the EU as a positive process.[72] With successive EU enlargements to the East in 2004 (including the three Baltic states) and in 2007 (Romania and Bulgaria) Russia has become increasingly more nervous about the possible impact of EU enlargement on its own economic interests and political projects. The creation of the Customs Union in 2010 with Belarus and Kazakhstan and the launch of the Eurasian Union in 2015 with its Single Economic Space, closely modelled along the EU's integration experience, have become the Russian President's main answer and his top foreign policy priority.[73] Such a union would economically and strategically only make sense with the inclusion of Ukraine, as the only other large country of the Commonwealth of Independent States (CIS) and with a significant industrial capacity.[74]

EaP AA/DCFTAs at Russia's Dispense?

However, the creation of the Customs Union and the announcement of the Eurasian Union happened long after negotiations on the EU–Ukraine Association Agreement had begun (March 2007) and the final deal on the Agreement made (October 2011). Throughout that period Russia had never asked for consultations with the EU with regard to the AA negotiations, nor raised its concerns bilaterally with Ukraine. And at no time did the Ukrainian side, independent of who was in power, ever call into doubt its intention to associate with the EU. At the same time one should recall that during the more than 2-year hiatus of 2011–2013, the EU's hesitation over whether or not to sign the AA with Ukraine, due to cases of selective justice against members of the previous government,[75] dominated the discussion on EU–Ukraine relations.

[72] The Kremlin, Moscow, Press Conference Following Talks with Spanish Prime Minister José Luis Rodríguez Zapatero, 10 December 2004, available at http://eng.kremlin.ru/transcripts/7741.

[73] See then Prime Minister Putin's remarks of 9 June 2009 at a meeting of the Supreme Body of the Customs Union of Russia, Belarus and Kazakhstan held at the level of the heads of government: "I would like to mention that the initiative to accelerate the establishment of the Customs Union was proposed by Kazakh President Nursultan Nazarbayev, who considers it possible to complete the basic procedures by January 1, 2010. We think so too, and have joined the efforts to implement this proposal." Available at http://archive.government.ru/eng/docs/4313/. See also article by then Prime Minister Putin (2011).

[74] See, for example, Adomeit (2012) and Halbach (2012).

[75] See Council conclusions on Ukraine, 3209th Foreign Affairs Council meeting, Brussels, 10 December 2012: "The Council reaffirms its commitment to the signing of the already initialled Association Agreement, including a Deep and Comprehensive Free Trade Area, as soon as the Ukrainian authorities demonstrate determined action and tangible progress in the three areas mentioned above, possibly by the time of the Eastern Partnership Summit in Vilnius in November 2013. The signature could be accompanied by opening for provisional application of parts of the Agreement." Available at http://www.consilium.europa.eu/uedocs/cms_Data/docs/pressdata/EN/foraff/134136.pdf.

Prior to August 2013, when the Russian trade restricting customs measures suddenly started, Russia had not formally raised any particular concerns in relation to the AA. Concerns seemingly existed earlier, which is best reflected in a study issued by the Russian-financed Eurasian Development Bank. This study, which was made available to the EU only in summer 2013, concludes that Ukraine's AA with the EU would have a severe negative impact on the Russian economy, notably "deterioration of the terms of trade throughout the post-Soviet area".[76]

Following the calls[77] to hold trilateral consultations between Ukraine, Russia and the EU, between October 2013 and March 2014 several EU–Russia consultations at expert and at senior official level have taken place.[78] In the context of the signature of the AA in June 2014, the EU also agreed to hold ministerial level meetings in trilateral format, the first of which took place on 11 July 2014, headed by Trade Commissioner De Gucht in Brussels, dealing with the implementation aspects of the DCFTA.[79] However, none of these meetings could placate Russian concerns. It has to be assumed that Russia's calls for trilateral consultations had as their ultimate goal the renegotiation of parts of the finalised and initialled EU–Ukraine AA/DCFTA, to take into account Russian concerns and possibly make it compatible with the *Customs or Eurasian Union*. Later, Russia has stated that the DCFTA was incompatible with the CIS-FTAs.[80] Renegotiation of the agreement was explicitly rejected by the EU, which called upon Russia to respect the sovereign

[76] See Eurasian Development Bank (2012), p. 29.

[77] See former Ukrainian Prime Minister Azarov's remarks of 17 September 2013; as well as President Putin's remarks at a press conference after talks held with Italian Prime Minister Enrico Letta of 27 November 2013: "I would believe it would be good to depoliticize this issue and agree with [Ukrainian] President [Viktor] Yanukovych's proposal to substantively and properly talk on all these matters in a tripartite format", available at http://sputniknews.com/voiceofrussia/news/2013_11_26/Putin-calls-for-depoliticizing-Ukraines-association-with-EU-7396/.

[78] In a statement issued on 25 November 2013, Presidents Van Rompuy and Barroso underlined the EU's readiness for consultations: "The European Union continues to stand ready to clarify to the Russian Federation the mutual beneficial impact of increased trade and exchanges with our neighbours, whilst fully respecting the sovereignty and independence of our Eastern Partners and the bilateral nature of Association Agreement and DCFTAs." See European Commission, MEMO/13/1052 of 25 November 2013, available at http://europa.eu/rapid/press-release_MEMO-13-1052_en.htm. At the EU–Russia Summit of 28 January 2014, the EU and Russia agreed to "pursue bilateral consultations at expert level on the Eastern Partnership Association Agreements and their possible economic consequences for both sides", see Statement by President Barroso following the EU–Russia Summit, European Commission—SPEECH/14/66, 28 January 2014, available at, http://europa.eu/rapid/press-release_SPEECH-14-66_en.htm. See also Remarks by President of the European Council, Herman Van Rompuy following the 32nd EU–Russia Summit, Brussels, 28 January 2014, EUCO 27/14, Presse 38, available at http://www.consilium.europa.eu/uedocs/cms_data/docs/pressdata/en/ec/140834.pdf.

[79] See European Commission (2014).

[80] In fact a Russia's governmental decree of 31 July 2014 foresees unilateral withdrawal of preferences under the CIS-FTA for the ratification of the AA/DCFTAs, invoking Annex 6 of the FTA safeguard clause. The measures entered into force end of August 2014, foreseeing the introduction of unilateral import duties for Moldova's main exports to Russia on the basis of the most favoured nation (MFN) regime.

choices of its neighbours.[81] This became in particular apparent at the January 2014 EU–Russia summit, which took place in a notably stilted atmosphere in light of recent developments. However, the Summit also recalled the shared longer-term vision of creating a common economic area between the EU and Russia,[82] for which it was agreed to first relaunch the negotiations on the New Agreement.[83]

It is fair to say that Russia has ignored for many years the possible impact of the EU's Eastern Partnership policy on Russia's relations with its own neighbours. Russia was rather focussed on its own new regional integration scheme. Back in 2004, President Putin welcomed the idea of Ukraine's EU accession and indirectly even hinted that this would have a positive impact on Russia's economy.[84] And when Russia reacted, it was too late to influence the substance of the new AAs in a realistic and sustainable way, notably since partner countries prefer the European economic integration model rather than the Eurasian one. Studies have also proven that economic gains from the DCFTAs with the EU are of more long-term benefit to the economies of Eastern partners.[85] Russia might have thought to have "won the battle" by successfully changing the mind of the then Ukrainian President and by using unprecedented propaganda efforts. But the longer term fight for Ukrainian citizens' hearts and minds was lost.

The massive pressure exercised on Ukraine led *de facto* to public outcry and a strengthened "Euromaidan" movement.

Ukraine and a significant majority of Ukrainians continue to prefer the path towards a European model of society and economy, as a way to overcome their system of corrupt and inefficient governance.[86] The European Union in turn has

---

[81] See statement of 25 November 2013: "the European Union will not force Ukraine, or any other partner, to choose between the European Union or any other regional entity", European Commission, MEMO/13/1052 of 25 November 2013, available at http://europa.eu/rapid/press-release_MEMO-13-1052_en.htm.

[82] See factsheet for EU–Russia Summit of 28 January 2014, which sets out "Some progress has been made in the negotiations [of the New Agreement] and both sides have on several occasions reiterated that they would like to develop even deeper cooperation and economic integration between the EU and Russia—and lay the foundations for a future common economic space from the Atlantic to the Pacific." Available at http://www.consilium.europa.eu/uedocs/cms_Data/docs/pressdata/EN/foraff/140784.pdf.

[83] In reaction to the fast unfolding situation in Ukraine, and in particular with regard to Crimea's illegal annexation, the talks on the New Agreement were suspended. See in particular point 4 of the Statement of the Heads of State or Government on Ukraine, Brussels, 6 March 2014, available at http://www.consilium.europa.eu/uedocs/cms_data/docs/pressdata/en/ec/141372.pdf.

[84] See The Kremlin, Moscow, Press Conference Following Talks with Spanish Prime Minister José Luis Rodríguez Zapatero, 10 December 2004: "If Ukraine wants to join the EU and if the EU accepts Ukraine as a member, Russia, I think, would welcome this because we have a special relationship with Ukraine. Our economies are closely linked, including in specific areas of the manufacturing sector where we have a very high level of cooperation, and having this part of indeed our economy become essentially part of the EU would, I hope, have a positive impact on Russia's economy." Available at http://eng.kremlin.ru/transcripts/7741.

[85] Movchan and Giucci (2011) and Prohniţchi (2012).

[86] The results of the 2014 Presidential and Parliamentary elections in Ukraine give evidence.

certainly underestimated the depth of feeling and force of power which Russia was willing to bring to the equation. This neglect was a common neglect of the EU-28. Throughout the past 10 years, notably since the 2004 enlargement, the EU has continued to struggle with a resurgent Russia which was gaining in importance as an economic but also a political partner, for example to solve regional conflicts further afield. In parallel, the EU also aimed to advance in deepening EU–Russia relations.

This mutual neglect led the EU's negotiators to underestimate the symbolism represented by the mere fact of Ukraine signing the AA with the EU and its turn westward becoming definitive. Russia's government in turn tended to exaggerate perceived negative consequences of such a step to the Russian economy, in order to preserve its wider geo-strategic objectives.[87]

Towards an FTA from Lisbon to Vladivostok?

There is an obvious need for better cooperation with Russia in the medium-term. The more progress that can be achieved towards a Common Economic Area with Russia or even the Customs Union, the less tension should exist in the relationship with Russia, by complementing each other's strengths and weaknesses and by building on mutual interdependence. Teaming up would make both the EU and Russia stronger for future global competition necessities. To achieve possible economic integration with Russia, a very similar method as the one already pursued with EaP partners should be used, since Russia seems to aim at very similar policy goals as the EU in terms of economic integration. This was outlined already in November 2010 by Putin himself when he presented his vision of an FTA from "*Lisbon to Vladivostok*".[88]

[87] On 27 August 2013, Sergey Glaziev, advisor to Russia's President Putin, warned in an interview to TV channel Russia 24 that signature of the EU–Ukraine AA will have "catastrophic consequences" for Ukraine. He indicated that if Ukraine prioritises EU integration, it will no longer be a strategic partner for Russia. After the AA signature the country will "disappear as an international partner, and will lose its legal personality in international law", as it will have to "agree all its actions in the trade field with the EU", he said. Glaziev reiterated the message in his interview to Kommersant daily on 3 September 2013 saying "By signing the AA (Association Agreement), Ukraine loses independence and ceases to be not just a strategic, but even a full-value partner (for Russia)".

[88] In an editorial contribution to the German daily *Süddeutsche Zeitung* of 25 November 2010, then Prime Minister Vladimir Putin indicated his vision for an economic area between the EU and Russia. See Putin (2010). See also President Barroso's remarks following the EU–Russia Summit on 28 January 2014, "Another way to reinforce our trust is to work jointly in one of our most important strategic and shared objectives: to create a common economic space from Lisbon to Vladivostok. It may seem a dream, but dreams can become reality", European Commission, SPEECH/14/66 of 28 January 2014, available at http://europa.eu/rapid/press-release_SPEECH-14-66_en.htm.

This will however require that not only Russia, but also its two partners in the Customs Union, Belarus and Kazakhstan, join the World Trade Organization and that all three will live up to their WTO commitments. It will also require that all Customs Union members demonstrate willingness to undertake significant and comprehensive trade and investment liberalising steps, to fulfil WTO criteria for an FTA.

However, there is one clear condition for the EU in pursuing such an approach in the longer term: Russia needs to return to the application of the Helsinki Final Act of 1975, to fully respect the territorial integrity and independence of its, and our, common neighbours. The EaP partner countries must be free to make the sovereign choices they wish to make and no one should impose its will by any form of pressure or even military force.

The EU will always respect free choices of countries wishing to join the *Customs Union*, as it has shown in reaction to Armenia's wish to join that Union and not to pursue the AA/DCFTA with the EU anymore. Russia should clarify its intention with regard to Ukraine and respect the country's political association and economic integration with the EU.

Eastern Partnership After the Vilnius Shock: Not Inclusive Enough, too Ambitious, Lack of Membership Perspective?

Against the background of increased Russian pressure on eastern partners and the Russia-Ukraine trade disputes in August 2013, followed by the Armenian decision of early September 2013 to join the Customs Union, the developments that took place just before the Vilnius Summit should not have come as a great surprise. Nevertheless, the Ukrainian government's decision to suspend preparations for the signature of the AA and the subsequent course of events came as a shock in diplomatic circles.[89] Throughout 2013, Brussels and other EU capitals were focussed on securing the support of Member States for the Ukraine AA, based on the conditions set out in the December 2012 Council Conclusions,[90] rather than concerned about a possible withdrawal by the Ukrainian side. Despite the very sensitive political context, there were high expectations that a political compromise would be found and the Agreement signed. Brussels was neither prepared nor

[89] Even China and Japan expressed increased interest to understand what happened.

[90] Council conclusions on Ukraine, 3209th Foreign Affairs Council meeting, Brussels, 10 December 2012, available at http://www.consilium.europa.eu/uedocs/cms_Data/docs/pressdata/EN/foraff/134136.pdf. See also Independent monitoring report, International Renaissance Foundation, Association with the EU: How Does Ukraine Fulfil the Benchmarks for Signing the Agreement?, 18 June 2013.

supposed to think of a "Plan B",[91] and EU officials faithfully prepared for signature of the Ukraine AA until the eve of the Vilnius Summit.

Following the rapidly unfolding post-Vilnius events in Ukraine, and notably in view of Ukraine's temporary U-turn, many political and academic voices, voiced criticism on the EU's EaP policy. In addition, Russia's massive pressures exercised on its neighbours and renewed East-West tensions, notably over the (supposedly unrelated) Russian illegal annexation of Crimea, led to a massive public debate over the EU's foreign and economic policy in its Eastern neighbourhood.

The *raison d'être* of the EaP and its Association Agreement dimension was questioned as being on the one hand too ambitious and expensive in terms of political, social and economic costs for the partner countries and on the other hand not timely, differentiated or attractive enough, notably lacking a real political perspective.[92] Although some hail the EaP policy as bold and innovative, others demand a complete re-write of the ENP's Eastern dimension. Almost all commentators agree that the Russian factor has to be better reckoned[93] in order for the EaP policy to become ultimately successful.

The conclusion was drawn that an intensified engagement with Russia is needed, as well as reflection on how to better factor in the Customs Union into the EU's Eastern Partnership policy and the accompanying Association Agreements. In broader terms, a reflection about the effectiveness of the ENP was launched with strong calls to revitalise the EaP, including in terms of offering a possible membership perspective and adequate financial assistance. There was also a consensus about a strengthened engagement with civil society. A re-definition of the EU's ENP with greater firmness, realism based on the EU's own interests and more attraction for its Eastern and Southern neighbours has been called for by many authors.[94] This usually includes also the call for a clearer policy vis-à-vis Russia and often also Turkey. All these considerations have been compounded by the Russian annexation of Crimea.

In view of a possible renewal and/or adjustment of the ENP and its Eastern Partnership under the new European Commission in 2014, one should take into account three main strands of criticism which are currently dominating the debate around the Eastern Partnership's bilateral dimension.[95]

The **first strand** argues that in Vilnius, the EU's Eastern Partnership failed since the policy neglected Russia's role as a strategic player in the region. It considers Russia's exclusion from the Eastern Partnership policy as a fundamental error.

[91] Remarks of Commissioner Štefan Füle to the press after the EU–Ukraine Cooperation Council in Luxembourg, EU–Ukraine: Good Progress but Still More to Be Done, European Commission, MEMO/13/605 of 24 June 2013, available at http://europa.eu/rapid/press-release_MEMO-13-605_en.htm.

[92] Filipchuk and Paul (2013).

[93] See, for example, Emerson (2014), p. 13; Stewart (2014); Popescu (2013).

[94] See, for example, Eneko (2014), pp. 6–7; Emerson (2014), p. 13; Stewart (2014).

[95] A review of the ENP started in autumn 2014 within the EEAS as well as the European Commission, notably DG NEAR, with the aim to propose recommendation by the end of 2015.

Since Russia was neither involved nor consulted, the EU was not able to anticipate or assess Russia's possible reaction to the Eastern partner's political association and economic integration with the EU. In addition, it is argued that the EU's approach to Eastern partners, including the AA/DCFTAs, was conceptualised as a zero-sum game, clearly against Russia's political and economic interest, in particular with regard to the Eurasian project. It forced Eastern partners to choose between "association" with the EU (Association Agreement) and "union" with Russia (Customs Union).

As long as the Customs Union requires one common external tariff regime for all its members, this rivalry of projects will continue to exist. The Eurasian Union will have to develop its own form of "Associated membership", respecting countries' choices. In fact, the EU genuinely never intended to enter into a geopolitical zero-sum game between East and West or to provoke rivalry with Russia over the so called "common neighbourhood" which includes all of the six Eastern partner countries.[96] There was rather an understanding that the Eastern Partnership could co-exist with the EU's policy towards Russia with its four Common Spaces of 2003 and related Roadmaps of 2005, including the numerous sectoral dialogues, the New Agreement negotiations since 2008 and, finally, re-invigoration of the Roadmaps by the comprehensive Partnership for Modernisation of 2010 with its manifold activities.[97]

The paradox in all of this is that Russia has quite successfully aligned many of its industrial norms and standards over the years with the EU's acquis. To add, Russia itself is interested in entering into a Free Trade Area with the EU—the very same policy goal it does not wish the EaP countries to pursue independently from Russia. This was also explicitly expressed in the EaP Vilnius Summit Declaration which states that the "effective future implementation of Association Agreements and, where relevant, DCFTAs, [. . .] will bring [. . .] gradual economic integration of partners in the EU internal market and therefore [. . .] the creation of an economic area."[98]

Taking into account Russia's perception of the EaP and in view of the events in the run up to Vilnius and shortly afterwards, one can argue that the assumptions and accompanying EU rhetoric was to a certain extent erroneous. The Russian pressure and determination of undermining the success of the AA/DCFTAs was

[96] See speech of Štefan Füle, former European Commissioner for Enlargement and Neighbourhood Policy, Moldova: At Comrat University about Myths and Benefits of Association Agreement, European Commission—SPEECH/14/57 of 23 January 2014, available at http://europa.eu/rapid/press-release_SPEECH-14-57_en.htm.

[97] See Progress Report on the Partnership for Modernisation, which was prepared in advance of the EU–Russia Summit on 28 January 2014, http://eeas.europa.eu/russia/docs/eu_russia_progress_report_2014_en.pdf.

[98] See relevant extract of the Joint Declaration of the Eastern Partnership Summit, Vilnius, 28–29 November 2013, Eastern Partnership: The Way Ahead, 17130/13, Presse 516, available at http://www.consilium.europa.eu/uedocs/cms_data/docs/pressdata/EN/foraff/139765.pdf.

underestimated, even if it manifested itself only very late in very massive ways, probably after all other means of influencing Ukraine had failed.

This can only be addressed over time by more closely aligning the direction of the Eastern partners' and Russia in the EU's Eastern policy.

The **second strand** of criticism claims that the EU's offer for Eastern partners was too ambitious without providing the partners with appropriate means to fulfil the associated obligations. The EaP's societies would not be in a position to live up to the important commitments "imposed" by the EU through the AAs. In the short- to medium-term the EaP countries would need to undertake crucial socio-economic reform steps, at a time where the impact of the financial crisis was still visible.

The EU asked simply too much from the partners when committing them to approximate to the EU's standards and norms by requesting them to approximate their legislation to the EU acquis.[99] This argument is popular among partner countries who would wish to qualify for the application of additional funding opportunities for adaptation to EU standards and norms similar to those of candidate countries for EU accession such as the Western Balkans or Turkey.

In fact, the main engine for undertaking the important approximation obligation to EU law was not imposed by the EU, but rather was an EU response to partner countries' own ambition. The EaP agreements as they stand are a result of negotiations, not impositions. One should also add that the EaP AA/DCFTAs are based on an asymmetry: EaP partner countries had the possibility to negotiate important transition periods (up to 15 years) for the transposition of the EU acquis into national legislation before they would be obliged to open their markets for selected EU goods and services. Taking into account the important investment costs for a country's transition, the EU stands ready to provide support to the EaP, as is intended in the "more-for-more" approach. However, the support is limited to the ENI funds until the end of the Multi-Annual Financial Framework in 2020.

At this stage, compromising on the level of ambition of EaP AA/DCFTAs is unlikely since the level of ambition not only represents a modern EU economic integration policy but it also provides partner countries with the long-sought effective economic blueprint for reform, thus helping our neighbours to overcome decades of stalemate and corruption-induced slowness in transforming their societies.

Ultimately, only the practice of active implementation and related targeted support will show whether the approach is too ambitious, and needs to be corrected. The future Association Councils will have the power to do so.

Finally, **the third strand** of criticism argues that the EU's offer to Eastern partners was not attractive and not differentiated enough.

This approach is based on the conviction that a carrot is indispensable to mobilise transformation in a country. Thus, only a membership perspective would enable the countries who wish to do so to undertake substantial transformative reforms. Without this perspective the transition towards sustainable and stable

[99] See, for example, Emerson (2014) and Stewart (2014).

market economies, based on a good system of checks and balances with the rule of law applied, would just not be possible.[100]

More differentiation[101] is already necessary now, since the EaP needs to become more targeted to cater for very different situations, ambitions and possibilities among the six EaP partners. An EU accession/membership perspective would be the single most powerful step to overcome inherent resistance in EaP partner countries to real reform and proper market opening. This is particularly relevant for Moldova and Ukraine. It would also make available qualitatively higher sums of financial support for structural reforms and adjustment. Russia may have involuntarily contributed to the greater prospect of realisation of such perspectives, following the illegal annexation of Crimea. In parallel, the EaP would need also to cater for the different ambition from countries such as Belarus, Armenia and Azerbaijan.

All these schools of thought will play a role in the review process of the ENP with its Eastern Partnership dimension under the new European Commission with the new EU High Representative/Vice President as of autumn 2014.

Conclusion and Outlook: Rethinking EaP in Different Terms

Taking into account the post-Vilnius developments, the EU needs to rethink its neighbourhood policy with regard to Russia but also how to present its EaP policy in a more inclusive way. An analysis of how to engage constructively with Russia while at the same time respecting the EaP countries' own and sovereign choices is warranted. Furthermore, Russia's role as an important strategic actor in the region needs to be acknowledged and a process ought to be started which would identify opportunities[102] for all relevant players—the EU, the Eastern Partnership countries

[100] See, for example, Nowak (2013); Filipchuk and Paul (2014), p. 2; Youngs and Pishchikova (2013). See also speech of Štefan Füle, former European Commissioner for Enlargement and Neighbourhood Policy, Time to Get Stronger in our Commitment to EaP and Reforms in Ukraine, SPEECH/13/1055 of 10 December 2013, available at http://europa.eu/rapid/press-release_SPEECH-13-1055_en.htm.

[101] See for example: Youngs and Pishchikova (2013) and Kaca et al. (2014).

[102] A first attempt to start a more strategic reflection about economic opportunities, implicitly also including Russia, was set out in the Vilnius Summit Declaration of 29 November 2013. See Joint Declaration of the Eastern Partnership Summit, Vilnius, 28-29 November 2013, Eastern Partnership: The Way Ahead, Vilnius, 29 November 2013, 17130/13, Presse 516, available at http://www.consilium.europa.eu/uedocs/cms_data/docs/pressdata/EN/foraff/139765.pdf.

This attempt was followed up at the 32nd EU–Russia Summit on 28 January 2014. At that occasion, President Barroso clearly indicated that the EaP is "not against someone, it is for something – it is about making the countries in our neighbourhood more prosperous and giving their citizens better living conditions. This is something that can only benefit our other partners, and certainly will not harm Russia. That's why today, also, we have agreed that we should pursue bilateral consultations at expert level on the Eastern Partnership Association Agreements and their

as well as Russia. In perspective, the creation of an economic area with the EU's eastern neighbours, including Russia, and contributing thus to the longer-term goal of a wider common area of economic prosperity based on WTO rules and sovereign choices throughout Europe and beyond could present such an opportunity.

Within this context, one should also clearly set out the possibility of a more differentiated Eastern Partnership: clusters of different cooperation areas to which each partner can adhere according to its own needs and possibilities. The partner country could combine the different elements offered under the political association and economic integration in its preferred way and choose the level of ambition and the goals to which it aspires in its relations with the EU.[103] The *menu* could also offer different depths of economic integration via a simple FTA for some partners or via the Deep and Comprehensive FTA for others. This differentiation is needed to maintain the Eastern Partnership as a framework for relations, taking into account the need and ambitions of Azerbaijan, Armenia and Belarus.[104]

Finally, the prospect of a membership perspective needs to be tackled. According to many observers, a conditional future membership perspective should form part of the EU's various offers proposed to Eastern partners on the *menu*. In line with the "more-for-more" principle, the EU is supposed to develop stronger ties and offer greater incentives to countries that make more progress towards democratic reform.[105] The successful implementation and enforcement of the AA/-DCFTA should represent an important aspect. The ambitious Eastern partner countries will need to have an important pull factor to overcome resistance to potential domestic reform when implementing the AA/DCFTA commitments and embarking on an irreversible transition process. For this set of countries, the next steps should hence result in a membership perspective. For the others, it could result in a possible integration via a purely economic area without the political project of full integration.

---

possible economic consequences for both sides. Our Eastern partners should be free to decide their own path." See Statement by President Barroso following the EU–Russia Summit, European Commission, SPEECH/14/66 of 28 January 2014, available at http://europa.eu/rapid/press-release_SPEECH-14-66_en.htm.

[103] See relevant extract of the Joint Declaration of the Eastern Partnership Summit, Vilnius, 28–29 November 2013, Eastern Partnership: The Way Ahead, Vilnius, 29 November 2013, 17130/13, Presse 516, available at http://www.consilium.europa.eu/uedocs/cms_data/docs/pressdata/EN/foraff/139765.pdf, which sets out: "In the framework of the European Neighbourhood Policy and the Eastern Partnership, the Summit participants reaffirm the sovereign right of each partner freely to choose the level of ambition and the goals to which it aspires in its relations with the European Union."

[104] To note that Armenia withdrew from the DCFTA in September 2013 and Azerbaijan was never offered a DCFTA since it is not a WTO member. Belarus has never entered in the bilateral dimension of the Eastern Partnership with the EU.

[105] The set of democratic reforms includes free and fair elections, freedom of expression, of assembly and of association, judicial independence, fight against corruption and democratic control over the armed forces. For the ENP review, see COM(2011) 303.

But in order to reach this differentiated stage of political association and economic integration, the EU must first communicate better, in a more political and professional way. Leaders and the broader public, administration, civil society and businesses, need to know what exactly is on offer in order to make the right choice when selecting the elements of the EaP *menu*. Only by winning the hearts and minds of citizens in partner countries, in the most interested third countries, as well as in our own Member States will this policy properly prosper. Hard facts and convincing arguments[106] will be the best answer to outright propaganda and manipulations, stoking up fears. The EU and its EaP partner countries need to become more effective in informing about the many new opportunities for citizens which political association and economic integration will bring.

For this all to happen soon, the first agreements with Ukraine, Moldova and Georgia started to be provisionally applied[107] in 2014 and will now have to be

---

[106] See for example the so-called "myth busters" on the AAs which were developed by the EU. These information sheets can be found on the websites of the EU delegations in Georgia (see http://eeas.europa.eu/delegations/georgia/documents/eap_aa/mythbuster_2_2014_en.pdf) and Ukraine (see http://eeas.europa.eu/delegations/ukraine/documents/myths_aa_en.pdf).

[107] Moldova ratified the AA on 2 July 2014, only 5 days after signature, and Georgia's ratification followed on 18 July 2014. The ratification of both AAs thus opened the way for provisional application of parts of the Agreements as of 1 September 2014. See Notice concerning the provisional application of the Association Agreement between the European Union and the European Atomic Energy Community and their Member States of the one part, and the Republic of Moldova of the other part, [2014] OJ L 259/1. Romania, Lithuania and Latvia were the first three EU Member States ratifying the Agreements and submitting their ratification instruments on 14, 29 and 31 July 2014 respectively. At the time of writing six additional Member States submitted their ratification instruments, notably Malta, Slovakia, Bulgaria, Sweden, Estonia and Denmark. For the state of play of ratification by all parties of the Agreement, see data base of the Council of the European Union, available at http://www.consilium.europa.eu/policies/agreements/search-the-agreements-database?command=details&lang=en&aid=2014045&doclang=EN for Ukraine, http://www.consilium.europa.eu/policies/agreements/search-the-agreements-database?command=details&lang=en&aid=2014001&doclang=EN for Moldova and http://www.consilium.europa.eu/policies/agreements/search-the-agreements-database?command=details&lang=en&aid=2014007&doclang=EN for Georgia. Ukraine ratified the AA on 16 September 2014 by the Law of Ukraine N1678-VII. On the very same day, also the European Parliament gave its consent on the Agreement. See European Parliament legislative resolution of 16 September 2014 on the draft Council decision on the conclusion, on behalf of the European Union, of the Association Agreement between the European Union and the European Atomic Energy Community and their Member States, of the one part, and Ukraine, of the other part, with the exception of the provisions relating to the treatment of third-country nationals legally employed as workers in the territory of the other party (13613/2013 – C8-0105/2014 – 2013/0151A(NLE)), see http://www.europarl.europa.eu/sides/getDoc.do?pubRef=-//EP//TEXT+TA+P8-TA-2014-0014+0+DOC+XML+V0//EN&language=EN. On 13 November 2014, the European Parliament gave its consent to the Moldova AA. See European Parliament legislative resolution of 13 November 2014 on the draft Council decision on the conclusion, on behalf of the European Union, of the Association Agreement between the European Union and the European Atomic Energy Community and their Member States, of the one part, and the Republic of Moldova, of the other part (09828/2014 – C8-0130/2014 – 2014/0083(NLE)), available at http://www.europarl.europa.eu/sides/getDoc.do?type=TA&reference=P8-TA-2014-0050&language=EN&ring=A8-2014-0020. Finally, on 18 December, the European Parliament also gave its consent to the Georgia AA. See European Parliament non-legislative resolution of 18 December 2014 on the draft Council

implemented and enforced. The many judgements which have been made to date should then be considered in the light of several years of actual implementation practice.

References

Adomeit H (2012) Putin's "Eurasian Union": Russia's integration project and policies on post-Soviet space. CIES (Center for international and European studies), Neighbourhood policy paper, No. 04, July 2012. Available at http://www.khas.edu.tr/cms/cies/dosyalar/files/NeighbourhoodPolicyPaper(04).pdf

Devrim D, Schulz E (2009a) Enlargement fatigue in the European Union: from enlargement to many unions. Real Instituto Alcano, WP 13/2009 - 10/3/2009

Devrim D, Schulz E (2009b) The Eastern partnership: an interim step towards enlargement? Real Instituto Alcano, ARI 22/2009 - 10/2/2009

Emerson M (2014) After Vilnius Fiasco: who is to blame? What is to be done? CEPS Essay No. 8, 21 January 2014

Eneko (2014) La place de l'Union européenne dans le monde, European Policy Brief, No. 20, March 2014

Eurasian Development Bank, Centre for Integration Studies, Ukraine and the Customs Union, Comprehensive assessment of the macroeconomic effects of various forms of deep economic integration of Ukraine and the member states of the customs union and the common economic space, Report 1, January 2012, p 29. Available at http://www.eabr.org/general/upload/reports/Ukraina_doklad_eng.pdf

European Commission (2014) Joint conclusions of the EU-Russian Federation-Ukraine ministerial meeting on the effects of implementation of the EU-Ukraine AA/DCFTA, STATEMENT/14/223, 11 July 2014. Available at http://europa.eu/rapid/press-release_STATEMENT-14-223_en.htm

Filipchuk V, Paul A (2013) Ukraine's European integration: between mayhem and opportunity. European Policy Centre, Commentary, 2 December 2013. Available at http://www.epc.eu/documents/uploads/pub_3974_ukraine_s_european_integration.pdf

Filipchuk V, Paul A (2014) Ukraine in deadlock – what next? European Policy Centre, Commentary, 12 February 2014

Halbach U (2012) Vladimir Putin's Eurasian Union, a new integration project for the CIS-region? Stiftung Wissenschaft und Politik, SWP Comments 1, January 2012 (English version of SWP-Aktuell 51, November 2011). Available at http://www.swp-berlin.org/fileadmin/contents/products/comments/2012C01_hlb.pdf

Kaca E, Parkes R, Sobják A (2014) Choosing our geography: 12 points to restore meaning to the eastern partnership, PISM Policy Paper no. 12 (95), July 2014

Karaganov S (2014) Russia needs to defend its interests with an iron fist. Russia in global affairs, 6 March 2014. Available at http://eng.globalaffairs.ru/pubcol/Russia-needs-to-defend-its-interests-with-an-iron-fist-16457

Langbein J (2009) The EU-Ukraine FTA: plus or minus? ICPS Newsletter "European Focus", November 2009, p 1. Available at http://www.girodivite.it/IMG/pdf/EF_November_2009_ENG.pdf

decision on the conclusion, on behalf of the European Union, of the Association Agreement between the European Union and the European Atomic Energy Community and their Member States, of the one part, and Georgia, of the other part (09827/2014 – C8-0129/2014 – 2014/0086(NLE) – 2014/2816 (INI)).

Lukyanov (2014) Принуждение к новому миру, 4 March 2014. Available at http://www.gazeta.ru/comments/column/lukyanov/5935113.shtml

Movchan V, Giucci R (2011) Quantitative assessment of Ukraine's regional integration options: DCFTA with European Union vs. Customs Union with Russia, Belarus, and Kazakhstan, German Advisory Group. Institute for Economic Research and Policy Consulting, Policy Paper Series PP/05/2011, November 2011. Available at http://www.beratergruppe-ukraine.de/download/Beraterpapiere/2011/PP_05_2011_en.pdf

Nowak B (2013) Time for the EU to Play Hardball with Ukraine, Real Clear World 17 (December 2013)

Popescu N (2013) "After Vilnius", European Union Institute for Security Studies, Issue Alert No. 40, 6 December 2013

Prodi R (2001) An enlarged and more United Europe, a Global Player – challenges and opportunities in the new century, speech to the College of Europe, Bruges, 12 November 2001, European Commission, SPEECH/01/528. Available at http://europa.eu/rapid/press-release_SPEECH-01-528_en.htm

Prodi R (2002) A wider Europe – a proximity policy as the key to stability, speech to "Peace, Security and Stability – International Dialogue and the Role of the EU", 6th ECSA-World Conference, Brussels, 5–6 December 2002, European Commission, SPEECH/02/619. Available at http://europa.eu/rapid/press-release_SPEECH-02-619_en.htm

Prohnițchi V (2012) Strategic comparison of Moldova's integration options: deep and comprehensive economic integration with the EU versus the accession to the Russia-Belarus-Kazakhstan Customs Union, Expert-Grup, Economic Analysis and Forecast Paper Nr. 3/2012, 7 June 2012. Available at http://pasos.org/wp-content/uploads/2012/06/Moldova-DCFTA_versus_RBK_CU_English.pdf

Putin V (2010) Plädoyer für Wirtschaftsgemeinschaft. Von Lissabon bis Wladiwostok. Available at http://www.sueddeutsche.de/wirtschaft/putin-plaedoyer-fuer-wirtschaftsgemeinschaft-von-lissabon-bis-wladiwostok-1.1027908

Putin V (2011) Новый интеграционный проект для Евразии — будущее, которое рождается сегодня, Izvestia, 3 October 2011. Available at http://www.izvestia.ru/news/502761#

Radeke J (2012) "DCFTA zwischen Moldau und der EU: Risiken erkennen, Chancen nutzen", German Economic Team in Moldova, Newsletter 15/2012. Available at http://www.get-moldau.de/download/Newsletter/2012/Newsletter_15_2012_GET%20Moldau.pdf?PHPSESSID=4f452cfccae425a76bfb65073263d3ce

Speck U (2014) Putins Aggression, Die Ukraine-Krise bedroht besonders Deutschland, Die ZEIT, 7 April 2014. Available at http://www.zeit.de/politik/ausland/2014-04/ukraine-konflikt-machtpolitik-postmoderne/komplettansicht

Stewart S (2014) The EU, Russia and a less common neighbourhood. Lessons Reinforced by the Vilnius Summit, SWP Comments No. 3, January 2014

Verheugen G (2003) EU enlargement and the Union's neighbourhood policy. Diplomatic Academy, Moscow, 27 October 2003. Available at http://www.cvce.eu/en/obj/address_given_by_gunter_verheugen_on_the_enlargement_of_the_eu_and_the_european_neighbourhood_policy_moscow_27_october_2003-en-be19f178-524b-4b69-902c-eb902079f45c.html

Woerhel S (2014) Ukraine: current issues and U.S. policy. Congressional Research Service, 7-5700 RL33460, 24 March 2014

Wisniewska I (2013) Eurasian integration, Russia's attempt at the economic unification of the post-Soviet area, OSW Studies No. 44, July 2013

Youngs R, Pishchikova K (2013) Smart geostrategy for the eastern partnership. Carnegie Europe, 14 November 2013

The European Union and the Accession of Russia to the World Trade Organization (WTO) in 2012

Meinhard Hilf

It was the main interest and fascination of Horst Krenzler to handle and shape the foreign economic relations of the European Union (EU). He served the EU Commission as the responsible Director-General for foreign relations from 1986 to 1996. This is a long period as this central function is very much aspired to by other leading Member States who are always interested in a regular rotation amongst them.

Ten years in this context is rather exceptional and testifies the extraordinary talents of Krenzler to handle conflicting interests with honesty and fairness on the basis of a deeply rooted interest and knowledge of international law relating to international trade relations. Though he started his studies in literature and political science he finally found his specific interest in public international law. He graduated at the University of Heidelberg in 1964 with a doctoral thesis on the "Provisional Application of Treaties under Public International Law". This thesis had been written under the supervision of Günther Jaenicke and Hermann Mosler, Director of the Max Planck Institute for Public International Law in Heidelberg. This subject shows Krenzler's deep affection for combining practical and theoretical elements in the resolution of conflicts. This early dissertation is still cited and has served as a reliable and important reference in the area of treaty drafting and handling. It is in this area where he found his satisfaction in the services of the EU Commission when drafting and handling innumerous international agreements and treaties as for example in the field of trade in textiles. Thus his numerous outstanding personal and professional talents qualified him to steer the newly founded and constantly developing European Union through the never calm waters of international trade relations.

M. Hilf (✉)
Bucerius Law School, Hamburg, Germany
e-mail: meinhard.hilf@law-school.de

C. Herrmann et al. (eds.), *Trade Policy between Law, Diplomacy and Scholarship*,
European Yearbook of International Economic Law,
DOI 10.1007/978-3-319-15690-3_19

Just before the end of his professional position with the European Commission he helped to realise the acceptance of the "European Communities" (EC) as an original member of the World Trade Organization which was created in 1994. His diplomatic skills were needed to convince all EC Member States as well as all other contracting parties of the GATT 1947 to recognise that all respective competences and powers in the field of international trade had finally been transferred to the EC. This has been confirmed by the European Court of Justice in its Opinion 1/94 of 15 November 1994 (OR 1994, I-5267) ruling that the powers concerning international trade in goods had been exclusively transferred to the EC.

One can only assume that Krenzler was likewise involved in clarifying the position of the EC regarding the proposed accession of China (1995) and of Russia (2012), becoming now the 156th member of the WTO. It is astonishing that these two events did not stir any significant attention. China's accession was discussed for 8 years after the formal application. The accession of Russia was initiated in 1993 and was decided after a period of 18 years, a period in which the dissolution of the USSR had taken place. The official documents of the EU do not reflect the importance of these events especially as there was no formal consent or any other formal involvement of the European Parliament. Only within the Working Party which had been established amongst the members of the WTO very intensive discussions took place as to the conditions Russia would have to fulfil in order to join the WTO. This Working Party had been established with 60 members participating thus having been the largest Working Party ever established.[1] It is obvious that the respective governmental institutions were regularly involved in the negotiations of the Working Party without, however, any general public attention as one would have expected.

Only inside the acceding states rather lively debates have accompanied the process of accession.[2] Especially in Russia, an intensive public debate followed the ongoing debates within the WTO Working Party. In the Final Report[3] these differentiated debates are well-documented: Here one has to distinguish two different stages: First of all, Russia had to negotiate 57 different bilateral agreements in the field of trade in goods relating to a number of special interests of the states involved. Only after those specific problems had been resolved, the given results had to be multilateralised or consolidated in view of the final consent of all members of the WTO.

This Report summarises the aspirations and problems which had been associated with the accession of Russia. A main part of this report deals with the internal measures which had to be taken with regard of the importation of foreign goods. Thus a new customs tariff had to be set up reflecting the average decrease of more than 25 %—or in absolute terms from about 10 to 7 %. The document sets out the many special rates and

[1] See Tarre (2007), p. 2.

[2] See in particular, International Trade Centre (2012).

[3] Report of the Working Party on the Accession of the Russian Federation to the World Trade Organization, WT/ACC/RUS/70 WT/MIN(11)/2, 17 November 2011.

the special time periods within which the final rates have to be applied. Of course, the Report does not show the applied tariffs which in reality are often lower than the tariffs indicated in the official schedules (so-called "water in the tariffs").

Exports duties shall be applied for 700 tariff lines as for example for crude oil, gas and metals. All together customs duties represent about 35 % of the federal budget.

Much attention had to be given to the less transparent "non-tariff barriers" which had to be dealt with in the Final Report. Russia had to guarantee a transparent and non-discriminatory system of non-tariff measures—such as SPS or TBT measures—which are common to all foreign trade regimes in the field of imports as well as in exports. In this context the Report refers to the alterations concerning the field of services for which a number of differentiated adaptations are foreseen for foreign providers of services in the fields of banking, insurance and telecommunications.[4] And finally, alterations and guarantees are summarised in the field of intellectual property rights and public procurement. Special rules are foreseen for trade operations with Belarus and Kazakhstan forming together with Russia a Customs Union (2010) and finally a single economic space (2012).[5]

In the end, the final accession package as adopted by the Working Party consists of the Report and the bilaterally agreed schedules of market access commitments in the field of goods and services. This package then had to be adopted by the Ministerial Conference of the WTO by a 2/3 majority. Finally, this package was adopted by consensus in December 2011.[6] As far as can be seen no other parliament—except the Russian Duma—was formally involved in this process though the accession will have a great impact for future economic relations. The accession became effective on 22 August 2012.

The absence of any parliamentarian involvement in these procedures of accession may astonish as the accessions of China and Russia will have considerable repercussions for international trade relations. Certainly, this lack of democratic legitimation can only be acceptable by understanding the relevant accession procedures in the sense that they include an anticipated approval of any future accession to the organisation.

It certainly is for the future to show the real effects of the Russian accession to the WTO. There were high expectations as well as uncertainties in the assessment of the future development of exports, imports as well as foreign investments. For lawyers it will be interesting to see to which degree the legalisation of foreign trade would have affected the internal legal order of Russia. In effect, any legal act in the field of foreign trade can be challenged before the relevant Russian courts. Final decisions then can open up the access to the dispute settlement procedure under WTO law by invoking an infringement of WTO law by Russia.

---

[4] For Russia's commitments in the area of services, see: International Trade Centre (2012), p. 11.

[5] Ehlers et al. (2001), p. 1.

[6] See WTO press release, Ministerial Conference approves Russia's WTO membership, 16 December 2011, available at http://www.wto.org/english/news_e/news11_e/acc_rus_16dec11_e.htm.

The first case against Russia is under way: The EU has filed a case involving a recycling fee which has to be paid only with regard to imported cars but not for cars produced in Russia. In addition vehicles imported from Belarus or Kazakhstan are exempted likewise as Russia is linked with these countries by a customs' union.[7] And Russia has filed its first cases under the Dispute Settlement Mechanism of the WTO.[8] And Russia is cooperating by acting as a third party in pending procedures.[9]

During the negotiations for accession Russia has confirmed that any violations of rights of foreign traders or investors may be challenged before Russian courts.[10] It will be seen whether this highly evolved system of judicial protection in the field of foreign trade law will contrast with the general judicial protection in other areas of general administrative law. The rule of law will tend to be applied on the same level in different fields of law. Especially in the field of protection of fundamental rights Russian courts will have to apply the respective rights under the European Convention of Fundamental Rights.

It would have been of particular interest to Horst Krenzler to follow and influence these developments in the field of international law as far as they are related to the trade relations of Russia and the European Union. In the future, these relations will be framed by the standards of the WTO and thus will strengthen the reliability of both trading partners.

References

Ehlers D, Wolffgang H-M, Schröder UJ (eds) (2001) Rechtsfragen der Eurasischen Zollunion, p 1

International Trade Centre (2012) Russia's accession to the WTO: major commitments and possible implications. Available at http://www.intracen.org/uploadedFiles/Russia WTO Accession English.pdf

Tarre D (2007) Russian WTO accession: what has been accomplished, what can be expected. World Bank, Policy Research Working Paper 4428, December 2007, p 2

[7] See *Russia—Motor Vehicles*, consultation request by the EU, WT/DS462/1, 11 July 2013.

[8] See EU—Cost Adjustment Methodologies and Certain Anti-dumping Measures on Imports from Russia, consultation request by Russia, WT/DS474/1, 9 January 2014.

[9] See EC—Seal Products (Canada), DS400; EC—Seal Products (Norway), DS401; China—Rare Earths (US), DS431; China—Rare Earths (EU), DS432; China—Rare Earths (Japan), DS433; US—Countervailing Measures (China), DS437; US—Countervailing and Anti-dumping Measures (China), DS449; and China—HP-SSST (Japan), DS454.

[10] See Report of the Working Party on the Accession of the Russian Federation to the World Trade Organization, WT/ACC/RUS/70 WT/MIN(11)/2, 17 November 2011, p. 127.

Part V
Trade Defence Instruments

Modernising the EU's Trade Defence Instruments: Mission Impossible?

Frank Hoffmeister

Introduction

Next to his many professional and academic achievements, Horst Günter Krenzler left his foot print also in the political world. He co-founded the European Liberal Democrat Party (ELDR)—renamed in 2012 Alliance of Liberals and Democrats for Europe Party (ALDE)—and the European branch of the German Free Democratic Party (*Auslandsgruppe Europa der FDP—AGE*) in 1969. Being the latter's first President since 1975, his advice on European integration matters was sought by the party and often heard. Still a long time after retirement as Director-General in the European Commission, Krenzler attended the Federal Expert Committee on Foreign Policy of the German liberals on behalf of *AGE*. The present author had the privilege to accompany him for several years at bi-annual meetings in Berlin, as representative of the Brussels-based German liberals. I remember with great admiration the thoughtfulness of his interventions in the Committee: whenever he took the floor, the other members recognised the great insight and logic of his positions, making it hard to contradict or even outvote his proposals. He brought the European political context into the debate and kept his passionate plea for more integration. As long as he was active, Krenzler's authority guaranteed that the FDP would remain the most Europe-friendly party in Germany.

When he left us in July 2012, I was assigned the impossible task to replace him in the FDP Committee. As the leader of the delegation of German Members of the European Parliament (MEPs), Alexander Graf Lambsdorff, noted in his obituary for

The views expressed in this article are personal and cannot be attributed to the European Commission.

F. Hoffmeister (✉)
European Commission, CHAR 4/130, Rue de la Loi 200, 1049 Brussels, Belgium
e-mail: frank.hoffmeister@ec.europa.eu

C. Herrmann et al. (eds.), *Trade Policy between Law, Diplomacy and Scholarship*,
European Yearbook of International Economic Law,
DOI 10.1007/978-3-319-15690-3_20

the party journal, Krenzler liked to cite Goethe as much as Adam Smith.[1] I am afraid that I cannot live up to this great humanist standard. However, I dare to intervene on matters of European policy in the great tradition of Krenzler. One of the topics, for sure, is the EU's trade policy, one of his old loves. The field, however, produces in itself a wide array of interesting legal questions.[2] Hence, for the purpose of this *Gedächtnisschrift*, I chose to write about a rather specialised sub-set, namely the modernisation of the trade defence instruments. I hope that going at the same time into the politics and the technical details of this topic would have pleased the great European liberal, Horst Günter Krenzler.

The Need for Modernisation

When Commissioner De Gucht assumed office as the EU's Trade Commissioner in February 2010, he received a mission statement from President Barroso. It contained a number of tasks, such as furthering the negotiations in the Doha Round, and bringing about deep and comprehensive free trade agreements (DCFTAs) bilaterally.[3] Interestingly, Barroso also expected De Gucht to modernise the EU's trade defence instruments (TDI). The Belgian liberal looked at this idea with some caution for a variety of reasons. First, the appetite for a TDI reform was not great among industry, trade associations, Member States and the European Parliament. In the January 2010 parliamentary hearing preceding his nomination, De Gucht was certainly not pressed to deliver such a reform early in his mandate. On the relevant question, he replied that the operation of TDI should be reviewed after the conclusion of the Doha Round. Moreover, many stakeholders had strong and mostly negative memories of the Commission Green paper issued in December 2006.[4] That reform proposal had soon got stuck in the Council as it was conceived as favouring import interests over producing interests.[5] Second, under the new Article 207 (2) TFEU of the Lisbon Treaty, any legislative change to basic trade rules fell hitherto into the ordinary legislative procedure. Starting one's work with the Parliament on such a controversial topic would not seem advisable. Third, as in many other policy fields, the gaining of practical experience with the implementation of the existing rules would give a better clue where a modernisation would make sense. Against that backdrop, the Commissioner decided to first build trust with the Parliament and Council through an even-handed application of the present

[1] Lambsdorff (2012), p. 23.

[2] Cf. Herrmann and Michl (2008), p. 81 and Hoffmeister (2013), pp. 385–401.

[3] On DCFTAs, see Hoffmeister (2014), p. 15.

[4] Commission Communication, Global Europe—Europe's Trade Defence Instruments in a Changing Global Economy, COM (2006) 763 final of 6 December 2006.

[5] For an excellent analysis of the Green Paper process and the reasons for its failure, see De Bièvre and Eckard (2011), p. 339.

rules. He thus wished to correct the image sometimes attributed to Commission practice under his predecessor Lord Mandelson (not counting the short interval with Lady Ashton and Mrs. Ferrero-Waldner at the helm of DG Trade) that TDI decisions in the European Union had become increasingly politicised.[6]

Accordingly, the years 2010–2013 were characterised by a steady handling of the incoming cases, where the Commissioner followed in almost all cases the proposals from the case-handlers, exercising political scrutiny mostly with respect to some very old cases. Noteworthy was, in this respect, his decision to terminate an expiry review on imports of Chinese lighters—against strong pressure from the French producer, BIC, to carry on the protection despite record profits of the company in the sector. The measures then expired.[7] De Gucht equally resisted pressure from huge import and downstream industry interests in the solar panel case. Here, despite a large number of opposing Member States led by Germany, he decided to impose provisional anti-dumping duties on Chinese solar panels in early June 2013.[8] Based on a Chinese offer for an undertaking presented in August, he was then able to lift the duties for those companies who respected a minimum export price within a certain numerical ceiling. That solution was accepted by the Council when imposing definitive measures in December that year.[9] In addition, there was no generous use of the Union interest test under Article 21 of the Basic Regulation[10] to strike cases down altogether. For example, De Gucht imposed provisional measures on consumer goods such as ceramic tableware[11] (the Council also confirmed this at definitive stage with a lower duty based on a revised Commission proposal)[12] even if this meant higher prices for consumers. Only in the *Termphos* case, concerning the import of white phosphorus from Kazakhstan, did he terminate the case on Union interest grounds.[13] In that case, an overwhelming majority of Member States had already voted against provisional measures in the Anti-Dumping Committee, because they would have been clearly disproportionate for the users in a number of East European member States, whereas the sole EU producer in the Netherlands had already become bankrupt. Finally, De Gucht was absolutely neutral when it came to judging the origin of the alleged unfair practices. He did away with an

[6] Tietje (2009), pp. 33 (43) observed an "increasing politicisation" of TDI proceedings around the time when the Green paper was issued.

[7] European Commission, Notice of Expiry of Certain Anti-Dumping Measures, [2012] OJ C 382/12.

[8] Commission Regulation (EU) No 513/2013 of 4 June 2013, [2013] OJ L 152/ 5.

[9] Council Implementing Regulation (EU) No 1238/2013 of 2 December 2013, [2013] OJ L 325/ 1.

[10] The term "Basic Regulation" refers to Council Regulation (EC) No 1225/2009 of 30 November 2009, [2009] OJ L 343/51.

[11] Commission Regulation (EU) No 1072/2012 of 14 November 2012, [2012] OJ L 318/28 (52), Recitals 218–226.

[12] Council Implementing Regulation (EU) No 412/2013 of 13 May 2013, [2013] OJ L 131/1.

[13] Commission Decision 2013/81 (EU) of 13 February 2013, [2013] OJ L 43/38.

informal moratorium not to bring anti-subsidy cases against China. Starting with the coated fine paper case in May 2011,[14] a number of subsidy cases against Beijing were accepted under his reign. Similarly, the United States could not expect special treatment, as witnessed by the decision to countervail US bioethanol exports[15] which was highly criticised on the other side of the Atlantic.

Finally, on the procedural side, Commissioner De Gucht revisited the role of the Hearing Officer in DG Trade. That post had been created in 2007 to facilitate communication between interested parties and Commission services in trade proceedings, and to offer mediation—on procedural issues—between interested parties and Directorate-General for Trade.[16] However, in administrative terms, he had been attached to the Director-General. In order to strengthen his independence and weight, Commissioner De Gucht decided to bring the Hearing Officer under the auspices of his Cabinet.

The Commission Proposal of April 2013

After roughly 2 years preparatory work, including an evaluation study, a public consultation of stakeholders and an impact assessment of different options, the Commission presented its modernisation package on 10 April 2013. It consisted of a Communication,[17] a legislative proposal to amend the two Basic Regulations,[18] and a DG Trade working paper with a set of four draft guidelines to clarify existing practice with respect to the choice of the analogue country, injury margin, expiry review and length of measures and Union interest.[19]

The Communication explained the rationale for modernisation by pointing to a number of economic challenges that have occurred since the last codification of the basic rules roughly 20 years ago. There was a need to respond to the growing practice of State-capitalist countries to distort international trade by way of subsidies, distortion of raw material prices by way of state interferences and the threat of retaliation. At the same time, the foreseeability and legal security for importers could be improved by procedural means. The basic idea behind this was to provide

---

[14] Council Implementing Regulation (EU) No 452/2011 of 6 May 2011, [2011] OJ L 128/18.

[15] Commission Regulation (EU) No 157/2013 of 18 February 2013, [2013] OJ L 49/10.

[16] See http://ec.europa.eu/commission_2010-2014/degucht/contact/hearing-officer.

[17] Commission Communication, Modernisation of Trade Defence Instruments: Adapting Trade Defence Instruments to the Current Needs of the European Economy, COM(2013) 191 final.

[18] COM(2013) 192 final. The term "Basic Regulations" refers to the above defined Basic Regulation, Council Regulation (EC) No. 1225/2009 on protection against dumped imports from countries not members of the European Community, and also Council Regulation (EC) No 597/2009 on protection against subsidised imports from countries not members of the European Community. Though adopted in 2009 in a codification exercise, their substance dates back to 1995 to implement the results of the WTO Uruguay Round.

[19] Available at http://trade.ec.europa.eu/doclib/cfm/doclib_section.cfm?sec=107.

for a pragmatic, modest change of the rules which would be balanced and offer interest for both the EU industry (and Member States with predominant producer interests) and importers (and Member States with predominant trading interests).[20]

In the legislative proposals, these political ideas were put into draft legal language. As both Basic Regulations have many provisions in common, the proposed changes concerned, as a rule, both instruments. The main elements thereof were grouped under five sections, namely transparency and predictability, fight against retaliation, effectiveness and enforcement, optimising review practice and codification.

Transparency and Predictability

The first item aimed at increasing transparency and predictability in particular before the imposition of provisional measures. Mainly responding to importer's interests, there would be an advance notice, pre-disclosure, and information about the activities of the anti-dumping and anti-subsidy advisory committee. The Commission also proposed introducing a 2-week[21] shipping clause. These are reasonable proposals as they allow EU importers not to be caught by surprise, having to pay duties on goods that were sourced from a country when it was not yet clear whether such products are actually unfairly priced.

Fight Against Retaliation

With the second item, the Commission drew lessons from the increasing practice of retaliation. As Commissioner De Gucht had opined in the TDI-modernisation workshop of October 2012 already, he was wary that companies would not dare to bring TDI cases to the Commission for fear of losing their business in the targeted third country. In order to counter-act such retaliation threat it was important for the Commission to activate its power to bring *ex officio* cases without a formal complaint from the industry. While this possibility already existed under the *lex lata*[22] in special circumstances, there would be a difficulty for the Commission to collect all the relevant data in the absence of cooperation by EU companies fearing retaliation. Hence, in order to make an *ex officio* case successful, companies should be required to cooperate with the Commission in such a scenario. Such a duty of cooperation is missing in the present law.

[20] COM(2013) 191 final, p. 2.

[21] The first draft of De Gucht's proposal had foreseen a 3-week shipping clause. The College of Commissioner's shortened the period to 2 weeks.

[22] Article 5(6) of the Basic Regulation.

Effectiveness and Enforcement

A main point of interest for EU producers was the third item on effectiveness and enforcement. Here, the Commission touched on the so-called lesser duty rule (LDR), an important "WTO-plus feature" of the EU's TDI system.[23] Under LDR, the EU compares the anti-dumping margin and the injury margin, and will always use the lesser one to determine the duty. This rule is not a concession to third countries, but serves as a safety belt that anti-dumping duties do not get excessively high and provide for overprotection. If, for example, EU only needs the prices of dumped imports to increase by 10 % to compete on fair terms with imports that were found to be dumped by some 50 %, the anti-dumping duty will nevertheless be set at 10 % as this is sufficient to re-establish fair competition between the EU industry and the exporters. While reaffirming this basic point, the modernisation proposal would nevertheless introduce two exceptions. LDR would not apply in anti-subsidy cases and in anti-dumping cases involving structural raw material distortions. The Commission argued that in those two scenarios, the active third country government involvement to help their own companies to outcompete EU producers with unfair means deserves a more principled reaction, i.e. the imposition of higher duties. The removal of LDR in these types of serious market distortions should also dissuade third countries from allowing or engaging in such trade distortive conduct.

Optimising Review Practice

The fourth item on optimising review practice dealt with a rather technical matter: what happens if an anti-dumping duty has been imposed for 5 years, and the EU industry launches a request for prolongation which in the end proves unsuccessful? The reply under the current regime[24] is that the duties remain in force during the time when the Commission deals with the request for expiry review (which lasts roughly a year or so). In other words: the EU industry receives an additional year of protection by the simple fact that it has launched a *prima facie* convincing expiry review request. In the Commission's view, that result should be corrected if the request turns out to have been unfounded. Following general principles of administrative law, duties whose collection proved to have no legal basis should then be retroactively reimbursed. This would also be coherent with the approach followed for new investigations: if duties were to be imposed at provisional, but not at definitive stage, any collected provisional duty has to be paid back. It is only fair to all operators that the same is done in the case of review investigations.

[23] Article 9(4) 4th sentence of the Basic Regulation. Cf. Müller et al. (2009), para. 14.03.

[24] Article 11(2) subpara. 1, last sentence of the Basic Regulation.

Codification

Finally, the legislative proposal contained a fifth item: targeted changes of the Basic Regulations in order to update certain provisions as a result of ECJ and WTO rulings.

The Fjellner Report in the European Parliament

In the European Parliament, the responsible Committee on International Trade (INTA) assigned the file to the Swedish Conservative, Christofer Fjellner. Being an outspoken free trader and having acted as the Parliament's rapporteur during the Mandelson reform, Fjellner was expected to favour import interests. However, stemming from the EPP faction it was felt that he might also be caught by the group's discipline not to go too far. Based on some questions put down in a working document of late October 2013[25] and after a joint workshop and hearing with Commissioner De Gucht on 7 November 2013 in INTA, he drew up his report in November.[26] Fjellner basically rejected the LDR exceptions, but also the optimisation of review practice. He showed some sympathy for *ex officio* cases but did not find it necessary to legislate on a duty of cooperation. In the end, he only agreed with the shipping clause from the Commission, proposing to model it, however, as "real" shipping clause similar to the one under the safeguard regulation. This would mean not to set a time-limit, but to allow duty-free entry of all goods which are on transit before the imposition of provisional measures.

Fjellner's report did not even muster the support of his own group when he presented it to the INTA Committee on 28 November 2013. The Committee voted so many amendments on 21 January 2014 that not much was left from the rapporteur's handwriting. Feeling outvoted, he then went to the Plenary which debated the issues on 4 February 2014 and voted on the next day. Against Fjellner's expectations, the Plenary confirmed and in some cases even went further than those INTA amendments. Some Plenary amendments openly favoured producing interests and may have been influenced by a perceived need of certain MEPs to show sympathy for industry ahead of the elections. The Plenary also tasked INTA to enter into trilogues with the other two institutions. However, in the absence of Council position the rapporteur brought the file back to the last plenary session of the Parliament in April 2014. The Parliament has thus taken its official position in the first reading which can be summarised briefly as follows.

[25] Working Document of 29 October 2013 on the Commission proposal, PE 522.838v01-00, available at http://www.europarl.europa.eu/meetdocs/2009_2014/documents/inta/dv/1008119_/1008119_en.pdf.

[26] Draft Report on the Commission proposal, PE 2013/0103(COD) of 11.11.2013, available at http://www.europarl.europa.eu/sides/getDoc.do?pubRef=-//EP//NONSGML+COMPARL+PE-522.895+01+DOC+PDF+V0//EN&language=EN.

Transparency and Predictability

On transparency and predictability, the Parliament unsettles the balance of the Commission proposal with the outright deletion of the shipping clause. Probably inspired by the *Solar Panels* case, it also pleads in favour of a duty to consult EU industry before accepting an undertaking offer from exporters. More reasonably, it proposes to recognise the role of the Hearing Officer, whose terms of reference are currently laid down in a decision of the Commission President[27] (only), in the Basic Regulation. To increase transparency, the Parliament also wishes to allow for a web-based access to the non-confidential file.

Fight Against Retaliation

The Parliament accepted in principle the Commission's second item, namely the need to fight against retaliation. However, when it comes to giving hands and feet to the idea, it falls short of strengthening the Commission powers: under the Parliament's text, the Commission cannot oblige a company to cooperate in an ex-officio case, but only issue a request to cooperate. Small enterprises would even be exempt from such a request. Some MEPs might have had the pending Telecoms case in mind when going over this item. In May 2013, the Commission had taken a decision of principle to launch an anti-dumping and an anti-subsidy investigation on mobile networks from China. However, the Brussels administration had also decided not to activate this decision immediately in order to negotiate with the Chinese government with a view to finding a friendly settlement. Interestingly, none of the three European telecom providers openly supported the action, while one even said in public that it would not cooperate in such an investigation. Clearly, the same company also tried to convince certain MEPs that a future duty of cooperation would endanger its position on that case, fearing that it would lose market share in China. In March 2014, the Commission publicly declared that it will not pursue the anti-dumping side of the case, while the countervailing investigation can still be opened if discussions with the Chinese side on this point were to prove unsuccessful.[28] Finally, in the Joint Committee meeting of 18 October 2014, China and the EU settled the entire case, leading to the abrogation of the decision of principel.[29] It remains to be seen how this development will influence the discussion on the modernisation proposal when it comes to the fight against retaliation.

---

[27] Decision of the President of the European Commission of 29 February 2012 on the function and terms of reference of the hearing officer in certain trade proceedings, [2012] OJ L 107/5.

[28] Commission Press Release, IP/14/339 of 27 March 2014, available at http://europa.eu/rapid/press-release_IP-14-339_en.htm?locale=en.

[29] Commission Press Release, IP/14/1182 of 20 October 2014, available at http://europa.eu/rapid/press-release_IP-14-1182_en.htm?locale=en.

Effectiveness and Enforcement

The key changes concern the lesser duty rule on the third item (effectiveness and enforcement). Carried by a majority of socialist, green and some conservative MEPs, Parliament asks to enlarge the scope of LDR exemptions considerably. In the future, the EU should not apply LDR when a case shows that key international labour or environmental norms are not respected in the third country, when the third country interferes with, for example, exchange rates or where the complaining EU industry consists of SMEs. These amendments raise legal doubts on the WTO front: could the Commission apply LDR towards one country, but deny it to another one on environmental or labour reasons without infringing the fundamental duty of equal treatment? How can TDI investigations show that certain labour or environmental standards have a direct influence on domestic or export prices? Moreover, they are politically not astute, as it would politicise TDI and cause heavy friction with third countries which may resent that their environmental and social policy is tackled by unilateral trade defence measures. These amendments thus carry the risk to turn TDI into a political tool, which was exactly the opposite of the modernisation objective. Whereas they are likely to be resisted by the Commission and the Council, the Parliament at least provides a useful definition of the LDR exception for structural raw material distortions.

Optimising Review Practice

Following Fjellner's questionable choice, the Parliament also does away with the proposal for reimbursement of duties for expiry reviews that do not lead to a renewal of measures. Without giving any reason why it is fair to keep duties collected without a proper justification, the Parliament simply maintains the status quo. Some advance the argument that "extra year" of protection of the industry compensates for the fact that it lasts at least 9 months after the complaint to get the first provisional protection. This, again, is a pure economic argument which runs against the legal consideration that the imposition of a duty should be based on the proper application of the law by an administration bound by it and not be achieved by a simple allegation from a private complainant.

Codification and Other Issues

Finally, while accepting the Commission's codification proposals, the Parliament also introduces a number of additional topics. It wishes to apply trade defence measures also in offshore platforms in the Exclusive Economic Zone and stresses the need for improved SME support. Procedurally, Parliament aims to establish a legal basis for Commission guidelines, and—importantly—wishes to cut down the time limit for provisional measures from 9 to 6 months. Moreover, in its view, the overall duration of an investigation should be shortened from 15 to 12 months. While appearing as a measure of making TDI more efficient at first sight, such a proposal risks undermining the quality of the EU's TDI procedure. Shortening the available time for the staff (which is already under strain following the cut of administrative expenditure in the Commission of 5 % in the coming years), would simply mean that crucial steps of quality control, such as on-the-spot visits prior to provisional measures would have to be abolished as well. This in turn, only makes provisional measures much more prone to faults, which could be attacked in court and thus does not help EU industry at all. A similarly "good" but probably not well thought through idea is the proposal to grant the right to submit complaints to trade unions, which even the trade unions themselves have not made. Such a right only makes sense, if the worker's representation wishes to bring a case against the will of the company's board. In such a scenario, a complaint is unlikely to contain all the necessary data on the injury side which the Commission needs to mount a successful case. So, in the end, giving a right to trade unions may make serve good election purposes for some MEPs, but it would not make a difference on the ground.

Assessment

In sum, the Parliament significantly changes the balance of the Commission proposal. Doing away with two important features interesting for importers (the shipping clause and re-imbursement of duties) and broadening the scope for LDR exceptions in a dramatic way can only receive applause from EU industry and some protectionist Member States. The EP position must thus be seen as largely tactical and—to a certain degree—adopted in pre-election mood. It will not facilitate the early adoption of the package, unless the next Parliament is ready to enter trilogue negotiations with a constructive position that focusses on amendments to the Commission proposal which are feasible and sound.

The Council Position

In parallel, the Commission discussed its legislative proposal with the Trade Questions Working Group of the Council. However, in contrast to the Parliament, the Council was unable to mandate the Presidency entering into substance with the two other institutions before the dissolution of the Parliament in May 2014. The old divisions between the free trade camp led by the United Kingdom, Sweden and the Netherlands on the one hand, and the more protectionist camp around France and Italy re-appeared. Moreover, the middle-grounders did not engage actively enough to bring about a Council mandate in time, arguing that the file does not demand particular urgency.

Moreover, the Council was sceptical about the Commission's intention to publish the four guidelines in summer 2014. In particular, some Member States led by France felt that two points in the draft Guidelines were too 'liberal' and needed counter-balancing.

First, they took issue with the Commission's wish to state that the notion of "Union interest" in Article 21 of the Basic Regulation allows taking into account other policy interests, if they have a demonstrable impact on the case. That point was already put in practice in the *Solar Panels* case, where the Commission verified whether the imposition of provisional duties would impede the fulfilment of the EU's Agenda 2020 goals on renewable energy.[30] While it is perfectly legal to recall this possibility in the guidelines, southern Member States saw this as an inopportune political attempt to broaden the scope of the Union interest test. Second, they also took issue with the observation in the draft guidelines that measures are regularly adopted for 5 years, but may be shorter in exceptional circumstances. Again, while the Commission can quote good precedent for this proposition,[31] the mere fact of mentioning 'exceptional cases' in a general guideline for Commission practice did not go down well with all members of the Council.

Accordingly, the Council asked the Commission to postpone publishing of the guidelines, echoing the position of the Parliament in this regard. While Commissioner De Gucht was not convinced of the substantive arguments against his draft guidelines, the Barroso Commission nevertheless conceded this procedural point. It thus left office at the end of October 2014 without adopting the controversial guidelines, thereby inviting the other two institutions to complete their work on the legislative proposal first. Nevertheless, and despite serious attempts of the Italian Presidency until the end of that year, the Council could not make progress on the draft legislation.

Conclusion

Seen from a distance, it appears that the second TDI reform proposal in the European Union after the Uruguay Round has again failed. Parliament dissolved in May 2014 and the Basic Regulations still stand where they basically were since 1994. Is TDI reform hence inherently a mission impossible in Europe?

[30] Commission Regulation (EU) No 513/2013 of 4 June 2013, [2013] OJ L 152/5, Recitals 257–259.

[31] Council Regulation (EC) No 1472/2006 of 5 October 2006 (*Footwear—China and Vietnam*), [2006] OJ L 275/1, Recital 326; Council Regulation (EC) No 261/2008 of 17 March 2008 (*certain compressors—China*), [2008] OJ L 181/1, Recital 143.

I do not think so. When compared with Mandelson's aborted green paper on TDI reform of 2006–2007, De Gucht's modernisation proposal of 2013 has already come quite far. Stakeholders did not attempt to "shoot it down", but generally accepted its careful preparation. Clearly, in the process, tactical positioning is inevitable. As argued in the previous sections, all the three institutions have followed their own rationale so far. In my view, the Commission put a moderate and balanced proposal on the table, which is sufficiently interesting for all sides to get "something" out of it. Parliament has understood the logic and shifted the balance in favour of EU industry in pre-election mood. Council in return will have to see the more long-term implications of some proposals and re-adjust. In my best guess at the time of writing, the mission will become possible when a narrow LDR exception and a reasonable acceleration of the procedures is combined with a meaningful shipping clause, a tame duty to cooperate in *ex officio* cases and some more transparency. This will still be more "pro-industry" legislation than the original Commission proposal, but it might be just pragmatic enough to satisfy all stakeholders. If all this happens under the mandate of De Gucht's successor, Commissioner Malmström, that would certainly constitute a good ex-post rounding-up of a largely successful performance at the helm of DG Trade from the Flemish liberal when it comes to steering the European Union's trade defence instruments. The chances may be slim, but they are still alive.

References

Alexander Graf Lambsdorff, Abschied von Horst Günter Krenzler, ELDE – Liberale Depesche 4/2012

De Bièvre D, Eckard J (2011) Interest groups and EU anti-dumping policy. J Eur Public Policy 18:3

Herrmann C, Michl W (2008) Grundzüge des Europäischen Wirtschaftsrechts, ZEuS 5

Hoffmeister F (2013) Aktuelle Rechtsfragen in der Praxis der europäischen Außenhandelspolitik, ZEuS 16

Hoffmeister F (2014) The deep and comprehensive free trade agreements of the European Union – concept and challenges. In: Cremona M, Takács T (eds) Trade liberalisation and standardisation – new directions in the 'low politics' of EU foreign policy. EUI Working Paper AEL 2014/1

Müller W, Khan N, Scharf T (2009) EC- and WTO anti-dumping law – a handbook, 2nd edn

Tietje C (2009) Die Gemeinsame Handelspolitik der EU im System des Welthandelsrechts: Ein Spannungsverhältnis zwischen fortschreitender Liberalisierung und zunehmendem Protektionismus. In: Pache E, Schorkopf F (eds) Die Europäische Union nach Lissabon

Price Undertakings in Anti-dumping Law: Recent Trends and Considerations from a Competition Law Perspective

Frank Montag

Introduction

Over his career in the European Commission's Directorate-General for External Affairs, the predecessor of what is now the Directorate-General for Trade and the European External Action Service, Horst Krenzler dealt extensively with trade defence and anti-dumping issues. This was when the author first came across him. This contact was the basis for Horst Krenzler joining the international law firm Freshfields Bruckhaus Deringer as an of counsel, after his tenure at the European Commission. During this time, the author had the pleasure of working together with Horst Krenzler on public international law, trade defence and competition law related issues. The interplay between trade defence and competition law has traditionally been hotly debated in the literature, and has recently become topical again as a result of the high profile investigation by the European Commission into dumping of solar panels from China. This article will examine the current status of this debate with a particular focus on price undertakings.

It has been extensively reported in the literature[1] that anti-dumping regulation has become a widespread tool used by both developed and developing countries aimed at—some say—protecting domestic producers against unfair practices in

The author is most grateful to his colleague Tone Oeyen, associate in the Brussels office of Freshfields Bruckhaus Deringer, for his valuable assistance in the preparation of this article.

[1] See e.g. Zanardi (2005), p. 1.

F. Montag (✉)
Freshfields Bruckhaus Deringer LLP, Bastion Tower, Place du Champ de Mars/Marsveldplein, 5, 1050 Bruxelles, Belgium
e-mail: frank.montag@freshfields.com

C. Herrmann et al. (eds.), *Trade Policy between Law, Diplomacy and Scholarship*, European Yearbook of International Economic Law,
DOI 10.1007/978-3-319-15690-3_21

international trade[2] or—according to others—as a weapon of protectionism lacking sound economic foundation.[3] A particular focus in the literature[4] has been the interaction between anti-dumping and competition law. Economists seem to agree that anti-dumping law interferes with the pursuit of the goals of competition law: whereas the final goal of competition law is commonly described as promoting consumer welfare and productive efficiency, the aim of the anti-dumping rules is to offer domestic industry protection against international price discrimination perceived as "unfair" if certain conditions laid down by the law are met, thereby effectively prohibiting low(er) cost foreign suppliers from participating in the domestic market. It has even been reported that the anti-dumping rules have been used by domestic producers to facilitate cartelisation on the domestic market by fencing it off from international competition.[5]

The purpose of this article is not to contribute to the debate on the conceptual tensions between anti-dumping and competition law. Rather, the focus is on a particular form of relief that is available under the anti-dumping rules and on the competition law questions that can arise in that context. Price undertakings are alternatives to the imposition of anti-dumping duties.[6] The European Commission has a long track record in reaching what can be described as an "amicable solution" to an anti-dumping investigation, i.e. accepting undertakings by exporters not to sell their products below a minimum export price.[7]

The article summarises the legal framework applicable to price undertakings and gives an overview of the pros and cons of price undertakings compared to *ad valorem* dumping duties. It describes the evolution in the European Commission's decisional practice before discussing how the determination of an appropriate minimum price and the monitoring of price undertakings may raise concerns from a competition law perspective. The article concludes with a description of the Commission's investigation into dumping of solar panels and the acceptance of a joint price undertaking offered by the Chinese exporters.

---

[2] This is the traditional view of the European Commission; see e.g. Commission Regulation (EC) No 1748/95 of 17 July 1995, *Peroxodisulphates (persulphates) from China*, [1995] OJ L 169/15.

[3] See e.g. McGee (1996), p. 87.

[4] See e.g. Pierce (1999–2000), p. 26; Vermulst (1999).

[5] See e.g. Pierce (1999–2000), p. 26; Messerlin (1990), p. 465.

[6] See below for an overview of the legal framework applicable to price undertakings under the WTO/GATT Anti-Dumping Agreement and the EU Basic Anti-Dumping Regulation.

[7] E.g. Commission Decision 81/663/EEC of 24 August 1981, *Potato granules from Canada*, [1981] OJ L 243/16; Council Regulation (EEC) No 228/85 of 29 January 1985, *Oxalic acid from Brazil*, [1985] OJ L 26/6; Commission Regulation (EEC) No 2800/86 of 9 September 1986, *Deep freezers from USSR*, [1986] OJ L 259/14; Commission Decision 2000/523/EC of 10 August 2000, *Certain malleable cast iron tube or pipe fittings from Brazil, Croatia, Czech Republic, Yugoslavia, Japan, China, Korea, Thailand*, [2000] OJ L 208/ 53; Commission Decision 1758/2000/ECSC of 9 August 2000, *Certain hot-rolled flat products of non-alloy steel from China, India, Romania*, [2000] OJ L 202/ 21; Commission Decision 2004/600/EC of 4 August 2004, *Polyethylene terephthalate from Australia*, [2004] OJ L 271/38; Commission Decision 2005/802/EC of 17 October 2005, *Potassium chloride from Russia*, [2005] OJ L 302/79; Commission Decision 2005/613/EC of 18 July 2005, *Polyester staple fibre from Saudi Arabia*, [2005] OJ L 211/20.

Price Undertakings Under Anti-dumping Law

Price undertakings can be described as "a form of anti-dumping measure whereby an exporting producer undertakes to increase its export prices of the product concerned to the Union to non-dumped or non-injurious levels."[8]

Applicable Legal Framework

The WTO/GATT Anti-Dumping Agreement (ADA)[9] foresees three types of anti-dumping measures: (1) provisional measures, (2) price undertakings and (3) definitive anti-dumping duties. Article 8 ADA provides that:

> Proceedings may be suspended or terminated without the imposition of provisional measures or anti-dumping duties upon receipt of satisfactory voluntary undertakings from any exporter to revise its prices or to cease exports to the area in question at dumped prices so that the authorities are satisfied that the injurious effect of the dumping is eliminated.

The possibility for an authority to accept price undertakings from (mainly) exporters has been implemented in Article 8 of the EU's basic anti-dumping regulation (EU ADR),[10] which largely mirrors the text of Article 8 ADA.

According to the ADA and EU ADR, a price undertaking can only be accepted once the authorities have made a preliminary affirmative determination of dumping, injury, and causation between dumping and injury. Negotiations about a price undertaking can be started at the initiative of the authorities or exporters. The only condition for an undertaking to be acceptable is that the authority must be satisfied that the undertaking eliminates the injurious effect of the dumping. The authorities however have significant discretion in deciding whether or not to accept exporters' undertakings offer. A price undertaking offer can be rejected by the authority when "*their acceptance is impractical*" or "*for other reasons, including reasons of general policy*". Exporters on the other hand can also not be forced to enter into a price undertaking. The European Courts have confirmed the wide margin of discretion the European Commission enjoys in accepting or rejecting price undertaking offers[11]:

> No provision of the basic regulation requires the institutions to accept undertakings which are offered by economic operators who are the subject of an investigation prior to the

---

[8] Van Bael and Bellis (2011), p. 420.

[9] WTO Agreement on the Implementation of Article VI of the GATT 1994, commonly referred to as the Anti-Dumping Agreement, [1994] OJ L 336/103.

[10] Council Regulation (EC) No 1225/2009 of 30 November 2009 on protection against dumped imports from countries not members of the European Community, [2009] OJ L 343/51.

[11] This has also been confirmed by the WTO Dispute Settlement Body, see WTO Panel Report, *US—Continued Dumping and Subsidy Offset Act of 2000*, WT/DS217/R and WT/DS234/R, para. 7.81.

> imposition of anti-dumping duties. On the contrary, it is clear from Article 10 of that regulation [Article 8 EU ADR] that it is for the institutions, in the exercise of their discretion, to decide whether such undertakings are acceptable. It is not open to the Court to find fault with a rejection of offers of undertakings, which was issued after individual examination and was accompanied by a statement of reasons which satisfies the requirements of Article 190 of the Treaty, where the grounds on which that rejection is based do not exceed the margin of discretion conferred on the institutions (Case C-240/84, *NTN Toyo Bearing and Others v Council*, [1987] ECR, 1809, paragraphs 30 to 34).[12]

The Commission has in the past indeed rejected price undertaking offers on different grounds, including concerns regarding the lack of effective monitoring (and associated risks of circumvention of the undertaking), the breach by exporters of previous undertakings, high volatility of prices, the risk of cross-compensation of prices etc.[13] On a few occasions, the Commission explicitly motivated the rejection of a price undertaking offer on the basis of its likely anti-competitive effects.[14]

Pros and Cons of Price Undertakings Versus Dumping Duties

Exporting producers have an obvious incentive to convince the authorities to accept a price undertaking by way of an alternative to imposing anti-dumping duties, as they directly benefit from the additional revenue resulting from the increased price. Anti-dumping duties on the other hand result in higher import prices without increased revenues for the exporter. Some authors have also argued that the prospect of increased revenues in the event of a price undertaking creates an incentive for exporters to invest in other, non-price aspects of their products.[15] Another advantage of undertakings is that they can be revised and terminated at short notice[16] and therefore provide greater flexibility than duties which, in principle, remain in force for at least 5 years. Accepting undertakings is sometimes also regarded as being easier or less costly for the investigating authority.

The main drawback of price undertakings—which has indeed been frequently used as a justification by the Commission for not accepting a price undertaking offer—is that they impose a high burden on the authority and/or the domestic industry to monitor compliance by the exporting producers. In addition, an exporting producer will need to ensure that his trading activities do not fall foul of the obligations agreed to in the context of the price undertaking with an authority in a foreign country. These monitoring obligations unavoidably result in additional costs for the parties involved.

[12] ECJ, T-97/95, *Sinochem v Council*, [1998] ECR II, 85, para. 119. See also ECJ, T-249/06, *Interpipe Niko Tube and Interpipe NTRP v Council*, [2009] ECR II, 383, para. 226 and 228.

[13] For a comprehensive overview of grounds on the basis of which the Commission has rejected undertakings in the past, please refer to Van Bael and Bellis (2011), pp. 424 et seq.

[14] See below for further details.

[15] Stegemann (1990), p. 268 (294).

[16] Undertakings usually contain a revision clause which facilitates a modification of an undertaking in the event of changed circumstances.

More conceptually, there seems to be an inherent tension between the concept of a price undertaking, which effectively sets a minimum price level for exporters, and competition law, the goal of which is to enhance welfare by stimulating price competition. It could therefore be argued that a drawback of price undertakings is that they increase the level of price transparency on the market and, in a worse scenario, are used as a conduit for the exchange of competitively sensitive information or even the creation of a price cartel.[17]

The Commission itself indicates that, in order to avoid any restriction of competition, the content of price undertakings is not made public.[18] Indeed, the text of a price undertaking is not published in the EU's Official Journal. The Commission decisions accepting price undertakings only contain high level information about the (appropriateness of the) price undertaking and do not disclose the core terms of the undertaking, e.g. the minimum price.

Evolution in the Commission's Practice Regarding Price Undertakings: "An Instrument of the Past?"

An analysis of the European Commission's decisional practice shows that the number of dumping investigations which are concluded with the acceptance by the Commission of a price undertaking has drastically fallen in recent years. In 2013,[19] the Commission imposed definitive anti-dumping duties in 12 cases, whereas it accepted a price undertaking offer by exporters in one (high profile) case (*Solar Panels*).[20] In 2012,[21] the Commission imposed definitive anti-dumping

---

[17] See below for further details.

[18] See the description of the types of trade defence measures available at http://ec.europa.eu/trade/policy/accessing-markets/trade-defence/actions-against-imports-into-the-eu/.

[19] European Commission (2013).

[20] The 2013 Commission statistics (Annex M) refers to two cases in which a price undertaking was accepted. However, for the purpose of this contribution, these cases have been treated as a single case, as they both relate to the anti-dumping proceeding concerning imports of crystalline silicon photovoltaic modules and key components originating in or consigned from the People's Republic of China. By a decision of 2 August 2013, the Commission accepted the exporters' initial price undertaking offer (see Commission Decision 2013/423/EU of 2 August 2013 accepting an undertaking offered in connection with the anti-dumping proceeding concerning imports of crystalline silicon photovoltaic modules and key components originating in or consigned from the People's Republic of China, [2013] OJ L 209/26). By a decision of 4 December 2013, the Commission accepted the exporters' amended price undertaking offer, following the termination of the dumping investigation confirming the provisional findings of injurious dumping and imposing definitive anti-dumping duties (see Commission Implementing Decision 2013/707 of 4 December 2013 confirming the acceptance of an undertaking offered in connection with the anti-dumping and anti-subsidy proceedings concerning imports of crystalline silicon photovoltaic modules and key components originating in or consigned from the People's Republic of China for the period of application of definitive measures, [2013] OJ L 235/214).

[21] European Commission (2012).

duties in two cases and not a single case was concluded with the acceptance of a price undertaking. The 2012 and 2013 statistics confirm a trend in the Commission's decisional practice of refraining from the acceptance of price undertakings and imposing more anti-dumping duties.

This trend has indeed been confirmed in a recent study by Armin Steinbach, which analyses, on the basis of the statistics published by DG Trade, the use of price undertakings—as opposed to the imposition of dumping duties—to settle anti-dumping proceedings in the EU in the period 2002–2012.[22] Steinbach reports that the frequency of price undertakings has decreased significantly from an average of more than 40 % of cases between 1981 and 2001, to 21 % during the period from 2002 until 2012. This average has declined further during the past years, as DG Trade's statistics show that since 2010, between 0 and 15 % of investigations resulting in the finding of dumping were concluded by means of a price undertaking.

According to Steinbach, different factors have played a role in this evolution. A first factor is the accession of Central and Eastern European countries to the EU in May 2004.[23] Following the 1994 European Council declaration of Essen, price undertakings became the Commission's preferred tool to remedy dumping from Central and Eastern European countries and Turkey.[24] Upon entering the EU, trade defence proceedings involving imports originating in these countries were no longer possible, as the CEE countries entered the single market and the common customs union. The increase in anti-dumping investigations against Chinese exports has, according to Steinbach, also had a negative impact on the frequency of use of price undertakings, as the Commission's decisional practice shows that price undertakings offered by Chinese exporters are only very rarely accepted. Concerns in relation to the ability to ensure effective monitoring of the undertakings, e.g. via certain guarantees offered by the authorities of the exporting country, are often also a reason to reject a price undertaking offer.[25] The recent acceptance by the Commission of a joint price undertaking offered by Chinese exporters in the solar panel case seems to be a remarkable exception to the general trend.

[22] Steinbach (2004), p. 165. Steinbach compares his findings to the empirical evaluations by Messerlin (1989), Moore (2005) and Zanardi (2004). See Messerlin (1989), p. 563; Moore (2005), p. 298; Zanardi (2004), p. 403.

[23] Rovegno and Vandenbussche also confirm that the use of price undertakings in the EU has decreased steadily in favour of duties over the past years and that this may be related to a shift in the countries being targeted by anti-dumping petitions, see Rovegno and Vandenbussche (2011).

[24] Van Bael and Bellis (2011), p. 421.

[25] See e.g. European Commission, *Certain prepared or preserved citrus fruits from China*, [2008] OJ L 350/35, para. 72.

Price Undertakings from a Competition Law Perspective

A price undertaking is usually described as a unilateral commitment by an exporter to increase its export prices to the EU.[26] Given their inherent unilateral nature, authors have therefore considered that price undertakings are not captured by Article 101 of the Treaty on the Functioning of the European Union (TFEU), which applies to the (anti-competitive) conduct of at least two undertakings.[27] This commonly accepted view has, however, been superseded by the Commission's recent acceptance of a price undertaking *jointly* offered by a group of cooperating Chinese exporters in the *Solar Panels* case.

Despite their (in principle) unilateral nature, the effects of price undertakings offered in the context of a trade defence investigation are inherently contradictory to the objectives pursued by competition law. Whereas one of the core objectives of competition law is the promotion of consumer welfare via the stimulation and protection of price competition, price undertakings lead to a high degree of price transparency on the importing country's market and often create a *de facto* fixed minimum price adhered to by exporters and possibly the domestic industry. Some have even argued that price undertakings "in fact establish Government-sponsored cartels"[28] and lead to "*de facto* private price or quantity agreements between foreign and EC firms".[29]

In the following sections, we will elaborate on the issue of information exchanges in the context of agreeing and implementing a price undertaking and on the increased level of price transparency on the domestic market resulting from the acceptance of a price undertaking.

Exchanges of Competitively Sensitive Information: A Conditio Sine Qua Non for a Price Undertaking?

The exchange of commercially sensitive pricing information in the context of price undertakings may occur at two stages: (1) when determining a minimum price which is acceptable for the investigating authority, and (2) when monitoring compliance with the price undertaking by the exporters.

[26] Van Bael and Bellis (2011), p. 433.

[27] Steinbach (2004), p. 165 (181); Perone (1995), p. 41.

[28] Vermulst (1987), p. 220.

[29] Messerlin (1989), p. 563 (568, 570, 578, 586).

The Determination of an Acceptable Minimum Price

Although, as indicated, a price undertaking usually takes the form of a unilateral statement by an exporter filed with the Commission, in order for the price undertaking to be workable in practice, the price increases the exporters are willing to agree upon should be more or less aligned.[30] This inevitably requires exporters to coordinate and discuss commercially sensitive information.

In the same vein, although they are officially not consulted by the Commission in the context of price undertaking negotiations, it seems plausible that the complaining domestic industry engages in discussions in relation to the minimum price increase exporters should agree to when offering a price undertaking.

It is clear that these (hypothetical) contacts among and between exporters and the complaining domestic industry would at the very least raise eyebrows should they occur outside the context of a price undertaking negotiation. As far as we are aware, until today, the exchanges of competitively sensitive information in the context of a price undertaking have not yet been scrutinised from a competition law perspective by a competition authority.[31]

In this context it is worthwhile referring, by way of analogy, to the case law of the European Court of Justice on Article 4(3) of the Treaty on the European Union (TEU) and the competition law rules. Article 4(3) TEU imposes an obligation on Member States to assist each other in carrying out tasks which flow from the Treaties, to take all appropriate measures to ensure fulfilment of the obligations arising out of the Treaties and to refrain from any measure which could jeopardise the attainment of the EU's objectives. The Court of Justice has concluded that a Member State can infringe Article 4(3) TEU in conjunction with Article 101 TFEU by maintaining in force legislation which can deprive the competition rules of their effectiveness.[32] Applying this so called *INNO doctrine*, the Court ruled on several occasions that by taking legislative or regulatory measures which effectively require or reinforce an anti-competitive agreement between private undertakings, a Member State infringes its obligations under Article 4(3) TEU.[33] It could be argued that in a hypothetical scenario where Member States have the power to investigate dumping, a Member State would violate its obligations under Article 4 (3) TEU in conjunction with Article 101 TFEU when accepting a price undertaking which goes beyond a unilateral commitment from an exporter and reflects the outcome of discussions between exporters (and possibly the domestic industry) on an appropriate minimum price level. In reality, Member States do not have

[30] Van Bael and Bellis (2011), p. 433.

[31] Van Bael and Bellis (2011), p. 434.

[32] ECJ, C-13/77, *INNO v Association des détaillants en tabac*, [1977] ECR, 2115.

[33] See e.g. ECJ, C-136/86, *BNIC v Yves Aubert*, [1987] ECR, 4789; ECJ, C-311/85, *Vlaamse Reisbureaus v Sociale Dienst*, [1987] ECR, 3801; ECJ, C-66/86, *Ahmed Saeed Flugreisen v Zentrale zur Bekämpfung Unlauteren Wettbewerbs e.V.*, [1989] ECR, 803. Note however that challenges on the basis of Article 4(3) TEU to national legislation where the final determination of prices remained with the Member State have failed, see Whish (2012), p. 220.

competence in the field of trade defence and the European Commission may consider that it is not bound by the duty of sincere cooperation laid down in Article 4(3) TEU.

Monitoring Compliance with the Minimum Price

Compliance with price undertakings is monitored both publicly by the Commission, as well as privately by the domestic industry and the exporting producers.

A price undertaking generally contains provisions regarding monitoring and reporting of the undertaking, according to which exporters are required to submit sales volumes and pricing information for exports of the products covered by the undertaking. The Commission will generally also foresee an explicit right to conduct inspection visits at the premises of the exporters. The frequent use of price undertakings in the past put a heavy burden on the Commission's scarce resources and this has resulted in criticism of the Commission for not taking monitoring of exporters' adherence to their price undertakings seriously.[34] The significant drop in the use of price undertakings in recent years should have positively impacted on the availability of monitoring resources and it seems therefore reasonable to assume that the Commission is serious about monitoring compliance in the—relatively limited number of—cases which result in the acceptance of a price undertaking.

The domestic industry and the exporting producers each have their own reasons to individually monitor compliance with a price undertaking. Exporters will want to ensure that they are not foregoing sales and the increased revenues which result from the price undertaking as a result of maverick exporters who undercut the minimum price of the price undertaking or use non-price incentives to increase their sales. The domestic industry has a clear interest in taking measures aimed at monitoring a price undertaking agreed to by exporters, independently of the public monitoring carried out by the Commission, as they will want to be certain that the price undertaking is adhered to. It has also been argued that, given the often limited market transparency, it may even be required for the domestic industry and the exporters bound by a price undertaking to communicate directly in order to clarify misunderstandings which may arise during the implementation of the price undertaking.[35]

It seems doubtful however that, even in the past when there was a lack of public monitoring and enforcement of price undertakings, a (perceived) lack of enforcement could justify collusive behaviour in private monitoring between competitors, domestic producers and/or exporters, which falls foul of the obligations under the competition laws.

---

[34] Stegemann (1990), p. 278. Stegemann refers to European Court of Auditors' annual report for 1987, which confirmed and criticised the lack of public monitoring of accepted price undertakings.

[35] Stegemann (1990), p. 278.

Competition Law Compliance

Although the risk of competition law enforcement seems relatively limited, competitors should be aware that when they discuss prices or other types of commercially sensitive information in the context of offering or implementing a price undertaking in an anti-dumping investigation, the fact that their discussions take place in a—at first sight—legitimate context, does in principle not shield them from the application of the competition law rules.

From a compliance perspective, it would thus seem important for a company that the boundaries of price undertaking discussions are defined upfront and that appropriate consideration is given to the restrictions arising from the competition law rules during any type of contact with competitors.

Increased Price Transparency and Reduction of Price Competition in the Market?

Although the details of a price undertaking offered by exporters in the context of an anti-dumping investigation are not published by the Commission, in practice, it can be assumed, especially in oligopolistic markets, that the domestic industry will become quickly aware of the minimum prices agreed to by the foreign exporters, as customers often disclose competitor prices when conducting price negotiations with suppliers. In such a scenario, a minimum price agreed to in the context of a price undertaking could easily become a reference price for the entire market and thereby reduce or exclude price competition. This risk seems particularly high in markets which are dominated by a few large competitors.[36] It is clear that such a scenario would be problematic from a competition law perspective. It has even been suggested that it might infringe Article 101 TFEU for a trade association representing the (complaining) EU industry to try to discover the minimum price agreed to by exporters in the context of a price undertaking.[37]

In a limited number of cases, involving oligopolistic markets, the Commission has indeed explicitly referred to the likely anti-competitive effects as a justification for not accepting a price undertaking. The underlying rationale for rejecting a price undertaking in each of these cases was that price differences continue to exist after the imposition of an *ad valorem* dumping duty.

In *Glycine*,[38] the Commission argued that "it was considered not to be in the Community's interest to accept the undertakings offered because of the effect these price undertakings could have in this case on the competitive situation and structure

[36] Steinbach (2014), p. 183.

[37] Lang (1987), p. 590 (606).

[38] Council Regulation (EEC) No 2322/85 of 12 August 1985, *Glycine from Japan*, [1985] OJ L 218/1.

of the glycine market", on which only a limited number of competitors were active. The Commission specified that "in a market where only a limited number of companies are competing with each other an alignment of prices resulting from undertakings of the kind offered by the Japanese companies, i.e. to respect the same minimum price, would reduce competition".

More than a decade later, the Commission used a similar argument in *Polysulphide Polymers*[39] to reject a price undertaking offered by a US exporter of PSP, arguing that "given the duopolistic supply structure of the Community market, price undertakings are not appropriate". The Commission also justified the rejection of the price undertaking as it would not have removed the Community injury and would have resulted in monitoring issues.

The oligopolistic nature of the European market (on the demand side) was also used by the Commission in *Manganese Dioxides*[40] in 2008 as a justification for rejecting a price undertaking offer by the South African exporter of electrolytic manganese dioxides (EMD), a product used in the production of consumer batteries:

> as there is only a limited number of EMD buyers in the Community market, there is a risk that any measure based on a minimum price could become a reference price on the market and thereby reduce competition, which would not be in the Community interest.

It is unclear how the above cited cases, in which the Commission rejected a price undertaking offer on the basis of competition policy considerations, differ from other cases where the Commission accepted price undertakings from the exporting producers in relation to oligopolistic markets. Some argue that the Commission's reluctance to take into account competition policy considerations in the context of anti-dumping proceedings, is related to its long-established policy of favouring the interests of Community industry over the interests of consumers.[41]

Solar Panels

For several reasons, which go beyond the high profile and political nature of the case, it seems appropriate to discuss the Commission's investigation into imports of crystalline silicon photovoltaic modules and their key components. The Commission's anti-subsidy and anti-dumping investigations in this case came to an end in December 2013, with the acceptance by the Commission of a price undertaking and the imposition of final anti-dumping and countervailing duties for exports which do not meet the conditions set out in the undertaking.

---

[39] Council Regulation (EC) No 1965/98 of 9 September 1998, *Polysulphide polymers from USA*, [1998] OJ L 255/1, para. 56.

[40] Council Regulation (EC) No 221/2008 of 10 March 2008, *Manganese Dioxides from South Africa*, [2008] OJ L 69/1.

[41] Perone (1995), p. 42; Steinbach (2014), p. 165 (183).

Procedural History of the Case

In September 2012, the Commission launched an anti-dumping investigation into imports of solar panels and their key components originating in China, in response to a complaint lodged by EU Pro Sun, an association representing more than 20 European producers of solar panels and their components.[42] Two months later, in November 2012, the Commission opened a parallel anti-subsidy investigation concerning the same products.[43]

In June 2013, after a 9 month investigation into alleged dumping, the Commission imposed provisional anti-dumping duties on imports of solar panels, cells and wafers from China. It thereby adopted a so-called "phased approach", according to which an initial dumping rate of 11.8 % was applied during the first 2 months, after which a higher (average) rate of 47.6 % was applied for the remainder of the investigation period. The phased approach was, according to the Commission, required: "*in view of the exceptional circumstances and, in particular, the need to ensure the stability of supply in the short term*", as "*a period with a lower duty will ensure sufficient supply to meet all the demand, while allowing the Union industry to adapt to the situation and increase the supply gradually*".[44]

In practice, the lower initial provisional duty was part of a broader intention of the Commission to reach an amicable solution to the solar panel trade dispute in accordance with Article 8 EU ADR, i.e. agree to a price undertaking offered by the Chinese exporters. Indeed, on 27 July 2013, Trade Commissioner De Gucht announced that the Commission was ready to accept a price undertaking offer submitted by Chinese solar panel exporters and to close the EU-China solar panel dispute on that basis.[45] Subsequently, the Commission concluded both the anti-dumping and anti-subsidy investigations in December 2013, when it confirmed the price undertaking and extended its scope to the anti-subsidy

---

[42] European Commission, Notice of Initiation of an Anti-dumping Proceeding Concerning Imports of Crystalline Silicon Photovoltaic Modules and Key Components (i.e. Cells and Wafers) Originating in the People's Republic of China, [2012] OJ C 269/ 5. With €21 billion-worth of imports of solar panels and key components for the EU coming from China, this is the most significant anti-dumping investigation by the Commission so far.

[43] European Commission, Notice of Initiation of an Anti-subsidy Proceeding Concerning Imports of Crystalline Silicon Photovoltaic Modules and Key Components (i.e. Cells and Wafers) Originating in the People's Republic of China, [2012] OJ C 340/13.

[44] European Commission, MEMO/13/497 of 4 June 2013, available at http://europa.eu/rapid/press-release_MEMO-13-497_en.htm.

[45] European Commission, MEMO/13/729 of 26 July 2013, available at http://europa.eu/rapid/press-release_MEMO-13-729_en.htm. The formal acceptance of the price undertaking is reflected in Decision 2013/423/EU of the European Commission of 2 August 2013 accepting an undertaking offered in connection with the anti-dumping proceeding concerning imports of crystalline silicon photovoltaic modules and key components (i.e. cells and wafers) originating in or consigned from the People's Republic of China, [2013] OJ L 209/26.

proceedings,[46] and in parallel, imposed definitive anti-dumping and countervailing duties.[47]

Under the agreed price undertaking, which, according to the Commission, covers approximately 75 % of Chinese solar panel exports to the EU, imports of solar panels and their key components will remain free of duty for an annual volume that covers part of the total European demand in so far as the price remains above a certain price floor. An average, residual anti-dumping duty of 47.7 % applies to imports by exporters who did not participate in the price undertaking or participating exporters who violate their terms, or to imports which exceed the annual volume determined in the undertaking.

Price Undertaking

Whereas a price undertaking in principle takes the form of a unilateral commitment by an exporter not to sell its products below a certain price floor, the undertaking in the *Solar Panels* case was offered jointly by a group of Chinese exporters. The Commission's initial decision accepting the Chinese exporters' price undertaking provides that:

> In order to ensure that the undertaking is practicable, the Chinese exporters presented a joint undertaking offer with one minimum import price for photovoltaic modules and one for each of their key components (i.e. cells and wafers).[48]

Although no details are publicly available regarding the method adopted to find a minimum import price acceptable for all exporters involved and the Commission and regarding the extent to which the Commission was involved in the negotiations between the exporters, it seems difficult to reconcile the concept of a single/joint minimum import price offer with the fundamental principles of competition law. Reaching an agreement on a single minimum price inherently seems to imply the exchange of competitively sensitive information between competing exporters.

---

[46] European Commission Implementing Decision (2013/707/EU) of 4 December 2013 confirming the acceptance of an undertaking offered in connection with the anti-dumping and anti-subsidy proceedings concerning imports of crystalline silicon photovoltaic modules and key components (i.e. cells) originating in or consigned from the People's Republic of China for the application of definitive measures, [2013] OJ L 325/1.

[47] Council Implementing Regulation (EU) No 1238/2013 of 2 December 2013 imposing definitive anti-dumping duty and collecting definitively the provisional duty imposed on imports of crystalline silicon photovoltaic modules and key components (i.e. cells) originating in or consigned from the People's Republic of China, [2013] OJ L 325/1; Council Implementing Regulation (EU) No 1239/2013 of 2 December 2013 imposing definitive countervailing duty on imports of crystalline silicon photovoltaic modules and key components (i.e. cells) originating in or consigned from the People's Republic of China, [2013] OJ L 325/66.

[48] Commission Decision (2013/423/EU) of 2 August 2013 accepting an undertaking offered in connection with the anti-dumping proceeding concerning imports of crystalline silicon photovoltaic modules and key components originating in or consigned from the People's Republic of China, [2013] OJ L 209/26, para. 5.

In addition, by implementing a single minimum import price, the risk seems higher that the minimum price becomes the reference price for the entire market, as there is no uncertainty about the price floor applicable to all exporters. One could even argue that the joint price undertaking results in a price cartel which affects around 60 %[49] of the EU solar panel market.

Based on its past practice in accepting (or rejecting) price undertakings, it would appear that the Commission's acceptance of the joint price undertaking in the *Solar Panels* case was mainly inspired by the politically high profile nature of the case and the tensions it gave rise to with the Chinese authorities. Indeed, the Commission could have easily rejected the undertaking offer in view of the high number of companies involved[50] or the high volatility in the prices[51] of the products covered by the investigation.

It is worth noting in this context that in February 2014, the German solar-panel maker SolarWorld and other solar-panel makers lodged an application to the General Court seeking the annulment of the Council Implementing Regulations of 2 December 2013 imposing definitive anti-dumping and countervailing duties and confirming the price undertaking offered by the Chinese exporters.[52] SolarWorld argues that the Commission's decision should be annulled because

[49] Around 75 % of the Chinese solar panel exports to the EU are covered by the price undertaking; Chinese solar panel manufacturers currently control 80 % of the EU solar panel market. See statement by EU Trade Commissioner Karel De Gucht on 29 July 2013 on the amicable solution in the EU-China solar panels case, European Commission, MEMO/13/730, available at http://europa.eu/rapid/press-release_MEMO-13-730_en.htm.

[50] More than 90 Chinese exporters participate in the price undertaking, see Annex to Commission Implementing Decision 2013/707 of 4 December 2013 confirming the acceptance of an undertaking offered in connection with the anti-dumping and anti-subsidy proceedings concerning imports of crystalline silicon photovoltaic modules and key components originating in or consigned from the People's Republic of China for the period of application of definitive measures, [2013] OJ L 325/214. The Commission has in the past already rejected undertakings because of the high number of companies involved, see e.g. Council Regulation (EC) No 397/2004 of 2 March 2004, *Cotton-Type Bed Linen from Pakistan*, [2004] OJ L 66/1 and (EC) 695/2006 of 5 May 2006, [2006] OJ L 121/14.

[51] Due to the high volatility in prices and the lack of correlation between prices of raw materials and those of the final products, the Commission held that no reliable indexation method could be established in the present case; the Commission therefore established an alternative method by using price reports and publicly available databases such as Bloomberg and pvXchange as a reference, see Commission Decision (2013/423/EU) of 2 August 2013 accepting an undertaking offered in connection with the anti-dumping proceeding concerning imports of crystalline silicon photovoltaic modules and key components originating in or consigned from the People's Republic of China, [2013] OJ L 209/26, para. 4. The Commission has in the past already rejected undertakings because of the high volatility in prices of the concerned products, see e.g. Council Regulation (EC) No 91/2009 of 26 January 2006, *Certain Iron or Steel Fasteners from China*, [2009] OJ L 29/1.

[52] Actions brought on 28 February 2014, ECJ, T-141/14 and T-142/14, *SolarWorld and Others v Commission*. An earlier action for annulment of the Commission's decision of 2 August 2013 was declared inadmissible as the Commission's Decision was considered no to be of direct concern to the applicants, ECJ, T-507/13, *SolarWorld and Others v Commission*, not yet published.

the minimum price in the undertaking is manifestly inadequate to remove the injury to EU producers, but also because the decision violates Article 101(1) TFEU "*insofar as it accepts and reinforces a horizontal price fixing arrangement*". The underlying rationale of this argument is that by accepting the joint price undertaking, the Commission is sponsoring a price cartel amongst Chinese solar panel manufacturers.

It will be interesting to see which position the General Court will take. Leaving aside the discussion as to whether the minimum import price under the price undertaking is sufficient to remove the injurious effect of the dumping, the decision of the Commission to accept a *joint* price undertaking by a large group of Chinese solar panel manufacturers raises the question whether the Commission can effectively implement a measure which, at first sight, seems to fall foul of Article 101 TFEU. It could be argued that the duty of sincere cooperation laid down in Article 4(3) TEU should not only apply to Member States to ensure compliance with the obligations arising out of the Treaties, but also to the Union institutions, including the European Commission.[53] From that perspective, one could claim that by accepting a joint price undertaking the Commission has accepted an anti-competitive agreement between competitors which falls foul of Article 101 TFEU, thereby infringing the duty of sincere cooperation.

Moreover, we would argue that the fact that the joint price undertaking has been accepted by the Commission, and that any anti-competitive conduct which may have taken place in the context of the determination of the joint undertaking could—arguably—be regarded as having been "rubber-stamped" by the Commission, does not necessarily shield the Chinese exporters from liability under Article 101 TFEU. By analogy, reference can be made to the General Court's judgement in *Steel Beams* and the Court of Justice's recent decision in *Schenker & Co*. In *Steel Beams*,[54] the General Court rejected the argument of one of the parties involved in the cartel that the Commission had itself initiated, and then encouraged, or at least had knowledge of and tolerated, the conduct it later held to be illegal, mainly because the Court found that the Commission had not been aware of all the exchanges of information between the steel beam producers. In *Schenker & Co.*,[55] the Court of Justice held that a decision of a national competition authority, holding that an agreement was not illegal under national competition law, cannot exempt an undertaking from being held liable for having engaged in an anti-competitive agreement.

[53] See above for further details on a Member State's obligations arising out of Article 4(3) TEU in conjunction with Article 101 TFEU. Lenaerts and Van Nuffel state that "the same mutual duties of sincere cooperation apply between the institutions as govern relations between the institutions and the Member States", see Lenaerts and Van Nuffel (2011), p. 153.

[54] ECJ, T-141/94, *Thyssen Stahl v Commission*, [1999] ECR II, 347.

[55] ECJ, C-681/11, *Schenker & Co. and Others*, [2013] not yet published.

Conclusion

The potential competition law risks which are inherently associated with the acceptance of price undertakings as a way of settling anti-dumping investigations illustrate that from a policy perspective, there is a need for further coordination between anti-dumping and antitrust policy. Although both price undertakings and *ad valorem* anti-dumping duties have a welfare impact on the domestic market, there seems to be less scope for competition law risks associated with *ad valorem* duties.

Companies need to carefully consider how far they go in engaging in discussions with competitors. Although there are, to our knowledge, no concrete examples of enforcement actions by competition authorities against anticompetitive behaviour associated with price undertakings under the anti-dumping rules, it seems prudent for companies who are serious about compliance to give due consideration to the competition law boundaries of price undertaking discussions.

References

European Commission, Anti-dumping – anti-subsidy – safeguard. Statistics covering full-year 2012. Available at http://trade.ec.europa.eu/doclib/docs/2012/december/tradoc_150133.pdf

European Commission, Anti-dumping – anti-subsidy – safeguard. Statistics covering full-year 2013 (2013 Commission statistics). Available at http://trade.ec.europa.eu/doclib/docs/2014/february/tradoc_152184.pdf

Lang JT (1987) European community anti-dumping and competition laws: their actual and potential application to EFTA countries. Tidsskrift for Rettsvitenskap 100

Lenaerts K, Van Nuffel P (2011) European Union Law, 3rd edn

McGee RW (1996) Antidumping laws as protectionist trade barriers: the case for repeal. Policy Analysis 14

Messerlin P (1989) The EC antidumping regulations: a first economic appraisal, 1980–85. Rev World Econ 125:3

Messerlin P (1990) Antidumping regulations or procartel law? The EC chemical cases. World Econ 13:4

Moore M (2005) VERs and price undertakings under the WTO. Rev Int Econ 13:2

Perone F (1995) Settlement of anti-dumping cases by price undertaking: the European community and United States practice. LL.M. thesis, McGill University. Available at http://digitool.library.mcgill.ca/webclient/StreamGate?folder_id=0&dvs=1415287018790~556

Pierce RJ (1999–2000) Antidumping law as means of facilitating cartelization. Antitrust Law J 67:3

Rovegno L, Vandenbussche H (2011) A comparative analysis of EU antidumping rules and application. Discussion Paper 2011-23, Institut de Recherches Économiques et Sociales de l'Université catholique de Louvain. Available at http://sites.uclouvain.be/econ/DP/IRES/2011023.pdf

Stegemann K (1990) EC anti-dumping policy: are price undertakings a legal substitute for illegal price fixing? Rev World Econ 126:2

Steinbach A (2004) Price undertakings in EU anti-dumping proceedings – an instrument of the past? J Econ Integrat 29:1

Steinbach A (2014) Price undertakings in EU anti-dumping proceedings – an instrument of the past? J Econ Integrat 29:1
Van Bael I, Bellis J-F (2011) EU anti-dumping and other trade defence instruments, 5th edn
Vermulst EA (1987) Antidumping law and practice in the United States and the European communities: a comparative analysis
Vermulst EA (1999) Competition and anti-dumping: continued peaceful co-existence? Available at www.ssrn.com/abstract=200616
Whish R (2012) Competition law, 7th edn
Zanardi M (2004) Anti-dumping: what are the numbers to discuss at Doha? World Econ 27:3
Zanardi M (2005) Antidumping: a problem in international trade. CentER Discussion Paper Series 85

Decision-Making in EU Trade Defence Cases After Lisbon: An Institutional Anomaly Addressed?

Tibor Scharf

Introduction

The Lisbon Treaty has led to the first major change in trade defence decision making since the adoption of the last consolidated[1] anti-dumping and anti-subsidy regulations in 1994, and arguably even since the inception of the trade defence regulations in 1968.[2] So far, whilst the Commission was in charge of the administrative investigation procedure from the beginning to the end, the Council adopted the Regulations imposing duties, amending or prolonging duties further to a review (or anti-circumvention) investigation on the basis of a Commission proposal.[3] In

The views in this paper reflect the author's view only and not necessarily those of the European Commission.

[1] But for the first time separated into two distinct Regulations for the Anti-Dumping and Anti-Subsidy instruments, Council Regulation (EC) No 3283/94 of 22 December 1994 on protection against dumped imports from countries not members of the European Community, [1994] OJ L 349/1.

[2] Regulation (EEC) No 459/68 of the Council of 5 April 1968 on protection against dumping or the granting of bounties or subsidies by countries which are not members of the European Economic Community [1968] OJ L 93/1.

[3] Council Regulation (EEC) No 2423/88 of 11 July 1988 on protection against dumped or subsidized imports from countries not members of the European Economic Community, [1988] OJ L 209/1, Article 12; Council Regulation (EEC) No 2176/84 of 23 July 1984 on protection against dumped or subsidized imports from countries not members of the European Economic Community, [1984] OJ L 201/1 as amended by Council Regulation (EEC) No 1761/87 of 22 June 1987, Article 12; Council Regulation (EEC) No 3017/79 of 20 December 1979 on protection against dumped or subsidized imports from countries not members of the European Economic Community, [1979] OJ L 339/1, Article 12 and Regulation (EEC) No 459/68 of the Council of

T. Scharf (✉)
European Commission, Legal Service, Office Berl 02/121, Rue de la Loi 200, 1049 Bruxelles, Belgium
e-mail: tibor.scharf@ec.europa.eu

C. Herrmann et al. (eds.), *Trade Policy between Law, Diplomacy and Scholarship*,
European Yearbook of International Economic Law,
DOI 10.1007/978-3-319-15690-3_22

practice, the Commission was, having conducted the investigation, privy to all the facts justifying proposed measure. The Council on the other hand (only) had at its disposal the duly motivated, but necessarily summarised.[4] Commission proposal and any additional explanations given to the Anti-Dumping Committee on which to base its decision to adopt (or not) the Commission proposal.

However, since 20 February 2014, the date of coming into effect of Regulation (EU) No 37/2014 (the "Amending Regulation"),[5] definitive trade defence measures are adopted by the Commission, subject only to some transitional arrangements.[6] It is therefore timely to consider not only the changes brought about by the Amending Regulation, but also to reflect on the nature of decision making in trade defence more generally. This paper will argue that the changes by the Amending Regulation in fact also address what could be argued to be, or rather to have been, an anomaly in Union decision making.

Decision making for Union Trade Defence Instruments[7] has so far been somewhat odd from an institutional point of view. Trade defence regulations imposing, amending or repealing measures are, as regards their nature and scope, of a general character, in that they apply to all the economic operators concerned taken as a whole. However, their provisions are none the less of individual concern to certain economic operators.[8] Advocate-General Jacobs thus qualified them as being of a "hybrid" nature.[9] They are imposed after an administrative investigation and following an administrative procedure by the Commission as foreseen by the Basic Anti-Dumping and Anti-Subsidy Regulations.[10] In that respect, they are more akin to antitrust or

5 April 1968 on protection against dumping or the granting of bounties or subsidies by countries which are not members of the European Economic Community, [1968] OJ L 93/1, Article 17.

[4] This not least as the information concerned is often of a highly technical nature and involves an elaborate economic and legal analysis (see Basic Anti-Dumping Regulation, Recital 28). Consequently, the Basic Anti-Dumping Regulation foresees that the advisory Committee be sent all "relevant" information, and of course not all information (see Article 15(2)).

[5] Regulation (EU) No. 37/2014 of the European Parliament and of the Council of 15 January 2014 amending certain regulations relating to the common commercial policy as regards the procedures for the adoption of certain measures, [2014] OJ L 18/1.

[6] Article 3 of the Amending Regulations foresees that the Amending regulation applies to pending investigations only in so far as the Commission has not yet adopted an act and/or no consultations have yet taken place and/or the Commission has not yet made a proposal of any sort. In other words, only pending investigations in the very initial stages of the investigation at the entry onto force of the Amending Regulation will be subject to the Amending Regulation's procedure.

[7] Both Anti-Subsidy and Anti-Dumping measures, but the present contribution will focus on Anti-Dumping measures.

[8] ECJ, C-75/92, *Gao Yao v Council* [1994] ECR I, 3141, para. 26; Order by the General Court of 12 January 2014, T-596 /11, *Bricmate v Council*, not yet published, paras. 23–30, in which the General Court summarises case law on individual concern of anti-dumping regulations.

[9] ECJ, Opinion by AG Jacobs, C- 76/01 P, *Eurocoton and Others v Council*, [2003] ECR I, 10096, para. 84.

[10] Where in this paper, reference is made to the Basic Anti-Dumping Regulation, this refers to Council Regulation (EC) No 1225/2009 of 30 November 2009 on protection against dumped

state aid decisions[11] than to the legislative acts more commonly adopted by Council regulations.[12] Yet, the Commission's role is, as held by the Court of Justice, situated in "the context of the Council's decision-making process"[13] and "forms an integral part"[14] of it. In fact, as the General Court commented recently, an anti-dumping regulation is not a legislative act since it is not adopted in accordance with either the ordinary legislative procedure or the special legislative procedure within the meaning of paragraphs 1 to 3 of Article 289 TFEU.[15] Yet, trade defence measures—at least measures imposing duties—entail implementing measures in so far as the duties they impose require collection on the basis of measures adopted by national customs authorities,[16] and in this sense differ from, for instance, Commission competition decisions.[17]

The set-up of trade defence decision making was also odd for a number of more general reasons:

- Trade defence is part of the common commercial policy[18]: yet the Treaties and case law, have—for nearly 40 years[19]—considered that external trade is a Union competence; the setting into practice of this policy rests largely with the Commission,[20] even if aspects of the commercial policy, such as international

imports from countries not members of the European Community (codified version) of 30 November 2009, OJ L 343/51.

[11] Like for competition decisions, the implementation of the common commercial policy—including trade defence decisions—was excluded from the comitology decision 1999, see Council Decision (1999/468/EC) of 28 June 1999 laying down the procedures for the exercise of implementing powers conferred on the Commission, OJ L 184/23, Recital 12 and Article 1.

[12] The Court of Justice recognised this ambiguity in ECJ, C-76/01 P, *Eurocoton and Others v Council*, [2003] ECR I, 10123, when at para. 69 it held that "anti-dumping proceedings are similar in several respects to an administrative procedure".

[13] See Order of 15.10.1986, ECJ, C-299/85, *Tokyo Juki Industrial v Council and Commission*, [1986] ECR, 2965.

[14] Order of the Court of 8 May 1985, ECJ, C-256/84, *Koyo Seiko v Council*, [1985] ECR, 1351, para. 3.

[15] Order by the General Court of 12 January 2014, T-596/11 *Bricmate v Council*, not yet published, para. 65.

[16] Order of the General Court of 5 February 2013, T-551/11 *BSI v Council*, not yet published, para. 53; Order by the General Court of 12 January 2014, T-596/11 *Bricmate v Council*, not yet published, paras. 72 and 75.

[17] But not necessarily state aid decision, as recovery of unlawful aid is done on the basis of a national procedure and the sums so collected do not go to the Commission, but return to the Member State concerned.

[18] See Art. 207(1) TFEU; see also Krenzler (2005), p. 801, which considered that the individual measures are measures of "trade policy" addressing individual cases. For a more general description of the development of Union competence in Trade see, Pitschas (2014), p. 209. See also, Pitschas (2014), p. 209 (217).

[19] The origins of this development go back even longer: Krenzler/Herrmann consider, in Krenzler and Herrmann (2013), para. 14, that already during the 1960, the Commission gradually started taking over GATT negotiations from the Member States.

[20] The Court of Justice held already in ECJ, C-41/76, *Donckerwolke and Others v Procureur de la Ré publique and Others*, [1976] ECR, 1921 para. 32: "as full responsibility in the matter of commercial policy was transferred to the community by means of article 113 (1) measures of commercial policy

agreements, need to be implemented and thus require Member State involvement.[21]

- Trade defence is about fair trading practices. In the internal market, there is no doubt about the Commission's exclusive role in enforcing these. Fair trading practices in the Internal Market, in particular the four freedoms of goods, services, persons and capital, as well as competition and state aid rules, are all provided for directly by the European Treaties. These are backed up by thousands of pieces of sector-specific internal market legislation.[22] The enforcement of both the Treaties and secondary legislation based on them is the exclusive realm of the Commission as guardian of the Treaties.[23]
- Enforcement of trade defence measures is intricately linked to customs law; yet the Customs Union, and with it customs law, is one of the oldest components of European integration,[24] and the Commission's administrative competence in it very wide.
- The division of competences as to trade defence decision making, with a final decision at ministerial level after an administrative investigation by the Commission, contrasts with the situation in a number of third countries such as the US, where Department of Commerce decisions on trade defence are taken at administrative level.[25]

Hence, Why Was the Trade Defence Decision-Making Process Set Up as It Was Until 20th February 2014?

There has been little attention given to this issue in literature,[26] presumably because trade defence law has been analysed more closely from the practical aspect of its actual working, which is of eminent practical

of a national character are only permissible after the end of the transitional period by virtue of specific authorization by the community." This in practice meant the Commission.

[21] And thus subject to the Council's approval for the negations and the signature and conclusion (the latter after involvement of the European Parliament), see Article 218 TFEU.

[22] Trade Commissioner De Gucht estimated these at 10,000 in his speech "Modernisation of Trade Defence Instruments" of 10 May 2012, available at http://trade.ec.europa.eu/doclib/docs/2012/may/tradoc_149424.pdf.

[23] Article 17(1) TEU.

[24] Krenzler and Herrmann (2013), para. 40.

[25] Müller et al. (2009), para. I.36.

[26] In fact, even the Basic Anti-Dumping Regulation contains no recital in any way dealing with the institutional side of the decision making. Rather, much like its predecessor version, Council Regulation (EC) No 384/96 of 22 December 1995 on protection against dumped imports from countries not members of the European Community, [1996] OJ L 56/1, it appears to take this for granted, only having a reference to "the decision-making process in the Community" in the context of disclosure (see Recital 33 in the Basic Anti-dumping Regulation, and identical Recital 30 in the prior version of the Basic Regulation). Hence most commentaries and books merely describe the decision making process without giving its institutional aspects much attention: see e.g. Krenzler

relevance,[27] rather than from the point of view of institutional theory. Furthermore, imposing trade defence measures by way of regulations can be explained partly by the fact that duties are collected by Member States' customs authorities which leads to the necessity to have recourse to regulations of a general nature. So this set up may have seemed logical.[28] But in fact it was arguably more the result of the Member States' wish to maintain control over an activity which is considered politically sensitive, and it was not really logical from a systemic point of view.[29]

Has the Mechanism of Trade Defence Decision-Making Been Problematic?

The least that can be argued is that the Member States' involvement has been both a blessing and a curse.

Generally, the criterion of Union interest, which gives a large degree of discretion for assessing whether or not imposing a measure is in the overall Union interest, is arguably best determined in taking into account Member States' views[30] and not only the Commission's case for Union interest based on facts as established during the investigation. Member States' views can round off this assessment by a more general political assessment. As a result, the measures taken may be seen to be the result of a more carefully calibrated political assessment. This however does not necessarily require the adoption of measures to be made by Council act.

Furthermore, in at least a few instances, measures, which should have been adopted on the basis of the fact-based investigation by the Commission, were not because of Member States' disagreements. The facts underlying the *Eurocoton* case illustrate this point: in that case, the Commission submitted a proposal for a Council

---

and Herrmann (2013), para. 23, footnote 3, which merely refers to a more specific publication (Pietzsch 2009); Arnold and Meindl (2014), K.I. para. 141 only describe the situation, as does Van Bael and Bellis (2004), pp. 3–7 and Van Bael and Bellis (2011), pp. 2–7, this time describing the new situation, as well as p. 19; whilst Baule in Krenzler and Herrmann (2013), AD-GVO 70, para. 19 again merely notes the tension; some discussion in Müller (2000), p. 195 (200).

[27] After all, there are about new 16 investigation on average per year, and up to nearly 100 measures in place at any one time (see "Trade defence Statistics Covering the First Ten Months of 2014", available at http://trade.ec.europa.eu/doclib/docs/2013/august/tradoc_151694.pdf; The recent investigation into Solar Panels from China—the largest so far—alone concerned some EUR 21 billion of annual exports from China, see European Commission, Press Release, MEMO/12/647 of 6 September 2012, available at http://europa.eu/rapid/press-release_MEMO-12-647_en.htm; see also Van Bael and Bellis (2011), p. 15.

[28] Trommer and Wenig (2014), KII para. 19.

[29] Müller et al. (2009), para. I.36.

[30] Which the Commission had to seek already before the Amending Regulation by virtue of Article 21(5) Basic Anti-Dumping Regulation.

Regulation imposing a definitive anti-dumping duty on the imports of unbleached cotton fabrics from a number of countries. Yet, the Council found that there was not the simple majority necessary for the adoption of the regulation proposed.[31] At the lapse of the maximum 15-months deadline allowed for the Institutions to conclude an investigation, the lack of a majority in the Council resulted in no decision being taken and the procedure being closed without measures. The reason behind the lack of a Council majority, and also for the lack of an outright rejection, was due to disagreement among Member States.[32] The Court of Justice considered this not only as a reviewable act, but—logically—construed the Council's lack of action as equivalent to an implicit negative decision lacking motivation.[33] It is difficult to envisage how the Council should have been in a position to motivate its decision, except by changing the Union interest assessment, this inevitably leading to questions as to the factual soundness of the resulting decision[34]: the Commission will have based its decision on the totality of the facts during the investigation, and the draft proposal for a regulation will have benefitted from an extensive inter-service consultation within the Commission.[35] The Council on the other hand, would have been under enormous time pressure to conduct a reassessment of the facts at the very end of the 15-months deadline and, due to the lack of agreement between Member States, necessarily coming to a differently assessment based on the very facts previously assessed otherwise by the Commission.[36]

Similarly, in the case of *Hot Rolled Coils*[37] the Commission proposed imposing definitive anti-dumping measures on imports of hot rolled coils originating in Egypt, Slovakia and Turkey. However, the Council did not adopt the proposal within the time limits laid down in the Basic Anti-Dumping Regulation. As a result, definitive measures were not imposed on imports from Egypt, Slovakia and Turkey. On the basis of the principle of non-discrimination, the Commission considered it had, as a result, to refrain from imposing measures on Bulgaria and South Africa.[38]

---

[31] ECJ, C- 76/01 P, *Eurocoton and Others v Council*, [2003] ECR I, 10123, paras. 6–10.

[32] This is hinted at in Opinion by AG Jacobs, C- 76/01 P, *Eurocoton and Others v Council*, [2003], ECR I, 10096, para. 14, where AG Jacobs quotes from the Council's press release revealing the French Delegation "once again insisted on the need for such measures to be taken".

[33] ECJ, C- 76/01 P, *Eurocoton and Others v Council*, [2003] ECR I, 10123, para. 67.

[34] See Davies (2004), p. 5; Vermulst (2010), point 9 and in particular 9-013 et seq.

[35] See Vermulst (2010), point 2-003 et seq.

[36] Müller (2000), p. 195 (201).

[37] Defined as flat rolled products of iron or non-alloy steel, of a width of 600 mm or more, not clad, plated or coated, in coils, not further worked than hot-rolled.

[38] See Council Regulation (EC) No 1615/2004 of 13 September 2004 terminating the anti-dumping proceedings concerning imports of certain flat-rolled products of iron or non-alloy steel, of a width of 600 mm or more, not clad, plated or coated, in coils, not further worked than hot-rolled, originating in India, Taiwan and Serbia and Montenegro, OJ L 294/1, Recitals 5–7, and corresponding Council Regulation (EC) No 1616/2004 of 13 September 2004 terminating the anti-dumping proceedings concerning imports of certain flat-rolled products of iron or non-alloy steel, of a width of 600 mm or more, not clad, plated or coated, in coils, not further worked than hot-rolled, originating in Bulgaria and South Africa, [2004] OJ L 294/3.

An arguably even more striking example is the saga of the measures against Chinese and Vietnamese shoes. In 2005 the Commission started an investigation into shoe imports from China and Vietnam, which led to the Commission adopting provisional duties.[39] So far so classic. Then however, the Member States essentially split in those supporting duties to protect their national shoe industry and those opposing duties in order to prevent the import price of shoes to rise and thus harming their retail interests. In order to reconcile the Member States, the Commission displayed creativity in proposing a novel approach to imposing duties by way of compromise: The Commission proposed duties being in place for two as opposed to 5 years, a novel delayed duty mechanism, lower duties than originally proposed and the exclusion of a category of shoes.[40]

Finally, the investigation into solar panels from China is a recent example of where Member States' divergent political interests had a heavy influence on the investigation, this leading to the then Trade Commissioner being reported in the press as warning Member States not to be unduly vocal before the Commission could even end its investigation, and calling for the Commission's role in trade defence to be strengthened.[41]

The rationale for attributing state aid control to the Commission, is also valid to an extent for trade defence: for state aid, exclusive competence was given in the Treaty of Rome to the Commission due to the necessity to have an independent referee. In order for state aid to be evaluated from an EU point of view, and to maintain a level playing field between the Member States, this task can only be performed by the Commission.[42] Also, the interest of Member States in retaining control over an area perceived to be politically sensitive is, whilst understandable from a political point of view, also detrimental to the credibility of trade defence measures adopted: precisely because of that reason, trade defence measures can easily be tainted by the perception of political as opposed to factual motivations, or even simply as protectionist measures.[43] The recent solar panel investigation mentioned above was an example of this, and the press reported, among others,

---

[39] For a basic description of the facts, see General Court in Joined Cases T-407/06 and T-408/06, *Zhejiang Aokang Shoes and Wenzhou Taima Shoes v Council*, [2010] ECR II, 747, paras. 11–36; ECJ, C-249/10 P, *Brosman Footwear (HK) and Others v Council*, 2 February 2012, para. 9.

[40] For a detailed account of the attempts at reconciling the various Member States' positions in Council, see Eckhardt (2011), p. 965, in particular point 3.2.

[41] Commissioner De Gucht, reported in European Voice, 30 May 2013, p. 7, as saying: "We all know that China is trying to influence and scare off member states. [..] the best protection for the member states is to say that this is the competence of the European Commission" and "if we in the EU do not stand together on this, then we will lose". See also European Voice, 5 September 2013, p. 9; Süddeutsche Zeitung, 30 July 2013, p. 18.

[42] Pesaresi and Van Hoof (2008), paras. 1.29–1.32, and 1.59.

[43] Davis (2009), which suspects a bias towards imposing duties, possibly due to a "political bias towards supporting declining domestic industries", this not least as the economic soundness of the Community Interest test is put into doubt.

Germany as being opposed to the measures, fearing retaliation as China's largest trading partner in the Union.[44]

The decision making procedure has been amended in 2004 as a result of the *Eurocoton* judgement as well as the *Hot Rolled Coils* investigation. Before the amendment, the Basic Regulations provided for a procedure under which the Council imposed definitive measures by simple majority. However "in the light of recent experience of the application of the Basic Regulations and in order to preserve the transparency and efficiency of the trade defence instruments",[45] it was considered necessary to revisit the way Community institutions work together. Before the amendment, a Commission proposal was only adopted if a simple majority of Member States voted in favour of the proposal. This had the effect that abstentions counted effectively against the Commission proposal. In turn, this could result in a situation where a Commission proposal would not be adopted by the Council due to the number of abstentions. In order to address this problem, the Basic Regulations were amended by requiring a simple majority of Member States in the Council to reject a Commission proposal for imposing definitive measures, and measures were then adopted by the Council unless it decided by a simple majority to reject the proposal within a period of 1 month after submission of the proposal by the Commission.[46]

This amendment already represented a shift in the balance of decision making. But the real shift had to wait until the Lisbon Treaty.[47]

The Lisbon Treaty brought about a more general change in decision making in areas in which the decision making takes place by so-called "comitology". This term refers to procedures under which the Commission executes its implementing powers delegated to it by the legislator with the assistance of so called "comitology committees" made up of representatives of the Member States.[48] Comitology was based on Art. 202 EC, third indent, and the idea that the Council could make the exercise of the powers which it confers on the Commission subject to certain procedures.[49] The Treaty on the Functioning of the European Union (TFEU) separated formally for the first time all acts that could be adopted by comitology

---

[44] See e.g. Traynor and Rankin (2013), Ellyatt (2013), and Bradsher (2012). See also e.g. the recent Solar Panel from China investigations: Nitzschke (2013).

[45] Council Regulation (EC) No 461/2004 of 8 March 2004 amending Regulation (EC) No 384/96 on protection against dumped imports from countries not members of the European Community and Regulation (EC) No 2026/97 on protection against subsidised imports from countries not members of the European Community, OJ L 77/12.

[46] Council Regulation (EC) No 461/2004 of 8 March 2004 amending Regulation (EC) No 384/96 on protection against dumped imports from countries not members of the European Community and Regulation (EC) No 2026/97 on protection against subsidised imports from countries not members of the European Community, OJ L 77/12 of 13.3.2004, Recitals 2–9.

[47] Vermulst (2010), point 2-012; Herrmann (2011), § 30, para. 42.

[48] See more generally, Craig (2012), chapter 5, p. 109.

[49] ECJ, C-16/88, *Commission v Council*, [1989] ECR, 3457, para. 13, with reference to Art. 145 (pre-Nice numbering).

measures into delegated (Art. 290) and implementing (Art. 291) acts.[50] The comitology procedure in place until the Lisbon Treaty no longer fitted this new distinction[51] and thus had to be reformed.[52] As set out in the Amending Regulation, after recalling in Recital 1 that trade defence measures were not subject to the "old" comitology, it was considered

> appropriate to amend those basic regulations in order to ensure consistency with the provisions introduced by the Treaty of Lisbon. This should be done, where appropriate, through the granting of delegated powers to the Commission and by applying certain procedures set out in Regulation (EU) No 182/2011 of the European Parliament and of the Council [i.e. the "New Comitology"].[53]

The Amending Regulation accordingly foresees that the implementation of the basic Anti-Dumping Regulation requires uniform conditions for the adoption of provisional and definitive duties, and for the termination of an investigation without measures, which should be adopted by the Commission in accordance with Regulation (EU) No 182/2011.[54]

Decision-Making Shift Brought About by the Amending Regulation

Under the rules now in force, the Commission remains responsible for the imposition of provisional duties after consultation of the Member States. The main change is that it is now the Commission which adopts definitive duties and no longer the Council. In fact, the Council as such is no longer involved at all in the decision-making process. Trade defence implementing decisions are now[55] taken by Commission decision.[56]

The Commission is assisted by an "Examination Committee"[57] composed of Member States' representatives, chaired by a Commission representative, much akin to the earlier Anti-Dumping Committee. However now, the Commission

[50] See also, Stratulat and Molino (2011).

[51] Craig (2012), chapter 5, p. 124; Stratulat and Molino (2011).

[52] Pilniok (2014), p. 62 (76).

[53] Amending Regulation, Recital 2.

[54] Amending Regulation, Annex, point 22, para. 2.

[55] Subject to the transitional arrangements set out at Article 3 of the Amending Regulations.

[56] See, for instance: Commission Implementing Decision (EU) 2015/110 of 26 January 2015 imposing a definitive anti-dumping duty on imports of certain welded tubes and pipes of iron or non-alloy steel originating in Belarus, the People's Republic of China and Russia and terminating the proceeding for imports of certain welded tubes and pipes of iron or non-alloy steel originating in Ukraine following an expiry review pursuant to Article 11(2) of Council Regulation (EC) No 1225/2009.

[57] Implementing Regulation, Annex para. 11, new Article 15 of the Basic Regulation.

submits to the Examination Committee a draft decision to be adopted by the Commission and no longer by the Council.[58]

Member States are still in a position to block a proposed measure, however they now have in effect to do so by qualified majority and after involvement of a new "Appeal Committee",[59] to which the measure is sent if a simple majority of Member States has opposed it in the Examination Committee. This represents a higher threshold as compared to the previous situation in which a simple majority against a measure sufficed for Member States to block its adoption.[60]

Another aspect of the Amending Regulation may also lead to a stronger hand for the Commission in practice. Whilst Member States are in a position to suggest amendments to proposals before both the Examination and the Appeal Committees until an option is delivered,[61] the Council has bound itself by a statement to the Amending Regulation,[62] which foresees that where it will suggest an amendment to a draft measure proposed, it will be one

> (a) which respects the deadlines in the Basic Regulations and reflects the necessity for the Commission to be given sufficient time to undertake any necessary disclosure procedure, properly scrutinise the proposal, and for the Committee to examine any amended draft measure proposed, (b) ensure that the proposed amendment is consistent with the Basic Regulations as interpreted by the Court of Justice of the European Union and with relevant international obligations; (c) provide written justification which will, as a minimum, indicate how the suggested amendment relates to the Basic Regulations and to the facts established in the investigation, but may also contain such other supporting arguments as the Member State proposing the amendment considers appropriate.

In practice this means that whilst the Commission has to ensure that its submitted text is finalised, there is limited scope for Member States to alter the Commission proposal for political reasons. Member States can now only reject the text essentially by arguing on the basis of the provisions of the Basic Regulations.

On the other hand, it remains the case that the Member States keep, through the possibility to block the measure—even if with an increased hurdle—a considerably stronger involvement in the adoption of trade defence measures than, for instance, in antitrust or state aid decisions, where they have no involvement at all.

The new regulatory regime also has foreseen a continuous involvement of Member States through the Examination Committee in so far as Article 15(6) of the Basic Anti-Dumping Regulation provides that the Committee

> may consider any matter relating to the application of this Regulation, raised by the Commission or at the request of a Member State. Member States may request information and may be exchange views in the Committee or directly with the Commission.[63]

---

[58] Van Bael and Bellis (2011), p. 7.

[59] Article 5(5) new Comitology Regulation.

[60] Article 9(4) Basic Anti-Dumping Regulation: a qualified majority was required in some exceptional cases, such as the Commission proposing termination without measures for the Council to overrule the proposal, see Basic Regulation Article 9(2).

[61] Articles 3(4) and 6(2) new Comitology Regulation.

[62] Amending Regulation, Statement on p. 48.

[63] Amending Regulation, Annex, para. 11.

The special nature of this wording is underlined by the Joint Statement by the European Parliament, the Council and the Commission attached to the Amending Regulation on Article 15(6): it was felt necessary to clarify that this is not a different decision-making procedure than provided by the new Comitology Regulation and justified by the "special characteristics" of the trade defence regulations.

An interesting question will arise where a case referred to the Appeal Committee fails to reach a decision within the 15-months deadline applicable for Anti-Dumping investigations. The new Comitology Regulation has stipulated deadlines for trade defence investigations before the Appeal Committee in Article 5(5) and further stipulates: "The time limits laid down in this paragraph shall be without prejudice to the need to respect the deadlines laid down in the relevant basic act", in other words to respect the 15-months deadline of Article 6(9) of the Basic Anti-Dumping Regulation. However there is no provision dealing with the case in which no agreement can be reached, and in particular who then decides.

Arguably, this is a lacuna which will result in a situation similar to the one at the basis of the *Eurocoton* case, except that now, it would be the Commission and no longer the Council, which, after the end of the 15-months deadline, takes an implicit negative decision, necessarily—or logically—lacking motivation.

Thus, has the Amending Regulation addressed the institutional anomaly? The answer must remain a lawyer-like "yes, to some extent". Yes, in so far as both investigation and decision making are now much more clearly in the hands of the Commission. No, in so far as Member States can still prevent the adoption of measures which are proposed on the basis of an investigation, even if with more difficulties than before. On the other hand, practice may well show that the new decision making process is, in effect, (even) more fact-based and less prone to obvious political bargaining. Accordingly, the trade defence system may well be on the way to become a more "normal" technical and administrative investigation in what is, after all, an alleged trade distortion to the detriment of a specific sector, contrary to the common interest. If so, this can only enhance the credibility of the Union's trade defence measures.

References

Arnold N, Meindl A (2014) In: Dauses MA (ed) Handbuch des EU-Wirtschaftsrecht

Bradsher K (2012) Europe investigates Chinese solar panels. New York Times, 6 September 2012. Available at http://www.nytimes.com/2012/09/07/business/global/eu-investigates-chinese-solar-panels.html

Craig P (2012) EU administrative law, 2nd edn

Davies L (2004) Anti-dumping investigation in the EU: how does it work? ECIPE Working Paper 4

Davis L (2009) Anti-dumping investigation in the EU: how does it work? ECIPE Working Paper 4

DG Trade (2014) Anti-dumping, anti-subsidy, safeguard. Statistics covering the first ten months of 2014, 14 November 2014. Available online at http://trade.ec.europa.eu/doclib/docs/2013/august/tradoc_151694.pdf

Eckhardt J (2011) Firm lobbying and EU trade policymaking: reflections upon the anti-dumping case against Chinese and Vietnamese shoes (2005–2011). J World Trade 45:965

Ellyatt H (2013) Wine vs. solar panels: China hits back at EU. CNBC, 5 June 2013. Available at http://www.cnbc.com/id/100790486
Herrmann C (2011) In: Terhechte JP (ed) Verwaltungsrecht der Europäischen Union
Krenzler HG (2005) Die Gemeinsame Handelspolitik nach dem Entwurf des Europäischen Verfassungsvertrags – ein Schritt in die richtige Richtung. RIW 11:801
Krenzler HG, Herrmann C (eds) (2013) EU-Aussenwirtschafts- und Zollrecht. Einleitung 10
Müller W (2000) Stand und Perspektive des EG-Antidumpingrechts Europäisches Wirtschafts- und Steuerrecht
Müller W, Kahn N, Scharf T (2009) EC and WTO anti-dumping law: a handbook, 2nd edn
Nitzschke M (2013) Europe must stand up to China's trade distorting practices. Financial Times, 12 June 2013
Pesaresi N, Van Hoof M (2008) In: Mederer W, Pesaresi N, Van Hoof M (eds) EU competition law, volume IV – state aid, book one
Pietzsch H (2009) Die Kompetenzverteilung zwischen Rat, Kommission und Parlament in den EG-Außenwirtschaftsbeziehungen
Pilniok A (2014) Struktur, Funktionen und Probleme der Expertengruppen der Europäischen Kommission: legitime Expertise oder unzulässige Einflussnahme? EuR
Pitschas C (2014) Economic partnership agreements and EU trade policy: objectives, competences, and implementation. In: Drexl J et al (eds) EU bilateral trade agreements and intellectual property: for better or worse?
Stratulat C, Molino E (2011) Implementing Lisbon: what's new in comitology? EPC Policy Brief, April 2011
Traynor I, Rankin J (2013) EU to impose anti-dumping tariffs on Chinese solar panels. The Guardian, 4 June 2013. Available at http://gu.com/p/3gb7p
Trommer S, Wenig F-H (2014) In: Dauses MA (ed) Handbuch des EU-Wirtschaftsrecht
Van Bael I, Bellis JF (2004) Anti-dumping and other trade protection laws of the EC, 4th edn
Van Bael I, Bellis JF (2011) Anti-dumping and other trade protection laws of the EC, 5th edn
Vermulst EA (2010) EU anti-dumping law and practice, 2nd edn

The manufacturer's authorised representative in the EU is Springer Nature Customer Service Centre GmbH, Europaplatz 3, 69115 Heidelberg, Germany. If you have any concerns regarding our products, please contact ProductSafety@springernature.com

Printed and bound by CPI Group (UK) Ltd, Croydon, CR0 4YY
30/09/2026
02225652-0017